D0806005

M U
ARCH

THE
MURDOCH
ARCHIPELAGO

THE
MURDOCH
ARCHIPELAGO

BRUCE PAGE

in collaboration with

ELAINE POTTER

SIMON &
SCHUSTER

London · New York · Sydney · Tokyo · Singapore · Toronto · Dublin

A VIACOM COMPANY

First published in Great Britain by Simon & Schuster UK Ltd in 2003
A Viacom Company

Copyright © 2003 by Bruce Page

This book is copyright under the Berne Convention.
No reproduction without permission.
All rights reserved.

The right of Bruce Page to be identified as author of this work has
been asserted in accordance with sections 77 and 78 of the
Copyright, Designs and Patents Act, 1988.

1 3 5 7 9 10 8 6 4 2

Simon & Schuster UK Ltd
Africa House
64–78 Kingsway
London WC2B 6AH

Simon & Schuster Australia
Sydney

www.simonsays.co.uk

A CIP catalogue record for this book
is available from the British Library

Hardback: ISBN 0 7432 3936 9
Trade Paperback: ISBN 0 7432 3937 7

Typeset by M Rules
Printed and bound in Great Britain by
The Bath Press, Bath

For Anne

Nor houres, dayes, months, which are but rags of time

CONTENTS

ACKNOWLEDGEMENTS

I must begin with an explanation of the title page, which states my own responsibility for this book while trying to acknowledge the debt it owes to Elaine Potter, long-standing journalistic ally. We intended a joint project. There was no falling-out, but the essentials of the Murdoch political system – of the News Corporation method, now straddling the world – turn out to lie deep in the Australian media culture in which I grew up, and in distortions applied to Australia's myths of origin. Restating those myths in a form closer to their truth requires some personal experience of their force, and in attempting this the work gained a character of personal inquiry which persists in its overall structure.

Elaine, with great generosity, continued nonetheless to lend her support, assistance and counsel – sorting out, indispensably, many aspects of the narrative. She is the entirely outstanding instance among many people who aided this project without gain to themselves, out of belief that News Corporation's impact on the democratic process is not sufficiently understood. (Elaine was present – one of those who resisted – when Murdoch took control of the *Sunday Times*, and she saw firsthand the subjection of a formerly independent newspaper.) Though the errors of the final product are mine its completion – thus any virtues it does contain – would have been impossible without her contribution.

I have exploited others also. I took many hours of Godfrey Hodgson's time resolving issues which arise in the boundary-layer where politics and news-media interact. John Menadue provided unique evidence about the institutional growth and present political influence of Newscorp. Jonathan Mirsky gave me access not only to his own deep knowledge of China, but also that of many other reporters and scholars. Jonathan

ACKNOWLEDGEMENTS

Kaplan, author of *The Natural History of Zero*, patiently steered me away from many errors in mathematical principle. Nor is this all.

Some guides cannot be thanked personally. The late George Munster's name comes quickly to mind: one aim of this book is to build on *Rupert Murdoch: A Paper Prince* which he wrote in the 1980s. Adrian Deamer, who expounded his family's experience of the Murdochs to me frankly but with remarkable dispassion, died in 2000. (I owe to him also most of my initial journalistic tradecraft.) I had hoped to learn greater detail about the period when that remarkable political reporter Tony Bevins demolished the Thatcher government's one-time media hegemony, but his dreadfully premature death prevented it. (As some compensation, an unpublished Bevins MS is listed in the bibliography.) Work on the book also gave me debts that can't now be repaid to Malcolm Crawford, John Grigg, Richard Hall and Eric Jacobs.

The scope of the Murdoch's Newscorp and the media industry it seeks to dominate is beyond any one writer's reach: this accounts for an extensive bibliography. But along with Paper Prince there must be particular mention of Thomas Kiernan's *Citizen Murdoch* (1986), Jerome Tuccille's *Rupert Murdoch* (1989) and *Stick It Up Your Punter* (1999) by Peter Chippindale and Chris Horrie. Everyone who studies the Murdoch phenomenon is in debt to William Shawcross's biography (*Murdoch*, 1992): true in my case in spite of reaching very different conclusions.

I have wherever possible used public record and open sources. But when Newscorp employees discuss their employer, or their employer's relationships with politicians, the concept of open discussion becomes shadowy. Very much the same applies to politicians where the subject is their government's relations with Newscorp. (Not that they are silent. Many hours can be spent in denials of the visible: in the examination of square wheels and round bricks.) As Paul Farhi of the *Washington Post* wrote when investigating Newscorp's tax affairs, Newscorp diffuses 'a very real fear' through its own organisation and a good many others. There are to be sure insiders who will help – some a little bolder than others – but the only appropriate course is general anonymity.

The names which follow are of people who were able openly to provide information. I must not suggest they agree with all or any of my conclusions: some, indeed, will powerfully disagree. That does not lessen my sense of obligation. Many properly possess titles like Lord or Professor: not to say both; not to say Senator, former Senator, and in many cases editor. But the handling of titles as between America, Australia and Britain gives enough trouble in the main text and here I have imposed an alphabetic equality which I hope does not appear to cancel gratitude.

Michael Adler, Jonathan Aitken, David C. Anderson, Johnny Apple, Murray Armstrong, Neal Ascherson, Paddy Ashdown, Lionel Barber, Steven Barnett, John Barry, Patrick Barwise, Don Berry, John Biffen, Chris Blackhurst, David Blake, Roger Bolton, Georgina Born, Peter Bottomley, David Bowman, Tom Bower, Pauline Boyle, Ben Bradlee, Patrick Brogan, Adam Brookes, Tina Brown, Gordon Brunton, Ian Buruma, David Butler, John Button, Neil Chenoweth, Lewis Chester, Pilata Clark, Tony Clifton, Ian Clubb, Kenneth Clucas, Alexander Cockburn, Richard Cockett, David Conn, Barry Cox, Alie Cromie, Don Cruickshank, John D'Arcy, Richard Davy, Tana de Zulueta, Gwen Deamer, Brenda Dean, Tony Delano, Meghnad Desai, Chris Dunkley, Paul Eddy, Andrew Ehrenburg, David Elstein, Gareth Evans, Harold Evans, James Evans, Richard J. Evans, Paul Farhi, Stephen Fay, Adam Finn, John Fitzgerald, Barry Fitzpatrick, Laurie Flynn, Michael Foot, Denis Foreman, Christopher Foster, Roger Gale, Don Garden, Richard Gentle, Nicholas George, Tony Geraghty, Peter Gillman, Ian Gilmour, Stephen Glaister, David Glencross, Geoffrey Goodman, Harry Gordon, Andrew Graham, Anthony Grayling, Roy Greenslade, Bill Hagerty, Ron Hall, Fred Halliday, Adrian Hamilton, Max Hastings, Peter Hennessy, Harry Henry, Michael Heseltine, Isabel Hilton, Christopher Hird, Matt Hoffman, Robert Hogg, Thomas Hogg, Anthony Holden, Brendan Hopkins, Mark Hosenball, Geoffrey Howe, Colin Hughes, Ken Inglis, Philip Jacobson, Oliver James, Peter Jay, Robert Jones, Andrew Joscelynne, John Kay, Peter Kellner, Phillip Knightley, Leszek Kolakowski, Daniel Korn, David C. Krajicek, Peter Lassman, John Lawrenson, James Lawton, Tim Laxman, Michael Leapman, David Learmount, David Leigh, Lawrence Lessig, David Lister, John Maddox, Margaret Maden, Tom Margerison, David Marr, Arthur Marriott, Andrew McKay, Tom McNally, Linda Melvern, Anthony Miles, Alex Mitchell, Mike Molloy, Edward Mortimer, Chris Mullin, Robin Munro, John Naughton, Pippa

ACKNOWLEDGEMENTS

Norris, David Nyhan, Sally Oppenheim, David Page, Alf Parrish, Chris Patten, John Allen Paulos, Julian Petley, Greg Philo, Henry Porter, Stuart Prebble, Peter Pringle, James Prior, Colin Pritchard, Alan Ramsey, Charles Raw, Moira Rayner, Nan Rivett, Geoffrey Robertson, Andrew Round, Suzanne Sadedin, Anthony Sampson, Michael Schudson, Andrew Schwartzman, Phil Scraton, Steven Shapin, William Shawcross, Chris Smith, Mike Smith, Hugh Stephenson, Sue Stoessl, William F. Stone, Stefan Szymanski, Suzana Taverne, D. M. Thomas, Claire Tomalin, Carol Tongue, Brian Toohey, Polly Toynbee, Donald Trelford, Jeremy Tunstall, Tunku Varadarajan, Steven Vines, Eric Walsh, Rosie Waterhouse, Gerry Weiss, Francis Wheen, Judith White, Phillip Whitehead, Andreas Whittam Smith, Robert M. Worcester, Gavin Yamey, Brian Young, Hugo Young, Gary Younge.

My agent, Michael Sissons is in a quite real sense the true originator of this book. As agent to Chris Patten, the former Governor of Hong Kong, he dealt with Murdoch's outrageous decision to remove Patten's book *East and West* from the HarperCollins list – by way of currying favour with the Beijing Communist regime. Michael was the tactician in the subsequent battle, which led to a humiliating defeat for Murdoch: demonstrating that Newscorp, for all its global reach, is not by any means invincible. He then steered this project through many vicissitudes, and to the extent it succeeds in explaining the Murdoch phenomenon, much of the credit it due to him.

Andrew Gordon and Martin Bryant at Simon and Schuster have been patient and supportive in dealing with quite unreasonable burdens, and David Hooper has provided sagacious legal advice throughout.

I am sure I am not being original in saying that Peter James is close to the ideal in text editors: combining most remarkably a gift for encouragement with a relentless eye for gaps in an argument.

The book is dedicated to my wife. Anne Page. It is in no sense an adequate return for her gifts to me, but it is something which would not exist without her strength and resolution.

INTRODUCTION

DYNASTS IN CYBERSPACE

FRYAR: Thou hast committed—
BARABAS: Fornication? But that was in another Country:
And besides, the Wench is dead.

CHRISTOPHER MARLOWE, *The Jew of Malta*

Rupert Murdoch denies quite flatly that he seeks or deals in political favours. 'Give me an example!' he cried in 1999 when William Shawcross interviewed him for *Vanity Fair*. 'When have we ever asked for anything?' Shawcross didn't take up the challenge. Rather, he endorsed Murdoch's denial, by saying that Rupert had never lied to him. Shawcross was far too tolerant, both in the interview and in his weighty biography of Murdoch.

This book will present sufficient examples to suggest that Murdoch is a poor witness on the character and history of the enterprise he controls. Not only has Murdoch sought and received political favours: most of the critical steps in the transformation of News Limited, the business he inherited, into present-day Newscorp were dependent on such things. Nor is there any essential change in his operations as the new century gets under way, and he prepares his sons to extend the dynasty's power on a new global scale.

It is a pity to criticise Shawcross along with Murdoch. But it is an important measure of Murdoch's manipulative capacity that he has more than once been able to persuade skilful, well-respected writers to

1

accommodate insolent misrepresentations which are convenient to his purpose.

Not long after *Vanity Fair* published, I talked to the official head of a major Whitehall department about the outcome of the British government's inquiry into the development of digital television. A detailed study had been commissioned from a committee headed by Gavyn Davies, chief economist of Goldman Sachs and – by virtue of his close personal links to both the Prime Minister and the Chancellor of the Exchequer – a greater figure in the land than any simple director of an investment bank with worldwide reach. The Davies Committee made recommendations which were firmly argued, backed up by sophisticated research – and highly displeasing to Rupert Murdoch and a number of his allies. The recommendations were then substantially ignored. Did that make sense? I asked the mandarin. Not at all, he said. But the requirements of 10 Downing Street were perfectly clear. Nothing was to be done which might upset Rupert Murdoch and his friends.

This veteran of the corridors of power was not lying or fantasising – and certainly not expressing surprise. His working assumption was that Tony Blair's government would strive to avoid any action likely to discommode Rupert Murdoch, and that only a naif would imagine otherwise. The one respect in which the '*Vanity Fair* position' corresponds with reality is that in Canberra, in some recent instances, the fear of Newscorp has been such that the company has been awarded favours without the bother of asking for them. Sumner Redstone of Viacom is reckoned one of the most influential corporate bosses in present-day America, and he does not deny it. But he has said that neither he nor anyone else he knows can bend governments to his will as Murdoch can.

Power is abused when the apparent rules of society become a cover for other arrangements, or when things every insider knows to be true can be coolly denied in public. The lines from Christopher Marlowe quoted in the epigraph focus attention on two important aspects of Murdoch's manipulative technique which determine the character of this story. First, most of the misdeeds involved are diluted across three political cultures – widely separated by their geography and their institutions, in spite of their common language. And there are important cases where altogether different cultures and histories are concerned.

2

Australians and Americans know little about the Westland scandal of 1986 which nearly demolished Margaret Thatcher's government; in Britain and America nothing is known of the 'constitutional coup' which displaced the Australian Prime Minister, Gough Whitlam, in 1975. Murdoch was a leading actor in both processes. *The Times* of London is perhaps the world's best-known newspaper, but in America not much is known about Murdoch's seizure of Times Newspapers in 1981 – or about the politics which helped Sky television become in the 1990s one of the world's most lucrative businesses. Similarly, Australians are un-familiar with the structure of American media law – still more so with the methods used to circumvent it, in order to establish the Fox network and defuse the subsequent regulatory challenges. Fox itself would not be in Murdoch's hands but for his critical services to Margaret Thatcher's administration – scarcely understood in Britain, let alone elsewhere.

Second, Murdoch is deft in forgetfulness, and in the separation of the past from its present-day meaning. In a properly observant world, his past destruction of editors would provide the yardstick against which the sup-posed independence of his contemporary editors would be measured. Murdoch, however, like Barabas, has noticed the powerful synergy between time and space – whatever happens to the universal effect of globalisation, as soon as we really need it?

But the main purpose here is to go beyond proving that Rupert Murdoch – like his father Sir Keith Murdoch before him – has dealt in political favours. Rather it is to analyse the qualities of personality which made father and son such formidable exponents of this trade. Intrigue is of course nothing new to democratic politics. But their use of news media, newspapers particularly, has no real parallel. By searching out comparisons between what happened to Gough Whitlam's government in 1975 and Margaret Thatcher's in 1986, we can begin to put Rupert Murdoch's role in its proper light – the one story illuminates the other. When they are placed within the continuum of Keith's and Rupert's activities – and put together with, say, the thoughts of Rupert's son James on human rights in China – we can see the development of a method which democracies would be foolish to ignore, even if journalists often accept it with cynicism, innocence or a gruesome compound of the two.

Such comparisons, though, are technically complex. For example, much of this analysis depends on comparisons between two countries ruled by 'responsible government' (Australia, Britain) in which an administration falls when it loses control of the lower legislative house. Leaving aside the fact that one of these countries has a unitary constitution and the other is federal, there is the fact that in America's federation 'responsible government' is absent. Broadly, the doctrine of the separation of powers is there to perform a similar role: preventing the decay of authority into autocracy and oppression. We have therefore to rely on the proposition that societies often achieve similar aims by dissimilar means. Both America and Britain, for example, place high value on the political neutrality of the army, and its acceptance of civilian rule. Yet there are radical differences in method. Personal nomination by a Congressman is the formal requirement for entrants to West Point – whereas, aside from some circumstance of parenthood, it would be unwise for a British applicant to Sandhurst to confess any sort of acquaintance with a politician. Still, the outcome of these processes is essentially similar.

Translations can be made with a little patience, even if the differences of constitutional language are more than might be supposed. The 'First Amendment principles' to which this book refers quite frequently derive obviously enough from the Bill of Rights which was added to the Constitution of the United States in 1791: 'Congress shall make no law respecting an establishment of religion, or protecting the free exercise thereof; or abridging the freedom of speech, or of the press; or the right of the people peaceably to assemble, and to petition the Government for a redress of grievances.' Of course these words were written by Americans in an American situation, but our working assumption is that they were written for and have validity in the world everywhere, and that the principles in the First Amendment generally inform the laws and customs of the other two countries chiefly concerned with this story, and where they don't they should. Clearly the same idea is to be found in the British statute which declares that an essential social need is 'the accurate presentation of news and free expression of opinion'. And there is an assumption that duties and obligations go with these liberties – that there is a bargain involved. Freedom is given on the principle that newspapers and broadcasters will exercise it, rather than enter into profitable alliances with the powerful – particularly the powerful in government.

Not that this is a uniquely Anglophone belief. It's important for later stages of the Newscorp story, in Asia particularly, to remember that the First Amendment was not introduced as a luxury for the nation that had everything. At that time the United States did not have very much, and what it had was at risk from an angry monarchy resentful of its liberties. That the monarchy in question was one within which American liberties had been often been born – and within which there existed freedom from slavery, which had yet to reach America – only shows that the dialectic of freedom was complex in the eighteenth century, just as it is complex today.

Liberal critics have long been accused of demonising media bosses, from which follows an argument that the Murdochs are of much the same ilk and shouldn't be demonised either. It is certainly the case that William Randolph Hearst, Lord Northcliffe, Lord Beaverbrook and others sought power and wielded some influence. But historians either doubt that their power was specific and instrumental or consider that, if it was, it was derived from the public roles which they attained. (All three of those named had something of the conventional politician about them, both Hearst and Beaverbrook actually by election.) Stanley Baldwin said in the 1930s that the harlot press lords sought 'power without responsibility', but he did not admit that they possessed it. And we shall see that at the time they did not. Rupert Murdoch is a different phenomenon, operating in special conditions. And he has changed real political outcomes by covert and strictly irresponsible manipulation. So, far from arguing that he resembles the old demons, we suggest he is something different and more dangerous.

Ideological mists must not be allowed to intrude. Murdoch's homely affection for the political right is not something he would indulge at the expense of his notion of corporate good practice. What matters to his organisation is a corporatist sense of partnership with holders or likely holders of political power. How they package themselves ideologically is largely their own affair.

There is nothing corrupt about news media taking a hand in the rise or fall of political power. The *Washington Post* in 1974 and the *Guardian* in the late 1990s contributed to the demise of particular American and British administrations; the Melbourne *Herald* did the same in the

Australian context in 1975. But in doing this they simply fulfilled their First Amendment task. So, at the time of the Army/McCarthy hearings in the 1950s, did the US television networks, and so did E. D. Morel and Henry Nevinson when they exposed King Leopold of Belgium's truly evil Congo empire and showed that slave-trading did not cease with the onset of the twentieth century (it has not, as a matter of fact, ceased yet). And Nelson Mandela's rise to democratic authority in South Africa owed something to the news media of the free world, as did the fall of the Soviet tyranny.

This in itself does no more than follow what *The Times* under Delane said in 1851: that the press lives by disclosure. But disclosure confers scarcely any instrumental power – it consists essentially of surrendering control, of giving something away. Rarely if ever can it secure benefits directly for an editorial group, whatever it may do in the longer term for honour and commercial prosperity. Short-term, it usually imposes danger and costs (ones likely to persist).

Newscorp is effective politically without having any battle-honours of the sort listed above. And it is effective *because* it has none. Murdoch in 1986 brought to Thatcher's rescue a reversed action of Delane's famous principle. There was a cover-up, of which he was aware, and which he did not disclose – because he was one of its instigators, and its disclosure would have endangered his business. Whitlam was brought down by a scheme which succeeded – but which was illegitimate, because it was mounted in secret. Murdoch was aware of what was happening, and did nothing to break the secret, because the outcome was desirable to him.

It may seem paradoxical that a media business should be feared – by politicians above all others – when it seriously lacks competence in the basic operations which justify the media's legal privileges and existence. But this is because its relationship with power is symbiotic and collaborative – contributing nothing to the dialectic of challenge and compensating response. And in many cases politicians find that such collaboration sits neatly enough with certain kinds of fear. This relationship may be considered the greatest danger modern society faces; if not checked, it fatally injures the capacity to deal with all other threats, rather as AIDS destroys our resistance to enemies we might otherwise repulse.

INTRODUCTION

Complaints about media systems often centre on instances of false assertion – something which certainly occurs, and has done from time to time under Murdoch. (There are the grotesque examples where the *Australian* claimed that the federal treasurer was under the influence of a 'Japanese agent', and the *Sunday Times* alleged that the Leader of the Opposition at Westminster was a KGB agent.) But it is not usually important.

Silence is what counts. When C. P. Scott said that every newspaper was something of a monopoly (at a time of media ownership more diverse than ours), and that comment was free but facts are sacred, he insisted that abuse of monopoly was as much a negative as a positive action: 'Neither in what it gives, *nor in what it does not give* . . . must the unclouded face of truth suffer wrong.' Or in Rupert Murdoch's own words: 'The basic premise of the democracy we live in must be the citizen's right to know, and if we do not publish what we know, if we know the facts that are in the public interest and are of importance and do not publish them, then we do not deserve our freedom.' So much for theory. Murdoch's lack of practical interest in disclosure is neither accidental nor episodic. It is part of the Newscorp business model, and when the Fox network suppresses *Strange Justice* (a tale of sexual embarrassment it might normally revel in, but which happened to touch the Supreme Court bench) or eases out reporters who look into Monsanto's impact on the environment, this relates to *The Times* in London diluting the truth about Murdoch's friends in Beijing.

We are looking into the corruption, over some 130 years, of media systems based in high technology – which have rightly been thought the brightest hope for enlightenment, liberty and entertainment. The harm done is not irreversible, but it is certainly serious. The Murdoch dynasty isn't solely responsible for the process, but it provides the exemplary case. And as the new century begins with new waves of technical change, the Murdochs are anxious to establish themselves as a cyberspace power – with expanded reach, but morals and techniques unchanged since Rupert's father was a propagandist during the world war of 1914–18, those critical years which one commentator described as 'the golden age of lying'.

The phenomenon they represent can't be understood in isolation, just as disease can't be understood without knowledge of the healthy body. The story therefore begins in the ideas that people like Jefferson, Delane and Camus had about the value and necessity of free media: illustrated in the record of newspapers like the *Washington Post*, the *New York Times*, the *Sydney Morning Herald* and – before Rupert engulfed them – *The Times* and *Sunday Times* in London and the *Herald* in Melbourne; and in the record of television networks like CBS and the BBC (if their truth-telling appetite is less than it used to be, that is part of the story). Their independence of government, Jefferson believed, was more important than government itself – even if he did find, when in office himself, that it was a difficult principle to live by.

Newspapers, television, the Internet and the Web are closely related descendants of the seventeenth century's array of discoveries in science, politics and technology. The link between today's discussions of electromagnetic bandwidth and Victorian advances in the economics of printing and communications is an obvious one. Subtler and still more important is the notion of truth as having a social value created by particular rules and manners: sometimes one must look outside the media histories, to works like Steven Shapin's *Social History of Truth*.

Web press and electric telegraph ended direct subsidy of newspapers and made commercially practical the independence that Jefferson desired. But in the mid-twentieth century great gains were eroded by great political mistakes: broadcast media were necessarily licensed, and governments used (still use) this to truck, barter and exchange with media bosses. Of this practice Murdoch is the supreme exponent. Erosion of analogue-era regulation leads smoothly into the claim – phoney as a matter of both law and technology, but preached busily by Rupert and the scions Lachlan and James – that digital regulation is both undesirable and *impossible*. In Jefferson's time it was assumed that press freedom would disinfect itself. By the mid-twentieth century there was ample reason for the British lawyer Hartley (Lord) Shawcross (less suggestible than his son) to warn that in the practical circumstances of industrial society freedom of expression needs strong defences against monopoly.

Our narrative confirms his warning. The gap through which Murdoch reached to seize the world's first independent newspaper (*The Times*) was exactly the one Lord Shawcross wanted the law to close. Today the Stanford University cyberspace lawyer Lawrence Lessig argues that the pseudo-libertarianism peddled by Murdoch and his friends masks a lust to regulate and control – for Newscorp's profit. Nobody, he says, can be neutral over the organisation of the Net and its related systems, any more 'than Americans could stand neutral on the question of slavery in 1861'. The liberties involved are not simply American: when we find Newscorp's greed and naivety combining with the despotism of Beijing, the story becomes one of worldwide danger.

The First Amendment provides the classic statement of the liberties which every democracy considers fundamental – and which are everywhere known to carry duties. Newscorp offers a no less classic case where those duties have been scoffed at and compromised for the sake of leverages enabling it to write its own rules on accounting, tax breaks, corporate governance and social responsibility. Professor Lessig will say that all the media giants offering urgently to escort humankind into the digital future should be regarded at least with caution. In the case of the Murdochs, the record suggests the offer should be rejected altogether.

Obviously 'the media' is a term covering many technologies and disciplines. It can be clumsy to make specific and inclusive definitions over and again, so when we refer to 'journalism' we generally assume it may be found in newspapers or magazines, in radio, television, books and websites. Similarly 'freedom of the press' does not necessarily refer only to printing machinery. When Rupert's father wanted to become the grand censor of Australia in 1940, he sought power not over newspapers alone. He added magazines, radio and theatres; television was omitted only because it had not yet reached that country. Both sides of the censorship argument appreciate that the means to free expression don't exist independently of each other.

'Editorial independence' is another term used frequently in this narrative. Journalists sometimes make it sound like an excuse for doing whatever they fancy and looking down on their commercial colleagues. It has been best put by Andreas Whittam Smith who founded a newspaper called the *Independent* and saw its finances ruined by Newscorp's lumbering progress. The notion of independence:

doesn't mean an absence of strong opinions, or the perfect balance of arguments for and against this or that. It doesn't mean a particular system of ownership. It is simply a promise to readers. That everything you find in the newspaper represents the editorial team's own agenda and nobody else's; neither the advertising department's, nor the owner's, nor any particular political party's, nor any business interests.

It is in fact a strenuous doctrine. As the Murdoch story shows, it is easier and often more rewarding to forget what the readers were promised, and let the highest bidder set the agenda.

How serious is the matter of freedom and independence of the press? One of the little problems of interpreting Newscorp is that it takes itself very seriously – until it finds itself in a tight corner. Then it typically asks everyone to lighten up, and to remember that we're only in the entertainment business. In reality, the condition of the news and entertainment media is a matter of life and death – something which becomes sharply apparent whenever the state uses deadly force against its own people.

This is something that happens only exceptionally in free societies. But a vital part of our argument says that to live by disclosure means dealing in the exceptional. Media organisations cannot demonstrate their value by routine activities, and establishing a scale for the exceptional requires examination of events as far separated in place and time as Bloody Sunday and Tiananmen Square.

1

A CONTINENT OF NEWSPAPERS, 1700–1960

> News as an element of interest in the Press has so far transcended all others since the construction of the telegraph that the force of a newspaper is now largely concentrated in that department.
>
> JOHN BIGELOW in his first editorial for the
> *New York Times*, 3 August 1869

> Yes, we do perceive her as sprawling and informal;
> even dishevelled, disorderly. That may be because
> we are still of two minds about militarism and class-systems . . .
>
> We darken her sky with our cities.
> She is artist enough to manage a graceful asymmetry;
> but we are more apt to turn crooks.
>
> JUDITH WRIGHT, 'The Eucalypt and the National Character'

Geoffrey Blainey, one of Australia's more provocative historians, once called it an improbable country – and this refers to more than the strangeness of the landscape and of its ancient creatures. Much of that, anyway, is disguised by suburbia; to Americans it can feel very like America, and to people from the British Isles very like the places in which they grew up. But, at second and third glance, variations emerge. There is, to begin with, no other place where the English and the Irish have formed the basis of society – together with a proportion of

Scots – and spent less of their natural energies in lacerating each another. And perhaps this unusual economy affected the national temperament. In England, stubborn determination is considered admirable. So also is flair, but a suspicion exists that they are incompatible. The most attractive characteristic of the Australian people is a notion that the two qualities go naturally together.

The Anglo-Celtic jealousies which trouble the British Isles remain visible in Australia, but their potency is reduced, and the nation's vitality suffers little from them. Enriched now with Asian and European components, it manages to be a strikingly cohesive society. Something of this can be put into American terms by recalling that in 1960 there was a soul-deadening debate about whether John Fitzgerald Kennedy – a Catholic – could properly become President of the United States. By 1960 Australia had long ago elected, not to say forgotten, several Catholic Prime Ministers, like 'Honest Joe' Lyons (whom we shall encounter in Keith Murdoch's company).

There are other complexities, which emerge from its unique status as a nation which is also a continent, and a remote one at that. Little more than two centuries ago, what existed here was a subtle, isolated civilisation which, with only neolithic technology available, had mastered a tricky, arid, often deadly environment – far the leanest of the habitable continents. This brilliant culture was so unfamiliar to the invading Europeans that they denied its existence. Having survived the decades during which they relied heavily on its aid, they told themselves they were colonising a vacant wilderness: *terra nullius*, in legal Latin. Even though the first advocate of this doctrine, Richard Windeyer, identified, piercingly, 'a whispering in . . . our hearts that tells us it is not so', *terra nullius* remained an assumption of Australian existence – until, with the last third of the twentieth century, the whispering became inescapably audible, with interesting effects on the trajectory of the Murdochs and those involved with them. Australian history is poignant because so much of it is about clear-sighted remedies for old injustices, and so much of it about blindness creating new, unnecessary ones.

Nineteenth-century visitors who accepted the simple wilderness doctrine were usually amazed at the rate of urban growth they saw. The *Port Phillip Herald* – ancestor of the paper which became Keith Murdoch's first command – started in January 1840, just after Melbourne's first buildings rose beside the turbid Yarra river. Some ten years later the city had a university, more newspapers, a spacious street-plan and principal buildings which were generally substantial and sometimes distinguished. Each of the six colonies which were to become the six states of federal Australia evolved as the hinterland of a dominant maritime city. New South Wales and Sydney started first, of course, but during the second half of the nineteenth century Victoria and Melbourne expanded considerably faster.

It was the newspaper publishing of Sydney, and still more of Melbourne – with an associated flood of books, magazines, poetry collections, pamphlets and printed ephemera of every sort – which most impressed that sophisticated Englishman Anthony Trollope in 1871. Trollope the novelist thought he had never seen a people devoted so furiously to written self-expression. He had previously examined – and mostly admired – America. Its newspapers, however, he thought slightly rustic. This was not the case in Melbourne and Sydney, where the journalism showed a metropolitan gloss which he liked. At roughly the same time, the British journalist Edward Dicey described 'the American' as 'a newspaper-reading animal'. The Australian, in Trollope's account, appears to have become, precociously, a newspaper-*writing* animal.

Trollope may be thought a reliable witness, for he noticed, in addition to the urge to publish, other durable national attributes, such as an addiction to competitive sport and a collective, hair-trigger resentment of alien criticism, however modestly offered. He records a country progress via several well-appointed homesteads, at one of which bugs invaded his belongings. Trollope thought he should mention this, but tried to avoid offence by suggesting that the insects might have joined him at an earlier staging-post. 'I don't think so,' was the unyielding response. 'You must have had them with you when you got there.'

Reasons for a headlong love-affair with what we now call the media are not too hard to find. Australia and New Zealand were the last-born infants of the West: technologies and notions of democracy which had been evolving with dramatic speed since the early seventeenth century often reached nineteenth-century Australia in full working order. Like the rabbit, they found few natural opponents. Also like the rabbit, they expanded without delay.

The newspaper is just such a case – until 1800 and later both its legal status and its content had been the subject of arduous experiment. In John Peter Zenger's famous case of 1735, American jurors had to consider whether seditious libel had been committed by publishing scandalous but admittedly truthful claims about the government of New York. Andrew Hamilton brought them out on what we today would call the right side. Even so, in 1773 a printer could be jailed for publishing the proceedings of the South Carolina legislature. No linear process in one country created the journalist's right to report the activity of government. As the historian Thomas Leonard observes, throughout the 1780s 'when Americans found a speech in their newspapers it was more likely to have been made in the Parliament of the kingdom they had rejected than in the assemblies of the new nation they had joined'.

Nor was this just a matter of law and politics, for issues of technique and style were also involved. Newspapers could be printed well before people knew what to put in them (just as it is easier now to generate a website than find a use for it). One of the first serious editors, John Campbell of Boston, conceived the immense idea of a newspaper as a record, but could not master the flow of events – by 1718 his arrears were such that he was publishing material twelve months old. Our casual trick of skipping to the most recent events was beyond him.

Australian colonists, rather more than a century later, felt no uncertainty about making a newspaper or asserting its rights. Great changes lay ahead of them, but they had arrived in possession of a pattern (one we can still recognise) and they wasted no time applying it. The *Port Phillip Herald*'s first issue promised 'the latest information of recent events', and inside two weeks it produced 'a long list of the wants and wishes of this community'. Should authority procrastinate over supplying them, said the paper grimly, 'we must . . . try what the power of the press can effect'. Attempts were made to import antibodies such as enabled existing privilege in Britain and America to delay universal literacy and universal suffrage – those notorious vectors of barbarism. Most came to grief: often amid ribaldry, like William Wentworth's attempt to create a hereditary nobility in New South Wales.

So – through an absence of inhibitions – the orthodoxies of present-day government first reached full growth as far as possible from where they germinated, and such a thing was surely improbable. When New South Wales, Queensland, South Australia, Tasmania, Victoria and Western Australia – separate self-governing colonies – became states of a federal Commonwealth in 1901, they were accustomed to manhood suffrage, complete (soon to be compulsory) registration, secret balloting and an assumption of electoral equality for women. Two years later, the first federal elections were contested under universal adult suffrage. Nothing so extreme had been in Lincoln's mind when he spoke of 'government by the people, for the people'. But it may be hard now to recall that 'democracy' ever meant anything less.

Did this breakneck expansion of citizenship produce barbarism? Not everyone, certainly, has admired the result. Another English novelist, D. H. Lawrence, turning up fifty years after Trollope, thought Australia the most democratic place he had seen, concluding that 'the more I see of democracy, the less I like it'. Within Australia itself there is a strain of conservative distrust for a supposedly reckless populace – curiously, because the country's political history, though quarrelsome in detail, has been remarkably stable overall – and this produces intermittent spasms of intense reaction, some of which become part of our story.

Considered commercially, democracy created an opulent market for newspaper and periodical publishing. Australia was arguably the first country in which the press was authentically popular – that is, formed part of the life everybody led. It was from early on a powerful and important industry, provincial only by virtue of its extraordinary geographic remoteness. Much of this was true also of New Zealand, but there is a distinction. Until quite recently New Zealand's population had a large rural component, but even before federation Australia was essentially urban.

Where the wealth serviced by Australia's harbour cities came from agrarian industry – and, with the mighty exception of gold, it mostly did – its operatives viewed the vast dry spaces as factories, and themselves as industrial workers. Wool production needed only a scattered workforce, and was hard to unionise. But unionised it was. The result of such processes was that in Australia even the minority living in rural circumstances shared urban attitudes, including a huge thirst for newspapers and magazines.

In 1883 Richard Twopeny produced his small classic of observation, *Town Life in Australia*. This life, he said, existed in what was 'essentially the land of newspapers. The colonist is by nature an inquisitive animal, who likes to know what is going on around him.' By this time the six colonies had some 600 newspapers. The major cities were rich enough to afford substantial railway networks and advanced lighting-systems, so that people found it easy to get papers, and comfortable to read them. Democratic politics – which often struck visitors used to a narrower franchise as raucous or worse – provided entertainment, and serious accounts of sporting events were staple material. Australia's first federal institution may have been its cricket team. When it took ship to the northern hemisphere in 1882 and crushed the horrified English, every detail was reported by the press back home, at a telegraph cost of about $300 a word in the country's present-day money.

And of course there was crime. Colonial society was not violent by most standards, but journalists made the best of the available action. It would be hard to outdo the assurance of the *Herald*'s two-column eyewitness account of the great bushranger Ned Kelly's execution in 1880, minutely detailing (in service to deterrence) the hangman's grim visage, the victim's last sardonic words ('Such is life') and the spasms of the dying body. But the Kellys were Irish, and the *Herald* – which believed itself popular with Irish readers – was careful also to record Ned's 'courage and address', his humane moments, and the 'surprise and amusement' he had caused by shutting two New South Wales cops in their own cells during the great Jerilderie bank raid. Demonstrations calling for his reprieve were scrupulously reported.

Twopeny wrote as an English gentleman rather than as a resident colonial and, while he approved the Australians' sporting enthusiasm, he thought their view of crime far too relaxed. How could members of the colonial legislature agitate for the reprieve of a criminal whose murders 'were not to be counted on the fingers'? – and do so just because the fellow 'had for over two years set the police at defiance'. But of course it was not only Kelly's criminal eminence that prompted the agitation. It was because the agitators too were Irish. And the point is that the

16

colonial power-structure, though dominated by people of Twopeny's background or similar, did not exclude the growing Irish middle class. It is not quite true to say that Kelly is remembered as a hero – for he was indeed a murderer – but he came to represent a belief that style and daring are admirable wherever they exist.

Twopeny wrote before the age of audited circulation figures, but he is convincing about the sheer popularity of the press (and he is supported by other witnesses): 'Nearly everybody can read, and nearly everybody has the leisure to do so. Again, the proportion of the population who can afford to purchase and subscribe to newspapers is ten times as large as in England; hence the number of sheets issued is comparatively much greater.' They produced, in many cases, great wealth for their owners – conspicuously for the Fairfaxes of the *Sydney Morning Herald*, with advertising revenues enviously described as 'rivers of gold'. (The gold flows still, but the Fairfaxes have dispossessed themselves by feud. Now Kerry Packer, Rupert Murdoch and other predators eye the abandoned inheritance.)

This was a press which was popular – and, in aggregate, prosperous – but Twopeny agreed with Trollope that it was mostly serious and reliable. There was strong competition between the numerous titles, but he did not think:

> the quality inferior to the quantity. On the contrary, if there is one institution of which Australians have reason to be proud, it is their newspaper press.
>
> Almost without exception it is thoroughly respectable and well conducted . . . Reports are fairly given; telegrams are rarely invented; sensation is not sought after . . . Neither directly not indirectly does anyone ever think of attempting to bribe either conductors of journals or their reporters; the whole press is before everything honest.

Twopeny contradicts himself a little in one or two instances – notably in what he has to say about the *Age*, the Melbourne paper on which Keith Murdoch began his career a generation later. And he wrote before the rise of John Norton's scabrous *Truth* chain – eventually bought by Rupert

Murdoch – which Cyril Pearl chronicled in *Wild Men of Sydney*. But it can fairly be said that Australian newspapers of the later nineteenth century show that the version of media history in which ordinary working people ignored newspapers until Northcliffe sought to reinvent them as juvenilia (saying that his readers were 'only ten') is misleadingly crude.

In 1889, seven years before Northcliffe launched the *Daily Mail* in London, the *Herald* in Melbourne decided that the standard format of the nineteenth-century newspaper was obsolete. This had long been a single sheet folded into eight broadsheet pages, with advertising on the 'outside' surfaces. The *Herald* developed a 'front page', with illustrations and headlines designed to seize the reader's attention without delay (the *Mail* did not get around to the same idea till it was aged rather more than ten).

Although the paper was editorially adventurous – excessively so, for some respectable folk – its first half-century was not a competitive success, and it was often near to closure. The man who made it the city's chief publishing business, taking the lead away from the *Argus*, eclipsing David Syme's *Age* – and becoming, to his great subsequent discomfiture, Keith Murdoch's first major patron – was Theodore Fink, who was born in Guernsey to German-Jewish parents and arrived in Victoria as a child in 1861. Fink's character displays the contradictions of urban Australia in classic form. He was, at the financial level, a fairly ruthless crook. But he was also a patriotic liberal, a man of literary sensibility and a serious advocate of social and educational reform.

He was subtle enough to see that journalists could not follow pharmacists, electrical engineers and other practitioners in the new skills of industrial society into becoming exclusive professions, like the law. A free society may limit the right to concoct medicines but not the right to concoct words, even if (as Kipling says), they are 'the most powerful drug used by mankind'. But Fink also saw that the communications industry – not his name for it – was developing professional requirements which the traditions of Grub Street and the procedure of a hiring-fair could not satisfy. He became one of the first newspaper managers to admit that his employees needed systematic training.

Fink opened a law practice in 1877, specialising in insolvency and electoral disputes – lucrative work in a state with a gold-driven economy and an expanding political franchise. During the ten-year land boom which got under way in 1880 he became an energetic speculator himself, and spent some of his profits on buying an interest in the *Herald*. He was certainly a smart, or over-smart, practitioner of law. But politics and literature fascinated him much more – he might have started out in newspapers had not his newly respectable family noticed that most journalists then lived precariously on payments-by-the-line and consoled themselves with whisky. At eighteen Theodore addressed a remarkable four-part lecture on newspapers to the members of the Jewish Philosophical Society of Melbourne, who may have learnt more than they cared to about printing machinery and New York advertising practice. Clearly, he understood the technical advances being made in American papers, though this was in 1873, ten years before Pulitzer's acquisition of the New York *World*. As a law student he produced reviews, verses and scraps of social news; and as a prosperous practitioner he found time to write for the *Age* (a weekly gossip column called 'Under the Verandah').

Then, during the panic which shook the financial world in the early 1890s, Theodore went bust twice inside twelve months. The detonator – the first Barings collapse – was in London, but the ferocity of Melbourne's local effect came from the rupture of a property-market bubble swollen over a decade or more. Its inflation owed much to absurd 'improvements' attached to savings legislation when it was imported from Britain: they allowed money subscribed in mutual societies for house-building to be diverted easily into generalised, often fraudulent speculation.

Fink escaped multiple bankruptcy by ruthless use of 'secret composition', an astounding feature of business law in Victorian Victoria, under which any group of creditors (often unrepresentative) could agree to clear all the liabilities of an insolvent (usually one with whom they were engaged in other business activities). The vote was by simple majority, taking no account of the volume of debt a voter might represent. Nothing then appeared in public records – and, though there was some contemporary gossip, the secret compositions made by Fink and various allies of his lay hidden until revealed by the work of present-day historians, chiefly Michael Cannon. A decent insolvency law, of course, is based on the equality of creditors. Really, this was just fraudulent preference legitimised.

Many details of Fink's manoeuvres remain obscure even in Professor Don Garden's most recent research on the Fink family. But there is no doubt that Theodore managed, most improperly, to insulate his *Herald* shareholdings from his creditors, and make them part of a new portfolio. In the aftermath of the busted boom there were more than sixty 'secret compositions', and many of the families involved – like the Baillieus – were counted then and later as pillars of the local business aristocracy. Nobody ever doubted that Sydney, the old penitentiary, was hazy on ethics. But, until modern research uncovered Melbourne's past, people liked to suppose things were otherwise in a city where the pioneers were businessmen rather than convicts.

In 1897 Victoria's financial regulations were modestly reformed, and secret composition was never again used with such bravura. Over the years, though, other and equally dubious means have been found to help powerful businessmen stave off the impact of their own recklessness. And a persistent component in the story of Australian media industries is the haphazard character of the country's financial regulation, a contradictory feature in a society where order and method are often valued highly. (The pinpoint organisation of the Sydney Olympics in 2000 surprised many people, but not those familiar with the country.)

Twopeny, writing just before the land boom broke, made it clear that the editorial honesty of the press existed alongside – or in spite of – a cavalier attitude to financial morals. Victoria, which was protectionist, he judged especially deplorable: 'In Melbourne the heavy protectionist tariff has brought about an almost universal practice of presenting the customs with false invoices so skilfully concocted as to make detection impossible. Within my knowledge this practice has been resorted to by firms of the highest standing.' The speculative nature of all business and the consequent frequency of insolvencies, he added, meant a generally relaxed attitude to business regulation: 'Even when there has been swindling, it is soon forgiven and forgotten . . . The fact is, that so much sharp practice goes on, that the discovered swindler is rarely a sinner above his neighbours; he has simply had the bad luck to be found out.'

Parallels have been drawn by Australian historians between the land-boomers of the 1880s and the eyeballs-out entrepreneurs who ranged the land in the 1980s, such as Alan Bond, Laurie Connell and Christopher Skase. Rupert Murdoch, who shared many of their follies, has survived – if sometimes narrowly – where they failed, because he has had superior access to overseas capital, and because he has been remarkably successful in restricting American understanding of his empire's actual characteristics. In March 1999 the *Economist* wrote that accounting standards in Australia, 'among the most lax of the developed economies', prevented Newscorp's financial performance – particularly its actual profitability and its extraordinary freedom from tax – being compared realistically with those of major international competitors such as Disney Corporation. If Australia happened to be a torpid backwater its deficiencies in corporate legislation and accounting discipline would not matter beyond its own frontier. But it is a society of much talent and energy which makes far more impact on the world than its remote location and modest population would suggest.

Professor Walter Murdoch – Rupert's great-uncle, and a cultural critic of some standing – once suggested that nations were like children buying sweets with limited pocket-money. Unable to indulge all tastes, each child indulges in the confection he or she fancies most. He argued that cultures, like individuals, can't have everything desirable: England, for instance, has no Olympian composer because the English binged on poetry. One might follow the professor and say that Australians have excelled in literature, sport, art and war – even politics, for this is a highly stable democracy. Financial regulation, however, seems rarely to have caught their interest.

In 1892 Fink was crossing the Atlantic, home-bound westward. Onboard ship, an American politician gave a bumptious after-dinner speech about the general superiority of his nation's institutions. Theodore offered his fellow passengers a witty rejoinder saying – he showed much familiarity with the America of the Gilded Age – it would be difficult indeed to rival America's rogues and speculators. The applause was generous. But Theodore just then was going home to repair his own estate via devices at which Jay Gould and his Wall Street comrades might well have drawn the line.

Fink was a man whose gifts were manifold, but whose self-awareness could be absurdly inadequate. This may be no more than to say he was a representative Australian of his day, a member of a society constructed on the the latest blueprints, but in a location so distant as to make realistic comparison between it and other models an unfamiliar exercise. In Theodore Fink there was a permanent tension between personal opportunism and social idealism. Keith Murdoch, one generation younger, was a rather simpler phenomenon.

Keith Arthur Murdoch, the second son of seven children, was born in 1885, when his father Patrick was minister of the Presbyterian church standing at William and Lonsdale Streets, on the north edge of downtown Melbourne. Patrick was thirty-five, and had been 'called' to Australia from his first appointment at Cruden on Scotland's North Sea coast. Two years later, he moved to Trinity Church in Camberwell, an eastern suburb several social rungs above its London prototype. There he preached for four decades, with a spell as Moderator of the Victorian Assembly of the Presbyterian Church, and then of its Australian Assembly. An important member of Trinity's congregation was David Syme, proprietor of the *Age*.

The Scots in Melbourne were fewer than the English and the Irish, but among influential folk – especially conservative ones – they were significant. The two larger communities contained many working-class families, recruited from the urban poor of the south-east of England and of Ireland. But Scottish migrants were often educated professionals, like Patrick Murdoch, an Edinburgh graduate, and his much younger brother Walter, who arrived with him and graduated from Melbourne. Walter, a literary scholar with an uncomplicated style, became the more eminent, and a university now bears his name.

Australia's conservative elite would have been a feeble thing without the Melbourne Scots – Sir Robert Menzies, its most effective leader, saw them as his personal tribe – and Patrick Murdoch had all of their characteristic connections and attitudes. Though he urged economic self-discipline in the manual classes, he was not the dour type of preacher. As a clubbable man himself, he was probably surprised to find that Keith was painfully shy, with a stammer which could render him incoherent. Keith did not want to follow Walter to the university, and told his parents that he had a 'calling' for journalism. They were disconcerted: though Patrick believed sturdily in a free press, the Murdochs probably cared no more than the Finks for its rank-and-file membership, and no sensible parent would advise a shy youth to become a reporter.

But David Syme was a friend, and in 1903 Patrick asked his help. The old Protectionist offered the minister's son a trial as a suburban correspondent in Malvern, adjacent to Camberwell. On Sir Keith Murdoch's own account some forty years later, it was not an enlightening professional start. The *Age* today is the urbane journal of the Melbourne middle class, kin to the *Guardian* or the *Washington Post*. It was very different when Keith began his career, and still exhibited many of the dubious qualities Twopeny had seen: 'The *Age* is a penny 4pp sheet selling 50,000 daily . . . Its inventive ability, in which it altogether surpasses the London *Daily Telegraph*, has brought it the nickname of "Ananias" . . . It is protectionist to the backbone . . . . and fosters a policy of isolation from the sister colonies.'

Syme's notions of political economy might seem remote from the experiences of a junior recruit, but that was not quite so. The devotion of the *Age* to protection had once been something of a radical, populist cause, founded on the argument that Victoria could not develop reliable employment without manufacturing industries, and that New South Wales persisted with free trade out of subservience to the City of London. It was not a wholly perverse argument in an economy which stalled at any dip in the world's appetite for primary goods. But Syme's pursuit of it had grown perverse.

Around the turn of the century a tide of nationalist idealism flowed for federation. Australians were often pleased to find this emotion in themselves, but not Syme. He thought free trade close to depravity – suicide and madness were among its consequences – and a nation embracing sinful Sydney was undesirable altogether. Newspapers are often damaged by proprietorial monomania: the *Age* which the eighteen-year-old Murdoch joined was editorially sclerotic and obsolescent, and was a harsh employer. Formally it wasn't even his employer – he brought in paragraphs from his allotted territory and got a penny and a half per line printed. This, as he said later, was sweating – a malpractice still common, in a business by then too profitable to need it. To be sure,

Australia's newspaper industry was not a particularly bad example. Indeed, reforms there were moving unusually fast, with papers like the *Argus* and the *Herald* in the lead. But they did not affect Keith Murdoch's formative years at the *Age*.

While nineteenth-century newspapers still used hand-set type and sheet-fed presses, the lineage system perhaps gave flexibility to a trade dominated by small, fragile organisations. But technology transformed operational speeds and made news the business of substantial industrial firms. A man setting type by hand could not outpace the creator of copy. But Ottmar Mergenthaler's Linotype – tested at the *New York Tribune* in 1886, perfected by 1890 – allowed type to be set at 2,000 words an hour, and few people, if any, can produce – as against transcribe – as many sensible words in a day while discovering and checking the facts on which they rest.

Presses which printed from a continuous web – not sheet by sheet – also became far more voracious: printing-output speeds went up by something like a hundred-fold in the last decade of the nineteenth century. John Walter I, who struggled to install *The Times*' steam-driven sheet-fed Koenig & Lomb press in 1820, would have been amazed to stand with Kipling in 1890 watching 'The Harrild and the Hoe devour / Their league-long paper bale'.

The newspapers these machines produced were not altogether changed from the *Port Phillip Herald*, so far as the page-image itself went. But, as their content and volume expanded immensely, so did their distribution, raising cash which fed back into further expansion. News, thought John Bigelow of the *New York Times* (quoted at the head of this chapter), would soon overwhelm every other activity in a newspaper. His note of surprise may itself seem surprising. But, not long before Bigelow's observation, newspapers filled much of their space with material rather like present-day lifestyle journalism. They still lacked the technical means to collect and distribute a comprehensive account of a city's diurnal business and its relations with the world. Newspapers, before the continuous-web press with its on-line folding systems, were like the Internet where high-speed digital transmission isn't available. They lacked bandwidth.

A history of the Australian Journalists' Association (AJA) describes the input side of industrialised journalism under a heading 'Slaves of the Press'. One example describes a Sydney lineage reporter sent to find a remotely located US consul at midnight: he had to walk back to town over rough country after filing eighteen lines of copy (the telephone was as elusive as the consul), and his net return on six hours' duty came – after paying his expenses – to threepence. In 1901 the daily paper in the prosperous Victorian city of Bendigo had eight wide columns, 22 inches long (representing no small bandwith): 'The chief reporter once covered a farmer's convention which began at 10 a.m. He finished his report at 3 o'clock next morning and was in a near-coma after having written $7^{1}/_{2}$ columns by hand [something like 8,000 words]. The editor . . . rebuked him for not having filled the whole of the page allotted to him for the convention report.' Such a regime virtually demands the inflation of material. At the same time, it penalises habits of inquiry and verification – in any case difficult ones to acquire.

What Murdoch did for six years as a 'stringer' for the *Age* was comb the streets of Malvern for suburban trivia, working mostly on his own. His sources were in police courts and municipal offices, churches and local businesses. Work often got into proof, only to be squeezed out in the final make-up: if so, he was paid nothing. Shoe-leather work of this kind was and remains a proper part of any reporter's training. But if it forms the staple element its effect will be destructive, for the journalist's pay is essentially controlled by people who supply or withhold the news he or she needs. For good papers, it was already outdated when Keith Murdoch began work.

And the twentieth century – though it brought new corruptions – did eliminate the idea that apprenticeship based on lineage would produce reliable reporters. Max Frankel's account of his career on the *New York Times* is a classic journalistic memoir, and his beginning as the paper's Columbia University correspondent in the early 1950s states the argument:

The pay was twenty dollars a week, nearly twice the cost of tuition. Unlike most newspapers' stringers – so called because they were part-timers paid by the measurement of a string, or ruler, at the rate of a dollar or two per inch – I would be earning only about fifty cents an inch, or a penny a word. But the steady income meant I could be trusted not to press for the printing of worthless news and not to pad every item just to enlarge my income.

The worst evil of the *Age*'s system was not just that it led to poverty – though often it did – but rather the kind of alternative to poverty that it offered. Murdoch could have joined the staff, after a trial period. He did not, because he could earn more as a stringer – something between £4 and £6, then a tolerable weekly wage – though that was a process of chasing volume, inevitably at the expense of other criteria. The money offered an escape route from the employer who so costively produced it. By 1909 Keith Murdoch had saved enough to buy a third-class passage to London and sustain himself during an eighteen-month search for work with more prospect of professional growth. He hoped also to find a therapist to treat his stammer, and had some thought of a degree at the new London School of Economics, which was interested in older students (he was twenty-four).

He was not necessarily looking for a Fleet Street career, but even some record of employment and experience in London might have been tradable on a return to Melbourne, providing a chance of work on one of the leading papers – the *Argus* or the *Herald*. In the event, none of his academic or journalistic hopes succeeded. When he returned to Melbourne, the *Age* kept a promise it had made to re-employ him – but this time as a salaried man, with a 30 per cent wage-cut.

Murdoch never sentimentalised his trainee days. At an AJA dinner just before the Second World War he said they were marked by overwork, underpayment and unhappy professional consequences: 'Looking back on those days I know that I would have been a better journalist had I not been sweated in my formative years.' Powerful inhibitions operated against unionising the 'slaves of the press'. The *Age* fired anyone suspected of such intentions, and journalists themselves were reluctant to follow a proletarian example.

Australia was not (and is not) a classless society, but class attitudes can be shifted by legislation. Wishing to reduce strikes by shearers and wharf-labourers, the new Commonwealth had built a system of industrial courts to try employment issues, and settle them by award. The courts gave registered unions an alternative to physical muscle, and journalists saw that they too could use it, however slight their class-warrior potential. Their requirement was to assemble a sufficient list of members for registration, and this was done on 10 December 1910 at a meeting in a basement café on Flinders Street, advertised only by word of mouth. The list – kept secret at the time – contained 210 signatures, and one of them was Keith Murdoch's.

In the complex, sometimes bitter arguments of the next few years Murdoch played no open part – pardonably, given the behaviour of the *Age*. Probably the decisive role in gaining acceptance for the Australian Journalists Association was that of senior executives on the more sophisticated papers – particularly James Edward Davidson, editor of the *Herald*. They were prepared to confront their fellow directors with the truth that businesses which were exploiting immensely productive technologies needed staff who were trained, educated and adequately paid – and that criticising payment by volume was not Red revolution. Davidson, as Murdoch and others agreed later, was a 'noble' character.

But an important share of the reformers' credit must go also to Davidson's boss Theodore Fink. He had been effectively the chief executive of the Herald business since the turn of the century, supervising its steady investment in powerful American machinery. The reformed speculator was no natural friend of unions, but he was a strong believer in technical education and training (to which he had devoted both academic and political energy).

What came out of initial confrontation and subsequent collaboration between the new union and the more technically advanced employers was an elaborate but pragmatic system for training and grading newspaper employees – a working ethos not lost today (though often imperilled), under which the content of a metropolitan newspaper should chiefly be the first-hand work of its own regular staff. Such an ethos is not uniquely Australian, of course – similarities with America, especially, are strong and obvious. But the legal empowerment of unions, the long background of literacy and of political engagement – plus devotional attitudes to sport and its reporting – made for particular local force.

Effectively, the union's demand was for human investment: Fink and his directors treated investment in equipment not as an alternative, but as a parallel activity. While negotiating with the new-born AJA, they were bringing three state-of-the-art Goss presses from America, and could reasonably claim that the machines, 'two octuple and one quadruple [when] set up in the office in 1912[,] easily surpassed anything of the kind then in Australia and were level with, if not ahead of, any relative equipment then in the world. Running together on a 16-page paper, these three machines print, fold and deliver 100,000 copies an hour . . .'

At this stage, just before the First World War, press technology began generating the architectural form that journalists have been accustomed to ever since, though a slightly later account of the *Herald*'s own development records an important difference between practice in London and the southern hemisphere:

> Extending well along the Collins-place front is the largest reporters' room south of the Line. In London and other places where a considerable portion of the local news is supplied by agencies serving all the newspapers, comparatively few reporters are employed. On *The Herald* there is an exceptionally large staff of them. Although much of their work is done outside, every member of the staff has his own place in the office and may do a good deal of his writing inside.

When Max Frankel started work at the *New York Times* four decades later, the neophyte campus reporter encountered similar architecture (dating this time from 1903), later describing 'the vast newsroom that stretched a full city block from Garst's chair at the City Desk'.

The technology of news has since changed further: the addition of colour, the replacement of letterpress by lithography; the discovery that news isn't necessarily connected with the printing of paper. But one shift which the big presses brought to news organisations remains with us today. They became teaching institutions – rather as the hospital, another great urban invention, had done earlier. They established the idea that journalism, like medicine, involves skills which must be learnt collectively, under a certain discipline, and to which sufficient years must be devoted.

At the heart of every industrial news system is a problem with no obvious solution – namely, how to make unpredictable events occur at orderly

28

times. This turns into a very practical question, which resounds through the story of News Corporation: how many – or, as Rupert Murdoch has usually asked it, how few – people are needed to make a news service? The answer requires experience, as Frankel records:

> Only slowly did I understand why even the worldly *New York Times* carried so much provincial campus news. Its large local staff was really needed only at odd moments, when planes crashed into the Empire State Building or New York's electricity suddenly gave out. Between crises, the locals were sent to cover insipid business lunches, charity dinners, and professional conventions, and their reports were supplemented by yet more trivia from dozens of suburban part-timers . . .

In relatively trivial – though useful – techniques of presentation, such as streamer headlines and half-tone display, the 'colonial' press was generally in advance of Northcliffe's model before 1914. Part of the Murdoch legend is that after the war Keith Murdoch was a carrier of advanced technique from London to Melbourne, and scepticism should be applied even to that. In the fundamental matter of training and organising news-gatherers, the antipodeans were far in advance.

British journalists were not fools, and plenty of them saw the value of importing the Australian grading system before the First World War. Northcliffe devoted his powerful influence to frustrating every such attempt; it would lead, he said obscurely, to 'jam-factory journalism'. The skills that Keith Murdoch acquired from Northcliffe during the war had more to do with the management of political intrigue than with the management of newspapers.

2

THE CONSPIRATOR AS HERO,
1910–1919

Clear and Round dealing is the Honour of Mans nature . . . Mixture of
Falshood is like Allay in Coyne of Gold and Silver, which may make the
Metall work the better, but it embaseth it . . .

FRANCIS BACON, 'On Truth' in *Essayes Civill and Morall*

'From a place you may never have heard of,' said the advertising for Peter
Weir's 1981 movie *Gallipoli*, 'a story you'll never forget'. It fired the first
stage of Mel Gibson's career, and for Australians and many others it
vividly expressed the Anzac myth, central to the Murdoch story.

Rupert was a principal backer. It was the film he 'really wanted to
make', wrote the Australian war-reporter Murray Sayle, noting its
London debut in the *Spectator*. Sayle reprised a much told tale in which
the Gallipoli campaign of 1915 becomes a sacrifice of the heroic
Australian and New Zealand Army Corps (the Anzacs) by degenerate
British staff officers, leading into a journalistic epic about the detection
of military blundering by two young reporters, Ellis Ashmead-Bartlett
and Keith Murdoch, who escape to London, break their security undertakings and (in Sayle's words) blow 'the whole story in the *Sunday Times*'.
This was the exploit which made Keith into an 'authentic Australian
hero', as Rupert's chief biographer William Shawcross puts it. It is one
with which the son has often and proudly identified himself – a matter of
daring and courage, where 'getting our boys out of Gallipoli' is a worthy

30

end, justifying rough-hewn means. But Sayle was not entirely wide-eyed about this tale. *Gallipoli* made him think there might be something dubious about this version of the Anzac legend.

Loss and horror dominate all memories of the First World War. But there are also idiosyncrasies, and interpreting Australia and its legends requires some insight into its experience of 1914–18. An American comparison might link Valley Forge with the Civil War battles – images of desperate heroism, overlaid with the emotions flowing from great changes of national identity. The Allied nation which volunteered its blood most freely in 1914–18 had just begun its constitutional existence. Its people were about a quarter Irish by origin; and families like the Finks, with origins on the German side, were not particularly unusual.

Violent anti-German sentiment gripped Theodore, and intensified when his first son Gordon was killed in the Gallipoli campaign. But the war also presented editorial and commercial opportunities, which he seized with fierce energy. In doing so he made the prosperity of the Herald business unassailable. Foreseeing the value of telecommunications, he made a deal in 1913 to join with the Sydney *Sun* in running a London bureau in the offices of *The Times*, with access to its British and world news. Although owned by Lord Northcliffe, the first of Britain's popular-press despots, *The Times* was still respected above all other titles.

War turned Fink's readiness to invest in communications and journalism into a master-stroke. The *Herald* produced war coverage which greatly outdid its rivals and enabled it (in Theodore's words) to make 'pots of money', endowing it with the financial stamina to make confident acquisitions in the 1920s and to survive in the subsequent Depression.

In 1915 Keith Murdoch was chosen by Fink to take part in the *Herald*'s wartime advance. Keith was good at cultivating influential elders – particularly the federal Prime Minister, Andrew Fisher, and Billy Hughes, soon to succeed him – and had attracted Fink's attention just before the war. He had left the *Age* to become the Sydney *Sun*'s Melbourne correspondent and had an office in the *Herald* building. Fink liked ambitious young men, and professional connection developed into domestic friendship: 'Theodore invited Murdoch home to meet the family, and Keith came to know Kate (Mrs Fink) quite well and to develop some acquaintance with the younger children, particularly Thorold [the second son] who . . . would later play a critical role in the relationship between Theodore and Murdoch.' Keith was a natural choice when the London bureau needed a new editor, and took ship in July 1915 via Suez. By this time the Gallipoli campaign was three months old, and Murdoch was about to achieve a curious distinction: great journalistic fame, based on words he never published.

The Gallipoli peninsula points south-west into the Aegean Sea from Turkey's short European coast. Between it and Asia runs the Dardanelles channel, linking the Black Sea to the Mediterranean. The Allied invasion started on 25 April 1915. Australians and New Zealanders, roughly 40 per cent of the force, landed at a point on the Aegean side later called Anzac Cove. The British 29th Division made the main attack, at Cape Helles on the southern tip; a French division joined them, after a feint at Troy. The aim was to destroy the Dardanelles defences, allow Allied warships into the Black Sea, knock Turkey out of the German alliance, link Russia to the West, and wreck the Kaiser's eastern wall.

This complex project had been agreed only six weeks earlier. The initial landings succeeded – surprising many commanders – but these were amphibious operations on a novel scale, and momentum soon decayed: the harsh slopes of Achi Baba and Sari Bair supporting stubborn Turkish defences. On 6 August, another landing was made at Suvla Bay, just north of Anzac, synchronised with heroic new attacks on Sari Bair. By the 15th these had clearly failed.

Two days later a note reached the Allied HQ on Imbros, an island some twenty miles off the peninsula. Keith Murdoch, in Cairo en route to London, had asked General Sir Iain Hamilton, the commander-in-chief, for permission to visit the front.

In the Gallipoli myth Australia often appears as a military innocent recruited by British warmongers. Alan Moorehead, generally a fine popular historian, says of the Anzacs that 'there had been no wars at all in their country's past'. Robert Rhodes James, the best British historian of Gallipoli, accepts this notion, as does the Weir movie. In fact troops from colonial Australia were in New Zealand for the Maori war of the 1860s, and in East Africa after Gordon's defeat at Khartoum in 1885. In 1900 Australians fought the Boers in South Africa, and helped to suppress the Boxer Rebellion in China.

By 1914, federal defence spending per capita was one of the highest in the world (just behind Britain and France). More significantly, training in the Citizen Military Forces – long a popular activity – became compulsory several years before the war. Much of this, begun as young as twelve, was managed through the education system, where teachers often held CMF commissions. Many of their military ideas Australia's generals and Labor politicians took from Switzerland; they also studied the American Civil War, which was seen as the principal modern example of a citizen soldiery in action. Australia indeed produced brilliant combat performances in 1914–18 – but they were not evoked by any impromptu bugle. Without being militarist in the European sense, the new nation had views on strategy which imperial London sometimes thought overvigorous, on naval issues particularly. Australia was not dragged into war in 1914, and not at all with its military eyes shut.

Though training was compulsory, only volunteers could serve in the Australian Imperial Force. The First AIF was certainly superb, selected from a society in which most young men knew some soldiering. But it under-estimated the effectiveness of new weaponry, and the Anzacs' tactics at Gallipoli were not ultimately more effective than anyone else's – even if in toughness and weapon-skill they matched any British regulars, and far surpassed the raw drafts supplementing them.

Just as its pre-history is clouded, there is still no clear-cut verdict on the Dardanelles Expedition's execution. Certainly vast blunders were made by everyone: Australians, British, French, Germans, Indians, New Zealanders and Turks. Twice Turkish inertia almost delivered Allied victory. Each time it was averted by minutes through Kemal Atatürk's genius – and he might have failed but for General Stopford's paralysis, when the August attack reached vital territory lying undefended.

Beyond doubt, though, the tactical lesson was that a line-abreast charge – then the normal infantry attack – could not survive automatic fire. The difference which then developed was between leaders like Plumer and Rawlinson (British) and, pre-eminently, Monash and Currie (Australian, Canadian), on the one hand, who devised radical solutions, and those like Douglas Haig, the British commander-in-chief, on the other, who (as we might say now) spent too long in denial.

Certainly the AIF, with its better-trained and relatively well-educated rankers and sergeants, was first on the Allied side to succeed completely with new techniques. But that was not at Gallipoli. And to imagine a divide between some blood-soaked 'establishment' brilliantly exposed by Murdoch and sacrificed colonial youth turns myth into corrosive fantasy. Many of the First AIF were anyway British born, recent emigrants to Australia in search of fortune and adventure. Syd Deamer, a compact, quick-witted young man born near the Old Kent Road with no father on his birth certificate, was typical enough. He was a gold-miner – a 'Digger' – though he only found sufficient to make a ring for the girl he would marry when (in post-war Melbourne) he became a journalist, and a colleague and rival of Keith Murdoch's.

The reporters accredited to the Dardanelles Expedition were among the first to find that in the wars of industrial society they might on the whole just be suppliers to elaborate propaganda-mills. It was a relatively new experience, for war correspondents – following William Howard Russell in the Crimea and the American Civil War – had usually achieved some independence.

Apart from the fact that the military authorities began to dominate both movement of reporters and their communications, newspaper chieftains such as Northcliffe and Hearst now supposed themselves to be political players, industrialists of information, with a role above government. And although the excesses of 1914–18 – the 'golden age of lying' – remain unequalled in the West, the distrust they created has never quite vanished.

Ellis Ashmead-Bartlett of the *Daily Telegraph*, who had covered the Russo-Japanese and Balkan Wars, had particular frustrations. The military authorities had allowed him a world exclusive with his account of the first landings, and his discovery of the Anzacs – volunteers who had stormed a rugged, unknown coast in darkness, something few regulars could have done – caused great excitement, and not only in Australia. At this level Ashmead-Bartlett's judgment was fair, though the excitement owed something to poor imperial sociology. The terms 'AIF' and 'Anzac' were novel, and early references assumed a savage vigour bred in wilderness. Ashmead-Bartlett later found that Anzacs rode electric trams more often than horses.

Larger flaws in his vision derived from obsessive hostility to General

Hamilton. There was indeed ground for criticism of Sir Iain – notably his failure to sack Stopford at Suvla – little of which survived censorship. But Ashmead-Bartlett's chief complaint was not inability to report the war: it was exclusion from its management. North of Helles, Anzac and Suvla the peninsula narrows at a spot called Bulair, which Ashmead-Bartlett considered vulnerable. But others also did, notably the Turks – who had been fortifying it since the Crimea – and one Gallipoli consensus is that the *Telegraph* man's idea was eccentric. Hamilton, who shared ideas freely with reporters, refused to take Bulair seriously.

Ashmead-Bartlett vented his pique by setting up on Imbros in grander style than the staff officers and other pressmen. He had quantities of wine for visitors and, while lecturing them on the general's errors, implied that the HQ facilities were too crude for a gentleman at war. Amused tolerance was the response from rugged and experienced colleagues like Henry Nevinson of the *Manchester Guardian*, whose memoirs described Bartlett issuing 'from his elaborately furnished tent dressed in a flowing robe of yellow silk shot with crimson, and [calling] for breakfast as though the Carlton were still his corporeal home . . . he had a way of loudly criticising the conduct of campaigns with an assurance that sometimes secured excessive respect . . .' Murdoch, arriving five months into the campaign, had neither acquaintance with the facts nor experience by which to judge them, and he gave this gilded figure unquestioning respect.

Murdoch had a personal assignment from the Australian Defence Minister, Senator George Pearce: to investigate delays in Cairo to the soldiers' mail. It did not require visiting Gallipoli, but Murdoch pleaded with Hamilton that doing so would be a 'privilege'. On receiving written assent to the censorship rules, Hamilton agreed. Murdoch arrived on 2 September, and at the start of a visit which lasted until the 8th spent several hours – perhaps a day – at Anzac, from which Suvla could then be reached on foot. He did not visit Helles, although Hamilton's staff offered transport. He dispatched to Melbourne some orthodox material about 'those great days, when men died charging with the light of battle in their eyes', adding, 'But the visitor now thinks he sees something even finer in this dying and suffering in full knowledge of war . . .'

At Imbros, however, he certainly heard Ashmead-Bartlett's regular jeremiad (so regular that men sometimes hid when its author appeared). Nevinson's memoirs refer to a notorious intention on Ashmead-Bartlett's part to get a 'strongly hostile' view of the campaign through to Herbert Asquith, the British Prime Minister: 'As usual, he had made no secret of that secret missive, but had read it aloud to various officers and correspondents, one of whom gave information about it to the Chief of Staff, so that the Australian who was carrying the manuscript was arrested on arriving at Marseilles . . .'

This, obviously, was Murdoch. The curiosity of this letter – which Ashmead-Bartlett published in 1928 – is that apart from fierce criticism directed at Hamilton and his staff, its contents generally are unsensational. It runs to about 4,000 words, many devoted to showing the Suvla attack a serious failure. Asquith and his Cabinet colleagues already knew that, and had issued a bleak statement to inhibit public euphoria. The character of 1914–18 war-reporting is shown by the fact that most newspapers produced triumphant headlines nonetheless.

Most of what Ashmead-Bartlett gave as narrative fact was sadly true – the Anzacs had lost heavily in attacks of near-suicidal nature, and dreadful conditions were sapping morale. But his obsession distorted his overall judgment. (Other sources show, for instance, that Hamilton was not universally 'reviled' by his troops.) The letter demanded instant removal of the incompetent Hamilton, and again touted the Bulair panacea. Ashmead-Bartlett's diary for 7 September says that Murdoch, desperately worried about the Anzacs, 'begged' him to write the letter. But he also says that supplication came from every side, so Murdoch perhaps was unique only in being an available courier.

Murdoch biographers have implied that Nevinson betrayed a valiant conspiracy, but what Nevinson really says is that no effort was made at concealment. In his diary Ashmead-Bartlett records persuading himself – and Murdoch too – that his letter did not breach censorship, as it was personally addressed to the Prime Minister: 'When Murdoch sailed I felt relieved for the first time. Although he is no great authority on military matters, he has seen enough to understand the position, and has been well coached . . .'

Murdoch took ship from Cairo to Marseilles, where he was arrested on 10 September and made to surrender the letter before proceeding to

London. As far as the military authorities were concerned, he was now in serious trouble. But he was arriving at a moment of political opportunity, and appreciated very quickly how to exploit it, finding in Northcliffe a sponsor to whom his own appearance was most opportune. The British Cabinet was a scene of factional strife. Northcliffe, in the background, was keen to participate, and matter discrediting the Dardanelles Expedition was just what he required.

Alfred Harmsworth had been Baron Northcliffe since 1905, and in 1915 was near the peak of his ability to inspire hatred, awe and editorial hero-worship. Sophisticates rated 'the Chief's' power as illusory, but rarely chose to test it. The *Daily Mail* was of course pre-eminent among his many prosperous inventions: *The Times* he had bought in 1908 to enhance his influence. In the late summer of 1915 Northcliffe – seeing himself as arbiter of the Anglo-German showdown he had long desired – was deeply hostile to the Dardanelles, and to the expedition's principal advocate, Winston Churchill. Victory, he thought, required concentration on the Western Front. Diversions were irresponsible, even treacherous. Asquith's reconstruction of his Liberal Cabinet as a coalition with the Conservatives had solved nothing, and Gallipoli was a focus for the belief that his leadership was insufficiently ruthless.

Keith's first contact in Northcliffe's empire was Geoffrey Robinson, editor of *The Times*, who swiftly told the Chief that an interesting witness had arrived, and provided introductions to Lloyd George, to Edward Carson – the Attorney-General, Asquith's harshest critic – and to Arthur Balfour – who had just taken over the Navy from Churchill. The men on the hillsides above Anzac Cove had become a touchstone of imperial politics

Northcliffe saw Asquith's vulnerability to suggestions that he might erode Anzac allegiance by misuse, and it seemed that evidence on just that issue had been suppressed. Northcliffe told Murdoch that if he held such secrets himself he would certainly use them, and then said, 'The matter has haunted me ever since I learned about it.' The question, then, was what these secrets might be. The Ashmead-Bartlett letter was beyond recall, and anyway it was more a hostile appreciation of Hamilton than a dossier of undisclosed facts. The need was for a shocking revelation, and Murdoch was ready to supply it.

On 25 September he finished dictating an 8,000-word letter, formally addressed to Fisher, the Australian Prime Minister, but delivered immediately to Carson, who secured Asquith's agreement to print it as a Cabinet paper. It is a striking document, derived from Ashmead-Bartlett, but supercharged by 'frantic and reckless' rhetoric (Alan Moorehead's term). Though twice as long, it gives less military information. Ashmead-Bartlett analysed Hamilton's operations in some tactical detail. Murdoch labels them disastrous, but mainly by generalisation. Oddly, he says that 'a strong advance inland from Anzac has never been attempted', though that is exactly what the August battles revolved around. He claims to have examined the peninsula thoroughly except for Helles, which he 'could not' visit.

Ashmead-Bartlett's attack on Hamilton and his staff was harsh, but was centred on their military judgment; Murdoch alleged a miasmic moral corruption. Allowing Hamilton to be a kindly incompetent he branded the others as 'unchangeably selfish' creatures appointed 'from motives of friendship and special influence'. This indeed was Bacon's alloy of truth worked together with invention. After such brief inquiries he could not have known whether appointments to the staff were corrupt – in fact they were not, and Murdoch never substantiated the claim. But it was obvious – and not even surprising – that some duds got into a force assembled in just six desperate weeks. Murdoch, writing in secrecy, turned a fair but obvious estimate into a startling, inclusive charge.

Where most observers saw amid the chaos at least some honest men confronting unprecedented military problems, Murdoch offered a simple vision of:

> high officers and conceited young cubs who are plainly only playing at war . . .
>
> What can you expect of men who have never worked seriously, who have lived for their appearance and for social distinction and self satisfaction, and who are now called on to conduct a gigantic war? I could tell you of many scandals, but the instance that will best appeal to you is that of the staff ship *Aragon*. She is a magnificent and luxurious South American liner, anchored in Mudros harbour as a base for the Inspector-General of Communications . . .

> Heaven knows what she is costing, but certainly the staff lives in
> luxury . . .

Officers on the *Aragon* were 'wallowing in ice' while wounded Anzacs
died nearby of heat and thirst. The *Aragon*'s incongruous comfort indeed
angered the fighting soldiers, and Murdoch's details could have been
legitimate, but for his pretence that the case was representative rather
than exceptional. He must have known that life on Imbros, at Hamilton's
insistence, was ruthlessly austere (his own informant being the sole
exception).

Compliments to the general's kindness went with an implication that
sloth or worse made him shun battle-zones:

> He has very seldom been at Anzac . . . The French call him the
> General who lives on an Island. The story may not be true, but the
> army believes that Hamilton left Suvla on August 21 remarking
> 'Everything hangs in the balance, the Yeomanry are about to
> charge.' Of course the army laughs at a general who leaves the
> battlefield when everything hangs in the balance . . .

This was absurd, as Hamilton was (in Nevinson's words) always 'restless
and unsatisfied unless . . . in the front line': 'an example of the rare type
which not merely conceals fear . . . but actually does not feel it'.
Hamilton perhaps spent too much time under fire. Murdoch's opposite
suggestion was a reckless smear.

Some of the ordure thrown at the Gallipoli staff still adheres – war
being a gruesome, ill-recorded business. But in an account focused on the
media professions it's apt to use Nevinson as a check – for Henry
Nevinson was one of the great reporters of the world, remarkable in the
wars he covered and the tyrannies he exposed for physical nerve and
moral perception: a radical socialist and soldier, a defender of suffra-
gettes, trusted by Irish revolutionaries and British generals alike.
Photographic film was never as sensitive to light as Nevinson to moral
corruption. He did not see it on Imbros, providing a rare instance of
robust negative proof.

But Murdoch's letter goes beyond saying that the British at Gallipoli were deficient. It reports the Australian performance not as superior – which overall it was – but as free of all blemish. This illuminates his technique and helps to explain his legend.

The 'Fisher letter' was not his first to the Australian government. Pausing at Cairo between Imbros and London he had written on 7 September to Senator Pearce about the mail problems which were his official task. The letter segues from postal to military advice, for the writer has 'had a thorough round of the Peninsula and talked a great deal with Hamilton & Birdwood'. He hopes Pearce will not think he is slavishly reciting their views in mentioning AIF blunders, which show:

> that old brigadiers should not be sent out. It is no place for a man over 50 years of age. Indeed, it is a place only for youth. Without doubt some of our brigadiers have cost us many lives through their ignorance and through their inadaptability to these extraordinary conditions. Monash and Hughes dashed their men against a high post here – Baby Seven Hundred – and they should have known after the first line went out that the job was hopeless. It was pitiful – fine Australian heart and soul and muscle wiped out in an impossible task.

Birdwood (though in Australian service) was, like Hamilton, British, and, seeing how corrupt British officers appeared by the time Murdoch reached London, it is odd that in Cairo they made good witness against Australian failure. But it is the substantive complaint which reveals most, the reference to a notoriously ill-planned attack in Monash's sector during May (a much decorated survivor called it his 'worst stunt' at Gallipoli). But Monash didn't make that plan – he implemented it only under strong protest. Maybe his technical reforms began in that experience; certainly his anger was well known at Anzac, and could not have been missed had Murdoch made decent inquiry before dispatching his blacklist. Luckily for the Allies, the 'old brigadier' survived.

The two documents are equal in ruthless fluency, but the direction of attack is reversed. The London text seeks to show all the combat burden falling on the Australians – because the British troops are 'feeble, childlike youths', poorly led and lacking resolution: 'I do not like to dictate this sentence . . . but the fact is that after the first day at Suvla an order had to be issued to shoot without mercy any soldiers who lagged behind or loitered . . .' Invention again is alloyed with truth. Always, in all armies, officers are empowered to shoot laggards if matters are desperate, and it was probably done at Gallipoli. A general order exhorting it would have been altogether more sensational: 'the fact is' that no trace of such a thing exists or ever did.

Given the wildness of Murdoch's allegations, why does the legend persist of 'the journalist who stopped a war', as Rupert's *Times* once called him – the reporter 'who got our boys out of Gallipoli'? Chiefly because he ruthlessly applied a simple template to complex events. The fragments of truth he blended into his document were stripped out of a richer context – one in which the drama of Gallipoli linked up with the world war's greater drama. But, when context is restored, it shows that what matters about Keith Murdoch is not what he allegedly got the AIF out of. It is what he contributed to the darker nightmare they got into after Gallipoli. His Gallipoli role was actually minimal, as was Ashmead-Bartlett's. Hamilton's command, in all probability, was doomed even before the two journalists met, in the aftermath of the August battles.

These involved two actions unlikely ever to fade from Australian memory – Lone Pine and The Nek, the emotional core of the Anzac tale. They were part of a plan intended to unlock the peninsula's complexities: diversionary attacks at Helles in the south; the new Suvla landings; attempts to take Sari Bair in the rear, after encircling night-marches by New Zealanders, Australians, Gurkhas and British Territorials. Lone Pine and The Nek were frontal assaults on Sari Bair, both appallingly risky, the second especially so, and were given to the Light Horse – an elite within the elite AIF – to attack dismounted.

The fate of this plan might occupy a book itself, but there are certain basic points. The British diversion at Helles was fought with sacrificial courage; Suvla was appallingly mishandled; the attacks on the reverse of Sari Bair worked only in part. Lone Pine, taking the Turks by surprise, was a bloody, brilliant success. Next day, 8 August, with everything else out of schedule, the Light Horse ran punctually into a consuming fire at The Nek. Though not one flinched, within minutes more than two hundred young horsemen lay dead within the space of a couple of tennis courts, leaving an indelible mark in their nation's consciousness. Amazingly, a few Gurkhas, New Zealanders and Warwickshires briefly held the crest of Sari Bair – before Atatürk personally led a counter-attack, which his staff considered hopeless. ('They were quite right,' he said – perhaps as close to a final Dardanelles verdict as is possible.)

Hamilton's staff were in fact a dedicated, brilliant group, and they concluded that his reaction to the August battles was unprofessional. They did not entertain fantasies about Bulair, or imagine he was dodging the action, but thought he fatally overrated the prospects of renewed attack. Reluctantly – for they liked him, and it was risky for career soldiers – they decided to tell the War Cabinet. They suggested to him that an officer should report personally to London, and Hamilton, innocently, agreed.

After some trial of conscience, Major Guy Dawnay agreed to go. Though young, he had a fine military record and elevated social connections which included the King and the Prime Minister. He left at the end of August. Robert Rhodes James' account quotes Major-General C. E. Callwell, the Director of Military Operations:

'Dawnay . . . was loyalty itself to his chief, but the information that he had to give and his appreciation of the situation were the reverse of encouraging.' He said clearly and firmly that the situation was grave, and even desperate. Ministers were impressed by the weight of his evidence and his transparent integrity . . . In all the history of the Gallipoli campaign there is nothing more surprising than the spectacle of this exceptionally competent young staff officer advising Ministers to over-rule the authority of his own commander-in-chief . . .

By the time Murdoch's letter reached Carson on 26 September Dawnay had already seen Lloyd George, Asquith and the King – whose influence mattered if he felt strongly about something, and who had been convinced by Dawnay that Hamilton's judgment had decayed. Lloyd George was already a Dardanelles sceptic. And, though Asquith retained some optimism, Dawnay persuaded him that the commander must change his mind or be changed. A decisive weight of opinion was against Hamilton by the end of September, and Asquith's main reason for circulating the Murdoch letter was probably that he feared that suppression might swell its importance.

The Cabinet's Dardanelles Committee met on 11 October, and decided to make further inquiries. These consisted of asking Hamilton to consider the prospects of withdrawal. Effectively he refused and, like his staff, the ministers found that unacceptable. On 14 October they decided that General Sir Charles Monro should take over and make new recommendations. Murdoch's letter surely did not help Hamilton. But without it he would still have gone.

Not that change of command was commitment to withdrawal: it did not 'get the Anzacs out of Gallipoli'. They remained till 20 December (the British 29th on their own held off the Turks until January 1916). This was because Monro, though a 'Westerner' by inclination, fulfilled scrupulously the demand for an impartial examination, and there were real arguments for both withdrawal and reinforcement. As late as 4 December Monro's staff expected orders for a new attack, with new resources. By that stage Hamilton's detailed rebuttal of Murdoch's wild charges – though little help to himself – had eliminated the letter as a serious influence on policy.

Withdrawal from Anzac and Suvla was ordered at last on 7 December 1915. Reverses in the Balkans – which the French and Russians considered first priority for reinforcements – seem to have been the proximate cause: certainly not whistle-blowing in the *Sunday Times*. Ashmead-Bartlett did give the paper an interview in October, but without Murdoch's colourful private rhetoric: 'I do not even know – what the future of the Dardanelles Expedition may be . . . [but] The time has come for us seriously to reconsider our position . . .' As much was being said in Parliament. On Boxing Day – *after* the Anzac withdrawal – the *Sunday Times* said Bartlett had secretly sent Asquith 'a very strong letter' via 'a well-known journalist'. It had been intercepted and its fate was 'wrapt in mystery'.

Still, one major figure believed in the impact of Murdoch's letter: Northcliffe, who had given it extensive private circulation. The Chief knew nothing of Dawnay, but he usually thought his own role in any matter pivotal. (A German naval bombardment near his seaside residence he saw as an attempt to decapitate the Empire.) Northcliffe was sure that Murdoch's rhetoric had aided his own rescue of 'those brave Aussies'. Thus for the rest of the war the *Herald*'s London editor was a member of the Chief's circle, where the Western victory formula was iron orthodoxy. Northcliffe in the Dardanelles matter was not a scientist criticising quackery, but a quack with his own panacea. It had three chief ingredients. The army must be 'left alone' – thus generals must be criticised rarely, and Field-Marshal Haig never. There must be limitless shells to batter enemy fortifications. And reinforcements must be provided on demand.

Application of this orthodoxy – beginning with the agony of the Somme in 1916 – was to kill roughly eight in ten of the 'brave Aussies' lost in the war. The AIF's special calvaries, Pozières and Bullecourt, offer sad evidence about wartime news media and Murdoch's claim to iconoclastic integrity. Pozières was fought in the central Somme battlefield through July and August 1916. Over seven weeks it cost the AIF 23,300 casualties – more than the seven months of Gallipoli – and maybe no more awful fight ever took place. Lieutenant J. A. Raws wrote that around him there was only:

> a charred mass of debris with bricks, stones and girders and bodies pounded to nothing . . . There are not even tree trunks left, not a leaf or a twig. All is buried, and churned up again and buried again . . . If we live tonight, we have to go through tomorrow night and next week and next month. Poor wounded devils you meet on stretchers are laughing with glee. One cannot blame them – they are getting out of this. We are lousy, stinking, ragged, unshaven, sleepless. I have one puttee, a dead man's helmet, another dead man's gas protector, a dead man's bayonet, my tunic is rotten with other men's blood, and partly spattered with a comrade's brains.

Lieutenant Raws did not live to read the accounts of this abyssal scene produced by Murdoch's London office. 'Men of the Southern Cross are merry in the trenches,' said a heading on 26 July. What could he have made of that?

Nodding occasionally to reality, Murdoch's coverage did mention 'desperate fighting'. But this occurred without severe consequences for the AIF, as in (24 July): 'Desperate fighting continues while villages are lost and won . . . Australians are engaged in the main battle area . . . marked by notable successes after most desperate fighting . . . Losses comparatively light . . . Pozières is a most important outstanding point in the Germans' second line.' On 25 July Haig was reported offering a special message about the Australians' very 'gallant, skilful and successful attacks', achieved with 'slight loss'. Quoted from *The Times* was a letter 'from a well-known officer' cheerily calling the Diggers (it was now their regular nickname) 'perfect devils of fighters, and splendid war material'.

On 21 August a report by Murdoch himself described the Pozières fighting under the heading 'Battle dramatic . . . Anzacs summoned in supreme moment'. The crisis of the whole offensive 'rested upon the Australians,' he wrote. Battlefield conditions offered 'many disadvantages' – not quite how Lieutenant Raws put it – but illuminated Anzac qualities all the better: 'It is of course a great honour. Of all the men in the British forces, the Australians have been chosen to do this most difficult and desperate task.' Through late August and into September the dispatches marched valiantly on: 'Allies advancing'; 'Anzacs win Mouquet Farm'; 'In battle inferno, Anzacs win glory'. The alloy by now scarcely included any truth – Murdoch's readers could not have known that this was bloodletting beyond experience, conducted for trivial advantage. Ending in November, the Somme battles gained about four miles, having taken no less than eighteen weeks to gain what had been judged worth a twenty-four-hour battle.

The AIF's war reached its low point in April 1917 during the Battle of Arras when the 4th Division, assigned to the British Fifth Army under Sir Hubert Gough, was asked to take the village of Bullecourt. Lacking artillery, Gough cobbled up a support-plan based on some tanks, which he thought might arrive. On the nights of 9 and 10 April the infantry lay in open snow-covered ground ready to attack, but no tanks came. They attacked anyway on the 11th and took Bullecourt – miraculously – only to receive not support but a mighty counter-blow. Of 4,000 attackers, 2,258 were killed, wounded or captured.

But Murdoch's office remained buoyant: 'Still blasting their way on,

British succeed everywhere'; 'Day goes well for us'; 'Anzacs win laurels . . . Two villages captured'; 'Wonderful scenes; headed by bands, men march to battle as if to a review'. On 14 April, headlined 'British consolidate gains', a sliver of truth emerged – Bullecourt was an attack 'delivered in bad weather, and over slushy snow'. In spite of 'consolidation', heavy counter-blows had compelled 'a withdrawal' – its extent was not revealed. Consolidation never occurred at Bullecourt. Triumphant advances and valorous attacks were meanwhile reported elsewhere. Had anyone cared to investigate, it would not have been hard to reveal the infantry's view of these escapades. Gough – responsible under Haig for both Pozières and Bullecourt – was widely disliked (not only by Australians) for his cheery outlook and casual planning. But Keith Murdoch was busy with matters greater than deficiencies in Western Front theory.

The killing-matches Haig directed in 1916 and 1917 were justified by a strong 'delusion' – the word is from John Terraine, his kindest biographer. In 1914 military arithmetic had seemed simple. Attacks with a mobile superiority of around three to one were expected to succeed. The Allies had the numbers, but machine-guns and barbed wire altered all calculation. Haig was not alone in hoping to demolish these obstacles with gunfire: he supposed that '[once] supplied with ample artillery ammunition of high explosive, I thought we could walk through the German line at several places'.

Shell shortage, indeed, had been publicised by Northcliffe to excuse failures in 1915. But it turned out that huge increases in artillery fire did not not increase pro rata the damage to well-made defences. Still, people knew how to make guns, and bombardment looked spectacular. Failures at the Somme and Arras suggested only the need for still greater bombardment of the Hindenburg Line. But men were consumed rapidly. And in February 1916 Britain imposed conscription. Australia's main 1914–18 idiosyncrasy was absence of conscription. Keith Murdoch spent much energy trying to change that, his journalistic activities being accessory to political services.

In October 1915 Andrew Fisher was displaced as Labor Prime Minister of Australia by Billy Hughes, a Welshman not unlike David Lloyd George – at least, in ruthless demagoguery. Fisher was appointed

Australia's official representative in London, but Murdoch became Hughes' unofficial personal agent. Apart from Hughes' distaste for Fisher, Murdoch had superior access to power and influence. Working at *The Times* linked him not only with Northcliffe's men, but with Lord Milner's Round Table group – great theorists of Empire, and organisers of the Monday Night Cabal, where removal of the Prime Minister was mooted, and where Lloyd George made circumspect visits.

Billy Hughes' chance of replacing Asquith in Downing Street – pre-empting Lloyd George, as it were – did not look as slim in 1916 as it does now. The 'Little Digger' (as he liked to be called) seems to have thought opportunity might arise if he could project himself forcefully into British politics. And this objective, starting with Hughes' arrival in London in March for an initial four-month tour, he and Murdoch took most seriously.

The anniversary of the Anzac landings made a platform for the Little Digger's eloquence. 'On the shining wings of your valour we were lifted up to heights we had never seen,' he told 1,000 real (rather gaunt) Diggers after a Westminster Abbey service: the royal family, plus bishops, generals, *The Times*, the *Mail*, the *Telegraph*, Lord Milner and every sector of the imperial order had joined in. Hughes stumped the land accepting city freedoms; joined the War Cabinet; dined with the King; and was everywhere seen as the kind of ruthless fellow needed in desperate days. Important people thought he should assume a high position in British affairs, Northcliffe examined his anti-Asquith potential, and Murdoch ensured that readers at home could follow it all.

But ruthless men in 1916 had to praise conscription, so Hughes was asked about Australia's stance. The best he could offer was a referendum in October. And with Murdoch's help, he thought he just might win. To the British the Australian system of compulsory training and voluntary service seemed illogical. George V's view of the referendum as an opportunity for voters Down Under to correct a simple error was widespread.

However, Australian logic can look more eccentric at first than at second glance, and this was such a case. The country had gone to war under social democrats who distrusted both militarism and pacifism; leaving citizens to moderate these extremes personally was a natural consequence, and it avoided conflict with the Irish (often ready to go, but hard to send). The notion that men exercising this democratic choice should already be trained soldiers reflects views on theory and practice still strong in the culture – peculiar maybe, but not perverse. Hughes and Murdoch knew that Australian opinion would not easily bend to the imperial pattern. Their idea was to use the moral credit of the fighting men, who would have votes – and Murdoch assembled teams of speakers to barnstorm the Western Front camps. It was assumed that the AIF would back conscription heavily, and, by disclosing this ahead of the civilian vote, opposition would be shamed. Just because 'spin-doctor' is a new name, let's not think the craft is new.

The British brass certainly hoped Australia would adopt conscription, so Murdoch assumed they would assist him with a clarion call to the ranks. It was not so easy. The Chief of the Imperial General Staff, Sir William Robertson, simply would not interfere in Australian politics. General Birdwood was thought to command the Diggers' respect (certainly they had his), but could not produce quite the exhortation desired. He complained to Haig that what Murdoch wanted seemed rather like ordering the men how to vote. Heftily nagged, he composed a strange document urging everyone to consider conscience and the safety of their families.

Haig then made difficulties about Murdoch's speakers having access to the troops – and we may think he was not just quaint. Men on active service were not a free audience, for pacifists and anti-conscription campaigners could scarcely be allowed, and Haig disliked the idea of a one-sided campaign with apparent official backing. He prohibited officers from making pro-conscription addresses, and only reluctantly permitted civilians to do so. Murdoch thought these scruples weird, reporting to Hughes, 'It was only by fighting his whole staff that I got him to agree to allow any meetings.' Those which were held went poorly: the men themselves were recalcitrant. Far from giving a ringing endorsement, the Army only just voted yes – and that victory depended on base units, and on the now quiescent Middle East. Among the Western Front men, the referendum was lost. Doubtless they knew how well-marked they were to die, but thought themselves enough to do their country loss.

One may dismiss the men of the First AIF as figures of a romanticised past, but it would then be hard to grasp both the strengths of the society which produced them and its vulnerabilities. One of these vulnerabilities is that its foundation myth protects uncritically any reputation so shaped as to tap its power. And it is a myth with a valid core. Contemporaries like Georges Clemenceau saw something exceptional in these five volunteer divisions from a small, remote nation, and so, passionately, did their commanders – by no means all Australians. Most striking was their collective selflessness: in awful crises, AIF units often gained numbers, through men absconding from rest areas – even bribing or overpowering sentries – to reach imperilled sectors. Conventions thought indispensable did not apply to them – they could not be shot for cowardice. But their resolve outwore armies with busy firing-squads.

We may also allow them political sagacity, for the doctrine of conscription and attrition effectively collapsed in the northern winter of 1917–18. Terraine is perhaps right to say that this is not a matter for mere denunciation, that it was a failure by thoughtful, honourable men confronting great complexity. 'Haig, his Staff and his chief subordinates were all involved together in a vast and tragic mistake . . .'

But, if some actors were tragic, not all were – certainly not the bull-frogs Northcliffe, Murdoch and Hughes. The Chief fancied that his intuition penetrated complex matters instantaneously, but, if that was ever true, it did not apply to the military problems of 1914–18. Murdoch too – as noted by his close associate Charles Bean, Australia's chief official war correspondent – needed little study before expounding military issues with confident force. The worst product of this was a theory, clad in vaguely racist terms, which treated the Anzacs as military athletes with no need for studious procedures. It obscured the AIF's real military virtues, and made Murdoch into a dangerous fool.

Whatever the arguments for conscription, the actual campaign of Hughes and Murdoch was an effort – though it was both ineffective and unscrupulous – to stuff a dubious imperial remedy down Australian throats. Murdoch claimed to be serving Hughes out of fierce Australian nationalism. But a nationalism which calls imperial sentiment in aid, and has to be restrained by the imperialists themselves, is so eclectic as to compel scepticism. Rejecting conscription, the Diggers were told, would lose them British respect. An argument of less nationalist validity could hardly exist, and it drew a stony response.

Hughes and Murdoch, however, can be understood better when imperialism is seen as close kin to the thing called globalisation now – simply
the label used when Europe had more power than America. Under
either name, there is a marketplace which attracts politico-cultural entrepreneurs interested in trading the lesser nations – or their assets – to and
from the metropolis. And in the Great War Australia's 'splendid war
material' was an asset for which demand outran supply.

Murdoch surmounted the presentational problems involved, not by
the coherence of his discourse, but because its absence did not trouble
him. He saw no contradiction in campaigning to drive more young men
into hells like Pozières and Bullecourt, equivalent – except for greater
lethality – to those which, by wildly denouncing them, he had used for his
own advancement.

For him the dead at Pozières had been chosen for an 'honour' by Sir
Hubert Gough – though the fate of the Light Horse he had lamented in
nationalist terms. Defending the anti-British chauvinism of his Letter
before an inquiry in 1917, Murdoch argued that in such a situation a
man of his birth could have done no other: 'I am always prepared to
offer everything I have to Australia.'

The Murdoch–Hughes relationship – with the reporter as the politician's propagandist ally – is a theme which continues into Rupert's
generation, though with relative advantage shifting, in accordance with
the dynasty's growing expertise. But what Keith was developing here
was another persistent component of the Murdoch political style: a
portable rhetoric of national commitment.

Historically, then, it's worth being clear that the doctrine Billy Hughes
preached was pseudo-nationalism, camouflaging hyperactive imperialism. Unlike genuine nationalists in Australia and elsewhere, he did not
want to abolish or moderate imperialism. He wanted to take it over and
intensify it. Notions of the war's purpose provide the clearest illumination. Douglas Haig, for example, believed its aim must be settlement
with a prosperous and peaceful Germany. Putting his military errors
aside, this may be seen as the minimum qualification for claiming (as he
did) to defend 'the freedom of mankind'. Murdoch's boss saw the war
simply as a crusade to ruin the German nation.

A national Australian army, conscript and subject to traditional military discipline, might have given Hughes enhanced imperial rank. Certainly he and Murdoch were not alone in thinking along such lines – and by 1918 volunteers were becoming hard to find. But what distinguished them was the recklessness with which they pursued the goal after it was clear that it would rend Australian society: patriotism, surely, cares more for the object of its affections. Their attempt inflicted notorious wounds on Australia. Less discussed are the possible effects on the Allied cause had they succeeded.

France in 1918 was bled nearly white. In Britain conscript reserves remained, but Lloyd George would not deploy them – for fear of the Western Front meat-grinder – and Haig's front was depleted. Strategy consisted of waiting for the Americans, and planning an aerial bombardment of Germany. But Russia's 1917 collapse had brought thirty German divisions westward. On 21 March Ludendorff struck at Haig's tired Fifth Army: this offensive, the 'Kaiserschlacht', which was intended to settle the war by separating the British and French, opened triumphantly. Whatever Haig's errors, he showed decisive moral insight by passing supreme command to the French and organising the 'Backs to the Wall' campaign of March and April. In this, he believed the AIF was crucial – a belief which was to give John Monash his moment in history, and Murdoch the occasion for a masterpiece of recklessness.

The AIF divisions were strong, but combat value alone was insufficient. The Canadians had that, but they were a drafted national army, and could not be thrown piecemeal into the vast, chaotic battle. The Australians, as Terraine says, were unique in scrapping 'their national ambitions and [letting Haig] use their divisions . . . wherever they were needed . . .'. Because Australia had not forced its men to go, it could tolerate the use to which they were put in extremity. Under the template Hughes and Murdoch sought, the AIF too would have been on the sidelines.

Haig sent Monash's 3rd Division racing to cover Amiens, the indispensable city, and at dawn on 27 March, with minutes to spare, they closed the gap. Haig's rising faith in Monash was confirmed. He never knew that Murdoch had advised Billy Hughes that Monash couldn't lead the AIF in its dynamic style of combat. The war, however, was by no means over. Time yet remained for the conspirator to gain his point.

Though the Kaiserschlacht faded, years of failure made it hard to believe that a way to break the front was now available. This was not the Australians' sole invention – though theirs was the pioneer demonstration. Nor did the chief inventors display the athletic Anzac-ness that Bean and Murdoch required. Sir Hubert Plumer was a portly, walrus-whiskered upper-class English Regular. Arthur Currie was a Canadian real-estate speculator who usually seemed to have borrowed his uniform. Only Monash – having a certain vanity – offered any military style, and he was a civil engineer. Though Monash tolerated rumours that in boyhood he had held Ned Kelly's horse during the Jerilderie bank raid – the AIF, after all, contained Irishmen – all three generals minimised bravura. Each can be imagined writing, like Monash to his wife, that every wartime day brought 'horror, fear and loathing'. They had no magic dogma, but a toilsome synthesis.

For instance, it was now seen that effective barrage must be brief – arriving accurately and unheralded. Shooting therefore could not start with laborious correction of errors in the guns, so electronic systems were devised to calibrate them in advance. Napoleon might have understood 1914 gunnery: not Plumer's by 1917. Fire-plans – plans generally – depended on exact information, gained by the new craft of aerial photography. It required slow, accurate flying, exposed continuously to fire – the trade in which Lieutenant S. H. Deamer won distinction, being noted in the official record for bringing back his shot-up RE-8 biplane, with its camera and observer, when badly wounded. Everyone hoped that tanks might suppress machine-guns. But they were slow, cranky and always being redesigned – tactical rules were hard to fix. The Mark V's arrival impressed Monash greatly – it had one driver, not four! – but trials were still needed to erase Bullecourt memories, and nobody knew how closely guns could support tanks without 'friendly fire' risks.

The chief paradox for generals used to older ways was that security, via swift execution, came from completeness of disclosure to the men taking plans into action. Just as it was the first mass-media war, it was the first in which data was vital, and photographers, map-makers, typesetters and lithographers were indispensable. The AIF were very adept in this, as theirs was a deeply literate society. But Monash was reckoned to be pre-eminent. Repeatedly, witnesses mention his gift for calculation and exposition. Workable plans interested the infantry, not military athletics.

On 12 May Haig promoted Birdwood to rebuild the Fifth Army; who should succeed to field command of the AIF? Birdwood consulted the chief of staff, General Brudenell White, an Australian Regular of outstanding quality. White said Monash at the 3rd Division had proved his worth: he was senior and gifted, and must not be passed over. White thus put aside his own claim – the only comparable one. Haig promptly endorsed Monash, and made White Fifth Army chief of staff.

On 16 May Murdoch and Bean heard this news with disgust. It was hardly worth winning the war, they agreed, should it occur with Monash heading the AIF. At once they began plotting a political reversal. Ministers in Australia approved Monash on 18 May, but the final word lay with Billy Hughes, in the US en route to London. Murdoch cabled Hughes on 20 May saying that the AIF did not want to be led by Monash, who would stifle their 'front line daring and dash'. This invention he then repeated in a dispatch to the Sydney *Sun*, meanwhile sending Monash 'hearty congratulations'. The general, undeceived, wrote that he distrusted and feared the journalist. Changeover was set for 1 June, but the Little Digger was not due till 15 June, and the conspirators reckoned the game would remain open after that. Thus intrigue and doubt persisted throughout August 1918, and the war's dramatic climax.

Murdoch's and Bean's tactics were consistent with their motivation. Both assumed self-interested ambition to be Monash's sole driving-force, a consequence of his undisguised Jewishness. The AIF in the field was a corps – a lieutenant-general's command – but proposals were being aired for a supreme Australian commander in London, ranking as a full general. It was a political idea, alternative to a Cabinet minister residing in London. Murdoch promised to support Monash's promotion to London as a full general – editorially, for his work was now read throughout Australia, and by lobbying Hughes – if Monash would quit the AIF command. Meanwhile, White was told that, if he offered himself in Monash's place, a campaign could get him back from the British Fifth Army. This was his duty, they said, to the 'true Australian type'.

It was crackpot stuff. Even by elimination of the proper candidate, succession would not fall neatly to White. There would be contenders among the divisional generals: Birdwood, hard pressed at Fifth Army, could not just wave goodbye to his chief of staff. And the misreading of Monash was total: his vanity was minor; he cared little about rank, and deeply about field command. The AIF wanted him, and the 'promotion' would have fooled nobody. Birdwood, fearing chaos, wrote that Murdoch aimed to be 'an Australian Northcliffe'.

The scene of this storm was no teacup. The Germans, Monash said, could still inflict 'serious reverses': bloody defensive fights punctuated June, and successful attackers – like the US Marines at Belleau Wood – suffered fearsome loss. But Monash never let his insecurity in command hamper preparation of the AIF for the attack which would lift the incubus of German defensive lethality. This was the masterly battle of Le Hamel on 4 July 1918, extending methods Monash had devised with Plumer in 1917. In hindsight it appears almost painless: in ninety minutes eight battalions of AIF and US infantry, with sixty tanks, penetrated 2,500 yards of German defences, capturing four times the territory a whole division would earlier have been sent to take (and never so readily).

But beforehand it did not look so easy. The plan relied on a minimal barrage, and an attack formation more wide-spaced than anything yet used. The AIF was now in Henry Rawlinson's Fourth British Army, and he wondered if the Australian planners knew what they were doing. Much rested on trust and hope. Haig worried about damage to the Australians – few other experienced troops remained – and still more about the newly arrived Americans, over whom General 'Black Jack' Pershing kept jealous watch. Only to the AIF infantry, perhaps, would the British tanks have ceded the necessary tactical control. It required much patient diplomacy from Monash.

Throughout this, Bean and Murdoch intensified their pressure, even though Monash had rejected Murdoch's 'explicit bribe' on 6 June. Bean chipped away at White with claims that Monash was exposing the AIF to danger ('Our men are not so safe under Gen. Monash as under you'). On 24 June, while Haig assessed the Le Hamel plan, Birdwood updated Monash on the intrigues – assuring him of support – and Monash wrote bitterly about fighting 'a pogrom . . . in the midst of all one's other anxieties'.

And it got worse. At the end of June, Bean boldly told White that

Monash had *accepted* Murdoch's suggestions on promotion. It was a well-aimed untruth, for White would not have dropped his own claim for anyone but Monash – to whom he sent a note asking if his faith had been misplaced. This reached Monash's HQ just before Billy Hughes' arrival. Hughes was prospecting for the hostility to Monash which Murdoch had reported, but he desisted on finding a major battle impending. He gave no straight answer when pressed on the command issue. He had grasped that Monash would not leave the field command by choice, and withdrew to await the battle outcome.

Next day Birdwood passed to White a personal reassurance about Monash's intentions. On 3 July, with the troops moving up to attack, Monash wrote in detail to White about his own resolve, and asked White if he was yielding to persuasion over the AIF command.

Then at 4.00 p.m. military disaster loomed. The US troops were withdrawn, because Pershing thought they were not ready. Monash told Rawlinson: no Americans, no battle. Was this so vital, Rawlinson asked, that Monash wanted him to disobey orders and get sacked? Monash said yes. However, the Americans (from the 33rd Division) disagreed with Pershing, and Rawlinson told Monash to keep going unless he heard otherwise. At 7.00 p.m. Haig on his own responsibility overruled Pershing. Le Hamel went smoothly ahead, and Pershing did not object to Independence Day celebrations in captured trenches.

It is unlikely that Haig would have acted as he did for any other corps commander. But the AIF was probably the most highly trusted formation on the Western Front, a disposition which would have ceased instantly had Murdoch and Bean managed to set its officers at each other's throats.

Le Hamel was vital because the belief in German defence was broken. It led on to the vast Amiens battle of 8 August which showed the Germans that their ascendancy was done (Ludendorff's 'black day of the German Army'). The 'Hundred Days' following were lit by Allied victories – Canadian, British, French, American – among which Monash's war-worn citizen–soldiers displayed transcendent qualities. Mont St Quentin, with the Victoria Cross won six times in three days, remains unsurpassed for 'front line daring and dash' – the final word on Murdoch the military sage.

Well before the Armistice, White and Monash had composed their relationship. White made it plain that he had never shifted on the AIF command: 'in case there is any suspicion lurking in your mind, may I say once and for all and very definitely that if the conspirators in this matter do happen to be General White's friends, they are not acting at the suggestion or with the approval of General White'.

The tactic which pits ambition against loyalty often triumphs, and Murdoch surely felt his initial confidence well placed: publicity and political access were in his command. Also in Anglo-Saxon military society a Jew then attracted prejudice which might even now be troublesome. But as it turned out there was no difference between officers who occasionally expressed antipathy to Jews (Birdwood, Rawlinson) and those like Haig and White who never did. Though White sacrificed most, they all supported the appointment they thought best in honour and efficiency. Maybe the Little Digger was right that the Anzacs' example lifted people above themselves. White said on the death of Monash that creating and preserving a fellowship, rather than winning battles, '[was] I venture to say . . . the outstanding achievement of the AIF'.

Had the Kaiserschlacht succeeded, or the AIF disintegrated in its supreme moment, the world's history would have changed – in momentous, complex ways. But we have a lesser question of media history: how could Billy Hughes' spin-doctor become the towering hero of the Murdoch biographies?

First, Australia's 1914–18 role was so classically heroic as to illuminate anyone connected to it. Lives were given in the same ratio as Britain's, but wholly without compulsion. Uniquely often, the AIF was for the Allies both bulwark against disaster and vector of success. But this was at bitter cost: six in ten of those who served were killed or wounded. Often those bereaved were people of English or Irish working-class origin, become Australian because British society had made them uncomfortable (or worse). It was plausible to them that their sons had died remedying the folly of imperial rulers – an unjust, but not a frivolous, view.

These circumstances produced the specially Australian version of the Great War trauma; into it, the half-secret tale of the Gallipoli Letter blended perfectly. Murdoch's wartime position as head of the *Herald-Sun* service made him the best-known byline in Australia, and it became notorious that he had written a powerful unpublished document, reputedly a denunciation of privileged corruption. Murdoch's own evidence to the Dardanelles Commission of 1917 suggested as much, though without substantiation.

His legend had ample opportunity to expand before the text of the Letter and the facts of Dawnay's mission became available, and by then another world war was three decades past. (The chief saviour of the Anzacs was exactly the kind of upper-class Englishman Murdoch spuriously accused of indifference to their fate.)

By contrast the 1918 conspiracy was truly secret, for Monash and White made no public complaint. Their magnanimity, Bean said, frustrated the plot – it also protected the plotters. Bean apologised, somewhat obliquely, in his final volume of the Australian official war history (completed during the new war, in which he saw anti-semitism for what it was). Murdoch neither acknowledged nor apologised for the escapade – never substantially described until Geoffrey Serle's life of Monash in 1982. Serle's suggestion that it was Australian journalism's 'outstanding case of sheer irresponsibility' passed almost unnoticed. By then Murdoch power over the country's news media had been exercised for decades.

What is perhaps the best-known study of war correspondents, *The First Casualty*, is by an Australian, Phillip Knightley. Describing Murdoch, it relates only the Gallipoli Letter tale, and suggests that 'if the war correspondents in France had only been as enterprising, the war might not have continued on its ghastly course'. This sustains Murdoch by contrast with the generals of 1914–18 – indefensible villains of popular culture. In truth, Murdoch and Northcliffe promoted the war's ghastliest illusions, and history increasingly finds the generals unfairly condemned. But it is specialised texts which identify Murdoch's political motives, anatomise the AIF's qualities, or show how trust developed between people as different as Haig and Monash. Stereotypes of class and nation remain easier to project.

The *Penguin Book of Twentieth-Century Protest* was edited by a present-day Murdoch executive, Brian MacArthur of *The Times*. There Keith's Letter accompanies works by Winston Churchill, Martin Luther King, George Orwell and Bertrand Russell. In that distinguished company Keith remains – for the Newscorp imagination anyway.

3

THE SOUTHCLIFFE INHERITANCE, 1919–1953

No word hostile to you has ever been uttered in Cabinet. On the contrary, all ministers realise only too well what the Government and the Party owe to the papers of your group.

J. A. LYONS, Prime Minister of Australia,
to Sir Keith Murdoch, 1935

The citizens of a free country have to depend on a free press . . . That is why the Constitution gives newspapers express protection from Government interference . . . It is also possible for the public interest to be defeated by the way a newspaper is conducted since the principal restraint on a newspaper owner is his self-restraint.

EUGENE MEYER, publisher of the *Washington Post*, 1948

The year 1931 was prosperous for Keith Murdoch, chief officer of the Herald and Weekly Times. His son Rupert was born, and Joe Lyons – who might be called the family's first prime minister – took office. Rupert certainly grew up aware of his father as a 'towering figure in Australian life' – the words of the British historian John Grigg – and since the Great War Keith and the *Herald* had travelled far. But the dynastic account in which he injected a comatose outfit with Northcliffe's expertise is untrue.

In 1918 Theodore Fink and his manager Arthur Wise were running a prosperous business, and planning post-war investment to exploit the national addiction to printed matter. Political and personal stresses were the problem. Fink admitted the skill of James Davidson, editor since 1911, but he did so only grudgingly, as he grew more conservative and Davidson did not. Davidson, the 'noble' pioneer of pre-war reforms, tried to develop a non-partisan policy, but abolishing the paper's editorial column only incurred the chairman's disgust. To any practised newspaper eye, Murdoch's letter sympathising with 'my dear Mr Fink' looks like a job application:

> I know you will be interested rather than indignant in my views – *The Herald* has always been curiously characterless as a journal. I know you have wished it otherwise . . . a newspaper should have some sort of a fighting platform, not necessarily political . . . *The Herald* has suffered from a lack of fighting and push . . .

Ejected in 1918, Davidson went to Adelaide, South Australia's capital, and did something Keith Murdoch never did. He created a paper, the *News*, which lasted many years – becoming the foundation-stone of Newscorp, in fact. His replacement, Guy Innes, didn't enthuse Fink. But Murdoch's presence in Europe was doubtless indispensable at the climax of the world drama.

The 1920 company accounts told of rising sales and work on new premises and plant. The site was in Flinders Street, classic newspaper territory, on the fancier fringe of downtown: a five-floor building was to provide ample editorial spaces, mahogany directorial quarters, advanced graphics-processing, and five rows of the latest Goss machinery. (Fink and Wise, canvassing examples, drew considerably on the *Chicago Tribune*.)

Melbourne's market offered most potential: Hugh Denison of the Sydney *Sun* meant to invade, and Fink meant to repulse him. Both saw Murdoch as a desirable acquisition: the Anzacs' saviour, admired by Northcliffe. (The Chief was by now eccentric enough to make his doorman head of advertising, but few comprehended his decline.) Keith adroitly kept his potential employers in the dark about each other. 'My mind is clear,' he wrote to Fink in September 1920, 'that I would like to do the work . . . if I come as Editor of the *Herald* I am to have complete and absolute sole control over the [editorial] staff . . .' While Fink was pressed for concessions, Denison was told he had the lead – being disabused (and enraged) in January 1921 when the *Herald* negotiations were complete.

Northcliffe gave a farewell party, and in September the new editor disembarked at Melbourne. *Smith's Weekly*, an astringent Sydney journal, reported Wise greeting him with a 'ready-to-wear expression of cordiality', and speculated about the general manager's prospects. Soon after, the Chief arrived on a world tour, and congratulated the Herald directors on Murdoch: their remaining duty was simply to support him. Next spring, when Murdoch demanded sole executive power, the board took this prescription, and Wise disappeared. Murdoch sent Northcliffe thanks (saying 'director after director' had been lobbied). But the Chief's mind collapsed before the letter arrived, and he died in August 1922, aged fifty-seven.

In command Murdoch cultivated something of Northcliffe's weighty manner – he liked to be called 'Chief' – but avoided the original's captious arrogance. He dressed carefully to make the best of his regular features, firm handshake and level hazel eyes. His manners were excellent, and he knowledgeably collected paintings, wine, furniture and books. The stammering youth was gone, and Melbourne knew little of his London conspiracies. He was a war hero, and the rising star of a substantial, cultivated family.

Naturally Monash and White were absent on 6 June 1928 when the Reverend Patrick Murdoch married his forty-two-year-old son to nineteen-year-old Elisabeth Greene, but General Harry Chauvel, dashing leader of the Light Horse, represented the Anzac connection, and the diva Nellie Melba shed glamour on an extensive congregation.

Keith and Elisabeth settled at Frankston, south-east of Melbourne, on a spacious farm named after Cruden in Aberdeenshire, location of Patrick's first ministry. Rupert Greene passed on grace and charm to his daughter. But he had a taste for gambling, which she hoped to eliminate in her offspring: they were to see her husband as their model. The children were principally her care, for Keith's workload was heavy, and extended well beyond Melbourne.

Grigg correctly identified Murdoch as a huge national presence. But it was less exact to call him the greatest 'editor and newspaper entrepreneur' in Australia's history. The *Herald* continued efficiently, but he was not an editorial innovator – pioneers like the political analyst A. N. Smith and the financial investigator 'Monty' Grover operated elsewhere. Nor was he an 'entrepreneur', if that means a creator of businesses. Takeovers were his métier, in an industry undergoing drastic rationalisation after luxuriant growth. Between 1923 and 1933 the number of metropolitan newspaper operators fell from twenty-one to six. Murdoch was the Herald group's tactician during this time; Fink the strategist, creator of a formidable financial and technical base. Their personal affection did not survive Wise's fall. But they collaborated over twelve years and three principal campaigns.

The first opponent was Denison, attacking with the *Sun News-Pictorial* – a bright morning alternative to *Age* and *Argus* grey – and then with an evening competitor for the *Herald*. The *Sun* found a profitable new readership; the evening, though it reached a creditable sale of 100,000, made no money in *Herald* territory. It closed in 1925, and Denison found his overheads crippling when borne by a single paper. Murdoch was authorised to buy the *Sun*, which slotted economically into the powerful Flinders Street plant. With Melbourne secured, Fink led a raid on Perth in Western Australia by a party of Herald directors. They bought, and sold profitably, an option over the *West Australian*. Murdoch managed the deal in return for an interest, which Fink thought provided his first substantial capital.

Though personally rewarding, Perth was not a purposeful corporate scheme. But the 1928 attack on Adelaide and the Bonython family's entrenched morning *Advertiser* certainly was. A tiny moribund competitor, the *Register*, was bought and put under Syd Deamer's editorial control. The ex-pilot, an intemperate, self-made intellectual – close to Fink, but sceptical of Murdoch's wartime role – was a tough newsman. The Bonythons, lacking competitive stamina, sold the *Advertiser* for a million pounds in 1929. The *Register* died, and Deamer returned to Melbourne as *Herald* editor, Murdoch becoming editor-in-chief and managing director. James Davidson agreed simultaneously a share-swap option over his evening *News*. It was activated on his death in 1930.

61

Connection to Queensland – Australia's Deep North – began through an association with the extraordinary John Wren, who built his illegal gaming empire from a desperate punt on Carbine for the 1890 Melbourne Cup. Monty Grover's riskiest target, Wren's ill-fame survives in *Power without Glory*, Frank Hardy's semi-fictional novel of Melbourne corruption. Diversifying to Queensland, Wren had acquired the Brisbane *Daily Mail* to run sporting promotions. Murdoch in the late 1920s bought its one rival, the *Courier*, and some of Wren's *Mail* shares. It took four years to produce the desired outcome: a merged *Courier-Mail*, run by the Herald group, though Murdoch and the shareholders he brought in (Fink included) were a minority. Wren's tacit and possibly unique admission was that he lacked the moral stature to function as a newspaper proprietor.

Ten acquisitive years thus made the Herald group the chief force in Australian metropolitan journalism. Melbourne produced a challenge in 1933, when the *Argus* launched the *Evening Star* against the *Herald* – at a bad time for Murdoch, who was immobilised by heart trouble. Deamer, however, was as vigorous in defence as attack. Keeping a taut news cover, he moved the paper successfully up-market, and in George Munster's words it was sometimes 'more reminiscent of the *Manchester Guardian* than the *Daily Mail*'. The *Star* died in 1936 without making any serious impression on the *Herald*.

But when Murdoch returned from convalescence the tension between editor and editor-in-chief intensified sharply. The terminal incident profoundly impressed twelve-year-old Adrian Deamer: Syd burst into the house swearing he would never speak to Murdoch again. The phone rang, and Adrian's mother announced that Sir Keith was calling. Syd hurled the phone through a window, and shortly after embarked the family for London, where other employment was found. Nobody knew just what had triggered the explosion, in which respect it resembled most rows involving Syd Deamer. But for once it had lasting consequences, because it occurred between men whose professional temperaments were profoundly opposed. To Murdoch, stories were a currency, and were most valuable when unpublished; by the 1930s he was an experienced practitioner of intrigue. Deamer's professional interest lay entirely in the day's disclosure, and whatever was on his mind reached his lips (or his newspaper) with virtually no delay.

The Australian Labor Party (ALP)* appeared as the country's natural rulers in Murdoch's youth (when he considered editing a party newspaper). But conscription split the party, and Murdoch had discovered conservatism before repair-work enabled James Scullin to take power in 1929 – exactly as Wall Street crashed. Scullin had no experience of office, and just two colleagues with a little: E. G. ('Red Ted') Theodore, ex-Premier of Queensland, and J. A. 'Honest Joe' Lyons, ex-Premier of Tasmania. Red Ted was a brilliant self-taught pre-Keynesian, not unlike Huey Long. Honest Joe was a schoolteacher and financial ascetic. Distrust was mutual.

On appointment as federal Treasurer Red Ted was accused of corruption – of having connections with John Wren. When he resigned to defend himself, Scullin made Lyons Acting Treasurer, and sailed for London to appease Australia's creditors. Thirty years later Enid Lyons recalled the Melbourne lunch-party where Murdoch moved smoothly to divide the government:

> 'Well, Mr Lyons, you will not be Acting Treasurer much longer. You will be Treasurer.' Joe said he doubted it; he doubted even if he could wish to be. 'Oh, but you will be. Scullin couldn't do anything else after what you've done in his absence, and after the way he supported you from London. Don't you think so, Mrs Lyons?' he asked, turning to me . . .

When Scullin found Red Ted freshened up sufficiently for reappointment, Lyons was upset – and aware of his potential outside the Australian Labor Party. Murdoch now helped the conservative Opposition's leader reach the conclusion that his day was done – at which Honest Joe crossed over into the job. Scullin's restored Treasurer treated the Depression with mild reflationary potions, and the Herald chain damned them as products of a shady financial background. Red Ted and Honest Joe were sternly contrasted throughout the 1931 election, with the result that Lyons' victory over Labor was widely (furiously, by the unions) attributed to the Herald group.

*Founded in 1900, the ALP was sometimes 'Labour' and sometimes 'Labor' till the American spelling was formalised in 1912. Australian usage otherwise is 'labour'.

In 1934 Murdoch became Sir Keith, and Lyons ruled in public amity with the Herald till his death in 1939. But a private altercation over federal plans for broadcasting diversity foreshadows Rupert's era of triple interplay between newspapers, government and electronic media. A limit of five radio licences for one company was proposed in 1935. Murdoch's group had seven: the scheme, he wrote to Lyons, demonstrated personal hostility to him. Not so, Lyons replied over five handwritten pages (briefly extracted at the head of this chapter). The Cabinet had only gratitude for him and his papers. For many years, gratitude had been all a politician could give a newspaper. But Murdoch's complaint and Lyons' fawning reply suggest a relationship with exchange-value on both sides. The Herald kept its licences. But what happens to such assets when gratitude decays?

Neither Fink nor Murdoch assembled a major block of the Herald's dispersed equity, using their resources instead to take various personal positions when expeditions were mounted under the group banner, acting usually in concert, but with assorted outcomes. Brisbane, though Fink shared in it, was essentially a Murdoch personal operation. The negotiations in Adelaide were Murdoch's, on behalf of the group. But Fink's private papers (which he left to Melbourne University) suggest much of the planning was his – plausibly, given Deamer's role.

The 'Murdoch press', subject of Lyons' affection and the unions' distaste, was something of an illusion. The *Courier-Mail,* the *Sun News-Pictorial,* the *Herald,* the *Advertiser,* the *News* (and many appendages) operated as a group, helpfully to editorial costs and overheads. But Murdoch's proprietorial control was limited to Brisbane. Within the Herald company, the relative influence of managing director and chairman depended on boardroom sentiment. During the mid-1930s Murdoch's stock rose and Fink's fell, as Theodore moved into his eighties without his editorial ally Syd Deamer. War then shattered a declining relationship.

That the Second AIF volunteered with fewer martial illusions was not the only difference between 1939 and 1914. Rather than denouncing 'England's war', the non-communist left worried about Robert Menzies, Lyons' successor, sympathising with London's appeasers. But Keith Murdoch's enthusiasm for Prime Ministerial propaganda remained undimmed. In June 1940, undertaking to relinquish all his editorial powers meanwhile, he became Menzies' Director-General of Information. He then asked Menzies for the means to correct media 'mis-statements', and received sweeping authority over the content of newspapers, magazines, radio and theatre. Outrage was universal – except among the Herald papers, allegedly now disconnected from Murdoch. They remained silent. Theodore Fink, eighty-five and unwell, called on the Herald directors to protest. Principles of editorial independence would be eroded, they said, were they to do so.

Dissociating himself from his own company's behaviour, Fink called the Murdoch regulations 'an infringement of the rights and liberties of the public'. His words were published everywhere – except in the 'Murdoch press'. Public opinion fiercely supported Fink, and Menzies jettisoned the Director-General's astonishing programme. Murdoch resigned in November and rejoined the board – perhaps a bittersweet victory for Fink, as its swiftness minimised the damage to Murdoch's reputation. On Anzac Day 1942 Theodore died, and Sir Keith succeeded.

The regular portrait of Sir Keith as author of Australia's first great media enterprise is over-coloured. Clearly he had a leading role, but even leaving Theodore Fink aside people like Davidson and Deamer were also significant and often more creative. Between Menzies' fall in 1942 and his restoration in 1949 Murdoch had little leverage in federal politics, for Curtin and Chifley, the intervening Labor men, despised him. But within the Herald group his personality expanded throughout the 1940s. His dress and manner were imposing – rather imperial, by local standards – and he usually had a promising young reporter assigned as his aide, to dispatch cases of wine to contacts, run confidential errands and tote his evening dress.

He apparently personified the company, so that people often took him for its owner, and nicknamed him 'Lord Southcliffe'. But his eminence owed much to the exclusion of the Fink era from corporate memory. Long-lived newspapers usually celebrate their history – but after the Second World War a distinguished career could be spent in the Herald building without discovering the men who had planned it. John Fitzgerald, one of Sir Keith's aides in 1950, rose by 1972 to the editor's office; there, he found an anonymous photograph of an elderly man. Eventually he identified Theodore Fink.

In 1995 – by then under Newscorp control – the papers left Flinders Street for a new tower block, and corporate publicity celebrated the bold physical investment on which seventy years of profitable publishing had been based. It was credited wholly to Keith, who had not even been in Melbourne when the work was set in train. In 1998 Professor Don Garden published a life of Theodore, using his private papers. People who had worked years for the business were intrigued – even moved – by its contents. But they found it reviewed only in non-Murdoch newspapers, of which few by then remained. People are often 'painted out of history' figuratively. But here there is a literal echo. In 1928 the portraitist Sir John Longstaff executed a painting of Theodore Fink for the Flinders Street boardroom. After Theodore's death it vanished, and has not since been seen.

Rupert Murdoch says he saw an exciting pattern in his father's life, and Keith certainly wished to prepare Rupert as a successor. That father and son shared a dynastic ambition is well attested. But in Rupert's recollection things did not begin quite so happily. His school disagreed with him, and he with it. Geelong Grammar – in the English, or New English, mould of Eton, or Phillips Andover – likes its inmates to engage with a collective ethic, and at that time it had two offerings: Christian social idealism (a speciality – its head, James Darling, being interested in theorists like Teilhard du Chardin); and team sports (Australia's overall secular faith, inclusive without reference to class, sex or cultural background).

Rupert thought sport pointless and Darling insincere. Few Australians, obviously, would share the first judgment, and perhaps none the second: Sir James faced complaints when he later chaired the Australian Broadcasting Commission, but no one else accused him of insincerity. Darling admired Rupert's mother for her concern with social values, and said the son had not inherited them. (Nor, for that matter, did her distaste for gambling transfer.) The formative experiences Rupert acknowledges are Oxford University, the *Daily Express* in its heroic period, and (obliquely) the *Herald* itself. Of these the *Herald* came first, though only briefly.

Sir Keith's bleak estimate of his own apprenticeship was accurate, David Syme's protectionist *Age* having been an editorial antique. The most significant passage in media history, says Professor Michael Schudson of the University of California, is journalism's transformation 'from the nineteenth-century partisan press to the twentieth-century commercial-professional press'. As he says, comparison of today's major newspapers with those of 1895 shows a professional, non-partisan pattern, where reporters rarely march 'in step behind an editorial line set by a publisher . . .'.

British journalists, apt to smile at the word 'profession', may doubt America's most rigorous media analyst (and 'professional' may not simply equal 'good'). But Schudson's account broadly matches Australian experience – illuminating the British, if only by contrast. It is certainly relevant to Newscorp, the democratic world's chief instance of journalists marching in step. If that is a historic reversal, Rupert's professional beginnings are the more interesting (especially given his later involvement with the Hitler Diaries and some other equally bizarre episodes).

Australia's newspaper reforms of 1910–14 set professional aspirations which afterwards grew steadily (even luxuriantly in 1945, when a training syllabus was proposed to include the rules of both Marxist analysis and the world heavyweight championship) and by the 1950s there was a settled process, known as 'cadetship', lasting roughly four years, centred on the role of the reporter. Belief in a native talent for this central craft is strongly held. Kay Graham of the *Washington Post* wrote from college wondering if she might display the good reporter's quality, 'given by God to a very few'; Sir Keith Murdoch looked anxiously for Rupert to display it. And in some people there is an unearthly capacity to penetrate and depict events. Stephen Crane was born six years after the American Civil War, yet veterans reading *The Red Badge of Courage* believed – famously – that they had served with him at Chancellorsville. Rather less famous, though, is Crane's remark made – to Joseph Conrad, with apparent relief – after testing himself against actual war in Cuba. He said: 'The *Red Badge* is all right.'

The reality is that the gift is rare, sometimes misleading: natural reporters cannot dispense with disciplined experience any more than musicians who have it can rely on perfect pitch alone. Training consists of testing the gifted, eliminating the self-deluded and teaching compe-tence (or humility) to the giftless majority. The first lesson is that fact-gathering is impossible; the second that something all the same can be done. It is always rough going. Arthur Christiansen, the transforming genius of the *Daily Express*, remembered his four years of English provin-cial reporting – of train crashes and witness payoffs, of trying to outsmart crooks and being heaved out of factories – as little but 'fright, nausea, hot embarrassment and near-failure'.

Induction on Australian metropolitan papers like the *Herald* was less Darwinian, but it took time – for the reporter's game is uncertainty, and the supply of it is sparse. Though labelled as 'news', a newsroom's throughput is largely predictable: events – though intrinsically unique – are processed for resemblances, and enough of these are always found to construct normality. This decent material is essentially stenographic. Presentation may render it as lavish features, editorials, even advertising, but the reporter's skills count only where ambiguity persists – in shadows inhabited by the living Elvis, crooked bankers and horses which talk. Most such items are fanciful: the norm – though crude – is not arbitrary. But young reporters find that, outside normality, truth is no special friend of likelihood. Many march on into the badlands of the Bible Code or *The X-Files*.

Mental defences – against both excessive caution and excessive credulity – can be practised. I was told that, if a man jumps from the tower of the Royal Melbourne Hospital and runs off unharmed on Grattan Street, I should shut my eyes and count the bricks he falls past. (The mentor, I think, was Adrian Deamer. The answer is about 950.) Assume also that if you can think it, someone will do it: a legless, bigam-ous chicken-sexer will pose as a priest to marry a new girlfriend to one of his wives posing as a male. (It was during my third training year: the girl refused to 'live in sin'.)

But, if doubts were everything, the small-town editor exposing injus-tice (walking out of step) would be non-existent instead of rare. Some reassurance comes from discovering that events are intractable. On my first day in the *Herald* newsroom (about four years after Sir Keith Murdoch died) the space abruptly filled with large men in working togs: wharf labourers, criticising recent coverage of federal wages policy.

Comment – the paper's faith in wage-restraint – they agreed was free. But recondite facts of industrial arbitration were sacred, and error had been committed. The printed outcome of their debate with the brass was highly abstruse, but not the lesson we beginners were told to draw – our own exposure to scrutiny.

This reduces any delusions that facts are the reporter's property (or invention: the classic allegation of authority). As experience proves the independence of events, the everyday reporter's task eases. It shifts from divining the truth to knowing what questions may reveal it; from that to discovering where those questions are being asked, and to the knowledge that threats and denials issued elsewhere are usually best neglected. The principle is universal, but risk and practice go best step by step. Here, the Australian newsroom offered exceptional training for much of the last century. As news agencies – powerful in the US, dominant in Britain – were marginal to its life, its first-hand work ranged from grassroots crime to national political shenanigans. This early exposure made the Australians, up to Rupert's time, the best – as Christiansen thought – of the reporters drawn to 'Fleet Street': an international village, sustained in London by the colossal revenues of Britain's popular press.

Training ended with a professional grade, though it rarely took the four full years as the course could be shortened by some 25 per cent where the trainee could show proven skill or graduate qualifications, or both. Rupert's, however, was reduced by some 90 per cent without either. George Munster in *Paper Prince* (1985) states that Murdoch was a *Herald* cadet 'for a few months' in 1950, between leaving Geelong Grammar and departing for England and Oxford. This time was served, as Munster dryly puts it, 'under Sir Keith's benevolent eye'. It might well have been impossible, given the impact of that eye, to make Rupert's brief experience even roughly normal. If not as distressing as Christiansen's, a cadet's first year was designed as an uncomfortable succession of menial tasks (like listing the movements of ships). But no strenuous effort seems to have been made in that direction anyway. Rupert began by turning up for work in Sir Keith's chauffeured car.

Murdoch himself has offered very few memories of the experience – even to William Shawcross, the biographer to whom he has given most aid. According to that account (it roughly agrees with Munster's) he spent about four months attending minor criminal courts in the company of another cadet, who had been at Geelong Grammar. Court-reporting ranked considerably above the first menial stage, but it wasn't something undertaken in pairs by old schoolmates. If someone couldn't handle a story solo, he or she did humble legwork for senior staff members, and underwent rigorous instruction.

Both Munster and Shawcross suggest that he wrote at least one court report, published anonymously. But the few months passed with no real trace; probably it was an embarrassment to everyone concerned. Certainly Rupert never reached the critical stage of solo assignments carrying a degree of risk for the paper. His 'cadetship' cannot have been anything more than playing briefly at journalism.

Newspaper managers do not need professional news-gathering skills, which is why – with some exceptions – they have in modern times done as Schudson says, and left reporters broadly to their own devices. Rupert Murdoch, however, is *the* exception: he intervenes strenuously in editorial processes, and even those who disapprove may suppose he does so on a basis of expertise. Indeed, Murdoch himself perhaps thinks so, for the *Herald* period became in his own later mind a genuine professional experience.

In 1979 he testified before the Australian Broadcasting Tribunal. The full circumstances don't matter till we come to issues of nationality and television ownership, but much of his evidence voiced his distress over being – as he saw it – subjected to unfair competition by the *Herald*, 'a company I used to work for', speaking as if he had given a period of loyal service to Australian journalism. It was in fact only symbolically true that he had worked for the *Herald*, but his vehemence suggests he attached substance to it.

A curious interlude demonstrates otherwise. Before Oxford, Murdoch had a short hitch with the *Birmingham Post* in the English Midlands, arranged through Sir Keith's acquaintance with Pat Gibson, chief executive of its controlling group. There Murdoch was rebuked for inattention by the *Post*'s editor Charles Fenby. On departure, he wrote to Gibson that Fenby was an incompetent, ripe for dismissal.

The urge for vengeance is odd, but more revealing is the written word as a means to it. Whether or not *Herald* training elevated character, it taught infallibly that a beginner who writes damaging words is their own likeliest victim: defamation must be utterly avoided till enough basic precision has been acquired just to write neutrally without heart-stopping repercussions (and that it comes quite slowly is one of Christiansen's points). Rupert's breezy libel on Fenby would have struck any real trainee on any newspaper as crudely suicidal. Its inaccuracy, luckily for him, was so gross as to make it ineffective – though forty years later Murdoch could recall it to Shawcross as a well-judged sally. Its significance is that Melbourne and Birmingham left him innocent of the reporter's tradecraft.

A good deal of this craft is only charms and amulets, but they help people cope with the peculiar insecurity of the work. Reporters cannot afford – are never finally allowed – much disengagement from the ambiguous situations they encounter. There is a famous pose of detachment, but it belongs, as most practitioners know, in movies, not in the world of experience where, as Professor Jane Richards has written, there are 'cognitive costs of keeping one's cool'. In an elegant piece of research she reported in the *Journal of Personality and Social Psychology* in 2000, her Stanford University team asked people to repress their emotions while viewing recorded matter known normally to be distressing. Successful reduction of distress – of involvement, that is – reduced, pro rata, the accuracy of perception and of recall: exactly the reporter's predicament.

Emotional tension is complicated by professional investment in the outcome of events – typically, turning out to be right requires things to turn out horribly for others. Max Weber, in one of the foundation documents of social science (*Politics as a Profession*), defined the reporter's existence as 'from all viewpoints, accident-prone', under 'conditions that put his self-assurance to the test in a way that has no match in any other profession'.

Training, finally, is an exposure sufficient to weed out those whose assurance remains inadequate and whose tensions are resolved (in a psychologist's term) by 'premature closure' – untruth being promoted, or truth suppressed, according to whether recklessness or timidity complicates the situation. Weber, pioneering the analysis of professions, put journalism firmly among them, but observed in it a unique lack of formal restraints against corruption. Deficiencies of integrity were not therefore 'astounding' – only the existence of more 'honest journalists than the layman can suspect'.

Technicalities such as libel apart, restraints upon newspaper journalism are indeed voluntary, and especially the submission of candidates to a test of quality. The underlying principle is Milton's 'liberty of unlicensed printing' in *Areopagitica* – a democratic essential, as Eugene Meyer, publisher of the *Washington Post*, says in our epigraph. But Meyer adds that the general principle allows a newspaper's controller to defeat the public interest in any particular. It would have been professionally 'intolerable', thought his daughter Katharine Graham, to make her own start as a reporter on the *Post*, and she went instead to Scripps-Howard's *San Francisco News*. Her autobiography reveals how she and Meyer sought to insulate the test of her capacities from the impact of his status. Newsroom grapevines probably hindered them somewhat. But in the Murdoch case no similar self-denial was even attempted.

At Oxford Rupert made his first important connection outside his immediate family – with Rohan Rivett, who had been at Oxford a generation earlier, and was running the Herald group's London office. Naturally a London editor would counsel the chairman's student son out of his own experience. But the Murdochs assumed a deeper bond.

Rohan Deakin Rivett passed a golden youth and brutal young manhood, going from school to Melbourne University and on to Oxford, as a gifted scholar and athlete. He had just become a cadet journalist in 1940 when he joined the Second AIF. Captured, he endured the Japanese oppression which locked many veterans into the emotional prison of White Australia. Rivett, however, survived as an advocate of opening to Asia and rapprochement with Japan.

His middle name puts him among the connections of Alfred Deakin, main architect of federation. Australian history recycles certain names frequently – Baillieu, Bonython, Boyd, Mackerras, Myer, for instance – manifesting not an aristocracy, but a durable bourgeois elite. Deakins and Rivetts are salient, for if Alfred organised the nation, his son-in-law, Rohan's father, organised much of its scientific and intellectual life. Murdochs and Rivetts made a subset of this network. Walter, the Reverend Patrick's scholarly brother, was Deakin's first biographer. Some AIF veterans might have suspicions of Sir Keith, but he was an intimate of prime ministers – and Elisabeth fitted exactly the Rivett tradition of graceful social concern.

Walter and Elisabeth saw Rohan in the way of an elder brother to Rupert, and an enduring professional ally. Sir Keith saw Rivett as an important corporate recruit. Their choices were fortunate: extensive correspondence reveals Rivett's uncynical trust in the Murdochs, father and son. He was not a toady, but something of a boy scout. His eclectic gallery of heroes – the British socialist Aneurin Bevan, the Australian Tory Richard Casey, the cricketing genius Don Bradman – readily accommodated Sir Keith, sole author of the Herald group. (The Finks of course had vanished during Rohan's war service.) Though Rupert castigates 'establishments', his own career germinated in the protective warmth of an Anglo-Australian elite.

Rohan and Nan Rivett's house at Sunbury-on-Thames became Rupert's refuge in England. Here nothing showed of Charles Fenby's would-be nemesis – Nan's memory is of someone engagingly puppy-like, and seemingly vulnerable himself. Rivett, who had much of the teacher in him, discussed British politics and newspapers with Rupert, and advised Sir Keith on Rupert's career and its dynastic implications. 'I know you are very worried about whether Rupert should continue his Oxford course beyond this June,' he wrote in January 1952. There was a 'very strong temptation' to have him in Melbourne 'so that he can work close to you and assimilate points from your experience . . . Against this, I know that if unable to finish his course there will always be a personal feeling of some dissatisfaction . . . at not holding the University degree.'

But domestic felicity is the principal memory, as in Keith's relationship with the Finks before 1914. There is Rupert turning up for some laundry or for a casual meal; entertaining the children David and Rhyl with nursery games and boisterous pillow-fighting; travelling with the family to Europe. In a letter written from Oxford after Rohan's move to Adelaide, Rupert conveys the flavour of the association:

> . . . I am sending by the same mail your shirts and pyjamas, for which many thanks . . . They saved me and it was extra kind of you to come good with them . . . [My letter] originally set out to tell you

1) how much I appreciate all the wonderful kindness you have showered on me over the last eighteen months, what great friends you've been to me and how much easier and more pleasant it's made life for me etcetera – all of which is meant;

2) to wish you all the best for Adelaide and find out how you're liking it and so on.

. . . very best love and kisses to Nan, David and Rhyl.

Given the way matters ended between them, it is no surprise that the surviving Rivetts remember Rupert's charm through a veil of pain. But they remember it nonetheless – like others in later decades.

Charm is not universally reported in corporate megastars. It has been since youth in Murdoch's case, even by people who think he has coldly betrayed them. Some consider it the quality that led them into relationships which became disastrous. Many find it hard to link the eager Oxford student – or the surprisingly attentive, self-deprecating executive – to the tyrant one long-serving editor (Andrew Neil) described under the headline 'RUPERT THE FEAR'. Still others puzzle over Murdoch, the virtuoso of kick-ass libertarianism, abasing himself before the gangster-bureaucrats of Beijing.

Yet the perception that authoritarian ruthlessness is apt to coexist with radical lack of inner assurance (and with the appearance of humility) has a solid pedigree. In Book IX of *The Republic*, where Plato considers the upbringing of tyrants, he sees their alternate modes as supplication and dominion: 'if they want anything from anybody . . . they profess every sort of affection for them; but when they have gained their point they know them no more'. Plato's description of the tyrannical character as fluid and yielding in search for power – as essentially without convictions – varies the older Greek picture of the tyrant as unflinching despot, pursuing substantive (not always wicked) politics. Plato seems to have drawn live from the corrupt, unstable politics of his day.

Modern investigators have sought to formalise such classical insights. Their foundation text is *The Authoritarian Personality* by Theodor Adorno and others (cited often as *TAP*) – much revisited, rethought, re-examined (even reviled) by social and political psychologists since its launch in

1950, and substantially updated in *Strength and Weakness* by William F. Stone, Gerda Lederer and Richard Christie in 1992. The *TAP* research, focused initially on far-right politics and anti-semitism, has expanded since to authoritarian and xenophobic attitudes of varied political colour. Theodor Adorno was one of the Frankfurt School stars exiled by Nazism, but alpha-listing slightly enlarges his role; another exile, Else Frenkel-Brunswik, did the pathfinding surveys with the Americans Daniel J. Levinson and R. Nevitt Sanford. Some of their Freudian theorising may have dated, but not its descriptive armature.

They identified authoritarian individuals via their expressions of hostility to nonconforming minorities – ethnic, moral or other – which are abused with as much enthusiasm as mainstream society allows. Anti-semitism is unacceptable in the mainstream today and so is rarely open. But alternatives abound – foreigners, drug users, sexual eccentrics – broadly, the usual tabloid suspects. Authoritarian intolerance has yielded much ground in modern societies. But, where it appears, it does not appear alone. Whatever the scale used, high-scorers display suggestibility – even gullibility – with a tendency to truncate complex argument and seize dogmatic conclusions. Personality centres on an adherence to convention which exceeds that of the conventional majority.

Genetic make-up, parental actions and social pressures have all been proposed as origins. What Frenkel-Brunswik and her successors demonstrate is that there are variations – however caused – in human capacity to endure ambiguity, and that authoritarian characteristics are found when that capacity is low. Authoritarians, for instance, feel implausibly victimised – Murdoch (he and his friends agree) is a hard-done-by multi-billionaire. Often there are bold promises, quickly forgotten: again, prominent in the Murdoch record. But most consistently reported is Plato's 'tyrant', oscillating between submission and dominion. The authoritarian perceives equality – which after all is an ambiguous state – as threatening. 'Object cathexis' is low: in plain language, principles are lightly held, though often strongly expressed.

For Plato friendship required a dialectic of equality. Of course there may be other definitions, and Murdoch does not lack long-term companions. Many, however, have been acolytes, subject to abrupt expulsion – journalists especially. Aggression is no necessary part of the authoritarian display; benevolence, indeed, may be conspicuous in assured, conventional settings. Rupert exuberantly romping with the Rivett infants accords with this. So does the magnate in later years discreetly aiding an old war correspondent – instances charming in themselves.

But an issue for those amenable to Murdoch's charm in testing conditions – where it may disintegrate without warning – is their degree of alertness to flattery. 'Authoritarian' and 'authoritative' are not equivalent – an executive trying to be firm and reliable may forfeit the advantage of 'charm'. The authoritarian essence is plasticity – a quality allowing others to see in Rupert Murdoch what they wish at that moment to see. Jean-Baptiste Clamence, Albert Camus' 'judge-penitent' in *The Fall* – having observed that a mental humiliation hardly matters if it enables one to dominate others – says of himself, 'I was considered to have charm . . . You know what charm is: a way of getting the answer yes without having posed any clear question.'

Sometimes people like Murdoch are supposed to have duplicate personalities – one aggressive, one emollient, the famous 'Jekyll and Hyde' notion. But Multiple Personality Disorder – if it exists – involves *dissimilar* multiples: typically, one conventional and one rebellious. Murdoch, whether dominant or submissive, displays conformist attitudes – separate modes of a single performance. Naturally one mode displays more vividly if time adds status to an authoritarian disposition. Even emperors are rarely powerful in youth, so this is a character which reveals itself in phases. And if we glance ahead, from Murdoch as student to Murdoch as a media chieftain, and to the Hitler Diaries fraud, we can see the difference status confers – and see its effect on professional formation.

High-level news-media errors are rarely simple. Inattention, crookery or blind chance usually interact, and certainly did in 1982 when the London *Sunday Times* – just absorbed by Newscorp – decided that these Führer 'diaries' were real. Calamitous presentation of the claim resulted, however, from a simple, honest error by Murdoch himself. The great scoop originated dubiously. The *New York Times* and the *Daily Mail* had rejected the story – and Murdoch's acceptance troubled his staff, for diaries and 'proof' derived from the same source. Their own expert was positive, thereby reducing doubt sufficiently to make publication tolerable. He then reversed himself, which the *Sunday Times* only discovered just after starting the presses.

The commitment could have been unravelled, but it would have been costly and messy. Murdoch's decision was as clear-cut as Russian roulette: keep printing. Such a decision is hard to parallel. Rarely does anyone with the aptitude acquire sufficient rank. The matter is not risk itself, but an urge, in its presence, to simplify. Among paths to editorial disaster, none is so direct. But it is discovered usually at the level of Albert, a *Herald* cadet-colleague of mine, whose scoop was 'delivery' of a ban by the Presbyterian Assembly on dancing in church halls. The reproductive effect for the Melbourne Scots – for whom such dances were an important sexual marketplace – should have raised doubt: 'deliver' turns out, in Presbyterianism's intricate democracy, typically to mean 'dump'. But, having his notes and his deadline, Albert took a clear-cut decision, as he did in all things. Another, soon after, was to find other work.

Some details of the *Sunday Times* and Nazism's legacy must come later, but we should briefly examine the débâcle's aftermath. Editorial investigation has little of the gambler's fatalism about it, because the participants believe that their tense engagement with fact is deciding the result ('cathexis' is just a term for the focus of emotional energy on a mental target). Thus failure produces a fierce recoil, and Murdoch's colleagues felt shattered, professionally humiliated. Murdoch was calm, not so much avoiding blame as seeing little to shoulder. The experience for him had *not* been intense. A bet had simply gone wrong. In businesses depending on public performance, shame is always a potential, often a real, danger to executive stability (try the words 'Wen Ho Lee' on a *New York Times* veteran, or 'Leyland slush fund' on one from the *Daily Mail*). As the Newscorp story develops, rich in editorial mishaps, the commercial value of Rupert's curious immunity may be found to grow.

Liberals often conflate 'authoritarian' with 'conservative', but in truth authoritarianism traverses the spectrum. Its values are consistent with each other only in lacking rebellious or deviant content, being jackdawed from the mainstream and stripped of the mainstream's tolerance. However, the Murdoch described by allies such as Irwin Stelzer is Rupert the Outsider, a rebel nothing like the tyrants in *Strength and Weakness*. Much of that case derives from struggles with the establishment – an unknown dragon in Rupert's youth. But part is from Oxford days, and the radical implications of student socialism.

Rupert's course was Politics, Philosophy and Economics (PPE), a replacement for the classical readings once used to polish captains of affairs. Some philosophers and economists disparage PPE's content, but they can hardly deny its part in what one Oxford voice called an 'extraordinary success . . . in educating people effectively for major positions in the outside world'. If it is superficial, it seems strenuously so: the two sizeable weekly essays can be remarkably eclectic and, if rhetorical aptitude exists, PPE will maximise it.

Murdoch notoriously decorated his room with an image of Lenin, which he and others serenaded intermittently with Soviet verse and addressed as the 'Great Leader'; he has described this, plausibly, as less than ideological. But Rupert's correspondence with Rivett records his less noticed membership of the Cole Group, then Oxford's most distinguished socialist society, led by Professor G. D. H. Cole (a designer of PPE), with members selected from the Labour Club rank and file. These activities have been presented (with Rupert's own indulgent smile) as the vague rebellion which usually evolves into conservatism. ('We are reformers in the morning,' said Emerson, 'conservers at night.') The Cole Group, though, was not vague: it toiled at details of administrative power, having bred a notable Labour Party leader (Hugh Gaitskell), a Foreign Secretary (Michael Stewart) and serried officials and legislators (some Canadian and Australian).

Today – when Lenin's image indicates a taste in graphics rather than ideology – it is hard to imagine that socialism was once a political juggernaut mounting Marxist guidance-systems, to recall that ambition sometimes preferred communism to investment banking, and that the left might be an alternative orthodoxy as much as an alternative to orthodoxy. If in those days rebel hearts warmed sometimes (misguidedly) to Lenin, they never did to Cole. Both the ruthless totalitarian and the democratic technician were manifestations of established power, and it seems fair to suggest power as the chief interest of anyone who managed to admire the odd couple concurrently. Though transient, Rupert's leftism hardly seems vague, and not at all rebellious. Mid-century socialists, though often admirable – as was Cole – were rebels only exceptionally.

Sometimes they said, 'Help bring about the inevitable' – the ideal authoritarian formula.

It's noticeable also that Murdoch the ex-socialist is very unlike a socialist – even unlike the social democrats he sometimes encourages electorally. In people undergoing Emerson's process the mature portrait *resembles* the youthful snapshot (social attitudes outlasting economic faith). Lately, Rupert's newspapers have had to abandon one or two of their favourite targets. But over the years few alumni of the Oxford Labour Club can have done more for homophobia and xenophobia. There is no evidence of the rebel in these early years. Nor is there evidence of conservatism, in the ordinary sense.

Sir Keith died in October 1952 just as the final academic year began. The Melbourne funeral was an emotional pause before the onset of arguments over inheritance which were to intensify during 1953. Rupert's degree was undistinguished, but that he concluded it surely proves resolution. When he returned to England, an essential relationship began: with Edward ('Ted') Pickering, editor-in-waiting at the *Daily Express*, and an old contact of Sir Keith's. In 2003 Sir Ted was still a director in Newscorp's British operation, occupying an office in the London HQ rather grander than the boss's own. Murdoch identifies Pickering as the first of his two chief mentors (his second, the late 'Black Jack' McEwen, enters in the next chapter). Pickering, a Fleet Street adept, introduced Murdoch to the curious environment – the curious professional model – which became an ideal incubator for his qualities.

The *Express* then reckoned itself the world's best newspaper, and a sale of four million broadsheet copies, on the basis of hard news brilliantly presented, made criticism difficult. British popular papers of the 1950s seem now like dinosaurs galumphing in a Jurassic arcadia. The lost possibility of such creatures evolving otherwise than into today's tabloid zoo owes much to Murdoch's character – and much, naturally, to their own.

The *Express* was by its proprietor Lord Beaverbrook (Max Aitken, 1879–1964) out of Arthur Christiansen, editor from 1933 to 1957: Beaverbrook, Hearst (1863–1951) and Northcliffe (1865–1922) being joint archetypes of the despot publisher – Welles' Citizen Kane, Waugh's Lord Copper. How real were their powers – Northcliffe's, for instance, which dazzled Keith Murdoch in 1915? Certainly politicians had no purchase on Kane or Copper, unlike the case when their originals were born. *The Times* was rare among early-Victorian papers in refusing bribes, but that became less of an eccentricity as technical advances steadily increased commercial independence. It was a significant moment when Captain Arthur Stevens of the London *Evening Standard*, finding that American Civil War telegrams were generating large profits, returned his regular envelope of Tory Party cash and instructions with the words: 'I will see you to the devil first!'

Hearst, Northcliffe and Beaverbrook were never bribed: the rotary press, said Northcliffe, was 'more powerful than the portfolio'. But when Owen Glendower says he can 'call spirits from the vasty deep', Shakespeare's sceptical Hotspur asks, 'Will they come?' The issue, notoriously, was tested in 1930, when Beaverbrook, and Northcliffe's brother Rothermere, tried to impose Empire Free Trade on Stanley Baldwin's government – assailing his candidate for a Westminster by-election with every armament of the *Express* and the *Daily Mail*.

Baldwin's response was a legendary stump oration. How curious, he said, that Hearst, Rothermere and Beaverbrook fancied newspaper ownership qualified them for political command – Rothermere, for instance, offering to support the Tories if allowed to supervise their policies and their Cabinet selection. In forming an administration, said Baldwin, he would have to tell the King, 'Sire, these names are not necessarily my choice, but they have the support of Lord Rothermere.' Repudiating the 'insolent demand', he followed up with a lethal soundbite provided by his cousin Rudyard Kipling, saying that what these newspapermen sought was 'power without responsibility – the prerogative of the harlot through the ages'.

In routing his enemies, Baldwin showed that a serious politician can crush direct invasion of electoral processes. But it is worth cross-referring the Lyons–Murdoch correspondence with less celebrated parts of his speech. The *Express* and *Mail*, Baldwin said, were only 'engines' for the 'desires, personal wishes, personal likes and dislikes of two men'. They represented no real interests – not even their famous ambition to save imperial commerce from foreign goods. He quoted sales material that the two managements were using to attract US advertisers, which claimed that with *Express* and *Mail* assistance many American brands had become 'household words in Great Britain', and he added, 'So much for the United Empire Party and Empire Free Trade!'

Beaverbrook and Rothermere were not serious – or not serious about Empire Free Trade in the way Keith Murdoch was serious about radio licences. In another way, the Beaver *was* serious: the way of the partisan past. He was an eighteenth-century pamphleteer, his business having grown so profitable through technology that he became his own patron. He patronised additionally much socialist pamphleteering by his ideological enemy and dear friend Michael Foot, later Labour Party leader; no more than Northcliffe did he use newspapers as a direct medium of exchange. But via his technical lieutenant Christiansen he brought about changes in newspaper practice ('black arts' he called them) which helped his successors, Rupert Murdoch especially, to do so.

When Christiansen joined Beaverbrook people understood what the front page was (Ben Hecht had already made it the title of a famous play). Christiansen reinvented it. Columns in Victorian hand-typesetting displayed the regularity of a Greek temple. But after on-line type-casting ('hot metal') arrived in the 1890s, headlines and illustrations expanded, and the classical structure decayed. Christiansen dynamited the ruins, recreating the page as free space – into which text and pictures flowed to generate any image necessary for projecting the events at his disposal. Though not alone, he was the virtuoso, creating a template which rules every British or Australian broadsheet, and influences many American ones. The *Financial Times'* version is the most staid, the *Independent'*s (or the *Australian'*s) most polished, but the aim is anyway Christiansen's – using the whole page (the whole paper) as a swiftly scanned meta-story about the package of stories offered. The size and layout of the human body make it less effective on the smaller, tabloid scale. Limitations of hardware and bandwidth still inhibit Internet emulation.

Electronic print technology actually favours such an intercourse of word and image. But juggling some 1,200 hot-metal castings per page demanded improbably assorted skills: visual grasp, mathematical insight, verbal wit, *Fingerspitzengefühl*. It was rather like bonding a wall from small bricks of varying size, while solving (against time) jigsaw puzzles moulded into the bricks. These arts made for a shift in editorial power-structure which, if not irrevocable, remains unrevoked, in Britain especially. They required an expanded corps of print-interface experts: 'the subs' (from 'sub-editor'), a subordinate role which was elevated by technical need.

With form and content integrated, the British newspaper product improved sharply. But its profession, never so much formalised as in the US or Australian case, split into antagonistic mysteries – for even those few with equal aptitude for subbing and reporting rarely had time to maintain dexterity in both. Positional power accrued to the subs, astride the output channel. Christiansen was the ur-sub, and his disciples – expert, office-bound, often happy to come in from the cold of primary newsgathering – invested the Fleet Street village. When Murdoch and his followers say British journalists are the world's best, they mean – the subs. To William Rockhill Nelson, making the *Kansas City Evening Star* famous in the 1880s, the reporter was 'the big toad in the puddle . . . we could get on pretty well without our various sorts of editors. But the reporter . . . is the only fellow who has any business around newspapers or magazines.' Nelson's Law had been modified everywhere by the 1950s. But the news-paper to which Pickering introduced Murdoch was close to repealing it.

The curiosity is that Christiansen himself admired great reporters for succeeding where he had not, and intended his 'black arts' for their ser-vice: 'Our Page One purpose is to give the hard, cold, complicated picture of real events in bright focus, as well as to project the human twiddly-bits that make for conversation in the pubs.' This hard, bright expertise fascinated reporters of Murdoch's generation throughout the Anglophone world, Australians especially. They were inclined to think highly of their own news-gathering – but felt that it might look best in the *Express*, attracting, perhaps, a line in one of the pungent bulletins Christiansen addressed to the performance of his team.

While Rupert wrestled with PPE, twenty-eight-year-old Adrian Deamer arrived in London with roughly that idea. Adrian had grown up while Syd edited Frank Packer's Sydney *Daily Telegraph*, and went to uni-versity set on circumventing heredity and becoming an architect. By the time he had done with the Second AIF and the RAAF, Syd, was a legend still but no longer a newspaper power. By the reversed dynastic logic of the Deamers, this opened journalism as a career for Adrian.

His record of five years with the *Telegraph* and the Melbourne *Age* persuaded the *Express* to offer a trial: an opportunity to survive among the pitiless men and women Fleet Street papers sent out during those days to hunt exclusives. In this he prospered, and led the paper with one of the nuclear defectors of those Cold War years. 'Newcomer Adrian Deamer gave us a useful beat on Pontecorvo,' wrote Christiansen approvingly on Adrian's story of an ex-Italian physicist en route to Moscow with another shipment of British weapons expertise. Deamer was encouraged to stay, but he could see that while the *Express* still gave a superb postgraduate class in news-presentation, its noontide was past. In 1952 he returned to Australia, not quite crossing paths with Murdoch – who arrived on a very different basis the next year – but taking with him skills which would help him, seventeen years later, save Rupert from corporate humiliation.

From this point onward the *Express* appears ingloriously in the background to the Murdoch story, but Christiansen's idea of popular journalism deserves a parting glance. A newspaper's business, he thought, was continuously to re-educate both its staff and its audience. Readers might be uninterested in opera, vintage claret, modern poetry or 'dry-as-dust economics', but 'It is our job to interest them in everything. It requires the highest degree of skill and ingenuity.' The *Express* approach to people in 'the back streets of Derby' contained neither flattery nor contempt; it saw in them a 'thirst after knowledge'. It had little in it of Northcliffe – a commercial, not an editorial innovator – saying his readers were 'only ten', and nothing of Murdoch's reply to a proposal that the *Sun* in its triumphal 1970s might attempt some current-affairs briefing: 'I'm not having any of that up-market shit in my paper.'

One flaw in the *Express* model has since undermined the entire popular project. Christiansen insisted on a principle that Hearst (and before him Horace Greeley) also stated: 'There is no subject, no abstract thing, that cannot be translated into terms of people.' It is true enough to be useful: we may take to physics better with Newton's apple than with orders to 'Consider the equation $F = MA$'. The *Express* strove to reveal everything through an exemplary victim, beneficiary or hero – of disaster, triumph or insight.

Yet some abstractions rendered in 'terms of people' intrinsically mislead. The image of one gaunt child may project the famine of sub-Saharan multitudes. But no such image of a murdered British child – singularly tragic – conveys the *absence* of multitudes: just the reverse.

Infanticide's decline in modern society is real, but stubbornly abstract. Newspapers' refusal to engage with abstraction and number corrupts popular reportage most visibly in crime and ethnicity. David Krajicek refers to 'the tabloidization of America', but the phenomenon is international, taking place over a half-century in which society has altered in ways which are unavoidably statistical.

No rigid distaste of audiences for mathematics is responsible for this – sports cover is numerate, and opinion-poll data is a tabloid staple when convenient. That popular papers, so far from modernising their discourse, have spent decades in regression is viewed by financial analysts as business realism, owing much to Murdoch's sagacious leadership. As we shall see, it has been accompanied by a vast decline in popular-newspaper sales – a curious sagacity.

Under a confident surface the *Express* at the time of Murdoch's 1953 tutelage was becoming a vessel of cranky obsessions, ruled by arbitrary power. Pickering was overseer of this process (though the ailing Christiansen held editorial title till 1957). The Beaver might not use his papers for business leverage, but Meyer's notion of self-restraint was equally remote. Rights to publish he claimed as rights to make 'propaganda' – and essentially he had always taken that view. In 1938, when Neville Chamberlain said the Munich Agreement surrendered only a 'faraway country', Christiansen felt sick, but Beaverbrook said harshly: 'Well, isn't Czecho-Slovakia a faraway country?' 'I agreed . . . and got on with my job of *producing an exciting newspaper*' (emphasis added). Admirably, *Express* philosophy said that 'important' was equivalent to exciting, never a lazy synonym for 'dull'. Less admirably, excitement was something editors could organise independently of its emotional roots, like engineers manipulating electricity irrespective of its generation.

But war, when it came, changed everything, and among the finest hours it enabled was that of the *Daily Express*. So far from returning to 1914–18's 'golden age of lying', Anglo-American journalism in 1939–45 was basically honest and frequently superb, and the *Express*, its technique fired by authentic emotions, operated at the cutting edge. Within the anti-Nazi framework, liberals, orthodox conservatives and outright socialists like Michael Foot could make common cause with Beaverbrook – an effect which did not end immediately in 1945 – and among them were some reporters of a quality hard to surpass, such as James Cameron, René MacColl and Alan Moorehead (certainly the Melbourne newsroom's finest product, able to unite literature and popular journalism as Crane had done for Hearst).

But by the mid-1950s propagandist orthodoxies were reviving: the Beaver was returning to his political home on the fruitcake right – the slice of it obsessed with Euro-corruptions – and the brilliant individuals, as they moved on, were rarely replaced. Reporters may make mistakes or even lie deliberately, but contact with their sources makes it difficult for them to be good propagandists. Amid oceanic uncertainty, a reporter will cling to any flimsy insight with the object cathexis of a mariner for an upturned boat. And when reporters deform reality, it may not be predictably. The *Express* solution, in the Beaver's twilight, was to treat its own reporting staff as a raw input for the creative subs' desk. I knew a man in the Pickering days who was well paid to write each day one paragraph only – whatever he liked, as long as it tarnished the 'Common Market'.

It had also become an advanced workshop of what management analysts wryly call 'creative tension'. Its shiny Fleet Street palazzo was nicknamed the Black (or Glass) Lubianka: the paper was fascinated by doings in the actual Moscow Lubianka, headquarters of the KGB, and ironic kinship with its own office politicking was implied. Life might be safe, but a job rarely so. The wise sub, it was said, looked around carefully before standing up to fart. It was a bleak environment for dissent, in that almost anyone might be swiftly replaced from the reserve armies in Britain's provincial cities. The memoirs of William Barkley tell the defining story of a colleague scraping acquaintance in El Vino's wine-bar, only to find himself talking to the stranger taking over his job the next day. His boss, confronted, could only mutter, 'But you weren't supposed to know.' 'Well,' snarled the victim, 'I used to be a reporter, and I picked it up around town.'

Nor was the *Express* unique. Guy Bartholomew of the *Mirror* set a moral datum by demoting men who left to fight Hitler. In later years the *Mirror*'s pub was called The Stab in the Back, and his dark spirit probably approved. 'Come over here – and bring your bollocks with you' was a howled reprimand on the *Mirror* subs desk well before its incorporation in the *Sun*'s disciplinary code.

It is argued here that a chronic natural insecurity dominates the reporter's occupation. Anyone who has done the work knows that nobody truly escapes being 'as good as the last story'. It may be surprising that sub-editorial cadres should have endured greater professional instability, for practice skews the natural risks of news-gathering away from them. Rarely invested in the unknown outcome of a particular investigation, the sub selects among known outcomes of many investigations by others (exceptions exist, but the principle is true). If, as in the observable Fleet Street case, subs' insecurities are as great as those of reporters (and acute as often as chronic) this owes less to chance and necessity than it does to corporate design.

Power, while individually fickle, has been loyal institutionally to the subs' desk – from which, as Roy Greenslade observes, the recent editors of major British newspapers have chiefly come. Honourable men are employed there (and women, though that reform arrived at glacial speed). But the speciality of presentation encourages some into a corruption classically enunciated by Bernard Shrimsley – one of Rupert Murdoch's first lieutenants at the *Sun* – in which journalists allegedly resemble a barrister making a case. A rich man, or corporation, is surely entitled under the law to have a cause selectively advocated.

This ignores the fact that the Bar accepts restraints which the *Sun* ignores. But it is anyway a difficult attitude for a reporter, who must retain some capacity for personal engagement on the ground. A test of the difference can be made by asking a barrister for the details of a ten-year-old case; more often than not, it will have been wiped from memory. The reporter's memory will often be highly detailed, even photographic, and a cross-bearing on the issue is provided by Christiansen's memoir, *Headlines All My Life*, in which he says that as editor he never kept a diary, because he thought the files of his newspaper would bring everything back to him. But, when he came to look, most of them conveyed nothing at all. His techniques were capable of destroying their own purpose: they had helped the *Express* to its reputation as a great reporting newspaper, but turned it within a decade or less into a mechanism which could be disconnected from reality at will.

Newscorp's standard counter to charges of tabloid degradation is that its papers do no more than was always done. And the characteristics of its decisive cash-spinners, the *Sun* and *News of the World*, indeed descend visibly from the *Express* – and to some extent from the *Daily Mirror* – of the days when Pickering imparted the lore of Old Fleet Street to Rupert. The same 'creative tension' appears, the same docile subs concocting 'exciting' newspapers, with a lack of restraint that can seem grotesque – though the grotesque was never foreign to the Street. The Newscorp flagship, observes *Stick It Up Your Punter* – the *Sun*'s very unofficial history – is and was a 'rip-off' from pre-existing notions.

Murdoch's defence is ironic, in the Greek playwright's sense of irony – truth more than the speaker knows or intends. The Newscorp tabloids indeed have not done anything more than was done when he started in the game. They have done less. The corruptions of the *Express* are visible, but today's Camerons and MacColls, the reporters of high quality, are nowhere to be found in popular newspapers. It is of course astonishing that they ever coexisted with Christiansen's boss, but an important curiosity about Beaverbrook distinguishes him from Murdoch: he never quit the losing side of a political divide. Indeed no resistance, to the Abdication of Edward VIII, the election of Labour, the independence of India or British accession to Europe, was authentically kaput until the Beaver joined it, and something similar is true of Hearst and Northcliffe. If Plato and Adorno are right that a tyrant sides only with prospective victory, the description does not fit them, despots though they were.

Orthodox accounts are that Murdoch 'took a job' on the *Express* in 1953 after his Oxford finals and before returning to Australia to join Rohan Rivett at the Adelaide *News*. This was not a position gained and held in the Deamer manner, nor did he make any comparable impact. Murdoch spent four months on the subs' desk under the aegis of Ted Pickering. Rather than a job taken, this was a hereditary favour via the late parent's connection.

It was no place for Murdoch to repair his lack of expertise. The *Express* may have been in lesser shape than its paladins thought, but it was still too sophisticated a scene for anyone not already expert to practise journalism seriously. In order to acquire anything of the qualities which remained in the *Express*, you had to be capable of working in its engine-room. For a visitor on the bridge, there was nothing to be seen except the efficacy of arbitrary power in a newspaper undergoing propagandist decay.

Besides the chief items of Sir Keith's will – the Adelaide and Brisbane papers of the Herald chain – what was Rupert Murdoch's inheritance? From the *Herald* and his own country's reporting tradition he was isolated by dynastic choices and circumstances, which accounts for Australia being journalistic *terra nullius* in the standard accounts of Keith and Rupert. Oxford, which he found intellectually stimulating, drew out his polemic dexterity. When Murdoch nowadays equates Western media regulation to the restraints of totalitarian China – representing both as erosions of the First Amendment, to which Newscorp defers out of respect for global diversity – something may be credited to those PPE essays.

Like the classical *Express*, Oxford offers much else. But if rhetorical fluency engages you, the facilities are superb, and even include vocational training for one newspaper department: the leader column, or editorial. John Douglas Pringle (a fine editor of the *Sydney Morning Herald*, and professional rival of Murdoch's) reckoned on the basis of his own degree that almost any Oxford graduate could generate leaders with an *Encyclopaedia Britannica* to hand: '[they] are a lot easier to write without experience and training than, say, a news report . . . it is rather like . . . being asked to write "not more than 500 words" on, say, the domestic policy of the Emperor Tiberius . . .'. As this suggests, leaders are operationally trivial – but they are nonetheless critical, because they are the currency in which politicians (unwisely) value newspapers. However shaky his grasp elsewhere, Murdoch has always coped ably with leaders.

Biographers present Sir Keith's personal heritage as Rupert's chief link to Australian roots, and a professionally challenging example. But by taking the father at face value, they greatly underestimate. For a journalist this could only be a heavy incubus. Keith's heroic national status depended on secret, untruthful smears against an English officer-class he actually toadied to when convenient. His real quality – as a conspirator reckless of national security – expressed itself in efforts to undo a true Australian hero. Something of his role in 1915–19 might be defended as that of a minor agent in largely misguided causes (any credit must be given to Hughes, his boss). Defending Keith the reporter is hardly possible: the First Amendment bargain, as he showed again in 1940, seems never to have crossed his mind.

In newspaper operations he was ambitious and shrewd, but rarely creative: jealous of skilful colleagues; adept in flattery and credit-poaching; a fluent, imprecise writer; essentially devious; 'cold and manipulative', in the words of the historian John Hetherington; a trader of insider secrets and favours, according to George Munster. He wanted to bequeath an empire, but it was one to which his legal and moral title was narrower than he made it seem.

The Adorno proposal is that disorders of authority arise out of failure to achieve critical distance from our parents – a failure the parents may enhance. This is only denied entirely by the few scientists who say personality is genetic. Mostly, it is agreed that some free will exists, which we must use to gain perspective, and to discover our parents realistically. As nobody finds exactly their desire, distress is likely: respect, or charity, an achievement. Whether the Freudian bestiary – id, ego, superego – is valid science or not, if psychology only restates the Greek tragedians on the fate of parents and children, the force of the Adorno proposal suffices. The struggle for independence is central, wrote Erich Fromm in *The Fear of Freedom*, both to normal development and to neurosis.

It was certainly Keith Murdoch's project to fashion Rupert Murdoch as a continuation of himself, personal and professional – that is, of his own character as publicly defined, and as loyally maintained by his wife. Dame Elisabeth Murdoch* – from every account a strong, generous character, recipient of more unforced respect than any other member of the family – holds intact the image of the hero she married when she was nineteen. To this example she has consistently and publicly insisted the heir should conform. In 1953, she gave him little choice about it.

Sir Keith considered in the early 1950s a variety of schemes for reshaping the 'Murdoch press' outside of, and competitive with, the Herald structure – including a partnership with the *Mirror* in London. At the same time several colleagues were scheming to eject him from the group, led by the managing director Jack Williams in the role of Keith during the Finks' latter days. Amid these intrigues, only one big move was complete at Keith's death – his purchase of the Adelaide *News*, owned by the group since Davidson's death. In part-payment the group received

*Lady Murdoch became Dame Elisabeth when she was awarded the DBE in 1963.

options over his far more valuable controlling minority in Queensland Press (the Brisbane *Courier-Mail*). Doubtless a chess game was halted in which both sides had seen several moves ahead.

Lady Murdoch, as she then was, became under the will trustee of the Murdoch estate, jointly with H. D. Giddy, finance director of the Herald group. Sir Keith had always regarded Giddy as an ally against Theodore Fink, and a Herald role in settling the estate was necessary: the trust structure would reduce tax liabilities, but some part of the Queensland value would be needed to meet them. (Settlement was not reached until 1961, which takes us into the next chapter.) The trustees could give Rupert control of the newspaper properties only if they found him capable of running them properly and making a 'useful life' in command of them. By the standards of the time and place – not arbitrary ones at all – no rational basis existed for such a finding. Responsibility may well be borne young; after all, Rupert was the age of (say) a flight leader in the Battle of Britain. But the pilot would have had valid training and experience. Rupert, on the other hand, did not meet requirements for the bottom grade of editorial responsibility in the company over which his father had presided. The trust had nonetheless to exercise a judgment – otherwise it, and its tax advantages, would be invalid.

There were some useful points of appearance and practice. A link with the *Daily Express* then conferred an éclat that now seems impossible to imagine, and that was provided via Ted Pickering. Also the *News*, the urgent case, was already in the competent hands of Rohan Rivett, a loyal friend to both Rupert and his mother – who much admired Rivett.

But essentially it was a hereditarian proposition. Elisabeth could say that Sir Keith had at the end thought Rupert a fit successor to himself. Sir Keith on the last day of his life received a letter from Rupert describing the British Labour Party conference – he was present as an Oxford student representative – and turning to Elisabeth said, 'Thank God, I think he's got it.' By no realistic standard could such a judgment rest on a scrap of private correspondence. But who better than Australia's dominant newspaperman to judge that Rupert had inherited his talents? Obsequies aside, Sir Keith's colleagues had their doubts about him both as journalist and as man. The widow, however, was universally liked and respected.

She did, however, make plain to Rupert that there could be no evading the emulation now due from him. According to William Shawcross' biography, there was a dialogue – shortly after Sir Keith's death – in which Lady Murdoch demanded Rupert repay her support by accepting his father's example, and his father's expectations. This was said by members of the family to have 'shaken him to his foundations'.

Ever since, Rupert's assertions of fidelity to the example have continued, ritualistically – though modified, over the half-century, to cope with Elisabeth's public distaste for a tabloid empire she clearly never foresaw. His mother took too much notice of his critics, said Murdoch when asserting this fidelity recently, in a long interview for the January 2000 edition of the *British Journalism Review*, and she was wrong, he said, to fear for Sir Keith's standards, summing up firmly: 'His ideals are my ideals.'

Connecting the ideal journalist–statesman Sir Keith with tabloid vigilantism and escapades like the Hitler Diaries is absurd – and the Anzac spirit accommodating itself to the pseudo-Marxist thugs of Beijing is still more disagreeable. But with the real man there is an acceptable fit, truth being ironic, as it is in the early speeches Sophocles gives to Oedipus. Keith was better than Rupert has been at appearances. But the son's political and organisational techniques resemble those of the hidden father in many substantial ways.

To become, as he did, a quite unprepared journalist–proprietor Murdoch had to adopt a respectable myth about his father. The validation he needed depended on the validity of the myth itself: his independence began in an act of submission. And this 'official' father has remained dynastically intact ever since, though not robust enough, in truth, to withstand any significant amount of the curiosity essential to journalism – a curiosity which must not be deterred by uncertainty about its destination. Investigation, like charity, begins at home.

None of this applies to Dame Elisabeth. First, the relationship of partners begins (more or less) with the independent capacities which a child is still constructing. Second, there was no professional resonance for her, no obligation of inquiry. If she preserved a deeply mistaken estimate of Sir Keith as a professional icon, it was not her profession. It left untouched her own life's work of voluntary service to the poor and disadvantaged.

Research and common sense suggest that everyone carries some authoritarian damage, but that most people grow up sufficiently poised for life's ordinary inconsistencies, not pursued by a need to dominate or submit. The Adorno team remarked that authoritarian people often function admirably where structure, responsibility and discipline enable them them to minimise the ambiguous – as judges, engineers, senior administrators. But the news business exists only to *seek* ambiguities. Such discipline as it has rests on expelling anyone suffering the authoritarian need to be certain before being right.

No sign exists that Murdoch has ever looked straight at Murdoch: biographies and profiles report, in common form, the heroic version. The diarist Woodrow (Lord) Wyatt was Boswell to the Newscorp elite from 1985 to 1997, and his record shows Rupert's table-talk reinforced still with strands from the Dardanelles jeremiad. It isn't a son's office to disparage his father, but in the Wyatt context the Murdoch of 1915 is invoked as Rupert's exemplary predecessor, scourging contemporary Britain with valiant truths. Here Keith succeeds in continuing himself, as a component of Rupert the synthetic iconoclast.

It would have been arduous in the 1950s fully to illuminate the mystery of Keith Murdoch (much military history, for instance, such as Serle's *Monash*, is the work of subsequent decades). But that there was enough to start on, few people in journalism or politics doubted: many, as Rupert knew, saw in Keith a cynical servant of established authority. It is not so hard now to learn that an English staff officer did most to reduce the Gallipoli débâcle; that Australian journalism owed little to Northcliffe's protégé; that the *Herald* was not really a Murdoch creation. Specialist histories, documents and old newspaper files link naturally to each other via strands of curiosity.

Such curiosity is anaesthetised among Murdoch's employees, to whom Keith remains 'THE JOURNALIST WHO STOPPED A WAR' (as *The Times* put it with sweeping naivety) and a classic voice of conscience. 'For courtiers to survive at the court of King Rupert,' wrote Andrew Neil, veteran of a decade's service at the *Sunday Times*, 'they . . . have to be adept at anticipating their master's wishes and acting in his interests' – but their adeptness is barely tested by the case of a dynastic record which is explicitly approved, and can be sustained largely by oversight (of review assignments and so on). In Australia, where the history lies nearest the surface, Newscorp is responsible for about three-quarters of mainstream newspaper employment. The simple discovery that, contrary to his claim, Rupert is not a second-generation iconoclast fails to be made.

Few people, probably, will doubt that Rupert Murdoch's personality is authoritarian, if only because his ruthlessness is paraded rather than denied. To explain its impact we must be clear that this is ruthlessness of a particular sort. The authoritarian, says Erich Fromm, has attributes that are commonly found: activity, courage or belief. But their expression is uncommon, because he gains the strength to act through adherence to superior power. The News story records the impact of a courageous, intrinsically insecure man on an intrinsically insecure profession – one he has studied to make more insecure, and which he has learnt to rule by 'terrorism' (Andrew Neil's word).

Murdoch's personal inheritance imposed a career on him, but stripped from his character the qualities it implacably demands. And whatever appearances may have suggested, the story set in context shows him – blunders aside – concerned in very little consequential journalism during many years' activity. As George Munster first noted, his papers are combative in style, not in substance: they do not evoke from state or corporate power the authentic backlash which, once felt, is never forgotten by anyone in newspapers or television. Instead we find a Newscorp doctrine that entertainment is preferable to news. It's not obvious that this is a useful preference, except insofar as some enter- tainment can be scripted and controlled, whereas all news is accident-prone. Still less obvious, initially, is how this fits a corporate obsession with politics, which after all is only news, though rarely of the most gripping type.

Having failed as as sinister farce on the Western Front in 1918, the Keith Murdoch plot against John Monash recurs time and again as effec- tive melodrama on Rupert's corporate stage, as ambitions and rivalries manipulated to produce dominance and submission. The son's improved results need not mean that media people are grubbier than soldiers, only that organisations may be more or less robust against the attack an active authoritarian is qualified to launch. The AIF was a volunteer elite, with a temporary existence; nobody joined it except for honour and nobody (literally) was doing it for a living. Its basis was a military bureaucracy –

helpful to residually authoritarian members – modified by a democratic and collective ethos. Shielded from much of the ambiguity of civilian life, it presented to Keith an impregnable target.

Newspapers and television companies we shall find in various ways less robust – inevitably so. The question is not whether each outfit investigated was ever invincible, but whether it and its members might have been less fragile, whether the sociology of the media industries allows for an ethic somewhere between Sir Jocelyn Stevens' cheery definition of 'the law of Fleet Street [as] every man for himself' and the selfless companionship of Charlemagne's paladins Roland and Oliver.

At this stage, let's note only that, when Murdoch set out, tests of professional suitability as strong as any a free society might use were in place, having developed in response to the rise of industrial journalism – the media, as we now say – around the start of the twentieth century. Rupert was insulated from them, and it seems clear that his father intended that to be so.

4

BLACK JACK AND THE STUDENT PRINCE, 1900–1971

La reconnaissance de la plupart des hommes n'est qu'une secrète envie
de recevoir de plus grands bienfaits.

DUC DE LA ROCHEFOUCAULD

Politics is the art of putting people under obligation to you.

COLONEL JACOB L. ARVEY

Rohan Rivett's removal from the Adelaide *News* in 1960 has been much
recorded, and justified by Rupert Murdoch as a poignant consequence of
his friend's professional instability. More truly, it is poignant as an episode
in which Murdoch himself approached real journalistic achievement –
and chose to retreat. Sir Keith had installed Rivett as a pathfinder for
Rupert, and after Keith's death it was a 'great comfort' to Elisabeth to
know he was there. Loyalty is a scarce commodity, and had Rivett not
supplied it generously the inheritance might well have come to nothing
when Rupert arrived and began to describe himself as publisher of the
News.

The paper had come into Murdoch hands as an undistinguished fragment from the Herald empire, overshadowed by the morning *Advertiser*.
The correspondence between Rohan and Sir Keith – now in the
Australian National Library – records much concern over replacing
group services the *News* had long relied on, and retaining able staff in an

editorial backwater. Plainly the Herald bosses were confident that without Sir Keith a leadership vacuum would develop, making the *News* ripe for repossession. In spite of energy and legal control, that was not something Rupert could have done much about in his first two or three years. He had too little experience. The memoirs of Sir Norman Young, later chairman of News Ltd, say that old hands called him 'the boy publisher': use of the US title – then meaningless in Australia – demonstrated that he had no authentic role.

But Rivett supported him totally, and amply motivated the staff. David Bowman, editor later of the *Sydney Morning Herald*, wrote at the time that Rivett was not 'the easiest man in the world to work for' but that nonetheless 'a couple of times . . . Melbourne . . . held out attractive bait that I rejected', because there was no editor of whom he might be as proud. Rivett's means were simple. The *News* addressed issues ignored elsewhere, and most notably ethnic ones, domestic and international. This was a time of editorial anaesthesia, when the Sydney *Bulletin* – fountainhead, once, of the nation's radical democracy – carried on its masthead the words 'AUSTRALIA FOR THE WHITE MAN'.

As Rivett's *News* showed no sign of dissolution, Murdoch had time to start learning his trade. In October 1953 the *News* reported the Murdoch estate's sale of Sir Keith's Queensland Press shares to the Herald group, stressing its own independence and the local residence of all its own directors – Rupert and Rohan included. Rupert would have been a Brisbane resident if he could have persuaded his mother to pay off the estate's taxes by borrowing against the *Courier-Mail*'s value, and keeping the shares. But he had to attempt a patriotism for Adelaide.

Lacking both gold and convicts, this was always the most decorous of Australian cities, but not always the oddity it had become by the 1950s. When the British scientist A. P. Rowe arrived to run Adelaide University he knew it as a considerable institution (training-ground of Marcus Oliphant, a pioneer of modern electronics). But Sir David Rivett's principles had vanished from this segment of Australian intellectual life: university policy-making came under Tom Playford, South Australia's premier – and very little in the state did not. Normal government, Rowe concluded, had been suspended. This condition can be traced to the Depression's devastating impact on South Australia. Sir Thomas – as he saw it – had personally rebuilt the state, and he ran it in corporatist style, via a tiny, obedient cabal. Rivett and Murdoch were not members. And in 1959 they became the focus of its loathing.

Ceduna, 490 miles north-west of Adelaide, is the last halt before the emptiness of the Nullarbor Plain, with Western Australia far away. The name may come from an Aboriginal word for 'resting-place': Ceduna four decades ago saw itself existing at civilisation's rim. On 12 September 1958, the body of nine-year-old Mary Olive Hattam was found in a cave beside the brilliant waters of Murat Bay; she had been raped, and battered to death.

Rupert Max Stuart, from a people then called Aranda in the northern interior, was arrested. He had travelled to Ceduna as odd-job man with a funfair – a representative young black of his time, living on the white world's fringe, a frequent drunk and brawler. He was illiterate, and scarcely articulate in English. But having agreed a coherent confession, he was taken to Adelaide and was scheduled to hang. Only the pathos of Mary's fate seemed to make the case unusual. However, the lawyers assigned to defend Stuart disbelieved his confession. Their appeals, though denied, generated disquiet.

In July 1959 Rivett met Father Thomas Dixon, a missionary to the Aboriginal peoples, Stuart's death-cell counsellor. Rivett said he did not think it a case for an anti-hanging campaign. Dixon, however, was suggesting a racist frame-up. Stuart both repudiated his confession and claimed he had been at work when Mary died. The sketchy police inquiry had not contacted Norman and Edna Gieseman, the funfair's owners, by now in Queensland. Dixon could find them, but had no airfare, and the execution was imminent. Rivett put Dixon on a plane with the *News*' chief crime reporter.

On oath, the Giesemans corroborated Stuart, justifying a simple, explosive headline: 'PRIEST: STUART HAS PERFECT ALIBI: Murder case bombshell'. Sir Thomas had to put off the hangman and commission an inquiry. Adelaide found itself a national, even international story – one London account invoked the Dreyfus case – and Playford found that not all South Australians shared his outrage.

Circumstances were ready to amplify the conflicting emotions stirred by race, paedophile savagery and the gallows. First, Australia's urban middle classes – with international experience broadened by two world wars – knew their society was a comfortably advanced one, and ignoring the gross exception created by *terra nullius* was becoming harder. But to outposts like Ceduna the disinherited blacks at their fringes were menacing, not pitiable. Second, capital punishment, having been intrinsic to the penal colonies, affronted progressive nationalists. But frustration had followed the early defeat of its military use. Though Red Ted's Queensland banned hanging in 1922, conservative state bosses like Playford were tenacious defenders. So execution was a geographic lottery, as it has become again in America. Long-damped journalistic sparks struck this volatile material.

Many Australian reporters had found exciting work in wartime, and many idealistic ambitions survived into the peace. But with the 1950s a competent blandness infected the editorial offices of Fairfax's *Sydney Morning Herald*, those of the one-time 'Murdoch press' and those of their chief rivals. Anti-communist stresses having split Labor's Catholic constituency, Robert Menzies monopolised federal power, and over a land where social dynamics had relied heavily on party contention, a soggy membrane of consensus spread.

To Jack Williams of the Herald group and Rupert ('Rags') Henderson of Fairfax, this was not unwelcome. They were preoccupied with commercial television licences and, being intimates of Menzies, knew his doubts about letting newspaper companies share in the new gold-rush. Even conservative journalists sometimes agitated public opinion deplorably, and Menzies was not sure they could be trusted with a new and potent medium. Discrepancies in the nation's ethnic arrangements were just the kind of thing Menzies thought better left obscure. The major newspapers and networks had noticed the Stuart trials and appeals, and had even reported Father Dixon's belief in missing evidence. None dared take the investigative initiative – least of all the *Advertiser*, essentially the Playford regime in print.

Rivett's 'bombshell' broke this dubious calm. Every editorial and legal eye in the country focused on Adelaide and its Royal Commission – where, to the bench's fury, Jack Shand QC, Sydney's deadliest cross-examiner, came representing Stuart. Meanwhile other cultural detonators were taking effect. In England, the idea of the 'establishment' had just been unmasked by the columnist Henry Fairlie, and to many reporters it seemed that a powerful chapter must be operating in Adelaide. The potent – but still undocumented – legend of Keith at Gallipoli came to life, establishing Rupert suddenly as a second-generation exponent of emotionally committed journalism.

Alan Reid of Packer's *Telegraph* found himself unique in not caring whether Stuart was hanged or not (it was 'a good story either way'). Writing privately, he reckoned he could hardly remember anything able to 'divide newspapermen the way this one did'. There was a 'wonderful study' in the:

> complex motives that animated the various individuals who surged and fought over the body of the incoherent Stuart [including] Rohan, firmly astride a white horse with a Crusader's glint in his eye, and Rupert, the young proprietor, delighted at the trouble he had stirred up and yet intermittently fearful as to what might be the outcome . . .

The three Commissioners told Shand they would not test the verdict – he had to shake their confidence in it. One having been Stuart's judge at first instance, and another – Chief Justice Sir Mellis Napier, Playford's senior disciple – on appeal, this was no surprise: just a manifestation of the Commission's scandalous composition. But here the *News* stumbled into hazard.

Sir Mellis – who clearly disapproved of newspapers offering evidence, however significant to justice – blocked Shand's cross-examination of the first police witness. Declaring that 'this Commission is unable properly to consider the problems before it', Shand walked out. Swiftly, the *News* had a poster on the street: 'SHAND QUITS: "YOU WON'T GIVE STUART FAIR GO"'. Murdoch devised a punchier replacement, which Rivett agreed: 'COMMISSION BREAKS UP: SHAND BLASTS NAPIER'. And this went fractionally too far: the Commission, though disrupted, was still in business, and Shand had subtly avoided a personal focus on Napier. To Playford's men such tiny errors invited prosecution of a newspaper which was promoting 'mob rule'.

Nine counts of defamation were eventually aimed at Rivett and News

Ltd, among them seditious libel, which the blunderbuss John Peter Zenger had faced in New York in 1735. As a judge in present-day Australia can be called a 'wanker' with impunity, Playford's repressive aspirations now seem absurd, but they were not quite so in his own time. That said, the *News* – with Murdoch taking control – backed off further than Zenger and his counsel Andrew Hamilton ever did.

Anticipating prosecution, the *News* ran an editorial by Murdoch, 'LET'S GET THE RECORD STRAIGHT'. It apologised for quote-marks on headline and poster paraphrases, and said 'SHAND BLASTS NAPIER' should have been 'SHAND ATTACKS NAPIER'. Defamation being a matter of content, not punctuation, and the gap between blasting and attacking being insignificant, none of this mattered. Murdoch's poster had been inaccurate – something not admitted – but no sane court would drive charges through so slight a factual crevice.

Unhappily, Adelaide's bosses just then were not quite sane, which was why Sir Tom saw criminality when Napier & Co. were criticised as judges of their own decisions. The *News* had an invincible right to report that, as interstate and international experts swiftly confirmed. But powers irrational enough to think otherwise were not to be appeased by apologetic trivia, and when that became clear, Murdoch decided that the *News* must abandon the principle. It denied editorially any intention to convey criticism of judicial actions.

Though journalists rail tribally against lawyers, experience tells them that a legitimate judicial system will recover from its excesses, and that the process is never accelerated by conceding on essentials. A decent respect for authority rests on a belief that it will come back to respecting its own rules.

But it seems likely Murdoch was concerned more to appease the powers of Adelaide than to maintain editorial credibility and legal principle. Once new lawyers had been found for Stuart, the Commissioners resumed work. And while they deliberated, Murdoch proposed a merger between News Ltd and the Advertiser group. News would give three new units of its own stock and some cash for four existing Advertiser shares. No votes would attach to the new equity – Murdoch began, and remains, resistant to modern capitalism's ideas about democratic equity – so that financial control of the Advertiser and its Herald shares would fall to him. This, along with the deal's price-tag – A£14 million when News Ltd had issued capital of only A£565,000 – made its acceptance implausible.

But non-financial aspects of the plan showed his determination to accommodate Playford's Adelaide, notably provisions for a trust to secure the *Advertiser*'s editorial character. Suitable persons to conduct it were identified as the Chancellor of Adelaide University, or the Chief Justice of South Australia. Just then, both offices were held by Sir Mellis Napier, who was revealing at the Commission a strong desire to suppress journalistic activism no matter how well justified. This scheme was rejected with a paragraph in the *Advertiser* suggesting that the paper was best run by local patriots and that Rupert was not one of those.

Anti-climax supervened at the Commission. The revised official case portrayed Stuart as a courtroom veteran and linguistic counterfeiter. But this made his frank confession still less plausible – unless gained by torture or other inadmissible means – and lack of forensic data was irreparable. The evidence would never have hanged a white Australian, and the *Telegraph*, pointing out from Sydney that discounting a black life might appear racist to Asians, probably chimed with the views of an embarrassed federal government. Stuart's sentence was commuted to life before the Commission's report. Months later his guilt was reaffirmed in that diffuse document, tabled with elaborate obscurity and barely reported.

The prosecution of Rivett and News Ltd in January 1960 was anti-climactic also. By this time even Sir Tom could appreciate the lethal recoil of seditious libel. It has to allege things so lurid as to capsize civil authority – indefensible even if true. But governments subject to election cannot admit that truth acts on them like holy water on the devil. (Essentially, Hamilton had used Zenger's case to launch the principle that allegations must be legally *disproved* in order to be legally suppressed.) And South Australia's social fabric visibly had not disintegrated over the notion that a Royal Commission could be packed: a judge free of previous involvement directed the jurors to ignore the sedition charge. They rejected seven other charges too, disagreeing on just one – which in June was quietly dropped. But by then Murdoch had shifted territory, geographic and editorial.

In Sydney – where News Ltd already ran a group of suburban papers – there had long been speculation about the *Daily Mirror*, weaker of the city's two evenings. On 21 May 1960 News bought Mirror Newspapers for A£1.9 million. Among the first people Murdoch told were the handful of radical journalists producing a small, influential journal, *Nation* – he is recalled charging up the stairs of their shabby office to shout: 'I've got it.' That they were his audience indicates how much the Stuart case had done to anoint him as the new bright hope of Australian journalism. But acquisition of John Norton's decayed legacy did not really point that way.

Richard Twopeny wrote that the Australian press was honest and unsensational 'almost without exception'. Ironically, those words were penned when Norton arrived in 1883, just as Norton was on his way to instigate a monstrous exception. Norton's *Truth* did – outdid – for the southern hemisphere the work of British organs like the *News of the World* and New York's *True Story* or (later) *Daily Graphic*. His journalism was as scabrous as anything of theirs, and his personal excesses overshadowed Hearst's. Norton, says Cyril Pearl in *Wild Men of Sydney*, was 'denounced many times as a thief, a blackmailer, a wife-beater and an obscene drunkard . . . [and was] accused of killing his oldest friend in a drunken quarrel'.

Truth became a weekly with editions in each major city. When Norton died in 1916, with Napoleonic statues clustered about him, it still had a certain livid vivacity, as he did have political ideas (identified by Pearl as proto-fascist). But by mid-century it offered little beyond routine court-house pornography. The *Mirror*, added in 1941 by Norton's son Ezra, widened the group's base, but was outgunned in the 1950s by the *Sun* – once Denison's paper, now Fairfax-controlled. Fairfax then ran Mirror Newspapers for several years – desiring to block abler competitors, and hoping to use newspaper companies as vehicles for television-licence applications. But the losses starved Fairfax's existing TV projects, and News Ltd's assumption of the burden was welcome in 1960. Rivett and Murdoch saw this investment dissimilarly.

Rivett's papers include an account of his sacking. On 7 July, just after the last defamation charge was dropped, he was typing an article when his secretary brought in two letters. 'I looked up to see she was in

tears . . . I finished the sentence on my typewriter and picked up the letters.' Both came from Murdoch in Sydney. One said in 180 typescript
words that Rivett was dismissed – for 'many' reasons it would be 'unwise'
to cite – and an acting managing editor, Ron Boland, was en route.
Rivett could become a 'star writer', or leave with eighteen months' salary.
This letter, Murdoch said, had taken much painful time to compose.
The other, handwritten, dwelt further on Rupert's distress:

> I have never loathed writing a letter more. In coming to this deci-
> sion to 'close your innings' as editor of The News I have not lost
> sight of your achievements – and our long personal friendship
> makes the whole thing impossibly hard. But there it is!
>
> I thought about getting you up here to tell you verbally first, but
> we can discuss it much better after you have had time to think it
> over.
>
> Sincerely, as ever,
>
> Rupert

The promise of reasons was unredeemed at Rivett's death in 1977.
However, Murdoch has subsequently been more forthcoming.
Interviewed for Channel 4's *The Real Rupert Murdoch* (1999) he said Rivett
had grown 'headstrong', and thus unreliable. William Shawcross, also
assisted by Murdoch, suggests rather similarly that Rivett was striking
leftish attitudes unsuited to the *News*. An 'impassioned' obituary of the
British socialist Aneurin Bevan crystallised matters, and Murdoch
ordered him out of the office that day.

This looks specious, because Bevan's news-value among working
people worldwide could then be likened, not intolerably, to Roosevelt's:
Adelaide has a large Labor population (to which Playford's Liberal and
Country League liked to offer a rural–socialist face) and *News* readers
would not automatically have recoiled from the subject. In detail it's
false, because the obituary – a response to breaking news – was the piece
on Rivett's typewriter when Murdoch's costive paperwork arrived.

Murdoch suggests his friend's professional marbles were adrift. But,
while the *News* never had an *Express* polish, its files display no gross
discontinuities under Rivett (nor evidence of another Murdoch

suggestion: renewed taunting of Playford over Stuart). The Bevan coverage was not smoothly presented, but completing it at all must have required steady professionalism.

Negatives are tricky. But Rivett's letters from readers and colleagues, stacking two inches thick, display none of the ambiguity usually seen if a departing editor has lost the plot. Their chief note is amazement that anyone able so to recreate an obscure publication should leave (by his own choice, a few assume, thinking no rational proprietor could desire it). David Bowman simply asked to be considered for Rivett's next paper.

Why offer, long after, an account discrediting Rivett as scatty and incompetent? It is a smokescreen over the real dispute: dispersal of the smoke reveals Murdoch's character in action, and a pattern not much varied since.

Among the papers is a letter to Murdoch on 28 May 1960, when the *Mirror* purchase was 'last week'. Clearly it is written after a hot personal exchange, one which Rivett says would have been intolerable 'except that I know you better'. He then deals calmly with the issues involved. A modest pay hike for the journalists' union (the AJA) had been awarded under the national arbitration system. The *News*, with record profits and buoyant sales, could easily afford it, but Murdoch – unlike the industry generally – was refusing to pay.

Rivett wanted to avoid confrontation at the *News*. Good staff now thought it an exciting paper, and the lure of bigger cities was resistible; denying a legitimate arbitration would imperil that. Rivett saw the *Mirror* purchase as a financial strain – which it plainly was – and warned against letting it erode the value of the *News*, potentially the kernel of a high-quality newspaper business. Much could be lost if staff felt they were going unrewarded to prop up Mirror Newspapers. (He did not say serious journalists thought the *Mirror* as toxic as it was unprofitable: that was notorious.)

Rivett's vision of News Ltd's future is best evaluated after penetrating further into Murdoch's. The contingent point is that it was neither eccentric nor reckless. Rupert's admirers might call it cautious or orthodox. But it was a fair business view, coolly put by a fellow director, concerning a shared responsibility. The evidence suggests that

Murdoch tried to shout down Rivett's doubts. When they were pursued with reasons, Murdoch didn't engage the criticism, but obliterated its source. 'Headstrong', the epithet projected on to Rivett, properly matched himself.

Murdoch's mother was more explicit, and more graceful, about the cost to Rivett of his own fidelity. 'My dear Rohan,' she wrote, 'I have always been so glad that you and Rupert were together in Adelaide. The connection she saw as having originated in loyalty to Keith, and it had been a great comfort to the family: the letter's implication was that she realised how much Rupert had depended on Rohan's friendship and support, and she 'could not bear to think that your close association with our own interests should hurt you.' But she thought it rather remarkable that the association had endured so long and Rivett perhaps smiled wryly at that. Rivett disappointed some colleagues by making no open protest. It seemed to concede justice to Murdoch, and to discredit the Stuart investigation.

The papers show he was concerned to improve his payoff (small even by the standards of the day). Murdoch's executive authority ran in practice to arbitrary sacking of an editor, but removing a director of a quoted company might require reasons. These he did not have, and Rivett avoided providing any by making statements likely to harm News at a delicate moment. He stayed punctiliously on the board till he was offered A£25,000 (about A£300,000 today). Maybe it was not heroic. Maybe Rivett, after the war, felt he had done enough in that line.

Altering editorial course usually takes time. Rivett's editorial soul remained in command on till 15 July, when the *News* tackled a Menzies description of White Australia as 'unaltered and unalterable'. The Prime Minister and his Migration Minister Alexander Downer insulted Asia, and imperilled Australia, said the *News*. 'In his . . . championing of a policy which is regarded by Asians as founded on racial prejudice, Mr. Menzies is . . . building up a reservoir of ill will which may one day be let loose on our children.'

Fourteen days later, the *News* decided the same Downer had made a 'statesmanlike analysis of Australia's migration problems'. There had been shocking words, but well-said ones. The Minister knew how to 'reorient his thinking to meet changing conditions' – was this a salute of equals? – and made the Menzies case on immigration with logic and common sense. 'As he said, to permit an admixture of Asian and European races to develop within Australia would probably result in tensions that would defeat all our efforts to retain the friendship of our northern neighbours.' His words ought to be noted in Asia. And to emphasise respect for orthodoxies in the new Murdoch press, the *Daily Mirror* ran the same editorial – simultaneously – under a masthead declaring itself 'THE INDEPENDENT NEWSPAPER'. When he removed Rivett, Murdoch still had no political connection like his father's. But he was developing the appropriate newspaper system: a man ready swiftly to accommodate external authority must allow no internal challenge to his own.

Murdoch's retreat and the demolition of Rivett's editorship reduced but did not cancel the value of the challenge to Playford's Adelaide oligarchy. In his 1962 account, *The Stuart Case*, K. S. Inglis said that the abuses of power were trivial in comparison with contemporary despotisms, but demonstrated that enough Australians understood the need to keep them trivial. Professor Inglis today would probably not modify his judgment that the line to a police state from a regime like Playford's, though long, 'is nonetheless continuous'. When Murdoch made his political breakthrough three years later, it was with a somewhat similar adept of conservative coalition-tactics. 'Black Jack' McEwen was a bigger man than Tom Playford, but no more particular about abuses of power.

Rivett remained active as a writer and broadcaster, but never edited again. Through work for the International Press Institute in Zurich he became a good friend of Harry Evans, who five years after Rivett's death agreed to edit *The Times* for Murdoch in London.

The Stuart case badly damaged the death penalty. Just a few more blows rendered it terminally unserviceable, and every state has now abolished it. The ethnic context of these events seems now implausible. Australia today includes much Asian 'admixture', and admits that the land had owners before Europeans arrived. For many people under thirty, the 'unalterable' thoughts of Menzies and Downer must sound like gibberish. Remedy for the wrongs done to the original inhabitants remains incomplete, but the attention focused on Rupert Max Stuart's case was one of the things which began the process.

Many people suppose Stuart died in jail. He survived, and fell again into trouble for boozing and brawling. Eventually he sobered up and joined his tribe's land-claim in Central Australia, becoming a steady member of the community. He never accepted the verdict against him, but long ago abandoned hope of changing it. 'Some people think Elvis is alive and I can't change that either.' Much knowledge of violent paedophiles has accumulated since the 1960s, telling us that without special supervision they nearly always reoffend. So the passage of years – added to the flimsiness of the initial evidence – suggests that Stuart was never any such thing

At Alice Springs on 30 March 2000 Queen Elizabeth II – still Australia's head of state – stepped for the first time on to Aboriginal land – that is, on to land which the Arrernte (Aranda) hold by a title now admitted to be older than her own. The chairman of the Central Land Council, Max Stuart, thanked her for coming so far to visit the Arrernte, and gave her a painting by one of the clan elders. Nobody told his story – an interesting project, perhaps, for the Adelaide *News* – but it would have involved revisiting the career of the paper's most distinguished editor.

No possessions matter more to a media business than a place in the history that starts (though not from zero) with Zenger. Delane's exposing of the railway-share swindlers in the 1840s, the BBC's 1956 reporting of Suez, the *Washington Post* in Watergate 1975 or the *Daily Mail*'s 1998 challenge to the Lawrence murder gang in London: these and many others can be recognised (and not necessarily ranked). Of Ron Boland, who served for many years in Rivett's place, his Newscorp obituary states that his proudest campaign defeated a prohibition against topless swimsuits – for men. 'Man's first faculty is that of forgetfulness,' said Albert Camus, 'but it is only fair to say that he even forgets the good that he has done.'

Before examining Murdoch's enthusiasm for the *Mirror*, we should step back and pick up the story of his broadcasting operations. These began in 1957 with a stake in the Adelaide radio station 5DN. Towards the end of that year applications were invited for television licences in Brisbane and in Adelaide. Sydney already had two commercial channels – Fairfax's Channel 7 and Packer's Channel 9 – plus the Australian

Broadcasting Commission (ABC). Similarly in Britain, commercial television (ITV) competed with the publicly funded BBC. But in Australia, as in the US, competition *between* commercial channels was a regulatory aspiration.

In Melbourne, the Herald owned Channel 7, and the *Age* a part of Channel 9. The two Channel 9s were network-sharing their output, as were the Channel 7s, but the regulators at the Australian Broadcasting Control Board (ABCB, distinct from the ABC) saw networking as an evasion of the competitive diversity they desired. At the same time, they were unsure that the lesser capitals (Adelaide was one-fourth Sydney's size) could support multiple franchises. Sympathy grew in the ABCB for licensing single operators ready to forswear networking. News busily encouraged this view, rebuffing interstate offers to assist in applying for Adelaide.

Three groups applied for Brisbane: one led by the Herald, one by Packer, and one by Fairfax (with Mirror Newspapers limping along in aid). Bidders for Adelaide were the *Advertiser* (that is, the Herald), Packer and Southern Television Corporation, 60 per cent held by News. Competitive hearings began at Brisbane, where Murdoch pleaded to make a preliminary statement.

His plea was that if Brisbane got two licences, it must set no precedent for Adelaide – where monopoly was essential. It was put to him that such a monopoly would have great financial value, and he agreed. But it would be valuable also to the public – for competition might undermine quality, and he cited evening papers as proof. In Adelaide, News ran a monopoly evening paper; it was infinitely better than Sydney's two competing evenings. This had some resonance: the *Sun* and *Mirror* – dealers in mayhem, synthetic or real – famously represented urban journalism's underbelly. But did anyone anticipate Rupert's advent two years later as the *Mirror*'s eager boss?

When the caravan reached Adelaide, News Ltd conjured up financial gloom. Even as a monopoly, Southern Television would take three years to reach a profit. In competition, it would lose more than half a million pounds over the same period (though Murdoch emphasised that he would not for that reason decline a licence). The ABCB's recommendation in July 1958 was for Brisbane and Adelaide to have one licence apiece, for an operator without interstate links or networking deals. Murdoch had campaigned shrewdly. His was the only application fitting the specification. But the specification did not fit the desires of the federal government, which waited until October 1958, and announced *two* licences per city. In Adelaide the *Advertiser* got Channel 7; News got Channel 9. This synchronised with federal elections, and was attributed generally to Menzies' decision to accommodate the East Coast moguls after all. Murdoch seems to have shared this view – and concluded that he must, by any available door, enter their club. The *Daily Mirror* was the best entrance ticket he could find.

Mirror Group Newspapers lost A£97,901 to 30 June 1961, making Rivett's scepticism of the previous year understandable. But his letters show that Rivett saw newspapers as enterprises profitable or otherwise in themselves. He did not conceive them as a means to government largesse.

Sadly competitive as the NSW-9 licence might be, Southern Television Corporation was already returning 40 per cent on its paid capital (after a small first-year loss). Frank Packer's purchase of the majority holding in Channel 9 Melbourne was the new industry's financial benchmark. He had paid A£6 for each A£1 share: the 500 per cent gain had taken four years, chiefly reflecting, in George Munster's words, 'the value of the licence issued by the government'.

Thus the role of the *News* and NSW-9 was to absorb the Sydney losses until Murdoch could gain more television revenue. When hearings opened in 1962 for a third Sydney licence, News Ltd came in as local publishers, with a new set-up and a rebuilt philosophy. The opposition was United Telecasters – several banks and industrial companies in alliance. Channel Ten Sydney, led by Murdoch, was also a syndicate, including two churches, two trade unions and the pastoralists Elder Smith Goldsborough. Along with religion, the proletariat and rural industry (not yet carrying the unfriendly agribusiness label) came Paramount Pictures, to guarantee content. News had the largest holding, but only 27.9 per cent.

Both syndicates celebrated locally made television, children's television, education and religion. (The Board's counsel said 'intangible qualities of character' should be remembered in evaluating these enthusiasms.) To Murdoch, on the stand for three days, the overarching issue was *competition*: its healthfulness, and his ability to supply it.

Inconsistencies were raised but they never fazed him. What of the blood-and-guts *Mirror* journalism he had deplored, as competition's outcome? His combat record against the Fairfax and Packer newspapers was just what qualified him to tackle their television operations. In the public interest, such monopolists must be challenged. And Ten, not United, were the team to do it.

It was put to him that he had bought the Sydney papers with television profits in mind – and Murdoch could hardly deny that Channel Ten promised just then to be more lucrative than *Truth* and the *Mirror*. But he applied his own gloss: he wanted the licence to be financial backing for his activities as a dedicated newspaperman. To argue that television revenues should be disposed so as to assist a paper which Murdoch himself had cited as a model of excess was the work of a rhetorical Houdini. Rivett, if still a director, could only have dissented.

Nor was the ABCB convinced. In April 1963 the Sydney licence went to United Telecasters, and Melbourne's third channel to the airline operator Ansett. Perhaps, as Murdoch believed, there was animosity on Menzies' part (for he had disliked the *Mirror* since Ezra Norton's time). The general effect was to intensify Murdoch's desire for a political alliance. The immediate response was a new tactical alignment.

Wollongong, fifty miles south of Sydney, claims now to be the world's greenest steeltown. In the 1960s it was highly ungreen, but one of its features was the lofty tower of Television Wollongong Transmissions Ltd (WIN-4), from which signals reached to southern Sydney. Few aerials received it: WIN-4 could not afford original production, and had little US material because the Sydney stations had corralled the distributors. In Newcastle, another industrial townscape to the north, NBN-6 suffered likewise.

In 1963 News Ltd bought 320,000 Television Wollongong shares and Murdoch took the ailing station in hand. In New York he bought 2,500 hours of programming from the network boss Donald Coyle for a million pounds; local and religious character it lacked, but it had Phil Silvers, Ben Casey and *From Here to Eternity* the serial. In June 1963 Murdoch told the Australian *TV Times*: 'There are two million Sydney viewers within WIN's range and we intend to go after them.' Sir Frank Packer did not wait for aerials to turn: he offered News a million shares (25 per cent) in

Television Corporation (Channel 9) and two slots on the board. Murdoch and Packer together then took control of NBN-6 Newcastle. Murdoch's Southern Television issued 150,000 shares to Packer's Consolidated Press, and News split its Wollongong holding with Consolidated.

What had become of Murdoch's competitive promises? They had been fulfilled, but not quite as a listener to the hearings might have expected. Murdoch had fought the supposed monopolists – but it turned out to be a preliminary to joining them. Feelings about monopoly commonly vary according to whether people stand inside or outside the system. Expression, however, may be inhibited – in engineering, 'hysteresis' describes the tendency for materials to a resist change of form, and most people display a psychic analogy. Murdoch from the beginning alternated between competitor and public monopolist – among other rhetorical configurations – with zero hysteresis.

All the same, the Channel Ten defeat left a distressing aftermath. Adelaide was still sustaining marginal operations in Sydney. More wheeling and dealing with Frank Packer was required to make News Ltd's share of television bounty provide real corporate comfort. Packer resolved to concentrate his print and television interests, by selling Consolidated Press to Television Corporation in exchange for 6.1 million units of new Television stock. Packer, already in command of Consolidated, thereby brought 62 per cent of Television into his control. Under the Packer–Murdoch deal Sir Frank, once he exceeded 42 per cent of Television, could not acquire more shares without offering an equivalent number to Murdoch. But this entitled News to only 1.2 million of the fresh issue. Murdoch would still have 25 per cent in the enlarged Television Corporation, but Packer would dominate it.

Murdoch instead exercised a right to return his shares to Packer at the market price, which brought in A\$3.3 million; Murdoch bought the outstanding stock in Southern Television, which was holding A\$2 million cash.* From the perspective of today's billionaire deals the sums seem

---

*The Commonwealth of Australia began producing its own currency, the Australian pound (A£) in 1910, and replaced it with a decimal system, the Australian dollar (A\$) in 1966. Although rates fluctuate, the conversion is usually around A\$1.4 = US\$1.0 = £0.70.

trivial, but at the time they were enough to make News' corporate position very secure. Murdoch began expounding to News executives his theories of global media investment and the coming primacy of entertainment over news. But, for this to be realised, the breakthrough into political influence had to be made.

Murdoch's difficulty for several years had been that of starting a liaison in a roomful of devoted couples. The Liberal leaders had all the editorial fulfilment they needed. Murdoch experimented with support for the Labor leader Arthur Calwell, but in its existing state the ALP had no prospect of power. Inspiration came when the *Mirror* political editor Eric Walsh identified Jack McEwen's potential. As leader of the minority Country Party in coalition with Menzies' Liberals, McEwen was Deputy Prime Minister – useful power, if not supreme. And Walsh knew there were no existing editorial attachments. It was a political connection which quickly became much more. 'Young Rupert', as Black Jack called him, found – in the words of McEwen's aide Bill Carew – 'something of a surrogate father', and a relationship very like that between Keith Murdoch and Billy Hughes.

McEwen, born in 1900, had long held major office via his minor party, and was a horse-trader of tireless skill – a match, perhaps, for Jake Arvey of the great Chicago machine, quoted at the head of this chapter. He and his followers were once called 'a faction in search of a party', accurately suggesting a minimal burden of philosophy. Resemblances to agrarian-socialists and to the farmer–labour parties of the US–Canada border never went much past Tom Playford's periodic gestures to Labor voters. Rural workers interested McEwen far less than urban manufacturers – to whom he offered protectionist insurance against the risk of liberal economics infecting the Liberals.

If the Country Party had ideological kin it was in European corporatism, where the state both controls the economic playing-field and participates among the teams. Corporatism of course was unlike the state-socialist model – where the state owned *all* the teams – but it was remote too from liberal-democratic ideals of an even-handed referee state empowered by the votes of an individual citizenry. In Australia as elsewhere the working democratic spectrum tends to mix such primaries as corporatism and liberal democracy. But there is a recognisable band, in which McEwen practised, where government is the business partner of deserving industries and firms.

Only in fascist versions is corporatism purely evil – free and competitive markets, after all, display some famous flaws. But its expression is remarkably like cronyism. The corporate tendency likes 'getting things done', with slight regard to constitutional niceties and libertarian issues. Politics centres upon fixing, and McEwen was a fixer who left no item to chance. He embodied both meanings of the word 'pragmatic'. Its modern sense fitted the undogmatic nature of his policies. But in his rigid public persona there was 'pragmatism' of the sort John Bunyan feared – censorious, and intolerant of dissent. In this he resembled (indeed admired) Billy Hughes, though few men could look less alike than the Little Digger and the massive ex-farmer.

Even with Labor divided, the Liberals needed McEwen, and 'Black Jack' was Menzies' name for him – supposedly after the leader of a Highland clan noted for ruthless cohesion and hard bargaining. And, like a Highland chieftain, McEwen held close to loyal followers. 'Young Rupert' was sufficiently one of those to think McEwen could become Prime Minister. Jack, a grim realist, probably knew otherwise.

It was a restless, impressionable time for Murdoch – not only because other newspaper bosses seemed to enjoy political rights thus far denied to him. His marriage to Patricia Booker in Adelaide in 1956 had not succeeded, and he had not met his second wife Anna. He wanted a substantial home accessible from both Sydney and Canberra. When he found Cavan, in the Murrumbidgee River catchment, McEwen assumed the delicate task of judging the worth of a sizeable rural property and arranging its anonymous, economical purchase. News Ltd's papers gave enthusiastic coverage to McEwen in the 1963 federal elections, but did so without visible effect. Obedient as the *News* and *Mirror* were, they carried no punch. For progress to occur, something quite different was required.

Though a national journal today, the *Australian* grew from other intentions. News Ltd accepted in the 1960s the conventional wisdom that Australia's geography, like America's, forbade the existence of a nationwide press. What Murdoch wanted was a political audience centred in Australian Capital Territory (ACT), the enclave where Canberra sits to prove that the federation is above the states – a habitat created for power-brokerage alone. He meant to proceed by ambush, but the selected victim ambushed him.

The main ACT title was Arthur Shakespeare's *Canberra Times*. It coped adequately with competition from Sydney, closest of the state capitals. Local assault by News would be different, though, and there was a vehicle to hand: the *Territorean*, a free sheet run by Ken Cowley, once a *Canberra Times* printer. Early in 1964 News Ltd bought the *Territorean*, and Murdoch told Shakespeare he was ready to buy the *Canberra Times* – or 'run you out of business'.

But the tactic once used against the Bonythons of Adelaide had been foreseen. Secretly in 1963 Shakespeare had sold an option to Fairfax, for exercise in just such circumstances. The paper's skilful young editor was Rohan Rivett's former lieutenant David Bowman. In May 1964 Fairfax made the experienced John Douglas Pringle (*Times, Guardian, Sydney Morning Herald*) overall boss, and provided new resources which Bowman energetically deployed.

News was denied swift local victory. The only alternative to retreat was for the *Territorean* – renamed the *Australian* – to add Sydney and Melbourne sales to its reduced Canberra potential, and achieve viable scale as an impromptu national. Technical impediments were many, as News lacked even the crude facsimile systems then available: interstate editions relied on flying stereotype 'mats' to Sydney and Melbourne, from an airport then often socked in at night. And editorial muddle marked the *Australian*'s birth and early life. Its first issue on 15 July 1964 would have carried the wrong date had not Eric Walsh dropped in and exercised a sharp pair of eyes.

Murdoch's editor was Maxwell Newton, then part-way along his trajectory from virtuoso economic analyst to fruitcake libertarian and pornographer. Having shone as a young editor of the *Australian Financial Review*, he might have shone again with a paper on the scale first intended. He was what the British call a 'journalist of opinion' – that is, organising broad news-cover was remote from his métier. And the *Age* and *SMH*, even if they remained dull, knew that business very well.

Though Murdoch appreciated Newton's limitations, he had little to suggest beyond misplaced borrowings from the old *Express* (star-gazing, an old-style gossip column). And his busy shirt-sleeved presence, far from damping editorial eccentricities, intensified them. Public curiosity about the notion of a national paper absorbed the initial print of 250,000. But by the end of the launch-month sales were at 74,782, and at 51,834 by November.

Newton's flair for insult, apt in a pundit, served poorly in an editor. Many free-market partisans might deplore tax revenue going into school-ing for religious groups. Few but Newton would mock it as 'saving Catholic children from the consequences of their parents' religious convictions'. Government service being a classic Irish-Australian aspira-tion, Peter Viereck's notion of anti-Catholicism as 'the anti-semitism of the intellectuals' resonates in Canberra with no need for translation from US usage: the harm a newspaper would suffer from similar remarks about Jewish families in New York could not be more acute.

And chronic harm was meanwhile caused by inept foreign cover, unforgivable in a capital city. These were the Vietnam years, and for Australia – a participant in the war – the issue had an urgency not unlike America's. The intricate Tonkin Gulf crisis set a tough test when the *Australian* was only a few weeks old. No newspaper in 1964 penetrated the truth of that crisis. But, as George Munster noted from contemporary reading, the *Australian* failed even to convey the scope of what was known: 'The lasting upshot . . . the Congressional resolution giving President Johnson the power to conduct hostilities without further reference to the legislature – was buried on an inside page . . . Newton and Murdoch decided what was important . . . neither was conversant with Asian politics.'

In March 1965 Newton sought much enhanced terms. Getting no eager response, he quit, telling *Canberra Times* readers that Murdoch's supervision had 'made it impossible to achieve . . . essential principles, aims and standards of quality'. Few thought the *Australian*'s faults were Rupert's alone. But he appointed no clear successor to remedy them. In 1965 Nationwide News Pty Ltd filed accounts suggesting that the *Australian* was losing about A£800,000 a year (its first and last separate accounting). In 1967 it moved base to Sydney, 'leaving the battlefield to us' as John Pringle remarked happily. Thus far, it was a disaster by ordin-ary publishing standards. By extraordinary ones, though, it was about to do vital service for Black Jack and his apprentice.

In 1966 Harold Holt succeeded Menzies as Prime Minister and Liberal leader. McEwen remained Minister for Trade, and Deputy Prime Minister. Holt was insecure, and the *Australian* suggested that McEwen might replace him. Few analysts agreed, and Murdoch's judgment attracted mockery – some of it from Max Newton. The ex-editor had become an economic consultant, and a publisher of newsletters in which he called McEwen's party an economic dinosaur, and Rupert a 'whippersnapper from Adelaide'.

The Country Party indeed was a fading power. But Black Jack still inspired awe in Canberra, because rumour said he had a special relationship with the Australian Security Intelligence Organisation (ASIO), roughly equivalent to the FBI or MI5. We now know rumour was accurate, and that Rupert Murdoch shared McEwen's advantage. ASIO of course was designed for counter-espionage (and won some battles with the KGB). But by the end of the 1960s it was suspected of burgling and bugging where no such enemies existed.

Above every rival Black Jack hated the federal Treasurer, 'Billy' McMahon. It was bad enough that McMahon was a dandified little lawyer with a party-going wife and affected, allegedly bisexual tastes. Worse, he was liberal economically: an enemy of protection. And worst, he appealed to those Liberals who saw the ALP reuniting and wanted to build a seaworthy Ark before the deluge.

Newton was a keen McMahon supporter – and the Trade Minister planned to strike at the Treasurer through this ally. Learning that Newton had a small consultancy with the Japan Export Trade Organisation (JETRO), McEwen's office called in the Director-General of ASIO, Brigadier Sir Charles Spry, codename 'Scorpion'. Spry's archives, opened under the thirty-year rule, provide a striking record of politico-editorial conspiracy, starting with a memo of 21 August 1967 marked 'Top Secret'.

JETRO:

On August 18, 1967, the Director-General discussed a plan of action against the abovementioned organisation. The Secretary, Department of Trade . . . had drawn the attention of the DG to the activities in Australia of the Japanese Government-sponsored JETRO and expressed the view that [it was] involving itself in domestic issues which indicated the possibility of subversion . . . inquiries should be made into the financial, and taxation, affairs of JETRO, Maxwell Newton and such other individuals as might emerge as being of interest . . .

Nothing 'indicated' subversion: Newton was simply briefing JETRO on trade policy. The true target, as events soon proved, was McMahon, and the project was the direct insertion of a secret state agency into the political process. The Scorpion's title for his file was quite frank: 'Spoiling Operations. NEWTON, Maxwell'. The extant documents are less frank about some of his excavations:

These [unidentified] papers have been seen by the DG. [Unidentified] suggests we hold them and I agree. Suggest they be made into a file. Also B1 and B2 should be told we have a file as they certainly will have one. B1 could well be dealing with something associated with JETRO not knowing we hold other papers . . . B2 knows of this.

Maybe the quarry knew something of it too. People who dealt with McMahon in 1967–8 thought he had become oddly paranoid about confidential telephone discussions.

On 17 December 1967 Prime Minister Holt vanished into heavy surf off a beach near Melbourne. The theories applied to this accident – from suicidal political despair to accounts of him as a Chinese agent fleeing by submarine – are only relevant as symptoms of the fever it generated in an already racked political community.

In Canberra on 19 December McEwen took the oath as Acting Prime Minister, and left for Melbourne, where Spry was ordered to meet him the same evening. Black Jack, now legally the Scorpion's chief, wanted to know what he had on Newton and McMahon. Holt's Liberal replacement, about to be elected, would replace McEwen. The contenders were John Gorton, a guileless landowner McEwen expected to control – and McMahon. McEwen had made plain already that he would not accept

117

McMahon. But his reasons, he said, must remain secret during a national crisis. McEwen had created appetite for disclosure which now it was imperative to feed.

Spry had to tell McEwen that surveillance of Newton had yet to produce anything of 'security significance'. On the world conference circuit, Newton had denounced Australian protectionism: McEwen thought the Treasury was subsidising him illegally. But no proof existed. An attempt to purloin official papers overseas was under inquiry – perhaps criminal, still unproven. Urgent messages were being sent out. Christmas, however, would reduce staff and delay confidential bags.

In New Year 1968, with the Liberal vote set for 9 January, McEwen decided to go with what he had, but not go public himself. On the night of 5 January Murdoch went to McEwen's suite at the Kurrajong Hotel in Canberra, and Black Jack gave him a package of material. Later, according to the Scorpion's notes, Murdoch called Newton and said: 'This is the whippersnapper from Adelaide. I suggest you read my paper tomorrow.'

The *Australian*'s main headline on 6 January was 'WHY McEWEN VETOES McMAHON: FOREIGN AGENT IS THE MAN BETWEEN THE LEADERS'. The text said McEwen knew McMahon to be in regular contact with an 'agent of foreign interests'. The agent was named as 'the former managing editor of this paper, Maxwell Newton', the 'interests' as Japan, represented by JETRO.

The *Australian* thus asserted what McEwen had purported to conceal: that the Treasurer was a treacherous 'cabinet colleague and coalition partner'. No sources or byline appeared – the story ran on Murdoch's word alone. The *Australian* still had no clear editorial command. Its staff, however, suspected that Black Jack was the actual author. Murdoch's headline-and-text package, though grotesquely false, may well have been believable at the moment to him. Credulity and conspiracy may go together – and 'truth' perhaps means 'whatever authority asserts'.

Corroboration was specious, but well timed. On 9 January, the day of the Liberal vote, the *Australian* published JETRO's contract with Newton in copious detail. This material could not have been legally obtained, and may fairly be assumed to be the product of ASIO's 'tax and financial' inquiries. By no sensible professional judgment did it justify the 'foreign agent' claim. But it had an official appearance, and political panic, not judgment, was in the saddle. McMahon, wrote George Munster, was found guilty 'by association', thus ensuring Gorton's victory.

In *Political Gladiator*, his biography of McEwen, Peter Golding records him as a young minister visiting a remarkable library in the outback ghost town of Borroloola. He opened a copy of *Curiosities of Literature*, by Disraeli's father Isaac, and a man standing alongside noticed the passage at which McEwen's finger pointed: 'A false report, if believed three days later, may be of great service to a government.'

Though journalists knew the story was spurious, they could not then uncover its origins. But the JETRO operation followed an undercover pattern in which action, however absurd, continues in pursuit of retrospective justification. Secrecy sustains hope. Thus the Scorpion's paperwork expanded, providing today a revealing overview.

Finding Black Jack's successor just as obsessive about Newton, Spry feverishly tracked any sliver of feloniousness. Accounts did at last turn up of Newton scavenging stray papers after a conference, *unsuccessfully*: now, Gorton was advised, the Crimes Act might apply. (Predictably, the lawyers disagreed.) And Newton's plans to start a newspaper in Western Australia were monitored for political character. An undated, unsigned note records the prospective editor asking prospective colleagues (1) their opinion of Gorton as Prime Minister and (2) whether McMahon might 'make a good Prime Minister': 'Source – Rupert Murdoch, phone from Perth.'

Most revealingly, Spry added a careful retrospective memo about the *Australian*'s JETRO story, after discussion with an unnamed journalist. The Scorpion seems to have suspected some personal animus on the part of Murdoch (shown in the 'read my paper' call). And the memo notes his belief that McEwen passed information to Murdoch (feeling it wise perhaps to record that it was not his doing: McEwen's papers show reckless determination to label JETRO a threat to 'national security'). In 1969 Gorton grew so frustrated as to order police raids on Newton's home and office. Their highly public failure to find pay-dirt ended the affair – bar one vengeful footnote. In the 1970 trade talks with Japan McEwen made it a condition that JETRO dismiss Newton.

In Canberra folklore the *Australian*'s January 1968 antics remained a shadowy episode – until September 2000, when Alan Ramsey of the *Sydney Morning Herald*, investigating recent security controversies, thought to compare the police operations against Newton. His inquiries unearthed the Scorpion's papers, and exposed the 1969 raids as the conclusion to a clandestine programme of secret-service abuse plotted months before the Holt crisis, conducted by McEwen and aided by the *Australian*. There is no other known case of a Cabinet minister using ASIO to develop character-assassination material against a colleague – nor any British or US equivalent. And Murdoch's role is hard to match.

McEwen's concoction could only be circulated via an uncritical conduit. For this it was essential to have a newspaperman he could entirely trust – or entirely dominate. Any competent reporter close enough to grasp what Black Jack was peddling would certainly have suspected – and probably penetrated – the real, explosive story about abuse of secret power. The untruth did McMahon some intended damage. But as Alan Ramsey observes, the truth at the time would have ruined McEwen. And Murdoch's gullibility, or professional naivety, was of a kind which cannot be separated from the ensuing benefit McEwen conferred on him.

Gorton in office eventually wore out even McEwen's patient powers. Before that, however, Black Jack was able to summon him in aid at a critical moment in the *News of the World* acquisition – which in 1969 projected Murdoch on to the world stage.

In 1968 six million British citizens bought the *News of the World* on Sundays. Though its slogan 'ALL HUMAN LIFE IS THERE' suggested a broad demotic sociology, the scholarship involved was rigidly selective. Therein lay the commercial attraction. Buying and distributing details of sexual eccentricity and violence was a business with steady, manageable costs. As the *News of the World* largely ignored the world, it required no versatile news-gathering systems. Christiansen might fret about creating interest in opera or economics – but not the *News of the Screws*. It knew what it liked, and so did every news agency and local reporter in the British Isles.

Sir William Carr and his family, with 52 per cent of the voting shares, controlled the business. They and it were pillars of Tory Britain. Mark Chapman-Walker, a former Conservative Party official, was a director, and the editorial page radiated patriotic domesticity. As Norton's *Truth* once did, it claimed to be society's watchdog ('the Hansard of the sleazy' said a Fleet Street veteran more candidly). But by the later 1960s Sir William's clan was split. His cousin Derek Jackson – a distinguished scientist and jump-jockey, beset by ex-wives – complained, not unjustly, about aimless diversification and declining core business. Nearly half the family shares were his; he wanted to sell. And Carr's health was failing, corroded by booze.

On to this scene in October 1968 burst Robert Maxwell, the most bumptious of modern swindlers, with a takeover bid. Sir William and his allies did not object to Maxwell as a swindler: remarkably, the City mavens had not divined the fact. But they supposed him efficient, socialist and foreign-born (that is, Jewish). Therefore the paper's editor, Stafford Somerfield, declared him unfit for a concern 'as British as roast beef and Yorkshire pudding'. Sir William, though, was still less fit to defend it, and no white knights volunteered. Anti-monopoly rules, if mild, encumbered the newspaper groups; Maxwell, on the other hand, owned no papers, and was a Labour MP, which the Labour government found congenial.

St Rupert and the Dragon (with the *Screws* as the maiden) was a script by Lord Catto of Cairncatto – scion of a Governor of the Bank of England, director of Morgan Grenfell, merchant bankers to the Queen, and London adviser to News. Financial elites in Britain and Australia interpenetrate: Catto had banking interests in Australia, used the Melbourne Club and knew Rupert well. Murdoch flew discreetly to London and on 21 October dined with Sir William's son William and his cousin Clive, who were charmed. Over breakfast, Sir William bridled at Rupert's refusal to unpack his armour for anything less than chief-executive status. But promises of executive slots for several Carrs calmed him.

Maxwell's takeover currency was equity in Pergamon Press, which he had expanded – inflated, rather – from a base in scientific periodicals. Four Pergamon shares would buy three shares of NOTWO (News of the World Organisation), making an offer worth £27 million, which News Ltd could not match. In Catto's ingenious counter NOTWO, which had 9.6 million voting shares, would issue another 5.1 million to News Ltd –

in exchange for Australian assets owned by News and guaranteed to add £2 million annual profit. News would have 40 per cent of the rebuilt NOTWO, which would be decisive when added to the votes of Sir William's loyalists.

This quasi-merger was unveiled at a press conference on 28 October. It would need ratification at an extraordinary general meeting, set for the New Year. Murdoch returned to Australia to collect the assets, and skirmishing became ferocious – the Sydney *Daily Mirror*'s investigation of Pergamon's encyclopaedia-selling drawing one of Maxwell's multitudinous writs.

The meeting on 3 January was indeed extraordinary, as a spectacle. Maxwell belched copious fire before releasing his prey. In truth, the outcome had been decided in advance by swift outlay of ready cash. The *Financial Times* reported that between Hambros (bankers to NOTWO), various Carr loyalists and Rupert's News Ltd, nearly all the uncommitted shares were beyond Pergamon's control well beforehand.

Operations by News in the London stock market required exchange-control approval in Canberra. Though such regulation was intrinsic to his protectionism, Black Jack could understand a special need when he saw one. Unfortunately, the 'Japanese agent' Billy McMahon was the Treasurer. McMahon's philosophy did not resist capital movements. But involved here were the resources of a business built largely on public licences granted for the development of Australian television. There were many valid reasons for McMahon to review News Ltd's uses of foreign currency – personal enjoyment apart – and publication even of an intention to do so would have been lethal.

McEwen decided to deploy Prime Minister Gorton's supreme power – but delicately, for overruling McMahon in the course of regular business would be counterproductive. Research by Bill Carew, McEwen's sure-footed press secretary, located a weekend in which McMahon would be absent from Canberra.

Then with careful timing – as Carew told Peter Golding – Black Jack called Gorton's official residence from his Kurrajong Hotel command post. 'John,' he said, 'we have a bit of a problem. Young Rupert Murdoch needs some foreign exchange out of the country and we can't track Billy down. Can you do it?' Gorton hesitated. Though unsubtle, he must have sensed oddity. But McEwen insisted it was urgent, and the paperwork complete: 'All we need is your signature.' Gorton replied: 'Righto, Jack . . . I'll come over to the Kurra. I am out of scotch. Have you got a bottle?' Black Jack, that master of detail, never forgot such things. 'So Gorton arrived. The papers were signed. Rupert and I were out in the garden. Gorton went off with his scotch. Rupert went off to buy his newspaper.'

Murdoch's London allies were not less devoted. Perhaps the City once showed gentlemanly restraint, but in the late 1960s, patrician financiers such as Morgan Grenfell certainly didn't. Like Hambros, the Carr advisers, they treated the City Takeover Panel – a toothless, voluntary body – with contempt. The Panel wanted to see bids decided by investors using equal quantities of rational information. There should be no tactics designed simply to forestall offers attaching more value to shares: NOTWO's plastic surgery and the pre-emptive share-buying were clearly of that type. The Panel, Maxwell expostulated, was presiding over a 'jungle'. That might have been so, a Morgan director later agreed, and Murdoch believed he could 'smell' the City's resolve to defeat Pergamon.

Ironically, bushwhacking Maxwell would have been superfluous had the *News of the World* or the Sydney *Mirror* (or any of the financial advisers) possessed real watchdog capacities. The truth – demonstrated by the *Sunday Times* shortly afterwards – was that most of Pergamon's value existed only in its over-cooked books. (Official proof that the truth was even worse did not preclude City help for later Maxwell swindles, and his reappearance in our story.)

Murdoch of course had been throughout the privileged protégé of both Black Jack and the Square Mile bluebloods. Yet within a few months he again saw himself victimised by political prejudice and social snobbery – thwarting, suddenly, his British television ambitions. His difficulties began with the *News of the Screws*.

Turning NOTWO's profitability around was largely a matter of not being Sir William. 'I am sober after lunch,' said Murdoch once, 'and in some parts of Fleet Street, that makes you a genius.' It was not a rating Sir William had aspired to for decades. Editorial philosophy was more complex. Six million copies per edition generated vast income – mostly as cash – but this was far from the peak of 8,441,966 in 1950.

The decline of British popular circulations, conspicuous as the 1960s became the 1970s, was associated with broad changes in media technology – most obviously, television's rise – and with changes specific to individual papers. Defects of the legal system had long aided NOTWO's trade in prurience and pragmatism (in the old grim sense). When public provision for criminal defence was inadequate, the stories of eminent murderers could be secured by paying their legal fees (the noose usually claimed them in the event, providing an exemplary denouement). Meanwhile police entrapment of homosexuals, contested divorces and unrestricted reporting of preliminary proceedings produced numerous injustices – and acres of low-cost copy.

As legal reforms were imposed and consolidated, the *News of the World* had to prospect elsewhere for deviant activity, and even before the arrival of News Ltd the results seemed encouraging – in fact, deceptively so. It was natural that involvement with sexual experiment and drugs should become easier to detect from the Swinging Sixties onward. It was ceasing to be deviant.

This helps explain, in social retrospect, why a newspaper once read by almost half the British population is read today by less than one-fifth (and the *Daily Mail* shows that popular circulations do not inevitably contract). Profit has been richly sustained, but on altered terms. Working inside legal notions of deviance, the *News of the World* rarely fell out with society. During the 1960s, a behavioural Berlin Wall was crumbling, and when tolerance widens, moral and editorial sensibility is needed to prevent exposé journalism becoming, not just offensive, but tediously irrelevant.

News Ltd took control in transitional times, and almost immediately a certain Christine Keeler turned up, with a recycled memoir of her part in the famous Profumo affair. Its publication was a defining moment for the corporate ethos of News International (as it soon became). Profumo in 1963 had been a scandalous classic, incorporating sex, espionage, high politics, low life and aristocratic excess. Its central disclosure – the sex-worker Keeler servicing both the Russian officer Eugene Ivanov and Britain's Secretary of State for War – was modest as a security issue, though it was sufficient to deflect charges of gratuitousness, whatever lush byways Fleet Street explored. And for overseas papers – notably Rupert's *Mirror* – it had been a bonanza without opportunity cost.

Its revival by the *News of the World* in 1969 provoked a backlash which staggered Murdoch. The Press Council (like the Takeover Panel) had no sanctions, but what strong words could do they did – with bishops and editorial-writers in support. Murdoch was skinned alive on David Frost's television show, and indelibly tagged the Dirty Digger by *Private Eye* magazine. The shock was worse because, briefly, his status as a privileged City dragonslayer had combined advantageously with the charisma of his nationality. Though prejudice is complained of – and insistently, from this moment on, by Rupert himself – the British have usually taken a generous view of Australians, crediting them – from Nancy Wake to Germaine Greer and Edna Everage – with talent and dash, particularly in Fleet Street.

Murdoch could understand the abrupt retraction of his welcome mat only in terms of low work in high places. Lecturing at Melbourne University in 1972, he said there was reason to suspect 'certain forces' in British society of 'coming together . . . to try to stop us because they did not want the public reminded of the events of 1963'. The real problem was that the events were so well recalled as to make blindingly clear that Keeler II offered nothing new – nothing making it worth while to exhume the corpse of Profumo's good name and slaughter it afresh. Recycled thus, the classic scandal was a non-story, a classic of gratuitousness – Murdoch's conspiracy theory being equivalent to the tale of McMahon and the secret agent. Perhaps it was credible to Murdoch himself in some similar fashion. No doubt he was furiously angry – perhaps panic-stricken – when the Dirty Digger reputation seemed to threaten his cross-media ambitions, just as another fat target hove in sight.

In 1970 London Weekend Television (LWT) was in a predicament like WIN-4 Wollongong's in 1962. The architecture of British commercial television was reckoned a great credit to the Independent Television Authority (ITA). Under a system of regional franchises – which competed and co-operated to produce network output – several companies, Granada perhaps most famously, had become highly profitable sources of original television.

To give further space to new ideas, the second licensing round (1968) split London into weekday and weekend franchises. Whether a lesser base harmed LWT has been hotly argued; certainly it missed its high programming targets, and by 1970 its finances were shaky. Major industrial and media firms held shares, but their board representatives were fractious and disengaged. Dr Tom Margerison, LWT's managing director, thought a non-executive newcomer with panache and leadership might refocus the board. He thought of Murdoch, and conceived the idea of arranging for the LWT shares owned by the General Electric Company to be transferred to the *News of the World*.

The ITA regulators were keen to stop LWT collapsing into the arms of the London weekday operator, Thames. But they also needed Margerison's undertaking that Murdoch – by now operating the *Sun* also – accepted the legal status of cross-media investment. Such investment was considered beneficial, because the risk of television draining profit from newspapers – and indirectly reducing media diversity – would be less if they held electronic-media shares. But the purpose would fail if editorial controllers of newspapers could control television output, directly subtracting from diversity. Margerison assured the ITA that Murdoch's contribution to LWT was to be business leadership, not programming, and reported to Murdoch that the transfer depended on this assurance. 'I said, I have given my word. He said "Yes, yes".'

In November 1970 General Electric (now Marconi plc) sold its LWT interests (7.5 per cent of the voting shares; 16 per cent of non-voting; 11 per cent of loan capital) to NOTWO. Murdoch replaced Arnold (later Lord) Weinstock on the board, and, according to Margerison, said at once, 'Now, what about the programmes?' Margerison said they must be left to the programme controller, Cyril Bennett. Unabashed, Murdoch started to attend programme meetings. When stopped, he took to gathering the participants privately at his house. Discovering this, Margerison angrily reminded Murdoch of the ITA undertakings, to receive the simple answer: '"Yes, but that was before I came." He had no thought of telling the truth, unless it was convenient.'

In December a one-for-three rights issue was needed to shore up the LWT finances. It was underwritten by NOTWO, which took up the issue alone. Shareholders like Pearl Assurance and the *Economist* were perhaps timid – as Murdoch sympathisers suggested – or perhaps sceptical about his leadership. The outcome was NOTWO putting in £505,000 for 35 per cent of the non-voting shares.

Over the midwinter, Margerison got a close-up view of the leadership
style he had imported to LWT – by way of frequent requests to visit
Murdoch's Fleet Street office. Whenever Larry Lamb, editor of the
tabloid *Sun*, was present with page-proofs, Murdoch tore Lamb ferociously to shreds. If Margerison offered to leave, he would be asked to
stay, and he concluded that Murdoch's domineering and Lamb's meek
acceptance were linked components of an exemplary display. But as
managing director he could still insist on the independence of programming. On 18 February, the board designated Murdoch chairman of an
executive committee to take command of LWT; immediately he dismissed Margerison. Anthony Pragnell of the ITA now declared that
changes in the company were such that had they been in place during the
licence competition 'LWT would not have got the contract'.

Much of the uproar which broke out in Parliament and press
expanded on the theme of the Keeler publication, and the nature of
News journalism. None of this was inspired, or needed to be inspired, by
the ITA: disquiet about the *News of the World* and the *Sun* was
autonomous and widespread – indeed, much of it was linked with accusations of dereliction by the Authority itself. Bernard Levin wrote in the
New York Herald Tribune that 'Americans who grumble about the feebleness
of their FCC can now stop grumbling . . . Britain's ITA is even feebler.'
To demands for a public inquiry into the handling of television licences,
the government replied that it was up to the ITA to sort things out.

The Authority's decision was to 're-interview' LWT, allowing six weeks
for a new submission to be prepared. And while this was discussed by the
shareholders, Murdoch demanded a meeting with (Sir) Brian Young,
the ITA Director-General. The Authority, he alleged, had been subject-
ing him to a campaign of 'character assassination': he had been
'pilloried' and accused of being unfit to control a broadcasting company.
The ITA's history *Independent Television in Britain* describes this as a 'ninety-
minute outburst' in which Murdoch asked the Authority either to
welcome him or to disapprove of him – and to do so in unequivocal
terms. In any case he 'required the Authority's co-operation in repairing
the gratuitous damage inflicted on his good name'.

It is remarkable that Murdoch should complain of 'character assassination'. But the significance of his own exploits against McMahon and

Profumo may be that he saw it as a perfectly normal device, which the Authority or any other body might employ for the sake of getting its way. In fact Murdoch's personal character was not something Brian Young and his colleagues considered. They believed they had to deal with a plain legal issue. There was nothing to prevent NOTWO holding shares in LWT, but under the Independent Television Act nobody could hold executive authority in a television company and control a major newspaper. Nobody could be exempted from the rule, and so Murdoch's fury at being labelled the Dirty Digger seemed to Brian Young quite misdirected. Character, under the legislation, could only be an issue if control came under discussion.

In a separate provision the Act did require the Authority to refuse television licences to persons of 'improper' character. No exact definition was laid down. However, a strong case might have been presented against Murdoch in 1971 based on the circumstances of the smear on McMahon, and the nature of his services to the Deputy Prime Minister of Australia. But the ITA was not examining Murdoch as a licence applicant. And the essential facts were anyway still secret.

As it happened, the London Weekend controversy ran out of steam quite promptly. John Freeman, who had been nominated originally as chairman only to be stolen by the government to be British Ambassador to Washington, was persuaded by David Frost to rejoin the company at the end of his diplomatic term. Frost, a shareholder in LWT, also helped to establish that the Authority was immovable on the cross-media issue. Murdoch then stated that he had never sought executive power at all. Under Freeman, LWT proceeded by orthodox stages to become a successful company and a good investment for News International.

But the interlinked episodes at the *News of the World* and London Weekend – the drama of acceptance and rejection – turned into essential components of the Rupert Murdoch myth. In this account the 'British establishment' decided to exclude Murdoch from any participation in British television, because of revelations made in his fearless newspapers about their degenerate behaviour. From this, his admirers have suggested, was born his drive to build satellite television, and escape altogether from such shadowy totalitarianism. Within this view, extended by Murdoch's followers into a corporate anti-ethos, there is no need to look at what the newspapers actually do, or indeed to respect doubts or criticism at all. In a battle against hidden and inimical forces rough methods may be required.

The passion Murdoch brought to his expression of distress gained him a degree of sympathy in 1970–1. Could he be so furious without there being something in it? The ITA's historian correctly denied that the Authority had instigated an attack on him, but thought he 'had cause for anger'. There is really no reason to think there was any more substance to Murdoch's complaint of being 'pilloried' than there has been substance to the contrasting views he has taken on monopoly and competition when trying to win licences in Australia.

A more credible notion is that Murdoch interpreted his studies with Black Jack McEwen as proving the truth of what he suspected – that laws and regulation never constitute a barrier, given sufficient influence with sufficiently powerful people. Any failure of a desired purpose must be due to an occult resistance not yet identified and won over. Notions of impersonal authority, the essential pillar of civil society, seem entirely absent.

Murdoch's conduct throughout the LWT episode suggests that he expected the ITA to drop its pedantic cross-media rules, and that he believed it would have, but for a conspiratorial prejudice against him. The 'character-assassination' tirade perhaps was a last try at smoking out the 'real' objection. In his own case, views could be adjusted to serve any necessary purpose – as he had shown – making it difficult for him to see that other people might be any different.

In the same process with Black Jack he had tested and proved an essential capacity. In his Melbourne University lecture – contributed to a series which commemorates A. N. Smith, Australia's greatest exponent of independent political analysis – Murdoch was particularly concerned to argue that tabloid newspapers of his own sort had been the Anglophone world's bravest enemies of repression. But he also dwelt generally on relationships between newspapers and politicians, and came to a most respectable conclusion: 'Politicians do not want watch-dogs – they want control . . . Their control.' The lecture conventionally states the newspaper's duty to refuse the politician's desire. In reality, Murdoch was already practised in the technique of handing over control.

5

TRADING TABLOID PLACES, 1969–1980

> The thing that hath been, it is that which shall be; and that which is done is that which shall be done; and there is no new thing under the sun.
>
> ECCLESIASTES, I:8

Not even Rupert Murdoch, its proprietor, or Larry Lamb, its editor, thought the first issue of the tabloid *Sun* looked like a success on Monday 17 November 1969. It was more than three hours late, after a night of editorial and mechanical embarrassments, not least the ceremonial starting of the presses by Anna Murdoch. Following some rather ill-tempered argument, she had been specially inducted as a print-union member, to allow her to punch the sacred button. This to begin with did no more than reveal one of the many electrical faults infecting the ancient machinery. It had been acquired with the *News of the World*, and seemed to resent the task of rolling out a daily paper after the Sunday was done.

Lamb was a seasoned tabloid practitioner, and his first product as an editor made him squirm. It was littered with misprints, battered type, ill-cropped pictures and uncorrected copy: the lead story, 'HORSE DOPING SENSATION', was 'exclusive' only in the sense that nobody else cared about it. Many inhabitants of the *Sun*'s squalid editorial floor assumed they had only a few weeks' employment in prospect; some eased their way through the night's hold-ups by swigging whisky from pint glasses.

When at last a few bedraggled first-edition copies made their way to the nearby offices of the *Daily Mirror* – the market-leader against which Murdoch was aiming the *Sun* – Hugh Cudlipp, the *Mirror*'s editorial director, distributed champagne. He had said the *Sun* would be no threat. Now he felt sure. But, unpromising as it first seemed, the impact of the Murdoch *Sun* directly revolutionised the British media industries – and via them, the world system.

Fleet Street in the 1970s was Rupert Murdoch's Klondike gold-strike (with Larry Lamb as Skookum Jim, the crafty native guide). The cash generated from it turned News into a world-scale organisation, and has nourished it through three decades of shifting fortune. The *News of the World* was a potent asset anyway, but it was transformed by the synergy between it and the *Sun*. And the *Sun* also provides his claim to editorial originality. Murdoch's reputation (in Britain especially) is that of a master-drummer of circulations. The dread of liberal critics, the esteem of businessmen and the awe of politicians all rest on the assumption that he 'knows how to run newspapers' and possesses 'an instinctive grasp of readers' demands'. Matters are not really so simple. But certain basic facts are dramatic indeed.

The *News of the World* had an audited average sale of 6,066,928 for January 1969, the month Murdoch took command. He claimed that envy generated much of the criticism directed at his Profumo rehash; supposedly, it 'put on 200,000 sales', and his competitors 'didn't like it'. In fact the records of the Audit Bureau of Circulations (ABC) show no real remission in the *News of the World*'s decline during summer 1969. The trend persisted over the next decade, and by January 1979 the month's average was down 20 per cent, at 4,785,710.

The *Sun* story is very different. When Murdoch agreed to pay the International Publishing Corporation (IPC) £800,000 for it in September 1969, its most recent ABC monthly average (June) was 964,156. Since 1965 it too had been in a decline, steepening yearly, having lost 6.0 per cent in 1965–6, 7.6 per cent in 1966–7, 10.0 per cent in 1967–8 and about 11.5 per cent in the last pre-Murdoch year. For later 1969 – a chaotic takeover interlude – there are no audited figures. But the circulation in November perhaps averaged 800,000. Then in 1970 under Murdoch the circulation averaged 1,600,000.

A settled decline exceeding 10 per cent year on year had become a year-on-year gain of 100 per cent. By 1978, many editions of the *Sun* were selling more than four million copies, and it had become the biggest-selling newspaper in Britain. This rebound and ascent is unparalleled in ABC statistics. It is a famous media legend, the basis of Murdoch's talismanic reputation. But why were the two cases so divergent? Why did his magic refresh the daily and not the Sunday paper? And had there not been big, even bigger, circulations in Britain before this? What kind of newspaper was the *Sun*? How was it made?

Obscure as it may have been to Sir William Carr, Rupert Murdoch knew without reflection that presses capable of turning out a huge weekly paper must not – however well worn – stand idle the rest of the week. He needed a weekday product to run with the *News of the World*, and there was not much doubt that it would have to be what universally we now call a tabloid.

Page dimensions don't altogether fix a newspaper's character. Indeed the *News of the World* at the Murdoch takeover consisted of broadsheet pages (some 40 centimetres wide by 60 deep) but they contained material radically more prurient than anything in the tabloid (20 by 30 centimetres) format of *Le Monde*. Nominally, a tabloid section of thirty-two pages accommodates as much text as a broadsheet section of sixteen. In practice, the big sheet is handier when deadline-heavy stories are arriving from the outside world, but it has no particular advantage in presenting material which is internally generated, or divorced to some extent from events. This need not be spurious or fantastical, as *Le Monde* shows with its sedate coverage of international affairs. But, supposing it is, no requirement exists to inconvenience readers with a broadsheet page. So by the end of the twentieth century the smaller page stood for a class of journalism, and David Krajicek's 'tabloidization of America' refers to a cultural divide, not a choice of press technology.

Just such a divide existed in Fleet Street at the end of the 1960s, but not as format; among daily papers only the *Mirror* and the moribund *Sketch* were physically tabloid. The distinction was between 'popular' and 'quality' newspapers, or (in Larry Lamb's words) between the 'Populars' and the 'Unpopulars'. A favourite conceit of Murdoch's is that newspapers differ only in that some sell more than others – the editorial commodity being similar, however dispensed. This is not so, and anyone in the 1960s or 1970s could see that it was not.

Visiting American journalists could identify one group of British papers which were rich in intrusive gossip, often skipped over weighty affairs, were heavily illustrated, and – staggeringly, from the viewpoint of anyone trained on (say) the *New York Times* – felt free to spike their news cover with political invective. Even though such characteristics were not always displayed to the same extent, this was a recognisable group. There was then another group working in roughly the same way as the *New York Times* (or the *Sydney Morning Herald* or the *Asahi Shimbun*). In the first group were the *Mirror*, the *Daily Express*, the *Daily Mail*, the *Sun* and the *Sketch*. In the second, *The Times*, the *Daily Telegraph*, the *Guardian* and the *Financial Times*. (It now contains the *Independent*. Veterans, in 1969, knew it had once contained the *Morning Post*, and that ghosts of both type were numerous.)

Sunday papers, whether or not allied with a daily, were divided in similar fashion. Any publisher would have seen in each group a distinct commercial anatomy. For the Populars, which in 1969 had a combined daily sale of twelve million, revenues were dominated by cover price. The Unpopulars, with sales of two-and-a-quarter million, covered less than one-fourth of their costs from cover price, compensating with a richer advertising stream. Neither kind of newspaper (then or since) survives without advertising. But relative dependence makes a big difference. Circulation income is stable, and quickly collected. Advertising income is volatile, and takes months to arrive. A successful popular newspaper, everyone agrees, is not hard to manage. There is disagreement about whether it is hard to create – a question we shall come to.

Two Populars, the *Sketch* and the *Sun*, were so derelict by 1969 that they sold less than the *Telegraph*, the biggest Unpopular (at 1.3 million). Murdoch and Lord Catto quickly learnt that the *Sun* was the one up for sale. In name it was only five years old, but history traced it to 1911, when it originated as a printers' strike-sheet. Named the *Daily Herald*, it had after the First World War a short, brilliant spell of socialist independence (including Will Dyson's cartoon of the Versailles statesman with the weeping infant named 'Class of 1940'). It then became the official organ of the British unions, and proved that dullness may take any political colour. A partnership between the Trades Union Congress and the commercial publishers Odhams Press then proved that readers can be gained for a dull paper by sacrificial promotion – it briefly topped the circulation league with two million.

Later it proved the hollowness of such gains, and in 1961 Odhams wearily sold the *Herald* – as part of a magazine deal – to IPC, who as owners of the *Mirror* did not need it. Their relaunch of it as the *Sun* in 1964 was followed by the sad figures cited earlier. Hugh Cudlipp, IPC's editorial director, was loath to fold it. He had hated ending another fruitless IPC investment, the once-famous Melbourne *Argus*, and was relieved when Robert Maxwell offered to maintain the *Sun* with reduced mechanical employment. Murdoch enlisted Richard Briginshaw – most devious of London's print-union bosses – to back his own counter-offer, by threatening that sale to Maxwell would lead to strike action against the *Mirror*. Briginshaw did not, of course, object to Maxwell's business morals, only to his suggesting – unlike Murdoch – that Fleet Street print shops were overmanned.

Murdoch and Catto got the *Sun* on deferred terms, but the £800,000 purchase cost was least among the problems to be tackled. It was bleeding perhaps £2 million a year, a flow which might destabilise the News/NOTWO deal unless swiftly dammed, and Murdoch decided the *Sun* should become a new publication on the first day he could take control.

He had to improvise bravely to create in seven weeks a daily-paper system at the *News of the World*'s cramped home – barely adequate for a news-averse weekly – on Bouverie Street, one of Fleet Street's newsprint-clogged southern tributaries. It was 'an awful workplace', as one of its veterans recalled, insanitary and smelly, 'with a low ceiling, poor lighting and cheap office furniture'. There were insufficient telephones and insufficient headline type. But the date, just, was met.

'REACH FOR THE NEW SUN', said the announcement on Launch Minus One; '. . . the most important thing to remember is that the new SUN will be the paper that CARES. The paper that cares – passionately – about truth, and beauty and justice.' These values were dubiously visible in the launch serialisation, *The Love Machine*, second novel of Jacqueline Susann, whose *Valley of the Dolls* had established her at world level in quasi-pornography. *Machine* concerned dark events within the psyche of Robin

Stone, a sexually voracious television executive apt to exclaim 'Mutter, Mother, Mother' at orgasm. Terminologically, 'orgasm' itself was disallowed in the new *Sun*, which dealt in circumlocutions like 'moment of fulfilment' or (with classical overtones) 'going for gold'. Murdoch did not care for an inclusive sexual gamut, and when Nicholas Lloyd, recruited from the Unpopular *Sunday Times*, produced a piece on homosexuality, his response was icy: 'Do you really think our readers are interested in poofters?'

Why not, if incest was on offer? – though *Love Machine*'s psychopathological import may have lost something in the *Sun*'s production system. In their comprehensive account *Stick It Up Your Punter*, Peter Chippindale and Chris Horrie suggest that the developed sexual style of the Mark I Murdoch *Sun* was best exemplified in The Great Knicker Adventure: readers were invited to apply for a pair of panties supposedly irrigated with Chanel No. 5. Anyway the gamut, narrow or not, was exploited without rest. The staff churned out:

> features like 'the Geography of Love' – where were the best lovers in Britain to be found?; 'Do Men Still Want To Marry a Virgin?'; 'Love 30—women of thirty talking about the facts of living and loving in middle years'; 'The First Night of Love' – with riveting details of the first time; 'Are You Getting Your Share?'; 'The Way Into a Woman's Bed'; 'How To Be a Cool Lover'; 'How to Pick a Mate' . . . 'Casanova Girls' featured . . . a Swedish woman of twenty-one who claimed to have had 789 lovers since her first bedding at the age of twelve . . .

Chippindale and Horrie's amazement at this catalogue blends with considerable reverence for Murdoch as the 'hands-on' proprietor:

> involving himself in every aspect of the business, shaping his papers down to the last detail . . .
>
> Before and during the launch Murdoch dominated the *Sun* . . . the journalists' trade paper, *UK Press Gazette*, reported how he had rolled his sleeves up and pitched in . . . 'It's bloody chaotic,' he chirped, 'but we're getting a paper out.'

His uncanny gift was for selecting not 'the best editor', but infallibly 'the right editor' – and Larry Lamb was certainly right in terms of accommodating Murdoch's dominating role. First-night troubles aside, Murdoch and Larry Lamb were able to make production of the *Sun* into a boyish adventure – exclusively boyish, for in those hot-metal days women could write for Fleet Street papers but not enter the composing room, the clattering space where subs and printers hacked out the final form of a newspaper around the 'stone' (actually an ink-soaked steel table). Lamb struck just the right note of rough flattery when Murdoch turned up to take a hand: '"I'll tell you one thing this paper's got that no other paper's got – the two highest-paid stone subs in history," Lamb joked. Murdoch grinned back . . .'

Over a few months the *Sun* evolved into a smoother product of which Lamb became defensively proud (until, later in the story, disillusion arrived). Defensive because it was junk, as a simple listing of its content shows. Why did it make Murdoch's fortune, when his dominion over the *Australian* produced a débâcle? Standard accounts give us a simple triumph of fresh thinking and colonial daring over fusty British backwardness, like a state-of-the-art southern hemisphere sports combine crushing half-trained English cricketers. John Menadue, the deft manager who kept News Ltd's Australian base in order while the *Sun* took off, gives a representative version in his memoir *Things You Learn Along the Way*: 'Fleet Street was in a sorry state of flabbiness and decline . . . In Sydney I was cheering from the sidelines. The boy from the colonies, the "dirty digger", was getting up the noses of the English Establishment.' That so thoughtful a man, later one of Australia's most accomplished public servants, should have considered this a valid analysis of his chief's activities shows how rarely the Murdoch story carries a contextual frame. To grasp what really happened it's necessary, as in any battle, to look over the hill and see what the opposition were doing, or failing to do.

Rather than a period of simple decline in British newspapers, the transition of the 1960s to the 1970s was one of multiple experiments, many of which remain prosperous today. The *Guardian* was part-way through the risky project of recreating itself as a national competitor (having lived more than a century inside the regional security of Manchester). At the *Financial Times* the processes were under way which have made it one of the very few international newspapers. In general, boldness animated the Unpopulars: the *Sunday Times*, having easily passed one million, was running investigations and narratives of a complexity once thought unsaleable, but achieving sales which are still its high-tide mark. While the new *Sun* spouted about truth and justice, *The Times* was exposing corruption inside Scotland Yard – as if Delane had returned to remind people why Abe Lincoln once called his paper a bigger force than the Mississippi River.

In Popular territory confidence was lower. The *Mirror* was over five million – still with a rising trend – but the *Express* and *Mail* were sinking, and the *Sketch* was on its deathbed. Reasons and causes were much discussed: experiments, everyone knew, must be made to find a new direction for popular journalism. As it happened, the experiment which was statistically biggest – involving the *Daily Mirror* – was most thoroughly mishandled, to Murdoch's crucial benefit.

The *Mirror*'s distinction as a daily paper was to have achieved working-class readership on a national scale – a phenomenon not truly paralleled elsewhere in the world. Britain's social layer-cake has always been exceptionally deep, and the populists of the Northcliffe and Beaverbrook eras, successful as they were, didn't penetrate quite to its base. Harry Guy Bartholomew, who did so with the *Mirror*, took up the methods of New York 'yellow-press' chieftains, and their savage tabloid successors of the 1920s, and used these on a population base six times the size of New York's. Much media history turns on the vast commercial numbers generated by interplay between Britain's complex social system and simple geography.

Francis Williams, a contemporary, described the methods Bartholomew used in the 1930s and 1940s to reach people who before had scarcely read newspapers. There was:

> a frenzied gusto in dredging the news for sensational stories of sex and crime and a complete lack of reticence in dealing with them . . . To this he added radical muck-raking, personal invective, 'live letters' that give [readers] a sense of participation in a warm, communal life . . . strip cartoons with characters with whom they [could] identify.

The men Bartholomew gathered around him for his purpose invaded privacy shamelessly. They embraced every stunt, however contemptible in terms of normal human dignity, the public could be got to swallow and set practically no limits on what was permissible in print . . .

But this scandalous publication took a part – arguably the most spectacular part – in a unique expansion of the newspaper marketplace. Between 1940 and 1957 Britain's population increased by 7 per cent, while newspaper sales increased several times over. Adolf Hitler's gruesome career had much to do with this: pre-war, the *Mirror* mocked the authorities seeking to appease the totalitarians; subsequently, using 'FOR-WARD WITH THE PEOPLE' as a slogan, it elected itself as a raucous kibitzer to the process of social reconstruction.

Momentum continuing through the 1950s and 1960s enabled the *Mirror* to displace the *Express* as the world's biggest-selling newspaper – even if some critics doubted it was a newspaper at all. Many front pages in September 1957 displayed Elizabeth Ekford's confrontation with the troopers at Little Rock, Arkansas. One which did not was *The Times*, still using small ads there. Another was the *Mirror*, which ran Jayne Mansfield (a sub-Monroe of the day), and asked, 'HAS THE BUST HAD IT?'

Hugh Cudlipp and his IPC colleagues did not imagine that their biggest property was immune to forces affecting its rivals. But they were nervously aware how well Machiavelli's caution to reformers – nothing is 'more dangerous to manage than the creation of a new order of things' – applies to a successful newspaper. Readers, to be sure, are conservative, but editorial executives more so, and for the reason sailors are: handling immediate contingencies gives them a liking for what seems to work now over what offers to work better tomorrow. When 'the initiator has the enmity of all who would profit by the preservation of the old institutions', organisational politics assumes Machiavellian intensity.

In search of a persuasive rationale, Cudlipp turned to Dr Mark Abrams, a celebrated pioneer of market research, social analysis and advertising science. Abrams, who shared Cudlipp's broadly left-wing views, was quite unlike the passionless image of his profession: he handled statistics with an oracular vision, and believed a sea-change was impending among the much tried British proletariat. Better education and economic advantage would produce a demand, already visible in the middle class, for journalism with more intellectual depth. Abrams' estimate has attracted much scorn. But a 'vivid and correct imagination', says the historian Sir John Masterman, may well antedate results 'though it sees clearly the course of future events'.

IPC's unhappy recreation of the *Daily Herald* as the *Sun* was in fact a first attempt to apply Abrams' notions, but in the manner of a respray on an elderly vehicle. As it was a failing newspaper, there was little internal resistance. But the staff ordered to attract the emergent working class was substantially the staff which had bored the available workers – and a good many of its members considered 'serious' a synonym for 'dull'. The launch sale of 3.5 million decayed at much the same rate – with extra noughts – as that achieved by the *Australian* at the same time in the southern hemisphere. A sad remnant was what passed to Murdoch five years later.

Cudlipp, however, persisted boldly, and in 1967 risked bringing his experiments into the *Mirror* itself, as a section called Mirrorscope – four and sometimes more pages containing current-affairs background material such as might be found in any efficient Unpopular. It tried to address questions of context, relevance and significance – questions journalism still handles poorly, and which popular journalism had steadfastly, often cynically, ignored.

Mirrorscope split the *Mirror*'s staff in two, shattering its ebullient culture. One party said the new section effectively insulted the readers' native judgment, the other that it was nonetheless an overdue reform. (Rare neutrals took heavy crossfire.) Today, we may think both sides had significant points. According to Christiansen's doctrine, newspapers endlessly encounter didactic requirements, but have to discharge them without didactic excess. This severe test of technique Mirrorscope did not always pass. Often it gave background to a foreground invisible to readers, for in ten years the *Mirror*'s basic news sense had not got far past Mansfield's bust. Mirrorscope exposed as much as supplied the need for reform.

All this might have been remedied had not the argument merged into the jostling for Cudlipp's favour – and succession. Soon it related as much to editorial philosophy and market research as the duelling of

Montagues and Capulets. Among the precarious, self-absorbed sub-editorial communities of Old Fleet Street, professional discussion frequently took such a course. Moderating the raw material of human competition is hard for any corporation: IPC, faithful to the anti-ethos of the Stab in the Back, hardly tried, and the Mirrorscope Wars capriciously stalled or wrecked several careers.

Larry Lamb, the *Mirror*'s chief sub-editor, was the biggest casualty, and in 1968 he quit to become Manchester editor of the *Daily Mail* – a bitter return to regional obscurity, after reaching the last few rungs of a national ladder. When Murdoch found him a year later he had, he admitted, a vast chip on his shoulder.

Born in 1929 to poor parents in a Yorkshire mining town, Lamb was exactly, painfully, a product of his times. Ironically, the man who made a monkey of Mark Abrams was a proof of Abrams' vision, for in Lamb's own belief his natural abilities justified aspirations more sophisticated than the popular newspapers of his day. School, which he left at sixteen, did just enough to stir Lamb's potential, but nothing to certify it. The odds against someone of his origin being educated even close to capacity were crushing by US or Australian standards, and can hardly be grasped in present-day Britain, where a third of students reach university or an equivalent level.

For people maturing in the 1960s and 1970s, graduate status increasingly was a passport to the journalism Lamb sourly called Unpopular – sourly, because the passport was linked still to narrow economic privilege. In his generation *The Times* still asked recruits about their private means; even in the next, an Oxbridge degree could lead straight to a *Financial Times* career after the drafting of a few top-of-the-head words and a chat with Sir Gordon Newton, the editor. His eye for quality was allegedly infallible, but someone like Lamb – who started as a clerk, and struggled for eight years to get any newspaper work – could scarcely be impressed. Ten years' sweat at the *Mirror* went into his rise to chief sub. The causes of his fall are obscure, but as later he both expressed loathing for Mirrorscope and claimed to have been one of its inventors, an arbitrary component seems likely.

Certainly his emotional need for an attack on the *Mirror* matched Murdoch's financially urgent requirement. The crew they enlisted in three frantic weeks contained numerous boozy derelicts, but the sober ones generally felt some less furious version of Lamb's own motivation. Roy Greenslade, one of the youngest members of the first draft, recalled them as 'ex-*Mirror* staff frustrated by failing to win promotion . . . or, like me, wannabes who saw it as a stepping-stone to the *Mirror*'.

Of Fleet Street's existing institutions the *Mirror* then was pre-eminently the one from which young men and women with few advantages but their talent hoped to profit – those who, in Anthony Delano's words, wanted from journalism 'classless acceptance, swift upward mobility – and glamour'. It was known to pay better than the papers demanding social or educational gloss, and to be free of the increasingly arcane obsessions ruling the *Express*. Though they had no wide professional culture, its aspirants were fiercely professional about (in Greenslade's words) the 'rigorous technical expertise' of the *Mirror* – which took popular broadsheet style to additional extremes of verbal compression and typographic inflation. The veteran Dick Dinsdale was only half joking when he said the ideal story contained three paragraphs and 'every paragraph, three sentences. Every sentence, three words. Every word, one syllable.'

Graphic devices were lavishly applied to such textual pellets: they were *italicised*, **CAPITALISED** (along with a font change), **emboldened**, reversed into WOBs or WOTs – white on black or tone – empha-sised with barkers !, stars ☆ and bullets ●, or enclosed in boxes , perhaps *shadow boxes* , before being wrapped up with headlines based (if possible) on puns or alliteration.

For most talents these procedures, under hot-metal technology, demanded sufficient personal investment to generate a strong craft pride. This often blended into contempt for anyone uninitiated, and resentment of anyone who might doubt their ultimate value. In expert hands, this style could energise the least substantial input. Actually, it made sub-stance almost irrelevant. Hugh Cudlipp himself liked to say, 'I could produce the paper with just Johnny Johnson and the PA' – meaning the routine news-agency feed from the Press Association, plus a single staff reporter to cobble up angles (though not even in hyperbole did Cudlipp mean a single sub-editor). But it always stood near the point where technique stops being the servant of content and turns into its master – becoming a complex way of presenting simplicities, not a way of

presenting complex things simply. Newspapers are not alone in such failings – the engineer Ettore Bugatti said that many cars expressed 'the
triumph of workmanship over design' – but newspapers cannot halt production while they rethink. The *Mirror*'s populist technique imposed a
narrow agenda – like the fancy perspective of a Mannerist painting
excluding real observation – and trying to reform it on the fly was a
confidence-sapping process.

What Lamb's drunks and wannabes turned out, from Day One, was
really the *Mirror* – the only newspaper they knew how to make – stripped
of Mirrorscope and all such troublesome experiments. The *Mirror*'s chief
columnist was 'Cassandra', actually Bill Connor: Lamb hired Connor's
son to write as 'Son of Cassandra'. The Live Letters page was recreated
as Livelier Letters. The famous strip-character Andy Capp – reputedly,
an archetype of the *Mirror* reader – was cloned by the *Sun* as Wack, and
Garth – not much less famous – became Scarth. 'FORWARD WITH THE
PEOPLE' – which the *Mirror* had dropped to seem less partisan – Lamb
pinned to the *Sun* masthead.

Shame usually inhibits mimicry among journalists, but not among
Murdoch's recruits – because they thought the *Mirror* belonged rightly to
them, and was turning itself into something alien. Murdoch was giving
them a chance to recapture it, though most of them probably – Lamb
certainly – overestimated the extent to which they would have property
in the victory, which very soon appeared spectacular. Sales of the *Sun* and
the *Mirror* during the 1970s moved in striking counterpoint, as Figure 1
shows. Clearly there is something more to the story, as the *Sun*'s rise was
steeper than the *Mirror*'s fall. But this was not due to the *Sun* reaching out
to new readers. Between 1970 and 1980 its average sale rose by
2,822,363, very close to the amount by which the other popular dailies
collectively declined in the same period, that is 2,825,658. (This includes
the loss of the *Daily Sketch*, which its owners killed in 1970 in order to
focus on reorganising their other daily, the *Mail*.)

Nothing occurred like the vast expansion led in previous decades by
the *Express* and then by the *Mirror*. Figure 2 portrays a market essentially
without growth, within which the *Sun* is substituting itself for the *Mirror* –
and taking over the market-leader position which before had made the
Mirror the natural beneficiary of other titles in decline. Then at the end

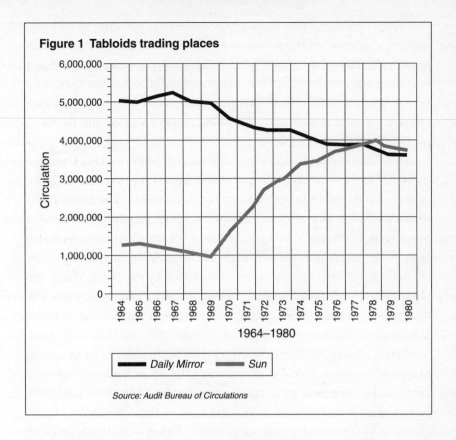

Figure 1 Tabloids trading places

Source: Audit Bureau of Circulations

of the period a general downturn commences, with the *Mail* alone maintaining a rising trend. This was a significant change in the situation of the popular dailies – though the popular Sundays had for some time been established in generic decay, and their combined sale fell 22 per cent between 1970 and 1980 (20,472,622 to 15,779,428).

During these years the IPC management behaved with staggering commercial folly. The company had undertaken a complex diversification programme, centred on a reverse takeover by its own subsidiary the Reed paper group. Making this agreeable to the City involved 'sweating the assets' heavily for revenue. Thus the *Mirror*'s cover price was kept high, averaging 15 per cent above the *Sun*'s between 1970 and 1980 – for a paper which usually had less than thirty pages when the *Sun* was comfortably over thirty. As the advertising quota was also kept high in the *Mirror*, the *Sun*'s essentially similar editorial content probably cost its

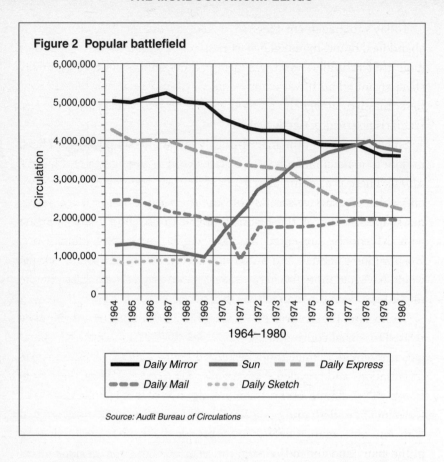

Figure 2 Popular battlefield

Circulation

1964–1980

Daily Mirror ▬▬ Sun ▬ ▬ ▬ Daily Express
●●● Daily Mail ●●●● Daily Sketch

Source: Audit Bureau of Circulations

readers about half of what IPC was charging. The group transformed itself into Reed International during 1970.

Derivative as the *Sun* was, it came with one marketing weapon new to Fleet Street: heavy television promotion, which Murdoch had practised for some time with News Ltd's Australian papers. Disliking the expense, Reed allowed the *Sun* to outspend the *Mirror* on promotion by roughly four to one. This may or may not have moved many readers directly, but the *Mirror*'s circulation staff had no doubt about its effect on the news-distribution trade. Big-circulation newspapers depend continuously on news-stand display and availability. Murdoch gave the news trade a higher percentage of the *Sun*'s lower cover price, which anyway made an effective incentive. Newsagents, already anxious about fading popular volumes, were disposed still more towards the *Sun* by its promotional activity.

Today's management theorists would say that IPC/Reed recklessly abandoned brand-maintenance when a major brand was trying to reposition itself radically – and was facing competition from a substantially cheaper imitation. It was commercial self-immolation. For the *Mirror* to suffer massive damage there was no need for editorial alchemy at the *Sun*. Plagiarism served perfectly well.

So far from fresh thinking, Murdoch and Lamb simply stepped back in time to make a newspaper as narrowly predictable as the traditional *Mirror*. There is a sentimental legend of its wit and vitality but it is not one which can survive scrutiny of *Stick It Up Your Punter* or a visit to the newspaper section of the British Library. Lamb himself, after parting with Murdoch, presented a less gung-ho retrospect than News Corporation's barkers and apologists have done: he estimated that he would have had more fun in broadsheet journalism. (Not implausibly, he might have been the man to fix Mirrorscope.)

To be sure, the *Sun* was denounced for innovations, but mostly they related to sexual convention. From November 1970 the first right-hand page presented a female nude; when added to a menu of Susann-style serialisations and recycled sex manuals (*The Sensuous Woman*, and so on) Lamb's Page Three Girl attracted many accusations of pornography. Certainly bare flesh and pounding blood were displayed and described with an extravagance new then to British dailies, but the realities of pubic hair (and indeed of orgasm) remained far too misty for real pornographers. The *Sun* went obsessively, but not deeply, into sex because it was a paper with a tiny editorial range, and no other subject can be revisited as often.

Essentially, Murdoch and Lamb emulated Bartholomew's tactics. But they were not extending a market – rather, they were competing for part of a saturated one – so the social dynamics and the consequences were both very different. The *Mirror* audience had been recruited from people who had not before used daily newspapers, so severe was their educational poverty (which is not to say their civil qualities were lacking). It is hard to believe that anything more demanding could have served them as a vehicle of entertainment and of elementary – but sceptical – news coverage of their rulers' activities.

However, by the time Murdoch's *Sun* rose an educational revolution was under way in Britain – far from a clean sweep of the injustices visited on Lamb's contemporaries, but still profound. In 1970 a third of school leavers had a C-grade or better in English, nearly a quarter had the same in mathematics, and they were participants in a rising trend. Modest enough in absolute terms, these grades require a capacity to analyse or create structured text and to manage the four arithmetic operations – abilities disseminated to some extent among those with lower grades and even with none.

Serious controversy exists over international comparison, and the rate of educational expansion. Less seriously, there are arguments about value, which in extreme forms assert either that this revolution has not occurred, or that it has degraded culture by having occurred (notions worth testing when 'dumbing down' debates enter the Newscorp story). But neither these controversies nor inconsistencies in the data obscure the gross pattern. By 1974, decisive progress had been made towards the present-day case, one in which 85 per cent of the population are educated to standards of literacy and numeracy which scarcely applied to 10 per cent when Britain's unique popular press was created.

At this point – and when it was already clear that nobody had to buy newspapers for elementary news – Murdoch and Lamb launched a paper which, as most journalists saw it, sharply reduced any demand made on readers' minds. Arthur Christiansen's son Michael became editor of the *Mirror* in 1970, and stated that view baldly: 'From the popular newspapers' point of view I think that Murdoch's arrival in Fleet Street was the worst thing that could have happened . . . The clock of journalistic standards has been put back ten to fifteen years.'

Lamb was enraged, particularly as Christiansen seemed to imply that the *Sun* was peddling gross erotica. Even if true, the charge would hardly have been one for the *Mirror* to prosecute. But Lamb did not try seriously to defend the *Sun* as a good newspaper for its time in any terms that journalists could engage with. Rather, he denied, and with moralistic zeal, that they had any business offering opinions on its qualities. The proper, objective test of a newspaper's quality, he said fervently to his staff – and to an appreciative Murdoch – was 'the number of people who bought it'.

And indeed that number is critical. Though literary theory may allow for the neglected masterpiece, newspapers are about circulation. But the complexity (Lamb must have known) is that the current sale of a news-paper doesn't predict its sale in a year's time (or in a decade's time) much better than stock-market prices predict the future – though circulations are at least less volatile than shares. Indeed, they are inflexible as a rule in the short term, and the *Sun*'s instantaneous break into the *Mirror*'s sale was evidence of something entirely unusual – of substitution, in fact, not editorial competition. Any opinion of a newspaper's quality – whether that of a journalist or not – is of course subjective. But so is cir-culation: the figures collect numerous subjective preferences – like other records of economic choice – and imagining that they impart their own objective character to the material they summarise is a crude fallacy.

And journalists have, finally, no other business but estimating their product's future value from present-day evidence. Circulation is an input, but a treacherous one, because the feedback it gives from editorial devel-opment is heavily lagged. Transient effects are quite frequent, as when heavily promoted serials 'put on' thousands of sales, but anyone analysing audited averages must be struck by the rarity of identifiable short-term impact. This insensitivity is easy to understand: readers, though quite as subjective, are far more laid back about newspapers than the people producing them.

Creative responses to ambiguous data, drawn from assorted social and technical sources, require collective thought and argument in any business. Though fond myths exist of the mastermind flying solo by gut, most creative editors – Ben Bradlee, Harry Evans, Charles Wintour – have been essentially collegiate, if sometimes imperial in style. But Rupert Murdoch's distaste for the collegiate runs deeper than style. Reports of him both as a charmer and as a bully refer to situations which are one on one (or hierarchical), and the evidence is that any rare editorial gathering with frank and level exchanges renders him confused or impatient. The copycat approach to producing the *Sun* was able to avoid anything like that.

What Christiansen tried to say was that Murdoch was taking market share by means which would erode the overall market. At the time his prophecy was dismissed as the product of self-interest. But from our longer perspective we can see the decay beginning in Figures 1 and 2 – the Abrams effect, as it were, kicking in at the border of the 1980s (though with many complications still to come). There were Cassandras less compromised than Christiansen, but they were ignored as thoroughly. Murdoch never supposed the tabloid style might grow sterile, or the *Sun* itself suffer destructive competition.

Christiansen should have blamed his own corporate colleagues no less than Murdoch – and probably did. Having compounded commercial negligence by complacency near to arrogance, they switched after roughly three years to dark despair about editorial development. Mirrorscope foundered by 1973; whether any of a rapid succession of editors might have solved the problem it represented cannot now be known, as none had backing enough for a serious try. The *Mirror* of the 1970s turned by degrees into an imitation of an imitation of itself – extreme humiliation, though worse lay in store.

Lamb's defeat of his old colleagues was complete in 1978 when the *Sun* overtook the *Mirror* – and, as his obituarists later observed, it had a meaning broader than personal revenge. 'Larry Lamb,' said the *Independent,* 'achieved more than any other journalist of his generation . . . he was the paramount influence on the course the British popular press has taken . . . Those who think tabloid standards have fallen precipitately . . . hold him largely to blame.' Curiously, no memorialist placed any blame for fallen tabloid sales on Lamb, though by the time of his death in May 2000 the facts were quite conspicuous.

Murdoch's success has been in more than one case the obverse of others' dereliction. But gaining market-domination in British popular newspapers was the decisive instance. Once it was established, he was close to fireproof financially. By the mid-1970s, Lamb estimated, News International (the old NOTWO) was producing annual net revenue at a rate equal to £125 million in today's values. It was at this time (1976) that Bruce D. Henderson of the Boston Consulting Group produced his famous anatomy of the 'cash cow' which every major corporation indispensably needs to 'pay the corporate overhead . . . pay the corporate interest charges and justify the debt capacity for the whole company'. News International ranks as an outstanding specimen – ruthlessly acquired, and ever since fiercely defended by any weapons Murdoch and his team find themselves able to manage.

For some inhabitants of Fleet Street its swift rise gave special pungency to schadenfreude generated by the *Mirror*'s fall – they could gladly reaffirm the famous axiom about never losing money 'by underestimating the intelligence of the great masses of the plain people'. Fleet Street happened about then to be rich in contrary evidence. The *Daily Sketch* (seen expiring in Figure 2) underestimated intelligence valiantly while losing heroic sums; more recently, billions have been lost estimating that people will buy anything a dotcom offers. However, the old saw survives on giving comfort rather than truth: anyone knows that seeking the reader's intelligence is arduous, but easier ways, if given specious respectability, may qualify as the path of duty. Its author was H. L. Mencken, who never detected popular intelligence, or (as he said) reason to change his mind on any substantial matter.

Such sentiments helped to dress up a commercial coup – merited in terms of energy and nerve – as something greater. The financial worth of News International was reckoned so overwhelming as to demonstrate lasting editorial achievement, based on supreme refinement of Mencken's Law. But the fact that capitalism has lived alongside free media far better than its rivals does not mean its valuations apply sensibly to news-media assets beyond the immediate term (communications infrastructures, like railways and the Internet, similarly escape its measure). Christiansen's time-scale of ten or fifteen years was tolerably accurate. But for some journalists, and most financial analysts, it was just too long.

Of course there were (and are) other assessments. One carrying liberal-left overtones suggested that popular newspapers all became culturally worthless – financial value aside – during the 1970s, and should face inevitable erosion in a society increasingly dominated by television. This can still attribute great potency to News, for Murdoch and his followers may be seen as strategists of damage-resistance – even as demoniacally skilful ones by those who find that some tabloid exploits make them gag. Such assessments subsisted readily together while circulation trends were still ambiguous. But we now know that the television environment has not been corrosive to all British newspapers. The *Daily Mail*, a Popular by history and technique, has grown steadily since its 1971 relaunch in tabloid format, and today enjoys its highest-ever sale. That progress can be seen starting in Figure 2. It requires more analysis when broadsheets enter the Newscorp story (along with terms like 'mid-market'), but may be taken already as a counter to inevitability.

Worldwide evidence now is that serious newspapers not only coexist with television, but in some ways benefit from the association. It's therefore important to establish at this narrative stage that a major part of the strategy Murdoch and Lamb initiated with the *Sun* was a hot, close embrace between tabloid and television – cohabitation, more than coexistence. Insofar as they added anything to the *Mirror* formula, it originated in their view that television was getting 'far less coverage than the huge role it played in . . . readers' lives warranted. The *Sun*, Lamb and Murdoch both agreed, would cover TV in great depth.' This was a resolution thoroughly made good – the origin of a practice in which television's fictions are reported with more intensity than most of the actual world (though mixed with incursions into the actual lives of the actors projecting the fictions). It was swiftly emulated, and during the 1970s a symbiotic relationship with television came to be accepted as fundamental to tabloid vitality. The question to be asked later in the story is whether television's effect on newspaper readership has been rather subtler in the long term.

Another important sequential point is that today's high levels of distaste for popular papers – whether or not justifiable – would have been hard to justify purely on Fleet Street evidence in the years 1970–80. Present feeling reflects the cumulative effect of things done to and with tabloids – primarily by Murdoch and his entourage – and many of those things happened elsewhere in time and place. Larry Lamb's *Sun* was crudely derivative, and many of its scoops were factitious. But it was never much like the Murdoch *New York Post*, a paper which the *Columbia Journalism Review* called 'a social problem, a force for evil'. Nor was it Lamb's *Sun* which the media commentator Raymond Snoddy said in 1990 had become a 'bigoted, foul-mouthed fantasy factory'. Lamb, who left the paper in 1981, was an unhappy witness of that progress.

But it of course it was never Lamb's *Sun* – it was wholly Murdoch's. There was no journalistic sense in which Murdoch had made the *Sun*, but he had made its editor, and never allowed Lamb or anyone else to forget it. By the 1970s the corporate style of News was fairly mature, and distinctive for curious practices which Murdoch developed as intrinsic to his authority. The first to become notorious were the phone calls. These any executive had to expect from any international location at any moment, and consisted from Murdoch's side of terse enigmatic questions and long, eerie silences. The effect, as John Menadue states, was to create insecurity in those who submitted – that is, everyone, for anyone who rebelled was disposed of. Free spirits occasionally tried out-silencing the boss. Most embarrassed themselves with their garrulity, says Menadue, and Murdoch collected many hostages to fortune.

Administrators, like Menadue himself or the finance director Mervyn Rich, were least affected as they were working in areas where the corporate agenda might be quite orthodox – or largely orthodox in professional terms. Rich and Murdoch from the early days of News conducted an intense crusade against corporate taxation, and many accountants might think it morally dubious. But they would not think of it as something counterproductive to doing accountancy at all – as it would be to make credit entries without matching debits.

Pressure fell mostly on journalists – placed anyway in the company's front line – for their equivalent of the accountant's double-entry rule was subjected to a contempt barely (if at all) disguised. At its best or its sleaziest journalism depends on exchange and interaction: events and individuals (the controllers of the system, as much as its subjects) must be interrogated continuously, with no judgment being immune. No other means exists to extract sense from the gabble of incident. Murdoch imposed from the top of News an arbitrary style, stripped to an unprecedented degree of all such dialectical qualities.

The tension the lopsided phone calls set up was enhanced by Murdoch's intermittent appearances at *Sun* edition-planning meetings, where he would promote story-ideas which Lamb – painfully, speechlessly – recognised as consistently 'wooden-headed'. Though they were rarely implemented – were uneasily forgotten for the most part – they were never treated to the brusque tests such gatherings exist to apply. As Chippindale and Horrie put it, 'Murdoch expected his every word to be listened to', but did not 'show the same interest in what Lamb and the others at the paper had to say. He would sit in meetings firing out questions into space and moving on to the next one before the people had a chance to reply fully. He would leave meetings without explanation . . . having lost interest in the topics under discussion . . .'

151

There was no operational need for Murdoch's appearances. But the remission of Lamb's usual way with inadequate notions – harsh, even brutal – produced a clear message. Other people's judgments could not engage with Murdoch's, but Murdoch's would take no coherent form and might (at some risk to fortune) be ignored, so long as they were not challenged. Beaverbrook's and Hearst's bizarre views were rarely arbitrary in this sense – not even Northcliffe's, until his clinically insane phase. Rather they were cut in firm relief: Beaverbrook freely employed the telecoms of his day to goad his editors, but occult silences were far from his style.

The dominion Murdoch imposed was nearly free of content – something apologists have emphasised, particularly veterans keen to testify that service with News involved (in their own case) no ethical discomfort. There is nothing very apparent as a Murdoch programme, they say, and what there is a little modesty can circumvent. The argument has appeared effective in some phases of News history, and in others it has seemed more like a suggestion that it wouldn't matter if the chairman of a hospital supervised operations without a mask. For the real effect was to demonstrate that basic editorial procedure ultimately had at News the status of a charade – a further stage in the expulsion of judgment which began at the *Sun* by displacing all estimation of quality and readership in favour of the pseudo-objective circulation theory (which Lamb, its promoter, would live to regret).

Even when the sub's reflexes have virtually abolished the reporter's – even with cynicism and incompetence lavishly supplied – an attachment to collective method inhibits journalists from acting nakedly as conduits of propaganda. Murdoch, who had done exactly that to oblige Black Jack McEwen, made plain that such attachment carried no weight with him.

And this empty domain was ruled by fear, efficiently distributed. The sessions between Murdoch and Lamb to which Tom Margerison had been an unwilling early witness developed into a ritual built around comparisons between *Sun* and *Mirror*. Murdoch:

would lay the papers next to each other and flick through the pages, complaining if he thought the *Mirror* had done better on any particular story. 'Why did you print this dreadful rubbish?' he would ask Lamb . . . 'What's all this crap about poofters?' he would enquire when there was a fleeting reference to homosexuality . . .

Any such reference, irrespective of substance, was apt to trigger a ritual joke: why did the sun never set on the British Empire? God, Murdoch pronounced, didn't trust the Poms after dark. *Stick It Up Your Punter* says he got a laugh with this initially – an easy one if so, for it was perhaps as old as the First AIF – 'but Lamb ground his teeth as it was endlessly repeated'. These sessions were wholly one-sided, their acrimony varying only with the chairman's mood, and Lamb was reduced to searching for ways it could be manipulated. He thought that Murdoch, a gambler, was superstitious and might be influenced by astrology. Thus the *Sun*'s stargazer had to 'doctor the Pisces entry to assure his chairman . . . that he would have a good day and to cast his bread upon the waters . . .'.

Lamb was not a supine character – indeed, friends saw in him a rage which was usually suppressed but never assuaged – and he believed strongly in his own capacities. But he could achieve no relationship with Murdoch other than subservience. And what Lamb had to endure he also imposed, perhaps inevitably. He said he hated to rule by dread, but it was the result: people called the passage outside his office 'The Giant's Causeway', after the Ulster landscape haunted by legendary ghosts.

The rise of the *Sun* and the rebirth of the *Australian* were parallel events, and illuminate each other. Of course in Australia there had been nothing to imitate – no concept of what a national newspaper might do – and after the Max Newton débâcle Murdoch could find no fresh editorial direction. John Menadue's evidence is that closure was only weeks away at times. It doubtless owed its reprieve chiefly to political utility (which meant that closure would have been a dangerous defeat). Some fiscal footwork helped: Merv Rich shunted the paper's deficit of A$20,000 a week ('a lot of money in the late 1960s') around cash-rich sections of the News group via a series of licences. And with the *News of the World* in the bag the losses looked much less daunting.

But, while Murdoch occupied himself in London, editorial salvation turned up of its own accord. Adrian Deamer, bored at the Herald group in Melbourne, had joined the *Australian* as assistant editor, and found it the most disorganised newspaper he had seen. The post-Newton vacuum Murdoch filled, after much delay, by appointing Walter Kommer, but Kommer was unwilling and asked Deamer to take over while he moved to the business side of News. Though not Murdoch's choice, it was both the best editor and the right one.

It appeared to many people then that Australia might have still more federal disparities than America, and still poorer prospects for nationwide publishing. Canberra seemed as remote to many Australians as Washington to Americans before the Second World War and the imperial presidency. New South Wales supported (as now) enough political mayhem for several sizeable countries, paying faint attention to other states (which reciprocated the ennui). And devotion to sport may be universal without unifying: Australia does not have as many regional sporting idioms as France has regional cheeses, but an editor might think so (and just then cricket, the one national sport, seemed in temporary decline).

In fact, the opportunity existed. There was an economic boom – part-fed by mineral speculation – and simultaneously a synergy between three issues with national content. There was the Vietnam War – breaking the tradition that only volunteers should fight in foreign wars. There was land ownership, with real legal challenges being made to the expropriation of the original Australians. And this was the crisis-point of apartheid's bid for world acceptance, making sporting relations with South Africa explosive. The combination tested Australian concepts of ethnicity, social equity, military honour and sporting decency further than existing newspapers recognised – and lifestyle, furthermore, was changing in ways their discourse barely registered. The *Sydney Morning Herald*, like the *Sun*, excluded 'orgasm' from its vocabulary, and was little better equipped for mature discussion of morality and gender.

Circumstances appropriate for creating a significant new newspaper are clearly unusual – it is another aspect of the accidental quality which Max Weber diagnosed in journalism. The final circumstance, perhaps least usual of all, is the presence of an appropriate journalist.

Adrian Deamer had been a reporter good enough for the *Daily Express* in its last bright phase, but his chief gift was for imparting architectural logic to a newspaper, edition by edition. Something of this he gained watching Arthur Christiansen packing news and features into the *Express*, but he knew he had started with 'a good eye', and technique for once was servant to the moment. What struck people about the *Australian* once Deamer took charge was its limpid structure – a simple paper to use, even when it presented a 'hard, cold complicated picture of real events'. It was not, for the most part, very opinionated about the nation's issues, but conservative politicians (of various ideologies) thought so, because it illuminated matters which obscurity improved for them. (Deamer's own views were left-wing, but he held that partisanship should never appear in news-columns, and only sparingly in editorials.)

Though promotion was modest, circulation, having sunk to 50,000 in 1968, effectively trebled, reaching 141,000 (in one audit period) in 1970; instead of humiliating losses there were increasingly frequent periods of profit. Not remotely was it a financial bonanza like the *Sun*, but by 1970 it was on the way to becoming a first-class property. And in spite of cross-readership with the deep-rooted Sydney and Melbourne broadsheets, this was essentially a new product in a new market, not a cheap substitute in an existing one. (There was a general slump in 1971.) 'The *Australian*,' wrote Professor Henry Mayer, the country's leading press historian, 'has created its own personality; it is a paper . . . about which people argue and to which some have a strong attachment. For the first time in many a decade here is a paper some of its readers feel they like . . . [and do not simply] find bearable . . .'

Technically, it was becoming pre-eminent. David Bowman, then on the *Sydney Morning Herald*, remembers that day after day the *SMH* news conference began with a sad admission that the *Australian* had found the dimensions in the day's news that everyone else had missed. Managers like John Menadue and Ken May (still wincing at the *Canberra Times* defeat) were equally pleased. But Murdoch was not. Although preoccupied in London, he took what opportunities he could to make that visible.

He used the same approach in Deamer's office as in Lamb's – flipping through a run of papers, picking out individual stories, and demanding for each one the editor's instant, detailed provenance. Technically, this is an absurd scale for assessing a daily paper, where decisions flow densely and reflect much random turbulence. In a real news operation, the editor

155

knows – should know – little more about individual stories than a divisional general knows about company commanders' actions. An editor must maintain an overall mental scan of the process, and many fail through excessive second-guessing.

The Murdoch inquisition was a technique of personal domination with zero professional relevance (as Larry Lamb knew). But it bounced off Deamer. Each time Murdoch asked why this story or that story made the paper, a roughly similar answer resulted: 'Christ, Rupert: I don't know. If you stick around while we're getting the paper out, you'll find out that kind of thing.' Nor was the telephone method applicable. It exploited the obligation people usually feel to succour a dying conversation. Deamer always put such things immediately out of their misery. All this might have been welcome among rugged colonials. But Murdoch found it distasteful, and fell back on grumbling that the *Australian* exhibited 'bleeding-heart attitudes' and apparently wanted to see 'the country turned over to the blacks'. Menadue says, 'Murdoch spent a lot of his life tugging it back from the left when he came under pressure from his business friends'.

In July 1970 Murdoch was in Sydney to announce the *Sunday Australian* – pointedly under separate editorial control. (It somewhat resembled the Newton *Australian*, and never prospered.) Departing, he summoned Ken May to the airport, and told him to order changes in the daily paper: removing or restraining columns and cartoons which had caused distress in the political class, and placing over Deamer as editor-in-chief a former golf columnist named Neal Travis, briefed to constrain new excesses. When May retailed these instructions, Deamer pursued Murdoch by phone, and asked, bluntly, 'What's this about Travis being put in over me?' 'That's something you'll have to work out between yourselves,' said Murdoch (who dislikes confrontation not initiated by himself). Deamer told Travis and May that he would ignore Murdoch's vicarious instructions and any personal ukases Travis might care to offer. Little of this had effect, because May feared that internal disputes might bring back chaos, and Travis had little relish for his task.

In June 1971 South Africa's Rugby Union footballers arrived to tour Australia, and when transport workers 'blacked' these all-white

Springboks the government offered to supply military aircraft. The *Australian* in a front-page editorial said this was a 'cynical misuse of Prime Ministerial power' which would 'divide Australia'. Murdoch, in London, declared furiously that this was the worst thing since Newton's attack on Catholic schools.

If he meant it, he was massively out of touch with his own country, for Australia was visibly, fiercely divided (in Queensland, core rugby territory, a state of emergency was declared). But he flew to Sydney set on tackling Deamer, and this time with deliberation. When the paper-flipping routine failed again, Murdoch at last said, 'You're not producing the sort of paper I want.' 'Rupert,' said Deamer, going to the heart of the matter, 'I don't think you know what sort of paper you want. So until you do I'll go on producing the paper I want.'

Murdoch withdrew to the Cavan homestead, and conferred over the next three days with Ken May, Menadue and Tom FitzGerald, perhaps the country's most respected journalist, and recently appointed editor-in-chief of News Ltd. None of these discussions identified actual issues of editorial performance; their aim was to discover whether enough executive solidarity existed to make removal of the editor embarrassing.

It did not. Menadue, in retrospect, is bleakly self-critical: 'As manager . . . my view would not have been decisive against Murdoch's clear determination. But I had influence and I didn't support Deamer as I should have . . . I have regretted it ever since . . . I was . . . keeping on-side with the boss . . .' Menadue's motives were not simple corporate ambition. He was a major figure in the opposition Labor Party, and deeply involved in switching Murdoch's support away from the decayed, long-victorious ruling coalition. FitzGerald also had unsimple motives: he owned the small, distinguished but uneconomic *Nation Review*. He thought a threat to quit might deter Murdoch, but if he had to fulfil it and lose his salary, *Nation* would die. He too later thought he had made a sad mistake. May, though he admired Deamer, was purely a footsoldier.

Murdoch now summoned Deamer, and said he must choose another job in News Ltd – an important one, of course. He seems to have been authentically puzzled when Deamer said, 'Rupert, you don't want me, and I don't want you.' The relationship of their families had taken much the same course in the second generation as in the first.

Back at the airport Murdoch met Owen Thompson, an assistant editor of the *Australian* who had just written to recommend himself for promotion. Thompson found himself made acting editor, and he asked, 'What's this about "acting", Rupert?' The meaning didn't long remain obscure, but executive succession at the *Australian*, the paper's chequered further history, and the last crossing of Deamer and Murdoch paths must be taken later in the story. A postscript to the Springbok case may be added, however, to illustrate the uses of controversy.

Non-union transport became available, whereupon the military option lapsed. The demonstrators halted no matches, but believed that their representations to Australia's cricket authorities influenced Sir Don Bradman's announcement that cricket against South Africa would cease until selection was non-racial. The debate included some pointed South African remarks about Australia's own racial record, which are widely thought to have benefited the Aboriginal cause. And on the thirtieth anniversary of the contested Springbok tour a rugby team of Aboriginal schoolboys toured South Africa by way of commemoration.

Deamer was right that Murdoch had no positive vision of what the *Australian* should be. But in another sense he clearly knew what he wanted: a vessel empty enough to ship any political freight considered profitable. With Deamer as editor the *Australian* could not have been used in the relentless pro-Labor campaign which Murdoch ran in 1972, when Gough Whitlam became Prime Minister of Australia. Subtler than his father, Rupert never echoed Sir Keith's boast that he had put Honest Joe Lyons into that job. He did not suppose he could personally create election outcomes. His concern was creating obligations, as he had successfully done with McEwen – but new ones, as Black Jack had become a figure of the past.

Eric Walsh, author of the Murdoch–McEwen alliance, set to work on its replacement with relish, as the ALP was homeland for him, and its general secretary Mick Young his intimate friend. Walsh, Young and Menadue, toiling like diplomats before a superpower summit, found Murdoch eager but Whitlam severely reluctant.

In July 1971 Menadue set up a dinner for Murdoch with Gough and Margaret Whitlam, Ken May, Tom FitzGerald and himself. It was awkward, because Whitlam wanted to discuss Deamer's very recent departure. Two months later the Whitlams spent a weekend at Cavan, much of which Gough devoted to admiring the columnist Mungo MacCallum, one of those whom Murdoch had decided was insufficiently respectful of politicians. Whitlam is huge, sometimes vain or ponderous, but with a core of irreverence. Murdoch is slight, restive, unaffected – except in command mode – but essentially conventional. They found it hard to see eye to eye in any way.

But the effort went on because the Liberals seemed utterly doomed, and for Murdoch there was the prospect of entering the ground floor of a new political structure. (It was not so for the Packer and Herald groups, Liberals immemorially; even the Fairfaxes, occasional users of a lower-case 'l', would be waiting in the street.) Some bonding there had to be, however. Young and Menadue succeeded at last with a cruise in Sydney Harbour, though at first 'we couldn't get Gough to be in it. "I'm too fucking busy to see Rupert, I'm too fucking busy" . . . We finally persuaded him that he had to . . . and Gough was courteous and relaxed. Rupert paid for the boat.'

Only 'some key people in the Labor party' put more energy into the campaign than Murdoch, says Menadue (who had to manage the *Australian* in parallel with the ALP campaign: Walsh actually moved to the ALP payroll). Murdoch turned out proposals for speeches and statements, sent to Whitlam through Menadue or Young. Whitlam used only a modest number. But, when he did, their currency was assured:

> I remember one press statement that Whitlam put out about the release of conscripts from jail. I was with Eric Walsh as he spoke to Mark Day, editor of the [Sydney] *Daily Mirror*. Eric said: 'It's a pretty good story that Gough's put out on conscription.' Mark said, 'Oh, it's old hat, isn't it? That's all been said before.' I remember Eric replying, 'You'd better believe it's new, because Rupert wrote it.' The story was carried.

Deamer would have killed it. But there were other election stories for which he would have found space – like the true nature of Businessmen for a Change of Government, presented as an alliance of neutral executives with concerns about the state of the nation so grave as to subscribe

159

for advertisements bringing them to public notice. It was a front, devised by Mick Young, with the aid of Walsh – who largely wrote the copy – and Hansen Rubensohn McCann Ericson, the ALP ad-agency. Murdoch, learning of it, saw no conflict with Walsh's earlier role as the *Mirror*'s political editor. On the contrary, he was 'attracted both by the advertisements and the intrigue surrounding the front we were using. He agreed that he would run the advertisements in his own newspapers free of charge and would pay for their placement in other newspapers . . .' Eventually the 'independent businessmen' ran A\$74,257 worth of advertising, most of it in News Ltd papers. This, with some additional cash, made Murdoch the largest donor to the Labor campaign, some way ahead of his close friend, business ally and poker companion Peter Abeles of Thomson National Transport (TNT).

From the campaign's start the *Australian* sailed as the flagship of Murdoch's Labor fleet, his other papers taking station in turn. They included now the Sydney *Daily Telegraph* and *Sunday Telegraph*, bought five months earlier from Packer, and when they came out for Whitlam some Liberals probably turned their faces to the wall. In short, the Murdoch organisation was slanted utterly in the ALP's favour during the 1972 elections. (There were no protests or walk-outs by the journalists' union, as when Murdoch changed tack three years later. The right has rightly taken the point.)

Enthusiasm came close to producing embarrassment. Work began at the *Australian* on the speech Murdoch thought Whitlam ought to give at the final rally. Menadue conferred anxiously with Mick Young: 'We've got a bit of a problem . . . Rupert wants the final speech to be his.' Baldwin might solicit a punchline from Kipling, but this was a text too far. Eventually some ideas and lines were used, and Young got Whitlam to thank Murdoch for his input. Clear victory on 2 December then swamped everyone in euphoria. Eric Walsh became Whitlam's press secretary; Murdoch gave a dinner in Sydney including the new Prime Minister and Kay Graham of the *Washington Post* (which probably confirmed the Nixon administration's idea that they had lost Australia); and in Menadue's seasonal card from the Murdochs Anna added to the Happy New Year wishes: '– nothing can beat the last, a Labor Government and a new baby'.

When Murdoch asked, 'How many seats do you think we won?' he meant News, not the ALP. He clearly thought enough had been done to earn a reward, and he nominated it via Menadue. He wanted to be Australian High Commissioner in London. This is somewhat like a US publisher becoming ambassador in London after endorsing the correct Presidential candidate. But for a true parallel the American publisher would have also to possess huge business interests in Great Britain, with obvious intent to expand them. US politics has yet to produce anyone with chutzpah enough.

Murdoch's diplomatic ambition qualifies the 'anti-establishment' radicalism which is supposed to animate him. It may be argued that there is no such thing as the British establishment – or, better, that the term is only an imprecise substitute for the 'ruling class'. But to the extent that such a thing exists, the High Commissioner for the Commonwealth of Australia belongs ex officio, doubtless ranking below the Archbishop of Canterbury, but comfortably above (say) rank-and-file Governors of the BBC. Murdoch's wish to join the club doesn't suggest any principled objection to its activities.

The appointment would have had enormous business value at that time, and that alone would have made it impossible for Whitlam. But the remaining importance of the incident is Murdoch's denial that it ever took place. John Menadue's account is quite specific:

> Murdoch raised the appointment with me and explained that if he was the High Commissioner he would put his newspaper and television interests in a trust so there would not be a conflict of interest. He believed also that he could influence other Australian media proprietors and avoid media flak . . . over the appointment . . .
>
> I raised it with Mick Young. The absurdity of it amused him. I put it to Whitlam on the phone. It was the Sunday morning a week after the election. We had a lengthy discussion . . . But Whitlam was adamant about Rupert for London. 'No way,' he said.

Menadue is a substantial witness. After leaving News he ran the Prime Minister's Department in Canberra, and then the Immigration Department; he was Ambassador to Japan and chief executive of

Qantas, the Australian international airline. His account makes it hard to take seriously Murdoch's claim never to have asked for political spoils. But it also makes clear that to Murdoch the Whitlam alliance seemed a disappointment – scarcely an alliance at all – and that was to have dramatic consequences.

6

MR MURDOCH CHANGES TRAINS,
1969–1975

We have to fulfil our role in the democracy. The basic premise of the democracy we live in must be the citizen's right to know, and if we do not publish what we know, if we know the facts that are in the public interest and are of importance and do not publish them, then we do not deserve our freedom.

RUPERT MURDOCH on Channel 9, Sydney (quoted in *The Age* 18 March 1976)

Gough Whitlam's rejection of the idea that Rupert Murdoch had the makings of an ambassador to the Court of St James's caused no immediate estrangement, but it pointed the way things would go. The personal connection which Murdoch had enjoyed with Jack McEwen would not be repeated with Whitlam, nor would his close relationship with the Thatcher, Hawke and Reagan regimes be anticipated. No intimacy developed, and so there was little to inhibit the war which broke out two years later, when Murdoch was seen, in his own words, as the man who 'tore down' Whitlam – as the destroyer of a political settlement he had helped to create.

Of course News Ltd's centre of commercial gravity was fixed in Britain by the early 1970s, and – election times aside – Murdoch's visits to Australia were growing ever more widely separated. When he did appear there, he began expounding to his executives a theory of media development with two principles which he saw as interacting. To John

163

Menadue he said that 'to be successful an English-language newspaper group had to be established in each of the major English-speaking markets . . . He also believed that, increasingly, newspapers and the media were about entertainment and less and less about news.'

Murdoch himself might be – obviously was – fascinated by political news. (To Menadue he appeared at the time to have some authentically radical instincts.) But he did not acknowledge that Western populations at large might share, other than trivially, his own fascination. Naturally, a journalist may find any kind of subject tedious or irrelevant. But it is very curious when he asserts that something he personally finds central is of declining interest to almost everyone else – and that there is nothing to be done about it.

Although Murdoch and Newscorp have done a great deal to further media globalisation – at least, to show that it can be pursued as a corporate strategy – it is not really a law of human development. And neither is the displacement of news by entertainment, though many glib formulas suggest as much. To say that 'globalisation' has increased is not much more useful than saying the climate has 'increased': the term covers a mass of phenomena, with contradictory trends profusely attached, and investigators are hard put to produce a net estimate.

It's obviously true that modern communications are swift and powerful. However, a fair argument can be made that the world's political economy was more close-knit in the days of Queen Victoria and the gold standard than is the case today. While some local sovereignty is being ceded to supra-national organisations like the European Union, devolution within every such organisation makes the world increasingly polycentric.

Media industries certainly show many instances of international ownership and control. But, as a contrary example, some of the most stable, successful newspapers are deeply rooted in locality – and these, usually, are the ones offering a sophisticated account of global events. The *New York Times* and the *Sydney Morning Herald*, which have between them more than three centuries of experience and profit, are not joined in any global corporation. But each presents the people of its home city with a tolerably detailed picture of the world beyond. The *New York Post*, the *Sun* and the Sydney *Daily Telegraph* are all run by Newscorp; only in desperation would anyone turn to them for global information.

And it remains true that most of the legislation which affects media businesses – liberties and protections, as well as regulation – has a local or national base. Desirable as it might be, there is no such thing as a globalised freedom of the press. The excellent freedom-of-information laws which Scandinavian countries apply are peculiarly Scandinavian. And British regulations which try to provide for a fair market in television products are British made, even if European influence in them is now evident. The 'media' are children of the nation-state – often of its municipal sub-divisions – and while the nation-state's death has been noisily prophesied its obituary is not yet required.

Rather than a perception about laws or processes, these were statements of Murdoch's corporate attitudes and desires. The notions he sketched out in the 1970s have since been elaborated – with the aid of assorted philosophers – into a doctrine with many effects, which dresses Newscorp up in a polymorphous supra-national identity. Sometimes Newscorp claims to knows what people need far better than their elected governments, and demands the right to serve those needs without interference. And at the same time, but elsewhere, Newscorp is quite happy for unelected powers to decide what the people may be offered, and volunteers to supply the appropriate stuff under official supervision.

But when first voiced Murdoch's globalist notions perhaps meant no more than that he lacked the temperament to build authentic newspapers – in Australia or anywhere else – and, having had brilliant financial success with his imitative adventures in Britain, he wanted to repeat the process on still larger territory: the US. He invaded America in the conviction – as sincere as any he holds – that British tabloid technique relates to effete American media practice in the way that Cecil Rhodes' Maxim guns related to the assegais of the Matabele.

The British expedition was roughly repeated, in that it began with acquisition of some declining down-market property – though the two papers in San Antonio, Texas, were of course tiny beside the *News of the World* – and then a new but highly derivative venture: the *National Star*, imitating the *National Enquirer* rather as the *Sun* copied the *Mirror*. The *Star* did not achieve the same swift lift-off as the *Sun* – the *Enquirer* vigorously protected its franchise as the original celebrity-spattered supermarket tabloid – but persistence eventually produced a profitable outcome.

165

Murdoch invested much personal energy in the project. It was, in a way, demonstration of his belief in the entertainment principle, and American commentators who found the *Star* a tedious rehash he denounced as 'snobs' and 'elitists'.

The *Star* has never had any political impact in America, but it affected the Anglo-Australian scene because it was important in shifting Murdoch's personal base to New York in 1973. Other factors were involved, and one was desperately sad: the wife of a News executive was kidnapped and murdered in mistake for Anna Murdoch, who consequently and understandably found London a distressing environment. Newscorp folklore adds to that true affliction the curiously Edwardian complaint that 'good society' had 'cold-shouldered' the Murdochs. Of course, such an entity scarcely existed in London's plutocratic 1970s.

Geographical separation between Murdoch and the Whitlam administration favoured an ideological separation. It must have become obvious that the government he had wished to represent as something like his own creation was very deeply disliked by powerful people in the United States. Richard Nixon and Henry Kissinger were in 1973 still the greatest of these – Nixon's regime was in the overweening moment just before its fall – but the feeling was not theirs alone. Coalition Australia had been a happy certainty for America's keenest Cold Warriors, particularly in the readiness of Canberra's overseas intelligence service (ASIS) to lend the CIA a hand with causes few other allies fancied, such as the harassment of Salvador Allende.

So happy was the Agency with the arrangement that its officers thought the Coalition must win the 1972 election, and it was a short step from disappointment to seeing Whitlam as another 'Marxist'. (He did terminate ASIS's Chilean links.) If Whitlam personally didn't return the paranoia, some of his colleagues visibly did and gave reason for unease about Australia's political reputation. Probably this had no profound ideological dimension, but Murdoch's nationalism, which he was otherwise keen to advertise, did not run to any sophisticated appreciation of the Australian–American relationship.

Eric Walsh and the ALP matchmakers tried hard to preserve amity, geography notwithstanding. At least Murdoch was in New York, which contained something Whitlam did deeply admire – the United Nations.

And in January 1974, when Whitlam was to address the General Assembly, Walsh seized the chance to set a dinner date. Navigating his hotel lobby that evening, Whitlam again exercised his talent for alienating Murdoch. He found David Frost free for the evening, and decided that the television inquisitor would be a more amusing dinner-companion. He told Walsh to move Rupert to breakfast. Whitlam probably didn't realise his offence – didn't realise that Frost was both the man who had begun (as Murdoch saw it) the 'character-assassination' causing his troubles at London Weekend, and then the one to step in and resolve the situation. Murdoch was doubtless relieved that News Ltd's investment did not vanish. But even a man less touchy than Murdoch might dislike being rescued by the apparent author of his distress. Walsh still recalls the postponed gathering as his least favourite morning meal.

Meanwhile, there were initial manifestations of a controversy with dangerous potential: the ownership and exploitation of mineral resources. News Ltd was a member of the Alwest consortium, led by Reynolds Aluminum of the US, which aimed to develop Australian bauxite deposits, but faced opponents inside the ALP. Some of these did not want the ecosystem harmed. Others wanted it harmed under purely Australian – indeed public – ownership. Their combination was irresistible, and in March 1974 the Cabinet rejected the scheme. Whitlam did not personally oppose Alwest, but it was remote from his style to explain that to Murdoch. 'Rupert wanted to be treated as a confidant, and Gough just wouldn't be in it,' says Menadue. The *Australian* chastised the government's natural-resources policy, and Murdoch described as 'irresponsible' the Labor sympathisers who suggested the paper was less than objective.

In November 1974 Walsh managed to bring Whitlam and Murdoch together for a dinner which passed off fairly amicably. It was held at the Prime Minister's official residence, The Lodge, and Murdoch was in Canberra to update on Australian politics. Publicly, amity was preserved. Privately, things were changing. During the same month, Murdoch presided at a gathering where the downfall of Whitlam's government was discussed, in terms remarkably close to the event which took place twelve months later. A curious drama of newspapers and constitutional politics was in the making. This of course was Watergate year: it was three months after Richard Nixon's resignation.

There are powerful similarities between the events of Watergate and the events known in Australia as the 'Dismissal', or more angrily as the 'Coup'. Also, there are vital differences. The great similarity is that newspapers, and the people running them, were decisively involved each time – as was to be the case in the British government's crisis of 1986 (see Chapter 12 below). But there were profound differences between the motives and conduct of these newspaper controllers.

Though there are Nixon sympathisers who cannot be reconciled, the Watergate investigations of the *Washington Post* can be – should be – represented as a case of First Amendment obligations discharged as properly as an imperfect world dare expect. Conspicuously, the threads running through the Watergate story are disclosure, civic courage and lack of foreseeable reward. There is a perfectly fair sense in which Watergate did enhance the commercial strength of the *Washington Post*, but only as the after-product of passage through a deadly seeming storm. And the Watergate process rested on an earlier decision in which the paper's financial existence was put on the line in defence of an editorial principle.

In June 1971 the *New York Times* began publishing the Pentagon Papers, the remarkable set of documents which proved that 'every administration after World War II had enlarged America's commitment to . . . South Vietnam and . . . hidden the true dimensions of the enterprise and its own abundant doubts about the prospects for success'. The Nixon administration obtained an injunction which halted the *Times* after three instalments, and began a prosecution under the Espionage Act. It was a furious, determined attempt to impose censorship on the American press.

At this point the *Post* also received a set of the Pentagon documents – and its own legal threats from the government. The paper's editorial staff believed with passion that the government's legal actions made it imperative for the *Post* to publish. But the circumstances were peculiarly risky, because the filing for the first public issue of stock in the Post company was just being completed. In one of them Katharine Graham, the publisher, had to warrant that no outstanding litigation was likely to reduce the value of the business.

The advice of the lawyers working on the issue was stark. Postponing the stock issue was scarcely an option, for it would heavily damage financial credibility. For it to go ahead, the routine warranty had to be given; but, if the paper then became involved in litigation with the government such as to damage its profits, investors could sue to get their money back – with ruinous consequences. Therefore, the Pentagon Papers story had to be suppressed. After intense debate with her editors, and a second set of lawyers, Mrs Graham chose to publish.

Both the *Times* and the *Post* defeated the government's legal actions, and far more easily than at first seemed possible. Not for the first time it was shown that the press in a democratic society does better to avoid the kind of backward step Murdoch took in Adelaide. From Judge Murray Gurfein, a famous restatement of the First Amendment was evoked: 'A cantankerous press, an obstinate press, a ubiquitous press, must be suffered by those in authority . . . This has been the genius of our institutions throughout our history.' Ben Bradlee's judgment is that, if Graham's decision had gone the other way, the Watergate process would not have been carried through, that the 1971 precedent was necessary to sustain morale when Nixon and Attorney-General Mitchell made their tolerably plausible threats to destroy the *Post*.

It is untrue to say that a newspaper's editorial independence conflicts permanently with its existence as a business. Rather, the business value of an authentic paper rests on its independence. But it is a curious kind of asset, one which can be preserved only by proving that in many quite probable circumstances it will be thrown away. It need not always be proved in such an extremity as the *Post* faced in 1971 – an accumulation of lesser precedents will often serve. For instance, the London *Sunday Times* revealed in 1964 that a television company controlled by the Thomson group – owners of the paper – had become a cover for gun-running and mercenary recruitment. Thomson absorbed the commercial harm without complaint; any other precedent would have inhibited the growth of the paper's investigative capacity, described below in Chapter 8. Such risk is the natural price of independence.

Though the *Post*'s editorial column under Mrs Graham showed Democratic allegiances rather than the Republican ones of her father Eugene Meyer – and it never endorsed Richard Nixon – no sensible reading suggests that partisan advantage significantly motivated its

Watergate reporting. The *Post*'s part in the fall of Nixon was central, but the mechanism involved was disclosure. The paper simply published, as swiftly as it could, everything it knew and reasonably suspected about the activities of the Committee to Re-Elect the President. Some of this was inaccurate, but more of it was correct. And quite certainly the *Post* never held any matter back to lessen or increase the likelihood of Nixon's fall. Murdoch in America watched the process, and by his own account thought Nixon was unfairly treated.

Disclosure may seem at first glance an act of power, but – as the Introduction states – it generally surrenders power. Once information is disseminated, its authors have slight influence on the effect produced. They can express opinions, but these carry no decisive weight. Not all who call themselves journalists subscribe to the ethic involved – though it is indispensable – and honourable people from other backgrounds may fail to grasp it.

John Thadeus Delane, under whose leadership *The Times* laid it down that 'the Press lives by disclosure', puzzled his political friends when he refused to see documents 'in confidence' – that is, as part of a deal – saying it would only trouble him when he gained the same information unconditionally. And Kay Graham describes in *Personal History* the bitterness caused when her husband Philip, as the *Post*'s publisher, suppressed a story of Ben Bradlee's about racial segregation in Washington swimming pools. By using it as leverage, Graham – formerly a lawyer – forced the city to desegregate its pools. Bradlee and his colleagues approved the end, as citizens, but considered the means professionally disgraceful. Mrs Graham – trained as a reporter – says that in her own time as publisher, after Philip's death, she never herself did likewise.

And disclosure imposes its particular emotional costs. There was a lonely period when the *Post*'s honest competitors could not imagine its Watergate story was true. 'Not even my most cynical view of Nixon,' wrote Max Fraenkel of the *New York Times*, 'had allowed for his stupid behaviour.' Was it in support of a fantasy, Mrs Graham, Bradlee and their colleagues wondered, that Nixon's promises to strip their company of its broadcasting licences and bury their paper in punitive litigation were being faced (the famous 'tits in the mangle' jibe)? On his re-election in 1972 there seemed every possibility that he could fulfil them. Instead, of course, came an electrifying drama – the classical proof that in a democracy disclosure can generate huge and unpredictable impacts. To this the Dismissal, and Murdoch's role in it, is a sub-text – one which illustrates the development of his method.

Though in substance a figure of the centre-left like Bill Clinton or Tony Blair, Gough Whitlam was temperamentally remote from their circumspection. His maxim in trouble was 'Crash through or crash'. It might have formed a bond with the gambler in Murdoch, except that Whitlam likes people to have firmly held views, and grows bored when they are not in evidence. Incaution often served him well. He became leader of the ALP because he dared to invade old sectarian minefields which others avoided (and which turned out to be inert).

In government, matters were more complicated. Much of the country's present-day social complexion derives from reforms which Whitlam forced through – and without him Australia might have become a coelacanth among nations. But doing so alienated the conservative elite which had ruled since the 1940s – and whose values are Murdoch's emotional default settings, whatever tactical populism he engages in. There were symbols involved, some with heavy sentimental content. Whitlam launched a civil honours system designed to compete with – and eventually replace – that provided by the English Court from its medieval inheritance. And as Canberra, like Whitehall, had been a place where a whole lifetime could be the run-up to putting KCMG or KCB after a man's name and 'Sir' in front of it, there was disquiet over substituting the mere Order of Australia.

Nor was that all of it. The novelist Patrick White had just won the Nobel Prize for Literature, and Whitlam – after much effort – recruited White as the Order's inaugural Companion. If he thought at all about White's open homosexuality, he was probably amused by the notion of picking off two orthodoxies with a single stone. Intricate fictions like *Voss* and *Riders in the Chariot* the Canberra mandarins were ready to leave to the Nobel committee. But it was another thing when the man declared as Australia's most distinguished citizen was – a *poofter*, and one refusing to conceal it. Symbolic degeneracy was accompanied by financial troubles – and in those days connections between sexual and fiscal immorality were widely assumed – dramatising the belief that Australia's economy was exposed to socialist disorder. There was a little justice in this, though from today's perspective the injustice is more apparent.

Whitlam's unforeseen affliction was the economic turbulence of the early 1970s, touched off by US deficits from the Vietnam War, and amplified by the 'oil shock'. The oil-producing nations quadrupled prices, and all the world's cash seemed to be flowing into Arabia. After fifteen placid years, the technicians of Australian finance had slight experience of managing under stress, and after twenty-three years in opposition the ALP's ministers had none of managing the technicians. But the period was one in which few governments handled themselves well.

In fact much timely change was under way, with effects persisting today: school, university and healthcare funding was reformed; progress on native land rights ceased being symbolic and started being substantial; sexual injustice was attacked; telling investments were made in arts and sports. But at the same time ministers with roots in the ALP's state-socialist past nurtured fantasies which they strove to hide from Parliament – especially Rex 'Strangler' Connor at Minerals and Energy. And officials mourning conservative hegemony acted as if obstructing their own government was the cause of civilisation. Overall it looked messy.

By early 1974, much of Whitlam's legislation was blocked by conservatives in the Senate (the upper house) after passage in the Representatives (the popular house). Boldly, he used a provision of the Constitution which provides for 'double dissolution' of both houses in a deadlocked Parliament, and fresh elections. They were set for May.

James Hall was now editor of the *Australian* (Owen Thompson had been right to worry about 'acting' rank when he vaulted into Deamer's shoes) and Ken May transmitted Murdoch's instructions: play it 'straight down the middle'. On polling day, consequently, the *Australian* endorsed nothing. One senior journalist wrote about his decision to vote for the Coalition. Another wrote 'Why I Shall Be Voting Labor'. Doubtless this 90-degree recalibration – after 1972's 180-degree bias – was refreshing to the Coalition. All the same the ALP easily won the House, with the Senate staying close balanced. However, when deadlock is followed by double dissolution and re-election, the Constitution allows a joint session of Representatives and Senators, where the more numerous lower house can override the upper. Thus Whitlam cleared the legislative logjam.

And it was now imperative for the government to get its act together. With this in mind Whitlam at last asked Murdoch for a favour – of a very unusual sort. He wanted John Menadue released from his role as manager of Murdoch's newspapers, so that he could become head of the Prime Minister's Department – the post known in Britain as Secretary to the Cabinet, and regarded in both countries as the preserve of mandarin bureaucracy. (The President's Chief of Staff is the nearest American equivalent, but due to the separation of powers does not have quite such pivotal influence.)

Murdoch was asked by Whitlam – unknown to Menadue – to promise reversion of employment. That doubtless was a concession Murdoch was more than happy to make, for Whitlam's request amounted to lavish fruition of a long-laid policy. Menadue had been an aide to Whitlam before joining News in 1966, and had always known his recruitment was political. 'I don't think Murdoch really knew what to do with me, but he wanted to be involved in the political process, and my background and contacts interested him.' Similarly to Woodrow Wyatt a decade later – a case in which Margaret Thatcher played the Whitlam role – Menadue was hired as the link into political structures Murdoch considered important. That he turned out to be an exceptional businessman and administrator was simply a bonus.

Murdoch now had his graduates organising the government and (with Walsh as press secretary) running its communications. The cloud over things, though, was uncertainty about Whitlam's longevity in power. Alongside Menadue several other talented outsiders were recruited to revive derelict official empires. But conservative discontent only increased at the sight of a radical government which might be efficient enough to deliver. Surely the Constitution did not allow such things?

Australia's Constitution blends from British and American elements a compound with explosive properties special to itself. Like America's, it consists of a specific document, with a court (High, not Supreme) deciding interpretation. With the nation creating the Representatives, and the states creating the Senate, American resemblances run more than skin-deep. Yet the Australian system at the same time resembles the British, in relying much on unwritten custom and moral precedent (more so in the 1970s than it does now). And in an essential respect it seems exactly British: the Australian executive is 'responsible', holding great and unseparated powers, which are instantly lost without a majority in the popular house. Here Representatives and Commons are close kin.

There is a curious myth that this Constitution was imposed from Britain. Actually, it is an intensely local growth with many democratic virtues. But the notion of the executive being subject to recall – something America's founders fenced round with numerous precautions – creates ambiguities in federalism, where states must be represented as well as people. One of Australia's federal architects said that if responsible government didn't kill federation, it would happen the other way round. And in the 1970s this looked a prescient call.

Checking the responsible government's health – and finding a replacement should it expire – are matters in which the British monarch claims inherited expertise, and can apply it as Australia's head of state. In practice, Elizabeth II puts out the Australian work to a resident governor-general, and, finding by the 1970s no call for aristocratic exports, her practice was to take a vice-regal nomination from the serving Prime Minister. Gough Whitlam, when this came up in 1974, chose Sir John Kerr, the portly, sociable Chief Justice of New South Wales. Sir John had a friend and admirer in Rupert Murdoch, who said that if younger Kerr might have edited the *Australian* (though people had begun to think about taking a number for that). But Whitlam also admired Kerr, saying he would change people's ideas about the Governor-General's role: prescience again.

In November 1974, within a few days of Murdoch's evening at The Lodge with Whitlam, there was a weekend gathering at the Cavan homestead outside Canberra: News Ltd cadres were summoned to feed the boss with political intelligence. At such a party eminent outsiders might be expected. It seemed the new Governor-General might drop in, and so he did. Sir John socialised generally, then settled down with Murdoch and a small group.

Queen Elizabeth's understudy then expounded some striking ideas about the job he had been in for about three months. He thought that, in a certain kind of a deadlock between the Representatives and the Senate, the Governor-General could use the monarch's reserve power to dismiss the Prime Minister – regardless of the will of the lower house – and that he might do so without warning.

The circumstance he envisaged was a refusal by the Senate to vote Supply, the legislation formally enabling a government to raise money and run its budget. In democracies, of course, the legislature usually controls executive spending – and in 1997 America suffered an extended crisis when the House of Representatives under Speaker Gingrich tried denying Supply to Clinton's administration. Again, there are American resemblances, and differences – because it had been assumed that the Australian Senate, though it might stop specific legislation, could not block enabling decisions on money, or refuse a Budget.

Inquiry, however, showed this to be just a custom, derived from a British one under which the hereditary House of Lords never refused money bills from the elected House of Commons. As their distaste for Whitlam grew, Australian conservatives noted that the Senate was elected, and might escape this British inhibition (though many of them, such as Sir Garfield Barwick, Chief Justice of the High Court, greatly admired British customs they found agreeable).

Sir John, while not wholly a drunk, was far from the judge in the sobriety metaphor, and never the reticent lawyer. ('An amiable, rorty, old farting Falstaff' was the novelist White's account.) All the same, these were startling thoughts for a representative of the monarchy. The reserve, or emergency, powers had their last British outing during the American Revolutionary era, and with results not thought encouraging.

Though there is no exact record of what was said at Cavan, Kerr's remarks were necessarily theoretical. As practical fact, the Liberals, the Country Party and their allies had not then sufficient Senate numbers to block the Budget. And even given the numbers, for convention to be so far defied as to dynamite the government there would have to be more than financial formality at stake. It would be necessary to portray the nation as being under threat from an iniquitous executive. And while Whitlam's public record was spattered with errors, 'iniquity' went too far.

Though Murdoch listened closely to Kerr – it was the kind of talk dedicated insiders love – there were no immediate consequences, and very likely he thought it premature to write off an administration within which he had such remarkable contacts. If at this stage he thought Whitlam deserved to be 'torn down', he took no steps towards it. (Furthermore Alwest was approved early in 1975 – though with heavy environmental conditions – and the *Australian* called it a late move the right way.)

But, anyway, the question of government iniquity was not one News Ltd's papers were equipped to address. Strong editorial teams aren't needed for campaign rhetoric (see 1972) or secret-agent fabrications (see 1968) – indeed, their presence makes such things difficult. As Watergate had just shown, revelation may destroy a government. But disclosure of wrongdoing in high office requires pertinacious reporters, led by executives who aren't worrying about one-way phone calls, and these are rare within the News culture. In 1975, however, most Australian newspapers were still outside News Ltd's control. An exemplary stroke of investigative journalism transformed the situation late in 1975. It had nothing to do with Murdoch.

'Strangler' Connor was a grandiose economic nationalist, holding that the Australian state must develop the nation's natural resources at top speed – while excluding foreign equity, such as the leaders of the Alwest consortium. The economic maelstrom made it impossible to find money for this by normal government finance, unless Whitlam could be got to sacrifice the government's social programme. The Strangler had earned his nickname among the coalminers of Wollongong, and other ministers often rated him an irresistible force. However, he knew an immovable object when he saw one, and rather than confront Whitlam he sought a way round him.

Like many fierce beasts he was naive outside his personal jungle, and he simply broadcast on the grapevine that he wanted financial stratagems. Almost immediately, his colleague Clyde Cameron – another old-style fixer, Minister for Labour and Immigration – said he knew two Adelaide opal dealers who suggested in deep confidence that certain Hong Kong contacts might find petro-dollars for Connor. Nothing makes quite plausible the political lunacy involved here, but it becomes faintly less baffling with the reminder that 'petro-dollar' just then had the properties of 'railway share' in 1840s Britain, or 'dotcom' almost anywhere more recently. Realism dissolved on contact. And as with railways and the Internet, there were slivers of truth within the fantasy. Oil being a commodity traded in dollars, the price-hike was making large dollar pools – mainly in Arab countries – whose owners needed investment prospects.

Even so, only a pair of obsessive politicians could have thought Tirath Hassarem Khemlani a competent broker in sovereign debt – nearly everyone else correctly perceived a small-time commodities dealer. Cameron and Connor were deeply impressed when he turned up for a secret meeting with them in Canberra on 11 October 1974. (The fact of its secrecy, though, *was* remarkable. The opal dealers' 'confidential' inquiries seem to have echoed throughout Asia's entrepôts, and Khemlani picked them up quite casually in Singapore.)

Of course the development of Australia's natural resources was a valid ambition – indeed, the oil crisis itself made that obvious – and Connor was not the only minister who thought the Treasury's orthodoxy might reduce the nation's opportunities. Connor argued that the Treasury approach was obsolete in a world where the centre of financial gravity was shifting, and he had enough party standing to generate trouble if not allowed to give his discovery a trial.

This does something to explain why on 13 December 1974 Whitlam, with his Treasurer and Attorney-General, signed papers authorising Connor – a departmental minister – to avoid official channels and negotiate loans to a value of US$4 billion (say $13 billion in present values). Success, some thought, would bury criticism – and failure would be Connor's problem. Thus codenames were devised to cloak the operation: Connor was 'Rock Phosphate' or 'Uncle'; the government's London lawyer was 'The Big Man'; Whitlam (only scantily informed) was 'The Father'. Money was 'Sugar'.

The Treasury officials had to be told, of course, that a consultant had been engaged to show them the way. Dutifully they enlisted their worldwide contacts to provide the government with background. It took time, for Khemlani was unknown to Wall Street and the City: he was a Pakistani citizen, trading from a London basement containing a camp bed, a bathroom full of drip-dry shirts, and a telex. (Telex then was advanced business telecoms: e-mail and fax were for specialists only.)

The Canberra rumour-mill had few facts to go on, but that has rarely inhibited it, and did not do so in this case.

In January 1975 the Strangler's senior colleagues grew nervous and revoked the US$4 billion authority. On 28 February a new authority for US$2 billion was issued, but questions were popping up in Parliament, no sugar was visible, and Connor's standing was falling fast. On 20 May, the second authority was revoked.

At this stage Labor's political fortunes were chilling along with Canberra's mountain air in the southern winter. Treasurer Jim Cairns – having survived the addition to his payroll of a thinly qualified woman friend – caught the loan fever, and wrote to a Melbourne executive suggesting he might profitably raise cash for Canberra. As a football-club president George Harris was not an obvious financial choice. As a friend of the Opposition's finance spokesman, he was a horrid political error.

And the *Australian* turned frosty with the weather. The order to 'play it down the middle' was abolished, together with the editor to whom it had been issued. Bruce Rothwell, one of Murdoch's right-wing honchos, took charge. Reporters found their bylines being excised and their stories rewritten to support an editorial stance favourable to Malcolm Fraser, the Leader of the Opposition. (Actual editorials required use of a sympathetic freelance, the swerve being too abrupt for the incumbent writers.) Whitlam himself said the cause was the Alwest environmental clauses, which had led the US backers to pull out. Perhaps that played a part; more likely Murdoch was repositioning with a view to Fraser's rising prospects.

Labor recovery, however, remained possible. John Menadue administered the nation's business as deftly as he had Murdoch's. Bill Hayden, replacing Treasurer Cairns, designed a popular and competent Budget. Clyde Cameron, the opal dealers' friend, gave way to the sagacious Jim McClelland, and spring arrived hopefully. If no more skeletons walked, the government might make it.

But there was Connor. In June he had written to Whitlam that all loan-raising attempts had ceased on 20 May. Trusting him, the Prime Minister gave assurances to Parliament, stonewalling all further questions. Rumours nonetheless persisted of the Strangler maintaining contact with Khemlani, sometimes lurking all night beside his ministerial telex. The Senate Liberals interrogated opal dealers, and officials of Connor's department, but unprofitably.

And there was the Melbourne *Herald*, still a vigorous, profitable metropolitan newspaper, with a substantial staff. It had recently acquired a new editor, John Fitzgerald, ready to back reporters capable of following a long trail and acting on their own judgment. His staff included a determined specimen of the type named Peter Game, who was a little obsessed with Khemlani. Inquiring in Hong Kong during June, Game picked up reports of Khemlani still in circulation with a mandate for US$8 billion – though the man himself seemed as elusive as the Flying Dutchman, and some thought no more real. Then Game got on the trail again in Singapore. He was a few days behind his man, but he located Khemlani's daughter, and left with her a letter suggesting that the *Herald* would provide an interested audience whenever the great loan story could be told. And this must have been persuasively drafted.

Game spent most of August reporting a revolution in Timor, but as he headed back to Melbourne on 4 September a call reached him at Mount Isa, Queensland. Khemlani, bound from San Francisco to London via Bangkok, was suggesting a rendezvous in Sydney. Game switched his destination. Hotel-room discussion in Sydney suggested that Khemlani was eager to talk – but he was formidably skittish. After six hours of preliminaries, he proposed restarting a few days later, possibly in Bangkok or London. It turned out to be London, and there Game became familiar with the basement HQ where Khemlani, clouded in tobacco smoke, punched telex tapes for his oil and machinery deals. On 14 September, just as Game began unravelling the Connor connection, Khemlani vanished, reappearing from West Africa on the 22nd with the announcement that he must instantly depart for a few hours in Hong Kong. This time Game, with his notebooks and tape-recorder, clung to him for the round-trip.

In Australia, political pressure was rising, because the death of a Labor Senator had given the Opposition upper-house control. It was now feasible for Malcolm Fraser to block Supply and deadlock Hayden's reforming Budget – the government's chief political asset. Could Fraser then compel his own double dissolution and new elections – likely to make him Prime Minister? Perhaps. But could it be justified? Fraser had said himself that without 'reprehensible' conduct an administration should run its elected term. And it was now some time, as a respected commentator noted, since the government had done anything truly silly.

Peter Game's own *Herald* was as conservative an outfit as any in the land, and on 3 October its editorial column, while conceding that the temptations of office were great, said Fraser 'should not yield' to them. Courageous refusal would 'prevent him from becoming the violator of immensely important principles of our democracy'.

In London, a few hours later, Game began drafting a three-part series about the Khemlani–Connor connection. On 7 October, when Game had transmitted his copy, Khemlani left for New York with several cases of documents. He said he was still working on the loan project, and would visit Connor in Australia. Next day, when the *Herald*'s main headline said, 'KHEMLANI TELLS: I've got Connor go-ahead', it became plain that the Strangler would provide no welcome mat. Confronted by Hayden and Menadue, Connor asserted (wildly) that Khemlani was lying and (with reckless accuracy) that his writ for criminal libel was being served. This last bluff co-opted Whitlam, who could only repeat Connor's denials.

It was Wednesday. Game and Khemlani arrived in Melbourne to spend the weekend in a motel with editors, lawyers, the Khemlani document hoard and Connor's writ – one more tryout for criminal libel, and one certain to terminate several journalistic careers if it did somehow serve its purpose for the Minister.

Game had brought home a courageous, skilful inquiry, one that bore comparison with Woodward and Bernstein's greater achievement. But there were long anxious hours while the lawyers wrestled with the unbelievable facts. (The *Herald* is run today by Newscorp, and has added no similar honours to its record.) On Monday, the headline was 'KHEMLANI REPLIES: EIGHTEEN TELEX MESSAGES'. The copy demonstrated that fundraising contacts had persisted after 20 May, that Connor had lied to Whitlam, who had thus misled Parliament. There had been elaborate precautions: phone calls via Connor's mistress, and a system to collect late-night messages from the ministerial telex. All were exposed. Next day's lead was 'CONNOR QUITS', and after that 'FRASER DECIDES: SENATE TO STOP THE BUDGET'. Clearly, it was reprehensible. Equally clearly, the fall of Whitlam and his replacement by Fraser seemed inevitable.

And now it was time for Rupert Murdoch to join the hunt. He arrived from America and immediately launched in the *Australian* a strident assault on Whitlam's administration – slanted to the same degree as 1972, but reversed in sense. There was no suggestion that inquiry or reflection might be in order.

The Senate Opposition, consisting of the Liberals, the Country Party and a few independents, blocked Labor's Budget on 15 October, declaring Whitlam unfit to govern. No Supply would be voted until Labor agreed to double dissolution and new elections. All this was clothed in rhetoric about constitutional rectitude and urgent need. But anti-climax ensued. Though concerned, the public displayed few signs of panic or zeal for fresh hustings.

One reason for this was that House and Senate had several times recently batted budgetary threats to and fro – always settling up, after tedious arm-wrestling – and people did not quite see the difference this time. It was particularly hard to take seriously the constitutional scholarship paraded by the *Australian* and other hot enthusiasts for dissolution, because Opposition control of the Senate rested on a fix of almost Soviet crassness. Senators, as in America, represent the states: additionally the Senate is designed to stabilise politics by working to a longer political cycle than the popular House. So, when mortality removes a Senator, the government of the deprived state nominates a replacement, instead of holding a new election – maintaining the Senate's distance from the politics of the instant. Under this principle, the nominee belongs to the party of the person replaced.

But the principle then existed only in the unwritten or gentlemanly part of the Constitution. (It is now set in stone.) The dead Labor senator was from Queensland, where the conservative government rated Whitlam's Canberra as lower than the Cities of the Plain and retribution far above gentlemanliness. Queensland nominated an obscure, elderly *defector* from the ALP, whose one qualification was malice towards his former party. When this occurred – in September, before Murdoch took the helm – the *Australian* had shared the general revulsion. If you thought about it, it was the kind of thing Strangler Connor might have done. Australians are sometimes unsure about the details of their constitution. But they usually can distinguish between statesmanship and appetite for office.

181

It soon emerged that the government had resources to operate without a budget for weeks, possibly months. There were differences about the placement of the deadline, depending on what the banks might be persuaded to do. But the most commonly agreed date turned out to be 30 November, which drained much drama from the situation. Might Whitlam find an exit from the trap into which Connor's arrogant dishonesty had propelled him?

His critics were many of course. But even conservative papers had doubts about using constitutional devices against a representative majority – notably the *Herald*, which had done the work and taken the risks to expose Labor's misdeeds. Most journalists saw the moment as demanding all the professional objectivity they could muster. The *Australian* displayed no such restraint, but neither did it take any risks. It participated as an engine of propaganda, and its motivation was apparent to all Murdoch's familiars. If the government did survive, Rupert Murdoch would get no more invitations to dinner with the Prime Minister. And now John Menadue, who had toiled to connect the engine to Labor's bandwagon, saw how readily other vehicles could be hitched up. He understood his old chief's new alignment because 'I had seen it at first hand three years earlier . . . It is like an addiction [with Murdoch].' The ALP had ridden a tiger, and now there was 'a price to pay'.

But perhaps Murdoch had declared too soon. As October advanced, the sense that the government must fall receded, for Fraser's problem was that his control of the Senate was fragile. The Coalition could win most votes; however, certain of its allies were irresolute on the great financial issue. If the government was unpopular, so was the prospect of social disruption should its payments be suspended shortly before Christmas, and opinion polls found that 80 per cent of voters thought Supply should be passed. (Newt Gingrich rediscovered in the 1990s that use of procedural devices to undermine an elected executive plays wretchedly with a democratic people.)

Senator Reg Withers, the Coalition's floor tactician, reminiscing ten years later, he said he knew all along that two among 'my blokes' were quite likely to 'collapse'. 'I would have lost them some time about 20 November onwards. I know I would have lost them in the run up to 30 November, but it wouldn't have been two then, it would have been ten.'

If 'twere done, 'twere best 'twere done quickly, says Macbeth – for Fraser it was quickly or not at all. But, if Whitlam failed to surrender, there was no more Fraser could do. Only the Governor-General could act. And Kerr's duty consisted of doing what Whitlam advised – short of using the emergency powers applied by George III. The more hysteria there was in Canberra's air, the more plausible an emergency might seem, and here the *Australian* worked hard. Regularly, in the second half of October, Fraser issued accusations that the government was abusing the Constitution and clinging to power illegally. Though other papers saw more serial rhetoric than significance, the *Australian* reacted each time with headline treatment – typically, on 27 October, 'WHITLAM ACTS LIKE A DICTATOR'. The paper's journalists had been depressed even before Peter Game had thunderously scooped them (and everyone else). Now its basic news judgment seemed to be unhinged, and an impressively large number of them signed a letter to Murdoch saying that the paper had become 'a laughing-stock'.

But it was not a laughing-stock to one significant reader. Sir John Kerr's memoirs show that he was closely engaged with the *Australian*'s coverage. Disclosure was not its leitmotif, but on 18 October it did attempt a scooplet, suggesting that without Supply the Governor-General might be personally stuck with the vast costs of the vice-regal establishment. Sir John rang Whitlam and complained that Murdoch's men were trying to unnerve him – asking in the same call if he could seek counsel from Chief Justice Sir Garfield Barwick. Whitlam reassured him about the costs, and 'advised' – told – him not to contact Barwick. The Prime Minister didn't know quite how hostile Barwick was, but he suspected.

The *Australian* essentially dealt in advocacy – a series of editorials and features canvassing the powers the Governor-General might use in ignoring Whitlam's advice and ejecting him from office. Presented in a mode of intellectual discovery, they were in fact playing the Governor-General's own thoughts back to him with embellishment and reinforcement. And as he studied them, the loquacious Sir John developed a new talent for discretion, indeed for dissimulation.

Whitlam's team had assumed initially that dismissal was an option, but when the Opposition produced a legal opinion arguing the case, Kerr described it to them as 'bullshit'. He did not reveal that this bullshit was essentially his own, laid out at Murdoch's house the year before and now rehearsed in the *Australian*. (Whitlam only learnt about the Cavan gathering much later.)

Traces of inside knowledge appear in the *Australian* coverage. Very few people knew about Kerr's desire to confer with the Chief Justice, yet on 24 October the *Australian*'s editorial urged Kerr to consult Barwick – irrespective of Prime Ministerial views. (Whitlam had a decent point which the editorial ignored: the High Court might become involved, and should not be canvassed in advance.)

Along with his legal theories, the Governor-General's self-esteem was buffed up. Since his appointment, Sir John's control of alcohol had notoriously declined – due, perhaps, to his new wife's hyperactive socialising – but the *Australian*'s profile on 25 October showed nothing of that. Two authors produced 'The Man in the Middle': Graham Willis' sources were Sir John's officials – who described a modern Pericles – and John Lapsley's were in unofficial Sydney, where White's Falstaffian estimate prevailed. Little of Lapsley made the cut. The paper produced a portrait so sycophantic as to convince many of the *Australian*'s staff that its outlook had parted from reality. On 28 October the in-house committee of the Australian Journalists Association (AJA) wrote to Murdoch that the paper's political coverage was 'blind, biased, tunnel-visioned, ad-hoc, logically confused and relentless . . . [characterised by]. . . the deliberate or careless slanting of headlines, seemingly blatant imbalance in news presentation [and] political censorship'. Seventy-five editorial staff signed, in spite of the known fate of dissidents inside News. Murdoch made no immediate reply.

Media critics, left and right, repeatedly assert that newspapers abuse power by manipulating electoral opinion. And surveys by political scientists repeatedly find the effects modest, even negligible (though recent, sophisticated inquiries suggest that this reassuring verdict may be slightly over-comfortable). But more potential exists for abuse – the Dismissal suggests – in manipulating protagonists within a political drama. This is harder to quantify, but probably no one who has seen a politician reading a newspaper (even a significant politician and an obscure journal) will much doubt the principle. Nor is it unique to politicians: for all of us, the tension of an event in which we participate raises the significance of anything written about it – and the writing only need be public in the least sense for the effect to intensify further. Really this is the obverse of the argument in Chapter 5, where sales figures show how modestly the editorial drama impacts on the disengaged. Reporters are engaged, protagonists far more so, and politicians are sensitised to coded messages and rapid feedback.

Realistically, perhaps, editorials should rank with postcards in real-world consequence, but realism and self-possession are early casualties in political war, where almost anything offering a pattern may be welcome. James Callaghan was only half joking when, as Britain's Prime Minister, he said he read the papers to learn what he had been doing. Kerr read the *Australian* to learn how right he was, and it succoured him every time. And the paper's other great task – Rupert Murdoch himself said this – was to sustain Malcolm Fraser, to help him 'keep his nerve' and uphold grand constitutional issues.

This process is distinct from disclosure, but political perception often conflates them. Lincoln, when discussing the power of *The Times*, probably didn't separate its revelations about free trade in foodstuffs (a bonanza for the Midwest constituency) from the actual vote against the Corn Laws. Similarly, people say the Watergate disclosures 'caused' Nixon's fall; in a lesser way, the present writer was said (with a colleague) to have brought remedy to victims of the drug thalidomide. What we actually did was reveal facts, on which others took action. Genuine journalism – Delane's disclosure – is rarely the efficient or final cause of anything, and certainly not the outcome of a political intrigue.

Aristotle's fourfold analysis of causation still helps in analysing a process. *Material* cause is the stuff it consists of; *formal* cause the shape in which it becomes visible; *efficient* cause is a deliberate act, as when parents cause a child's birth; and *necessary* or *final* cause is the intention towards which actions move – the extension of a family, the death of a political regime. The Dismissal's material causes were the conduct of Rex Connor and the structure of the Constitution, its formal cause the shape that material was put into by the *Herald*'s investigation. The efficient cause was Fraser's refusal of Supply. The necessary cause – the aim – was removal of Whitlam's government.

Disclosure by general principle isn't an efficient or final cause of

185

outcomes, because its effects are not steerable. Inherently, it creates new situations (often, cascading disclosures) with complexity rising as dissemination expands. But highly selective disclosure is different. It may potentiate rhetoric and persuasion. It may be steerable; it may turn journalism into effective propaganda for an efficient cause.

Propaganda may include an element of fabrication. But in modern conditions the rationing of information will better serve a necessary cause. The famous remark of C. P. Scott about free comment and sacred fact includes a perception Jefferson and Delane never had: that a newspaper always has 'some character of a monopoly'. The papers Jefferson thought more important than government were many, ephemeral and subsidised; out of their largely mendacious Babel he hoped (warily) truth would emerge. Delane realised that his steam-driven, telegraph-fed Thunderer was changing things, but it was not yet clear that the world would support only a limited number of such beasts.

Scott, a pioneer of the commercial–professional newspaper, knew that the *Manchester Guardian* and its equivalents would grow stable and efficient by becoming fewer and by developing regular audiences – by growing large enough, indeed, that real people would rarely have time for more than one. To Scott the reader has a contract for general disclosure, making *suppressio veri* as evil as *suggestio falsi*. The newspaper must taint news neither 'in what it gives, nor in what it does not give, nor in the mode of presentation'. He could have added that *suppressio veri* draws little risk, and requires little more professionally than lack of competence and volition. A fabrication always presents some risk – even if needed for a few days only – and truth is never quite simple, since it is much easier, as every reporter finds, to know things than to make them known in public. But the great point is that the more strictly truth is rationed the more its effects may be predicted.

The staff of the *Australian* at 28 October thought it was losing its credibility with 'well-informed people'. But the protesters did not realise that the definition of a well-informed person – as in political Canberra, third quarter 1975 – was about to shift dramatically.

The Dismissal's outstanding feature is the secrecy of its execution, making it one of democracy's most paradoxical happenings. When Sir John Kerr invoked the royal powers on 11 November 1975, no one in

Buckingham Palace, 12,000 miles away, had the slightest premonition. And hardly anybody in Australia did. Rupert Murdoch was among the rare exceptions. In the amazed aftermath the Queen's Secretary, Sir Martin Charteris, said to an Australian diplomat in London, 'If faced with a constitutional crisis which appeared likely to involve the Head of State, my advice would have been that [the Queen] should only intervene when a clear sense of inevitability had developed *in the public* that she must act' (emphasis added).

This blows away the fine-spun legalisms used later in Kerr's justification. Emergency powers require an emergency, and there was no such thing. It also focuses on public knowledge, and the part information-media play: a democratic emergency can exist only in newspapers and on television screens. And one of the few certainties about the Dismissal is that the public had no information at all, let alone enough to develop a 'sense of inevitability'. Most people thought the prospects of an emergency had been *receding* for some time. Nor was this just a popular view. Nearly every professional in a highly sensitised political community thought likewise. Even in the *Australian*'s news pages, the story was fading out in the lead-up to the 11th.

It is known that Kerr's decision to dismiss Whitlam became set on or about 6 November. Perhaps it was because of pressure from Fraser, who had been promising to accept any decision the Governor-General made and changed on that day to saying that if Kerr did not impose double dissolution he would be attacked for having 'failed . . . his duty to the nation'. Whatever his reason, two personal fears acted on Kerr. It might seem plain that, if he thought Whitlam's behaviour truly dangerous, he should issue a warning and allow time – however nominal – for a change of course. In 1932 Sir Philip Game, Governor of New South Wales, told the state Premier Jack Lang that his financial operations were illegal. When Lang persisted, Game called new elections.

But Kerr feared that his Prime Minister, if warned, might dispose of *him*. Though removal didn't lie in Whitlam's own gift, he could request the Queen. And unless Whitlam had simply no plan to resolve the deadlock – was being irresponsible beyond debate – she would almost certainly ask for a fresh nomination. Kerr confided his fear to Sir Roden Cutler, currently New South Wales' governor. But Cutler, a traditionalist war-hero, was unhelpful. If great issues were truly in play, then risks must be faced and chips must fall – one's own job didn't count. Kerr reacted by more thoroughly concealing his views from the Prime Minister.

But, no less than Whitlam did, he feared Whitlam's enemy Barwick. Legal gossip said that the Chief Justice thought the Prime Minister's fall a most desirable end. Publicly, however, he seemed to deny the means. For months, conservatives had been petitioning the High Court to invalidate Whitlam's 1973 voluntary dissolution – and in turn the House and Senate joint session. That would restore the great logjam, so the Court had been focusing on dissolution law. Little finally came of this, but at 6 November 1975 it was known that Barwick's opinion – though unpublished – was anti-dissolution. If he had found some great pitfall, a government appeal might expose Kerr to the Chief Justice's savage intellect. It was a predicament out of some Jacobean betrayal-melodrama like *The Devil's Law-Case*. Sir John would have to take the *Australian*'s advice and talk to Barwick. But if he was seen at the High Court in Sydney, Whitlam would know attack was imminent. He set himself to fulfil his public role by clandestine means, an oxymoronic aim almost nobody divined.

Simultaneously with Kerr's 6 November resolve, Whitlam's team settled their plan. Under the Senate's normal cycle half its seats were ripe for re-election: they would recommend to Kerr that he set a voting day. This sweetly married constitutional propriety to political advantage, as territories previously unrepresented were due for inclusion – areas where Labor would do well enough to restore Senate control. It would be formally put to Kerr on Tuesday 11 November. But nobody made it a great secret meanwhile.

On Friday 7 November John Menadue got a call from Rupert Murdoch, suggesting lunch. When they sat down, with Ken Cowley in faithful attendance, Menadue was surprised to find Murdoch quite sure that Malcolm Fraser would shortly be Prime Minister. For once, it seemed, his old boss was telling last week's tale, or even older: Fraser's chances now were surely receding. Menadue quoted the half-Senate plan.

Murdoch was unmoved. Before Christmas, he said, there would be a general election, and Fraser would win. Menadue knew well that the ALP would lose if it had to fight without a Budget – and that Murdoch, now Fraser's ally, understood that well. But he still saw no plausible mechanism. Then Murdoch displayed his intimate knowledge of the Opposition's tactics. A few weeks earlier, Fraser had revived the accusation that Menadue's appointment was a case of 'jobs for the boys': threatening that all the officials appointed in such unorthodox fashion would be dismissed from government service by a Fraser administration. This had been copiously reported, notably in the *Australian*. Now, said Murdoch over the lunch-table, Fraser's attitude had changed. Once Whitlam had been disposed of and the new government established in office, Fraser would appoint Menadue as ambassador to Japan. This, of course, is for Australia an appointment of great importance: also, a Murdoch knew, one which would have powerful appeal to Menadue, who had undertaken several missions to Japan for Newscorp, and was fascinated by the country.

The immediate effect it produced on the head of the Prime Minister's Department was absolute bafflement. He could understand neither Murdoch's certainty of a regime change nor the prediction about Japan. Nothing, however, appeared in the *Australian* to suggest anything remarkable was in train. Prime Minister and public continued to assume things were winding down.

At the weekend, Sir John Kerr left Canberra for a public tour, within which his mission to Barwick was hidden. Supposedly it was a search for artworks to enhance the national collection, and by Sunday night it brought him to the vice-regal premises in Sydney. Barwick visited secretly in the morning, and told a much relieved Kerr that if he would be bold he could shortly have supportive written opinions to take back with him to Canberra.

These were partly concerned with modifying responsibility, by arguing that the Australian executive should control both Houses. But more dramatic was Barwick's advice that Kerr could dismiss Whitlam without warning and instantly end the Parliament's life. This radically eliminated the doctrine of public involvement. (Barwick's royalism appears to have been most selective. But a story about news media is concerned even more with idiosyncrasies relating to secrecy.)

On this same Monday Whitlam and Fraser were both in Melbourne at the Lord Mayor's banquet, after which they returned to Canberra in the Prime Ministerial aircraft with Phil Lynch, a Fraser colleague. Menadue, meeting the flight, heard Lynch say to Fraser, 'Do you think he knows?' At the time Menadue didn't link it to Murdoch's predictions. At 9 a.m. next day the party leaders met to reconsider the Supply. Fraser said the Opposition would yield if Whitlam would call a general election. Whitlam said he would advise the half-Senate election, arranging to meet the Governor-General at 1 p.m. for that purpose. When Whitlam arrived, Kerr handed him a brief letter of dismissal. Fraser at almost the same moment began forming a caretaker administration to call a general election and put basic Supply through the Senate. Never before, said Whitlam, had 'the burglar . . . been appointed as caretaker'.

And then came something like Charles Stuart's ghost walking in the southern light. The House of Representatives at 3.00 p.m. voted no confidence in the caretaker executive. Kerr's office agreed an appointment for Mr Speaker Scholes to put this before the Governor-General at 4.45 p.m. But Scholes arrived only to learn that Parliament had just been prorogued. As a mere private citizen, he was shut out. So by the slenderest margin a confrontation of elected and vice-regal authority was averted – and how had all this been done so briskly? The proroguing of Parliament is a sizeable exercise, requiring a battery of official actions by the Prime Minister's Department and others. Fraser had hit the ground running with great speed and precision. Of the many errors lying in wait none was made, and even one might have unravelled everything. (The Labor majority included many republicans, but that would not have stopped a recourse to the Queen had time allowed.)

It was Menadue's department which organised this. Whitlam's 'boys' had in fact been an administrative success – younger officials did not much regret Sir Humphrey's departure – and Menadue especially so: the Prime Minister's Department under him was a sharp, efficient, cohesive outfit. At some time in the last days before Dismissal, Fraser must have seen that expeditiously closing Parliament and arranging elections would require an official team in place – that trying to install a new one would risk fatal delay. So he decided to consider Menadue and all Whitlam's appointees as legitimate public servants, appropriate for further appointments – exactly the message Rupert Murdoch conveyed to Menadue at lunch. And now a familiar phenomenon recurs. Murdoch remembers the lunch. But he cannot remember anything of the discussion which shows that he understood Fraser's planning.

Immediately after Kerr's move, Menadue was with Whitlam and a sizeable group at the Prime Ministerial residence, where the no-confidence motion was being drafted for the House. His office called to tell him the new Prime Minister demanded his presence; he left the meeting and started on Fraser's problems immediately. Menadue didn't tell Whitlam where he was going – an omission which troubled him in later years – and Whitlam, doubtless preoccupied, asked nothing. Of course, the last thing he had read about Fraser's plans for all his appointees – probably the *Australian*'s story – was that they faced instant dismissal. Murdoch, in contrast to his angry staff, had been sensationally well informed. But not so his readers. Even advocacy had vanished from the *Australian* in the lead-up to 11 November.

Interviewed by Peter Bowers of the *Sydney Morning Herald* in 1995, Menadue agreed that the Murdoch meeting predisposed him to accept Fraser's summons, as he knew it would not be a command to clear his desk. Murdoch, in contrast to his angry staff, had been sensationally well informed. But not so his readers. Even advocacy had vanished from the *Australian* in the lead-up to 11 November.

Murdoch said the *Australian*'s great interest was 'the Constitutional issue', but post-Dismissal this evaporated. The 'real debate' became the economy, which it illuminated with a lead story about sharply rising unemployment. Everywhere else *falling* unemployment was correctly reported: the *Australian* had reversed things by ignoring the seasonal adjustment it usually understood quite well.

The bias Murdoch's paper showed in the 'real debate' probably had little effect on the election – anyway a foregone conclusion. But it deserves comment because of its extent, and the defence of it he eventually produced. The table below is based on a contemporary study made at La Trobe University, and while the classify-and-measure technique isn't subtle, neither is the case examined. There need be little surprise about Labor's zip score in the right-hand column of the first section. This includes the pages openly labelled as opinion (op-ed pages, in US practice). In most papers, though, non-byline news – routine news, the left-hand column – is typically least biased. In the *Australian* at this time it was more biased than bylined news stories, where some play of opinion is usual in Australian and British papers. This betrays internal resistance: some residual difficulty always exists in manipulating copy to which individuals' names are attached. Anonymous coverage can be much more plastic.

	Non-bylined news	Bylined news	Editorial and news comment
Material in column centimetres	15,865	4,255	5,085
Percentage favourable to Coalition	45.2	13.0	56.3
Percentage neutral	33.4	51.14	43.7
Percentage favourable to Labor	21.4	26.4	0.0
Unclassified	0.03	9.46	0.0
Total space given to election coverage (col/cm)		25,205	
Total space judged favourable to Coalition		10,587	
Total space judged neutral		7,494	
Total space judged favourable to Labor		4,514	
Percentage of total coverage judged favourable to Coalition		42	
Percentage of total coverage judged neutral		30	
Percentage of total coverage judged favourable to Labor		18	

n.b apparent discrepancies in the two lower sets of figures are due to 'Unclassified' not being included.

The election was set for 15 December. On Tuesday 9 December the AJA members at the *Australian* voted to stop work for a fixed period, in protest against bias which they claimed was ethically unacceptable. Next day, the Arbitration Commission ruled that ethics could be a valid industrial issue, and suggested that Murdoch and his principal aides should meet the AJA representatives. Murdoch told his staff that if they disliked the editorial line he was imposing they should set up their own newspapers. It was an argument rooted in Jefferson's time – though not in his ethic – and in the notion of an infinity of newspapers. It ignored today's real industry of relatively few franchises, and economies of scale allowing efficient newsgathering – Scott's scrupulous monopoly.

The idea that in modern conditions media biases can somehow be cancelled out by multiplicity of sources is of course spurious, but it is a favourite rhetorical workhorse of Murdoch's, and one which has had some political impact. (It recurs later in the context of British and American television.) The true point is that media businesses in a modern economy can be sufficiently profitable to operate without subsidy. But this still involves a duty of attempted impartiality, which in this case was ignored with exceptional arrogance. The meeting broke up in recrimination. Having made their point the journalists returned to work.

Fraser was delighted with the *Australian*'s performance and invited the editor, Leslie Hollings, to become his speechwriter – perhaps thinking, wrote George Munster, that the editor decided the editorials. Hollings declined.

During the election campaign Menadue had the leisure to write up extensive notes about the crisis, which enabled him to retain a clear memory of Kerr's attitude and of the 7 November lunchtime which has departed from Murdoch's recollection. His relations with Fraser followed Murdoch's prediction exactly: after nine months' loyal and competent service he was made ambassador.

The visible causes and consequences of the Dismissal were modest. Of course Strangler Connor's activities were beyond any democratic excuse, but he was anyway ejected before the crisis. Labor's economic sins were never as wicked as they looked, and the restored Coalition found it difficult to do any better. Less visibly, harm ran deep. Malcolm Fraser – long retired, and personally reconciled with Gough Whitlam – has doubted his own wisdom in taking Kerr's commission. The manner of the Dismissal, he concedes, damaged Australia more than any of the constitutional nightmares it was allegedly averting.

That there was unwisdom also on Whitlam's side – and something of arrogance – is perfectly plain. His government could well have collapsed, even have been dismissed, without Kerr's astonishing ambush. But, had a 'clear sense of inevitability' preceded the use of emergency powers, such a result – however painful and divisive – would not have carried the freight of deception and legalistic intrigue which characterises 'November 1975' – something impossible for losers to forget or winners to justify, and which might have fatally harmed a less resilient democracy.

That Sir John Kerr, principal author of the crisis through his inability to distinguish discretion from deception, confessed no doubt about his role is unsurprising. Murdoch considers his own role was perhaps significant – but also expresses no regret.

Menadue's charge is that Murdoch's conduct amounted to 'abuse of power'. And this is obviously true in a general sense. Murdoch had the power to control the *Australian*'s content, and abused it, as in 1972, by producing indefensibly unbalanced coverage. But the special and perhaps decisive abuse was that the *Australian* revealed less than its proprietor knew about the events it purported to report.

That the use of emergency powers in advance of an emergency was plotted by several people is obvious, the principals being the Governor-General and the Chief Justice, and Fraser some time ago ceased to maintain that Kerr's action was as surprising to him as it was to Whitlam. Conspiracies rarely have well-defined plans and explicit membership – which is why they appear in history, more often than not, as cock-ups – but beyond Kerr, Barwick and Fraser there were others who knew or suspected much, and Murdoch was clearly one. Very likely he did not know everything – if he did, we may be sure he has since forgotten – but that he understood the Fraser camp's tactical scheme is plain. The details of the ambassadorship were too specific to be guesswork.

The story of Fraser's new attitude to – new long-term role for – the head of the Prime Minister's Department should have been in the *Australian* some time in the week ending 9 November. Menadue's account makes evident the level of confidence Murdoch had in his story. It was, if benchmarks are needed, a better-found story than the nonsense about liability for the vice-regal costs or – making an earlier parallel with Murdoch's journalism – the involvement of Treasurer McMahon with foreign agents.

But Murdoch's instinct was not to publish, any more than his father's had been. It was to dole out an insider's tale in just the way likeliest to aid his partisan cause. Menadue did not see himself as a mere Whitlam henchman, but as a public servant with a duty to any formally appointed Prime Minister, and it was in that capacity – not out of hope for a glamorous ambassadorship – that he organised the prorogation. But that was the essence of Murdoch's lunchtime story: Fraser had accepted the legitimacy of Whitlam's officials, and expected to work through them. A real reporter would have gone public with that – it was quite a scoop, in fact – leaving the actors to make of it what they might.

Would it have changed the outcome? It is hard to think Kerr's secret could have survived, for that was the nearest of near-run things. Whitlam's Treasurer, Bill Hayden – a detective in pre-political life – was almost certain that Kerr was deceiving Whitlam, and for him the story would have confirmed a plot in hand. It would surely, have led to other stories, and then the events of Tuesday would have unrolled otherwise, for the Speaker and his majority, given the slightest advance warning, would not have let themselves be moved so readily off the stage.

The anger of ALP loyalists who believe Murdoch 'tore down' Whitlam has usually focused on the biases of the kind shown in the La Trobe research. But they should rather have recalled 'Silver Blaze', the story in which Sherlock Holmes searches for a missing racehorse, and draws Watson's attention to 'the curious incident of the dog in the night-time'. The doctor protests that surely the dog did nothing. 'That was the curious incident,' remarks Sherlock Holmes.

The surest thing is that Murdoch's entire participation represents an approach to First Amendment tasks utterly unlike the standard set at roughly the same time by the *Washington Post*. His was centred on rhetoric, concealment or selective disclosure in aid of a final cause. The political payoff for Murdoch was not something simple and immediate, like Jack McEwen's help with the *News of the World*. His relationship with Fraser in office was not much closer than his relationship with Whitlam had been. All that he gained initially from being on the winning side was a narrow escape from the losing one. But the later outcome shows us that the true symbiosis of Newscorp and politics was in train.

To add to his repute as a circulation magician, the Dismissal gave Murdoch the name among politicians of a kingmaker and un-maker (something British exploits would soon enhance). The ALP's leaders saw 'the media' – along with Kerr and Barwick – as the cause of Whitlam's fall, and Newscorp as the media's cutting-edge. We know this was grossly oversimplified, because Murdoch's partisan operations would never have begun without the prior effect of disclosures he could never have organised. But the conclusion Whitlam's successors Bob Hawke and Paul Keating drew from the Dismissal included little subtlety. It was never to fall out with Rupert Murdoch, and on the contrary to find ways of appeasing him.

With Labor returned to office in the following decade, we shall see them assisting Murdoch into monopoly influence over Australia's metropolitan newspaper industry. Told in Chapter 13, the story shows well that monopoly insulated Murdoch from the moral hazards of its purchase: a primary example of the process in which politicians, by making a fantastical estimate of Newscorp power, confer on it increasing substance.

Many details of Murdoch's Australian record were obscured from public view in Britain and America during the years when he gained similar – if less comprehensive – power in those countries. But because the public were unaware, it should not be thought that the politicians who helped him over legal obstacles also were. Murdoch was welcome to the political elites of the northern hemisphere not because they were naive about his business model but because – like the ALP – they thought it promising.

The title of this chapter is of course adapted from Christopher Isherwood's fable *Mr Norris Changes Trains,* set in Berlin between the world wars. Mr Norris is adept in trading and betraying allegiances. He isn't presented as actively wicked – the narrator finds a certain charm in his freedom from shame. To Mr Norris, it does not matter with whom he does business, only that he can somehow do it. Allegiance for him is purely tactical, and people suppose they are using Mr Norris. But he is a practised operator and they often overestimate their own skill.

7

AN AMERICAN NIGHTMARE,
1801–1980

You cannot hope to bribe or twist
Thank God, the British journalist.
But seeing what the man will do
Unbribed, there's no occasion to.

HUMBERT WOLFE, *The Uncelestial City*

... of those men who have overturned the liberties of republics, the
greatest number have begun their career by paying an obsequious court
to the people; commencing demagogues, and ending tyrants.

ALEXANDER HAMILTON, founder of the *New York Post*

Many journalists (practising and academic), media commentators and
political spokespeople hold that news and entertainment media in
America – by extension, in the world – have declined in quality over the
past thirty-odd years. The majority position is generally pessimistic, and
sometimes apocalyptic: going so far as to doubt the survival of democratic institutions which require an informed, conscientious citizenry. A
smaller, more cheerful group claims that things have improved, that dull,
self-important journalism has given way to a streetwise populism speaking directly to the people in language they enjoy and understand. This
method has been successfully cross-bred into television.

A sub-text of the argument is that many of the tabloid techniques

197

involved were imported to America from Britain – or re-exported, perhaps, from Fleet Street to their place of origin in New York. One side speaks of a corrupt miasma, and the other of a keen and bracing wind. If there are excesses, say the optimists, they represent a turbulence which has always existed – a cost of liberty which cannot damage a robust people. Where the two sides agree is first that Rupert Murdoch has been central in the process, and second that the decisive phase began with his purchase of the *New York Post*, America's oldest surviving newspaper, in 1976, and his startling reconstruction of it, imposed the following year.

The points of agreement between the admirers and the critics of Murdoch seem well based. But it is remarkable that a newspaper which has never made money in his hands – has been for the most part desperately unprofitable – should have had such a seminal impact. If nothing else, it shows that the Murdoch story involves complexities: the *Post* could not exist within a publishing organisation oriented towards profit-making by conventional, rationalistic means. It is when talking about the *Post* that Murdoch has said that running newspapers is not, basically, about profit. It is about 'making the world a better place' – not a stance he is famous for defending.

But the statement calls for something more than incredulity, given a consensus that the *Post*'s influence outdoes its slight economic prowess. Clearly Murdoch has made adherents, and at the very least some attempt must be made to grasp what his concept of a better place may be. All the same, the power and extent of the Murdoch empire has not been enough to convince many media analysts of this altruistic purpose other than those actually on its payroll. Many, probably, would go along with the swingeing judgment of the *Columbia Journalism Review*, which in 1982 described the *New York Post* under him as no longer 'a journalistic problem [but] a social problem, a force for evil'.

Calling a newspaper other than the *Völkischer Beobachter* evil may appear melodramatic. But precedent exists in New York's combative past. One of the most formidable of the *Post*'s great editors, Edward Lawrence Godkin – though using a Victorian idiom – produced a century earlier a very similar denunciation of what was in his day called 'yellow journalism', and which both he and the *CJR* would certainly have thought equivalent to Murdoch's output: 'A yellow journal office is probably the nearest approach, in atmosphere, to hell, existing in any Christian state. A better place to prepare a young man for eternal damnation than a yellow journal office does not exist.'

The *Post* seems to have been the first Murdoch paper to attract quite so unsparing a verdict. Larry Lamb's *Sun* (the Mark I version) was called scurrilous, irresponsible, pornographic (frequently) and many other things, but not with any deliberation 'evil' – and nor were the ratbag follies of the early *Australian* and the Sydney *Daily Mirror*. Not until the Kelvin MacKenzie (Mark II) *Sun* of the 1980s do we encounter an equivalent loathing.

It's stimulated by protean characteristics in the case made for the defence. First, 'darkly playful', but sentimental: the *Post* experience is described as a (physically) reeking chaos ordered by intermittent bullying where images of rotting corpses are privately hoarded, and display ('HEADLESS BODY IN TOPLESS BAR', and so on – see p. 223 below) is optimised for callous glee. Amid this, we're told, jovial togetherness breaks regularly out – like the gothic critters of Hieronymus Bosch rendering a chorus from *Oklahoma!* Second, furiously proletarian and resentful: Murdoch denouncing the *Post*'s critics (especially those from Columbia at the other end of town) for being 'snobs' and anti-democrats. Third, high seriousness: this is a newspaper nearly as old as the Republic, offering not just a 'bracing start' to New York's day, but a tireless attack on abusers of the public trust. Fourth, towering pretension: surely it is unique for a paper's headlines to be praised for their pure 'trochaic rhythms', or its text by reference to the literary theories of D. H. Lawrence? Some of this can be rendered as a family quarrel among New York institutions with competing notions of journalism – American ones, naturally, but with resonance beyond America. Uncles from Fleet Street, often unsavoury and arguably evil, have been heavily involved.

The first attribute of the *Post* is the aura of its creator – one of the indispensable geniuses who built the US Constitution. Alexander Hamilton happened to be a journalist of dramatic originality. The newspaper historian Edwin Emery calls him 'one of the fathers of the American editorial. His perspicacity, penetration, powers of concentration and clarity of expression were those of a premier editorial writer.' This even understates Hamilton, who also was a brilliant soldier, lawyer and administrator, and who established both the financial system and the naval security of the youthful Republic – even if he was a lesser pistol shot than Aaron Burr.

But his essential contribution to the liberty of news media – one with impact far beyond his own time and nation – was consolidating the Zenger truth principle, first constructed by his namesake Andrew Hamilton to deflect corruption's antique blunderbuss, the law of seditious libel (see Chapters 1 and 4 above). This was part of Hamilton's extended quarrel with Thomas Jefferson (elegantly proving the value of conflict between quality opponents). Though Jefferson in 1787 had famously rated the liberty of newspapers as more important than the reputation of government (see Introduction above), he saw things a little otherwise when president, and in 1803 he persuaded New York State to indict Harry Croswell for seditious libel. Croswell, editor of the *Wasp*, had alleged that under Washington's administration Jefferson had bribed an editor to defame the president. Croswell was not allowed to defend his report by trying to prove it true.

A six-hour exposition by Hamilton – usually thought his finest – failed to rescue his fellow editor, but it split the appeal bench, and in 1805 the state legislature adopted his argument, making proven truth a statutory defence to any defamation claim. In 1812, the Supreme Court abolished seditious libel as a cause of action in the federal courts. These were for Hamilton posthumous victories, thanks to the fatal duel with Burr in 1804, and in their own time they were not absolute. But that does not reduce their importance even slightly, for the principle he established – even if only imperfectly observed – underpins the accountability of government, the saving grace of Western power.

The *New York Evening Post* started life on 16 November 1801, with William Coleman as its nominal editor, but Hamilton plainly in charge. It promised to avoid 'dogmatism' and to:

> diffuse . . . correct information on all interesting subjects . . . being persuaded that the great body of the people of this country only want correct information to enable them to judge of what is really best . . . all Communications, therefore, shall be inserted with equal impartiality . . . we never will give currency to anything scurrilous, indecent, immoral or profane . . .

Hamilton was of course a federalist – a conservative – but his central allegiance was to free debate, and under William Cullen Bryant (editor for fifty years, with gaps, from 1829) the *Post* evolved as a major vehicle of liberalism, supporting Lincoln, and giving fair hearing to organised labour when that was a quaint idea.

However, the most vehement – and effective – campaign of Bryant's successor, Godkin, was his assault on sensationalist ('yellow') journalism. He declared war as editor of the *Nation* magazine, and extended it when he went to the *Post*, gaining the support of other journals like *Collier's Magazine* and the *Dial*. Given today's Murdoch connection, this is a sizeable curiosity. Godkin, according to Emery, was an editor of striking austerity: 'He disliked sentiment and color in the news, and he would have liked to have kept all news of crime and violence out of the paper.'

The history of sensationalism is often over-simplified, and particularly in accounts agreeable to Murdoch. William Shawcross' biography, in leading up to the *Post* takeover of 1976, conflates nineteenth-century phases with twentieth-century ones, and suggests that American newspapers right up to Second World War days were tabloids largely staffed by boozy sociopaths. On such a base, the antics of the post-1976 *Post* appear in lesser relief. The true story is involute, and not yet done: the twists and turns are hard to compress without distortion. But, on a fair argument, the ancestry of American sensation does trace to Britain. That is, New York's first cheap newspapers, beginning with Benjamin Day's *Sun* in the 1830s, took their lead from London's police-court sheets. Day's co-owner George Wisner was an Englishman who had developed his relish for mayhem among the Bow Street Runners.

The journals written and read by people like Hamilton and Madison varied of course in quality (though rarely has magnificence been closer to being routine), but their subscribers were prosperous merchants and professional gentlemen. A reference to 'the people' did not mean 'proletariat', for few members of such a class existed in American cities until a third of the nineteenth century had passed. It was only as their numbers increased that pay-as-you-go 'penny papers' like the *Sun* appeared to provide them with both information and entertainment. Though media analysis may treat the two functions as separate (even contradictory) their ultimate relationship is a subtle interplay, similar to that between truth and fiction. Earlier chapters traced something of this in reporters such as Stephen Crane and Rudyard Kipling, and should include adulterated cine-history and present-day documentary scams. Subtlety, however, scarcely entered into penny-paper operations.

When Richard Locke wrote in the *Sun* a three-part account of daily life on the Moon he knew perfectly well his 'information' was fraudulent, and the intimacies provided about aristocratic passion across the Atlantic must also have been on-site concoctions. Day and his followers rummaged through experience like infants in a bran-tub, and used anything they found – inconsequential or fabricated – so long as it seemed likely to be startling.

But to improve radically on this method was actually hard. Untruth in an early-nineteenth-century newspaper might or might not be reckless, but was anyway endemic. 'Insertions' (articles or stories) had to be based largely on letters, and excerpts from other journals delivered by irregular mails. Verification was rarely possible outside an immediate locality, and the real origin of much content inevitably unknown. In *The School for Scandal* (1777), Snake says that because the paragraphs he plants for Lady Sneerwell are always composed 'in a feigned hand, there can be no suspicion whence they came', and for several decades after Sheridan's time things changed little. *The Times* in London was developing an organised news staff, but its wealth as yet had no parallel. James Fenimore Cooper complained in *The American Democrat* (1838) that most of what the new urban classes might find in a newspaper would be misleading, but often for no more reason than the ordinary editor's slight 'means of ascertaining the facts'.

Day startled his contemporaries most thoroughly by showing that the literate poor made a profitable audience. But he only started things. It was in the second half of the century that growth of circulations became explosive – and alarming – through the interaction of demographic change and electric press technology. America's urban population increased by half during the hectic 1880s, when Joseph Pulitzer's *New York World* recorded the first quarter-million sale – reaching 1.5 million during the next decade, with William Randolph Hearst hot in pursuit.

Briefly, but not unfairly, the offence of these rich and growing organisations was that they were acquiring ample resources, technological and financial, for 'ascertaining the facts' about most things under their inspection, and they showed small interest in doing so. They appeared to use their energies mostly in competitive pursuit of freakish events, and belabouring political opponents. As the potential to clarify them improved, the boundaries of truth and fiction actually became more, not less, confusing, and this to Godkin and his allies was unforgivable – along with the grasshopper attention-span induced by the search for sensation. Novelty is of course an essential element of news. But, where it overwhelms all others, stories actually blot out their predecessors, and the newspaper's frame of reference shrinks rather than expands.

America and Australia shared during this period near-complete literacy – a generation ahead of Britain – but Australia was less polyglot, less unequal, and for the most part less turbulent politically. Its urban culture, if far from innocent, was less violent – less dynamic, some might say – perhaps accounting for the comparative restraint which Trollope and Twopeny observed in its newspapers. Maniac concoctions like those of John Norton and the Wild Men of Sydney were somewhat outside the mainstream in Australia. But in Pulitzer's and Hearst's New York they often dominated it.

According to Professor Hazel Dicken-Garcia the first book devoted entirely to editorial failings in the US was *Our Press Gang; or, a complete exposition of the corruptions and crimes of the American Newspapers* (1859), in which Lambert A. Wilmer identified fourteen types of dishonesty, incompetence, bias and recklessness. He initiated a vigorous debate, though it took some time to move from complaint to remedies. The word 'ethics' appeared for the first time in 1889, and the first 'code of conduct' was proposed the year after.

Pulitzer's role, in the end, was pivotal. He was far too intelligent not to be moved by the press critics. Indeed, he admired Godkin and his work at the *Post*, but feared that such austerity would deprive him of the mass audience he craved. Pulitzer thought that with sufficient sales the *World* could be more powerful than the Presidency, and said, 'I want to talk to a nation, not a select committee.' Scarcely anyone can have been called a 'bundle of contradictions' with better cause than Joseph Pulitzer. He might denounce ethnic injustice almost in the moment of directing opportunistic abuse at Mexicans, Spaniards or any other outgroup rendered unpopular by the flux of events. Relentlessly pursuing gain, he asserted that his heart was entirely with the poor. And he mourned the bloodshed of war, though it is hard to think of anyone apart from Hearst who did more to encourage it editorially.

Above all, Pulitzer's journalistic persona was schizoid. His intellect, certainly first class, was committed to precision, objectivity and persistence. Regularly, he lectured his staff about the duty to carry each story to a conclusion before galloping after others. He himself had been a fine reporter for the *St Louis Post-Dispatch*, before becoming its proprietor. But when competitive stress afflicted him – which was often, after he bought the *World* from Jay Gould – these ideals showed fragility. 'Accuracy! Accuracy! Accuracy!' was his favourite injunction. But exceptions were apt to be made if a competitor seemed to excel in riots, fires or hangings. He liked headlines to be spiked with melodrama or alliterative titillation – preferably both, as in 'DEATH RIDES THE BLAST'; 'LITTLE LOTTA'S LOVERS'; 'DOES REV. MR TUDOR TIPPLE?' or 'BAPTISED IN BLOOD' – and his staff devoted much time to working up communications from condemned murderers and wronged servant girls. (The 'Yellow Kid', identifying the whole genre, was a cartoon infant published by Hearst as well as Pulitzer, technically notable because his smock used newspaper colour for the first time, in the *World*'s comic section during 1889.)

In the last decade of Pulitzer's life (the first of the new century) the *World* grew rather calmer, but did not radically alter. Pulitzer's response to Godkin's reproofs was a resolve to reform, not his own journalistic generation, but subsequent ones, and to this he made a decisive contribution when his will (1911) endowed the School of Journalism at Columbia (Alexander Hamilton's university, as it chanced). The assessment of Murdoch's *New York Post* as injecting 'evil' into the city thus came from another New York institution which the *Post* itself had prompted into being.

Like his admirer Theodore Fink in Melbourne (see Chapter 1 above) Pulitzer acknowledged that the communications industry made by the nineteenth century would become a threat to its own society if ruled solely by political partisanship and commercial opportunism. It needed journalists with enough education and training to develop tolerably consistent means of dealing with complex events, and the last period of

Pulitzer's life saw the change which Professor Michael Schudson has most clearly identified – from the political–partisan press to the commercial–professional model. The Columbia School, indeed, became a major agency in developing and consolidating the process, though it was only the most famous element (and not the first) in a wider movement. Synchronising neatly with expansion of American universities, the demand for journalistic education led to a nationwide establishment of journalism schools, graduate and undergraduate. It may be sentimentally remembered, but the route from copy-boy to editor has not since been heavily trodden.

Perceptions of journalism as a profession – and one in need of some intellectual apparatus – were not uniquely American. In Germany at the same time Max Weber began work on the huge inquiry into newsgathering and its ethics which he hoped to make the capstone of his career as a social scientist. Our understanding of our media industries might be more coherent had he succeeded, but the project was wrecked by the First World War and Weber's early death in 1919; in English we have only the few penetrating observations cited in earlier chapters (a mass of German material is still being edited). The system which developed in Australia relied less on vocational teaching in universities than did the American, and more on workplace-based training. But it had similar professionalising aims.

Standard disproofs of journalism as a profession rely on its lack of self-regulating privileges, and the curious status of its members – a caste of influential 'pariahs', as Weber noted with fascination. Some of this loses force as 'real' professions begin to surrender many of their immunities. And for Weber the essence of a professional activity is not so much the ability of initiates to protect themselves as the asymmetry of information between them and their clients: consumers of news still have little more chance than a doctor's patients of decoding statements compounded with dishonesty. (A 'yellow press' trick which attracted particular loathing was sensationalised medical news – today a fairly rare offence.)

Most of these efforts at education and intellectual inquiry can be seen as attempts to turn Pulitzer's aspirations into reliable practice, into rules against deception as a means to entertainment or political leverage.

'Objective' journalism was a specially American outcome – an almost pedantic collating of alternative viewpoints, with estimates of their relative value forbidden, at least in theory; and at the twentieth century's midpoint it had largely captured the American newspaper. It is a style easily – even unwittingly – caricatured, and extreme forms can be demolished philosophically by anyone carrying the intellectual firepower of a popgun. Still, if one has to disentangle real events, a slab of US reportage bearing its stolid imprint can be very welcome (somewhat like the BBC World Service, also scorned at times for a dowdy balance). It did not produce flawless news coverage in any medium. But it hard-wired into several generations of American reporters a belief that some evidence should support any statement offered to the public.

The gap between this notion and Murdoch's sophisticated 'Fleet Street style' is defined by an account of his lieutenant Steve Dunleavy briefing a *Post* reporter on development of a story about AIDS being spread by kissing. (The witness is Steven Cuozzo, an enduring *Post* veteran, who sees Murdoch and Dunleavy as journalistic demi-gods clothed in mutual admiration.) 'When [Joe] Nicholson protested that the supposition had yet to be proven, he was taken aback by Dunleavy's scoffing retort, "Let's not be too technical, mate – it's a good yarn."'

The sensationalist wave didn't recede evenly from twentieth-century America. In the 1920s, indeed, it produced a deluge exclusive to New York – again with British origins.

The *World* and its competitors were broadsheets. The modern tabloid – a half-broadsheet page built around pictures, not words – was a Northcliffe development for customers several social pegs below his *Daily Mail* readers. His *Daily Mirror* swiftly achieved a lucrative million sale, and Northcliffe thought a similar formula would capture New York's immigrant working class. His friend Joseph Medill Patterson (of the *Chicago Tribune* McCormick clan) was convinced, and launched the *Daily News* in 1919.

Briefly in the 1920s, war between the *News* and its imitators – chiefly the *Daily Graphic* – outdid even the yellow decades. The phenomenon was more egregious because newspapers (and now radio systems) were in general moving the other way. The conflict reached its gruesome apex in 1927 with the Ruth Snyder execution. On the day Mrs Snyder was electrocuted for killing her husband, the *Graphic* put before its readers her final thoughts before she was led to the chair that 'sears and burns and FRIES AND KILLS . . .'. However, the *News*, smuggling in a camera, managed to show her receiving the current. This enhanced sales by some 20 per cent on the day, and 750,000 individual copies of page one were flogged.

But the waters did subside. The tabloid rivals of the *News* – the *Graphic* above all – were financially catastrophic, and after their collapse the paper's own news values slowly calmed. Sensational populism didn't vanish. But during the decades straddling the Second World War it ceased to dominate the US media system.

The New York wars had more lasting impact in Fleet Street. As we saw in Chapter 5, their furious example was Guy Bartholomew's inspiration – if the word suits him – when he rounded up the British working class and propelled the *Daily Mirror* towards the world's largest circulation. (Post-Northcliffe, it had ailed.) This may seem culturally bizarre, but Atlantic cross-currents often are: what could be less plausible than a bunch of middle-class Brits naming themselves the Rolling Stones and recycling the blues to America? By the 1970s, Rupert Murdoch was eager to do some re-recycling, and saw good reason for his enthusiasm.

While building his New York base around the *National Star*, Murdoch turned his defence of its supermarket concoctions into a claim that mainstream American journalism was anaesthetising itself – he, by implication, being the fellow to wake it up. There were good observers who conceded his first point (if never the second). Max Frankel, later editor of the *New York Times*, records that its best reporters were in this period often driven 'close to resignation' by editing so oppressive as to resemble censorship. New social and political patterns were replacing a long post-war consensus, and reporting them often required more than a simple tour of the certified positions. This courted accusations of non-conformity, and while there was nothing especially American about media top brass dreading such a prospect, there was about the solution they attempted – a mechanical 'objectivity', almost stenographic in character, with sheets of editorial boilerplate obscuring any gleam of judgment. Frankel and some of his colleagues envied the British *Economist*'s 'concise and dispassionate' analysis of their own country enough to consider starting their own version of it – and found from its

US editor that 'her best articles were merely rewritten from our dispatches'.

The *Times* is today more heterodox, to its stylistic benefit. But the *Economist* incident cross-references the comparison Murdoch was dwelling on – the presentational superiority of British journalism over American. It is valid only as a very broad comparison, with multiple exceptions. And it relates to a complexity he bypasses – the greater relative strength of American reporting. But in the 1970s Murdoch wanted simply to argue that (a) US papers were systematically dull, and (b) they were dull because, unlike himself, they cared little for social and political legitimacy. This he dressed up in class analysis of a kind, telling American newspaper publishers in 1977, 'A press that fails to interest the whole community is one that will eventually become a house organ of the elite.'

'Elite' is a key concept in Murdoch discourse. An elite newspaper generally is one which is not a populist tabloid, or one not operated by his own company. (Under the second term, a Murdoch broadsheet may be less elitist than a tabloid in other hands.) Over the years he has stated his case against elite newspapers in variorum, and extended it to television, but a core version can be distilled. Elite newspapers are dull because they despise the tastes and ignore the needs of 'blue-collar workers' or 'ordinary people'. Elite journalists are 'snobs'. Snobbery makes them incapable of attracting a popular audience, so they resent the egalitarian success of tabloids. Resentment motivates their condemnation of his methods. Like all snobs, elitists are unrealistic; they should be brought down to earth, not least because of their affected concern for social reform, liberty and the people's rights. Their talk about making the world better is a sham.

Just as he and his newspapers respect and serve popular tastes, they are the people's true defence against the power and corruption of elites. 'Serious' journalists are too comfortable inside the status quo to do anything for the masses who enjoy the tabloid newspapers which attract so much hostility for their sensationalism. But, for Murdoch and his followers, the hostility of the elite is welcome. The tradition of the Muckrakers, he says, is an old and honourable one, and Murdoch types are happy to be its populist successors, exposing the selfishness and hypocrisy of power wherever it exists.

Like the Gallipoli Letter – decked out similarly in class-war rhetoric – the diatribe has a rough plausibility but rests on a spurious history. Murdoch put it this way in one of his more extended essays: 'It was not the serious press in America but the muck-rakers, led by Lincoln Steffens and his *New York World* . . . who challenged the American trinity of power – Big Business, Big Labour and Big Government.'

Some modern research challenges the *scholarship* of Muckrakers like Lincoln Steffens, Ida Tarbell and Ray Stannard Baker: only Murdoch could suggest they were not part of – most of – the serious press of their time (1904–12). The Muckrakers exposed city bosses and oil companies in magazines like *McClure's* and *Collier's*, which didn't at all resemble the *Sun* or *News of the World* – and were tough critics of contemporary papers which did. They sometimes worked with yellow-press paladins – when they got them to be serious – but Steffens didn't own, edit or work for the *World*. If the *Sun* can be justified via the Muckrakers, Sairey Gamp trained under Florence Nightingale.

The Fleet Street style Murdoch desired for America came of another pedigree. Britain was only lightly touched by the notions of training and professional education which shaped American and Australian news-gathering in the twentieth century. It did not stop the country producing its full share of brilliant reporters and editors: Henry Nevinson, C. P. Scott, Elisabeth Wiskemann, Clare Hollingworth, René MacColl, Harry Evans, Kate Adey – some celebrated, some known best to discriminating insiders (and more turning up still). But it certainly caused Britain to out-produce heavily in cynical hacks – predominantly inept, but sometimes darkly skilled.

Some of the story we have traced already: presentational ingenuity suppressing reality, in a culture dominated by subs where only a minority of journalists believe they carry any professional obligation – broadly, the US situation reversed. Baldwin's 'harlot' speech had its crunching effect because the image of the press lord and his ductile entourage was already embedded in public consciousness: Humbert Wolfe, writing *The Uncelestial City* at the same time, represented journalistic mendacity as orthodoxy, *not* as corruption. His work is mostly forgotten, but not the lines quoted at the head of this chapter. Hearst of course had his lordly ambitions. It is just that in the US context there were more countervailing forces.

Generally Britain's mass newspapers in their period of hectic mid-century growth recruited from survivors of the provincial sink-or-swim ordeal that Arthur Christiansen describes (augmented sporadically from Oxbridge and the Antipodes). Entry standards were modest, to allow for lavish wastage. Talent has always seemed abundant in Britain, permitting a substantial cynicism about training and supportive instruction. There have been organisational exceptions (such as the armed forces), but until recently newspapers have been much better at exhorting other industries to improve than doing better themselves.

Of course there were those who survived with a crystalline sense of truth – James Cameron, for instance, after whom Britain's premier award for journalistic courage is named. Cameron, among other things, quit a glamorous job at the *Daily Express* just because it began telling deliberate lies, and he was thought most eccentric, as his autobiography makes clear. There were far too few Camerons to change either the public's estimate of the British journalist or the view within popular newspapers that truth was a matter for the boss to define.

The social and political environment which once nurtured this huge press was changing fast when Murdoch joined the Fleet Street scene. Consequently, much of it was disintegrating by the 1970s. Often the rise of television is cited to explain the collapse – and now is a good moment to zap that shopworn alibi, as Figure 3 does very effectively. Newspapers were at saturation point in the 1950s; the progress of television towards a similar status never produced destructive competitive pressures. Some there were, of course – but a fair hypothesis is that there were too few people in the newspaper business with enough intellectual address to organise any better response than a down-market plunge, made at the least opportune moment in terms of the overall trend of British society.

Murdoch was able to pursue it without complicating inhibition. He had double immunity against the idea of dealings between news media and consumers being anything more than the most basic contract. He had not undergone the processes of selection and training developed in his own country (having qualified by the laying on of parental hands) and had triumphed in Fleet Street among and through people contemptuous or resentful of all such philosophies.

Figure 3

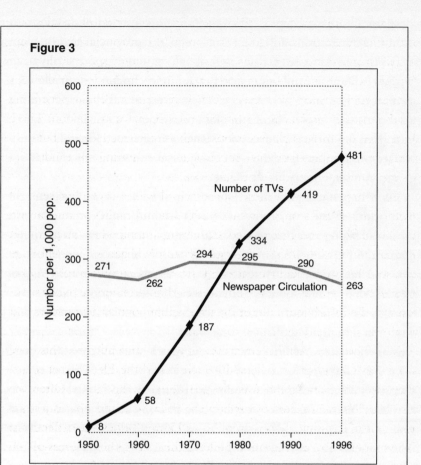

This data shows a mild decline in newspaper sales in OECD countries, not significantly related to TV growth. Much of the recent fall is concentrated in Anglophone countries: without them newspaper figures are better. Circulation is most resilient in Scandinavia, where television is universal, Internet usage is very high (like educational attainment) and tabloid publishing is minimal. Source: Pippa Norris (Shorenstein Center, Harvard): *A Virtuous Circle* (2000)

America presented a chance to repeat that triumph – the supermarket *Star* was reconnaissance-in-depth – and Old Fleet Street's mortal convulsions threw off recruits abundantly. Roger Wood, for instance, editor of the *Star* after James Brady, was one of the technicians behind the first, abortive *Sun*, and then one of many editors given a brief try at curing the

211

desperately ailing *Express*. (These were scarcely triumphs, but surely Murdoch could transmute men too.) And to augment Fleet Street there was his own Antipodean supply out of the old Norton tradition in Sydney – Dunleavy pre-eminently. Brady found Dunleavy 'wonderful'. 'If you wanted a miracle cancer cure, a flying saucer, a Hollywood scandal, or a rip-off of a forthcoming book in the guise of a "review", what we called an "el thievo", Dunleavy was your man.' Dunleavy did have a philosophy, and could define it: 'If it's accurate, anything goes. If the reader buys it, it's moral.' Accurate. Now there's a word.

As it happened, American journalism did reshape itself during the final third of the last century. It hasn't become ideal (or stopped the *Economist* taking good money from the American ruling class). But newspapers, in Frankel's words, ceased to be mainly 'expositors of government policy . . . We saw ourselves as more accountable to our readers than to our sources.' That distinction the London *Times* originated in the nineteenth century – and, as the next chapter will show, forgot in the twentieth. 'In the generation before ours,' Frankel went on, 'it was enough for Arthur Krock to interview President Truman to qualify for a Pulitzer Prize. In our time, the prize went to Woodward and Bernstein for planting dynamite under Richard Nixon's throne.'

From Pulitzer's accessory bequest, the Prizes, we gain a narrative portrait of the Republic's journalism. Since 1970, they have been won most often for exposing corruption: which was a sin of elites (who else gets the chance?) when Ida Tarbell dealt with Standard Oil, and still was when Bethany McLean punctured Enron in 2001. But no award has gone to a paper under Murdoch's control, though the *Post* persistently claims to be a terror to abusers of the people's trust.

Across the border dividing paranoia from conservatism, some say the Pulitzer awards – even the whole media – are an elite–metropolitan fix. Fixing a selection process so elaborately generalised would be tough, but it is true that, as in the Olympics, most medals go to the big teams. Since 1970 the ten papers with double-figure scores have 218 out of 416 mentions: the *New York Times* with forty-seven is followed by the *Washington Post* (twenty-nine), the Associated Press (twenty-one), the *Los Angeles Times* (twenty), the *Philadelphia Inquirer* and the *Wall Street Journal* (nineteen), the *Chicago Tribune* (eighteen), the *Boston Globe*, *Miami Herald* and *Newsday* (fifteen).

It's scarcely political – few liberal papers outscore the arch-conservative *Wall Street Journal*. But it's disseminated – the group taking more than one prize is twenty-three strong, and while some are grand titles (*Atlanta Constitution, St Louis Post-Dispatch*), not all are (*Akron Beacon-Journal, Orlando Sentinel, Pottstown Mercury*). And seventy-one papers, mostly small, have scored at least once: the *Berkshire Eagle, Fort Wayne News-Sentinel, Gainesville Sun, Odessa American* and *Xenia Daily Gazette* hardly belong to a metropolitan elite. Most of these prizes were for tackling local, sometimes vicious power-abuse. Anyone who understands journalism – or community life – knows that such action demands civil courage of a daunting order.

Though Murdoch likes his papers to generate a hyperactive look, they aren't usually allowed generous budgets for the purpose. Even so, the *Post* must be better resourced than the *Xenia Daily Gazette*. How can all that activity, over thirty furious years, have struck no enemy of the people anyone else can recognise? How did it all begin?

Dorothy Schiff, who took control of the *Post* in the 1940s and turned it into a tabloid – in size, not style – enjoyed fair success until the later 1960s. The paper empathised with liberal Manhattan, and enjoyed an evening monopoly, but it was one that did not develop with its times. Its news-gathering was honest, but stuck in the mechanical style, and its editorial package relied heavily on columnists – often distinguished, but too many, and too often syndicated. (Evening papers which stay profitable do so by covering their patch.) And Mrs Schiff's years weighed on her. Clay Felker, the urbane founder–editor of *New York* magazine, who had begun steering Murdoch around upper-class Manhattan in the mid-1970s – seeing the Oxford-alumnus aspect, and taking it for the full Murdoch – confided that she might consider a sale.

She was ready to consider, reluctant to decide. Mrs Schiff was fond of her paper, and thought Murdoch's use of it might be unlike hers. But his attention seemed to veer towards the London Sunday-paper market – as the distinguished *Observer* came up for sale – and it compelled her to think that his offer could not be kept on ice. And it was not just tempting, it was staggering. Murdoch was ready to give $32.5 million (about $100 million now) for a newspaper shedding both money and readers. He had acted likewise (if on a lesser scale) with his San Antonio purchases. The value of a newspaper is classically a multiple of its earnings. Not in New York or Texas were there earnings visible. So the *Post* justified only the kind of bargain-basement price which had been paid in London for the *Sun*. In accountant's terms, therefore, Murdoch was paying lavishly for the *Post*'s 'goodwill' – more plainly, for what he thought he could do with a real newspaper franchise in the world's most fabulous city.

It was a deal an American company could not have financed, because in the US accounting 'goodwill' is not a bankable asset. But News Ltd – though renamed News Corporation – was registered in Adelaide, and under Australian accounting it could treat the goodwill of its US acquisitions in much the same way as tangible assets. Nor were the Commonwealth Bank and its associates in Australia likely to quibble about the worth Murdoch attached to them. He was the tabloid alchemist who had converted base Fleet Street elements to gold. If he had promised to raise the *Graphic* from the dead – and Mrs Snyder with it – they would not have doubted him.

Murdoch was very excited indeed. He described having the *Post* as like having both the *Sun* in London and the *Mirror* in Sydney. He saw enormous changes to be made – columns to be scrapped, layouts to be reconstructed, reporting to be 'improved'. It was a stupendous opportunity. As it would seem, he owed it to Clay Felker's introduction, but the favour attracted no return. Laying the *Post* aside for a moment, he bought out *New York*'s shareholders and ejected Felker – who said the experience modified his conception of friendship.

The *Post* deal closed in November 1976. On the 26th of the month a stranger tracked two New York girls walking home from the movies. Catching up with them, he muttered something, and fired several shots, wounding both. Donna DeMasi recovered well. Joanne Lomino was rendered paraplegic.

Though he was still a mystery to the police, this was the third New York shooting escapade of David Berkowitz, who became known as 'Son of Sam'. Five weeks earlier he had killed Rosemary Keenan and wounded her friend Carl Denaro. And before that, on 29 July 1976, as Donna Lauria and Jody Valenti sat in a car outside Donna's apartment, a man peered into it, then took a .44 Charter Arms Bulldog revolver from a paper bag and fired all five chambers at them. That, too, was

Berkowitz. Donna died. Jody survived and was able to give some account of her attacker, though not of the unusual weapon.

Thus the 'Son of Sam' story, taken to define the *Post*'s new, hard-boiled and ruthless character – the story Spike Lee turned many years later into a movie about urban hysteria – was already far advanced, if still clothed in mist, by the time Murdoch took over his new paper.

On 30 January 1977, as Christine Freund sat with John Diel in his car, two shots pierced the windscreen. She died, but he survived to describe loosely a young male attacker. Ballistics this time did identify a .44 Bulldog – suspected in the earlier cases, and a gun unlikely to appear often. The NYPD feared this might be a serial madman, and the evening of 18 March made them sure. Virginia Voskerichian was killed while walking home from Barnard College, and a complete Bulldog bullet matched the earlier ballistic material. A witness got a good look at the killer – white, dark-haired, twenty-five to thirty, medium build.

The police held a press conference, described their unidentified quarry, and began organising Operation Omega – bigger than anything they had done before, involving more than 300 detectives and costing in today's prices \$2.75 million a week. This had become a serious metropolitan crime story. And nobody who depended on the *New York Post* would have been aware of the fact, or of the degree of menace New York faced.

The first of two or three striking headlines which Murdoch's team produced for the case was

NO ONE IS SAFE

FROM SON OF SAM

on 1 August 1977. And this is remembered as a classic item of alarmist sales-drumming (for of course serial murderers, horrible as they are, never pose a significant threat to people in general). Less often remembered is the timing. 'Sam' had by this time committed his last murder; the *Post* had taken so long getting hold of the story that the tocsin sounded only days before it was redundant.

In media folklore Murdoch's *Post* advent resembles a shirtsleeved Assyrian descending like a wolf on the fold. Shawcross describes 'Dolly Schiff's staid liberal backwater' abruptly changed to a 'roiling, clamorous torrent of news, mostly conservative opinion, and hucksterish entertainment'. And without Larry Lamb sharing the charge, this was editor-in-chief Murdoch's own show. Steven Cuozzo, the devoted eye-witness, has Murdoch transfixing New York with revelations of 'human emotion as a topic for serious consideration – even when that emotion reflected the dark side of the human psyche . . . The street-brawler publisher and the street-brawling city proved a combustible mix.'

If so, it hung fire for the first six months of 1977. Entertainment was there ('101 THINGS YOU CAN DO FOR FREE IN NY') and flecks of conservative opinion. But when one reviews the pages with an eye to newsflow, it hardly seems torrential – rather, it's intermittent and erratic. The noun might be 'trickle'. If Son of Sam was then fighting a 'one-man guerrilla war' against the city (that is how the subsequent assertions of the Murdoch team added up) then the *Post* wasn't covering it. In July it was trying to start a 'war' of its own against arson gangs, and lamenting public indifference to the issue. 'The *Post* has in the last week told of mindless destruction by arsonists – gangs who burn for the fun of it, greedy landlords who pay hoodlums to burn buildings to collect insurance . . .' A $500 reward was offered to counteract apathy, with a two-page spread (supplied from the trade magazine *Firehouse*) explaining 'how the underworld turns fire into profit'. This looks like a newspaper peering around for big stories and not finding them.

To be sure, inhibitions existed. Murdoch had recruited several subs adept in Fleet Street style, and as early as January one showed the way with a tale of capital-punishment protesters 'storming' the Utah jail where Gary Gilmore was being shot (in restoration of the American execution). Authority's repression of violence against its own violence made a piquant mix – blended from reports of a *peaceful* protest. Maybe executive editor Paul Sann knew he was blocking progress when the sub said it would 'juice up' the coverage, but he demanded a rewrite without juice.

Murdoch's strategy was to add a morning edition, head to head against the *News* – tough work, for its circulation was roughly two million against half a million. The team certainly needed a big story, and in the event the story found them, but through the pages of the *News*.

At 3.00 a.m. on 28 April Berkowitz came upon Valentina Suriani and Alexander Esau in a parked car. He shot each of them twice –

Valentina dying instantly, Alexander after several hours – and left a demented note, addressed to Captain Joseph Borrelli and signed 'Son of Sam'. Two days later the *News* columnist Jimmy Breslin received a letter, crazy but not illiterate, signed likewise and reading (in part), 'Hello from the cracks in the sidewalks of NYC and from the ants that dwell in these cracks and feed in the dried blood of the dead . . .' When the *News* ran it in May – after discussion with the police – the edition sold out immediately. The '.44 killer' had for months been a big story in the *News*; now as 'Sam' he was incandescent melodrama. The paper doesn't seem to have spiced it with invention. But with a correspondence between lethal madman and its star columnist there was no occasion to.

In July Murdoch drafted Wood and Dunleavy from the *Star*, and what Cuozzo calls the 'real fun' began. The *Post* had to find its own angle – the standard tactic of ignoring a competitor's story was out of the question. The NYPD understandably feared that the killer, having become a celebrity, would attempt something on 29 July, the anniversary of his first attack, and heavily publicised the danger. Both the *Post* and the *News* provided major coverage. But essentially it was the story-so-far.

Nothing happened. Then at 1.45 a.m. on 31 July Berkowitz found Robert Violante and Stacy Moskowitz in a car at Gravesend Bay, Brooklyn. He shot Robert twice, Stacy once; she died after thirty-eight hours in hospital, while the doctors discovered he was blinded, and their parents shared a bleak vigil amid intense media pressure. This 'inspired one of Dunleavy's memorable acts of competitive mischief' (Cuozzo), when he found a doctor's smock and entered Violante's hospital room posing as a 'bereavement counselor', which:

> naturally enabled him to score an exclusive interview with the grief-stricken family . . .
>
> It was this kind of Dunleavyan effort, Murdoch chuckled at the time, 'that gives the young reporters confidence'.

Dunleavy's account of the ordeal of the families wasn't perfectly exclusive, but it splashed over two pages of the *Post*. Some of the text must have challenged its readers:

So he goes to a movie in Brooklyn and this.' Neysa this .44 guy that did it. And this might says: "You know Stacy wasn't scared of this guy because she is a blonde. I suppose it is Wouldn't it be terrible for other kids of there sound terrible bit I hope it is the guy were two of these madmen running around?"

. . . Jerry know what the doctor is telling the press: "I know, I know it doesn't look and Neysa. Their boy is running the same good for her." Teresa and Pat comfort Jerry race.

Sic. Robert Lipsyte, an ex-colleague, has noted that Dunleavy's words, devoted to 'frenzy', aren't 'orderly, measured or intelligent'. Gibberish, though, is rare. The cause was production incompetence: the stone-sub getting cut-lines badly scrambled. It happens, but not often at such length in the hot pages of a major newspaper. The arts of Christiansen's *Express* were black perhaps, but they were always artful.

On the first day of August the *Post* moved fully into big-story mode and declared Sam a universal menace. It was an alarmist gem of sorts, but it created a problem. The paper clearly had no real information to offer – a regular difficulty with murder stories. There were simple ways to stoke alarm, like crediting the .44 Bulldog with invincible ('awesome') lethality (its forensic significance, its rarity, came from being notoriously inaccurate, thus allowing some victims their lives). Dunleavy produced speculations (baseless) about the cops letting Sam escape. There were sidebars about Britain's 'Yorkshire Ripper'. Combing the archives produced 'THE WAVES OF FEAR', a series indicating that figures like Sam were New York regulars. 'The .44-caliber killer is not the first human monster to hold the city a hostage to fear . . .' Adding force to this text was a picture of the shoes of Frances Hajek and her boyfriend, victims of the 'Lipstick Killer', in 1937.

Four days into August the *Post* led (exclusively) on Carmine Galante, America's 'most powerful Mafia chieftain', deciding that his own daughter was not safe and joining the hunt for Sam. If anyone was reassured by Galante putting 5,000 'soldiers' on the case, they must have been troubled next day when the police collared him for another matter. Murdoch of course wasn't, for he knew the lead was spurious, as he told Thomas L. Kiernan lightly. The confession has an interesting background.

Kiernan wrote a book about Murdoch which began as a co-operative biography, but relations grew hostile over discussion of Murdoch's editorial tactics. Kiernan failed to see that 'We didn't have anything else' justified a fraudulent lead, especially in the Son of Sam context. *Citizen Murdoch* (1986) is considered deeply unfair in *Post* circles.

Elmer 'Trigger' Burke from the 1950s and Francis 'Two-Gun' Crowley from the 1930s provided the final Waves of Fear on the same day. Neither case was remotely relevant, suggesting the cupboard indeed was bare. Now Dunleavy showed the way again with his celebrated Open Letter, offering Sam therapy in exchange for surrender. He began by saying he had been 'stunned, shattered and angry' when embracing the Moskowitz parents three days earlier. (He omitted mention of his role as a 'bereavement counselor'.) 'But it's time to put aside anger . . . and make a genuine, lasting appeal to the man who calls himself "Son of Sam".'

Many people had called the *Post* claiming to be the killer. None had been authentic, but 'chillingly' the possibility existed, so Dunleavy made:

> a straightforward and genuine appeal to the 'Son of Sam' to give himself up. Call us, and we pledge that together with the New York City police, perhaps the finest department in the world, we will see that you will be given the best help this city can afford.
>
> We know you are intelligent, no matter how monstrously misguided you might be. We know you have suffered and we feel for you . . .

The electric chair was a thing of the past. What the *Post* wanted was to find the real causes of the tragedy in Sam's troubled mind:

> By turning yourself in to us now, we feel that not only would it bring an end to the slaughter, it might also give the world an insight into what triggered this terrible nightmare.
>
> Help us help you to help the city to once again sleep in peace. Call us.

Berkowitz made no response, but the *Post* anyway came up with its own theory about the trigger and the nightmare. And it was one justifying tracts of ready-made copy which required no strenuous recyling into factual guise. Four years earlier Lawrence Sanders had produced a novel, *The First Deadly Sin*, about a crazed New York publisher butchering people for thrills. What about Sam having developed his lethal mind-set by reading Sanders? Naturally the *Post* must introduce everyone swiftly to this potent text – 'COMING NEXT WEEK!'

It's your kind of reading.

His name was Daniel Blank . . . he prowled the city, picking out his victims . . . Don't miss the digest of this thriller starting Monday in the *Post* . . . Police think Son of Sam may have modelled himself on the aimless killer [it describes].

Sanders is a writer of some account, but the digestion clearly did something to his dialogue, especially in the metaphysical exchanges between the killer and his morbid girlfriend. "'I'm not talking about evil for the sake of evil," said Celia. "I mean saints of evil – men and women who see a vision and follow it."' He wanted her to know just how profound the vision thing was for him: "'When . . . I . . . saw him walking toward me I thought yes, now, he is the one. I loved him so much then, loved him. And respected him. That he was giving. So much. To me. Then I killed him."' These serious considerations of human emotion were suitably illustrated. Had there been even a scintilla of truth in the publishing pretext it would have been an insane act. But elsewhere in the *Post* a news-stand man was quoted saying, 'Fifty copies of anything about Sam go like hotcakes in 10 minutes.'

It wasn't a novel which led the NYPD to Son of Sam, but a parking ticket collected near the Moskowitz–Violante shooting scene. Arrested on 10 August, Berkowitz admitted all his crimes (killing six people, blinding one, paralysing another, wounding seven less seriously). Remorseless, and relishing celebrity, he was jailed for 364 years.

The *Post* of 15 August devoted fifteen pages to recording a twelve-month 'war' which it said Berkowitz had waged against New York. This appeared to centre on a major personal communication from 'Sam' to the paper, with his own account of the psychological processes which had turned him into a serial killer (Sanders being superseded). These were not just notes like the *Daily News* had received, but seemingly his autobiography:

By David Berkowitz
The man the police say is Son of Sam

How many readers penetrated this fakery is unknown. Notoriously, the material was cobbled up – without participation by Berkowitz – out of letters sent to a girlfriend years before and sold to the *News* as well as the *Post*. They were certainly the letters of a bombastic misfit, with a disagreeable interest in weaponry. Not by any stretch were they the story of his homicidal activities in New York.

This seems an embarrassing circumstance, but the interesting point is that Murdoch has never been much embarrassed, either on his own behalf or on the *Post*'s. Questioned by William Shawcross, he said, 'I didn't write it, but I certainly approved it. I think it was wrong. But that's hindsight.' In another explanation, he implied that the critics just haven't had to take the heat: 'When you get in there at 3 o'clock or 5 o'clock in the morning, you've got five minutes to make an edition, and you're trying to choose between two headlines, it's easy to make a mistake.'

We're being offered a slippery pronoun: when Murdoch says he didn't write 'it', the impression is of a quick slip in a stressful second, a small enhancement gone just too far. But making a tabloid edition isn't a five-minute process, it's an extended architectural operation – which is why broadsheets are better for hard news. It aims to produce a sledgehammer ensemble which can't be misunderstood at the hastiest glance. There's evidence that Murdoch's production team weren't quite as slick with detail as Old Fleet Street liked. But if we look at the actual presentations of 15 August 1977 it seems they got the basic message into solid shape. For an experienced newspaper executive to suggest that only 'hindsight' revealed to him a possible impression that the *Post* was offering the personal story of a famous killer is grotesque. Most likely they knew what they were doing, and hoped to get away with it, though that calculation must have involved a large amount of professional naivety.

Since that hot, apparently terrifying summer of 1977, New York has suffered ordeals which make us think again about the entire notion of a

221

city being at threat from 'guerrilla warfare'. But, leaving some recent nuances aside, the *Post* remains pretty much the same newspaper, working in the same way. After two interludes in other hands, it is back with Rupert Murdoch, and still losing money. Its relevance, as both its friends and its enemies say, is now in its imitators more than in itself.

Where does a detailed look at the *Post*'s treatment of the Son of Sam story leave the *Columbia Journalism Review*'s accusation of 'evil'? Lately, that word has been much used in cases where it is undoubtedly appropriate. The first impression one gets from the record, overwhelmingly, is of lavish incompetence, and this frequently disarms. Most of the attacks on Newscorp are put in terms of its ruthless skill, and the deadly intuitions of its boss. In earlier chapters it's been suggested that such a picture may be overdrawn. But earlier chapters don't contain anything as absurd as the *Post*'s attempts to peer into the mind of Berkowitz and exploit him as a celebrity. If a newspaper proprietor is effectively represented as Dracula, an evil reputation will surely accrue. But will Dracula still seem evil if he can't make his false teeth fit properly? Isn't he just a clown?

Certainly a lot of what the *Post* was up to – 'competitive mischief' and so on – looks immediately like clowning. But on any closer look it's obvious that the raw material of this clowning was the pain and agony of real people. Just as obviously, the belated two-week pursuit of Son of Sam was exploitative. To be sure, that's true of much newspaper work. But there is something additionally chilling about exploitative behaviour married to childlike professional clumsiness. The *Daily News* coverage doesn't look very pretty in today's retrospect. They didn't make things up, and they didn't wildly inflate the threat from Son of Sam. But neither did they step out of their tabloid role and remind the citizens that the real risk to any individual New Yorker from Son of Sam was utterly negligible compared to the ordinary chances of urban life. They were, all the same, observing limits.

Murdoch and his *Post* team, with their wild calls to panic, their Mafia fantasies and their ludicrous psychological theorising, saw no limits except what they could get away with – and even that they couldn't competently judge. Dunleavy said as much: 'Anything goes.' He did, of course, nominate accuracy as a constraint, but this didn't mean anything when Murdoch thought the headlines needed 'juicing up'.

Steven Cuozzo, having spent his working life at the *Post*, has developed several lines of defence for its style, which he considers to be inspired wholly by Murdoch. One – the proposition about making human emotion a topic for 'serious consideration' – explodes on contact with *The First Deadly Sin* and its 'angels of evil' used as a means to comprehension of the Berkowitz murders. Another claims that Murdoch's *Post* has brought to journalism a 'dark playfulness' which sustains people amid the pressures of modern life. Here D. H. Lawrence is brought in with a variant of his 'intentional fallacy' thesis, in which subs juicing up headlines may unconsciously assist the American people to purify their emotions.

Cuozzo's examples generally resemble the sort of black humour cops and nurses use – but privately – to release stress. Incivility apart, parading it weakens the release, but for Cuozzo anything's grist to the headline mill, most of all the rather notorious *Post* item: 'HEADLESS BODY IN TOPLESS BAR'. He was pleased that a friend in the *National Review* could expound its metaphysical wit and (yes) 'trochaic rhythm' conveying 'appropriate ancient truth about sex, violence, and death'. Otherwise it might just be turning a murder into a joke – thus being pretty callous somewhere. Of course murder mostly affects people who can't object to becoming joke material, but busybody critics do exist, and Cuozzo suggests that 'dark playfulness', tinged with classicism, has helped the *Post* and its boss to see them off.

An effect of 9/11 is to make this kind of hokum more transparent. The *Post* would not dare to attempt 'dark playfulness' in respect of anything close to Ground Zero. Public black humour, in reality, applies only to those nobody troubles much about, or are for some other reason no danger to the wits who devise it. The *Post* mixture displayed in Cuozzo's celebratory history is exploitative enthusiasm, incompetence, ruthlessness, institutional toadying and an operational inability to distinguish fact from fabrication – topped off with some pseudo-intellectual bullshit. It doesn't seem so far-fetched to call such a newspaper 'a force for evil'.

That it hasn't – so far – worked any better than the *Daily Graphic* is striking, because it has been allowed to try three times longer. Had it been simply a newspaper operating in the marketplace it would have disappeared long ago. But at some level it has worked for Murdoch, and in the first place this seems to mean some personal gratification. However rigidly he controls them, none of the other Newscorp titles have given him so unencumbered a domain – here was no Lamb, no Deamer actually setting the operation in motion. An observer can only say: how clearly it shows, in the sheer awfulness of the paper, and its inability to extract a living – let alone a fortune – out of the city Murdoch appeared to take by storm a quarter of a century ago.

Yet he speaks of 'making the world a better place', which must in some sense mean producing the kind of newspaper he wanted to see. In 1988, when his first period of ownership ended – under cross-ownership rules that he and certain allies have since buried – he presented every *Post* executive with a gold Tourneau watch, engraved on the back, 'My thanks and appreciation – Rupert Murdoch'. One of the executives said, 'That's the first time an owner retires from the company and buys the employees a gold watch.' It is also reported that after a long, sad farewell dinner he 'cried like a baby'. Perhaps he did. But along with the sentimental attachment to his own journalistic creation there goes something rather harder: the fact that the *Post* was Murdoch's political bridgehead in America, and without any sentiment at all that would have made the losses a good investment.

And this is the working principle of the entire Murdoch machine. Whatever his ambition may have been, he did not turn the *Post* into a good newspaper, even in the limited sense that the *Sun* is a good newspaper: rich, that is, admired for its circulation success, and feared by competitors within its own declining territory. But the *Post*'s value, as it has turned out, is in its lack of quality, its entire dependence on Newscorp to pay its way, and the absence within it of any reporter who might doubt Rupert Murdoch's right to determine the truth as the *Post* ought to see it. It is an American newspaper which has turned the clock back as near as possible to the way things were before one of its own editors persuaded Pulitzer to change, if not quite his own ways, the ways of his successors. And it's an indication of how politicians essentially see newspapers that the *Post*'s political leverage isn't cancelled by its louche character.

Without the *Post* – or some equivalent source of political leverage – the coup which brought the Fox network into being would not have been possible. In that part of the narrative the *Post*'s wider influence on the American news media is examined further. But, in view of the paper's claim to be carrying out a historic mission set down by Alexander Hamilton, something is required here.

Steven Cuozzo again is the lead spokesman of a curious case. Roughly speaking, it claims that Murdoch's *Post* restored to American newspapers – and then transferred to television – a disposition to ransack the world frantically in search of sensation and celebrity news. A great virtue of this approach, to Cuozzo, is its total incoherence (including a cavalier approach to fact) and he quotes Neal Gabler as defining a 'tabloid worldview' to perfection: 'in place of facts marching in neat ranks, conveying the essential orderliness of things . . . a jumble of words and images conveying the essential disorderliness – CHAOS'.

Via gymnastic interpretation of *The Federalist,* the origins of this worldview are ascribed to Alexander Hamilton – which of course confirms the *Post*'s duty to expound it. To call this preposterous isn't quite enough, for the first issue of Hamilton's paper contained a reflection on news values which not only demolishes those of the present-day *Post*, but raises issues which are still challenging to anyone engaged seriously in media work. It assumes that the desire of newspapers for extraordinary events is due to pressures of the marketplace, and continues:

> Surely extraordinary events have not the best title to our studious attention. To study nature or man, we ought to know things that occur in the ordinary course, not the unaccountable things that happen out of it.
>
> This country is said to measure seven hundred millions of acres, and is inhabited by almost six millions of people. Who can doubt, then, that a great many crimes will be committed, and a great many strange things will happen every seven years! There will be thunder showers that will split tough white-oak trees, and hailstorms that will cost some farmers the full amount of twenty shillings to mend their glass windows – there will be taverns, and boxing-matches, and elections, and gouging, drinking, and love, and running in debt, and running away, and suicide. Now, if a man supposes eight or ten of twenty dozen of these amusing events will happen in a single year, is he not just as wise as another man who reads fifty columns of amazing particulars . . . ?

Strange events are facts, and as such should be mentioned, but with brevity and in a cursory manner. They afford no ground for popular reasoning or instruction, and therefore the horrid details that make each particular hair stiffen and stand upright in the reader's head, ought not to be given.

Hamilton observed that 'America' was not a concrete personal reality, but a set of measurements presented in documents, newspapers primarily. For himself he had not only outgrown Owen Glendower's sensibility, but had seen just how 'columns of amazing particulars' could be devoted to maintaining its existence: and producing an abstract fantasy.

Hamilton was a man of his time who often saw piercingly into the future. The questions asked in the first *New York Evening Post* are part of the technical background to the next part of our story, which describes Rupert Murdoch's alliance with Margaret Thatcher, and the further development of his political method.

8

TIMES AND VALUES, 1819–1981

For herein lay the most excellent wisdom of him that builded Mansoul: that the walls thereof could never be broken down nor hurt by the most mighty adverse potentate, unless the townsmen gave consent thereto.

JOHN BUNYAN, *The Holy War*

Man may smile and smile but he is not an investigating animal.

JOSEPH CONRAD, note for 1920 edition of *The Secret Agent*

I: Attempting independence

As often as it has been suggested that the acquisition of *The Times* and the *Sunday Times* by Murdoch's News International was made possible by political influence – the influence of Margaret Thatcher – it has been denied. The ministers in charge have said, plainly and to Parliament, that they took the decision on their own, and that the Prime Minister had nothing to do with it. Suggestions that the accounts of Times Newspapers were misrepresented continue to be rejected by News Limited spokespeople and by Peter Stothard, editor of *The Times* from 1992 to 2002.

We shall see how seriously these denials are to be taken. But the assets Murdoch acquired should be described before looking at how he went about the business. It has already been shown (see Chapter 5 above) that his rise to leadership of the popular newspaper market had more to do with the failings and neglect of others than with creative originality on his part. This is still more clearly the case with Times Newspapers: the failings involved being not just commercial and editorial, but deeply political also, and by no means limited to Margaret Thatcher and her party.

The two chief assets of Times Newspapers in 1981 were papers with distinct histories, the longer and more original belonging to *The Times*. It may fairly be called the prototype of all real newspapers, which of course is why the *Irish Times*, the *New York Times*, the *Times of India*, the *Straits Times*, the *Cairo Times*, the *Los Angeles Times* and many others derive mastheads from it.

In its prehistory it was called the *Daily Universal Register* but little of that is relevant to today's media industry. The period which most matters is referred to in an earlier chapter (Chapter 6), that is, the first half of the nineteenth century, when the paper's owners and editors used the most advanced technology they could find to free it from the need for subsidy, political or other – to make it *independent*. Between 1814, when it installed its first power-driven machinery, to the 1870s, when it was pioneering rotary presses and automated typesetting, *The Times* was at the cutting edge of its industry.

Some journalists – even editors – express disdain nowadays for the technology of communications, suggesting that their essential activities occur on some more elevated plane. That does not seem to have been the way people on *The Times* saw things under Thomas Barnes (editor 1817–41) and his successor John Thadeus Delane (editor to 1877), but more important than their drive for independence via technical advance was their use of it to work out a relationship with the governing power of their society. Their technology gave substance to the great discovery of Machiavelli and the Florentine republicans, that a free people may be, not a passive weight upon a nation's rulers, but a reservoir of strength. 'The enduring contribution of Barnes,' wrote Harry Evans – whose editorship of *The Times* Murdoch abruptly truncated – 'was to conceive and organise a newspaper not as a means by which government could influence people, but as one by which people could influence government.'

The vital element, a news staff trained to provide reliable accounts of contentious issues, was largely Barnes' own. Not much more than the

Prime Minister of the time, Lord Liverpool, did Barnes like the theories of the radicals who in 1819 planned a huge demonstration for voting rights at St Peter's Field in Manchester. But he sent John Tyas to cover it because the man was independent and 'about as much a Jacobin, or friend of Jacobins, as is Lord Liverpool himself'. Because Tyas, like a good operator, got himself physically close to the speakers, the troopers sent to disperse the crowd – who conducted the 'Peterloo Massacre' – threw him into jail. But Barnes got a report from another Manchester journalist, and followed it up in great detail as soon as Tyas freed himself and started writing. Eloquently, *The Times* denounced the fact that 'a hundred of the King's unarmed subjects have been sabred by a body of cavalry . . . in the presence of those Magistrates whose sworn duty it is to protect and preserve the life of the meanest Englishmen' – and its basis in fact made the eloquence devastating. ('Peterloo' was sardonically adapted from the recent triumph of Waterloo: eleven of those wounded at the hands of their own state died.)

During the twentieth century, discussion of *The Times* mostly centred on its leader-writers – its dealers in editorial opinions – but in that early zenith it was foremost a reporter's newspaper. A later *Times* generation said that Delane – perhaps its greatest editor – wrote 'nothing', meaning he wrote reports, not editorials. The famous leader saying 'the press lives by disclosure' was composed with his approval, but he spent most of his own time actually chasing the disclosures: revealing that the Corn Laws were going; exposing crooked railway promoters; devising fancy ways to get William Howard Russell's dispatches from the Crimea and the Civil War to London faster than the military could transmit their own information. 'The degree of information possessed by *The Times*', wrote Lord John Russell to the Queen, 'is mortifying, humiliating and incomprehensible.'

It is hardly enough to say that in the mid-nineteenth century *The Times* dominated British journalism; when Lincoln compared it to the Mississippi it largely was British journalism, and a model for much of America's. All the more curious, then, that it should decline into something which a hundred years post-Lincoln resembled a shabby ornamental pond more than the Big Muddy.

Central to this decline was antiquarian elitism. When the tide of low-cost readership began flowing at the close of the Victorian era, *The Times* offered itself as the least, not the most, advanced product available. It declined to compete for the attention of readers from the new middle class, on the deeply mistaken view that they were bound to remain passive spectators of society's affairs. Readers of *The Times* ceased to be uniquely informed, except about the views of its leader-writers, and the contributors to its letters page, giving it the air of a club journal rather than a commercial newspaper.

Northcliffe's takeover of 1908 was like a rich industrialist buying an old castle as a setting for country-house parties, and after its passage into Astor hands during the 1920s its connections with anything as populist as disclosure vanished – no ministers had to apologise to the monarch for 'mortifying' exclusives in *The Times*. When young Claud Cockburn defected from his family's legal tradition, they could only deplore his decision to join *The Times* as 'in the last analysis' going into journalism, and even that seemed overstatement in the Appeasement years. Of course the Tory government's contemporary spin-doctors bewitched the British press generally. But *The Times*' surrender was an especially abject betrayal of its founders. The paper's reverence for Stalin's USSR after 1941, coming so soon after the favours it offered Nazism in the 1930s, confirms that its conservatism was not political, but technical and professional: its design and layout and its reporting were unspeakably bad throughout that period. However, the radical triumphs of 1800–70 had not been political either, certainly not party-political; chiefly, they had been technical and professional too – in other words, the development of power-printing had allowed the circulation to be increased and revenue to grow, which in turn enabled the paper to recruit and train a staff of skilful reporters.

In twentieth-century decay *Times* journalism was absorbed into the Whitehall bureaucratic process. When in 1946 a story almost disclosed that *the Cabinet operated sub-committees*, the Cabinet Secretary represented successfully to the editor that such indiscretions hindered 'efficient discharge of public business' and must cease. Delane of course had thought his readers entitled plainly to the truth, not 'such things as statecraft would wish them to know', and on the particular issue of Cabinet committees – which of course were heavily used for the secret assignment of power – the present writer and Professor Peter Hennessy were able some years later to follow Delane's specification.

But, in spite of decay, the ideal of an independent, critical record seemed redeemable, and not only to journalists. Don Cruickshank, for instance, was a recruit from McKinseys in the 1970s and was briefed to rebuild commercial systems at *The Times*. He recalls a sense of being engaged in work with a national significance. By then, in late hope of wider readership, ideas were being tried which would have been daring in 1914 and timely in 1940 – running, on 3 May 1966, to a *news front page*, which asserted, with ill-chosen prominence, 'LONDON TO BE NEW NATO HQ'. After a half-century spent getting small-ads off page one, replacing them with such a turkey undermined the claim to be 'authoritative' – if rarely first – and cast doubt on hopes that *The Times* could learn by itself how to adjust to the times. The decision was made to merge with the Thomson Organisation and the *Sunday Times*, an arrangement which promised well, but went horribly wrong.

The history of the Sunday paper was rather like that of *The Times* in reverse. Its period of conservative conformity was in the past, and its 1960s and 1970s under Denis Hamilton and Harry Evans aspired to Delane's example (consciously, on Evans' part). When the Canadian entrepreneur Roy Thomson bought the paper in 1959, it retained the air of modest distinction it had worn fairly consistently since its launch in 1822. In 1915 it had interviewed Ellis Ashmead-Bartlett with results which impressed Keith Murdoch, if few others. Between the wars it had gained a name for fine criticism, mainly through the work of Desmond McCarthy, amplified in the 1950s by Cyril Connolly and others. Its reviewers could be quite feisty, notably the Oxford historian Hugh Trevor-Roper – though surely no one foresaw his impact on the investigative reputation which the paper would later develop.

Its great rival, and sole competitor in the Sunday quality market, was the *Observer*, which for most of the 1950s had grown faster, and looked like taking the lead early in 1956, when both papers were selling about 600,000 copies. As people recall it, the *Oberver*'s liberal philosophy seemed to fit the time better; the 1960s social revolution was visible on the horizon, but perhaps hazily to the *Sunday Times*. Later in 1956, Britain, France and Israel – in secret collusion – invaded Egypt to regain control of the Suez Canal. British society was convulsed, and the *Sunday Times* took the standard conservative position of war as a patriotic duty. The

Observer was among the contrary voices, which were few. In retrospect, almost no one cares to defend that dishonest attempt to grab an obsolescent waterway, but at the time moral courage was needed to tell the nation's masters they had lost the plot. The upward curve of *Observer* sales flattened, and that of the *Sunday Times* steepened: by 1959 it was selling 900,077 to the *Observer's* 677,856.

Newspaper circulations are often mythologised – as we have seen in the case of the *Sun* and the *Mirror* – and maybe Suez was not the sole cause of slippage at the *Observer*. The *Guardian*, quite as sceptical in its Suez coverage as the *Observer*, expanded its daily readership throughout the 1950s with no sign of a midway hiccup. All the same, the story is still cited to explain the fact that newspapers don't often care seriously to challenge the knot of power which twines around the core of any society, however democratic. Doing so is not the same thing as directing tirades against the political party in office, or criticising an entity which can be found well categorised as 'the state' in political-science texts. Nothing is quite so neat.

But there is a brand of opposition that journalistic operations encounter from time to time – not very predictably – which usually includes bureaucratic and elected power close-coupled, and may join itself in various ways with legal prerogative, an excited public opinion, corporate interests and perhaps a well-shrouded criminality. (A dash of cronyism is very usual.) Of this one can say it is different at each experience, but utterly recognisable always. Properly it is not state power, but it has no proper name. It is a remnant of powers which existed prior to the democratic state, and before criminal libel was defused, a primitive thing which never quite dies, and remains in many countries horribly alive.

In the British case, looking back several decades, the list of challengers is rather short: the *Guardian*, the *Daily Mirror* and the *Observer* can be included, and parts of the television system on occasions discussed in Chapter 12 below. After Thomson's acquisition, the *Sunday Times*, while keeping its conservative editorial column, both consolidated its commercial leadership in the Sunday market and became – especially through the work of its Insight investigative team – the most consistent British opponent of primitive power. The reasons for this were more technical and professional than political (which means, incidentally, that absence from the list of challengers is not necessarily due to a deficit of honour). They have to do with what began in the 1960s to be called 'investigative' journalism – a word Delane doesn't seem to have needed – and with the preference of Roy (later Lord) Thomson for having journalists develop journalistic products.

An ability to produce disclosures of its own has simple commercial value to a newspaper which only publishes weekly, and this has become more so with the long rise of competitive media. But there is a well-established philosophy of media work which inhibits development of 'investigative' reporting, by conceiving it as an optional extra. Charles Moore, editor of the *Daily Telegraph* from 1995, expressed this view when writing that in spite of his admiration for the work of some journalistic muckrakers, newspapers should recognise 'a higher aspiration than exposing corruption, although one that is perfectly compatible with doing so. It is to tell people the news, and to interpret it in a way they find interesting, honest and helpful.' This implies a body of stuff, 'the news', existing objectively and essentially uncorrupt, the newspaper's business being to collect and distribute it, perhaps remedying obscurity or urging a case. And like any durable illusion, it makes good sense most of the time – certainly if one looks at really well-organised sports coverage such as the *Daily Telegraph* offers.

But sport is a special, enclosed universe. The idea of the 'news' in general as having objective existence surely grew up since the organisation of sophisticated news agencies in the later nineteenth century. The vital date is 1868, when 120 British newspapers co-operated to form the Press Association. Today the lacework of agencies is developed so far as to enable broadcasters and newspapers to retail 'news' which they have little or no part in originating. 'Interpretation' may mean nothing more than the packaging used to put a brand image on a commodity which other retailers get from the same wholesale co-operative source.

Things were not like that when Barnes organised his coverage of the Peterloo Massacre. The 'news' did not exist for a newspaper unless it made its own arrangements, and they were investigative by nature. The 'commodification' of news – about which much more has been written since the rise of the Internet – isn't in itself either deplorable or avoidable. International coverage, particularly, would be impractical without

233

Reuters, the AP, Agence France Presse. But the fact that modern societies generate vast quantities of information which can be circulated without much contention over its meaning does not mean there is such a thing as the 'news'.

There are limits to the ingenuity with which commodity news can be repackaged and retailed (the decline of the *Daily Mirror*, seen in Chapter 5 above, had much to do with Hugh Cudlipp's over-indulgence in the practice). The limits are reached more quickly as volume falls; this becomes very clear to anyone editing at weekends, when populations have more time to consume news, but produce less of it. An obvious development for a commercial–professional newspaper trying to distinguish its brand is to look beyond commodity supply and develop its own material. Some of this can be done by buying serialisation rights and by hiring specialist writers, by advising about cooking, cars or investment: and some of it by 'investigative' journalism, which essentially is journalism in which the reporters are closely involved with the subject matter and share in the uncertainties, emotions and unpredictable accidents of which their stories consist.

In essence it is far from new. The American poet Randall Jarrell observed that when Queen Victoria or any of her ministers (like Lord John Russell) wanted to tell lies, they did it for themselves, as they had no media consultants; equally, if the newspaper which then annoyed them so much wanted to know something, it had to find out for itself (elements of the professional background to this were sketched in Chapters 3 and 6). In many news organisations the objective fallacy runs deep, making it hard to create a staff with investigative skills.

There is a story about a *Daily Telegraph* piece on the crash of an airliner caused by a fire in one of its two engines. An executive imported from the *Sunday Times*, toiling over the copy-flow, found two sequential paragraphs which contained survivors' quotations – and placed the fire each time in a different engine. Not even a 'but' moderated the contradictions. His plea that the conflict must either be resolved by inquiry or acknowledged in the text was dismissed as 'getting reporters to comment on *the facts*' (emphasis added). Later when a government minister stated that eyewitness reports were contradictory and would be looked into, the *Telegraph* quoted him. No investigative outcome will result from reporting 'the facts' in this passive way (an impoverished version of the American 'objective' method). The engagement with fact must be an active one, and must be selectively destructive.

In spite of a favourite belief of politicians, no radical discontent with society and its authorities enters into this – radical discontent applies only to the story. Generally, investigative reporting requires a confidence running close to faith in society's adherence to rational, impersonal rules, because resolving alternatives involves an imaginative (and often real) testing of evidence – typically, trial under civil law, which cannot presume innocence, and must finally choose a side. 'Disorders in relation to authority' interfere with this process, which requires respect for authority – if qualified and wary – and a belief that it will eventually honour its own rules. Anyone lacking this will find investigation's pressures intolerable, and shed them prematurely.

Related temperamental issues run through the gathering and training of staff. Many people will face real physical danger sooner than the social distress of picking at the lies of a swindler who troubles to make himself agreeable – as Conrad says, we are not investigating animals – and only slowly is it learnt that soft questions always have hard consequences somewhere. And it is then difficult, once a staff is trained and motivated, to exert much control over the issues it engages with. These tend to choose themselves. Something may be done by sticking to 'stings' and witness-purchases. But these in the end are only extensions of chequebook journalism, with the defect that any significant villainy tends to have a significantly larger chequebook, non-monetary immunities, or both. Though pop stars, actors and athletes remain vulnerable, their sins grow less riveting as readers grow less naive – the consequence for Sunday tabloid sales we noted earlier (see Chapter 5 above).

The real problem again is one of temperament. Any reporting risks damaging some of its subjects. But investigation, insofar as it is specialised, is developed with that specific intent. Andrew Neil – editor of the *Sunday Times* after Murdoch's takeover – tells us he was never happier than when leaving the office with an edition under his arm calculated to ruin the breakfast of someone rich and powerful. Three points about this are striking to an investigative reporter. First, you usually have something worse than a spoilt breakfast in mind. Second, whatever the stakes, they rarely fall so neatly; as a rule there's some sporting chance of copping porridge-burns yourself. Third, it shouldn't always be in a cause you feel happy about.

Nobody with an aptitude for genuine investigation fails to see that it ineluctably does harm, and only hopefully does good. And insensitivity on that score degrades the capacity for emotional commitment on which accuracy depends (see Chapter 3 above). There are few good ways to deal with this other than a version of the 'cab rank' rule used by the English bar: accepting cases as they come, and exercising little choice. A good team therefore acquires underdog causes, or gets locked into daunting engagements by being confronted with lies too aggressive to ignore.

People reporting the 'news' could move on from exchanges with the epic swindler Maxwell, in the way Tony Jackson of the *Financial Times* described:

> Some months before Maxwell's death, it began to be rumoured that his holdings in Maxwell Communication and Mirror Group were partly pledged as collateral against private loans. Since this was plainly crucial to the whole ramshackle structure of his empire, I phoned him to put the question . . . he flatly asserted that none of his shares was so pledged. As we now know, they almost all were. I was fairly sure he was lying . . . He was correct in assuming I would not undertake a long investigation on the off-chance of proving it.

The Insight team could scarcely have ignored the lies Maxwell similarly put to them – and continued meanwhile to make profitable game of lesser fraudsmen, wine forgers, negligent doctors and assorted gunrunners. So throughout the 1970s Insight's resources were heavily taken up by bruising encounters with Maxwell (who died without going to jail, but would doubtless have stolen many millions more but for being harried by the *Sunday Times*, and then by the courageous work of the author Tom Bower).

According to Weber's principle, journalism must have an accidental character; investigative work enhances the accidental, and makes it dominant. Financial costs may be less erratic than managements sometimes suppose (much of the material is naturally exclusive, rather than properties having to be bought at auction). But, if political costs matter, they are certain to be high. The investigative department, in its quasi-random progress, will pick up the state as a target (or part of some target combination, potential or actual) very consistently, just because the state and its limbs ramify much further than any other element of a modern society.

Choice may start things moving, but accident regularly supervenes. Harry Evans indeed chose to pursue the Philby story, not imagining there could be ferocious official objection to discussing the career of a man known already to have defected to Moscow and who had surely told all to the KGB. Then, with inquiries barely begun, Lord Chalfont, representing the ruling party (Labour) and the always ruling bureaucracy (Foreign Office section), delivered a ukase (secretly) about national security and the pressing need for secrecy respecting Kim Philby. The *Sunday Times* team would be prevented from (a) learning anything, and (b) from publishing what they would not be able to learn.

Chalfont's challenge, which offered no proof of risks to security, suggested the existence of a major story. The paper found many sources of information – its own contributor, Professor Trevor-Roper, provided much critical detail. He had encountered Philby during his own wartime intelligence work. Interviewed, he gave a brilliant historian's sketch of the secret world and its denizens, laying bare many of the deficiencies Soviet espionage exploited. It took, of course, many weeks and much travelling to substantiate the record of treachery. Much information the officials strove hard to bury. But often their earthworks were illuminating.

Secret outrage was immense when the *Sunday Times* disclosed that the Secret Intelligence Service had (a) chosen a once suspected Soviet 'sleeper' to run its anti-Soviet section and (b) made him its resident with the CIA, thus blowing both services simultaneously. Vengeful whispers were circulated that the reporters involved must be communists. One secret mastermind alleged that Kim's potential as a double-double was being ruined. The Foreign Secretary, flown with drink, told Lord Thomson that he might be stripped of his peerage if he did not restrain his subversive employees. The 'Cambridge spies' became icons in the literature of espionage. Certainly no harm and perhaps some good came to national security by disclosure of incompetence. (In those Cold War days covert political smears were basic Whitehall psywar, and probably did some damage.)

Philby became a celebrated revelation. The roughly contemporaneous story of national security and the seamen's union never did, though its keynote phrase – Prime Minister Harold Wilson's 'tightly knit group of politically motivated men' – has lived on. The union launched a strike which was highly damaging economically. Wilson alleged that its leaders were bent on leftist subversion – not on better wages for Britain's ill-paid seamen – and this unscrupulous fabrication, on the part of a Labour leader, gained swift media impact. The *Sunday Times* reported that no evidence of subversion existed, challenging Wilson to prove otherwise. His officials alleged that there was much sinister material up the Security Service's sleeve, but after tense argument nothing was found but hairy armpits. (One of the tightly knit group, John Prescott, later became the United Kingdom's deputy prime minister.) Official manipulation of news media often exploits the fact that a negative-proof call is always a dangerous call, and even when successful it is basically a non-story. But the investigative challenge – though far less rewarding than Chalfont's – was scarcely any easier for the *Sunday Times* to duck. (The *Daily Mail* also took it up, to similar effect.)

Over some fifteen years Insight developed methods based around each team member having an embargo over all copy produced in a collective task. Where evidence must be robust, consensual practice forms a kind of internal jury, and members of a group are bonded in the process of defining a common truth. The thalidomide scandal – involving children deformed by drug action during their mothers' pregnancy – showed the inverse action of this principle among the coalition which sought to suppress the *Sunday Times*' story.

Deviant power, as already suggested, is typically an ad-hoc grouping, and often some members have been deceptively persuaded of a danger to their own legitimate beliefs. At the heart of the scandal was a hard-hearted company – Distillers, manufacturers of thalidomide – but its most powerful supporters were misinformed, not hard-hearted. Judges and eminent scientists believed that thalidomide had been developed with highly sophisticated tests. Exactly the opposite was true, but Distillers sustained a myth by their own ignorance of their business: they were whisky makers dressed up as a drug company, like the impostors who put on white coats and are sometimes taken by doctors to be their colleagues.

Recycled regularly by news media – including at one point the *Sunday Times* itself – by lawyers and scientists, the myth developed substance, making the claim that huge injustice had been done seem itself like injustice by exploitation of populist emotion. Of those involved in the myth journalists were perhaps most culpable, having most obligation to be sceptical – to look back and count bricks. In any event, Distillers' coalition unravelled fast wherever truth impinged on it.

A curious intervention by Rupert Murdoch threatened the effort to win tolerable financial compensation for thalidomide's victims. Their pathos made the issue unavoidably emotional, and it became a national controversy. Through the *News of the World*, Murdoch secretly began distributing posters containing violent abuse of Distillers. This had the unintentional effect of seeming to give substance to the company's claim that it was the target of a conspiracy in which the *Sunday Times* and the children's families were involved. Fortunately the courts accepted that there was no connection, and the anonymous crusade fizzled out.

Though the *Sunday Times* produced great impact under Harry Evans, his precursor Denis Hamilton established the operating framework – one quite distinct from Murdoch's subsequent version. The principle was editorial decision-making separate from Thomson commercial interests, though like the 'Chinese walls' against conflicts of interest in banking it could not be perfectly observed. This made personal example decisive – equally, the 'walls' in a bank will be as porous as chief-executive demeanour suggests they should be. Hamilton, as editor of the *Sunday Times* and then as editor-in-chief of Times Newspapers, was rigid at vital moments, which allowed practical relaxation at others. Two cases – the ex-SAS gun-runners, and the Mussolini forgeries – illustrate his approach.

The first, in 1964, produced a backlash as startling as in Philby, but one which developed late. A group of SAS veterans had a private army and weapons-supply business, rented out to assorted political groups around the world. Their personal links with the official military and diplomatic services were enough to convince some Arab governments that this was the British state in covert action. Inquiries eventually showed the head of the business to be Colonel David Stirling, the founding spirit of the SAS, who initially claimed immunity from disclosure on the grounds that he was serving British national interests (his own profit being fortuitous). But he changed ground deftly when he saw that this might lead to the dangerous prospect of an official inquiry.

He then revealed he was working with the Thomson group on television franchises overseas, and that one of the companies channelling his military work was jointly owned with Thomson. The story was ready for press. Stirling, however, was confident that embarrassment would kill it. But Hamilton's only editorial instruction to the Insight staff was 'Ensure this has adequate display.' Those five practical words were more effective than any tract on editorial morality. Colonel Stirling was shown that attempting to turn his Thomson connection into pressure merely guaranteed attention. (He had also brandished his rank, which Hamilton, a brigadier, didn't.) Of course the Thomson group, which knew nothing of Stirling's military enterprise, had to write off the television investment.

The Mussolini affair came along, in early 1968, after Hamilton's move to editor-in-chief. He found that the Thomson Organisation had agreed to buy – for about £2.8 million in today's money – the dictator's 'diaries', depositing £150,000 cash (£1.7 million, as it were) before finding that, like the Hitler Diaries of 1982, they were forged. It was a rare case of a Thomson commercial deal done over the editorial team's head. By the time this was put right, the deposit was gone for good.

Amid great tension it was decided that, once Hamilton had taken a deputation with the grim news to Lord Thomson, the story would be given to the *Sunday Times* – but of course it would make things worse should thick whitewash appear on it. Just on press-time, the hand of Hamilton's successor Evans was seen to alter the correct '£150,000' to '£100,000'. Words like 'integrity', 'suppression' and 'prerogative' flew about, dripping adrenalin. 'Have a heart,' said Evans at last. 'He took it pretty well. But finally he said "How much?" And they just told him "Six figures".' In Roy Thomson's regime, this classed as significant breaking of walls.

A much fingered cliché says that the Troubles in Northern Ireland trace back to Cromwell's time – maybe to Finn MacCool's. In fact the province was largely calm in the mid-1960s: the IRA had officially renounced violence to pursue Marxist theorising. Political scientists and reporters knew that instability was developing, through Protestant determination to keep gerrymandered control of Catholic areas. But London ministers thought Ulster a faraway province of which they chose to know little. Then in 1969, without looking much ahead, they sent the Army to absorb turbulence caused by the Ulster statelet's incompetence, and the IRA reappeared as the ferocious Provisionals. The years since have desperately tested the military, political and editorial institutions of the British Isles – and the fever remains undulant, only slowly declining. A part of our story concerns the ongoing collateral damage.

Ulster for British news media took over, as it were, from Vietnam, replacing pages heavy with massacre stories like My Lai and harsh portraits of strutting US generals or bewildered politicians. Counterinsurgency came home. Suddenly it was Britain's own army being accused of crimes, against people who were legally subjects of the Queen. It was British soldiers being murdered by men whose relatives could well be neighbours of their own.

The *Sunday Times* and Insight were naturally drawn in because there were few 'facts' – little uncontested 'news' – about internment and hunger strikes, bombs in pubs, and shootings where some people saw 'innocent victims' and others saw 'terrorist suspects'. This did not stop servants of the media finding simplicities, though the frankness of one man from the *Daily Mail* was unusual: 'Why should I go and talk to some old women on a wet street corner when I've got a perfectly good story from the Army?' Insight assumed that in a cloud of witnesses truth could yet be found.

As this is written the Saville Commission is trying finally to settle the events of 30 January 1972, when the 1st Battalion of the Parachute Regiment fired on a crowd in Londonderry, killing thirteen of twenty-nine people hit. Catholic sources claimed that the 'Bloody Sunday' deaths were deliberate – product of a plan approved by the British Cabinet to lure the IRA into combat and decisive defeat. One *Sunday Times* reporter filed a story within days stating that case boldly, and naming the officers responsible.

Not since Peterloo had there been a comparable British event. Bloody

241

Sunday stands alongside modern instances like Sharpeville, Tlatelolco, Lhasa, Kent State and Tiananmen Square – small death-tolls beside Hiroshima or the World Trade Towers (eleven at Manchester in 1819; three or five hundred in Beijing in 1989). But their distinction is that they are instances of authority killing its own subjects when they exercise that famous 'right . . . peaceably to assemble, and to petition . . . for a redress of grievances'. They are characterised by a special sense of shock, and occur in the moment when hostility has not yet ruptured trust, before the descent into ethnic cleansing or uninhibited war.

Except that the government denied that such had been the case in Derry. Officially, the Paras had been faced with armed men who fired first; it had been a legitimate response to deadly attack. The *Sunday Times* neither published the story of murderous intent by Prime Minister Heath's Cabinet nor accepted the official account – though enormous pressure went towards legitimising it, pressure which extended to corruption of the legal system. The government set up a tribunal under Lord Chief Justice Widgery, and it accepted many dubious, even absurd official claims – such as that the Paras had killed many IRA men whose bodies and weapons had been spirited away by their comrades. By such means, Lord Widgery constructed a verdict which shamefully endorsed the official fabrication, and became a significant barrier on the terrible road back towards civil existence.

Insight, after talking with many old women and soldiers, after combing hospital records and examining forensic data, published a 12,000-word report which said that Widgery was wrong: that the attack on the Paras was largely if not wholly fictional, and their shooting was 'out of all proportion . . . [and] reckless in the extreme'. That at the time was a tough call for reporters to make against the Lord Chief Justice, the Cabinet and a good deal of misled British patriotism. Now, the Saville Commission's work – in the Ulster peace process – is showing that it erred only in caution. It is clear that the Paras had high-level backing for their Derry operation, though the lethality was reckless more than deliberate – suggesting that the *Sunday Times'* suppression of the initial story was correct (though the US Army in Vietnam might not have got the benefit of the doubt).

The merger creating Times Newspapers loaded into one corporate vehicle a noticeable part of the history and hopes of Britain's democracy – a significant proportion of the assets likely to work as counterweights to abuses of power. Their history briefly set out is a benchmark against which to measure performance under Murdoch. The protection available for the protective assets themselves was Britain's competition and merger legislation. This exhibited admirable principles and serious operational flaws – built into it by one major party, and exploited by the other. Most political systems have a tradition of appointing expert commissions (Presidential or royal) to find remedies for actual or impending disasters. When ignoring advice, legislators like it to be the best available.

In 1961, a Conservative government was so alarmed by deaths and marriages in the newspaper industry as to set up a Royal Commission on the Press under Sir Hartley (later Lord) Shawcross. Looking back to the work of an earlier inquiry (1948), the Commission warned bluntly that 'the nation would be in danger' should the control of major newspapers become highly concentrated. It found that some sanguine people thought this unlikely to happen – but said that if they proved mistaken the knowledge might arrive too late for remedy. The Commission did not say just how much concentration might be safe. But the tenor of its report suggests a threshold far lower than has since been overstepped.

Rather than wait and see, the Commission recommended pre-emptive action, putting effective restraints on merger-and-acquisition activity in the newspaper industry. The law already presented conditional barriers against the controllers of valuable newspapers selling out to their competitors. Industrial societies vary in their attitude to market-concentration: the British principle is that monopoly may be lawful if shown to generate economic returns which benefit consumers. But in the case of newspapers a second principle says that no increase in economic efficiency can justify reduction in diversity.

The Shawcross Commission's recommendations focused on practical enforcement of these principles. Naturally, there was little to be done about an economically worthless, irredeemably unprofitable title. Eminent or not, it would have to go to any purchaser interested. But Shawcross practised commercial law, and knew how flexible value, profit and corporate structure could be in the hands of businessmen and their advisers. The Commission insisted that in merger proposals *newspapers*, not *newspaper companies*, must be considered. Otherwise, determined sellers might pop a rich paper into the same corporate shell as a loss-maker, and claim exemption for the 'uneconomic' company.

The next question was: who should investigate and pass judgment on newspaper-merger issues? The Commission was certain it would be wrong:

> to follow the pattern of the Monopolies and Restrictive Practices (Inquiry and Control) Act 1948, under which an advisory body reports to Ministers but leaves the ultimate responsibility to Ministers and Parliament. The question whether a specific transaction should or should not be allowed to take place is, in our opinion, essentially a matter which should not be under the control of Parliament or the subject of party political considerations; it should be kept entirely free of Government responsibility or political association.

Shawcross and his colleagues recommended creating a Newspaper Amalgamations branch within the High Court, on call at any time to deal with proposed changes of ownership. This was a neat practical idea, requiring little in the way of specialised staff. The High Court has a regular body of judges who handle commercial and financial issues every day, experienced in commanding expert witnesses, analysing documents, giving decisions – and enforcing performance.

The provision they wanted was essentially simple: one demanding a pause for inspection whenever a sale of newspapers is proposed which will reduce diversity within a market. The sale may be approved, but only if there is no reasonable likelihood of danger to the public interest in presentation of news and expression of opinion. Quite often there isn't. Very low levels of competition have been allowed in local and suburban newspapers. Most report the town hall decently, and offer space for the community's disputes. What Shawcross proposed was a means to apply these principles when higher stakes lay on the table.

A Newspaper Mergers section appeared in the 1965 Monopolies and Mergers Bill, by which time Labour had replaced the Tories. The

Secretary of State for Trade, Douglas Jay, conceded that political decisions were scarcely acceptable. But he rejected the High Court scheme
because the issues might not be 'justiciable'. This was mumbo-jumbo. A
'justiciable' matter is one a court is capable of handling, and the primary
issues in a newspaper merger all concern the financial state of the businesses involved. Such things are the daily work of the High Court, and
were they not 'justiciable' the economy would collapse. The secondary
questions of accuracy and censorship concern – bluntly – the honesty or
otherwise of newspaper bosses, and a courtroom is one of the few venues
rigorous enough for that. There was no decent reason to reject the Royal
Commission's advice. It seems fair to assume simple distaste for loss of
political leverage.

The Secretary of State decided that in spite of Shawcross' warning his
successors would send newspaper mergers for examination to the
Monopolies Commission, which would provide recommendations for
ministerial action. Anthony Barber for the Opposition thought the judicial approach would have been better, but that all might be well if the
operational problems were carefully considered. Some of these were
apparent from the first, and it is hard to believe any care was spent on
them.

A recommendation of the Monopolies Commission (now
Competition Commission) is almost binding on ministers, but it has
nothing like the swift reflexes of a commercial court. It must assemble a
fresh panel for every inquiry – reasonably enough, since it may have to
study industrial products from antibiotics to x-ray lasers. (The newspaper
industry, if morally byzantine, is not in that sense complex.) And these
panels dissolve once their recommendations are made; they have no
capacity to follow up their work or check whether undertakings given to
them are being honoured or disregarded.

Jay said Parliament could not make proprietors maintain a newspaper
long if disposing of it better suited their financial desire. And his legislation foresaw that for unprofitable cases even the three or four months of
Monopolies Commission reference might be too much. Nonetheless, the
principle was supposed to be that a newspaper has social value – someone who has decided, for whatever reason, to give up running one should
no longer have the right to decide its future. And so the legislation made

reference to the Commission compulsory for any newspaper which could be considered a 'going concern'.

This at least was a concession to Shawcross. The going-concern test is a much cleaner measure of economic value than current profitability. The auditors of a company may call it a going concern – however worthless – so long its owners will guarantee its debts. But this has only formal significance. Substantively, a business is a going concern if its assets and goodwill are worth more when kept together than when sold separately. The one situation in which merger approval could be given without investigation was that of a newspaper with no such value – one with assets which would fetch more if sold separately.

The debating record makes very clear why Parliament did not give discretion in the case of newspapers losing money at the time of sale. Members saw that economic fluctuations, bad management or mishap can turn a good business for the moment into a loss-maker. Further, an illusion of unprofitability is easily produced by switches in accounting philosophy, such as the treatment of returns on equity. The going-concern concept is clear, robust and in familiar use by accountants handling businesses in financial difficulty. It stimulates diversity where that is considered the essential purpose of the market; it makes it harder to stitch deals which concentrate power in fewer hands. The law's principles had been refined admirably. But, without practical enforcement and public understanding, laws are readily corrupted. And nothing was done about that.

The creation of Times Newspapers Limited (TNL), to run both *The Times* and the *Sunday Times* as a subsidiary of the Thomson Organisation (via Thomson British Holdings – TBH), was the first issue for Jay's new legislation. It was sent to the Monopolies Commission, investigated comprehensively and, somewhat reluctantly, approved. Times Newspapers, it was agreed, would have several non-executive 'national directors' to protect the independence of the editors. The standards and undertakings involved then would have disqualified News International and Rupert Murdoch from buying Times Newspapers in 1981. But, had they been enforced, the sale would anyway not have arisen: the Commission was led to expect no change in ownership until 1987 or later.

Much pseudo-history has gone into alleging that the precipitate, illegitimate sale to Murdoch was imposed on a worthy Thomson management by labour intransigence, that it was the only chance of saving something of the trust assumed in 1966. The London print workers of the time supported some of the nastiest, least competent union officials imaginable. But suggestions that this was the rare – the unique – case of perfectly asymmetric industrial morals derived at best from ignorance, and more often from gross self-exculpation. The efficient cause of the Thomson management's fall was incompetence by certain of its leaders. Had the facts been known, even Mrs Thatcher's government might have found it hard to leave the fate of democratic assets in such reckless hands.

It must be quickly said that little of this attaches to Lord Thomson himself. By the time of the merger he was an old man, with much assorted success behind him. He had built newspaper and radio businesses in North America. In television, oil exploration and colour publishing he had found 'licences to print money' where others saw only risk. He had enabled the rise of the *Sunday Times*, and this was so great that it realised his longstanding ambition to own *The Times*.

The merger was not a rescue. For both papers it was an option and not a requirement, and for this reason the Commission was basically reluctant to see the *Times* business taken over – its accounts at that time showed a profit, which has never since been the case. Thomson was grilled quite hard about editorial independence, and about risks to the independence of reporting and opinion. But in this respect there was an impressive lack of anything to be said against him, and though one member dissented, the majority had no concern.

The MMC believed that *The Times* could reverse its decline while remaining separate. But the majority accepted that quicker progress might be made with access to the capital resources and publishing expertise which had made the *Sunday Times* so formidable. It was an attractive idea, and the downside risk appeared remote: 'Lord Thomson and his son told us that, if it proved necessary in order to keep *The Times* in being, they would be willing to put at its disposal the whole of their personal fortunes in this country.' The unequivocal sense of the pledge given to the MMC was that *The Times* would be provided with any necessary development capital, and, while no precise development plan was laid out, such investment would continue if necessary for twenty-one years.

No serious effort was made to fulfil these pledges. According to the *History of The Times*, Lord Thomson's real intent was to spend no more than £5 million over five years. It is unlikely he was still sufficiently 'hands on' to know that such an amount was altogether inadequate to make *The Times* into a daily newspaper compatible with the *Sunday Times* – and that so far from improving *The Times*' economics it was likely to worsen them, as indeed it did. But the Organisation's senior executives cannot have been similarly unaware. The promises made to the MMC, says the *History*, were 'reckless'.

Something should be said about *The Times*' history: this is Volume VI, *The Thomson Years*, written by the historian John Grigg (Lord Altrincham) and published in 1993. Like earlier volumes, it contains lengthy accounts of editorial policy-analysis. But in this case they are interspersed with highly detailed passages on business operations. Grigg had comprehensive access to records at a time when the Murdoch management, having been in charge for eleven years, probably cared little about the reputation of their predecessors. Few contemporary documents reveal as much about news-media management. Grigg does not suggest, of course, that Thomsons' financial loss in TNL was insignificant. But he does show that Thomsons brought it on themselves, by failing to make realistic investment plans for development of *The Times*, and trying to compensate for this by setting short-term targets.

In the last year of independence *The Times* lost £3,000 on its daily publishing and made £149,000 from its three weekly supplements with their specialised advertising (chiefly educational) and other trading activities. The daily paper's sale in the second half of 1966 averaged 273,248 – about 10,000 behind the *Guardian*, then six years into the process of turning itself into a national newspaper. The *Sunday Times* in the same period averaged 1,236,007.

Having assigned his formidable lieutenants William Rees-Mogg and Harry Evans to edit *The Times* and the *Sunday Times* Hamilton set up his overall editorial and commercial strategy. His objectives were a *Sunday Times* with more pages, and a *Times* with circulation comparable to the *Daily Telegraph*, then as now the giant of broadsheet dailies, selling 1,354,146. An earnest of success, he thought, would be raising *The Times*' circulation to 400,000 in four years; and he outdid his aim, for it reached

401,315 in the first half of 1968. This was in some ways more startling than the lift-off of the Lamb–Murdoch *Sun*, because the growth of the *Telegraph* and the *Guardian* was only modestly reduced.

It was also a disaster, which turned the small, break-even *Times* business into a much larger and unprofitable one. This was not unforeseen: it was predicted in writing by Harry Henry, the Thomson Organisation's marketing director. If a newspaper has any qualities – and *The Times* was a famous product – sales can usually be boosted by giving more pages for the same cover price, and this, plus heavy promotion, was the method used. But a 'quality' newspaper means one where advertising is the main source of net revenue: if it cannot be turned into higher advertising rates, larger circulation means larger losses. To achieve a profitable balance sales may have to fall. Henry warned that readers in the ABC-1 social class were too few to allow rapid growth in the *Times* advertising base with the *Daily Telegraph*, *Guardian* and *Financial Times* as well-established competitors.

TNL did not lack able individuals and good systems. By Fleet Street standards – in which MBAs and other qualifications were rare – its budgetary procedures and marketing operations were rather competent. But strategic warnings like Harry Henry's were met with inertia. Corporate self-criticism did not run to the notion that Hamilton, after many years of success, might have made a profound mistake. Both the *Sunday Times* and *The Times* were stern critics of incompetence in British institutions. But where the symptoms occurred internally the usual recourse was to work around them – developing, naturally, a culture of double standards. When Henry was eased out in 1971 his awkward perceptions about the condition of *The Times* went with him. Though his dissent was expressed in marketing language, it could have been put into other terms: emulating the *Daily Telegraph* was not a sufficient editorial ambition to restore *The Times* to life.

During the 1970s it became painfully clear that the Sunday paper needed much bigger weekend production resources than anything the daily paper could justify. The habit grew – it was scarcely a policy – of using casual workers. Few, naturally, had loyalty to the *Sunday Times* and some looked on a fat edition like Drake studying a Spanish galleon. A discontinuous workforce and an insistently continuous product is an obvious recipe for ruining management authority – and the authority of union leaders, apart from workplace representatives (shop stewards). But the mismatch of the papers made it hard to avoid – the more so as *Times* sales drifted towards lower, more realistic levels. It began to seem exceptional for the *Sunday Times* to achieve a clean print run.

By 1971 Hamilton was under severe pressure, and he agreed with Gordon Brunton, chairman of TNL and of Thomson British Holdings, to reduce himself to editor-in-chief. Marmaduke ('Duke') Hussey was imported from the Mail group as TNL's chief executive, and was vividly advertised by Brunton as its saviour – a perception difficult to explain. Mike Randall, who had been an able editor of the *Mail* before joining TNL, was present when Harry Evans imparted the glad news about Hussey to an executive group. Asked for a sketch of his old colleague, Randall said prophetically, 'If you're looking for a blundering amateur to run the whole business into the ground, you've got him.' Randall didn't suffer Henry's fate. But he was not consulted again.

During the Second World War Hussey had a short, brave military career, when it appears he evolved his social manner. He spoke to union officials in the breezy way of officers to rankers in expensive regiments (not something universal in the Army, and certainly not by the 1970s). One of his first encounters with an alleged firebrand was at a social occasion, and he took the chance to put the fellow at his ease: 'Merry Christmas, Fitzpatrick!' Barry Fitzpatrick, after a thoughtful pause, replied, 'Merry Christmas, Hussey.' Interaction never improved significantly. Industrial relations, in spite of Brunton's prophecy, steadily worsened. Brunton's path to supreme command in Thomson British Holdings had not closely involved him in newspaper operations. His colleagues saw him as a salesman, and he seems to have taken Hussey's industrial expertise for granted.

The Thomson assumption had been that *The Times* would be profitable by the mid-1970s, but it was stubbornly losing about a million pounds yearly. The *Sunday Times* could sustain TNL, but, peering ahead, Brunton and his colleagues saw no financial light. Even if Roy Thomson's urge to invest in *The Times* had been inflated to the MMC, his affection for the paper translated into tolerance for its losses. The Commission had been told that his heir felt the same. But when Kenneth

Thomson succeeded in August 1976 he made clear this was not so. From his Canadian base he put increasing pressure on his British executives to get *The Times* into profit. The deadline was hazy, but certainly closer than 1987.

In 1978 they decided that the solution was a dramatic, one-off cost reduction, by immediate, simultaneous introduction (a) of wholly new electronic print technology, and (b) of wholly new working conditions with enforceable guarantees. These would be imposed by a threat to close the papers down. In April 1978 Hussey wrote to the five major print unions with an outline plan. Redundancies would not be compulsory. But if any negotiations were incomplete by 30 November the whole workforce, journalists apart, would be fired, and publication cease until they were. The aims made sense. Electronic composition was overdue, and financial executives like Donald Cruickshank thought industrial relations were so chaotic as to make planning impossible. A fresh start was needed. The tactics were insane. It would be hard to find a parallel, though the Light Brigade has been mentioned. Management theory conventionally forbids tackling two complex objectives simultaneously. But that was nothing.

Hussey's plan as sold to Brunton assumed that financial pressure on the union side would become intolerable within three months – and then *get worse*. The facts were exactly opposite, were common industrial knowledge, and arose from the conditions Hussey sought to change. Many of TNL's workers were freelances, getting income from several newspapers (and from other work, like taxi-driving). They would suffer a reduction of earnings only during the first phase of the lockout, and would then earn more as other publishers raised production to fill demand caused by the absence of the Times titles. Hussey had got TNL's competitors to promise not to do so – for three months. Failing victory within the deadline – an impossibility – TNL would suffer rising financial distress, while the unions' position grew steadily easier.

Some of these print workers were unattractive characters (though nothing like as many as claimed by Brunton, Hussey & Co., who obviously knew little of them). But for the commanders of TNL to claim that their woes had real authors other than themselves was like complaining about Russian cannonfire in the Valley of Death. Amazed spectators saw that at the time. Grigg's *History* reveals more: when the policy of agreement-or-else was declared in April 1978, no proposed agreements existed. After Hussey's démarche, teams of managers and consultants began working up proposals for fifty-four negotiating units, to be presented to the union branches ('chapels') from October onwards – work, Grigg observes, which 'might with advantage have been undertaken at an earlier stage'.

According to James Evans, later chairman of TNL, its line executives did not think the shutdown serious until just before it happened, which is not surprising. Thus six months passed in supposing the workforce might agree – under a futile threat – to a set of generalised principles with consequences which were not known in detail; and these were replaced by an array of detailed agreements demanding total acceptance within weeks. Many of the first drafts were so clumsy as to invite – to compel – immediate rejection, even by the pacific National Union of Journalists.

This was a wretched enough gamble with just a business at risk, and not the public interest which had been trusted to Thomsons in return for fulsome promises. Thomson British Holdings was (and is) controller of many other assets with a public dimension: as a North Sea oil operator, as a recipient of airline landing-rights, as a publisher of regional newspapers and directories. If those operations had departed similarly from reality, stiff criticism might have been expected in the *Sunday Times* and *The Times*.

But the editors were loyally silent, having succumbed to the ubiquitous rationalisation about sinful unions and the panacea of cost reduction via technology. The unions were surely irresponsible. But the central problem at TNL was absence of an editorial purpose for *The Times* such as to make it viable in a commercial partnership with the *Sunday Times*. Two decades later, neither the unions nor any constraint on technology exist, but *The Times* still cannot meet its broadsheet competitors without subsidy – now provided by Newscorp. *The Times* was founded as a high-tech newspaper, but by people who knew that technology is only effective as implementation of an editorial idea. However competent a business may seem in its ordinary mechanism, chieftains inadequately supplied with criticism will run it into the ground. Media businesses, vendors of criticism generally, rarely keep any for themselves.

Brunton and Hussey surrendered in November 1979 and publishing recommenced with just a few manning reductions. They added some profit potential, but nothing to justify £45 million spent, chiefly in cash (£138 million today).

II: Independence surrendered

Meanwhile the Callaghan Labour government had been tossing on its deathbed, while the Conservatives promised new laws to restrain the rampant union activities which had laid it there. During the lockout James Prior, the Tory employment spokesman, was canvassed for an endorsement of the lockout's aim: he decided TNL's leaders must extract themselves from the trench they had dug. But *The Times* and the *Sunday Times* awoke to a new political scene, for Margaret Thatcher won the general election of 3 May 1979.

While democratic systems persist, no government does only harm. Comparing the ratio as between governments is contentious and beyond our present purpose, but it it should not be too much to say of Mrs Thatcher's regime that the good it did was damaged to an unusual degree by the way it worked and the rigidity it developed. Its media life was part of this, and is part of our subject.

Initially Mrs Thatcher, leader of her party, was also leader of an out-numbered faction within it. Memories of a later ascendancy often obscure the fact that the Tories who won the 1979 election were largely moderates, or – like the economic spokesman Geoffrey Howe – temperamental moderates allied to 'Thatcher's People' over specific monetarist aims. The True People had a vaster agenda, in which normal Tory urges like squeezing public expenditure were replaced by an ambition to abolish it. Their enemies were, famously, the Wets – to be overcome thoroughly, but without loss of purity.

Some True People were Cabinet ministers, like Sir Keith Joseph and John Biffen, probably her closest acolyte of these early days. But most were not elected (and often not Tories at all), like the software millionaire Sir John Hoskyns, who ran Mrs Thatcher's think-tank, and the columnist Woodrow Wyatt, once a Labour MP. Important among them was Larry Lamb – representing Rupert Murdoch, the *Sun*, and heroic inputs to the electoral triumph.

Murdoch's attachments to power are the natural consequence of an authoritarian disposition. But the method of Murdoch's mentor Black Jack McEwen was subtle: he selected among powerful factions the one where attachment would best supply need and most evoke gratitude. Thatcher's People, anxious to gain results and eschew compromise, needed things the Murdoch editorial technique could bring to the government context as well as the electoral one.

A Cabinet of course has a public form. Every Prime Minister makes it somewhat of a façade by cultivating subsidiary committees and ad-hoc networks. Mrs Thatcher, on abundant testimony, went far in that direction, building a personal apparatus congenial in terms of policy but unusually remote from the public structure she was responsible for. This created a need for customised media presentation based on torrential leaking: Howe (though an ally) measured the incontinence against his time in the previous Tory administration, and was alarmed. Lord Prior describes Larry Lamb's plumbers at the output end:

> Margaret developed a technique for getting the right-wing popular press [that is, the *Sun*] to have a major lead story on some matter coming up for discussion in Cabinet that morning. The headline would be something along the lines of BATTLING MAGGIE UNDER ATTACK FROM WETS. The issue would then be unfolded in terms of being pro- or anti-Maggie. The Cabinet would hold its discussion and everyone would say how shocking it was that there had been a leak this morning, which simply must not be repeated. An edict would go out that no one, but no one, was to give any indication of the decision which had been taken.

Next day the *Sun* would penetrate security, and announce a victory without contradiction.

Sir John Kerr had been glad to find in the *Australian* constitutional ideas developing similarly to his own, and Mrs Thatcher's People were reassured by reports of a Cabinet in which their outlook was generally prevalent despite the real Cabinet's unsatisfactory composition. And when reverses did occur, the method could still provide. In October 1980 Prior recalls:

at the time of the cabinet discussion on public spending, the *Sun* proclaimed: 'Premier Margaret Thatcher routed the "wets" in her cabinet in a major showdown over public spending. She waded into the attack . . .' This was not what had happened . . . When the *Sun* finally reported a month later that the Prime Minister and her Treasury team had not secured the cuts they had sought, its headline typified the view that Margaret was somehow separate from her own Government: MAGGIE AT BAY: Tories baffled as the battle for £2 billion extra cuts is lost.

'The Tories' – that is, the Cabinet majority who had voted against the cuts – were not of course 'baffled'. It was just the *Sun's* way of mitigating reality. Within this special political framework the Prime Minister could compromise without having to take demeaning responsibility for it.

It is curious that political propaganda should succeed more with participants than with spectators, but reassurance is an important commodity to closely engaged political groups, and forms part of the demeanour of the embattled leader. All the same it has limits, even in the hands of a team like Larry Lamb's. John Hoskyns in the latter part of 1980 wrote pessimistically to a friend about the Prime Minister's progress: 'I believe she is in a rather fatalistic mood, feeling that we've missed the boat on trade union reforms, lost the first 18 months on public spending. The colleagues, officials, banks, etc are all "no good".' These were early days, however, and Murdoch only had the *Sun* and *News of the World* to put behind the cause.

At TNL the first half of 1980 was actually euphoric because the papers had reopened with amazingly little harm, and the *Sunday Times* recorded near-record sales. All the same, command was reorganised. Hussey followed Hamilton to the sidelines, leaving Brunton, via the holding company, wholly dominant. With editorial executives excluded, James Evans, formerly TNL's lawyer, returned from Thomson Oil to serve as TNL chairman. If not briefed for a sale of the papers, says Grigg, 'he was the sort of cool, detached professional under whom such a step could more easily be taken . . .'. Distanced from Hussey's débâcle, Brunton was securing exits. By August projections showed that resurgent sales would not prevent a £13 million loss on the year (much of it relaunch costs). Then, as Don Cruickshank's financial team tackled the strenuous task of recovery plans for 1981, a strike was called at *The Times* – by the journalists, whose salaries had been paid throughout the lockout.

The folly was trivial compared to the exploits of the chieftains themselves. But it was as if Napoleon had trudged back from Moscow to find Josephine twined around a Cossack. Denis Hamilton's bitterness was all consuming. At the end of August 1980 Brunton secretly gathered a few advisers, including James Evans, for dinner at his Elizabethan mansion, left them briefly while he called Canada, and returned to say that Ken Thomson had decided to get out. Neither editor was told until 20 October, two days before the revelation that both papers – due to huge losses – would, unless meanwhile sold, close for good in March 1981. James Evans had found his detachment tested by keeping silent for two months among colleagues striving with recovery schemes. The editors immediately decided they would try to buy the papers separately. But the sale, in timing and method, was loaded against them – deliberately so.

Little remained by now of the undertakings which had once persuaded the Monopolies Commission. *The Times* had been ruined, not revived, and the superb *Sunday Times* made vulnerable. One promise had been kept: editorial independence. So honour survived for the moment. Brunton – assuming, says Grigg, 'unfettered power' – now set himself to dispose of that, by selling to the man who would predictably terminate independence. Murdoch was his choice.

Here the Shawcross newspaper court deserves a backward glance. It would have agreed the TNL merger, but with undertakings of legal force. And, as TNL breached them, there would have been no 'unfettered power' for Brunton: indeed, the law – undertakings aside – excludes the failed management of a major newspaper from selecting its next owner. The point may seem harsh, as the failings were unmalicious, the financial pain real, but it needs making because Brunton's bill of sale – dumping exclusive blame glibly on the unions – seized the right to conduct an 'open and responsible' sale of 'great national newspapers' by methods actually secretive and arrogant. It was unlawful. But the law had no protector.

Murdoch certainly wanted the *Sunday Times*. He had followed the suspension closely, and Brunton had sent Hussey to discuss its progress with him in June 1979. Brunton's close relationship with Murdoch was quite recent, and its context was the board of the Reuters news agency, where they were doing some goldmining together. TNL and TBH (through its regional papers) were big Reuters shareholders, and Denis Hamilton was chairman; Murdoch became a director in 1979, representing the Newspaper Publishers Association. (His tabloids had a few shares.)

Reuters had long lived – usually breaking even – as a trust handling world news on behalf of the British and Commonwealth newspapers which controlled it. But in 1980 it was commencing a profit explosion driven by the boom in financial data, and Brunton was among the directors wishing to split the trust and market Reuters. The Mail group (Associated Newspapers), also a big shareholder, sought to keep Reuters as an asset for the general news industry rather than as equity for institutional portfolios. (They were accused then of obstruction, though Reuters' condition today suggests prescience.) Murdoch was on Brunton's side – and eventually matters turned out the way they desired, though not until after the Times deal had been consummated.

Pre-Reuters, the two had been in contact over Newspaper Proprietors business, and Brunton suggested Rupert would be 'tough and straight' at TNL. Of course Brunton's adjective-selection would look somewhat exotic within months of the handover, but he probably meant only that he was doing business happily with Murdoch and fancied doing more. Underneath the adjectives, it went rather further: Associated Newspapers could well compete for one or both Times papers. And besides disrupting arrangements at Reuters, that could inflict severe collateral damage on Brunton.

Any bidders seriously analysing TNL could see an argument that two newspaper businesses had been bodged together in such a way as to breed a sickness affecting them differentially. The *Sunday Times* was ailing, but still robust. *The Times* was catastrophically sick – it needed to be sold separately as a title, closed, and restarted on a new basis. Few likely *Times* buyers really disagreed. Associated's Lord Rothermere said bluntly that simple continuance of *The Times* would be insane. Unhappily, Brunton required a madman. The papers had to go (and surely Brunton himself

257

would if the papers didn't). Deadline March. But *The Times* had to be sold in running order, to someone reckless enough to keep it running.

Ken Thomson did not want a reputation as 'the man who closed *The Times* of London', and he believed that sale to anyone intending closure – however temporary in plan – would have that effect. So, if no one saved him, he would close it anyway. This irrational precondition exploded all the nonsense about a 'responsible' sale. But it had a kind of logic if one took *The Times* to be not a real newspaper, but a symbol, a vial of reputation-concentrate. If reorganised, it would be something else – perhaps nothing like the reputable *Times* of London, and Thomson would get blamed all the more. (He had of course intended no permanent closure in 1978, only Augean laundering.)

Reputation is a peculiar commodity. If Thomson could sell some, there would be more for him to keep. It seems to have been Denis Hamilton's hunch that Murdoch might be a buyer – might take *The Times* as an extra with the *Sunday Times*, which he visibly desired. Even before the sale announcement Hamilton had discussed the papers with Murdoch in some detail when they flew together to the Reuters October board meeting in Bahrain.

At this time, Murdoch's public character was in transition. It inspired loathing very widely – most intensely, perhaps, in New York (see Chapter 7 above), with London a close second. Outside Australia it did not much inspire fear, or project an aura of invincibility. But outside Australia, Murdoch had not yet shown his ability to alter the rules of the state. Fox, Wapping and Sky were scenarios still unwritten. To be sure, he ran some bullying newspapers, and the *Sun* seemed to be a rising political force. But people who take themselves seriously often know too little about popular newspapers to judge them. There is something lawyers call the 'boys will be boys' defence, and eminent folk in business or politics often thought Murdoch's sins fell within it. Murdoch expressed a similar thought more aggressively: anyone agreeing that his *New York Post* was 'a force for evil' must be a 'snob'.

Of course publishers and journalists, like the Times Newspapers people, had no need to believe this. They could easily learn the truth, and even had a duty to do so. In a few hours one reporter with a notebook and a telephone could list the items of concern: Murdoch's cowardly removal of Rohan Rivett; his tergiversating over over television licences; his McMahon smear; his callous Profumo rehash (and its paranoid justification); Adrian Deamer's arbitrary ejection from the *Australian*; the raid on London Weekend; the gross political campaigns of 1972 and 1975 (first fawning, then dumping on Labor); the (literally) incredible Son of Sam escapade in 1977. And there was a live-study available: Ronald Reagan's 1980 bandwagon was on the home turn, and of its partisan outriders none whooped and hollered like the *New York Post*.

This was a clouded reputation by any standard – and darker in the Australian case, where fears existed that News Ltd's disregard for ordinary corporate restraints might be untameable. On 26 September 1980 the Australian Broadcasting Tribunal disallowed an attempt by News to obtain clandestine participation in ATV-10 Melbourne. Murdoch's company had operated through a subsidiary of his friend Peter Abeles' Ansett transport group. Judicial review had to be invoked to frustrate the attempt. The High Court of Australia then ordered the Tribunal to look behind the corporate mask.

Shortly before that, in seeking control of TEN-10 Sydney, Murdoch had given the Tribunal a famous battery of assurances which had turned out little better than those offered by the wolf to Little Red Riding Hood: the two instances gave News a look of frightening ruthlessness. As damage-reduction, News was preparing a case for the Administrative Tribunals Appeals system during 1981. It occurred to Murdoch, or to one of his advisers, that it would be a good moment to acquire some high-quality assets. As he was to say in his appeal next year, nobody would be allowed to buy *The Times* who had anything wrong with him. Brunton, Hamilton and their colleagues were not offering *The Times* and *Sunday Times* to Murdoch because his record was that of a suitable owner. Rather, he was a totally unsuitable owner who would look a bit better with *The Times* in his stable. This of course is not what they told themselves, but they weren't investigating animals.

At the end of November, Thanksgiving weekend, Murdoch decided to to go for both papers. He called Richard Searby QC in Melbourne, his contemporary at school and Oxford, now counsel to News Ltd, and in London Lord Catto of Morgan Grenfell, veteran of the *News of the World* and *Sun* campaigns. They would be the negotiating team. On

8 December Brunton arrived at Catto's apartment and was pleased to hear they were offering for both papers, with *The Times* as a going concern. Next day the board of Reuters met, and contemplated its glorious profit growth – some 800 per cent on the year – after which Murdoch asked Gerald Long, Reuters chief executive and the man considered the genius of the bonanza, to move over to TNL once it was secured. Reuters, apparently, had solved the industrial problems of electronic data-entry and Long was the man to transfer this feat to newspapers.

Here were golden prospects, with Reuters heading for a flotation – that had become Denis Hamilton's retirement ambition, to compensate for several years' disappointment – and Times Newspapers being restored to profit by Long's technical–industrial expertise. There could even be provision in the deal for Thomsons to share in the prosperity which had thus far been frustrated. December and early January were busy with exchanges between Murdoch and Thomson interests – but privately. Publicly, it was an open race.

Competitive offers were arriving, of course. But the only thing with real potential to unravel the package was the prospective bid for the *Sunday Times* by Harry Evans, to which threats and contempt were therefore applied. The power, Brunton explained to the editor, was wholly in his, Brunton's, hands. Was there no question of the Monopolies Commission? asked Evans. No, a loss-making company would be exempt, said Brunton with sincerity – showing that Shawcross had foreseen just how his mind would work. Brunton may not have wanted Murdoch exposed to any real test of just how 'straight' he was.

Harold Matthew Evans, then fifty-two, usually called Harry, had made the *Sunday Times* into one of the most admired papers in the world. An editor, said Adrian Deamer in an earlier chapter, needs 'a good eye', and this was a gift strong in Evans, combined with a vivid textual style and narrative sense. Some of his staff knew more about production minutiae, but his estimate of what risk could be taken with an edition was matchless on the big occasions. The type of journalist (not rare on *The Times*) to whom technical skill implied cultural poverty sometimes patronised him. He was working class by birth, and began his career without a degree. But he went back to get his MA from a good university, and few tried to patronise him twice.

His chief distinction was proven readiness to face challenges capable of denting or smashing an editorial career (a small selection has been cited). This requires not just courage – which in the plain sort humanity hardly lacks – but the scarcer alloy of courage with skill, sometimes labelled moral courage. Weber identified the accidental quality of journalism; skill is required to steer a paper regularly to where the accidents are, and not incontinently wreck it.

After many successful years the connection between Evans, the staff of the paper and the *Sunday Times* itself was so close that disposing of it against his resistance was scarcely practical. But, more than that, it had developed as the best available instrument for penetrating the armour around vehicles like News and drivers such as Murdoch. The unique opportunity Evans had – and let slip – was to interrupt Murdoch's progress, not just by denying him possession of the *Sunday Times*, but by denying him the freedom from its scrutiny consequential on possession. Evans has judged himself harshly in this respect. But before canvassing other judgments we should see how the odds stood against him and reach the endpoint of his fourteen-month interaction with Murdoch.

As 1981 started, and Britain's political and legal systems began to engage with the fate of two Times titles, the 'responsible' sale developed farcical qualities. These derived from confusion over the law and undulations in the worth of the goods offered. To achieve Brunton's aim, the *Sunday Times* had to be both profitable and not profitable. The October announcement had displayed no doubt: it was 'very, very rare for a paper as profitable as the *Sunday Times* to come on the market'. Naturally a decent price must be obtained for a major asset. The Thomson Organisation, though family controlled, had many public shareholders. On the other hand, huge losses were the justification for sale, and for evasion of Monopolies Commission scrutiny. Subsequent reports referred to annual losses of about £15 million (£40 million today) and by the New Year the public had not been told how all this fitted together.

However, the prospectus developed by Warburgs (now SBC Warburg), investment bankers to Thomson, was more specific, and of some quality. Its basis was a series of trading analyses for both papers, made by Don Cruickshank, who was both TNL finance director and *Sunday Times* general manager. His McKinsey experience gave him comparative skills unusual in the industry – he was a chartered accountant as well as a Manchester MBA, and his appointments since indicate ability (board level at Virgin, Pearson and the NHS; chairman of the government's banking inquiry, the Year 2000 project, and Scottish Media; chairman of the London Stock Exchange).

Ian Clubb, the Thomson group finance director, another chartered accountant with an impressive subsequent career (chairman of First Choice), examined all the work before it went to Warburgs. Clubb was sure of its precision: most of it came from audited years. It showed that the *Sunday Times* had traded profitably for fifteen of the past seventeen years, often in a feeble economy; only those years touched by the shutdown had actually been loss-making ones, and the shutdown had left its marketplace vitality untouched. The picture was of a nearly unkillable business, which in decent trading circumstances could keep TNL in the black even if *The Times*' steady record of trading loss persisted. Warburgs projected that TNL could make £8 million trading profit in its next financial year, and £16 million by 1983.

The prospectus was completed in November 1980. Assiduous efforts were made to keep it secret. When prospective purchasers had access, they had to guard its contents with zeal from any employees of Times Newspapers, and Evans obtained one only by insisting. 'Commercial confidence' was ritually invoked, but the document contained little which needed to be confidential or which should have been so in an 'open' disposal of nationally important properties. The primary message was that some stretch was involved in calling TNL unprofitable; to lose serious money, strategic misjudgment had to be applied (as indeed it had been). And that calling the *Sunday Times* 'profitable' was a great understatement.

But a secondary message undermined the entire basis of the Brunton–Murdoch deal, by showing that bidders who sought to separate the two papers had logic on their side. Warburgs had quite naturally sought analysis considering the two newspaper businesses separately and this, Cruickshank says,

> was something we had not really done before, because the whole assumption had been joint management. What it showed us was that the *Sunday Times* was far more profitable if separated from *The*

Times, and was a very different business with a different readership. It was possible to run them together, but certainly more profitable to run the *Sunday Times* without *The Times*.

In the relationship between the two papers as it stood, *The Times*' contribution to overheads did not make up for the losses it contributed to TNL. The implication was that both papers would be stronger with *The Times* operating separately on a smaller scale.

Of fifty bids on the table at the start of 1981 just a handful demanded serious attention. Associated Newspapers and the Sea Containers transport group both had substantial proposals to buy, close and relaunch *The Times*, and the consortium Journalists On the Times (JOTT) wanted to buy the title for a nominal sum and start afresh. All, essentially, were sighting shots, including Murdoch's – the only one ready to maintain the dubious TNL edifice. The bid entered by 'Mr Harold Evans . . . and his close associates on the staff of the *Sunday Times*' was the one Thomson and News most needed to neutralise, and in January Murdoch applied his personality to the task. The large, bearlike Brunton had been minatory with Evans, to little effect. Murdoch was effusive, attentive, flattering, enthusiastic, gossipy and (finally) effective. When he looked back at their relationship, over a period of acute distress, Evans recalled that in Murdoch's presence it was barely possible to believe he would break his word and 'away from him it was barely possible to believe he would keep it'. The courting display was of a kind customary with Murdoch, and Evans was ill equipped to resist. He has written that he did not have 'a settled view' of Murdoch's character; the analysis here suggests that Murdoch has little in the way of settled character.

In his years at the *Sunday Times* Evans had usually been slow to settle his own estimate where issues of character occurred. This was more than proper distaste for denunciations based on a half-dozen clippings: he was not quick in making use of others' experience. Evans had been a close friend of Rivett's; he was acquainted with the Deamer example, and in general with the Murdoch record. But the fluid switch of mode he had not personally encountered.

A reporter or investigator learns to trust at least some stories of wrongdoing where he was not personally on the receiving end; if he doesn't, the practitioner soon becomes another victim. But in his long service as editor this had not been Evans' specialist activity. He had been a friend, supporter and impresario of investigators, but not one himself. In the case of Robert Maxwell, Evans needed several opportunities to settle, by personal experiment, what witnesses had already proved – that every promise was worthless. Maxwell did little harm, because his furious threats against Evans activated other defences in a basically resolute character. Murdoch, far from threatening, asked effusively for trust – for co-operation, for aid. And Evans scarcely weighed the evidence showing that in this game there would be no supplementary chances.

Both Brunton and Gerald Long had floated the idea that Evans' duty was not to protect the *Sunday Times* from Murdoch, but to join him in resurrecting *The Times*. Murdoch made it a proposition over lunch at his apartment in Eaton Square on 15 January, and elaborated at dinner two days later, with Anna Murdoch and Evans' partner Tina Brown present. Brown thought life with Rupert might be 'enormous fun' (admittedly, by comparison with the later Thomson era). The tactics were gross. They worked – they subtracted urgency from Evans' own bid – by acting on his entirely genuine qualifications to become pre-eminent in the record of his profession: author of the *Sunday Times*, and saviour of *The Times*. Murdoch let him draw the picture himself.

In design, the Evans bid had never matched its potential. Its constructor was Bernard Donoughue, who had advised Harold Wilson in Downing Street and later investment banks in the City; at this point he was writing leaders for the *Sunday Times* and working for the Economist Intelligence Unit. Lord Donoughue's performance in the retrospective-occupation test suggests an uncertain guide to the kind of moral jungle enclosing Evans: later in the 1980s he prospered as a colleague of Robert Maxwell's, and even working for the paper which eventually disclosed it didn't enable him to grasp the man's dishonesty. But on the grounds that he 'knew his way around the City' Evans asked him to find a bank to handle the bid, and Donoughue found Morgan Grenfell, who were willing to work unpaid.

Using Murdoch's investment bank was almost as inept as it sounds. Theoretically, conflict couldn't arise because the Evans bid was meant to come to life when Murdoch's reached the Monopolies Commission –

and Evans, like many politicians and commentators, still thought that that must transpire. Morgan Grenfell would then swap the Jolly Roger for the White Ensign, while Murdoch demurely walked the plank. Realistically, it was absurd. Thomson and News clearly intended to beat off referral if it became a threat, and Morgan Grenfell would be joined in the battle. Meanwhile it made Evans and Associates look unreliable.

The prospective *Times* editorship having taken effect, another classic Murdoch display further eroded the barriers he faced. This was produced for the Vetting Procedure, a sad burlesque of a Monopolies Commission inquiry, which Thomsons mounted to reduce public demand for the real thing. It utilised the 'national directors' of Times Newspapers, the eminent non-executives appointed to impress the Commission in 1966. Assembled with the TNL editorial brass, they were to study Murdoch's character and – should it pass – negotiate with him a constitution for TNL under which they would get enhanced power to guarantee the independence of its editors. On the chosen date, 21 January, only three were available: Hugh Trevor-Roper (Lord Dacre by this time); Eric (Lord) Roll, economist, mandarin and banker; Sidney (Lord) Greene, a trade unionist. Evans and Rees-Mogg joined the panel, with Denis Hamilton as chairman.

Participants had to agree they would publicly support the guarantees if they were judged attractive. The trap could not have been plainer, and the night before Cruickshank and Donoughue implored Evans to pull out and denounce the procedure as a fix. Evans disregarded them, saying that if the guarantees were truly onerous Murdoch must either (a) refuse them, and withdraw or (b) agree them and be powerless.

The vetting became a show-acquittal of Soviet crudity, if gentlemanly tone. Murdoch's demeanour was submissive, and no question was disobliging. He sought to give the meeting a little of his background. Sir Keith had educated him from youth in the traditions of editorial freedom. He had not initially been able to afford the 'best and greatest' newspapers (this was as close as things got to a mention of the *Post* or the *News of the Screws*), but he believed he was creating one in the *Australian*. His respect for the two great papers he was now buying was immense, as it was for their offshoots such as the *Times Literary Supplement*. (Why, he had just been in Oxford and found his old tutor with copies of the *TLS* right back to his own time in the college.) Yes, he had heard of editors being given political orders or made to run vendettas. These were abhorrent practices. 'If there is anything of value in newspapers it is the goodwill position they have in the community . . . At all times there must be editorial independence.' No credibility was attempted: Murdoch's performance would have looked soppy in *Little Women: The Movie*, and was nothing like Rupert the Rebel, sacker of establishments. But on it the panel erected a media-statesman image.

On the constitutional question, Murdoch absolutely agreed that editors could be appointed and removed only with the national directors' approval. Was he surrendering power in this respect? asked Evans. Indeed he was, said Murdoch. Yes, certainly each editor would have the right to an agreed budget, and freedom to operate within it. Yes, he would be brave about legal threats. Certainly journalists must receive instructions only from their editors, though he would like to walk the newsroom sometimes to make a 'personal focus of loyalty'.

This was victory, thought Evans, though he was a tad worried about the ease of it. Next day, Thursday 22 January, at a rather rowdy press conference, Brunton, sharing the platform with Murdoch, Hamilton and Evans, announced that *The Times* and *Sunday Times* would now be transferred to News International 'as a whole and as a going concern'. Murdoch said he had agreed powerful guarantees, notably that editorial instructions could come only from editors.

He wasted no time illustrating the 'focus of loyalty' principle. On the Saturday he arrived on the *Sunday Times* news floor while the paper was going to press. There was an interesting leader in which Evans said the excellent guarantees much reduced any need for a Monopolies Commission reference. Murdoch thought it could be sharpened at just one point – and Evans wasn't in sight. Quickly he marked his proof, and handed it out for typesetting . . .

The vetting panel were not naïfs. They were used to trading points back and forth against resistance – to performance falling something short of agreement. That agreement and performance might have no relation to each other was beyond their experience.

The price was £12 million (£28 million today), less than the freehold property was worth. After £20 million aggregate profit for News,

Thomson would receive for ten years a quarter of the annual profit exceeding £5 million. It was a wondrous bargain. But obstacles remained.

A few days earlier there had been an exploratory meeting at the Department of Trade. Murdoch and his counsel Richard Searby discussed the Monopolies Commission issue with John Biffen, the Secretary of State for Trade, his deputy the Minister of State (Sally Oppenheim) and officials. Biffen was newly installed by Mrs Thatcher in place of the wet John Nott, but he did not have good news for her chief newspaper supporter. Grigg records that the men from News 'had a clear impression that the deal would be referred; the two ministers seemed unlikely to budge on the issue'. This must have come disagreeably after Brunton's confident assertions. Probably the officials saw no reason why a sound purchaser should worry about following the Roy Thomson precedent. But Murdoch had told Brunton all along he would not.

A Monopolies (or Competition) Commission inquiry is ponderous, as Shawcross had seen, but it is also daunting, once launched under the newspaper provisions of the empowering law. The panellists are recruited openly, with little chance of fixing. The question is mandatory, and must be resolved. Is the deal one which 'may be expected to operate against the public interest, taking into account all matters which appear in the circumstances to be relevant and, in particular, the need for accurate presentation of news and free expression of opinion'. Roy Thomson's failure to get unanimous clearance in 1966, even with a perfect record, put the bar impossibly high for Murdoch.

Though advisory in form the answer has an effect of compulsion. Acting on it the Secretary of State steps, theoretically, out of the political role into a 'quasi-judicial' one, which must be discharged 'reasonably'. This does not imply that all political decisions are unreasonable, only that quasi-judicial ones are subject to appeal, like those of a judge. Approval for a deal 'expected' to harm the public interest would be *un*reasonable, and reversible by judicial review – like the Australian Broadcasting Tribunal's attempt to see no evil in the ATV-10 case.

Most comment at the time was far more pro-referral than the *Sunday Times* leader which Murdoch checked over, but generally took it as optional – which it is for the vast majority of mergers. The legislation's compulsory nature in respect of newspapers – Jay's 1966 legislation sub-sumed into the Fair Trading Act 1972 – largely escaped notice. But Biffen clearly had been advised that approval 'shall not be given . . . until after the Secretary of State has received a report on the matter from the Commission'. Nor, of course, was there anything in Brunton's idea that the losses of TNL were relevant. That illusions of discretion still clouded judgment three months after the sale announcement proves the ill-effect of there being no active, non-political enforcement of newspaper law.

The Act provides for just one case in which reference can be avoided: 'Where the Secretary of State is satisfied that the newspaper concerned in the transfer is not economic as a going concern'. The 'satisfaction of the Secretary of State . . .' This was a chink through which partisanship might reach to give Murdoch and Searby a different answer.

Biffen was celebrated, as a minister and a Parliamentarian, for high intelligence and minimal personal initiative, sure to follow official advice in the absence of any overriding imperative set by the Prime Minister. Lord Howe's memoirs draw a wryly affectionate picture of a man for whom 'the word was all, action at best secondary and at worst extremely painful, to be avoided at all costs'. His skill in finding the words suitable to the Prime Minister's will was seen by colleagues as the key to their rela-tionship: Biffen, as Lord Prior puts it, did not then have a separate political existence.

The man the Murdoch camp turned to in their hour of need certainly understood that relationship. Murdoch was of course aware through Larry Lamb, if no one else, of Mrs Thatcher's strong regard for him, but their personal acquaintance was still slight. The go-between was Woodrow Wyatt, with whom the Prime Minister consulted weekly, and who considered it one of his duties to increase the number of 'pro-Margaret' newspapers. Wyatt's diaries record that he spoke to the Prime Minister at Murdoch's 'request' and that in consequence she 'stopped the *Times* acquisition being referred to the monopolies commission, though the *Sunday Times* was not really losing money and the pair together were not'.

The record is somewhat complex, but not open to sensible doubt. Wyatt began keeping his daily, secret journal – for posthumous publica-tion – in October 1985. The text cited occurs in the entry for 14 June

1987, not as a casual anecdote, but rather as an operational parallel in extended accounts of lobbying for and against Monopoly Commission decisions on another newspaper (*Today*, now defunct). It shows that these operations were quite professional:

> Rupert rings . . . the deal about *Today* is nearly completed. They are writing a letter to the Secretary for Trade . . . He will let me know when the letter goes and if any help is needed in making sure the Monopolies Commission is bypassed. I told him that Mrs Thatcher knows about it because I have spoken to her. He says, 'I expect she's spoken to David Young.' [Lord Young of Graffham was Secretary of State for Trade and Industry, 1987–9.]

It also shows the coarsely partisan character of the manipulations. In 1986 Murdoch wanted *Today* referred – to stop a pre-emptive purchase by Maxwell, a Labour supporter – and Wyatt laid out the strategy for the Prime Minister:

> *Thursday 12 June.* Ring Mrs T just after 8.00 a.m. I say, 'We don't want *Today* to fall into the hands of our enemy Maxwell' . . . I say to Mrs T that the reason why it should be referred to the Monopolies Commission, if it is Maxwell alone, is that whereas Rupert was the only person offering to save the *Times*, a number of people are prepared to have a go at saving *Today* . . .

For 'save *The Times*' one could read 'save Gordon Brunton' – other saviours existed for the paper. But Wyatt in these conversations focused on broad aims like 'having another pro-Margaret newspaper' much more than developing the Prime Minister's knowledge of media economics. The account of his talk with her on 14 June 1987 suggests that in 1981 she got the idea that both papers were unprofitable, even if he knew better. But without doubt he imparted to her Murdoch's urgent desire to prevent referral. When have we ever asked for anything? was Murdoch's rhetorical question to his agreeable biographer William Shawcross (see Introduction above).

On Friday 23 January, two days after the 'guarantees' procedure, formal application was made for approval of the transfer, with exemption from Monopolies Commission inquiry under Section 58(3) – the going-concern clause. Biffen had been several days on business in India, and was still on the way back on Friday. A number of those listening to Biffen in the House of Commons concluded that his officials were conducting a substantial inquiry into the *Times* and *Sunday Times* businesses during his absence – the basis on which things changed in Murdoch's favour. In fact they were wrong to do so. Sir Kenneth Clucas, head of the Department of Trade, did not look into the matter at all while Biffen was away, and the chief accountancy adviser, Sir Kenneth Sharpe, never became involved.

The financial data and analyses which Cruickshank had compiled for Warburgs were in the Department's hands – supplied by Ian Clubb, probably on the previous Monday, 19 January – and were examined by an accounting officer named John A. Knox. The figures had not been modified in any respect, and in both Cruickshank's and Clubb's view they showed very clearly that the *Sunday Times* was a most profitable business. (Obviously TNL and *The Times* were in a different condition.) No discussion or inquiry came back to either of them from officials: all relations with the Department were handled by Brunton, who had no accounting qualifications.

However, Brunton was asked to provide some further information – not surprisingly, in view of his public statement that the sale was 'as a going concern'. He contacted the Thomson auditors Price Waterhouse (now PricewaterhouseCoopers – PwC) and asked them 'certain questions'. Sir Gordon will not say how they were framed, as they were 'confidential', and there is no evidence from PwC from anyone who worked on the Thomson account at the time. The auditors provided a good deal of material – some of which Biffen later used in Parliamentary argument, though without appearing to convince any independent person that it was relevant to the Monopolies Commission issue – and in this they certainly included a statement that TNL and its subsidiaries were not going concerns. This must have been true from an auditor's viewpoint, as their extensive liabilities were no longer to be guaranteed by the Thomson Organisation.

On Saturday, while Murdoch was checking out the *Sunday Times* leader column, Biffen went to stay with friends in the country. Over the week-end he caught up with his official papers, but does not recall that they included anything about Times Newspapers. Doubtless he saw from the public prints that it had become a hot issue during his absence and would have to be tackled when he got back to the office.

On Monday the decision was made – without question as a matter of urgency, but disagreement exists about where it was made, and the Whitehall geography bears on its legitimacy. Sir Kenneth Clucas told me that it was made in the Department under the 'quasi-judicial' theory, and therefore cannot have gone to Cabinet, where it would have become 'political'. Indeed, this is the cornerstone of Sir Kenneth's belief that the Prime Minister would have held strictly to her legal training, and been quite above politicking such as Woodrow Wyatt describes. However, the fact is that it did go to Cabinet, showing his view to be over-idealistic.

There was a meeting at the Department in the early afternoon with Clucas, Biffen and Knox. Remarkably, Sir Kenneth says this was his first personal acquaintance with the matter. Neither he nor Lord Biffen remembers any detailed accounting argument – or claims to have been in command of any at the time – but both agree that the opinion of 'the auditors' was crucial (Price Waterhouse being a magic name). Biffen says that he looked Knox firmly in the eye and asked if he was certain that the words 'not a going concern' had been used.

If Sir Kenneth's view of this as the decisive moment was correct, one would expect Biffen to have Murdoch called in and told the news. Instead, Biffen went shortly after to the E (for Economic) Committee of the Cabinet, clearly without telling his Permanent Secretary. (Lord Prior recalls this occasion as a full Cabinet meeting, but E contains all the principal ministers, making it virtually identical.) Biffen told the gathering that Times Newspapers did not constitute a going concern; as he puts it, the committee 'considered' this and then 'decided that the bid could go forward'. Prior recalls that the Prime Minister remarked approvingly, 'This is a decision John is taking in his quasi-judicial capacity.'

The phraseology, however, Prior regarded as mumbo-jumbo. Like Lord Howe he considers that Biffen did not then have any will distinct from the Prime Minister's – Biffen's decisions were hers made in another form. Prior was unaware of any restriction on merger approval and feels sure most ministers were quite as innocent. He took it to be a political decision, cynically made to supplement the government's press support. He did not like it, but thought objection would consume political capital to no effect.

There had been no 'investigation', and demanding one would have taken 'quasi-judicial' resolution much greater than Biffen's. The auditors' going-concern language had been picked up from Brunton's discussion with Price Waterhouse and passed through to the Cabinet as a cover for a political fix. The Royal Commission's warning proved true: diversity fell victim to the lobbyist, and the Cabinet assented to the breaking of a law which it did not know existed.

Biffen could not bear personally to announce his change of mind, and a slightly resentful Clucas had to do it. Murdoch and Searby arrived between 5.00 and 6.00, and received the news decorously enough. Outside by the lift, however, Sir Kenneth found them rubbing their hands with more glee than he liked. His evening engagement was at the Australian High Commission, but Clucas neither understood his invitation nor recognised the occasion. It was the Australia Day party, and he spent the evening dodging Murdoch, who seemed eager to thank him.

Next day Biffen applied his principal abilities to a Parliamentary dress for the outcome. It was hard to show that the *Sunday Times* was somehow not the exceptionally profitable item Brunton had described for sale. He did his best with its recent losses, but as everyone knew about the shut-down nobody was impressed. The Opposition were furious, and his own side glum. Two Tories, Peter Bottomley and Jonathan Aitken, put in devastating attacks. But Biffen was resolute within his own domain of the word, and Evans, in the gallery, felt sickened as one of the world's finest editorial properties – more his creation than anyone other's – was portrayed as a wallowing derelict ripe for salvage. And when Biffen moved off the tricky area of profit and value, it got worse.

Evans had played a complex game, leaving others to urge reference – expecting their success to unmask his own bid – while staying onside with an enlightened Murdoch who, if successful, would give him *The Times*. This ended up giving the Secretary of State an invincible formula against every difficulty with the Fair Trading Act.

Biffen told the House he was not just clearing *The Times* and *Sunday*

Times for salvage; he was also protecting their liberties by means far better than marketplace competition. Guarantees had been given by Mr Murdoch, whose enforcement Biffen would now assume, as a legal duty for himself and his successors. And were they adequate? He would turn to authority greater than himself, for Mr Harold Evans had said, 'No editor or journalist could ask for wider guarantees of editorial independence on news and policy than those Mr Murdoch has accepted . . .' The Opposition motion was to compel reference. Five Tories voted for it. But the majority went with Biffen, as the Whips commanded. And now they could feel good about doing it to help a great editor.

The grotesque edifice was nearly complete. But there was a shudder in its gimcrack legal foundations which briefly appeared lethal. People on the *Sunday Times* had never thought their paper needed Murdoch. They wanted to see *The Times* saved, but noticed that those who claimed that the package deal was the sole possible means were the masterminds who had crashed TNL. The vetting charade troubled them. But when the leader-changing episode ensued, and was in turn followed by Biffen's performance, they decided – sooner might have been wiser – to investigate the law for themselves, instead of trusting the people supposed to be responsible for the paper. The task was deputed to four men: Magnus Linklater, the features editor, who had the widest executive experience (subsequently he edited the *Scotsman*); Eric Jacobs, who had worked for several years as the paper's labour editor and had negotiated frequently as union representative for the journalists; Charles Raw, a financial investigator of almost legendary skill and integrity, probably best known for dissecting Slater Walker's spurious investment empire; and John Barry, later defence correspondent of *Newsweek*, then the Insight editor – brilliant, mercurial, a fluent speaker and a fast student of multi-disciplinary questions. But without their paper they were only a band of private citizens. How could they take arms against legal abuses committed by Whitehall at the behest of two international corporations? Indispensable fortune began by offering a top-class legal team almost ready-made (a present any veteran of litigation will appreciate).

Arthur Marriott had acted for the *Sunday Times* as a partner in one of the major law firms handling its libel work. And Marriott (who became one of the rare solicitor QCs) had just then started his own practice: he could take the case personally without the huge overhead of his old firm. Immediately Marriott booked as advocates Geoffrey Robertson (later a QC) who was familiar with the Australian use of judicial review, and Leonard Hoffman QC (later a Lord of Appeal). All three had worked together before, often with investigators from the *Sunday Times* – it was a combine the opposition could not match quickly, if at all. Barry's swiftness in grasping and expounding legal concepts made him an effect-ive link between the lawyers and the journalists.

Hoffman in their first conference said the law was plain: if the *Sunday Times* had going-concern value, application for judicial review would succeed, and the court could order Biffen to refer Murdoch's bid. But judicial review, though solid in principle, was not then familiar in Britain. The case would be sensational, and no judge would relish thwarting the government. So an eminent accountant would have to be found to testify unequivocally against the Secretary of State.

Fortune intervened again. Raw called Gerry (Gerhardt) Weiss FCA, then Britain's best-known insolvency practitioner – and Weiss had been following the debate. Biffen's position was absurd. Weiss would testify to that – and having examined the available figures for the *Sunday Times*, he gave an affidavit saying that as the paper's receiver he would propose to sell it as a going concern. Were he to close it down at once, he would expect to be sued for negligence.

Hoffman said this brought success almost to certainty. On 30 January, a hundred *Sunday Times* staff gathered and John Barry made an inspira-tional speech urging them to stiffen their sinews, summon up their blood – and file suit. Only six voted against following into the breach. The application was listed for Monday 9 February. As the days ticked by, Murdoch could do little to save his bid – now laden irrevocably with prestige – except implore Evans, unrestingly, to persuade his journalists against litigation. Seemingly, Murdoch did not grasp that his own craft had achieved its aim of dividing the editor from his staff.

But as emotional pressure rose, fear, uncertainty and doubt worked hard for News, Thomsons and the government. Confusion about the state of the law was too deep to be dissipated in the few days available. James (rather than Harry) Evans struck a shrewd blow by taking John Barry aside and proffering the 'advice' that Biffen would only ignore a

Commission report. James Evans had enjoyed great respect as the *Sunday Times* staff lawyer, and Barry seems not to have aimed off for an old comrade's new obligations. With the lawyers actually on his side, he remained so gung-ho that they tried to inject a little doubt: unhappily, he did not reveal the chimerical doubt imparted by Evans.

Many rumours insisted that costs were ballooning. A TNL staff lawyer distributed a memo suggesting personal bankruptcy as a consequence of resisting Murdoch. Marriott had advised that cost commitments were modest for the immediate action, but the hectic process of documenting the case allowed no moment to circulate that information. Essentially, a brilliant campaign had been improvised, from several amazing strokes of fortune, but time did not exist to provide it with a clear-cut objective and chain of command. (With an editorial succession imminent, many senior executives were playing cautiously.) Friendly pressure for briefing from politicians seeking to counter-attack Biffen added more distraction. (The Labour leadership came out in support, though the print union bosses lobbied hard for Murdoch.) Eventually Harry Evans managed to set up a meeting for Murdoch on Saturday 7 February.

Murdoch talked with Barry, Raw, Linklater and Jacobs in two separate sessions. He was accommodating, but had only tokens to offer. There was indeed little to add to the guarantees – if you liked that sort of thing they could hardly be wider. He offered to add working journalists to the national directors. He did not threaten to win the lawsuit; he only threatened to surrender. If the case went ahead on Monday, he said he would pull out. And that, he alleged, would be the end of *The Times*.

At about 6.00 p.m. the four reported back to a meeting of some eighty colleagues. Jacobs, who had never pretended to be other than a cautious warrior, preferred to accept Murdoch's faint concessions and withdraw the action. Linklater and Raw thought they were reporting some minor gains, and that there might be something much more interesting after a successful application on Monday. They had not expected Murdoch to say he would pull out, but it did not after all impress them. They thought Jacobs would go with the meeting, which they assumed would vote to go ahead. Probably it would have but for John Barry – who, unknown to them, had changed his mind as dramatically as John Biffen.

Barry launched a passionate appeal for withdrawal, stunning

everybody present. Costs were frightening, Biffen would be unmoved, and Murdoch had made all the concessions he ever would. Murdoch was untrustworthy, yes, but also invincible – a great white shark, merciless and deadly. Resistance was futile. And he himself, anyway, was now leaving the paper. It was rather as if Henry V had made it from the Harfleur breach to Agincourt, only to say that those gentlemen in England now abed were smart fellows and he proposed to join them.

For a gathering racked by insecurity, it was shattering. Linklater and Raw were personally resolute, but they were men whose style ran to irony, not eloquence. Unprepared for Barry's scintillating collapse, they could not stem the panic it unlocked. Such was the dégringolade that no proper count was made of the majority for withdrawal, but it was certainly large. Twelve people voted against. Among many crimes they were accused of was digging a grave for *The Times*, so they had a Gravediggers T-shirt made.

Naturally Rupert Murdoch and his admirers see nothing regrettable in the process which put the *Times* idea – not just *The Times* newspaper – into his hands. That assessment is best made after looking at what Murdoch did with it, at what he did to the *Independent* newspaper (unborn in 1981), and at other consequences. But there are probably more people in the media business who feel regret or outrage. Our claim is that Murdoch was never invincible in the matter, and succeeded only because enough townspeople gave consent – in Bunyan's imagery – to ramparts being dismantled. Their motives were various, and some hardly grasped what they were doing. Sir Gordon Brunton and his lieutenants gave no real sign of a concern beyond placating their boss Ken Thomson. They produced boilerplate about 'responsibility' and 'great newspapers' but this can hardly be taken more seriously than a chat with Milo Minderbinder about the value of the Bill of Rights.

Hamilton was a great editor who had created much of what was now abandoned. He got the challenge of reviving *The Times* wrong; somehow the error embittered him, and became self-replicating. There were managers and journalists such as Cruickshank, Linklater and Raw who kept their heads and did all that lay in their own power to repair the defences. So did some politicians, particularly the Tory dissidents (that list, of course, includes Jonathan Aitken, as a reminder that none of us gets it right every time).

Harry Evans has said bluntly that during the *Times* sale he made the greatest mistakes of his professional life – critically, to disregard the warnings of Cruickshank and Donoughue on 20 January and throw away an invincible position by supporting the so-called vetting. The trap was baited with an ambition, but not a dishonourable one. John Barry only threw away a forlorn hope – but he did so by bolting at the prospect of its success, and if his colleagues had been able to foresee that eccentricity they would have saved him from the overhot ambition of leading it. Few speeches have done more for the myth of Newscorp invincibility. However, Bunyan's hard idealism should be put against the circumstance that most of these people were strung out after months of stress and confusion – itself just the racking up of a two-year sequence of catastrophes. Only at the last did it become dimly apparent that there might be legal defences against a political scam which they knew was happening but at that time could not prove.

For walls to be used by a city's defenders they must be visible and in good repair, as well as cleverly sited. Similarly with laws. If not, they fail in their aim of keeping within tolerable limits the quantity of moral courage society must consume in sustaining itself. Arthur Marriott had looked ahead, knowing that success in the 9 February application might lead to further action demanding large costs from members of a well-paid but insecure group. He wrote to the Attorney-General, Sir Michael Havers, suggesting that he take over the litigation, in his role as guardian of the public interest – the interest of how far the law might protect competitive supply of news and opinion.

In that role an earlier Attorney had sued the *Sunday Times* on behalf of the public interest in knowing whether the law protected thalidomide's makers from certain devastating criticisms (it did not). Marriott made no direct comparison, but wrote, 'We are aware that it is unprecedented . . . to assume such a role in adversary proceedings aimed at upsetting the decision of a Government Minister', but important issues were at stake which might be pursued 'in both the Court of Appeal and the House of Lords by the Secretary of State, Thomson's and News International . . . You may agree that litigation of this importance should not be conducted on a financial knife-edge, and should not in any event be aborted through lack of funds.' This was a slightly tongue-in-cheek first shot in a campaign Marriott thought might evolve in many directions; it would have been important to make it hard for the Thatcher administration and its allies simply to bury the *Sunday Times* protest in legal fees. (Had the battle been joined, Woodrow Wyatt's interchanges with Mrs Thatcher would have made his diaries even more fascinating.)

At this point the world of *Catch-22* is a valid comparison, though not through Minderbinder. We can imagine Yossarian himself giving a 'respectful whistle' as he appreciates the symmetry involved when the people protecting the media's freedom are the people who least want the media free to embarrass them. That's some catch, Yossarian might say. It's the best there is, answers Doc Daneeka.

9

VIRTUALLY NORMAL, 1650–1982

Most of what we are told about the world is likely to stand in broad agreement with what we already know, and indeed it is hard to imagine a stable situation in which very much testimony amazed or astounded.

STEVEN SHAPIN, *A Social History of Truth*, paraphrasing
Locke, *Essay Concerning Human Understanding*

News, news, news – that is what we want. You can describe things with the pen of Shakespeare himself, but you cannot beat news in a newspaper.

ARTHUR CHRISTIANSEN, editor of
the *Daily Express*, in a staff memo

an essential emblem . . . of those who sit in the top tier of the machine [is the] comfortable belief that nothing really serious ever happens.

JOHN MAYNARD KEYNES, *Essays in Persuasion*

Harry Evans records that during his brief editorship of *The Times*, which began on 18 February 1981, a memo came from Rupert Murdoch asking, 'I wonder sometimes what we would lose in all our papers if we simply shut the New York office down. There would be moments of loss, but they would not be fatal . . .' James Evans, Gordon Brunton's chief lieutenant in the selling of *The Times* and the *Sunday Times*, once looked back and said, 'Whatever you say about Rupert, he knows how to run newspapers. You may not like the way he does it. But he knows.'

Many publishing executives, bankers and journalists, assuming a sagacious air, have echoed James Evans. Clearly though, anyone who has been around major newspapers since youth and still wonders about keeping the New York office has a curious attitude to running them.

Naturally the question occurs in principle to anyone with a talent for the trade, immediately he or she starts training. We saw a young Max Frankel encountering them at the *New York Times* (Chapter 1 above) and they are formidable. News is infinite, resources limited. Obviously there are places where having your own people is poor value, and using the product of the news agencies will be best. But nobody, having once got to grips with news-gathering, wastes time speculating about New York being such a case. New York is indispensable, not simply for its own drama (which, to be sure, the agencies will cover assiduously), but because it is a space into which uniqueness from everywhere in the world is gathered, and where ten minutes of a reporter's time is likelier to have exclusive value than decades spent almost anywhere else.

This chapter and its successor, dealing with the clash between Harry Evans and Rupert Murdoch, describe a conflict between incompatible notions of what a newspaper is: between newspaper and pseudo-newspaper. On the argument of the previous chapter, Times Newspapers could have escaped the grasp of News had Evans acted otherwise. But that he admits, and it leaves a basic circumstance unchanged, giving a benchmark quality to their quarrel. Though someone *might* edit a newspaper better than Evans did before his Murdoch encounter, few have come near doing it as well.

At the same time, Murdoch's standing is also formidable, in James Evans' terms at least. Even if the rise of the *Sun* was less magical than mythology suggests, Newscorp still presents as an impressive edifice. Many people inhabit it, considering their own activities blameless and effective. They may defend, even admire, their boss. Many take Murdoch's part, as does the biographer William Shawcross, over his conflict with Harry Evans. They see a puzzled, misunderstood Murdoch, and a demented or self-serving Evans – anyway, one who, having mislaid Jerusalem, mislaid also his right-hand cunning. But the impressive structure depends in vital places on sham and self-deception; its inhabitants practise the form of journalism more often than its reality, and their failings are explicable.

There are other accounts of Newscorp's rise, and one of them should be eliminated quickly. Often it is cited as a sub-text of Gresham's Law, the assertion that 'bad money drives out good' – bad money, that is, has a Darwinian advantage shared by bad journalism, television, movies and mental artefacts generally. In news and entertainment, success and quality are inversely related. Quality needs support from grubbier products. You may not like it, but it works. And some like it. Murdoch's supporters don't contest the law structurally. Rather, they recalibrate quality – like Gerald Long telling people at the *Sunday Times* that Rupert would be unhappy if they failed to see 'excellence' in the *Sun*.

Gresham has many followers. One can find a commercial director of the *Observer* saying that its rising quality 'of course' will not improve sales, or the Director of the National Centre for Social Research saying that the 'economic principle' of Gresham's Law gives bad survey research competitive advantages over good. A British Cabinet veteran (Roy Hattersley) says that under a Gresham's Law of Politics edifying speeches are expelled by crude appeals to self-interest, another (Chris Smith) that suitable policies may one day reverse the Gresham effect.

Thomas Gresham, goldsmith, and adviser to Elizabeth I, was interested in currencies, but he left us no 'law'. Henry Dunning MacLeod's *Elements of Political Economy* (1858) stated in Gresham's name that 'where two media of exchange come into circulation together the more valuable will tend to disappear'. Or: if coins of identical face-value contain different amounts of gold, those with more will be melted and sold for cash. Someone who called Adam Smith and Ricardo 'worthless' surely wasn't all bad, but he was barking up an insignificant tree. The philosopher R. G. Collingwood pointed out that 'The "best" money, in the sense in which Gresham's Law uses the term, is the worst' because, to the extent that it has value other than symbolic, it isn't money, but a commodity. Some museums exhibit old Malay money consisting of tiny cannon: if rejected as coin, they might still enforce transactions. But, once in action as weapons, they must have lost exchange-value.

MacLeod's Observation – obsolete in a world of electronic cash – does not prove that bad newspapers enjoy natural advantage over good ones. It only restates the Mencken sneer as pseudo-economics. It was well established in the 1980s as a moral parachute for journalists – who can be blamed for obeying a law? – and a camouflage for bankers, who often dislike newspapers for what is best in them. The idea of television going inevitably bad is more recent – at least in Britain, which long believed that television could and should be good. Gresham is useful only because Collingwood's refutation prompts us to look carefully at what news media actually do.

The starting point is that most editions even of a good newspaper are mediocre, with dull news and commonplace features. Arthur Christiansen rightly says – in one of the epigraphs to this chapter – that you cannot beat news in a newspaper. But Shapin, following Locke, is also right that there is never much of it about; news media are the product of stable industrial societies, and where stability exists not much can be astonishing. And then Keynes points out that the important people may ignore such examples as exist. For these three reasons – as honest professionals know but rarely say – what appears mostly is a virtual newspaper, a simulacrum of the real, rare product.

Administrative, financial and cultural difficulties follow – for one reason, because our rationalistic business models assume an intent to produce steady flows of products, each of consistent quality, with use of resources optimised. Clearly cars, computers, butter and lampshades are made in such a way. The car business would look different if only rare uses involved a genuine automobile. Circulation records prove, by their limited volatility, that newspaper sales generally are not transactions over a single issue. But, while this readership patience helps, news media remain a trickier management problem than cars or lamps. A world which allowed newspapers to optimise both content and production would be too contrary to exist.

Obviously enough news is a break from some kind of pattern, and the fact that the pattern shifts does not say otherwise – it illuminates the point, and the problems which go with it. In Britain, for instance, child murder has become in recent decades exceptionally rare – and therefore more newsworthy. The exceptional coverage of child murder then creates false perceptions of the crime itself becoming more frequent. For some of us, covering Northern Ireland was wretched in a reverse sense: as deaths increased in number, their news value declined. And the Nobel economics laureate Amartya Sen has drawn attention to the news value of starvation. Spectacular justification for the First Amendment principle exists in the fact that true famine – as in China in 1959–61 – has never afflicted a nation with free media. But, as he says, self-congratulation should be sparing. Regular malnutrition persists, dully, in places where the media are free.

News media, like life insurance, are offspring of the Age of Normality, with its roots in the seventeenth century, its flowering in the eighteenth and nineteenth centuries, and its seeming dominion in the present. But they bear traces of belief-systems vastly older. Earlier times had weaker, unformalised notions of the normal and the probable. Physical stability was exceptional even for the rich. People lived amid bizarre, millennial events – assumed commonly to be under occult control. When St Augustine wrote *On Christian Teaching*, he included a detailed, coldly logical attack on astrology. Today, that would be an eccentric act for a famous intellectual analyst, but in the fifth century people's lives could be badly damaged by astrological hokum. Stargazing for us has minimal resonance; not even with the support of Nancy Reagan (or, in his desperation, Larry Lamb) can it much influence affairs. But newspapers offer it still – reminding us that communications systems maintain as well as explode delusions.

Shakespeare, in early-modern times, created people of both occult and rationalistic disposition:

> GLENDOWER. . . . At my nativity
> The font of heaven was full of fiery shapes,
> Of burning cressets; and at my birth
> The frame and huge foundation of the earth
> Shak'd like a coward.

HOTSPUR. Why, so it would have done at the same season, if your mother's cat had but kittened, though yourself had never been born.

Hotspur's is the dry tone of social science – the intelligent ruling-class citizen of our epigraph from Keynes – saying: I think you will find there really is no substantial problem. Shakespeare (like Keynes) doubtless

283

penetrated both illusions, as Hotspur's rationalism doesn't avert a sticky end.

For normality, though useful, and now ubiquitous, is not a profound conception. Around 1830, as the West's love affair with data-collection gained pace, Carl Friedrich Gauss assembled several mathematical tools developed in the previous century to create the 'normal' distribution and its famous – or infamous – 'bell-curve'. Gauss himself did not rank this among the works which bracket him with Newton and Archimedes. By his account, it might almost be called the 'trivial' distribution. It is the mathematics of the case with little news, in which hearts beat evenly, breathing is automatic, and atmospheric CO_2 harmless – in which the government is not being entirely truthful, but isn't shooting anyone.

It relates the *average* (mean) of a series of observations to the variance within it, and says that if most instances fall inside a range based on the square root of the variance, then they may be taken to delineate a real process, and the 'outliers' ignored. Gauss wanted a rough-and-ready way to decide that *this* is forest, *this* a negligible tree (to remove trivial errors from a particularly boring survey task he had been stuck with). Society has made altogether more of it.

Gauss and his mathematicians rendered the physical and social worlds tractable, by showing that an aggregate – the molecules of a fluid, the citizens of a nation, the readers of a newspaper – may be well understood without much knowledge of its individual components. For physicists and engineers, statistical mechanics and the allied disciplines based on this discovery underpin all our productive technologies. And social scientists commonly refer to 'the law of large numbers': no one can imagine a modern state without it; no one can avoid the impact Adolphe Quetelet's *Treatise on Man* created by persuading us to be governed according to Gaussian principles, with trends and circumstances universally sampled, predicted and managed, 'much as we can enumerate in advance the births and deaths that should occur'.

In *A Mathematician Reads the Newspaper*, Professor John Allen Paulos observed that Quetelet's proposal of 1842, since its great welcome by the Victorian administrators, now 'applies to sociology, sports, sex, political science, and economics, which may be thought of as a kind of social statistical mechanics'. Complaint and controversy has naturally accompanied its march, and its effect on our beliefs about facts and news. The assumption that data conforming to a bell-curve *must* represent a reality – such as a racial deficit in intelligence – has had to be refuted (for Gauss only said may, not must). Reporters clinging to older ways often refuse to see street gossip as inferior to an opinion-pollster's random sample. Mostly they're wrong – but not always, for Quetelet claimed too much, saying:

> we pass from one year to another with the sad perspective of seeing the same crimes reproduced in the same order . . . Sad condition of humanity! The part of prisons, of irons, and of the scaffold seem fixed . . . as much as the revenue of the state. We might enumerate in advance how many individuals will stain their hands in the blood of their fellows . . .

And we might get it badly wrong. The 'law of large numbers', in many contexts – especially the human – is only a sophisticated rule-of-thumb, and is not ineluctable. The modern Central Limit Theorem creates such a law, but that applies *only* to a universe of identical, totally independent agents – nothing like the place we inhabit, which under normality's mask, the artefact of our technologies, remains as weird and mysterious as ever.

Quetelet's heirs overstate both the continuity of affairs and the fixity of norms – neither taxes nor murderers are just what they were in 1842. The revenue of the state is bigger precisely because the predictive methods he advocated enable it to perform functions it once could not. Consequently, a real news business lives with a conundrum it never quite solves. It must recognise that there are scarcely any events which properly cause amazement or shock – without reclining into the fantasy that nothing, after all, does occur. Indeed, it must chase tirelessly after authentic disclosures – the more spectacularly important because of their rarity. It is a strenuous process and costly, though not always in monetary terms.

None reaches a complete solution. Some, for assorted reasons, don't try. These are pseudo-newspapers, and, to take an obvious case first, most tabloids answer the description. To say the *New York Post*'s belief-system is obsolete isn't enough. Under Murdoch, it has regressed to the condition of Owen Glendower (boasting about its founder, Alexander Hamilton, but ignoring his thought).

Very often Northcliffe's solution is taken, defining news as 'anything out of the ordinary' – though it was obsolescent when Northcliffe coined it about a century ago. It may look straightforward. When a child is abducted, sexually assaulted and murdered, the instance is 'out of the ordinary' in that virtually all children spend virtually all their time without suffering such tragedy. But murder as an event, even of a child, is ordinary – Quetelet got that right – and furthermore is rare. All the same, a sizeable human aggregate, or catchment area, will offer a flow of instances. These, provided nothing is said about scale and proportion, can be projected as matters of concern across the entire catchment area: the public will quickly imagine a matching population of murderers, and pack its schoolchildren into cars by way of safeguard.

A trade in news may thus be driven by gathering it on one human scale and distributing it on another. And for a title – how about *News of the World*? Moral glosses for this business are often sagaciously crafted, along the lines that every individual counts, and didn't the poet say the bell tolls for everyone equally? But the tabloid trade would look different if it took Donne's bell seriously and believed that 'all mankind is of one author, and is one volume . . . because I am involved in mankind'.

Assembling packages of pseudo-news is straightforward, particularly in a centralised society with an uninhibited agency trade – the British case supremely. While labelling rules control beer and sausages, newspaper producers apply 'the freedom of the press' and say nothing about their ingredients. It does not really need the talents of Hugh Cudlipp or Larry Lamb to marshal some commodity news and spike it lightly with exceptional items to make a 'virtual' newspaper which – unless some real news turns up for comparison – can be distinguished from the genuine article only by expert scrutiny. It will seem to be all action. But most of its testimony will be in broad agreement with what we already know, and anything amazing or astounding is likely to have the character of voyeurism.

Competitive markets assume that consumers can estimate the utility of what they buy, and this may well produce quick feedback when a product is used regularly for its main purpose. Cars do get driven – a product which merely resembled a car could not survive for long. But, if cars were driven just rarely, some ingenious constructor might well produce pseudo-cars, or virtual cars, with much reduced effort. And the condition applies to news media, especially newspapers – as a condition of their existence. Problems would arise with pseudo-cars once they were actually driven. But, depending on the frequency of these journeys, this might not trouble an adroit manufacturer, enjoying an easier life and better net revenue while more earnest souls sweated over genuine engines and suspension. Of course the market overall might decline, as customers became forgetful of the real driving experience.

And this we find in newspaper markets which Murdoch dominates. Typically Murdoch achieves increased market share – and frequently high net revenue – within markets suffering overall decline. Some crucial Newscorp titles are in absolute as well as relative decline, such as the *News of the Screws*. Not Gresham's Law. Just demand and supply, moving rather ponderously.

But the pseudo-newspaper can have a less frenzied manifestation than the tabloid one. The Quetelet world is awash in data, of which a good deal has to be processed – for lack of closer knowledge – under the head 'news'. John Bigelow was quoted observing that the stuff got rather out of hand with 'the construction of the telegraph'. Little of this is news in the sense of astounding – not even the chunks consisting of sports results, celebrity interviews, stock prices and government handouts (as against traffic signs, sewage-purification records and raw census returns). But the most extensive labour in a news business is handling it. Consequently it may seem the essential part. Human organisations readily assume that what they mostly do is what mostly matters, even all that matters – and sometimes they are right to make that assumption. But there are counter-examples, like the Victorian Royal Navy, which laboured so at beautifying its ships that gunnery practice declined into ceremony. This makes newspaper-like stuff – the supposedly objective 'news' discussed in the last chapter – but does not make newspapers. It has long been possible to disseminate it without them, and becomes more so with each extension of the Internet.

If news is abnormality, would it make sense to produce a newspaper only when there is something abnormal to report? No, because the norm requires active maintenance – something has been said in Chapter 3 of the newsroom procedures involved. The ground-bass message of a well-run newspaper has to be 'NO CHANGE TODAY' in order to make the exception recognisable: 'BIG NEWS TODAY: EVERYTHING CHANGED'. And these of course are only ideal statements. In practice there must be a scale with well-understood intervals. In the commercial–professional newspaper a display scale is not a decoration or a frivolity, but – as Christiansen showed – the message-bearing integument.

When Harry Evans took over *The Times*, the chief influence on its twentieth-century design was still the typographer Stanley Morison, who made the absurd claim that a 'scrupulously conducted' paper must not extend a headline across more than one column. It prevented the paper developing an efficient headline style, and the attempt to do without attracted a famous parody:

SMALL EARTHQUAKE

IN CHILE:

NOT MANY KILLED

The effect of Morison's rule was to prevent anything serious happening in *The Times*.

Real news is not something out of the ordinary. It is a change in the meaning of ordinary, a crack in normality's mask. The epigraphs heading this chapter inspect the issue of novelty – of news – from three viewpoints. Shapin's *Social History of Truth* describes natural scientists (specifically the early members of the Royal Society) developing the first reliable means to separate rare, amazing truths from fables and travellers' lies. The story has many threads: the equal necessity of trust and scepticism; the design of etiquettes to distinguish challenges to veracity from challenges to honour (or duels). Along with some borrowings from law, this is the foundation of the investigative method. It contains the paradox of discovery – knowing that not many things are astonishing has enabled us to penetrate some way into those which are.

Arthur Christiansen was a pioneer in the business of selling news and had some of his most effective years (1930s through 1950s) when newspapers were small and the world almost intolerably newsworthy. Even so, he wanted more than he could get. He represents an industrial need for novelty, and the techniques he devised to make the most of events might be assembled – in their corrupted form – as a *Social History of Untruth*, in which obsolete belief-systems live on.

Keynes' remark is about novelty and the governing class – in which he was a visiting member. These are the people diligent enough to master the administrative systems derived from Quetelet, for whom news is at least a nuisance, and often a threat to their enormous powers. (One must remember that prior to normality which the nineteenth century brought to everyday life in Europe and America serious or unpredictable events were incessant, and nobody was exempt.) Keynes, a probability-theorist before he was an economist, understood that normality is only an illusion, but an illusion to which power naturally adheres.

Journalism's business is putting itself in the way of accidents – looking for interruptions and breakdowns in the Quetelet world. A broadsheet which minimises their occurrence is not less a pseudo-newspaper than a tabloid which maximises them by its ruthless ignorance. But, if these breakdowns are only intermittent, the pseudo-broadsheet may be hard to identify – it will look like the real thing most of the time. To distinguish between newspapers and their simulacra something else must be taken from Weber: the theory of ideal types. 'Ideal' here refers not to ethical aspiration, but the construction of benchmarks. Just as there can be an ideal type of a university or an extermination camp, there can be an ideal type of a newspaper and of a pseudo-newspaper.

As logical abstractions of social science, ideal types are never exactly realised in the world (even the abstractions of natural science are a rougher fit than we tend to think). There are no pure embodiments of Weber's 'Protestant Ethic', 'charismatic leader' or 'exemplary prophet'. But perfection is not necessary – the extermination camp has been realised sufficiently for recognition, though the examples are rendered impure by slight traces of humanity.

The ideal type of a commercial–professional newspaper will exhibit characteristics recounted in earlier chapters. It will have a propensity for seeking and analysing accidents: sufficient resources (that is, physical and intellectual) for dealing with events outside the normal range. This propensity for discovery and analysis will be independent of any opinions which may be advanced in editorials – it has a flexible and inclusive agenda. Such a list can be elaborated, but a simple, crucial test of whether the newspaper's core propensity is effective and independent has been prefigured in the last chapter.

If it is effective and independent, it will bring the controllers of the newspaper from time to time into substantial conflict with the governing powers of the day – by disclosing shifts of reality which power finds unwelcome. The occasions will generally not be predictable, and will sometimes bring real danger. Similar considerations will apply in broad-casting. In a pseudo-newspaper the principles apply in the reverse sense. Conflict with authority brought about by the paper's own propensity for accident will be rare, even over long periods, and substantial risk hardly ever an outcome. However, this is only the negative side. In the ideal type of a pseudo-newspaper there will be active support of governing power, to the extent of assisting with official propaganda.

Actual newspapers will only approximate to these ideals more or less closely. But the distinction between the types will not occur within the range of normal events, because of the abnormal, intermittent charac-ter of journalism. News media are not the only organisations which present this problem of distinguishing the spurious from the authentic. Armies may be much the same, because they too practise their trade only intermittently, differing in this from hospitals, schools and commercial airlines.

Practitioners often repress the harsh fact that journalism's significance is so intermittent. But there is an up-side: when a newspaper does con-trive to distinguish itself in *abnormal* circumstances, the impact on readers will be greater, and more enduring. This explains the durability of some media titles – 'brands' if business terms work better – and their place in communal memory. To illustrate by the extreme, any educated sense of British citizenship eventually includes traces of *The Times*, Peterloo and voting reform; similarly, histories of the Presidency will always include the *Washington Post*.

A real newspaper depends on having resources over and above its 'normal' requirements, but nobody knows quite how large they need to be. How frequently should the *New York Times* expect aircraft to crash into the Empire State Building was Max Frankel's question in the 1950s, before anyone had to ask whether they might be aimed at it (see Chapter 1 above). Classically, editors and publishers fight about the size of the margin, but not about its existence. As the optimising theories of ortho-dox business offer little real help, the problem has to be solved empirically – by hunch plus experience.

Costs at least can be controlled by empiricism. Major outcomes in general can't be. Effective use of resources in decisive, accidental moments depends on quick, independent decision-making by reporters and editors – subject only to such rules of truth-finding as they have learnt. Time spent trying to estimate the consequences of inquiry must be kept to a minimum, or it will clog the process. For this reason the absolute quantity of resources is less important than how they are organ-ised emotionally. We defy augury, says Hamlet, when at last doubt is replaced with action: if it be not now, 'tis not to come, yet it will come. The readiness is all.

Murdoch's distinction, displayed in his reflection on New York, is that he expects to run newspapers on a 'normal' basis: if there are a few things missed, what does it matter? For this reason Newscorp papers are frequently run with stripped-down news staffs and massive use of agency copy. In the tabloid market, the lack of any real journalism can be filled by chequebook journalism and staged pseudo-events (such as the *News of the World*'s endless 'stings'). These may be quite expensive, but such expenditure is predictable, and therefore easily managed, both finan-cially and politically – give or take an occasional Profumo misjudgment.

A few days before Harry Evans took office at *The Times*, William Rees-Mogg wrote a valediction in which he called Rupert Murdoch a 'newspaper romantic' – he has always fancied a piquant phrase, and sometimes more than the available evidence justifies. More realistically he saw 'the shades of the prison house close round Mr Harold Evans (and even cast a somewhat fainter shadow over Mr Rupert Murdoch) . . .', suggesting that his own fourteen-year editorship had not quite been a barrel of fun.

It made Rees-Mogg himself into a national figure, by exhibiting his talent for controversy, which was eccentric – but more so than his sub-stantive views. Most of his positions were those of a liberal conservative – he was a swift enemy of Enoch Powell's attempt at racial politics – only spiced with economic fancies. Even before going to *The Times* Rees-Mogg 'took the position that a government which had responsibility ·

291

without sufficient power was decisively worse for society than its opposite. He thought [a serious] paper should reflect this view . . . should be ready to offer government its support in the never-ending struggle to prevent events sliding out of control.' This was support over explicit policies, and it could include trenchant criticism (Rees-Mogg's estimate of George Brown, deputy to Prime Minister Harold Wilson, as a better man drunk than Wilson sober put many respectable eyebrows into spasm). But his basically conventional outlook made him the wrong person to remedy the ailments of the world's archetypal newspaper.

These were connected not with policy debates, but with a definition of journalistic purpose infecting the core of its staff, a notion that *The Times*' essential function was 'to serve the governing class of Great Britain' (not even the elected administration!). Members of the staff wrote just those words in rebuke to consultants who suggested the paper ought to think more about service to the reading public. That was in 1957, during a last-ditch defence of the news-free front page, but the attitude remained manifest up to the time of Murdoch's takeover. (It was in principle his own view of a newspaper's relationship with the governing class, though he came to it from his own direction.) Of course a newspaper designed for people who believe – according to Keynes' testimony – that nothing really serious ever happens will be near to the ideal type of a pseudo-newspaper.

Rees-Mogg's attempts at modernising *The Times* were denounced in a tone very similar to that of the front-page diehards, in a round-robin letter drafted by the famous leader-writer Owen Hickey. It said of some fairly mild (and perhaps confused) attempts to alter the paper's organisation that the:

> general effect of what has been done, and of the manner in which it has been done, has been to diminish the authority, independence, accuracy, discrimination and seriousness of *The Times*. These are chief among its essential values. To the degree that they are lost *The Times* departs from its true tradition and forfeits the principal editorial factor in its commercial success.

Reaction might be defined as conservatism in defence of the non-existent, and the content of the 'White Hart' letter, as it became known, made a fine example. *The Times* had at that point (1967) not enjoyed real 'commercial success' for at least a generation, which was exactly why it had fallen into the Thomson Organisation's arms. Its special 'authority' was confined within its own hermetic world.

But the list of signatories (at the White Hart pub off Fleet Street) was a rather different matter. Rees-Mogg's fury at the patronising tone seems to have stopped him asking why it should be signed both by Robert Jones, one of the country's pioneers of financial investigation, and by 'Sandy' Rendel, the old-style diplomatic correspondent whose 'authority' had moved NATO from Brussels to London and made a bad joke of *The Times*' first news front page. *The Times* was still host to an idea not yet dead, and two quite different newspapers were represented among the White Hart signatories: one which had just published a groundbreaking account of corruption at Scotland Yard; another which considered such things, if true, unlikely to please dwellers in 'the top tier of the machine'.

It was Rees-Mogg's task to close one down and revive the other, but he was essentially a leader-writer when *The Times* needed an expert in the organisation and management of news systems. Rees-Mogg left the system essentially unchanged, and for Evans to change. Evans had formidable production skills, but he had long been running a well-oiled weekly operation with the aid of first-class specialists like Ron Hall and Don Berry. Though *The Times* had more good reporters and analysts than it deserved, there was nobody remotely in the Hall–Berry class to support an editor running a six-day operation and needing off-line time to reconstruct it. Of the two closest companions he did have, one was his own choice, the other that of his 'romantic' boss. Both were disastrous.

His deputy, Charles Douglas-Home, Evans selected from a somewhat limited field. He had not tried at the *Sunday Times* to teach himself the tricky art of working with a strong deputy, and was content to have in the role Frank Giles, an easygoing man with strong conventional values but little notion of how to defend them against conventional attack. This had been, until the Murdoch crisis, a reassuring, gentlemanly relationship, and *The Times* provided a candidate with some resemblance in terms of social exterior.

Douglas-Home had been the candidate of the *Times* traditionalists as Rees-Mogg's replacement, though with no chance of success against Murdoch's need to transplant Evans. He was the nephew of an aristocratic minor Prime Minister, with a professional record bright alongside Uncle Alec's, but not dazzling. Most of it had been spent on *The Times*, lately as home affairs editor. Untroubled by retrospective loyalty to a regime in which he had been a principal, he plied Evans with details of deficiencies he claimed to have seen in Rees-Mogg.

His talent for detraction went beyond gossip. Four years earlier he had given a startled subordinate (Brian MacArthur, the news editor) a secret dossier on the private lives of the *Times* reporters. One of its subjects found the investigative craft to uncover it, and read such things as his own complaint about depression due to working conditions being ascribed to 'chaotic' sexual activity. Douglas-Home apologised and promised to destroy the files – remarkably, there was nothing about this on his own record, and Evans only learnt of it months later, when the dossier turned out still to exist. Sex was not its only subject, for another reporter was classified 'not a gentleman'. Timelier disclosure might have set Evans reflecting on Surtees' rule that 'the man who talks about being a gentleman never is one'. On the face of it Douglas-Home – who died in 1985 – seems an absurdly unsuitable senior executive. There are friends who fiercely defend his memory but the basic facts are hard to smooth away.

Murdoch's appointment of Gerald Long as managing director of Times Newspapers was based on the assumption that Long had wrought the economic miracle of Reuters – particularly where it rested on the solution of labour problems by applying computer technology to the news business. Long, who had a bristling and macho style, was – or presented himself as – an authority on French cheeses, wine and gastronomy generally, about which he lectured his new colleagues at ostentatious length. Murdoch, brought up on the usual upper-class notion that the wine ought to be good but you shouldn't fuss about it, endured this in the belief that he had got the industrial-relations genius to revolutionise the production of his newly acquired broadsheets.

Being Murdoch, he reacted adversely once fact demonstrated otherwise some months later. Long devoted much energy both to gastronomical journalism and to refining TNL's boardroom cuisine.

When in February 1982 he published a treatise on rare French cheeses during a painful struggle for company-wide redundancies, Murdoch shut the kitchens down completely.

The assumptions about Long seem to have been over-hasty – whatever his part in converting Reuters from news agency to financial-data bonanza, it had little to do with labour relations. The official history of Reuters says that early in his period as general manager he handed over staff management to Brian Stockwell, 'a quiet, popular man, responsive without being weak . . . Brian joined in 1938, and acquired wide experience as a journalist and manager in London and overseas . . . Stockwell began by negotiating the introduction of a graded salary structure of all employees. This suited both management and trade unions . . .' Stockwell also negotiated joint manning of computer installations, and by his retirement in 1976 Reuters' industrial relations seem to have been as solid as TNL's were flaky. John Lawrenson, who wrote an unofficial history of Reuters, describes Long as a bully with a gift for sycophancy and self-promotion, the bristling manner a cover for insecurity.

As sycophant, Long made it his business to promote the general proposition that Murdoch was a 'much misunderstood man', rendered impatient only by delays in the pursuit of excellence. As bully, he dumped on individuals held to be maintaining the roadblocks. Conspicuous examples were Thomson–TNL grandees whose exit was not complete. Evans was disturbed to watch the growth of a double act in which Murdoch designated targets and Long brought down abuse or humiliation on them. Denis Hamilton was supposed to remain as chairman of the TNL holding board and as a national director: Murdoch groaned at Hamilton's 'long-windedness'; Long promised in schoolboy language to 'bag' him. The routine went into action at Rees-Mogg's farewell dinner:

> It was the first time I had been with Murdoch and Long together. It was bad news. They egged each other on in cynicism and mockery . . . That night Tina wrote in her diary:

>> I was disconcerted by Long with his Lucky Lucan moustache and impenetrable inward stare, and I was unhappy about the savagery with which he and Murdoch rubbished William

Rees-Mogg and Denis Hamilton. I stuck up for Hamilton by saying he had good taste in people and once had the courage to appoint Harry. Murdoch ruggedly conceded this. Long just reiterated, 'He's a bloody pompous old fool.'

The gastronome's weapons were ready. When Hamilton wanted to work through lunch in his seventh-floor office and sent for a tray, Long decreed that service should stop at the sixth floor. Many such small humiliations were added until Hamilton was 'bagged' late in 1981. Animosities, Evans recognised, were hardly new to the media industry, but here they were 'cultivated like tropical plants' – with a devotion even greater than in the old Fleet Street jungle.

The third person critical to Evans' prospects was his own replacement as editor of the *Sunday Times* – co-beneficiary of the 'guarantees' supposedly entrenched as law. These would hardly work unless they were applied in an equal spirit at both papers. It quickly emerged that the *Sunday Times* as a whole was classed fair game. Long stalked its premises in Murdoch's wake, diagnosing epidemic excellence-blockage, and a product judged 'flabby', 'unexciting' and lacking the 'element of surprise'. 'Rupert says so and I agree.' Rupert, however, had agreed the choice as editor of Frank Giles, who embodied just the qualities of which he furiously alleged himself to be the nemesis. Giles was a traditional diplomatic journalist: public school and Oxbridge by mould; entirely decent by aspiration; upper-middle class by birth, marriage and connection, with only modest technical grasp and a visible dislike of stories apt to frighten the horses.

This was like Dirty Harry denouncing a squad of cops for being insufficiently ruthless and street-wise after placing them deliberately under the command of one of those gentleman-detectives who populated 1930s novels. It was an irrational choice to succeed Evans. There were several prominent candidates – Hugo Young and Don Berry being most obvious – for the *Sunday Times* was not the demoralised part of TNL. But exactly so: its staff had shown resistance. And while the guarantees remained credible, any chance of a recurrence had to be eliminated – a priority easily outranking editorial momentum. Just how well candidates such as Young or Berry might have turned out is hard to say. What is sure is that any one of them would have been stronger than Giles, whose professional vulnerability offered every opportunity for ruthless manipulation.

Both Long and Murdoch would turn up in Giles' office to apply the standard editor-destabilising techniques – zapping through an edition, tossing surly, random questions. When Giles' executives were present some care had to be taken over the instructions-to-journalists rule, but impact could be enhanced by insulting manners, as when Murdoch arrived for the celebration of Giles' first issue: 'Giles asked Murdoch if he would like a drink and went on his knees to the low refrigerator by the door . . . "Bitter lemon" said Murdoch irritably, striding over the kneeling body of his editor . . .'

Loutishness during the courtship phase – rather than Murdoch's natural good manners – would of course have aborted the whole deal. Long, led by Murdoch, followed up diligently by insulting staff members as 'lead-swingers', 'expense-padders', 'Trotskyites' and 'communists'. Any properly qualified editor for the paper would have tuned up its work-ethic – which just then had slipped a few notches (without Leon Trotsky's intervention). But Long's campaign was intended to show that the editor actually chosen could not protect his staff from abuse. Frank Giles, Murdoch bizarrely claimed, was a communist. And worse, said Long, his knowledge of wine, gastronomy and the French language was lacking. Giles' French accent was probably the better, but it was not a point he saw fit to trade.

Murdoch spoke gleefully of 'terrorising' Giles: in a world of guns and bombs, we need some care with the language of office-warfare. There was of course no physical terror involved, nor need one suppose Giles short of the courage to face that. Most of the destructive effect was gained by crude discourtesy – that is, by use of tactics Giles would never consider using in return. The parallel is that armed terror also works by exploiting restraints which its victims consider binding. The result, anyway, was effective softening up of the other guaranteed editor. At this point it's relevant to notice that Murdoch had nominated to the national directors his old mentor from the last dark days of Beaverbook, Ted (Sir Edward) Pickering.

Under Rees-Mogg *The Times*' leader-column had not shown overall Thatcherite enthusiasm, but because of his personal view it approved of monetarist economics – thus counting as friendly if not One of Us. Evans set out to make the theme of his own leader-writing a 'weaning' of *The Times* away from monetarism. The implications he did not fully grasp in advance, and even in retrospect they may be hard to imagine.

Economics had been Evans' university subject and he had maintained a detailed interest. He saw the subject in technical terms rather than quasi-religious, ethical ones – that is, he shared the outlook general among the field's professionals. But the true Thatcherite monetarism which ruled Britain in the early 1980s was of a fundamentalist purity seen almost nowhere else – certainly not in America, where it had originated in the technical scholarship of Milton Friedman. In America monetarism was influential, but a technique among techniques. It never became the loyalty test it did in 1980s Britain (Friedman himself grew troubled by Thatcherism's total absorption in the quantity theory of money). That pure faith is now forgotten like the beliefs of the Albigensians, and economic policy debate once again is largely a pragmatic discussion of means. To reproduce the monetarist zeal the editor of *The Times* walked into, one should think of today's globalisation debate.

Quite swiftly Evans realised that Murdoch's technical editorial skills were not just less than his own, but far from being in the same league. Apparently he had believed the famous story of the shirt-sleeved creator of the amazing *Sun* – which of course had been a copy of the *Daily Mirror* assembled by its former chief sub Larry Lamb. He seems not to have looked closely at the *New York Post*, and never saw the lamentable pre-Deamer *Australian*.

Murdoch knew enough to be a deadly kibitzer in a tabloid set-up run by skilled people long inured to deference. There is a strongly held belief among tabloid journalists that making up a broadsheet is easy. So it is if the ambition is nothing more than grey vertical columns and minimal illustration. The kind of active and flexible broadsheet Evans wanted for *The Times* is far more difficult, because the text has equal rights with the display. 'Murdoch proved to be much less of a technician than I thought he would be, unsure of type-faces and liable to mix up off-the-stone time (printers finished) and set-plate time (foundry finished, and on the machines ready to roll).'

He found Murdoch adept in discussing the marketing of new publications and sections, but less effective on the question of content for them. He was not 'an ideas man in that sense', and lacked 'the pure editorial flair of Denis Hamilton, who was always dreaming up handsome and ambitious series for the *Sunday Times* review front and colour magazine'. None of this need have mattered in the case of a non-interventionist proprietor and a smoothly running product. But this was a proprietor carrying a charismatic editorial reputation – and with whom the editor needed to interact minutely about the reconstruction of a famous but dangerously sick newspaper.

Evans had to overcome inertia accumulated over decades in *The Times*. His deputy and his managing director scarcely understood the task, and were flawed characters; his *Sunday Times* colleague was a decent man under destabilising attack. He intended to apply some perfectly orthodox and sensible criticisms to the ruling policy of the government without being aware that he was committing blasphemy. His cell in the prison-house was likely to be chillier than Rees-Mogg's.

10

CASES OF CONSCIENCE, 1981–1982

When I Want Your Opinion, I'll Give It to You

RONNIE SCOTT, title of jazz recording

There is no such test of a man's superiority of character as in the well-conducting of an unavoidable quarrel . . .

SIR HENRY TAYLOR, *The Statesman*

Whatever his surrounding constraints *The Times* was an exhilarating experience for Harry Evans for most of the first half of 1981. His last three or four years at the *Sunday Times* had not been ones in which much new ground could be broken, and after Ken Thomson's decision to pull out there would have been no way to remain without a bruising and principally defensive battle.

In the first few months at *The Times* there was nothing from Murdoch but encouragement and praise, even when Evans himself was distressed by the paper's performance. When not absent in New York, Murdoch was preoccupied with the *Sun*, which was being out-down-marketed by the newborn tabloid *Star*. His counter-attack was to bring the Mark II *Sun* into being under Kelvin MacKenzie. It's worth remembering that those of the great and good who welcomed or reconciled themselves to Murdoch's acquisition of *The Times* had yet to see that remarkable publication.

There is every reason to think Murdoch genuinely saw in Evans a pliant technician ready to project the proprietor's political desires effectively. Something like it had been his experience with Larry Lamb – and his old mentor Pickering simply saw the Beaverbrook–Christiansen relationship revisited. Differences, it seems, were overlooked – such as that Larry Lamb was authentically Thatcherite (agent, indeed, of Rupert's conversion). Lamb actually thought it was for his sake Mrs Thatcher had given Rupert *The Times* – for which he would have left the *Sun* very cheerily. Instead he was transported to the *Australian*.

To Shawcross Murdoch said that Evans' entire attitude to him was one of 'Tell me what you want, and I'll do it.' If so, each misread the other, setting up an unavoidable quarrel. Evans was capable of misplaced enthusiasms, and his presence at *The Times* proved that. He had a huge over-investment in believing Murdoch was not the political camp-follower he had been warned about – and he had some personal propensity for telling people what they might like to hear. But all this was as superficial as the vanity Rupert's father had hoped to exploit in General Monash. Beneath it, Evans was a dedicated professional journalist with a formidable record owing nothing to Murdoch.

All the same, matchmaking was tried. Evans received a gold-embossed card inviting him to dinner at 10 Downing Street with the Prime Minister in honour of the French President, François Mitterrand. 'I told Murdoch, expecting that he would be there. No, but he seemed to know already about my invitation. "She likes you," he said of Mrs Thatcher.' The editor of *The Times* was courteously received on the Prime Minister's own table. But if she felt a strong affection for him she managed to control it. Handsome is as handsome does, she probably said to herself.

The near-assassination of President Reagan on 30 March 1981 was the new editor's first big night. His handling of it was highly successful, but it challenged the paper institutionally, sowing a resentment easy for Murdoch to cultivate when he realised matters were not going to plan. A chief rubric of *Times* conservatism called it a (or the) 'newspaper of record', with an equivalent proposition that 'Nothing is news until it has appeared in *The Times*.' If the idea was that a newspaper should range widely, should not leave stories hanging and should have an index, there can be little complaint. But essentially it begged all the questions of what should be recorded and how, with looming beyond them the problem of 'how it should record what others insisted on concealing'. At its worst, a 'newspaper of record' formula justifies indiscriminate accumulation, repetition and contradiction. (The method is ancient: 'I have made a heap of all that I could find,' wrote Nennius of his ninth-century collection of Celtic lore, and it was obsolete even then, for Bede in the seventh century had been criticising sources and synthesising narrative.)

On the night of the Reagan story Evans threw away the 'normal' front page (framed before the news broke) and gave its whole area to Reagan. Inside, he created a second 'front page' for the routine news. The Reagan coverage used a picture sequence six columns wide, and ruthlessly divided narrative from explanation; wherever possible repetition was cut out or dealt with by cross-reference. It was a hectic project, disconcerting to everyone who still thought one front page excessive.

Murdoch, phoning from New York, said his intelligence system told him *The Times* had outdone all other papers – had been 'the best in the Street'. Evans circulated this widely, which was perhaps natural, but it was also unwise. Letters arrived in some profusion complaining of the un *Times*-like character of the 'Reagan special', and Evans was left in no doubt that many of his staff agreed. Illustration had caused special offence. 'Some people on *The Times* regarded photography as a black art of tabloid journalism.' To be sure there were minor errors. The headline 'HONEY, I FORGOT TO DUCK' perhaps over-estimated the British currency of Reagan's witty quote from the Dempsey–Tunney fight. But what mattered to the *Times* conservatives was not the impact of the coverage on readers – which turned out to be beneficial to the paper when the evidence came in – but the fact that its production involved skills they didn't possess, admire or understand. And if the *Sun*'s proprietor liked it, so much the worse. They did not realise that Murdoch scarcely understood any more than they did. Anyway, neither he nor they would care about each other's motives when the time came to combine against Evans.

As accident dictated in that year, events followed each other in a procession vivid enough for Christiansen himself. There were the fierce inner-city riots of Brixton and Toxteth; near-disaster for the Columbia space shuttle; the Israeli air-attack on Iraq's nuclear reactor; the shooting of the Pope; an intruder in the Queen's bedroom; the assassination of

Sadat of Egypt; the introduction of martial law in Poland. Amazement created by the news was multiplied by the spectacle of the editor creating:

> pages myself, working with the subs into the small hours . . . I am sure I made errors which were gratifying to all who observed them [but] I was sure there was a better way than doing what *The Times* would naturally have done, which would have been to assign separate headlines to stories that were not distinct, but simply came from separate sources [that is, from different agencies and correspondents] so producing overlap and repetition . . .

These subs were not the clitc assault-troops of popular Fleet Street, described in Chapter 3; they were humble non-coms who looked up to an officer-class of leader-writers, area editors, specialist writers. And *The Times* at some time past had come to resemble those regiments in which 'Carry on then, sar'nt-major' covers many unglamorous operational necessities. Generally the officers lived a daytime life, leaving the non-coms to carry on through the night without their participation or supervision. Very frequently, parts of the 'record' simply went missing.

Central to Evans' achievement at the *Sunday Times* had been making use of the display-language derived from Christiansen's *Express* – without the corruption in which subs treat reporters' work as raw material for free-standing invention. Often, advantage was taken of a five-day deadline to allow his staff to switch between the two roles, or perform them in parallel. Active display, honestly run, does not create news. But it creates a propensity to look for it – provided the system has resources enough to handle the accidents coming its way.

Like Adrian Deamer, Evans was a meticulous text-handler, who rarely made errors except through exhaustion or lack of support – but that was a most serious contingency. The paper did not really have enough subs to check, edit and organise its fifty columns of text in routine mode, let alone enough to seize exceptional opportunities. 'It was something Murdoch affected never to understand, giving a sardonic chuckle as he surveyed the troglodytes and asking when I was getting rid of them; and perhaps he did not understand it, since all his experience had been of tabloids with a tenth of the text.' Evans was too charitable, for a large part of Murdoch's experience had been with the broadsheet *Australian*. And in that case too his eye had not been accurate.

Human resources apart, much of the physical layout was inadequate – the sign of a newspaper which had passed long years in passive mode. People who needed to work close together were far apart. Difficult as it might be to credit, there was no intercom system; even more extraordinary, internal phone numbers were unlisted.

> I thought at first that the [news]room layout, sanctified by a decade, would have some logic . . . But . . . finding there was none, I asked for the room to be reorganised . . . one or two senior people, however, had the same attitude to change as the readers who resented the invention of the camera . . . It took me four months of shuttle diplomacy to have the desks at *The Times* sensibly grouped.

Machiavelli today might say that moving executive furniture is a Prince's riskiest venture. Certainly the reservoir of ill-will deepened.

Newsroom routines – and sometimes their absence – showed traces of 'newspaper of record' doctrine in its corrupt, circular form. Late copy was appended to existing stories, rather than incorporated through rewrites. And there was no procedure for regular comparative checks on competing news media and agencies. A doctrine that nothing is news till it has appeared in *The Times* easily becomes a doctrine that it need not appear first in *The Times* – and then, in the last hermetic stage, need not appear at all. Journalists should scan opposition sheets with well-hidden dread. At *The Times*, Evans found, there was a tendency to do so with contempt, which presented itself in a suit of intellectual rigour, deceptively tailored: 'The story in another newspaper is not a scoop; it is a shallow misinterpretation, a base fabrication, and if it is neither of them, it is something we had months ago but the night staff had failed to realise its importance.'

The news trade always contains enough fakery, sensationalism and plagiarism to give the ploy some effect. A paper's specialist writers, armed with expertise in particular subjects – law, medicine, science, education and so on – can employ it with deadly effect against an editor who has no spare time to investigate the background. Specialists should be a newspaper's most dependable source of unique material, but they can most easily become creatures of routine, and prisoners of their expert sources. When Evans discovered, though, that his science correspondent was unavailable to cover the scheduled re-entry of a Columbia mission known in advance to be at risk, he decided the syndrome had gone too far.

Fred Emery, an energetic reporter, was given the task of eliminating passivity from the specialist writers' group. He was unpopular with Murdoch, because in covering the takeover he had asked questions judged over-energetic. Now he grew unpopular internally for demanding that the specialists work a Sunday roster and that some of them change jobs. Evans says he was told that specialist appointments on *The Times* were made for life. It is difficult to believe, but some of the incumbents held views no less remarkable. "'From the readers' point of view as distinct from specialised people in the field," one of them commented to Emery, "it is difficult to see the importance of scoops. The quality of writing is more important.'" This states the pseudo-newspaper principle in almost ideal form: implicitly asserting that, once the normal has been dealt with, all duty is done. It inverts plain truth, for in any field the 'specialised people' are mostly the local chapter of the governing class and, as Keynes suggests, their lust for scoops is indeed tiny: those they like are internal messages irrelevant to the governed classes. What does matter to the unspecialised – the readers, the governed – is what people in the field do save us from most of the time: rogue pharmaceuticals, rising pollution, collapsing buildings, officials being pressurised. Scoops are *all* that matters – the other stuff is there to determine how much they matter. But unreadiness is all. Scoops are not found by those who know better than to look.

Clearly, said Douglas-Home, there was a gap between old and new at *The Times*, and he added, 'I pledge myself to be the bridge.' There were undoubtedly two newspapers in one office, as there had been at the time of the White Hart letter. But which was old and which was new? Arguably, what Evans was doing was releasing a very old one – the still-powerful idea of *The Times* – from a pseudo-newspaper top-hamper. It certainly seemed to come alive quickly, to the detriment of Murdoch's hope that cordial relations would grow from the Downing Street dinner.

Seven days after that dinner the excessively energetic Emery produced a copy of a letter written on 10 Downing Street letterhead and signed by Mrs Thatcher's husband Denis. It was addressed to 'Dear Nick' – Nicholas Edwards, the Secretary of State for Wales. It had been written in 1980, and asked for a planning appeal over a housing estate in the Snowdonia National Park to be accelerated. Mr Thatcher declared an interest as an adviser to the developers. Passing this letter on to his officials, the Secretary of State had written, 'The explanation had better be good and quick, i.e. this week.' Thatcher's clients had since won their appeal, and the result was still in 1981 a focus of disquiet in Wales, because Whitehall had overruled the Snowdonia National Park authority.

Evans and Murdoch were dining at Woodrow Wyatt's house when the first edition arrived containing the story. Murdoch 'looked miserable and said nothing'. Every other newspaper followed up *The Times* – which had not for some time been a familiar event. Indeed, Lord Shawcross wrote to suggest that *The Times* once would not have stooped so low. The government spin was that everyone could write to ministers from their homes, and 10 Downing Street was Mr Thatcher's. He had not used crested, Prime Ministerial stationery. *The Times* wrote a leader saying that Caesar's husband must rise above suspicion. The only way to avoid publishing the story would have been to avoid finding it. Lord Shawcross was right to say that *The Times* in recent years had managed that omission with ease.

The big running story was the state of Britain and its economy. And whatever its internal tensions, *The Times* was making progress there. Ivor Crewe, a distinguished psephologist, produced a study of the government's mid-term position which showed Mrs Thatcher as the least-popular Prime Minister since polling began – indeed, as the leader of a minority in power. It also reported Michael Foot as the least popular Opposition leader, but that did little to improve the way Tory politicians felt about Crewe's piece. And this was not passively 'reporting the news'. It was probing under the skin of events and looking for changes in norms. The same was true of a series on attitudes among young people which took many weeks to complete. It was founded on scepticism about the government's argument – a central plank in Thatcher's platform – that unemployment resulting from the recession of the late 1970s was socially neutral, and did not affect the fabric of the nation.

Serious inner-city rioting enhanced such scepticism and made *The Times'* work timely.

> The conclusion was that unemployment was breeding a lumpen-proletariat in unique and dangerous isolation. Young people sympathised with the difficulties of the police. Nearly half of them thought they had been too soft with the rioters, only 12% too tough. But no less than 30% thought violence was sometimes justi-fied to bring about political change. They were depressed at not being able to find work . . . Mrs Thatcher was disliked by 70% . . .

Even if the government did not agree about the effect of the recession, they wanted it to be over.

Sir Geoffrey Howe, Mrs Thatcher's Chancellor of the Exchequer, had prophesied at the beginning of 1981 that mid-year would see an upturn in the economy. It did not arrive. David Blake, the economics editor, analysed data from the Central Statistical Office showing that output had fallen for the sixth successive quarter. This was an embar-rassment for the Chancellor, Blake wrote. Brian MacArthur – Evans had promoted him from news editor – was in charge of the paper on the night, and he made it the lead story: 'RECESSION GOES ON WITH SIXTH DROP IN OUTPUT'.

Failure of the upturn to materialise did not enable the Labour Party to damage the Tories, but the framework was shifting, with the formation of an alliance between the old Liberal Party and the new Social Democratic Party (the origin of today's Liberal Democrats). Running the resonantly named William Pitt in a by-election at Croydon North-West they triumphantly ejected the Tories (demoting Labour to third).

> It was a triumph as well for MacArthur and Emery. They organised *The Times* coverage so resourcefully that we were on press except-ionally early with the result and a full analysis . . . Readers of the *Telegraph* and the *Guardian* in comparable circulation areas got either no result in their papers or a skimpy report . . .

The competitors thus recorded this setback for the government less visibly than did *The Times*.

But where an upturn could be seen amid the economic gloom was in the sales of *The Times*. At the start of 1981, things had been quite nasty. The bloated sale of 400,000 at the beginning of the 1970s had been allowed to decline to a more sustainable 297,738 by the time of the shutdown. Times Newspapers spent heavily on relaunch promotion, and the *Sunday Times* returned undamaged. But *The Times* slowed badly in 1980 as promotion tapered off and January 1981 averaged 276,903, down more than 50,000 from the 327,576 of January 1980. There was not (and is not today) a clear thesis about a profitable level for circulation of *The Times*. But decline at that rate would soon eliminate any need to discuss it. It continued through the first quarter but then – without promotion – the monthly averages started catching up with the 1980 numbers. June was only 5,686 down from June 1980, and July was 4,064 up on July 1980 (there is of course a seasonal fluctuation in newspaper sales). By the third quarter it was clear that the downward trend had been broken, and in the best way possible.

As Christiansen said, you cannot beat news in a newspaper. Circulation trends, we know, do not change direction easily, and usually show less effect than people hope from one-off sensations and promotions. But when there is a lengthy run of big events, and a famous title responds distinctively – providing insights others don't – there is an excellent prospect of response, and everything suggests this happened between *The Times* and its readers.

A number of the *Times* staff took little pleasure in this turnaround. (Some of the specialists were still complaining about life being 'chaotic', which never sounds right in a journalist – like a banker moaning over high interest rates.) Murdoch and Long showed even less pleasure in *The Times*' editorial performance. Long went first into the attack, presumably having a lower profile than Murdoch as a guarantee-buster, though plainly acting as his agent. The David Blake lead 'RECESSION GOES ON' was the principal target of a two-page 'Private and Personal' memo to Evans. The headline of the story, Long said, might 'otherwise be expressed as "Sir Geoffrey Howe is a liar/idiot"'. This was fantasy. No sane journalist or politician would have read it as calling Howe a liar, any more than one member of the Royal Society would have called out another for challenging experimental results. To be sure, Howe could have done without Blake's assiduous statistical inquiry, but it was another case in which the story – written quite impersonally – could only have been different by remaining undiscovered.

Long's discontent took him into still stranger territory:

> This broadside on the unfortunate Chancellor, while not unde-served, seems to me again to be largely irrelevant unless some journalist seeks personal gratification in bringing the Chancellor down . . .
>
> The whole tone of the *Times* story is that the figures prove that the recession has not ended.

Of course nothing so vague as 'tone' was involved. Blake's story said in plain words and figures that the recession had not ended. Nor was it a 'broadside'. Given the facts, the headline could scarcely have achieved purer neutrality. But Long insisted on seeing it as part of a propaganda campaign permeating both news and opinion pages, designed overall to 'criticise the Government and to consider its economic policies mistaken'.

Under the statutory constitution of *The Times*, it was not the managing director's business if the paper did or didn't criticise the government's economic policies. It would be his business, of course, if the editor's notion of a package of accurate news and free opinion should turn out radically unsaleable. That can lead to very tricky debates about fair and foul means of making a paper pleasing to its readers. But in this instance the readers were increasingly happy. What Long was talking about was making *The Times* more pleasing to the government, which is not a legit-imate aim for a managing director or anyone else around a newspaper. Evans made no reply: '. . . I was determined to go on with a proper reporting job, however many memos and threatening scowls there were. It might satisfy Murdoch and Long if *The Times* suggested the recession was over or Mrs Thatcher was doing well in the polls, but that was not what the news happened to be.' Indeed it was not. A lift in SDP–Liberal support was clearly the sorest of points.

The Croydon by-election coverage had diverged fractionally from the ideal commercial–professional model: part of the advance plan had been lining up Shirley Williams, matriarch of the SDP–Liberal Alliance, for a comment. On the night her piece, understandably exultant, was run on the front page – MacArthur and Emery would have made a better call by running it inside. By the time Evans spotted the problem moving the Williams piece would have cost *The Times* its exclusive coverage, so he took no action. Next day Long caught Evans on his car phone, and there were no congratulations for beating up the opposition. 'He wanted to know why there were ten paragraphs on the front page by Shirley Williams and Rupert would want to know . . .' There was, of course, no 'why' and Evans didn't offer one. It was just a bum call made under pressure. The question essentially resembled those Adrian Deamer had swatted away as witless when Murdoch threw them at him in Australia. Not much real experience is needed to know that a basically accurate broadsheet newspaper always contains 'noise', in much the same way that honest scientific measurements do (any flawless bell-curve is usually a phoney).

Paradoxical as it may seem, if a newspaper is to be decently precise it cannot be very tightly controlled, nor its content be rationally explicable throughout. To quote Professor Paulos again (*A Mathematician Reads the Newspaper*) it must cope with real systems characterised by 'sheer size, intricate connectivity, sensitive dependencies, self-referential tangles, random juxtapositions, and meaningless coincidences . . . uncharted and nonlinear interactions', and doing this successfully does not mean indulging sloppiness, but it means devolving – irreversibly – a great deal of ground-level control. Different editors choose differently but all of them know that there is a point where tighter control over minor points increases errors in major ones. The more complex the newspaper and the more active its news-gathering, the less rigid its organisation has to be.

The only papers which can be read in the nit-picking sense of Long's question are those of totalitarian societies – the sort of sheet Kremlinologists used to scan for a few paragraphs, a few words, 'meaning' that a party bigwig had risen or declined. These exact journals contain no picture of the real world at all. Long and Murdoch had shown by the third quarter of 1981 that 'accurate' as in 'presentation of news' meant to them 'likely to please to the government'. What about 'free expression of opinion', the other public interest under their care?

The 1981 Nobel Prizes were announced simultaneously with the Tory Party conference, and the winner in Economics was James Tobin of Yale, for his work on financial markets. He was one of the world's great authorities on the link between inflation and unemployment – the main theme the Tories were to debate. When someone gets a Nobel Prize just as the ruling party happens to be discussing his particular subject, the conjunction can hardly avoid appealing to anyone interested in the free play of opinion. When *The Times* planned its coverage some unknown genius proposed the idea of getting Professor Tobin to write a piece about British economic policy. Evans approved, and Tobin delivered.

The professor suggested in firm but generally mild language that Mrs Thatcher was conducting an interesting experiment which he viewed sceptically: 'The idea that you leave money supply to determine employment and everything we want is burying your head in the sand . . . The public never believes that unemployment is a solution to inflation and they are right. It's crazy.' Murdoch, who was meeting Evans at his house for dinner, did not just disagree with Tobin's view. He was outraged that it had been canvassed.

The outer limits of 'free' opinion are hard to set, but if the concept makes sense at all an eminent, mainstream US academic commenting on British public policy must be near to its core. Murdoch, scowling at Evans, thought otherwise: 'Why d'ya run that stuff?'

'Well, it's timely.'

'And it's wrong! Wrong! What does he know, anyway?'

Evans cited the Nobel award, and Murdoch flashed back, 'Intellectual bullshit!'

Free debate doubtless could include classing the whole Nobel economics canon as bullshit – but that would take out Milton Friedman (1976), F. A. Hayek (1974) and others much quoted in the Thatcher cause. Evans' attitude was that *The Times* should look at the opinions freely on offer in the world, and make choices roughly representative of them. Murdoch's was the one he had imposed on the staff of the *Australian*: opinions not consistent with his allegiance of the moment were free – to go elsewhere.

Murdoch has strong rhetorical skills, but prefers using them on an unchallenged floor, like a bad judge or schoolteacher. Evans now realised with some alarm that his chairman had little capacity for handling an interactive discussion with a consistent theme. There was

> no relish for anything more than a couple of colliding assertions . . . He got restless or tetchy with any attempt to engage him further. If he could put the name of a personality to any observation he disliked, he pulverised whosoever it was as a wet, an intellectual or a creep, and that was the end of it.

It was not a happy evening (Evans had not realised that Anna Murdoch would be absent from the dinner – he had already discovered Murdoch's wife as a moderating influence). 'Tina later remarked that she had never seen anyone so hunched up with resentment as Murdoch. Tobin had trodden on sacred ground.' Specifically, he had advertised to the Tory conference that Murdoch's control over *The Times* was less than absolute. The editorial technician, seemingly, had some political programme of his own.

Actually the problem was in the first place technical and professional, not one of specific political sympathies. *The Times* was moving away from the pseudo-newspaper and towards the real type. To the degree it did so the frequency of its collisions with the governing class – in both news coverage and opinion coverage – grew quite naturally. There was essentially nothing an editor of Evans' type could do about this; a similar pattern would have occurred whatever the party in office. And Murdoch, with his ingrained preference for accommodating power, would have been offended. But dramatic charge was added to the 1981 situation, because the factional leader Murdoch was attached to still did not have an entirely secure grasp on power.

At some point as 1981 turned into 1982 Murdoch concluded that the editor of *The Times* might have to be driven out. Naturally a case had to be assembled, even if it was only of the specious kind which Burke suggests will do very well with a mob for its second. There was a mob available at *The Times*, though a rather decorous one. Political indiscipline could not be a charge – or not openly so. The initial one was budgetary mismanagement, which firstly had the advantage that everyone around *The Times* knew by the latter half of 1981 that its finances were a mess.

Secondly, in projecting the blame on to Evans, several sturdy archetypes were available. The ruthless businessman who understands where every penny goes is a notion as familiar as the tart with a heart of gold. And the brilliant editor lacking financial skills comes not far behind.

Actually the financial mess had little to do with Evans. The *Sunday Times* experience neither suggested that cost-control was his leading gift nor exhibited any major disasters. But that was in a context of regular, detailed budgeting throughout the Thomson group, where unwise courses might be chosen, but compasses and sextants did exist. *The Times* operated with no budget whatever for all but two months of Evans' period – in total defiance of the guarantee that editors would work within an agreed financial structure. Evans had to take an unfamiliar craft through turbulent waters, while rebuilding large parts of it. He had to steer on by-guess-and-by-God dead reckoning, and the professional marvel is that he stayed on course at all.

Murdoch and Long had started their management programme at TNL by firing, first, most of the account executives who understood and gathered in the company's revenues, and then most of the bean-counters who tracked its costs. With them went the knowledge required to develop a budget. Rather than analysing a flawed and highly complex business, Murdoch's prime concern seems to have been keeping what data there was in his own secretive hands. To the chief accountant David Lawson he said, 'You are working for me. You must show figures to nobody.' And after a short period of producing numbers for Murdoch, Lawson was fired. TNL's financial operations then turned effectively into a sub-division of News International, the old *News of the World* company controlled by News Limited (not yet called News Corporation). Executives from the *News of the World* took over revenue-earning.

Long then undertook to create a new framework for *The Times* on the 'zero budgeting' principle, which starts by assuming no spending requirements and constructs a new set from basic principles. In any newspaper the task is formidable, for lack of any useful theory on maximising resources. Empirical knowledge is indispensable, and most of it had been fired. Long had no experience except of a steady-state news-agency business, and Murdoch's chief earners were tabloids with minor news-gathering requirements, simple production costs and cash-dominated revenues. This was the context in which considerable management and editorial time was devoted to the issue of whether *The Times* might be able to dispense with an office in New York – since it only made a difference at quite exceptional moments.

Meetings of the new board of Times Newspapers were rare. Long's method was to assemble an executive group in his own office without even the formality of a table. The agenda was minimal, and minutes exiguous, much time being consumed with Long expounding management principles – but giving no details of the new budget. Indeed, the notable absentee at every meeting, wrote Evans, 'was documentation . . . After a few meetings, I asked for figures. "I'd like to know how we're getting on" . . . Long sighed. "Wouldn't we all. There's no management here. It's hopeless."'

Long, who had the reputation of a budgetary expert, was clearly troubled, but not Murdoch – for the moment anyway. Between non-meetings, Evans raised with Long the need for a policy on revenue-generation – the linkage between cover price, circulation and ad-rates which decides whether adding sales to a broadsheet newspaper means pain or gain for the profit-and-loss account. The managing director shrugged and said, 'Rupert likes to do these things himself. And he knows a lot more about them than I do.' Perhaps he did – though a correct setting for *The Times* has not since been found – and simply did not care to discuss the process. The chairman's intermittent appearances produced no visible attempt at policy development. 'Murdoch's own board-meetings were even more cursory than Long's. "Yeah, yeah, well let's all get back to work, there's a lot to do" . . . He shied away from talking strategy or money . . .'

Just as Larry Lamb and his *Sun* executives had done, Evans, Long and their colleagues found they would have to do without any consecutive discussion of *The Times* and its requirements: 'The conversations were sometimes jumpy. "Johnson's a scream" (Frank Johnson, a rising sage of the right). "Know anybody to follow Akass at the *Sun*?" "Got any ideas who might edit the *News of the World*? Present editor's too nice . . ."' After one meeting Evans did find Long in possession of a covered document which apparently set out financial details for *The Times*. But, when Evans asked to see it, Long hesitated: '"Rupert is very funny about figures. You must not say you have seen this." He lifts the corner for a quick peep.' The editor of *The Times* had a peep but it did not reveal whether any substantial data existed. 'Rupert works by weekly figures,' said Long. 'He takes them on the plane with him. I've told him it's deceptive. But who are we to argue with him? He's very successful. He has a brilliant financial brain . . . He just says tell everybody to spend less.'

It appears from this that Murdoch was still running on the Merv Rich weekly sheet as developed from the Hoyts cinema chain. It was obviously a soundly made system which provided well for arbitrary rule of a cash-rich tabloid newspaper business (which essentially News International remained). But, as Long clearly knew, it could not deal with the problems of a quality-newspaper business in serious strategic and tactical disarray. After his dismissal, which followed Evans' without long delay, he gave a less glowing judgment. Everything, he told William Shawcross, rested on the fact that Murdoch was a 'gambler' who 'had a martingale. Mostly it worked.' Martingales – various forms exist – are systems for playing roulette. They all depend on doubling up losses.

Some time in the latter part of 1981 Long gave up trying to be a serious chief executive of Times Newspapers or to produce a real budget. His chairman kept virtually all the information in his own hands, and Long said that it was difficult – perhaps impossible – to stand up to such a remarkable personality. (His final disappointment came when Reuters went public and he received none of the shares issued to make the executives who had stayed on very rich indeed. Hamilton or Murdoch might have helped him, but for different reasons neither chose to.)

Perhaps Evans shares some blame for the budgetary mayhem in that he did not protest to the national directors somewhere in the third quarter of 1981. By then Murdoch and Long were indefensibly remote from their promises. During September Murdoch bypassed the board with a memo asserting generally that costs were 'intolerable', adding that any fee above £100 must be submitted to the editor or managing editor and anything above £1,000 to the managing director. He also said that he would be checking everyone's expenses personally. This meant effective editorial control for Long, under Murdoch: Evans would not be able to start any non-routine operation on his own authority, or even commission an opinion poll. Evans thought that going to the national directors would

315

end all possibility of a working relationship with Murdoch. Remarkably, he did not yet see that he was already facing an unavoidable quarrel. But, having defied all the evidence to get this far, he could not yet turn back.

He called Murdoch in New York and said he could not edit the paper without a budget, and refused to go to Long to get approval ad hoc for routine editorial decisions. This démarche produced only a brief, disjointed reassurance: 'Sure we'll get your budget in place. This is temporary until we do . . . Talk it over with Gerry. What's [Tony] Benn up to?' And so Evans did go on without a budget – and without seeking cost-approvals from Long. He realised almost at once that this implicated him in the budget fiasco, but he still believed that the guarantees gave him security against dismissal. By this time, serious alarm was infecting most of the staff – subject to rumour and counter-rumour about 'intolerable' costs and their consequences.

When a dispute with one of the print unions briefly closed the paper the trading losses of *The Times* were estimated by some people at £10 million annually and others at £20 million, with variations between. At the start of November Evans asked Long for monthly indicators, even if they were only sketchy. But no – the real information was in the chairman's hands and the managing director, again, could not demand it. Long could only report on Murdoch's own requirements: 'Rupert says he wants 30 per cent off staff all round immediately. 30%! He's in great form by the way, says *The Times* is doing very well.' The compliment was perhaps Long's addition: he believed in keeping up morale. It was months since Evans had heard a kind word for *The Times* from Murdoch himself, and in December radical discontent became apparent.

Long and Evans were commanded to dinner with Murdoch and the advertising and circulation bosses. The project under discussion was raising the sale of *The Times* to 400,000 without delay. It was straightforward, said the chairman: expand sport; start bingo; kill the Diary; cut back business news; throw out the women's features. Nigel Grandfield, the group advertising director, followed up by suggesting a new approach to leaders: short and snappy, with harder views. The approach – perhaps a rough copy of the *Daily Mail* without its skilful appeal to women – struck Evans as insane. Long seems to have kept his own counsel, though by now he was calling the executive floor a 'madhouse'.

Next day Murdoch resumed his offensive, comprehensively attacking the business section in a meeting with Evans and Mike Ruda, the TNL advertising director. A swift, unprofitable redesign of the paper took place as Murdoch chopped out space for sport. 'What do you want this crap for anyway? Two pages is plenty for business news.' Ruda had many times told Evans that the business pages generated revenue which the paper would otherwise lose. Now, under pressure from Murdoch, and licking his lips nervously, Ruda retreated from his previous – obviously truthful – real view. Evans concluded that the discussions were really about having the editor of *The Times* take arbitrary instruction in front of witnesses. At the first available moment he sent Murdoch a handwritten note saying he would not accept such behaviour. In retrospect Evans thought that Murdoch's basic resolve to dispose of him formed shortly after. And this seems likely.

In early January 1982 Evans made a personal visit to America, returning on the 7th to find that the chairman had been complaining about 'leftist' headlines, and was demanding to see him. Murdoch was in full, very characteristic attack mode. He accused Evans of going absent without leave, and of lacking all political conviction. The administrative and the moral deficiency were pursued equally, though it must have been plain that the first could only be trivial and the second, if true, devastating.

Evans eventually had to photocopy the memo giving notice of his trip, which had somewhere been overlooked. Political amorality could not be so easily disposed of. Murdoch seems to have conceded that Evans had been stubborn about monetarism, but something else emerged: the editor lacked all convictions, because now there was only one conviction which mattered. This involved arguing for all hostility short of war against Moscow – there must be no tolerance for dealings with a government which oppressed its own people and the peoples of nearby states. As this became, over the following weeks, a principal strand in Murdoch's complaint against his editor, it should be made clear that Evans and his chief foreign leader-writer Richard Davy took no remotely pro-Soviet view. They argued only that limited co-operation with Moscow would better serve Western interests.

Ideological dispute rumbled on in a context of rising panic over costs and redundancies. Late that January Long produced an accountant's report saying that editorial spending was over budget by £2 million: it was £9,710,600 'compared to Mr Murdoch's budget of £7,723,000'. The excess must be immediately cut out. The appearance of a 25 per cent budget overspend of course did heavy damage to the editor – but what astonished him was to hear that a 'budget' did after all exist.

Gradually, in the small print, facts emerged. In 1980 the budget had been £7,364,000, which would have been £8,615,880 in 1981 prices (inflation was 17 per cent). So the £7,723,000 which Murdoch had set at some time – in secret – represented a large cut in real money. It then turned out that £600,000 of the £9,710,600 were group costs never previously charged to *The Times*. Increased editorial spend in real terms was £400,000, which was extremely modest for a newspaper being extensively remodelled. Evans says he was glad to have some real figures to work with at last. But he must have had some sense of an endgame getting under way.

In January the guarantees were twelve months old, and now Murdoch struck decisively against them – dropping entirely that persona with which the vetting committee had discoursed on family tradition and old Oxford days. There had been no new insurrection at the *Sunday Times*. But neither had there been any emergence of a natural representative for Murdoch, despite liberal use of creative tension.

Frank Giles had been appointed with two joint deputy editors, of whom the more promising Murdoch at first took to be Ron Hall, editor of the magazine section. The other, Hugo Young, was a political analyst who had visibly criticised the government. Hall, once a *Mirror* sub, was reputedly a good example of an apolitical technician, the chimera Murdoch was always seeking. Hall had been told by Murdoch – with emphasis from Long – that if he 'used his elbows' to achieve practical dominion over his colleagues he would be seen favourably – and might hope for substantive rank. Somehow Hall had not seized the Darwinian moment, and Giles was relying considerably on the suspect Young.

However, Murdoch had a good feeling about Evans' *Times* discovery Brian MacArthur – 'bushy-tailed' and keen to please. He decided to put MacArthur in as senior deputy editor at the *Sunday Times*, demote Young and fire the too-fastidious Hall, with Peter Jackson of the *News of the*

World put into the magazine. Of course he had undertaken that '4(b)(iv): The editor of each newspaper shall retain control over the appointment, disposition and dismissal of journalists', and Biffen had entrenched it as law, to be supervised under his authority by the national directors of Times Newspapers. When Evans learnt about MacArthur he did not see how it could be done. Grinning, Murdoch said, 'I'll tell the National Directors . . . Frank Giles has asked for it all.' On 13 January the directors were to meet for lunch. The day before Giles was sent for and ordered to make the announcements, presenting them untruthfully as his own.

This might seem a perilous series of inventions – the editor of the *Sunday Times* had not even met one of the recruits 'asked' for. The straightforward course for Giles would have been to reveal to the national directors that the chairman was conspiring to procure a breach of his statutory obligations. The result for Murdoch might not have been terminal but it would have been damaging. But after a wretched night Giles decided to sacrifice Hall – a colleague of many years' standing, but not a friend – and keep some face. He would insist on meeting Jackson – nominally – before announcing the discovery of his talent. And he would insist on keeping Young as first deputy.

Giles tried to see Murdoch before the directors' lunch, but the chairman was engaged. Long offered to go in and mediate. He emerged to tell Giles that he could have lunch with Jackson right away. But MacArthur as first deputy was compulsory. And demotion must be conveyed to Young as his, Giles's, personal idea. Otherwise, the chairman would say Giles himself must be fired, for impeding a vital commercial decision. It appears that something could have been cobbled up about promotional matter in the magazine. To Giles this made it a matter of saving his own head. Certainly he saved no face, for the fabrications paraded were unimpressive, produced with deep reluctance, and did not convince either victim. The quarrel was not one Giles could have avoided – he had been ambushed with it. He cannot have thought he conducted it well. But he got a call from Murdoch thanking him for being helpful on a difficult day.

As one reflects on Murdoch putting this business through, it is worth looking back to his father Keith and the 1918 plot over the field command of the AIF (see Chapter 2 above). Doubtless the fate of an army and a battle is more than the fate of a newspaper (even a famous one) and the will of Parliament. Does it seem likely, however, that either Murdoch would have anything but discreet respect for the other's bold technique – irrespective of the outcome sought or the result achieved?

With the guarantees made out to be (in Murdoch's words) 'not worth the paper they were written on', it took only another two months to wrap up the Evans editorship. Technical success was not denied at all. News Corporation's annual report called the circulation turnaround 'extremely gratifying' and celebrated the achievement in detail. The accusations which were developed were budgetary incompetence, political vacuity – with varied emphases for variant audiences – and defective leadership skills. This last was manifest, said Murdoch, because the staff were 'up in arms': many were hostile to the editor, and very few supportive.

Of course this could not have been otherwise. Probably Murdoch himself vaguely knew that the resentment incurred in turning around a paper like *The Times* could not yet have dissipated. It was perfectly in line with Machiavelli's Law of Newspaper Reform – 'the initiator has the enmity of all who would profit by the preservation of the old institutions, and merely lukewarm defenders in those who would gain by the new ones' – but some of the national directors seem to have been much alarmed. Collectively, they were themselves rather lukewarm about novelty – they had not, after all, been appointed for their radical sentiments. Three had taken part in the Vetting Procedure in January 1981 – the historian Lord Dacre, the banker Lord Roll and the trade unionist Lord Greene; Lord Robens had been a Cabinet minister, widely thought to have been a possible Prime Minister; John Gross was a literary journalist of great intellectual repute; and the Murdoch appointee Sir Edward Pickering had never shown any appetite at all for modernisation.

In any case, the mood was not left to itself. Both Murdoch and Pickering made extensive morale surveys among staff – the more readily after some clearing of the way by Evans' deputy Charlie Douglas-Home. When discussing his appointment as deputy, Douglas-Home had impressively stated to Evans the view that Murdoch (whom he called a 'monster') always seized power over an institution by separate dealings with its leaders. To protect *The Times*, therefore, they must neither of them initiate a meeting with Murdoch without forewarning the other. It was his condition of acceptance, and they shook hands on an agreement to act always in unison.

Late in 1981 Douglas-Home took leave to work on a personal project, but he learnt from Evans of the situation developing at the office. In February 1982 he returned a day early – without contacting the embattled editor – and conferred with Murdoch. His thought was that much good would be done if the chairman spent more time on the editorial floor. 'Rupert,' said Douglas-Home, 'you're a warrior king who should lead us from the front.' Not surprisingly, Evans' view of his deputy changed abruptly, but of course too late. Feedback soon disclosed the theme of Murdoch's interchanges with the staff: 'Harry doesn't know how to lead, does he?' The warrior king's own answer seems to have been easily visible to those he questioned.

Journalism's essential insecurity was racked up to a specially high notch in that place and time. For many years, the pseudo-newspaper principle had been dominant in *The Times* – 'normal' journalism and its routines had protected many of its staff from the accidental, unpredictable character of their profession. This produced a degree of personal assurance – complacency, some might say – even if the paper's entire financial structure was fragile. Evans, for the best part of a year, had been tearing all that up, and moving the people of *The Times* back into the world of competition, scoops, accident and uncertainty.

But the new personal challenge and stress had not been compensated for by any new structural assurance. On the contrary, the paper was losing more money than ever before – how much no one quite knew – and this allegedly was due to or connected with the frantic and unwelcome activities of Evans. If survival were possible, it would be at the price of many people's jobs. It was quite untrue that the financial disarray was the editor's fault, but its sheer existence would have taken effect whatever the cause. Where a newspaper is well run and tolerably profitable, the intrinsic professional stress can be kept within reasonable limits. Where two types of stress are present together, they potentiate each other, as psychoactive drugs will do.

In the circumstances of *The Times* Murdoch was unlikely to receive many challenging answers to his propositions about leadership and the popularity of the editor, or to his repeated direct complaint that 'The paper has no conscience.' The context of this was intense and continuous news about the great test of will in Poland, where nationalism was reasserting itself against Soviet tyranny. 'Conscience' was a kind of coded banner under which the Anglo-American right – Reagan and Thatcher supporters – claimed the ownership of freedom's struggle. Of course support for Polish and East European liberation was practically universal among the Western democracies – there were no substantial voices in favour of appeasing the totalitarians, only differences about means. 'Conscience' was a claim to exercise monopoly of morality in respect of foreign affairs.

Occasionally Murdoch drew an unwelcome response. 'Harry's fine,' the business news editor, Denis Hamilton's son Adrian, told him. 'The paper's fine. It's the management that's the trouble. It doesn't know what it's doing.' The usual thing in this kind of drama – specified perhaps in the *Handbook of Corporate Skulduggery* – is for the target-figure to fall briefly sick. He or she then receives affectionate phone calls at home, advising a solid break in order to get properly well. This happened with Evans in the first week of February and he went home leaving Douglas-Home to supervise a story which to him was exactly representative of the new *Times* journalism he wanted.

Its core was a letter written roughly twelve months earlier by the government's chief medical officer of health, during a secret dispute about lead in automotive fuels. Concern over brain damage to children from atmospheric lead pollution had long been growing, and America, Australia and Japan had decided to ban altogether use of lead in fuel. But the British government, without public discussion, had decided that a *reduction* would suffice. Sir Henry Yellowlees' letter – to all the departments concerned – said that the research behind that decision was out of date, and seriously understated the risk from lead. The latest work, Sir Henry thought, showed that its use at any level exposed several hundred thousand British children each year to significant chance of brain damage.

It was a story of breakdown in the Quetelet world. Naturally the old projections showed that lead-induced brain damage did not normally occur – occurred, that is, but at a tolerable rate. For the oil industry, the motor trade and their Whitehall regulators this was how things should be. But new surveys had convinced three major Western governments that normality was not, after all, acceptable. What had been thought normal was actually a situation where something quite serious, bad and avoidable was happening. Circulated confidentially, the letter had not modified policy. (There is a difficulty in feeling the sickness or death of several hundred thousand children – not named, generally not born. One might hear at this point Christiansen saying, 'It is our duty to interest them in everything.')

It was Sunday 8 February. Douglas-Home was running the paper. He chose as the main story a routine dispatch about the American Budget. The Yellowlees letter was also on page one, but at the next day's conference the old *Times* values were applied to the question of following it up. For Evans the letter was just the start of a process which should uncover the research which had changed Yellowlees' mind and the new research that might now be under way. What was now happening in America, Australia, Japan? What political input had there been in deciding against a ban? All this, without doubt, would mean some arduous inquiries, addressing questions to important people which they would find painful and perhaps impossible to answer. Was the story of lead pollution a *campaign*, the news editor wanted to know. Douglas-Home asked him what he meant. 'I mean, do we go beyond normal news values?' 'No, we don't.' The story of lead pollution faded out of the newspaper of record while Evans was indisposed. Britain continued using leaded fuel until 1990 when it was entirely prohibited.

For most of February the survival of *The Times* was in public doubt, Murdoch saying that unless 300 staff – including 46 journalists – were removed the paper would close. Evans returned to his office to find that other newspapers were speculating about his imminent departure. Ritual denial was circulated by Times Newspapers: 'Reports . . . that Harold Evans is about to be replaced as editor of *The Times* are malicious, self-serving and wrong. Mr Evans's outstanding qualities and journalistic skills are recognised throughout the world . . .'

Murdoch wrote to Evans about the central role of intellectual consistency in the practice of serious journalism.

My chief area of concern about the paper is one I have raised with you several times: the paper's stand on major issues. Of course it takes attitudes, but I fail to find any consistency in them, anything that indicates the clear position of conscience that a great newspaper must be seen to hold. Just what that position is, it is your duty to define, and it cannot be defined by me. But it must be defined with clarity and authority and even repetition.

Put like that, was it much to ask? Enough hints, suggestions and exposition had been offered to make known what 'clear position of conscience' meant. A few days earlier Murdoch had sought out the chief leader-writer, Owen Hickey, and – without quite 'instructing a journalist' – had described in detail the foreign policy which *The Times* could suitably advocate: terminating all trade and diplomatic relations with the USSR to procure social implosion there. Of course Murdoch could not actually write it down, just as he could not have given Giles written orders. It had to be Evans' own idea.

The difficulty was the pure nonsense involved. Not the policy of economic and social warfare itself – a coherent enough scheme favoured by the hawk minority in London and Washington – but the assertion that *The Times* lacked clarity with respect to it. The leader column had rejected it as 'apocalyptic'. Perhaps one day the West should 'gamble with the stability of the entire continent' but right then *The Times* wanted a policy of selective sanctions and pressures for the liberation of Eastern Europe and Russia (perceptible, in hindsight's luxury, as correct).

Text and conversation together make the position quite explicit. It is reasonable to think that if Evans had produced two or three vehement leaders (repetition was required) switching *The Times* to a new anti-Soviet policy he could have gone back to 'producing an exciting newspaper' like Christiansen after Munich. (It would have been abrupt, but not more so than the Adelaide *News* reappraising White Australia.) Doubtless there would be other arguments – monetarism perhaps – but peace for now. Instead Evans wrote back to Murdoch asserting the solidity, details, clarity and so on of *Times* leaders on the USSR and a raft of other issues. His basic message was that he planned to be consistent about all of them.

Personal interchange at *The Times* now grew conspiratorial. Douglas-Home assured Evans that he was not after the editor's job – it was outside his capacities, and he would never work for 'that monster'. But a little later Evans heard of Douglas-Home saying to the economics editor David Blake, 'Don't bother with him [Evans]. He's finished.' What was all this? the editor asked his deputy, and got the reply: 'Yes, let's face it, you are finished. You're not getting on with the proprietor.'

Much of Evans' time was now devoted to searching the staff for people willing to leave, to make up the cuts required to save the paper. When the *Spectator* revealed the names of three who had chosen to depart Murdoch seized on the evidence of failing leadership: 'I am frankly disturbed by the decision of Messrs Hennessy, Berthoud and Berlins to leave you.' That the chairman's charge against his editor should be inconsistency was ironic. This was Murdoch's propensity to attack from any direction, without himself admitting any need for coherence – something which Long had taken for irresistible force of personality.

Douglas-Home then wrote to say that he too wished to go after two or three months. Evans asked him to reconsider, and to keep it private until the immediate crisis was past. The information reached Murdoch anyway. And Gerry Long, with his kitchens zapped and most of his powers stripped away, revealed that he would soon be 'having a change' and suggested that the editor, surely, must be miserable and ready to resign. Not at all, said Evans, editing *The Times* was an enjoyable challenge. He certainly was not going to give himself up as a last offering for Long to take to Murdoch.

On 9 March Murdoch sent for Evans and demanded his resignation. Murdoch centred complaint on the emotional state of the staff: they were 'in chaos', and the editor was highly unpopular. Part of this emotion was actually the responsibility of Murdoch, part of it Evans had properly brought on himself, by chastising the Old Times with scorpions. The insouciance with which the chairman conflated the two causes dismayed Evans, and he realised that quickly separating them would be hard, even impossible. Criticism of the staff is never pretty in an editor, and the national directors – first judges in the matter – had a collective affinity with the Old *Times*. Being representative rather of the governing class – in a fairly limited sense – than the nation, they did not instinctively loathe passivity in journalists. Evans did not know that Murdoch had already offered the editorship to Douglas-Home – who also had his affinity with the Old *Times*, and had been refreshing it.

According to Evans' account the chairman seemed to find the interview highly painful, suggesting that it was harder for him than for Evans and coming close to tears. This, though consistent with the tone of his correspondence with Rohan Rivett, was sharply different from the jaunty air of Murdoch setting out to terrorise Giles. However, for all the odds against Evans, forcing the editor's resignation was a risky undertaking. If Evans chose to fight, and found the means to do so, the case against him would not withstand real inspection.

Evans withdrew to consider his position and was approached by Douglas-Home, who said, 'He had me up before you. He offered me the editorship of *The Times* and I have accepted.' Evans pointed out that the office was not yet vacant, and asked how he felt about betraying his editor. The reply was: 'I would do anything to edit *The Times*. Wouldn't you?' Perhaps it had looked like that. Certainly Evans had failed to see things which Murdoch had done to others. But there were things Harry would not do to himself for the sake of editing *The Times*.

The question was whether he could and should fight Murdoch for the right to do it freely. Would resistance trigger a structured inquiry by the national directors? That context might bring out their considerable qualities: Robens had come close to being Prime Minister; Dacre was a major historian; among them only Pickering was simply a placeman. They might not all like Evans, but they understood evidence and Murdoch's dubious claims were unlikely to deceive them long. The national directors, though, had no organisation. Even settling on a volunteer to act as chairman and co-ordinator, Evans realised, would occupy agonising time. There had been discussion of fine principles in the origin of the guarantees; there had been no discussion of procedure and contingency (echoing the case of the Royal Commission). The editor would have to make and argue his own case: he would have to build the courtroom and construct the procedure. And he would have to do it while producing a newspaper every day – with a deputy behind him declared as a ruthless opponent.

Thus if he fought to defend his formal ability to edit *The Times*, he would be deprived – perhaps already had been – of the ability to do it well, and the ability to do it honourably could not persist long. A simple, often forgotten point is that no edition of a major newspaper appears without doing damage to a good many individuals, and usually to causes also. For an editor of Evans' quality to continue in nominal, disputed control of *The Times* would be little different from a mariner taking a ship to sea without having it under proper command.

And so, after reflection, he resigned. Nothing in his experience had 'remotely compared to the atmosphere of intrigue, fear and spite at Murdoch's *Times*'. Discovering that the quarrel with Murdoch was unavoidable had taken so long that the odds against him were insuperable. But he did not compromise his own character in conducting it. The budgetary and personnel-management complaints were spurious in a commonplace sort of way. More remarkably, Evans was charged with having been an effective technician lacking conscience or conviction – exactly what Murdoch actually wanted – and was executed for having been innocent of the charge. Kafka could not have made it up.

It is not surprising that Murdoch and Pickering did not get what they wanted, but revealing that they were crude enough to suppose they might. The amoral editor who creates a brilliant newspaper may be defined as an ideal type, but manifestations are very elusive. We know the Christiansen–Beaverbrook example was in their mind, and Christiansen did produce rising sales while deferring to the Beaver's zany politics. But had they not looked at the *Express* circulation, and seen what happened when journeymen like Pickering attempted to do the same? (see Figure 2 on p. 144) Special factors, of course, permeate the *Express* case. Beaverbrook was a freakish despot, but not a calculating weathervane. Many of his beliefs he supported all his life; Christiansen shared at least some of them, and so trivially were they rewarded that something of conscience must have entered into them. Enough, perhaps, has been said (see Chapter 3 above) to show that Beaverbrook and his one great editor, working in unique circumstances, were a unique combination.

And where were the repeat examples? Had nobody noticed that Larry Lamb believed the nonsense spouted in the *Sun* (in any case no very original feat of journalism)? There is no difficulty of course in being an amoral technician and losing sales (as the circulation figures show) and no certainty that qualities of any sort will lead to success. But it is a curious idea that a man or woman could edit a newspaper with technical facilities engaged, but conscience and emotion in neutral – no more plausible than the emotionally blank reporter, a figure disposed of earlier in the story.

In the specific case it was very odd to suppose Evans was or could be like the ideal type required. Possibly his conscience was imperfectly adjusted (as most are). Like anyone performing in public Evans had displayed error and inconsistency. To many colleagues who had applauded him at the *Sunday Times* it had been difficult to see how he managed to admire Nelson Mandela as well as Henry Kissinger. He had taken over a Tory – if liberal Tory – newspaper, and was himself not a Tory: perhaps that had created some over-complicated positions. But to suggest that Evans was without conscience was ludicrous. To suggest it in the context of resistance to totalitarianism was only possible for people quite unable to grasp such issues.

11

PATRIOTIC LIKE A FOX, 1979–1985

Patriotism may be the last refuge of a scoundrel; but since all of us are
to some extent scoundrels we are foolish if we get rid of our last refuge.

REBECCA WEST, *The Meaning of Treason*

'I am very proud and grateful to become an American,' said Rupert
Murdoch on the morning of 4 September 1985. He had just taken the
oath at the District Court in Lower Manhattan, renouncing all allegiance except to the United States of America, and promising 'without
any mental reservation' to support its laws. The practical significance of
the oath was to make Murdoch acceptable in US law as controller of
the Fox television network. But it was taken also as a symbol of something new in the world: the arrival, said *New York Times* columnist
William Safire, of global man, a cosmopolitan equally at home in
Sydney, London and New York. If so, this wasn't the cosmopolitanism
once imaginatively linked to the brotherhood of man. Another New
York columnist, Jimmy Breslin, pointed out that national antagonisms
were a staple of Murdoch's newspaper operations. By the 1980s
Murdoch had become a significant figure in three systems of
Anglophone national politics, and the path to American naturalisation
included some complex interactions between patriotism, journalism and
partisanship.

In America, a central feature of the years 1976–85 was the solid failure of the *New York Post* as a newspaper. This did not destroy the legend

329

of Murdoch as a tabloid genius, perhaps because it succeeded simultaneously as a political instrument, and wiseacre minds conflate the achievements. Though the *Post* once sold a million during its Son of Sam period the trend line until 1981 was similar to Dorothy Schiff's paper. The real news coverage was no better, and headlines of 'dark playfulness' (or brutality) didn't alter that. The *Post* fascinated (and still does) the communications elite, but the columnist Pete Hamill – attracting much punitive ire – once said it was like the fascination of watching someone throw up at a dinner party. To the intelligent middle class generally the paper could not connect. Bingo, the ancient gambling game revived as Wingo in 1981, added 500,000 sales. Costs, however, rose in line, and the annual loss of some $30 million did not change.

But the *Post* was a switch on the city's political control panel, profitable or not, and Murdoch studied intensively to use it. When he claimed to have elected Mayor Koch, Koch dutifully agreed – deferring so zealously that Murdoch was called, gratifyingly, the 'real mayor'. No city before had made Murdoch so much at home as New York, and this accounted for the vivid (later awkward) interview in which he told Alexander Cockburn of the *Village Voice* that to 'live and love' anywhere else was unthinkable.

The relationship with Ronald Reagan didn't match Koch's case, but was crucial to Newscorp's development. In 1980 the *Post* was intensely Reaganite. The Republican banner on an old Democratic fortress was so conspicuous that no evidence was needed for major electoral impact to be assumed. The President personally thanked Murdoch and presented a large plaque which became the focus of the *Post*'s celebration dinner.

In 1984, by which time Newscorp owned the Chicago *Sun-Times* and Boston *Herald-American* as well as the *Post* and the Texas papers, a more elaborate programme was possible. Murdoch's territories were rich in the 'blue-collar Republicans' which Reagan's strategists aimed at. The special component was a savage personal campaign, led by the *Post*, against Geraldine Ferraro, Walter Mondale's Democratic running-mate. It was devoid of original investigation, and came when the Democrats were anyway doomed. But again it was conspicuous, and Reagan's second term confirmed Murdoch as a spokesman of partisan American nationalism.

In the same late-1970s-to-mid-1980s period the *Sun* shifted its character, and modified Murdoch's position in the British political cast. It did not learn to live with commercial failure like the *Post* – that would have been ruinous to Newscorp – but an intimation of mortality brushed it. By 1981 sales had fallen to 3.5 million from a 4.0 million peak in 1978.

The *Star* had been launched by *Express* Newspapers in 1978 as a regional tabloid. Moving to national distribution in 1981 it achieved a million circulation, chiefly at the *Sun*'s expense. It didn't just imitate the *Sun*, but imitated what the *Sun* had done to the *Mirror* – down to promotional television technique and an undercut cover price. Sir Larry Lamb (the knighthood was a reward for Tory campaigning services) called it a 'cynical marketing exercise'. Murdoch responded by matching the *Star*'s price (a 2p drop to 10p), by setting up an expensive bingo scheme, and by removing Sir Larry in exchange for Kelvin MacKenzie as editor.

MacKenzie himself acknowledged that the *Sun*'s sales resurgence might have been as much due to the bingo and cover-price effect as his dramatic editorial style (the Mark II *Sun*'s circulation graph is best analysed with 1990s data included). But MacKenzie, stimulated by Murdoch – 'the Boss' he worshipped and simultaneously dreaded – changed the British tabloid concept more profoundly than Lamb did. And this, perhaps, might not have happened but for Murdoch's years at the *New York Post* – because the Mark II *Sun*, though much cleverer than the *Post*, and variant from a basically effective model, resembled it in being produced virtually without professional restraints, and being able to cross the border into dangerous fiction without knowing it had.

The new *Sun*'s advent roughly coincided with the Falklands War, and as that was a crisis of survival for Murdoch's patron Margaret Thatcher it was natural that the *Sun* should set out to fan British patriotism into a blaze on her behalf. But in the course of this project, Murdoch and his team began to rank themselves as judges of who in Britain counted as true and traitor people.

The *Sun*'s least-admired Falklands headline began in a crude news-handling error. When the war began MacKenzie and his crew had little experience of handling swift, complex happenings in faraway places, and they started with some amazing blind luck, which rarely helps.

A very familiar trap in war coverage derives from a habit – or art – sometimes called 'leaning it forward'. Naturally there is an interval of some six hours between the editing of a daily paper and its delivery, during which the events described within it can move considerably. The art is in creating something to last for several hours into the future – tricky during a shooting war, as genuine battles rarely come off quite as anyone plans.

On 23 April 1982 the *Sun*'s correspondent in Buenos Aires, David Graves, sent a very cautious report that British forces were approaching South Georgia, the outlying island where Argentina's invasion had begun. Recapture might be imminent (his Argentine military contacts suggested). The *Sun* subs turned this into a stunning front-page lead:

INVASION!

Britain's counter-invasion forces swept ashore on the stolen island of South Georgia yesterday . . .

They then phoned Graves to tell him MacKenzie was delighted with the great exclusive – and please send more details of the fighting. Of course he didn't even know there was any.

Still, by the time the paper hit the streets the Royal Marines really had taken South Georgia, and the *Sun* office concluded that war coverage was a breeze. They celebrated by announcing that the *Sun*'s man with the carrier fleet would paint 'UP YOURS GALTIERI' on a missile and sign it; this was illustrated with a shot of a Polaris ICBM. (The Royal Navy didn't fancy the idea, but the *Sun* later claimed a non-nuclear device had been launched carrying suitable words.)

However, this was really a foggy kind of war, with British reporters and businessmen active in Argentina, and battle confined supposedly to an 'exclusion zone' around the Falkland Islands. On 2 May a British submarine sank the Argentine cruiser *General Belgrano*, drowning roughly a quarter of its crew. Not only Argentines were outraged, for she was outside the zone, and a naval antique. In Britain, which has long-standing ties with Argentina, there was distress, and while the Royal Navy felt justified, it avoided triumphalism.

Not so the *Sun*. There was an exuberant reaction to the first wire-reports of a hit on an Argentine ship, and long before serious detail was available the front page had gone away under a vast main headline:

GOTCHA

with more in like spirit:

> Our lads sink gunboat and hole cruiser . . .
>   WALLOP; they torpedoed the 14,000-ton Argentine cruiser *General Belgrano* and left it a useless wreck . . . its 1,000 crew needn't worry about the war for some time now . . . The ship was not sunk and it is not clear how many casualties there were . . .

This was mostly guesswork. But by the time the first edition was out it was clear there were many dead – and not combatants as defined under the British government's rules. MacKenzie himself was shocked, and rebuilt the front page for later editions with more guesswork and less glee: 'DID 1200 ARGIES DROWN?'

But he was worried about updating Murdoch. Even some of the team had wondered if 'GOTCHA' was excessive – Murdoch might think so too, and now it seemed the facts of bloodless triumph were illusory. Peter Chippindale and Chris Horrie, in *Stick It Up Your Punter*, report a first-hand account of the exchange:

> . . . Murdoch strolled out on to the editorial floor, where MacKenzie caught up with him. 'I wouldn't have pulled it if I was you,' Murdoch said in a casual way. 'Seemed like a bloody good headline to me.' MacKenzie protested. 'A lot of people have died, Boss,' he said. 'Maybe our own people have been hurt. We don't know yet.' But Murdoch assured him: 'Nah, you'll be all right,' walking off apparently unconcerned.

The death-toll turned out to be 368 – victims of the fact that a sea fight never fits well into boundaries drawn by land-based politicians. Within the *Sun* those troubled by 'GOTCHA' kept silent; elsewhere it was called reckless, incompetent, brutal or all three. But Murdoch had liked it, signalling that the limit was not yet.

The war was not unpopular in Britain – some Tories were quite thrilled. But even in 1939–45, when approval was near-absolute, the country had continued to be a democracy at war, where the government's actions were regularly challenged – and that custom persisted in 1982. Mrs Thatcher clearly did not like it, perhaps even less than Winston Churchill. But like him she had to endure it. The *Sun* now came forward to set her free.

Murdoch had installed as chief editorial writer Ronnie Spark, a *Sunday Express* veteran and old Oxford acquaintance. Spark was supposed to stabilise the flighty MacKenzie, and in this spirit he wrote a leader declaring, 'There are traitors in our midst.' The *Sun* 'does not hesitate', he went on, to state that the BBC's defence correspondent, Peter Snow, was guilty of 'treason', and so were the editorial writers of the *Daily Mirror* and the *Guardian*. Snow had impugned the British government's veracity by quoting Argentine communiqués, and the two newspapers had criticised its refusal to negotiate. Treason is of course the worst crime short of genocide, and so the *Sun*'s words caused deep, deliberate offence.

But even when produced by allies of the government they could not cause fear in a country with its legal system intact – as Britain's of course was. Though criticism has often been hobbled in times of stress (with varying success), not even the Star Chamber took it as proving an intent to rupture allegiance to the state and assist its enemies.

Murdoch's promotion of this kind of gaseous melodrama poses the question of what part nationality and patriotism play in his own character – of whether he understands what allegiance means to people generally. The primary evidence comes from his native land, and it means stepping back a few years from the Falklands, to when he was challenged on the exact point – on the depth of his national loyalty and whether it could be relied on.

On some accounts national, regional or particular sentiment hasn't much significance in a period of corporate globalism. Doubtless there are complex reasons for the vitality of this general notion, in the face of massive disproof from formal research and pragmatic experience, but one of its sub-texts springs from a simple motivation. It argues that the ownership of media business no longer has any political or cultural effect, and it is admired by investment bankers. There can be more merger deals on an unbounded playing-field.

Obviously national feeling is scarcely less potent – or potentially dangerous, as the Falklands showed – than it has been throughout the modern era. Personal expression, naturally, varies. In the Australian case it doesn't usually run to the hand-on-heart manifestations Americans relish, or to British pomp-and-circumstance. Self-mockery is rarely far distant – this is an identity first articulated by an all-convict company, opening the Sydney Playhouse in 1796 with 'True patriots we, for be it understood / We left our country for our country's good.' But intensity of feeling is no less – may even be greater – and includes an exceptional collective sense, still tinged at times with paranoia. In church-going terms Australia is close to pagan, and increasingly multi-cultural, but with little detriment to the Anzac 'lay religion'. For an Australian sports team there is nothing affected about using the Gallipoli battlefield as a bonding-place, and only slight knowledge of the culture is needed to know that it strongly protects from suspicion any statement of patriotism.

During the 1970s the assumption had grown in Australia that Rupert Murdoch was turning into an exile. It is a common rite of passage in a nation where migration has always been multi-directional, and by that time it no longer caused angst in itself. But an exile is different from an absentee landlord, and by the end of the decade many people were seeing Murdoch in that light, with implications of erratic action based on fading local knowledge.

What brought the issue to definition was a dispute over the TEN-10 Sydney television licence, which News had failed to win in 1961 – a failure due in Murdoch's view to a Prime Ministerial veto by Robert Menzies, which was due in turn to News having given editorial aid to Labor in the 1959 federal election. (This aid looms larger in Murdoch's memory than in the record. On the other hand the inconsistency of Murdoch's licence applications was marked, and Menzies could certainly have found non-partisan justification.) On 29 April 1979 the 1961 winners United Telecasters sought and gained a routine licence renewal. Two weeks later the *Australian Financial Review* reported that News was acquiring 48.2 per cent of United – effectively, control. Vendor and emptor denied having had these plans at the licence-renewal moment. They suggested that the Australian Broadcasting Tribunal should nod the deal through.

The Australian Labor Party, and several citizen groups, immediately protested before the Tribunal. Senator Gareth Evans said, for the ALP, that the deal was an 'unhealthy aggregation of media ownership': News owned four Sydney papers (the *Daily Telegraph*, *Sunday Telegraph*, *Daily Mirror* and *Australian*). This advance to monopoly, he said, would join bad practice to bad, for both United and News had 'appalling track records . . . in respect of . . . bias and distortion'. And control, it seemed, would be illegally exercised from outside Australia. The Television Act didn't require licence-controllers to be citizens (the US position) but specified in Section 92D that anyone holding 15 per cent or more of a licensed company must reside in Australia. And Evans thought Rupert Murdoch was a New Yorker – even flamboyantly so – when not resident in Britain.

Hearings began on 4 July, the News lawyers opening with the storm-in-a-teacup ploy. Mr H. Nicholas doubted there was such an entity as the 'Murdoch newspapers' complained of. And Mr Murdoch was not personally making the application, so there was no need for the Tribunal to hear from him. Did it even need to hear protests against this simple share-transfer? The Tribunal rejected this. A News executive stated that Mr Murdoch would some day return to Australia – but clearly it was insufficient. Nicholas changed tack: Mr Murdoch was exiled, perhaps, but not by desire. When, aged thirty-seven, he had 'left Australia's shores' he had done so, at his company's direction; after time in England, he had been moved to the US, 'again, because the News Limited board so desired'.

Rupert as the board's humble cipher may have been less convincing than suggestions that the application didn't involve him or that there were no 'Murdoch papers'. Counsel shifted a gear: Mr Murdoch might rarely be present, but he was always Australian at heart, and resident emotionally.

More than once, Mr Nicholas recited the case. There was the Cavan homestead outside Canberra, Mr Murdoch's address on the electoral roll. He voted in state elections. He had an Australian passport. His children had Australian passports. He had his investments in Australian companies. (True, of course, but their business was mainly overseas.) Cavan, and offices in Sydney, contained valuable personal property. In Australia he had 'brothers, sisters, mother and so on'.* It might be of interest that the family home was maintained by Dame Elisabeth in Victoria. Mr Murdoch's stated intention was to remain what he rightly considered himself to be – an Australian resident. The High Court had said a person could reside simultaneously in different places; this was in accordance with modern facilities, allowing men of commerce to span the globe with ease. 'That they may do so, and in fact do so often, does not mean that thereby they must sever their links with home or be denied their Australian birthright and inheritance, or become less an Australian.'

But Senator Evans doubted that patriotic emotion could perfectly cancel geography for the purpose of Section 92. Mr Murdoch might well retain his passport. 'He may even remain a Digger at heart . . . the question is whether he lives here . . .' Mr Nicholas was losing ground. For the concept of emotional residence to compensate for so small a physical component, some powerful statement was required – hardly issuable by proxy. Having read the transcripts, Murdoch arrived on 26 July, apologising for his initial non-appearance. He then offered a display of national feeling rarely surpassed in passionate solemnity.

And he came in shooting. Television owned by newspapers never showed bias: 'In Australia . . . the only stations that have suffered serious criticism on their handling of news and special events have been the stations not associated with newspapers. I refer of course especially to the ABC.' The shot was characteristic, for it was his own newspapers which did the criticising. He eloquently agreed that aggregations of media power afflicted Australia. But he, Murdoch, was not the problem. He – if but permitted to be – was the solution. He was battling 'those great monolithic newspaper and television companies' – Fairfax and the Melbourne Herald group.

My life has been spent fighting them, starting with a very small newspaper, standing up to attempts to push me out of business at

* There is no male sibling to support this moving passage.

337

the age of 23 in Adelaide; but I kept it alive through my own skill and effort, a second voice in that city and it is still there and still strong as a newspaper, giving the people of Adelaide an alternative voice. [Adelaide today has no alternative newspaper voice.

The same in Sydney: I came here only after John Fairfax had bled the *Daily Mirror* dry and, as you would well know, through great effort, perseverance and help from many people we have made the *Mirror* last.

In addition to that, I started the *Australian*. I am now accused of not being an Australian. Who in this room can say I am not a good Australian, or a patriotic one? Who else chooses to be battered and bruised ten months of the year in being an Australian, when it would be a lot easier not to be one?

Why being Australian was so arduous, he didn't say. But he told the chairman, Bruce Gyngell (who had worked in British television, and would soon return), that it was an ineradicable allegiance:

You will remember . . . your happy experiences in London, yet you chose to remain in Australia just as I did, because I love this country, because my wife does and my children do, and I bring them here at every opportunity. Who else goes on building an Australian company around the world employing more than 15,000 people with opportunities throughout the world for my fellow Australians? Who else has risked his every penny, his reputation and his career in fighting for what he believes is right for this country? Who else has risked everything to establish a national newspaper across the length and breadth of this nation? No nation this size or age at this stage of its development has had national media before. But Australia has. It is a time when it is searching for identity and purpose. Sooner or later we have to do some uniting in this country. I started the *Australian* 15 years ago as a dream and nearly $30 million has gone into making that dream a reality and I certainly did not do it to come here today to be called a foreigner or to be punished for standing up to the entrenched monopolies of this country. The story of News Limited since 1954 has been fighting these other great media establishments which have gone to any lengths to try to stamp me out. You will remember a company I used to work for was rather active in that at some stage, at many stages.

This referred to his brief passage under Sir Keith's benevolent eye. But his chief concern was present enemies – lurking ubiquitously, running a unique 'gutter campaign' against him. Fairfax's senior editorial officer had promoted the scurrilous thought that he, Murdoch, had tried to make somebody Prime Minister. Eventually this man – in fact the well-known journalist Max Walsh – had written it in the *Sun-Herald*.

I know that you are sophisticated men, that you would not normally be influenced by those things, that you know how these things are done, but nevertheless these things must be said because they have other avenues. Mr Walsh I am referring to, of course. His wife is a very trusted and senior officer of this tribunal.

That was irrelevant, said chairman Gyngell. Murdoch was glad to hear it. But the problem still was two great companies owning 'over 75 percent of the newspapers in this country and God knows how much of the television and the radio'.

The difference now is that one great company does so – Murdoch's – but in 1979 he was the man promising to avert the consummation of monopoly. Such a disaster would ensue only if the Tribunal were to place handicaps on News Ltd.

I am a competitor establishing competition and if you, I submit, Mr Chairman, are going to suggest that News Limited should not have a television licence in this city, you will see the press develop in this city the same way it has gone in nearly every other city of the world since television came into being . . . Already in Australia we have monopoly daily papers in three states, all in the one monopoly – Queensland, Western Australia, Tasmania. If you want that to happen in Sydney, so be it. But that is the position and I thank you for indulging me in stating my feelings about Australia and my feelings about this issue of competition.

This was the democratic dress of media cross-ownership: Murdoch's newspapers needed television revenue to survive and sustain diversity. 'I believe it is one of the most important things for the maintenance of democracy that we should have newspapers and as many as possible. The written word is fundamental . . .' In fighting for democracy, he knew he had to face anti-competitive practices. Fairfax, making record profits from television, were using them to sell newspapers at a loss and 'engage in predatory competition against News Limited'. Taken with the later record, these denunciations of monopoly and predatory pricing are benchmarks against which to check whether Murdoch's statements ever meaningfully reflected his intentions.

The protestors (who thought he would be absent) did not suppose his grip on TEN would be anything but tight. Murdoch's concern was to suggest that it would be relaxed – just a few News executives joining the board. Asked if he had 'any views as to the situation of the remainder of the board', he replied:

Yes, several of them are known to me, Sir Kenneth Humphries, for instance. I asked him and he agreed to represent the public interest in the first Channel 10 company that we proposed back in 1962. I think that he has done a magnificent job in steering this company through very difficult waters . . . I know some other members of the board, whom I respect but it would seem from the results of the company, the ratings, the service it is giving the public, that it would be madness to contemplate any change at all. Contrary to what might have been said privately or feared, there is much rumour about this in the industry: I wish to give an assurance to the tribunal that no change is contemplated at all.

His company was 'long steeped in the traditions of journalism and interference and non-interference'. And in twenty years he had not given directions over the operation of a television business. That startled the chairman: 'Can you say that you have never interfered with the news and programming of a TV station controlled by News Limited?'

'Since I relinquished my role as managing director of Channel 9 Adelaide back in 1959 or something I can say that absolutely.'

Gyngell asked him to think back to Wollongong, 1963. Didn't he construct WIN-4's service with programming bought from the US?

'I am sorry, I was on the board – I was thinking of Adelaide. Yes, when we first bought WIN-4 and saved it from bankruptcy.'

Gyngell, saying he had asked his question for the record, made clear that he didn't like Murdoch's answer: 'Bear in mind that you are under oath'.

'I thank you for reminding me about Wollongong, and there was a period of a very few months, but as you remember I subsequently joined the board of Channel 9 . . .' By then, of course, Murdoch had, for good or ill, decided the entire character of WIN-4, as we saw in Chapter 4.

Senator Evans asked about newspaper command practices, and Murdoch said he was certainly consulted by his editors. They talked at length on great issues such as elections. Evans persevered:

Sometimes it goes much further even than that, does it not? Can I ask you whether this is an accurate statement, this very familiar passage from the *Village Voice* in 1976:

In 1972 I ran all the election policy of my papers in Australia and got deeply and far too deeply involved. Looking back we did some dreadful things to the other side.

Later on:

In 1975 I changed my mind. It is true I did come in and turn our newspapers around.

Did you say that?

The writer, said Murdoch, was an irresponsible Stalinist. But the alleged ideological flaws of Alexander Cockburn of course had not misinformed the *Voice* readers about Murdoch's politicking in 1972–5 (see Chapter 6 above), and when Evans persisted Murdoch conceded having been 'involved' – and proud of it. Television, he said, he would not use similarly. 'I view the television station as a public licence and there is a duty there to remain impartial at all times.' Not that the ABC did, he added.

He was asked also about London Weekend: hadn't he dictated programming, and dismissed executives? It had been just a two- or three-week action, rescuing LWT from bankruptcy. As programming it produced only *Panorama* and *Upstairs, Downstairs*. (These were famous shows: the first was in fact a BBC flagship; the second was commissioned by LWT after his time.) There was no bankruptcy or other trouble at Channel 10 and so there would be no question of 'marching in and firing everybody'. (Notoriously Sir Kenneth Humphries and most of his team were dumped once Murdoch's men were in place.)

Mr J. W. Shand QC, leading counsel for News, suggested that the company's CEO should expound his 'citizen status' – not his residential status, the actual issue before the Tribunal. 'I regard myself as an Australian,' said Murdoch.

> . . . I carry an Australian passport. My children are Australian. I pay my taxes in Australia. I have a home in Australia. It has all my personal belongings in it. It is lived in by no one but myself . . . I certainly intend to come back to this country and certainly when my children are old enough to leave home I trust I will in fact put them through Australian universities. I choose to have them with me. I think that is very important, more important than proving some point at the moment by separating and breaking up the family.

Senator Evans, cross-examining, could not learn much about how much time Murdoch spent in Australia: a 'fair amount' in 1977; most of 1972; not much of 1970–1. Evans quoted what Adrian Deamer had written after leaving the *Australian*:

> [Murdoch] is an absentee landlord visiting Australia for short periods three or four times a year and making snap decisions while he is here, often based on incorrect or incomplete or misleading data.

> . . . I ask you to comment on its accuracy?

[Murdoch answered,] Mr Deamer is a very good journalist with a very good phrase . . . I would say it is most inaccurate. I have never lost my touch, my love for this country or my involvement. I have been totally involved in this country and everything that goes on in this country whether or not I am physically on certain days here.

However, said Evans, Mr Murdoch held a green card issued by the US Immigration Service – and had done since 1974. Did not that mean the US thought him a permanent resident? It was just a necessity of working in America for an Australian company, said Murdoch, enabling him to avoid innumerable visa applications.

You do not dispute my characterisation, admittedly in general terms, of the procedure and of the status of this particular card?
It gives you residence.
Permanent status?
I did not say that. It does in fact give me the right after a number of years to American citizenship, which I have not taken up, but I chose to remain Australian.
Can I just pursue this point, Mr Murdoch? You do recall having applied for an immigration visa in the United States?
I applied for a green card.
You accept my statement that in order to get a green card you must have first got an immigrant visa: you do not get them any other way?

Mr Shand found the line of interrogation objectionable: it was asserting facts about immigrant status, rather than questioning. 'I will proceed to the next point,' said Evans.

Mr Murdoch, you have said at a number of places throughout these proceedings you are an Australian by instinct and inclination. It is the case, is it not, that your possession of a green card does entitle you to citizenship status after five years of such possession of that card; is that correct?
I have been told that.

343

So on the basis you have put to us quite recently, a few moments ago, you are in fact almost now entitled to apply for citizenship should that be your desire?

Yes. But I think I have stated many times it is not my desire.

It is not your present desire. I was thinking of a desire which [it] is possible you could formulate in the near future?

I cannot imagine it.

News Ltd's argument, said Evans, was that the meaning of 'resident' was largely determined 'by considerations of Australian-ness and emotional and intellectual attachment . . .'. It was this, he said, rather than the challenge by the ALP, which brought into issue Rupert Murdoch's basic feelings about his country.

And these, Shand now said, were literally inalienable. Shand's final submission suggested that to reject the share-transfer would amount to denying Murdoch's nationality. Section 92D had no purpose except excluding aliens from control of Australian television. And 'is it even vaguely rational to suggest that Mr Murdoch is an alien, an outsider, a non-resident? Put in that way, which we suggest is the common sense and realistic way, the question only permits one answer: he is an Australian by derivation, by nationality, by career, by citizenship, by conduct . . .' The attachment, in short, was so vibrant that he resided metaphysically whatever the physical facts. (Surely Shand must have been tempted by Burns – 'My heart is not here / My heart's in the Highlands, a-chasing the deer' – but he held off.)

In August 1979 the Tribunal gave approval, saying, 'On the basis of advice received and the evidence before it, the Tribunal is of the opinion that Mr Murdoch cannot be regarded as being in contravention of Section 92D.' A lawyer cannot see 'mental reservations' in a client. But if Shand had stated the reality – that Murdoch was Australian, but open to offers – it would have been hard for the Tribunal to find as it did and allow further expansion of News into Australian television.

Media sophisticates were not surprised when the deals of 1987 – his descent on the Herald group – showed that Murdoch's desire was not to free Australia from monopoly, it was to impose one. But even they were startled in 1985 when he exposed the frailty of his patriotic bond. Why should it matter? To some people on the left – where Murdoch has intermittent appeal – patriotism anyway invites deception. And the transcripts suggest that in applying a rhetorical kiss-of-life to the corporate case he possibly fooled himself. But this kind of illusionism has serious consequences for news media, and explains something of Newscorp's international behaviour.

Patriotism is the presentable member in a turbulent family of synonyms. Nationalism has its good points, but it is often a chaotic nuisance, and once corrupted to jingoism or chauvinism is noxious. If Rupert Murdoch couldn't see much wrong with 'GOTCHA', most people could. Racism, the extreme case, now has few explicit defenders.

George Orwell proposed to consider traditional emotions in the light of immunology, arguing 'that patriotism is an inoculation against nationalism, that monarchy is a guard against dictatorship, and that organised religion is a guard against superstition'. Pure rationalists may be shocked, but Orwell, who thought collective allegiances indispensable, also thought they unavoidably contained darkness, the national manifestations especially (leaving monarchy and religion aside). Rebecca West, turning Dr Johnson rhetorically on his head, said there is a scoundrel in all of us, and that a patriotic vacuum would contain nothing likely to moderate collective passions – generated in what the biologist Edward O. Wilson called the 'hardwired part of our Paleolithic heritage': 'The human brain evidently evolved to commit itself emotionally only to a small piece of geography . . . For hundreds of millennia, those who worked for short-term gain within a small circle of relatives and friends lived longer and left more offspring' – even when the net impact shattered their chiefdoms and empires.

In the Johnson original, patriotism is a scoundrel's refuge because he will mine its irrational components for gain whenever he sees no better way forward (reckless, in West's version, or ignorant of his own state). And patriotically coloured sentiment will certainly sell newspapers and television – Fox News has been following the method with particular enthusiasm since 9/11. Though the figures show it isn't invincibly effective, it is undoubtedly an easy journalistic path.

Classically, personal gain is the point where patriotism parts from its synonyms: patriots are typically at odds with the object of their loyalty –

warning, upbraiding, sometimes rebelling. Nationalism, running more to flattery, can pursue advantage with less handicap. In either case the engagement is irrational, but patriotism takes it to be made with a society subject at least partly to reason. It is not-for-profit, non-negotiable and non-transferable. But crucially it is additive, as in Burke's classic conservative version of the development of loyalties: 'To be attached to the subdivision, to love the little platoon we belong to in society, is the first principle (the germ as it were) of public affections. It is the first link in the series by which we proceed toward a love to our country and to mankind.'

A dangerous world needs extension of that series, allowing group identities to reinforce – not destroy – each other, and individuals to acquire new allegiances without cancelling their initial ones (become naturalised, that is, though for refugees the original nation may be lost). 'Every civilised man,' said the patriot Kipling, 'has at least two home countries, one of which is always France' – clearly seeing no reason to stop at two. And increasingly we don't: notably in Europe, that old arena of hatreds.

Rupert Murdoch apparently spoke of this when he said that becoming American didn't end his being Australian. But, if he understood it, why is the Newscorp house-style rancid chauvinism? To be sure, Jimmy Breslin of the *Daily News* has never admired the boss of Newscorp, but he was not just fantasising when, writing of Murdoch's advent as his fellow citizen, he said, 'We are a mixed population and he tried so blatantly to use race to sell [the *New York Post*] that he became known as "Tar baby Murdoch".'

This isn't limited to tabloid print. *The Times* may segue from a heavy joke about German cars as 'adaptable off-road vehicles crashing through the Ardennes' into a fantasy about new plans to put Deutschland über Alles. A *Sunday Times* man defends a still barmier farrago about Germany by asserting (alongside a picture of himself in a steel helmet) that his victims probably want to 'send panzers over the border and shoot the editor'. The News Corporation assumption is that staunch patriots want this stuff: that the Chinese like to think the US deliberately attacked their embassy in Belgrade, or Americans that US bombs don't kill Afghans. The relevant Murdoch networks oblige, and the *Sun* continues feeding a supposed British appetite for predatory refugees. (Nicolas Chauvin, the original, at least confined his flattery to Napoleon.)

A diagnosis on Orwell's lines can explain this through Murdoch hoking up and then trashing his Australian national attachment. He could do so because it had never been felt deeply enough to inoculate him against its various corrupt forms. The bravura of the performance (marred only by a touch of paranoia) derived not from depth of attachment but from its lightness – the fluid qualities of an authoritarian personality showing through again. A patriot might have produced the hokum at the Tribunal (though most would have been embarrassed), but that would have made the later Manhattan courthouse ceremony all the more impossible. Someone who hasn't seriously felt an allegiance can of course readily acquire others. But it will be far more difficult to understand why those who have experienced the emotion feel disgust at its exploitation. Furthermore, those to whom patriotism is real never represent it as a dispensable handicap ('Who else chooses to be battered and bruised . . . in being an Australian when it would be a lot easier not to be one?').

Generally people find that their national allegiance – whether or not multiple, like Kipling's – is a stable attribute of their personality, even if they dislike ceremonious patriotism. Both an eighteenth-century statesman and a contemporary biologist tell us that the roots of this emotion are primitive and not to be played with. Burke added to his message a statement that the public systems which assist the development of real allegiance – and today he would doubtless include newspapers, television, schools and churches and probably everything down to sports clubs – constitute 'a trust in the hands of all those who compose it; and as none but bad men would justify it in abuse, none but traitors would barter it away for their own personal advantage'. The next part of the story is about Murdoch bartering his own nationality away, which he did in a complicated fashion. 'Traitor' is of course a very hard word. But the *Sun* chose to insert it as emotional spice into a passage of political flattery.

Construction of the Fox network seems to most witnesses to have been Rupert Murdoch's most striking operation. A widespread view, as it got under way, was that it could never work because of the number of regulatory barriers which impeded it and which would have to be shattered or circumvented. He was already rated as a world-class exponent in this branch of political science, but Fox established him as the supreme virtuoso.

After a remarkably profitable 1970s, placing *Star Wars* within contemporary mythology, the long and adventurous career of the Twentieth Century-Fox movie studio was by 1985 in a tangle. It had been taken over during 1981 by two oil-and-gas entrepreneurs, Marvin Davis and Marc Rich. Rich made for Switzerland in 1982, slightly ahead of the Justice Department (remaining there in well-padded exile until Bill Clinton notoriously pardoned him as a final Presidential act). Davis was not much aided in running the studio by the fact that his absconding partner's half-share was frozen by government application to the courts. In particular it did not help with finding new finance for the debt-sodden enterprise.

Davis had by 1984 got back more than he put in, but had decided that Fox's long-term problems were somewhat beyond him. He invited Barry Diller, who had established a brilliant creative reputation at Paramount, to join him, but they found they could not agree either about what movies to make or about how to raise cash for making them. Diller aroused the interest of Michael Milken, the junk-bond financier, whose career was just then close to its apogee (that is, the point in orbit most distant from earth). Attempts were made to assemble a proposition, but for assorted reasons it collapsed.

One shaft of light appeared at the start of 1985, when the Justice Department decided that Davis could buy Rich's frozen half-share. On 21 March 1985 it was announced that News Corporation would take over the ex-Rich holding from Davis. Rupert Murdoch was one of a number of people who believed that Hollywood studios should become prize assets for television network operators, and that made 50 per cent of Fox worth $250 million.

In the same week Milken was holding a week-long Los Angeles conference for borrowers and lenders using his 'high-yield' bond business at Drexel Burnham Lambert. It is still remembered as the 'Predator's Ball', the representative episode in what ranked, until the dotcom bubble, as the most thrilling modern instance of financial unreason. But of course the criminal charges later laid against Milken, his friend Ivan Boesky and various subordinates were unimagined in 1985. It was a happy throng discussing the gushers of speculative cash being tapped to fuel immense deals in news and entertainment media.

Barry Diller gave a cocktail party at the end of the conference at which the chief guest was John W. Kluge, whose Metromedia Company owned seven television stations in prime locations around America. Michael Milken knew that Kluge wanted to sell some parts of Metromedia, perhaps including the television stations. With Rupert Murdoch and Marvin Davis present, Diller asked Kluge to lay out the position. Kluge said that the licences in Los Angeles, Chicago, Dallas-Fort Worth, Houston, and Washington DC were certainly available. New York and Boston could be, but discussions were under way with the Hearst Corporation. As it happened Kluge and Murdoch were well acquainted. Kluge had long since advised to Murdoch to get into American television, and now he was serving up just that opportunity on a grand scale.

Next day there was a negotiation meeting, which produced an outline proposition under which Fox would take over the Metromedia stations – though the basic Newscorp–Fox deal, including a very necessary injection of cash for the studio, still had to be put to bed. Metromedia's price would be $1.05 billion for the five stations, or $2 billion with New York and Boston included. Murdoch said he only wanted the two-billion deal, which would give access to a quarter of America's television audience.

Diller thought the price (equivalent to $3.2 billion today) was crazy, but Murdoch told him not to worry about it. The point was to work up momentum before some competitor got on to Kluge. The idea of mating a television network with a movie studio was great, but not unique – Ted Turner was already working on his own combination. Diller saw the force in that, but, price apart, he could not see a path through the legal canebrake.

First there were the cross-ownership rules, preventing a newspaper owner from controlling a television station in the same location. Newscorp now owned not just the *New York Post*, but also the *Boston Herald* and the *Chicago Sun-Times*, all in prime sections of the Metromedia territory. Did Murdoch really want to give them up? The way to deal with cross-ownership, Murdoch said, would be to get a temporary waiver from the Federal Communications Commission (FCC) and find a permanent solution later.

A more serious regulatory hurdle concerned the entire philosophy of the deal, and the basic design of American television. With the aim of inhibiting concentrations of power, it had been given a highly sub-divided structure, containing hundreds of stations, often locally owned. Most of them could not afford to make their own drama, soaps and news, so they had to buy supplies in. To maintain sub-division, limits were set on the number of stations which any one company could control. The networks could increase their audiences by making deals with affiliated stations, which bought some of their programming and thus enabled the networks to increase advertising revenues. But they were barred from having a financial interest in material produced for distribution to affiliates. The whole point of putting Fox and the Metromedia stations together was to exploit such a financial interest – indeed, to *facilitate* the concentration of power. But there was a way through, very characteristic of Murdoch.

The FCC would have to let Fox classify itself as a 'mini-network' if the stations were restricted to fifteen hours of network broadcasting per week – at this level the financial-interest regulations didn't have to be followed. This would do for a start, and once things were up and running the FCC would find it difficult to prevent the network time expanding beyond fifteen hours. Indeed, after it had been done the rules could surely be changed to provide retrospective legitimacy. Murdoch's long-standing technique had been to accept explicit regulations in any form demanded and then undermine them by implicit practice, covertly if necessary. If it had failed at London Weekend Television, it had been a complete success at Times Newspapers and elsewhere. The central socio-political achievement of Newscorp has been to get this tireless form of backtracking ranked as commercial genius by financial analysts and bankers.

But beyond this there was the biggest, most obvious point. The American media law said that anyone controlling more than 25 per cent of a television system had to be not just a resident (as in the Australian case) but a citizen of the United States. It was 'not a problem', Murdoch told Diller reassuringly. It was something he could 'take care of'. Diller liked the deal (at this prospective stage, anyway). But he did not see how it could be pulled off given Murdoch's nationality.

Fairly soon the answer to that seemed obvious, as Murdoch ceased his official Australian existence by accepting the oath of allegiance – without a backward glance at his flowery rhetoric just a little earlier. It was somewhat less obvious that the deal required Murdoch to remain Australian in one highly important sense, even after the legalities. This was important to what Arthur Siskind, Murdoch's principal lawyer, later called 'an extraordinarily complicated and very unusual financing'. The Fox operation was not one News could have carried through if it been an American corporation. Success, when finally achieved, consisted of Michael Milken's junk-financing capacity coupled to Australian conceptions of accounting. The regulatory preconditions for it, as Murdoch foresaw, were not so difficult.

In July 1985 News announced that the Metromedia stations would become the basis of a new Fox national network. This was unsurprising news to the Reagan administration, and was welcome on both general and particular grounds. Generally, Mark Fowler, the FCC chairman, wanted to deregulate the media industries – a standard Republican position, as it tends to favour big money, which is a (arguably, the) Republican constituency. This could best be justified by saying that increased competition met regulation's goals more efficiently than regulation, and a new, fourth network obviously was competition. Regulation shouldn't stand in its way.

The particular reason for welcoming the new network was that its moving spirit was Murdoch. Reagan and his colleagues thought highly of what Murdoch's papers had done for them in the Presidential campaigns of 1980 and 1984, and believed that it qualified him admirably to run a national TV network. Probably they did not envisage the *New York Post*'s unsuccessful journalism crossing the species-barrier into television, and the vision anyway might not have troubled them. Their priority was correcting the leftist bias of the existing system (something not visible to foreigners, nor always to native eyes).

Thomas Kiernan, when working in 1985 on what was meant to be Murdoch's approved biography, formed the opinion that Murdoch's hopes at one point extended to a complete, unprecedented waiver on the citizenship rule. The authorised project collapsed when Kiernan rejected Murdoch's concept of editorial independence, and in the following year he published *Citizen Murdoch* entirely without approval. Murdoch, he wrote, had, 'after all, grown accustomed to receiving special favours from the governments of Australia and Britain when faced with sticky regulatory hurdles. Why not the government of the United States, particularly in view of his six years of devoted service to the Reagan inner circle, which for all practical purposes, controlled the FCC?'

Margaret Thatcher's government indeed had boldly ignored the British newspaper law for Murdoch's sake, but the Reagan people were not quite so steely, and thought the Democratic opposition would be galvanised if Murdoch had it so easy with US television. Still, one completely vital concession was made. Had the FCC obeyed its own rules, Murdoch's application would not even have been considered. Three years earlier, Efren Palacios, who had applied to run a station in Texas, was told, 'Although your application for citizenship is pending, you are not yet a citizen and, thus, you are statutorily barred from holding a broadcast license.'

Perhaps even someone as sophisticated as Barry Diller did not quite see that Murdoch ran the kind of newspapers that politicians really found impressive – not ones where 'support' means a well-weighed editorial endorsement, and discreet slanting of a news story here and there. In the famous words of Congressman Jack Kemp, Murdoch's *New York Post* in 1980 had 'used the editorial page and every other page necessary to elect Ronald Reagan President'. This was a little ridiculous, like senior British politicians making the *Sun* an adjunct to the Cabinet secretariat, or Murdoch – further back – trying to establish how many seats News had won for Gough Whitlam. But, as innumerable veterans testify, much high-level politics is about perceptions, illusions and morale-boosting – which newspapers can provide especially well, provided they perform their real tasks badly or not at all.

Mark Fowler was the incoming chairman of the FCC in 1985, and when Murdoch sought approval for taking over the Metromedia licences Fowler found the head of Newscorp to be a man of 'enormous vision'. Fowler's objective was to neutralise regulation and over four years he stripped his Commission of about 70 per cent of the rules it had been applying to broadcasting. Murdoch also met James Quello, appointed by the Republicans as one of Fowler's commissioners, and revealed his readiness to become an American citizen. Quello at once made clear that he was fully behind Murdoch's campaign to become one of the major players in the world media game. Diller wondered whether there might be some problems for Newscorp's television holdings in Australia now that Murdoch wasn't going to stay Australian after all. Worry about that later, Murdoch said.

To deal with the cross-ownership issue, the FCC suggested a two-year waiver, which would allow Murdoch comfortable time to arrange sale of the papers. Murdoch accepted, though he had hoped for more – especially in the case of the *Post*. The Chicago *Sun-Times* was sold almost immediately for $145 million, which was doubtless satisfactory, as it had been bought for $90 million in 1983 (and, although it was profitable, the time to recreate it as an efficient political instrument had not been found). The *Post* Murdoch was anxious to hang on to in spite of its towering losses; it was those losses which enabled him to do so for a long time, as nobody cared to buy it, and forcing the closure of newspapers could never be a popular option for the FCC. Murdoch's widely shared opinion was that the *Post* had made him into a force in US politics, which surely came under the head of 'making the world a better place'.

The FCC also considered, as was its duty, the question of whether News Corporation was able to finance the creation of Fox in a safe and proper manner. It ruled favourably, and without any very close inspection, which ten years later was to cause some anxious moments for many of those concerned. The financing in truth was a heroic task, and began on a stressful note. The deal worked out with Kluge was for Fox to pay $1.55 billion for six stations (Boston having indeed been sold elsewhere). Almost immediately, Marvin Davis decided to pull out altogether: he felt that as things were developing the space between Murdoch and Diller was too small for him (it would before very long prove too small for Diller). This immediately doubled the basic cost for News – and in addition Davis had to be bought out, for another $334 million.

Not that the Fox project was the only big-ticket purchase being made at the time, because Murdoch had agreed to pay $350 million for the Ziff-Davis magazine group. Altogether Newscorp had to raise new debt of $2.7 billion to make things work. And there was good reason to think it was well worth doing: ten years later News controlled, as a result of the outlay, businesses worth about $40 billion, a tenfold return after allowing for inflation.

But the Fox deal and its auxiliary items was not remotely within the capacity of a US company of similar size and construction to News Corporation. In 1985 it had net assets of $166 million according to American accounting rules, and had bank covenants under which its total debt could not be greater than 110 per cent of that asset value. This meant it had a credit limit of about $180 million, entirely dwarfed by the scale of its Fox requirements.

Here the saving circumstance was that News had an Australian identity altogether more persistent than that of its proprietor. It was of course registered in Adelaide, with its shares listed initially on the Adelaide exchange, and traded principally in Sydney. Its existence in New York – the market where its share price really mattered – was by way of ADRs (American Depository Receipts), which are documents that banks create in the US to show they have traded particular shares to order on an overseas exchange. Murdoch's personal equity in News, held through a variety of Australian private companies, has varied over the years between 50 and 30 per cent but it has always been sufficient to guarantee personal control.

To many people News looks like a large American public company. For purposes of decision and control, it rather resembles a privately held Australian concern having a large but disseminated public shareholding. It is in truth the corporate persona of its proprietor, Rupert Murdoch, irrespective of his nationality. In its dealings with the Securities and Exchange Commission, News insists firmly on its foreign status, thus ensuring disclosure requirements minimal by comparison with its US equivalents.

And in 1985 Australian nationality was its decisive resource, beginning with asset values. Murdoch and his finance director, Richard Sarazen, considered that the company's newspaper titles were gaining value, and between 1984 and 1987 they put an additional $1.5 billion against them in the Australian balance sheet. The value of a newspaper title is of course a goodwill item and (as we have seen) this does not count as an asset in American accounting – which anyway does not allow a company to revalue assets upwards. Sarazen's action raised Newscorp's credit capacity by $1.6 billion.

It was a huge advance, but it did not close the gap. To do that,

Newscorp raised another $1.15 billion from Michael Milken and his intrepid investors at Drexel in Los Angeles. But of course this could not be done by issuing anything actually called 'junk bonds'. Even with Milken's reputation at its astronomic 1985 level, the FCC would have balked, and nor would the bankers stand for further additions to debt.

In truth the money was a loan (and, as turned out later, a loan on very onerous terms). But it was reported in News Corporation's accounts as an issue of preference shares. Under a bizarre feature of Australian accounting principles, anything labelled as preferred stock – even if it has all the real attributes of debt – can be treated as shareholders' funds, or equity, and becomes an asset instead of a liability. So by increasing its debt, News acquired the capacity to borrow still more. This was Siskind's 'extraordinarily complicated' financing.

At this point, Australian paradoxes should be briefly recalled. By the mid-1980s Australia's economy had long outgrown its simple base in primary production and protected manufactures. It was diverse, it was generally buoyant, and it had a financial sector with powerful banks well able to syndicate big corporate loans – the Commonwealth Bank, Murdoch's long-term supporter, being prominent among them. But by US standards it was barely regulated: the need to do so had only just become visible, and efforts to meet it were encumbered by interstate rivalry. Exploiting the situation just then were various financial bushrangers who (on their scale) were capable of making Mike Milken look demure (and mostly went to jail for much longer terms). Amid all this, modernising corporate law, tax systems and accounting rules seemed implausible; though the work is now under way it remains incomplete. In 1985 the national mood, never entranced by business, ran more to wry amusement than alarm.

But what drove all this complexity? If the deal was intrinsically good business, could not Newscorp have raised genuine equity rather than junk? In theory yes, but it would no longer have been Newscorp, which is dependent for its value on Rupert Murdoch's arbitrary rule. Admirers consider that this equips it with unique entrepreneurial brio, likely to be suppressed in the culture of an orthodox public company. But there is a good case for saying that arbitrary rule furnishes it with quite different essential attributes.

First, there is its unique capacity to make political alliances, based on Murdoch's ability to turn newspaper support on and off. There are many biased newspapers, but hardly any can modify their bias on command. Doing so means hiring journalists who either have no individual judgment, or will suppress it: the resulting work is usually mediocre, often bad, and sometimes disgraceful. Murdoch's strength here is that he doesn't know or doesn't care about the difference, and it would be hard to be so cavalier except in an absolutist regime. And more important is the executive technique which exploits an alliance once made. Young radicals may think otherwise, but the number of business executives who can consistently undertake to do one thing and then pursue a quite different course is limited. Again, it is a behavioural pattern which ortho- dox companies can pursue only for a limited time – and a débâcle like Enron proves, does not contest, the point.

With the money on the way – at no risk to Newscorp's command structure, risking only its financial stability – the actual mechanism for controlling the new television system could be set up. The Metromedia stations were put into Twentieth Holdings Corporation, which had a small quantity of voting stock. Barry Diller and Rupert Murdoch took up 75 per cent of it, shared equally between them. Twentieth was an American company, but its major capital was in the form of non-voting shares, 99 per cent owned by the Australian company News Corporation. So this was Australian ownership, but the control was in the hands of two American citizens. The FCC had no difficulty in approving the set-up.

However, it was not quite as simple as that. News Corporation, under the articles of Twentieth Holdings, could at any time force Murdoch and Diller to sell to it all of their voting shares. So in the ultimate case the final power over the Fox network belonged to an Adelaide company which was controlled by an American citizen through a number of other Australian entities. Ten years later several FCC officials maintained that the Commission did not understand this subtlety – which meant that whoever exercised ultimate legal control over Fox had to do so from out- side America. Essentially Fox's reply was that if the officials had not grasped the point it was due to their own inattention. Whatever the rights and wrongs of this – which must be taken later in the story – it was another complex strand in the remarkable fabric of Fox.

And not the last. Drexel Burnham Lambert had severe difficulty getting their investors lined up. Some other big deals had begun to turn nasty, and the notion of junk finance relabelled as preferred equity was a puzzle even to veterans of the Milken trail.

Murdoch believed that his London newspapers would enable him to meet the immense interest bills created by the Fox deal, because he was setting up a plan capable of extracting another $150 million of annual profit from them. This was the celebrated move of all the papers away from their decrepit, union-dominated presses and into a new, purpose-built non-union plant with up-to-date electronic composition and lithographic presses. Desultory negotiations had been going on with the unions for several years, but without progress – a situation blamed by Murdoch's managers on union cantankerousness and by the unions on Newscorp's lack of interest. It is true that the two huge tabloids were so profitable intrinsically that the inefficiency of the plant was not, until 1985, a crucial issue.

Now it was, but there was no time for negotiation or uncertainty – Murdoch had to have the extra revenue without delay. Therefore the plans for a sudden, unanswerable coup had to be laid in deep secrecy. Nobody could be told about the profitable future, and certainly not Milken's punters.

However, Milken was able to point to the Fox deal, full of splendid possibilities, but rather further off. Eventually, the $1.15 billion was going to make News into a massively valuable company, and out of this, presumably, came the idea of tying the repayment system to the share price: after 1989, for every dollar that the share price rose above the March 1985 base, another 15 per cent would have to be repaid – and this did the trick. 'This . . . must have seemed like a good idea at the time,' wrote the Australian financial reporter Neil Chenoweth (who uncovered most of these details in *Virtual Murdoch*), 'as long as News Corp didn't do anything to make its share price spike up. It turned out to be a spectacularly effective way to tear up money.'

The year 1985 ended with Murdoch getting acclimatised to his new status as a US citizen. But by this point everything depended on a relationship with the British Prime Minister.

12

MARGARET THATCHER'S HEROES, 1982–1989

> If the journals were a novel, the heroine would be Margaret Thatcher ... and the heroes would be Rupert Murdoch and Lord Weinstock.
>
> SARAH CURTIS, in her introduction to
> *The Journals of Woodrow Wyatt*, vol. 1

> 'We've got to get her out of this jam somehow. It's looking very bad.'
>
> RUPERT MURDOCH, to Wyatt, 14 January 1986

Margaret Thatcher's political administration and Rupert Murdoch's business empire both went through defining crises in the New Year of 1986. The two events interacted, and with results which turned out in the end rather better for him than for her – casting interesting light on the relative advantages of media power and political power.

The financial connection between Murdoch's great Battle of Wapping and the birth of the Fox network in America has been acutely pointed out by Neil Chenoweth – and was quoted at the end of the previous chapter. But he may have gone a little far in suggesting that it was the British social system which unravelled in consequence. Rather, it was a part of the system called the Conservative Party, which at the time of writing has yet to recover.

Murdoch's father Keith worked in direct personal contact with Billy

Hughes, Joe Lyons and Robert Menzies. Similarly Rupert's 1960s apprenticeship with Black Jack McEwen was direct and personal. In the 1970s and 1980s a business operating multi-nationally needed more complex linkages, and Murdoch successfully developed the ability to work through others, like John Menadue and Larry Lamb. Of course Menadue – the man through whom the eventually destructive link between Rupert Murdoch and Gough Whitlam (see Chaper 6 above) was established – was never Murdoch's instrument alone, and Lamb considered himself, if not very credibly, an independent editorial power.

Woodrow Wyatt, who succeeded Larry Lamb as Murdoch's chief link with Margaret Thatcher, was much more completely the courtier (which means lobbyist in present-day terms) and, as the editor of his journals suggests, a personal acolyte. The 1980s in Britain were a decade of hectically coloured political events, and are treasured by a good many people as the country's second- or third-finest hour. Serious-minded comparisons have been drawn in which Margaret Thatcher is Elizabeth Tudor – Gloriana – and Rupert Murdoch the splendid pirate Sir Francis Drake. Wyatt indeed saw it like that.

Politics as historical melodrama turned out to be an expensive occupation for the country as a whole. Britain began the period with a functioning Conservative Party – one capable either of governing the country or of providing an effective Opposition – and emerged some years later with an inharmonious fringe movement in its place. The operations of the modern-day Sir Francis turn out to be closely connected with this transformation – a story which concludes with the chronicler Wyatt in a disillusioned condition, though that denouement isn't reached in this chapter. Wyatt, unlike Murdoch, was a true believer in the Thatcher cause.

It seems to have been Harry Evans who introduced them, at a dinner party given in 1969 when his most adventurous years with the *Sunday Times* were still to come. Evans then felt a mixture of sympathy and curiosity towards Murdoch, who was enduring resentfully the worst of the Profumo backlash (see Chapter 4 above). Much of the evening was taken up with Wyatt's passionate defence of the Vietnam War.

Wyatt was a man of causes, to which he brought pertinacity and polemical skill but, as time passed, an increasingly erratic judgment –

something demonstrated, if not otherwise, by his estimate of Murdoch as a man of similar outlook to his own. Operating under that illusion, he was able to do much essential good for Murdoch which the hero would have found hard to secure by himself. Lord Wyatt – as his heroine eventually named him – was like a soldier who, having secured one spectacular and righteous victory, spends subsequent years in search of others, without paying much attention to the features of the battlefield or the nature of his opponents. He distinguished himself initially as an opponent of communist dishonesties which others on the British left preferred to ignore.

Woodrow Wyatt was born in 1918, a descendant of Thomas Wyatt, the chief architect of Worcester College, Oxford, from which he graduated in law just before the Second World War – and, though a generation intervened, he felt connected to Murdoch through their college. When he became a Labour Member of Parliament in 1945, he seemed one of the likeliest of the upper-middle-class war veterans recruited to socialism by the Great Depression and their experiences in the anti-fascist war. But he sharply reduced his standing with Labour by heretically opposing the nationalisation of the steel industry in 1951. At that time the party believed in state socialism as a cure for the British industrial system's ills just as passionately as the Thatcherites later believed in privatisation.

As this is written – as the British public contemplates the festering state of its nationalised–privatised rail infrastructure – it is hard to recall why either side felt so sure it was discussing the real point. But the passage of time detracts only slightly from Wyatt's stand in his other early cause. He was centrally involved in exposing the Communist Party's illegal control of what was then the Electrical Trades Union (ETU), one of the country's biggest organisations of skilled workers. This drawn-out battle began when Wyatt was a Labour MP and continued when he became a BBC television presenter after the loss of his seat in 1951.

The communist minority in the ETU gained and held control by their proficiency in ballot-rigging. They were dislodged by lawsuits which right-wing members of the union fought, and by journalistic disclosures – many of them Wyatt's, via the BBC's *Panorama* programme, the *New Statesman* magazine and the *Daily Mirror*. The victors then imposed a regime not much less draconian than that of the communists, which was deeply resented by left-wing unions who were not communist themselves but had been reliant on policy support from that direction. Many chose not to notice that the ETU right, if rebarbative at times, was not illegitimate.

The effect of this on the ETU was to create a relationship of contempt with the rest of the union movement – this would make them eventually into the footsoldiers of Murdoch's 1986 war against the print unions. The effect on Wyatt was to shift his political standpoint towards the Manichaean right, from which he increasingly saw any liberal or social-democratic view as incipient communism, fit only for denunciation. This by stages enlisted him in support of causes such as the elimination of a crypto-communist 'Mafia' alleged to control the BBC; the racially neutral character of apartheid; the unharmful character of tobacco (especially with reference to cancer); and the prospect of swift victory in Vietnam if Western backsliders could just be silenced. He became a recognised eccentric – though one with a wide political connection, because many people thought him entertaining, and some saw that he had the courage of his eccentricities.

None of this made him a Tory – after Labour proscribed him he never joined another party. But it made him a devotee of Margaret Thatcher, when he became convinced in the 1970s that she would blow away 'the soggy consensus which had lain like dank fog over Britain and her politicians since 1951'. He was not quite right, for 'consensus' means uniformity of opinion, and Mrs Thatcher turned out to have a sturdy affection for it. But he was right that the kind of consensus she wanted to impose was a new one, and not soggy. He became one of her admirers before the 1979 election (see Chapter 7 above), and then one of the circle of informal advisers she consulted regularly once she was Prime Minister – and whom she usually cited to her Cabinet colleagues as 'my people'.

To Geoffrey Howe, who was Chancellor of the Exchequer and then Foreign Secretary, it sometimes seemed as though Mrs Thatcher 'was Joan of Arc invoking the authority of her "voices". The Prime Minister was understandably reluctant to reveal the balance of her telephonic kitchen cabinet. Quite often, I suspect, the voice was that of Woodrow Wyatt – which she may have thought sufficient reason for cloaking it in anonymity.' Wyatt's own very persuasive account – discussed in Chapter 8 – was that he played the crucial part in her determination to protect News International's purchase of Times Newspapers from the Monopolies Commission in 1981.

In 1983, after a long period writing for the *Daily Mirror*, he agreed with Murdoch a contract to write each week two columns in *The Times* and one in the *News of the World* – where he was billed each Sunday as The Voice of Reason. Charles Douglas-Home, editor of *The Times*, and David Montgomery, editor of the *News of the World*, were involved with these arrangements in trivial detail alone. Remuneration was discussed with Murdoch or with News International managers, and editorially Wyatt was quite independent of such modest independence as the two editors themselves possessed.

In October 1985 Wyatt began keeping his very detailed diaries, recording regular weekend phone conversations with the Prime Minister, and intermittent meetings. They also show that whenever Murdoch was in London he and Wyatt made personal contact, and often discussed Prime Ministerial opinions and intentions. In the years since, Murdoch has suggested when convenient that his connection with the Prime Minister was (like his acquaintance with Sir John Kerr) fragmentary and episodic. But this is tergiversation – the diaries reveal a sturdy, continuous link, which it was Wyatt's task to maintain and enhance as far as the crowded schedules of his two principals allowed.

If there is similarity between the roles of Wyatt and Menadue, there is a major difference as well. Where traffic in the Whitlam case had been largely one-sided, respects and confidences travelled in both directions between Thatcher and Murdoch. Whereas Whitlam didn't care to 'share his thoughts with Rupert Murdoch', Mrs Thatcher was ready to do so – in person, where circumstance allowed, and otherwise through Wyatt.

29 December 1985 . . . I asked her whether she would like to come to dinner again. She said 'Very much.' 'Who would you like to have with you?' 'Oh, just one or two people . . . What about Rupert Murdoch? I like talking to him . . .'

Wyatt would have strongly resented being called a 'lobbyist' – for he had once done serious service as a journalist – but that was exactly what he became. During the whole of Mrs Thatcher's reign he had access of a kind which those who openly acknowledge their activities can only dream about (and, though Murdoch was his chief client, there were several others).

As Howe's description shows, the Prime Minister was discreet about the relationship, and Wyatt himself made his arrangements clandestine as far as possible; though he liked to talk himself up in other matters, he took care not to boast about his calls to Downing Street. Neither Thatcher nor Murdoch knew about the diaries until after Wyatt's death, and, although members of the Cabinet were aware that the 'voices' exercised influence – and that Wyatt was a prominent one – they knew very little about the details. Wyatt's picture of Margaret Thatcher is affectionate throughout. He cannot endow her with Elizabeth Tudor's polymathic intellect, but she seems warm, and sometimes amusing – it is not a toady's relationship. And Murdoch, most of the way, indeed shows in a heroic light. But even in the first volume of the diaries, largely triumphal, there are moments where the frailty of Murdoch's attachment to the true faith – a major theme of the third volume – makes itself uncomfortably visible to Wyatt.

For example, like the Prime Minister and other of her advisers, he believed there was a vast, Augean task to be undertaken in cleansing the BBC of decadent leftism, before relaunching it as a grand vessel of private enterprise. When the BBC chairmanship came up in 1986 he therefore hoped for a modern Hercules to be appointed. At the time the job was in the Prime Ministerial gift with no trace of public accountability, and she gave it to Duke Hussey, then performing minor tasks for Murdoch at Times Newspapers.

Wednesday 1 October . . . a message to speak to Downing Street urgently. The Prime Minister wanted me to know before the official announcement . . . that Duke Hussey was to be the new Chairman . . . I was shattered . . .

Wyatt's immediate, horrified thought was that Murdoch must be responsible, must have cynically unloaded on Downing Street the man who had reduced the *Sunday Times* and *The Times* to the sad condition of takeover fodder (see Chapter 8 above) and had been kept on, as Wyatt thought, for the sake of charity – now opportunistically terminated. But reassurance came almost immediately:

> Rupert rings in a great state: 'Has she gone mad? What a disastrous appointment. He (Hussey) was quite useless here and the only thing he was fit for was to run things like the Hampton Court entertainment . . . They will make rings round him. The BBC Mafia must be absolutely delighted . . .'

Murdoch's conspiratorial suggestion was that Hussey's royal connections (his wife was a lady-in-waiting to the Queen) must be grooming him for a peerage. But a few days later the subject came up when Wyatt was helping the Prime Minister with her speech for the Tory Party conference.

> When I told her that the Duke Hussey appointment was a bad one, disastrous like the two previous ones, she said, 'I wouldn't have done it if I hadn't had a strong recommendation from Rupert.' I was amazed and said, 'But he rang me up asking whether you'd gone mad . . .'
> 'Good Lord,' she said. 'Well, he told me he was a very strong man, what had happened at *The Times* was not his fault . . . Otherwise I wouldn't have made the appointment.'

Wyatt, nothing if not persistent, caught up with his boss four days later, as Murdoch was taking flight for California.

> I tackle him about his having recommended Duke Hussey. Strange. He denies it, says he didn't mention his name . . . I said, 'Are you sure you didn't say anything about Duke Hussey?' He seemed evasive and giggled a bit. I said, 'Why did she get the strong impression that you did?' He says he doesn't know. I think she is telling the truth and not Rupert . . .

It seems unlikely that Thatcher or Wyatt were mistaken about what was said – and the exchange disposes of suggestions that the Murdoch–Thatcher bond was in any way trivial. The giggle, perhaps, is a rare manifestation of Murdoch's inner amazement at the suggestibility of politicians.

By the middle of the 1980s, as Murdoch's business operations moved towards the great Wapping turning point, Mrs Thatcher and her small but ascendant section within the government had gained a degree of influence over British news media which Lord Shawcross and his Royal Commission colleagues – working a decade earlier – might well have thought dangerous. This influence they owed for the most part to the Murdoch alliance, which Wyatt administered. That it didn't become still greater – even absolute – was due not to any lack of ambition, only to complications the allies failed to foresee. But it is important to notice that their motivations were not quite uniform, and the case of the BBC illustrates this. Alfred (later Sir Alfred) Sherman, a Thatcher Voice in good standing, wrote of the BBC in 1984:

> There has never been a justification for its existence. It was formed during an authoritarian mood following the First World War. Justifications adduced for state broadcasting and state control of broadcasting (and until a few years ago for state monopoly of broadcasting) are identical with those used in communist and other dictatorships for state monopoly of the press.

To equate the BBC with Soviet broadcasting systems because of nominal resemblance in formal structure is like calling the USSR a democracy because of the elaborate constitution it used to parade (as Sir Alfred perhaps did in his communist period).

Murdoch could happily go along with the rhetoric – elements of it occur in his recurrent assaults on public-service broadcasting – but we may be sure he never shared Sherman's cock-eyed sincerity. Dictatorship and state monopoly do not repel him, provided Newscorp can cut a deal with the system. Outfits like the BBC, however, under any political or economic system, are competitors which it is important to undermine – because of their inexplicable creativity, if nothing else. The majority of witnesses agree that Hussey, as encore to his performance at Times Newspapers, did extensive (luckily non-fatal) damage to the BBC.

During the reign of Harry Evans, *The Times*' tradition of critical sympathy with the government of the day had suffered interruption – more as a matter of troublesome news coverage than actual editorial opinion. That, of course, ended with his departure, but not by way of return to the older attitude. Subservience was the new thing.

Richard Davy, who was in charge of foreign affairs editorials when Charles Douglas-Home took over from Evans, recalls that the newspaper's staff knew quite clearly where instruction came from:

> Murdoch had let it be known that Charlie was a temporary editor, which did not suit Charlie at all, so he was eager to please.
>
> We were soon given to understand that no criticism of Margaret Thatcher or Ronald Reagan was allowed. Other changes followed. Strange interpolations crept into leaders on their way to the printer, often reversing the sense.

On serious newspapers, journalists never surreptitiously switch agreed meanings of copy during the production process – if only because that way madness lies. And the atmosphere Davy describes indeed seems febrile and neurotic:

> From having been personally critical of Zionism Charlie now supported 'my friends the Israelis', as Murdoch called them. Foreign aid became bad. Towards Moscow, balanced analysis was replaced by denunciations of the 'evil empire' that echoed Washington's line at the time.
>
> Charlie was so insecure that even when he was away he would phone in to have the leading articles read to him. Neither of the two previous editors had done that, so we felt demeaned. Once he called me from a phone box on the Scottish moors. Suddenly I heard a yelp and a clatter as the receiver fell, followed by the sound of birdsong. After a few moments he returned, breathless, to explain that he had left the handbrake off and his car was about to roll into a loch.

Douglas-Home's behaviour suggests that the proprietor's flip-and-zap technique was being applied to him effectively. ('I give instructions to my editors all round the world,' said Murdoch. 'Why shouldn't I in London?') Where there had once been analysis there was now 'a personal opinion passed down from on high', says Davy, who thought Murdoch 'was not really interested in issues, only in positioning his papers to win allies in high places'. Nominally the statutory provisions for the independence of *The Times* remained in place. But they could hardly be cited by Douglas-Home, had he wished to do so, because he owed his job to having helped subvert them. What he did do was behave humanely towards those like Davy, who preferred to leave rather than learn the new obedience.

It is hard to believe that Douglas-Home's short period in command brought happiness: for much of the time he was courageously bearing a painful disease, and when it killed him in October 1985 Murdoch appointed Charlie Wilson, who had spent most of his career in popular newspapers, and maintained the simple allegiance with apparent enthusiasm.

The capture of *The Times* was part of a process, naturally, and Wyatt must have been pleased with the spread of 'pro-Margaret' editorial attitudes. The *Sun* offered no pretence of independence. Lamb in his latter period argued occasionally with Murdoch; his successor Kelvin MacKenzie said once that if the Boss told him to print the paper in Sanskrit he would readily do so.

To be sure the *Mail*, *Telegraph* and *Express* papers were independent of Murdoch, and were constituted differently, their adherence to the conservative right due rather to conviction than to corporatist tactics. But it limited them no less in Thatcherite times as a source of countervailing opinion (they were better qualified ten years later, when Murdoch rediscovered social democracy). And partisan opinion anyway is not the critical item in the capacity of professional newspapers to challenge governments. Penetrative reporting – independent of editorial stance – is what matters, as examples from the *Washington Post* and the Melbourne *Herald* have shown. In the Telegraph and Express groups, for different reasons, that technical propensity was modest or declining. More existed at the *Mail*, but masked by Thatcherite commitment – the principle of judgment distinct from ideology never having been strong in Northcliffe's old territory. The *Independent*, founded to restate it, was only preparing its launch during the countdown to Wapping.

The *Mirror* was experiencing the saddest passage in its editorial history, and the *Financial Times* was sticking close to its specialist ground, avoiding investigative action as a board-level policy. A formal left–right analysis rarely describes newspapers adequately, but as a practical matter the potential for sceptical inspection of the Thatcher administration in the mid-1980s centred on the *Guardian* daily and the *Observer* weekly – that is, newspapers with a technical facility which partisanship had not disabled – and on television, insofar as its non-partisan constitution was sufficiently strong.

For a decade or more, the *Sunday Times* had generally been the most penetrative media outfit the government and its connections had to reckon with – which does not mean the *Guardian* and *Observer* were supine, or that there were not strong, independent minds elsewhere. But they were used to competing against a well-organised, determined, even dominant rival. Now, in situations concerning Downing Street or its allies, competitive pressures were replaced by an unfamiliar isolation. In few trades is competition a genuine comfort. But journalism which the government dislikes is certainly an example.

Some energy has been spent denying that the *Sunday Times* during the Thatcher years ceased offering any serious check to the state power in Britain. The denial has particular vigour in *Full Disclosure*, the memoirs of Andrew Neil, the paper's editor from 1983 to 1995. Neil's account is one of being commissioned by Murdoch to restore a moribund, even corrupted, newspaper of slender investigative capacity. He briskly restores its health and soon has it 'ruining the Sunday breakfasts of the rich and powerful', Margaret Thatcher's included. 'Up to a point, Lord Copper' is the response in Evelyn Waugh's *Scoop* when the proprietor of the *Daily Beast* drives reality from the field. More accurately, it was during Neil's watch that this major newspaper changed character and would later become capable of spouting official propaganda – a transition certainly linked to the influence of Rupert Murdoch.

The *Sunday Times* after two years under Murdoch was in professional trouble. Much of this was due to manipulation of its editorial structure (see Chapter 8 above). Still more harm had been done by the Hitler Diaries fraud – a shattering humiliation which requires separate discussion. More than any other British paper it depended on an investigative reputation to sustain the value of its brand and motivate its staff. Nobody had expected Frank Giles to succeed in that direction, and the attempt to generate a replacement by natural selection had failed. Andrew Neil was Murdoch's deliberate choice once he was able to make it with an effective free hand – and it was a long-term success, in a role more complex than Lamb or MacKenzie were needed for. Many people would identify Neil as the most impressive journalistic figure to develop under the Murdoch aegis.

Energy, physical and intellectual, was (and remains) his distinction. Having begun (after Glasgow University) as a Tory Party researcher, he progressed to the *Economist* and became a fluent television presenter in the 1970s. His first contact with Murdoch was as a television consultant, and a wide-ranging, forceful mind made him a good prospect to edit a Sunday broadsheet. But his experience was in opinion-dealing, rather than first-hand reporting and production technique. His conservatism he saw as rebellious nonconformity (at Glasgow, he refused to smoke hash), making him enthusiastic for Thatcher's revolution: something which doubtless engaged Murdoch. But Neil could not become a tabloid cheerleader with selective targeting policies. The *Sunday Times*, if it did not seem to imperil the Prime Minister's coffee-cups, would lose much of its value.

Neil's view of investigation was ideologically tinged: he thought the Insight team were left-wingers, so assumed they would have some ideas attractive to him. On inspection, he liked nothing, and disbanded Insight. The list of leftists bad at investigation readily disproves Neil's assumption that politics directly generates the required talent – but it does not include Christopher Hird, the Insight editor of the time. Hird's string of successes – pre- and post-Neil – suggests that Murdoch's new editor began without much idea of what a nascent investigation looks like.

Neil restarted Insight eventually with altered principles and results which we shall come to later. But in the meantime Mrs Thatcher denounced him in Parliament, and Neil presents this, with some enthusiasm, as the consequence of an 'exclusive' *Sunday Times* disclosure which opened the Thatcher family to criticism, as did the Welsh real-estate development in Chapter 10. It is his citation as that unusual creature, an independent Thatcherite. But it was only an exclusive up to a point.

In 1982 Mrs Thatcher, visiting Oman, Britain's Persian Gulf ally, used the moment to lobby for Cementation Ltd, a British firm bidding to construct the Sultanate's first university. The bid succeeded – Britain meanwhile restoring certain cuts in aid – and the Prime Minister was once more 'batting for Britain'. But nothing was said about Mark Thatcher, the Prime Minister's son, visiting Oman simultaneously as a consultant for Cementation – and joining her in a reception at the Sultan's summer palace, beyond media view. British officials disliked seeing mother and son jointly promoting a commercial cause – particularly as Mark just then was living at 10 Downing Street. Mark's marketing company received a substantial payment for aiding Cementation, and during 1983 rumours began to reach journalistic antennae.

But turning rumour to fact is usually arduous when it concerns the use of high, reflected power. This work was done not by the *Sunday Times*: it was David Leigh and Paul Lashmar of the *Observer*, who produced on 15 January 1984, after three months' pursuit, a front-page lead which was indeed exclusive: 'MARK THATCHER AND A £300M ARAB DEAL'. The paper's editorial, headed 'The case of Caesar's son', said Mrs Thatcher's response to the story might cause more 'disquiet' than the story itself.

This referred to the rage evoked (unattributably) when the *Observer*, in pre-publication etiquette, asked Downing Street for comment or rebuttal. Nothing was said of the facts – only that reporting them would be treated as scurrilous partisanship. Donald Trelford, the editor, realised this was browbeating designed to deter all questioners, and choosing to ignore it gave him and his staff a lonely start to 1984: their story, for some weeks, grew more not less exclusive. Many editors, said Ronald Dworkin, Oxford's professor of jurisprudence, were too ready to 'down tools once someone powerful tells them that the public has no right to know'.

The *Sunday Times* was silent till 12 February, when it interviewed Mark Thatcher. Under the heading 'PUT UP OR SHUT UP', Mark expanded on the government's allegations of malicious trickery. Downing Street, said the *Sunday Times*, saw the *Observer*'s inquiries as 'a politically inspired "psychological" campaign to get at the Prime Minister through her son'. This coverage conveyed sufficient flavour of privacy assaulted for Number 10 to circulate it to broadcasters. (Tastes vary on conflicts of interest. In the same issue a powerful leader on satellite television didn't mention Newscorp's Sky investment.)

But the *Sunday Times* staff seem to have found Number 10's embrace no more agreeable than being scooped on territory so often their own. And as the *Observer* persisted, so did the reporters of Mark's interview, Barrie Penrose and Simon Freeman: eventually 'a contact' told them Denis Thatcher was signatory to the bank account of Mark's firm. This addition didn't turn Oman into a public-interest issue: plainly it always was. But this was an item the paper simply had to print. Otherwise – even if staff didn't walk out – the story would do so, generating massive discredit. On 4 March Penrose and Freeman had a front-page headline: 'DENIS SHARES MARK'S OMAN ACCOUNT', with some acid quotes about the quality of Mark's consultancy. (Nobody, in the *Sunday Times* or else-where, suggested the father's involvement went beyond loyal counsel for a son's unsteady business.)

Unctuous editorialising mitigated this disclosure. The *Sunday Times* had not been among those 'leaping on every excuse to keep the story alive'. It would not join such a campaign: Mark's interview had been its sole earlier reference, and though there was now 'embarrassing' matter on page one, it probably came to 'much ado about little'. The govern-ment had been too secretive. But frank disclosure would repulse the detractors.

Ignoring this humble suggestion, the Prime Minister turned fero-ciously on the *Sunday Times* which – by tactical incaution – was offering an opportune diversion. Sourced to a nameless 'contact' the bank account story looked like traffic in personal data filched from financial institutions: a thing hated by the public. And use of a false name in the inquiry – venially, in truth – sanctified additional outrage. Now, Thatcher told Parliament, there *was* a matter of public concern: 'methods of impersonation and deception' had been used to gain 'information about a private bank account which was subsequently published in a national newspaper'. (Mark's business affairs were by contrast private and irre-proachable.)

Heavily – if unfairly – lacerated, the *Sunday Times* silently abandoned disclosure's cause. The *Observer*, however, pressed on with new news of Mark's doings in the Middle and Far East. And finally on 1 April its lead story was 'MARK QUITS CEMENTATION, DOWNING STREET – AND UK'. He was leaving to become the American representative for Lotus cars, giving up his Downing Street flat. And claims that all had been beyond reproach were given up also. Mark had been 'naïve . . . not to see that people I regarded as friends would use an association with me for their own ends'. Now he would stand on his own feet. The *Observer* ran its story at some length. A paragraph in the *Sunday Times* said Mark regretted embarrassing his mother.

Neil presents the episode as his *Sunday Times* pursuing truth, however disobliging to the great. Really, it came late to the pursuit, with manifest reluctance; operated with ineptness troublesome to those properly engaged; and withdrew with the outcome undecided. Neil tried far harder than MacKenzie or Douglas-Home to prove essential journalism possible within the Archipelago's boundaries: his book gives every sign of genuine belief, and some of effect. But calling a counterproductive follow-up an 'exclusive' demonstrates the poverty of instances available.

Mark Thatcher's Oman deal was peripheral to the Murdoch newspapers' dealings with the Thatcher administration. The Westland crisis and the controversy over *Death on the Rock* represent the main thread.

If, as in the Murdoch case, political journalism consists of maintaining sympathetic relations with authority, then the Westminster lobby system has matchless attractions. It has been turned to account by skilful and diligent reporters, but it is a system designed to enable the government to write its own coverage and have it distributed with an independent appearance. It was set up by Ramsay MacDonald's Labour government at the end of the 1920s, in response to the right-wing bias of the London press. It was based on the perception that to many humans comfort outranks prejudice. Thus if confidential arrangements were made to provide a restricted number of correspondents with non-attributable stories for easy collection, much of their content would insinuate itself even into hostile newspapers. ('The best story,' said Hunter Davies classically, 'is one that gets you home in time for tea.') Tory successors like Neville Chamberlain enhanced the system, and its role in mobilising the British press (not only *The Times*) for Appeasement is chillingly described in Richard Cockett's book *Twilight of the Truth*.

Similar practices exist, of course, in all media cultures. But in Westminister great attention was paid to making information unattributable and restricting journalistic membership. Rigorously unsourced stories suit both the government and its interlocutors, enabling the first to disavow unlucky fabrications and the second to apply any editorial spin thought useful. In the Westland dispute, which reached its crisis on the afternoon of 24 January 1986, when Mrs Thatcher found herself saying, 'I may not be Prime Minister by six o'clock this evening', both techniques showed to full effect.

It is sometimes said that societies are vulnerable chiefly through their good qualitics, and the lobby is a case: it draws on the British gift for trust within small, close-knit groups – colleges, regiments, clubs. In praise of the system Lord Howe once described a moment in his period as Foreign Secretary when he and his officials, in transit, forgot a small, essential statement. The lobby did not report – as they could have – a 'gaffe', but issued suitable sentiments in his name. An American or Australian reporter might see the amiable gesture as clearly as Howe did, but see also a relationship ripe for exploitation by Murdoch's kind of newspaper.

Naturally the lobby proper is not-for-profit (Appeasement's artificers at least were not in it for cash). But by the mid-1980s the formalised, secret news-media lobby was – like every limb of government – encircled by a very commercial, half-visible penumbra of political consultants, public-relations operators and unregistered urgers. Some of these involved themselves in the Westland story alongside elected representatives, journalists and officials.

By providing its staple food the Prime Minister's press secretary dominates the lobby. Mrs Thatcher's Bernard Ingham did so exceptionally because he had the News papers as core support, and only isolated challengers. The post is held usually by an able, not outstanding, ex-journalist and Ingham fitted the pattern: aged forty-seven on joining Thatcher, he had entered government service from the *Guardian* labour staff at thirty-five. He developed into one of the most flamboyant incumbents – reputed, in harness with the *Sun*, to be able to promote issues and terminate ministers at command.

And he was a bold exponent of his great weapon of office – the right of selective display over the entrails of government. Britain's Official Secrets law – born of a crackpot Edwardian spy scare, and still not decently reformed – supports a presumption that all official business is secret unless official exception is made. Other democracies have diluted or reversed this insane principle – and the courts have riddled it with holes – but it was potent in the 1980s and remains so today. 'I regard myself,' said Ingham, 'as licensed to break that law as and when I judge necessary; and I suppose it is necessary to break it every other minute of the working day . . .' The leak as political weapon essentially consists of selective disclosure. Protected by unattributable status and distributed by a complaisant press, it gave Ingham and his boss great – if not quite predictable – leverage.

When chief executives of nations are rated for power, we sometimes forget to distinguish between gross and net: between the total power of the nation and the amount of it in the chief executive's hand. Obviously the economic and military force of the United States is matchless, so the President is routinely considered the world's most powerful individual. But America's constitutional structure limits the extent to which the President's will goes unchecked. A dictator in a fair way of business has in some respects more liberty than America's chief executive. Great Britain is an intermediate case.

The Prime Minister is in charge of an economy which is about fourth largest in the world, and a society generally stable and resilient. Its experienced military force is capable of distant deployment. Outside America France is the only equivalent. And what power Britain has is close to the hands of the Prime Minister – more at the Thatcher zenith than now, because some Westminster business has gone to the assemblies of Scotland, Wales and Northern Ireland, and some to the European Community. Nothing moderates the sway of the British chief executive even as much as the Australian states modify the central authority of Canberra, and the distance from America's federal and separated structure is enormous. Globalisation has not yet turned even the Anglophone societies into copies of one another. For such reasons the office of Prime Minister has been called an 'elective dictatorship' – though it is surely a 'responsible' one as well. But this invites the question: responsible where, via what machinery? And this returns us to the Westminster lobby.

Of course the responsibility is to Parliament, but it is not owed by the Prime Minister individually – it is the collective responsibility of the Cabinet. Bagehot's *English Constitution* cites Lord Melbourne as producing (dryly) a classic formulation: 'Now, is it to lower the price of corn, or isn't it? It is not much matter which we say, but mind, we must all *say the same.*' The Thatcher Cabinet found that difficult. The principal bar to elective dictatorship is that a group of ministers, meeting regularly and minuting their discussions, agree to speak consistently to Parliament when their policy is scrutinised. It is, of course, fiction that they hold identical views – collective responsibility rather is a statement of what the administration's members can defend with varying enthusiasm. But it prevents government condensing into a single, arbitrary will.

It was hard for the Thatcher Cabinet to meet Melbourne's requirement because, in Lord Howe's words, it dwelt in a 'leak-driven world' – there is of course a similar account from James Prior cited in Chapter 8. Howe had served in Edward Heath's Tory administration, and says leaks were then so rare that he recalls no example. The Heath Cabinet could spend a day on economic scenarios '– some of them deeply gloomy – without seeing them splashed all over the newspapers. Margaret Thatcher and her colleagues were never able to do the same.' Howe believes that the fish-tank condition of the administration did heavy damage, still unrepaired, to basic democratic processes – to open thinking within the government, and between government and people. Rational discussion, in his argument, requires participants who know what audience they are speaking to, and need not fear the use of selective confidentiality for its tactical effect. 'A truly plural democratic society cannot hope to survive without a renewal of confidence and trust between government and media.'

Lord Howe's point is obviously serious. But our story suggests that the harm he sees was caused by an extreme *over*-confidence – within part of the government and a dominant part of the media. 'Trust' may not be the right second term, but 'mutual dependence' might do – making a good fit, also, for the link between News Ltd and the honchos of the ALP in the previous decade. Relationships in the boundary layer dividing journalism and politics have been subject to plenty of argument, and a good case can be made that in twentieth-century Britain they were generally too close, trespassing on the separateness which adult growth requires. And explanations can be guessed at – such as the mid-century wartime consensus.

But for the Thatcher team the boundary had no significance wherever drawn. Their world's only division was between Us, a votive band, and Them, an inertial mass. Temperamentally Mrs Thatcher was far away from Lord Melbourne's remark that he did not know whether people's good or bad intentions did the greater harm. Certainty reigned. 'The "Thatcher Revolution" is working: there is still much to be done, but it is happening,' wrote an exhilarated admirer. The language was representative, as was the fact that it came from a knighted long-service bureaucrat – for the revolutionary jacquerie were largely unelected officials and advisers. Fewer and fewer, as the 1980s progressed, were ministers of genuine standing in the Prime Minister's own party, and the administration developed as an autocracy, with deadly internal strains – Westland being a decisive station on the way.

The Thatcher government comes into this story as the largest material cause in the rise of Newscorp. I attempt no general assessment of it, beyond suggesting that much of its record might have been written by another Tory government – or by Mrs Thatcher's, served and organised otherwise – and certainly not all of it was wrong. During its time, for instance, other revolutionists offered themselves, such as the miners' leader Arthur Scargill, who proposed an insurrection to be followed by nationalisation of the news media. The present writer is grateful that Mrs Thatcher defeated him, and, while others might have done as much, the credit is hers.

Lord Howe suggests that sometimes the Prime Minister was served too loyally and too well by unelected supporters. He means officials. But it is still more true of her media allies. The *Sun* liked to say of the 1979 election, 'IT'S THE SUN WOT WON IT'. Psephologists quibble. But the creation of a constitutional crisis over the fate of the small helicopter firm Westland might well be headlined 'IT'S THE SUN WOT DUN IT'.

Explaining the interaction of the Thatcher and Murdoch enterprises during the later months of 1985 and the first weeks of 1986 requires a time-sliced narrative. But the essential is that the Prime Minister became involved in a mortal duel with her Secretary of State for Defence – one she neither expected not desired – just after Murdoch set in motion his plan for disposing of his London workforce and shattering their union leaders. He was committed irrevocably before he realised that the Prime Minister might not be there to assure his victory – which accounts for his remark to Woodrow Wyatt cited at the head of this chapter.

It is a fair bet that for most of 1985 Murdoch was far too busy financing Fox to think much about United Technologies, where he was a non-executive director. United's subsidiary Pratt and Whitney is one of the Big Three aero-engine makers, and via Ansett (the airline investment he had tried to use to gain Channel 10 Melbourne) Murdoch carried weight in antipodean aviation. But a lesser part of United Technologies, Sikorsky Aircraft, builders of the Black Hawk and other famous helicopters, decided in 1985 to pay £30 million for its small, bankrupt British competitor Westland Aircraft. This sum (£55 million today) was welcome to Sir John Cuckney, a City proconsul installed as chairman to rescue something for Westland's bankers. Admiral Sir Ray Lygo, chairman of British Aerospace (BAe), thought it was a lot for a sackful of liabilities, and suspected that Sikorsky must intend penetrating the European defence market.

His calculation reveals why a minor deal had high explosive potential: Westland stock's value, if any, was a function of European defence-procurement politics. Sikorsky, sagaciously, hired the best bomb-disposal talent: GJW Ltd, pioneers of Westminster commercial lobbying, plus Gordon Reece, chief author (after herself) of Mrs Thatcher's image. Reece (he was about to become Sir Gordon) had coached her through the arduous process of lowering her public speech from soprano to contralto, and in doing so became a personal friend. How could Sikorsky lose?

On 21 September 1985 – just after Rupert Murdoch became a US citizen, just before plans for the new Fox network were announced – the British Defence Secretary, Michael Heseltine, met Bill Paul of Sikorsky and 'the scales fell from his eyes'. Heseltine concluded that the Sikorsky deal, though nice for the banks, did nothing for Westland's shareholders, and nothing for the British taxpayer, who had put large sums into Westland, only to provide a European launch-pad for Sikorsky. He thought alternatives should at least be canvassed, and made doing so his responsibility.

Heseltine was then at the height of his powers, which have not often been equalled. As a self-made multi-millionaire his free-market credentials were beyond challenge, but he was at the same time zealous for government action any time markets seemed to go astray. He was a natural enthusiast, in which he resembled many True Believers – but, unlike them, he was a natural moderate philosophically. The combination was unsettling. Indelibly he was Them, not Us. He was just then enjoying the glow of achievement, having helped complete the deal for the multi-national Eurofighter (it is now in service), and he thought a similar consortium might buy Westland and expand it to build a forthcoming military helicopter, the EH101.

Expertly blending reason, pressure and chutzpah, Heseltine brought the National Armament Directors (NADs) of Britain, France, Germany and Italy to London on 29 November. They roughed out a procurement policy for the EH101: a very suitable supplier could be Westland, reorganised by BAe, Messerschmitt-Bolkow-Blöhm of Germany and the Italian helicopter specialists Agusta. Sikorsky of course could compete. (And Bruce Springsteen could apply to conduct the Berliner Philharmoniker.) The achievement much impressed Cabinet colleagues – not only Geoffrey Howe and Nigel Lawson, but Thatcherite trusties like John Biffen and Norman Tebbit. It was an unwelcome surprise for the Prime Minister, but not yet a crisis.

Tension meanwhile racked up on the Wapping front. In October *The Times*' lead story had been union agreement to discuss manning arrangements for work at the new but still-idle plant. Officially, this had been equipped to produce a new paper called the *London Post*. Murdoch put up a tough set of demands at November's end, which the unions rejected on 9 December with suggestions of their own and requests for a new meeting. Murdoch told them they had no 'God-given right' to work at Wapping, and made it clear that he could run the plant with members of the Electricians Union. (This connection had been made in great secrecy by Woodrow Wyatt earlier in the year.)

A basic point about the Westland row is that there was little in the underlying merits. The helicopter would be – has been – built anyway. 'Anti-European' and 'anti-American' epithets were tossed about, though with slight justice: the aerospace industry is heavily American, but

European interests then as now persist, and transatlantic co-operation is routine. (This time FIAT of Italy allied its helicopter division to Sikorsky.) Certainly the swift construction of the consortium was a fine example of Heseltine's organisational creativity, and it delighted Westland's institutional shareholders: counter-bidding might restore value to an equity long despaired of. Cuckney, on the other hand, had done patient work which would go to waste should the consortium drive Sikorsky off and then vanish, leaving his banks (who had no equity upside) unpaid. The real argument concerned the rules of Cabinet government and media lobbying. And the limits of Prime Ministerial power.

Initial exchanges were quite mild. On 16 December *The Times* stated, in the oracular lobby style, that reports of Cabinet support for Heseltine 'are wrong . . . Ministers believe the European offer . . . is a hollow one.' This meant that Ingham had told *The Times* it was hollow. The leader-writers of the *Financial Times*, supported by the *Daily Telegraph*, thought it solid enough to pursue.

It was a curious situation. The power to decide between Sikorsky and the consortium lay with the Westland shareholders – just a stock-market judgment, in theory. In fact the relative value of the bids depended on the sentiment of the British Cabinet: not quite whether it liked, but whether it would go along with, or fail to stop, the NADs–EH101 scheme – now acquiring Euro-interest – and anyway to what effect. The shareholders had to evaluate the lobby's output, market-sensitivity added to the political.

Obviously the Prime Minister was hostile and this put some truth into Ingham's claim of declining support. The Cabinet rank and file quite liked the NADs idea, but hated the risk of Cabinet civil war. In early-December discussion the Prime Minister laid down that the correct, collective policy could only be silence and strict neutrality. Nothing should be said to encourage or discourage Sikorsky or the consortium. It was an argument impossible to oppose: all variorum views must remain Officially Secret.

Informally, unattributably and, on his own exposition of the law, illegally, Bernard Ingham then briefed the lobby that Heseltine was isolated, that the consortium was Euro-moonshine and Sikorsky the hands-down winner. Though unattributable, it was utterly transparent.

Woodrow Wyatt – pitching in for Sikorsky via his *Times* column – found himself talking to Lord Prior, now an ex-minister with a watching brief on defence as one of Arnold Weinstock's directors. Prior and Weinstock saw trouble ahead for the Prime Minister, and Wyatt was plaintive.

> Wyatt: Why should it affect her? Her position is absolutely neutral – leaving it for the board and the shareholders to decide.
> Prior: She should tell Bernard Ingham. That's not the press stories he's putting out . . .

Ingham's dominance of the lobby – gift of the Murdoch papers – was a weapon of tempting power, but dangerously visible in use. And its target was a master of close Whitehall combat, now seriously enraged. Heseltine believed that Thatcher's officials were bending the rules to keep Westland off the Cabinet agenda (the claim was and is disputed, but the minutes he produces are hard to dismiss).

Ingham's briefings were not enough to counter all the shareholder fears Sikorsky had to deal with: would Westland under US control become 'non-European', and ineligible for bonanzas like the EH101? On 30 December Westland addressed this issue in a letter to the Prime Minister – what was the government's view? Cuckney was nervous of the response, but Gordon Reece, Mrs Thatcher's good friend (indeed her Christmas guest five days previously), assisted in the drafting. Murdoch had just announced that as union talks had 'broken down' he was bringing Wapping to 'operational readiness'.

A collective reassurance for Westland was tricky. Downing Street's first effort said Sikorsky ownership would make no difference provided Westland kept its UK domicile. Heseltine consulted the Solicitor-General, Sir Patrick Mayhew, the Cabinet's acting legal conscience with the Attorney-General away. Were Number 10 going too far: was this 'material inaccuracy'? The phrase has a dark, fraudulent flavour, but Mayhew thought yes. There must be qualifications: Westland *could* lose some Euro-business. The Prime Minister conceded, but then qualified the qualification: the government would 'resist to the best of its ability' any such Euro-discrimination.

Heseltine had to leave it there. But when the next day's selective briefings gave Westland a simple all-clear, he decided the gloves were off and got the consortium side to write some patsy questions to him. To these he replied on his own responsibility that there were 'indications available to HMG from both the other governments and the companies concerned that a Westland link with Sikorsky/Fiat would be incompatible with participation by that company on behalf of the UK in the collaborative battlefield helicopter and NH90 projects'.

This gobbledygook hit Downing Street like the rhetorical equivalent of a helicopter gunship. But, appallingly, it broke no collective rules – it was essentially the language which Mrs Thatcher had conceded in her own letter, and which had been excluded from the highly selective briefings. Now, unless Heseltine could be zapped, Westland's shareholders might bolt. Counter-strike was essential, and the Prime Minister's team applied themselves to this throughout the weekend of 4–5 January 1986 (Woodrow Wyatt phoning in as Sir John Cuckney's emissary).

Two, surely, could play 'material inaccuracies': if Heseltine had not checked his letter with Mayhew, perhaps there was something wrong with it? And, traced on Saturday evening, the Solicitor-General agreed it might contain misleading statements. A fine circularity now enters, because Mayhew seems to have been reading *The Times* – which was reflecting the Number 10 view. The parallel department for Westland's affairs was Trade and Industry. Its Secretary of State, Leon Brittan, asked Mayhew, at Mrs Thatcher's behest, to put his view urgently in writing.

First thing on Monday, Mayhew wrote to Heseltine: there seemed to be 'material inaccuracies' in what had been said to the consortium. He, Mayhew, thought European attitudes mixed, and he advised Heseltine to write again with corrections. The letter was copied to Number 10 and to Trade and Industry. In the afternoon, Heseltine sent information which convinced Mayhew that no correction was required.

But by then the leakage tap was in flood – though extra pipework had been installed, suggesting extreme peril had been detected. A junior press officer at the DTI, on the instructions of Leon Brittan, told the Press Association that 'material inaccuracies' had been found in Heseltine's much-publicised letter. For reasons explained later, no clear chain of command was established by inquiry, though the immediate assumption – never seriously challenged – was that Brittan acted at Number 10's command.

Once the magic words were in the public domain, Bernard Ingham's boys were let slip – and so consistent had been the anti-Heseltine briefings that he may not have needed to say very much to them. The *Sun*, as always, did him proud. Its headline was 'YOU LIAR', on a story which said 'Battling Maggie' had caught the Secretary of State for Defence in a devious Euro-scam. It probably baffled the *Sun*'s readers (no briefing on chopper procurement was offered them). To Cuckney and Sikorsky it perhaps looked like the US Marines. But Number 10 seem to have realised that leak had turned to dreadful flood.

All this went far beyond off-the-record chat about Cabinet headcounts. The Law Officers advise the whole Cabinet, as both professional lawyers and ministers of the Crown – Mayhew's counsel had been sought under double confidence, as it were. Then his advice had not just been leaked – for crude factional purpose – but selectively leaked, and blown into an insane tabloid libel against one of his oldest colleagues who was a close personal friend.

Murdoch had no hand in the matter – other than his responsibility for the creation and maintenance of the *Sun* apparatus, and its assignment to open-ended support of Downing Street. The piece of anti-journalism involved is hard to parallel, in that cursory checking would have shown that Mayhew was really making an inquiry – not an accusation – and one which had been satisfied before publication. The style, though, traces perfectly to the McMahon incident (see Chapter 4 above) now manifest as the attribute of a system.

Mayhew's anger was intense – that of his senior, Attorney-General Sir Michael Havers, maybe greater. Havers was returning from illness to find that the government's propagandists had embroiled the Law Officers in a scandal which attacked the basic principles of their office. He simply wanted the police called in, and criminal charges laid. He could do this on his own authority, he reminded Number 10.

When Cabinet met on Thursday 9 January the Prime Minister declared that all ministerial statements about Westland must be cleared with her. Heseltine interpreted this as a licence for Ingham and Cuckney to say what they liked, with others having to remain silent. There was, he said, no Cabinet decision justifying this – indeed, there had been no substantive discussion of the issue. He would not serve in a Cabinet subject to arbitrary power. And he walked out. Suddenly, visibly, the Prime Minister was in danger.

Her regime survived, as we know, for four more years – the means are part of our story. But it survived as an organism increasingly damaging to itself and to the party it represented. Occasionally, history presents itself neatly. The item on the agenda after Westland was the poll tax, in its second incarnation – the project which was to bring rioters on to British streets and ruin the government. The loss of Heseltine from the Cabinet decisively weakened the moderates who hoped to impede that juggernaut by discussion and collective responsibility.

Now Westland thus far was a most spectacular story. There was a limit to what the daily papers could do with it – it was sprawling, complex, space-hungry. But it was magnetic Sunday broadsheet matter, bringing together major constitutional issues, high technology and huge personal drama. The question of the Prime Minister's survival was simultaneously the question of whether she was eroding responsible government and substituting personal rule. The *Sunday Times* of Hamilton and Evans had built much of its reputation on such material. But that weekend's *Sunday Times* carried only orthodox coverage of Whitehall and the Westland shareholders meeting: Insight did not try to penetrate the political tempest. It also carried, though, a large front-page announcement that an extra section of the paper would be printed in Wapping next week. Brenda Dean, of the SOGAT union, took this to mean that Murdoch's plans for a confrontation were live, and she was perfectly correct.

Every proprietor had a case against the London print unions. They were anarchic, irresponsible and hostile to efficient technology, and if it was true that they owed much of that to interaction with managers like Duke Hussey, it might explain but scarcely exculpated them. Certainly, therefore, Murdoch had a right to official support in the event of union resistance – inspired by bad faith – to his plans for an efficient new printing centre. But that is not quite the same thing as the right to a crushing victory, set up by his own pre-emptive bad faith and enforced by a blank cheque on the civil power.

The public face of the Wapping project was what Murdoch called 'sensible and reasonable' demands for industrial reform, such as legally binding production agreements. In the climate of 1986 Brenda Dean and her union colleagues got little but scepticism for their view that his real aim was 'to provoke a conflict which he believed [he could] win due to his political standing with the government'. In lawsuits at the time, the unions could never produce proof that Murdoch was determined to avoid a settlement. The Wyatt diaries, however, make the position entirely plain:

> *13 January 1986* . . . He wants them to go on strike . . . He has a new problem in that the unions are scared and reluctant to strike. If they did he can sack everyone and print with five hundred and twelve people he has lined up who have already learned to work the presses at Tower Hamlets [Wapping]. That would be instead of the four or five thousand currently employed . . .

The high levels of staffing at the old Fleet Street plant indicate just how lately News International had acquired its active interest in new technology and efficient manning. Apart from the short-lived hope that Gerald Long would bring some Reuters magic to TNL (see Chapter 9 above) the News management had been entirely part of the old Fleet Street style – and much favoured consequently by union chieftains.

Now Murdoch wanted to shuck off his old workforce as cheaply as possible and get the maximum possible return from his new plant immediately. Every penny was needed for the outrageous Fox financing, and every moment of time needed for setting up the new American network. Patient and humane reorganisation of News International's production system was a luxury not to be considered. Murdoch's aim was to retreat into Fortress Wapping with retrained electricians in place of printers. There was much tactical craft in the plan. But it involved depriving 5,000 employees, mostly long-serving ones, of their living via a process of duplicity.

As Wyatt makes clear, it was recognised as a 'high risk' course which would depend on unquestioning and almost unlimited support from

London's Metropolitan Police – a force, uniquely in Britain, then directly under central government control.* Every employer in Britain is of course entitled to police protection if the actions of disgruntled workers endanger a business operation, but not automatically if a confrontation is brought about as part of a deliberate plan. If every firm in Britain were to treat its workers with the provocation Murdoch intended, there would be no cops available for any other duty.

There was no doubt in Wyatt's or Murdoch's mind that Thatcher would back them without asking questions about their tactics and motivation. She accepted Murdoch's heroic character as thoroughly as his newspapers projected hers. She has since been a loud advocate of the story that News International's aim at Wapping was an apocalyptic battle to free the British press from union dictatorship.

However, the Battle of Wapping's heroic aims had been achieved before it began – that is, the industrial scene had already altered sufficiently for newspapers to employ advanced printing technologies. The *Independent*, a completely new title – manned in good part by editorial escapees from Murdoch's *Times* – did not start publishing till later in the year. But its production arrangements, all in unionised plants, were already in place as part of its fund-raising operations at the end of 1985. Some of the credit was due to the government's new labour-relations laws, some to extended negotiating by managements more patient than News International. The *Independent* story is taken further in Chapter 13 along with details of Wapping's aftermath. What we need to remember as background to Westland is that the battle as fought had little to do with reform of the British media system and much to do with the financial desperation of Newscorp.

Almost every day in January brought fresh twists, turns and crises in the Westland saga – and the staff of the *Observer* had the strange experience of running on a classic Sunday broadsheet story without a breath of competition from the *Sunday Times*. The *Observer*'s coverage was chiefly the work of David Leigh and Paul Lashmar, and without their energy little systematic knowledge of the affair would have emerged. But it was

*Control of the Metropolitan Police was devolved to the Greater London Authority in 2000.

a story on which they might have expected the *Sunday Times* to field six or seven people against them.

Downing Street's first damage-limitation success was persuading the Attorney-General to accept a leak inquiry by the Secretary to the Cabinet instead of the police. Leon Brittan was assigned the task of stonewalling Parliament meanwhile, but Wyatt and Murdoch (like other observers) were unimpressed by his performance and by Downing Street's denial of any connection with the 'LIAR' headline.

> *14 January 1986* . . . Rupert says 'We've got to get her out of this jam somehow. It's looking very bad.'

While Murdoch's desire to rescue the Prime Minister is well recorded, the diaries do not show him reflecting on the *Sun*'s contribution to her distress. Nor is he heard extolling – in the manner of the epigraph to Chapter 6 – the right of citizens to be told what the rulers of the land have been up to.

There was better news from the unions. Frustrated by Murdoch's rigid negotiating stance, they were balloting their members on strike action. Less good was the Westland front: on 17 January the shareholders voted to hold out for improved offers.

> *18 January 1986*. Rupert . . . rang about 9.00 a.m. to say he'd been up till 2.45 a.m. supervising the printing of the extra section of the *Sunday Times* at [Wapping]. A great new plant with maximum security. He said the police were ready in case there were pickets and they had riot shields stored in the warehouse nearby and every now and then a police helicopter came over to see that there was no trouble. 'I really felt secure.'

Fortress Wapping, at least, was garrisoned and ready. Murdoch advised Wyatt's wife Verushka to buy Newscorp shares.

On 19 January Wyatt, Verushka Wyatt and Murdoch arrived at Chequers for Sunday lunch with the Thatchers, reflecting as they rolled up the drive on the security arrangements of the Prime Minister's country seat – modest in comparison with Wapping's. They found blazing logs, champagne – and an uneasy Prime Minister. 'It's been a bad week,' she said, though Woodrow's denunciations of Heseltine in *The Times* and the *New of the World* had 'cheered her up'.

I tell Margaret that Cuckney thinks it could be six weeks before they get the new Sikorsky–Fiat scheme through. 'Oh dear.'

Wyatt's diary entries are supportive of Thatcher throughout, but also realistic – without giving the lie direct he assumes (and reports Murdoch as assuming) that her claim to be unconnected with the leak is not credible. The question which exercises them is whether it can survive investigation until the Westland issue is neutralised. Even discussing the affair, clearly, makes the Prime Minister nervous:

'Are there precedents for the internal inquiry report not being published?' Margaret said, 'Yes' . . . She looks worried but I think is reluctant to say much more . . .

Knowing Murdoch less well than he did, Wyatt thought, she might be constrained by fear of old professional loyalties and think 'erroneously he might put something in his newspapers'. The suspicion was of course unjust, or at least misplaced. Later the same day Murdoch rang Wyatt:

'I've had an idea. I think I shall try to get United Technology to buy fifteen per cent in Westland. That should fix the vote permanently in favour of the Sikorsky–Fiat deal' . . .
As poor Margaret was saying, how on earth can we have been wasting so much time and effort on this tiny little company which is of no account in our affairs.

Rupert's idea contained the essential solution, as we shall see, but it did not work immediately.

Mrs Thatcher's next week was worse, while Murdoch's plans fell smoothly into place. On Wednesday 22 January the unions announced that their membership ballot had authorised strike action at the old News International premises if no settlement could be reached on operation of the new Wapping plant.

Leon Brittan was now suffering irredeemable damage. Additional to leakage he was accused of improperly pressing the consortium to withdraw. In retrospect his behaviour looks very like that of an honourable man failing in dishonourable tasks. At the time, the Commons distrusted his every word. On Thursday the 23rd the Cabinet Secretary, Sir Robert Armstrong, submitted his report. Nothing of it was published except his recommendation that the Prime Minister herself should interview Brittan. Sir Robert had found two potential culprits, but did not fancy deciding their share of responsibility. The story was now close to the heat at which governments can melt.

On the same day the unions and Murdoch met for the final time. Brenda Dean says that almost any concession was on offer, but News did not want to deal. Wyatt wrote that Murdoch found the meeting 'highly satisfactory. They've refused to negotiate on lower numbers at the old centres and he refused to discuss any of them going to Wapping. So the strike looks almost certain . . .'

On Friday afternoon Leon Brittan told the House of Commons with great brevity that he had made regrettable errors and was resigning from the government. Equally briefly, Mrs Thatcher said the errors had been made without her knowledge. Amid rampant scepticism, an emergency debate was set for Monday 27 January.

By 7.30 p.m. the printers at News International's old centres were on strike, and production of *The Times* and the *Sun* was lost. But Wapping was ready to produce the weekend's papers, the *London Post* camouflage being thrown aside. There was an editorial glitch because several distinguished *Sunday Times* journalists refused to transfer, notably Don Berry, the senior production executive. Berry may have endured more print-union hassle than anyone alive, but it did not reconcile him to active deception of an existing workforce.

And two other things happened without making traces at the time, one at the Stock Exchange and the other in Whitehall. Just prior to Brittan's statement there was an afternoon negotiating session in the private secretary's room at 10 Downing Street. It involved the Deputy Prime Minister (William Whitelaw), the Tory Chief Whip (John Wakeham), Mrs Thatcher's main Civil Service aide (Charles Powell) and Bernard Ingham. The Foreign Secretary, Geoffrey Howe, was there on behalf of his friend Leon Brittan, and from time to time Mrs Thatcher herself. A remarkable description of this meeting is given in Lord Howe's memoirs, *Conflict of Loyalty* (1994), in which he records Mrs Thatcher's remark that her period as Prime Minister might be over by 'six o'clock this evening'. She was recognising that the House of Commons suspected it was being deceived about the Cabinet's operations, and was at the limit of its tolerance.

Brittan was about to confess. He refused to deny outright that others had been involved; the question was whether his statement would be so drafted as to let ambiguity persist. Howe, present to do his best for a friend who was being hung out to dry, makes clear his assumption that the leak had been agreed with Number 10. He obtained a promise that at some point reasonably soon his friend would be reconsidered for 'high office'. This, he says, was sufficient to avert an outbreak of 'candour'. It was an extremely fragile story, but enough for Mrs Thatcher to survive past six o'clock.

Somewhat earlier in the day David Mortimer, finance director of the Australian freight company TNT, rang from Sydney to buy 2.6 million Westland shares, the most which could be bought without public announcement. A sudden passion for helicopters hardly explains the investment, but a connection with Wapping does – TNT was the contractor secretly engaged to move the Murdoch newspapers out of the new plant. The connection was close indeed: Sir Peter Abeles, Murdoch's close poker-school companion, was boss not only of TNT but also of Ansett Airlines, through which Murdoch had tried to capture Channel 10 Melbourne. The plan to wrap up the Westland controversy via United Technologies couldn't have worked: its subsidiary Sikorsky was already buying as fast as the rules allowed. Sir Peter, it seems fair to assume, was persuaded to assist a Prime Minister in a jam.

Meanwhile, from their new home, ringed by policemen and union picket-lines, the Murdoch newspapers spread encouragement.

26 January 1986. He says *The Times* will be friendly tomorrow, probably, and the *Sun* will be very friendly saying 'Well, what do you want, someone like Galtieri [the Argentine ex-dictator] to run the country?'

That was the *Sun* doing its best thing. But the *Sunday Times*, arguably, made a greater contribution by not doing its best thing at all. The question of what lay behind the almost absurdly implausible statements of Mrs Thatcher and her ex-minister it continued to leave to its old rival, the *Observer*.

In the emergency debate on the 27th Mrs Thatcher made a long, cloudy address, revealing nothing about Cabinet leakage but offering humility in quantity unfamiliar to the House. Wyatt, listening anxiously, divined that she was less than frank, but was relieved that questioning in Parliament and press was not intense. It was resolved to refer inquiries to three select committees of the House (Defence, Civil Service and Trade and Industry).

> *27 January 1986* . . . Rupert rings from his car at nearly midnight.
> 'I'm just going through the picket lines . . .' He thinks Mrs Thatcher
> has done well and says that *The Times* is favourable for tomorrow.

Mrs Thatcher remained at serious risk – she would 'fight them all the way', she told Wyatt – but intensely so only as long as Westland's fate continued in play.

The question was whether the constitution's rules against arbitrary power had been breached – and, in particular, with an intent to shift a stock market outcome. These were not matters easy to dispose of with three select committees engaged, but a responsible government – responsible for government appointments, after all – has ample stonewalling facilities within Parliament's own system. The difficulty was to optimise them while the Westland contestants continued to exchange blows outside – demanding editorial attention and inflaming back-benchers.

In this situation the London Stock Exchange and the press represented what separated power there was. And in the market remarkable things were happening: Westland's shares, worthless only recently, were now at 100p, and heading for 140 in intensive transactions. Whether this trading was politically motivated was a question to which the *Observer* devoted much attention in its issues of 3 and 10 February, but at that time it could find no evidence. It was one of many questions ignored in equivalent issues of the *Sunday Times*, whose proprietor had instigated at least some of the trading, specifically to assist the government.

By 12 February, when Cuckney called his next meeting, six purchasers acting through overseas nominees had acquired another 20.33 per cent of Westland – more than enough, with TNT's and Sikorsky's own purchases, to secure victory. The consortium, Wyatt wrote, complained 'at the irregularities under which shares had been bought by supporters of Sikorsky–Fiat's deal . . . However the matter at last seems finally settled.' At any rate, the wench was dead. The Parliamentary committees learnt little about Downing Street's activities – without pressure from press and public, their interrogation of the executive rarely succeeds – and the crucial fix in the private secretary's room stayed secret.

It might be said that a businessman dependent on a government would straightforwardly expect newspapers under his control to help that government out of a jam – by any action or inaction within their power – and that a public interest in accurate presentation of news cannot prevail over nature. But, as we have seen, British law does insist on the principle – at least in the case of newspapers developed by other hands – and Eugene Meyer has been cited (see Chapter 3 above) suggesting that it must prevail if democracy is to survive.

Not that this is just a matter of friendly opinion and editorial inertia. Here the newspaper controller participates in covert moves to help the government avert scrutiny. We can't say that the *Sunday Times* in its old competitive role would have brought to light the exchange of promises before Brittan's resignation statement (or would have provoked a rival into doing so). Misfortune and incompetence – the accidental quality of journalism – can always explain a failure to crack the hottest running story in town. They scarcely justify a failure to notice it – still less the fact that one of its hottest elements was Newscorp's own product. At any time after the 'LIAR' headline, evidence of the Westland vote being fixed as a cover-up on the government's behalf would have altered history's path.

And here is the core of Murdoch's operation. For a completely hands-off proprietor it might be acceptable to lend some private aid to a struggling Prime Minister. But Murdoch's essence is intervention: he is editor of all his newspapers whenever the moment is crucial, and all Newscorp's routine output comes subject to that rule.

We don't know of any orders making the *Sunday Times* quiescent in the Westland episode (as likely once as Francis Drake ignoring a laden galleon). But by this Murdoch period specific orders were hardly needed. Andrew Neil, then editing the paper, was quoted earlier on the command system: 'courtiers . . . at the court of King Rupert [must be] adept at anticipating their master's wishes'. Readiness is all – but readiness to a purpose, unlike that of the Scotts, or Meyers. Murdoch himself descried a political crisis engulfing his patron (A NASTY SMELL AT NO. 10, in the *Observer*'s words). His *Sunday Times* thought the government might be hiding things, but it was matter for the 'so what files': such fevers might be cured by sending the Cabinet to Baden Baden. We should not think it fortuitous that Newscorp's fate was linked with the government's: this was implicit in Murdoch's policy since Keith's days. This is the pseudo-newspaper in close to ideal form.

The unions fell into Murdoch's trap blinded by two miscalculations. They did not believe the Wapping plant could produce the papers effectively – eventually, they proved to be half right about that – and they thought that if it did they could prevent distribution by their own physical presence. That meant picketing on such a scale as to become, in effect, obstruction and intimidation. The plant's new machinery was highly efficient, and it met the demand – at the price of producing large areas of *The Times* and *Sunday Times* days ahead of their nominal publication date. There was a long-term effect on editorial character which in the immediate context was negligible.

The enormous Metropolitan Police presence – like nothing before seen at a single industrial site – swamped the pickets and guaranteed passage for TNT's trucks. It did not take long for the frustrated print workers and their allies to become involved in violence, often on a disgraceful scale. There were many tit-for-tat arguments about whether police or pickets were the more blameworthy, but the truth was that the mass-picketing tactic was one for which little public patience remained.

The unions were not much accustomed to being morally in the right, which like most things takes a certain amount of practice. If they had kept the strike weapon in reserve, and pursued Murdoch patiently through the courts – as Brenda Dean seems to have wished – they could have won a remarkable victory, which would have benefited many others besides themselves. As it was, they delivered Murdoch the financial bonanza which enabled him to pay for Fox and many conquests beside.

The Thatcher administration also seemed victorious, in that it escaped from the Westland crisis untouched by any effective challenge. But a consequence was that the practices which had caused the crisis continued in operation without modification, taking the Cabinet further and further away from collective process, closer to arbitrary rule – and thus becoming intolerable to its most substantial members. Margaret Thatcher's personality was not one likely to find collective responsibility easy. But it was the presence of a grossly servile press which offered her the fatal option of evading it.

Michael Heseltine was only the first major figure in a generation of Tory leadership which had to expend most of its political capital in opposing a notion of government quite remote from the traditions of their party and deeply unattractive to the British electorate. What the Conservatives have found is that collective responsibility is a habit easier to lose than to rebuild. It might be argued that the trade unions, who were Murdoch's enemies in the Battle of Wapping, have not suffered as much long-term damage as those who thought he was their friend.

The Westland–Wapping case was about the inactive, negative form of pseudo-journalism. There is also the positive form, and the relationship to official propaganda. The Anglo-Irish relationship has had many bad years, but not many worse than 1988. In February two British soldiers lost their way among a Republican crowd in Belfast; they were dragged out of their car, stripped and beaten to death. Distressing images of their naked bodies appeared on television. Mrs Thatcher and her ministers were furious. The media – television in particular – were sustaining terrorism by providing 'the oxygen of publicity' to Sinn Fein and the IRA. (Later in the year it was made illegal to broadcast the words of spokesmen on the Republican side – an approach the apartheid regime had once used, and most communist dictatorships.)

At about 3.30 p.m. on 6 March 1988 in Gibraltar British SAS troops shot dead Danny McCann, Sean Savage and Mairead Farrell, members of the IRA who had arrived in the colony to mount a serious bomb attack. Fairly certainly it was aimed at the weekly guard-mounting ceremony and would have caused appalling slaughter. Prevention was a coup for the Security Service: it had penetrated the IRA's plan.

The Foreign Secretary is responsible for Britain's overseas territories, and Sir Geoffrey Howe (as he then was) described the incident to the House of Commons on 7 March. He was able to prove that the IRA trio had brought a bomb with them – though not that it had been set up when they were killed. All three had been found to be unarmed, which raised the question of whether the SAS men had been right to shoot. Under the rules of engagement unarmed suspects should have been challenged and given a chance to surrender. No British government has ever sanctioned a 'shoot to kill' policy for dealing with Irish terrorists. In this case, the firepower employed left little to chance: McCann and Farrell were both hit repeatedly, and Savage perhaps sixteen or eighteen times.

The Foreign Secretary said they had been challenged verbally, and had made 'suspicious movements', not gestures of surrender. For many people, that was quite enough. Under the moral asymmetry of the Troubles, the IRA had no scruples about shooting to kill, and were cavalier or worse about civilian casualties. Nonetheless the asymmetry and the 'yellow card' rules restraining British firepower were intrinsic to Britain's claim to be engaged in police action, and to refutation of the IRA's claim to be at war. That unarmed people confronted by armed men should refuse to surrender was puzzling, and an editorial in the *Daily Telegraph* called the government's account 'contradictory'.

> Unless it wishes Britain's enemies to enjoy a propaganda bonanza it should explain why it was necessary to shoot dead all three terrorists on the street rather than apprehend them with the considerable force of police and SAS . . . deployed in the locality . . . It is an essential aspect of any successful anti-terrorist policy to maintain the principles of civilised restraint [otherwise] terrorism is succeeding on one of its critical aims: the brutalisation of the society under attack.

The question of challenges was a legitimate and urgent issue for news media. Like the Bloody Sunday story which the *Sunday Times* had taken up in 1972, it concerned deadly force used by the power of the state. It was taken up by the current-affairs team of Thames Television, holders of the London weekday franchise. In Gibraltar their researchers, led by an experienced reporter named Julian Manyon, found serious evidence inconsistent with the official facts. Claims that the security team had reason to think there was a device ready for detonation were thought unconvincing by a recently retired and highly decorated British bomb-disposal officer. More significantly, nobody who heard or saw the shooting heard any challenge.

Mrs Carmen Proetta said she had a clear view of the entire incident and insisted that what took place was utterly unlike the official account. It began with a police car stopping suddenly:

> and the doors were open, all of them . . . three men came out dressed in jeans and jackets . . . guns in hand . . . They did not say anything, they didn't scream, they didn't shout . . . These people were turning their heads back to see what was happening, and when they saw these men had the guns in their hands they just put their hands up . . . but there was no chance. I mean they went to the floor immediately; they dropped.

Mrs Proetta was the witness with the most striking testimony, but others gave detailed evidence which suggested purposeful killing rather than legal arrest. Essentially they said that McCann, Savage and Farrell had made no threatening movements, and had been shot repeatedly when already down and past resistance.

Thames Television developed from this and other evidence a forty-five-minute documentary which was scheduled for the ITV network at 9.00 p.m. on 28 April. Its presenter was the highly experienced Jonathan Dimbleby – and, although it raised the possibility that the killings had been unlawful, it did not draw that conclusion. It made clear that the SAS team had been faced with a group of terrorists certainly intent on murder, and had eliminated them without any harm to the civilian community. It was entitled *Death on the Rock*.

The programme went out in spite of the dispatch to the Independent Broadcasting Authority (IBA) of a strong letter in which the Foreign Secretary asked that it be held over pending an inquest in Gibraltar.

There is no doubt that Howe, Margaret Thatcher and other members of the government were passionately angry about the actions of both the producing company and the network authority, though they put their complaint in terms of massive risks to the legal system (which no independent lawyers could subsequently identify).

This outrage was amplified in the newspapers. '"TRIAL BY TV" ROW OVER IRA KILLINGS FILM', said *The Times*; 'STORM AT SAS TELLY TRIAL' said the *Sun*. Among dailies, only the *Guardian* reported it in another light: 'IBA REJECTS GOVERNMENT GAG ATTEMPT'. The *Daily Mail*'s Geoffrey Levy said the film accused the SAS of cold-blooded killing under the personal direction of Mrs Thatcher, and that *Death on the Rock* itself amounted to 'execution without trial – the very thing [it was] exposing to the world'. The programme, he said, should not have been transmitted. This was a forthright opinion, strongly argued, but not shared by all editorial writers: the *Telegraph*, the *Guardian*, the *Independent* and the *Evening Standard* all thought transmission justified. Some of the individual commentators spattered their rhetoric very wide: an ex-member of Mrs Thatcher's private office wrote in the *Evening Standard* that most of the British people had 'no time for the cringing, limp-wristed antics of the wet liberal pacifists in the TV establishment'.

The *Sun*'s attack, headed 'BLOOD ON THE SCREEN', was in a special class, and started on the 'quivering, geriatric' chairman of the IBA, George Thomson. But

> the overwhelming guilt belongs to the Thames company. They are supposed to be a British concern and they derive their income from British advertisers.
>
> Their audience is made up of British men and women. If that audience is diminished in the next few months by bullets or bombs in Ulster or in the rest of Britain some of the blood will belong on their hands.

The Prime Minister and the Foreign Secretary attacked Thames and the IBA in more restrained language, but with equally manifest anger. Mrs Thatcher was reported, privately, to be 'beyond fury', and comments recorded by Woodrow Wyatt more than support that estimate.

396

Action then intensified. Several tabloids picked up a freelance story about connections between Carmen Proetta, the most prominent *Rock* witness, and an escort agency called Eve International. 'SHAME OF THE SAS SMEAR GIRL', said the *Star*, and the *Daily Express* said 'TRIAL BY TV CARMEN IS ESCORT GIRL BOSS'. The *Sun*, though, produced the most striking version of this common material, headed 'THE TART OF GIB'. The text said that Mrs Proetta was an ex-prostitute with a criminal record in Gibraltar, and that she and Mr Proetta shared anti-British attitudes. *Death on the Rock* was in the *Sun*'s view simply 'a piece of IRA propaganda. Its only purpose was to discredit our Security Services.'

So far all this, if not quite fair enough, was more or less what any programme critical of the government might expect from the government's tabloid allies. But on 1 May the *Sunday Times* produced something quite different – a heavily displayed spread attacking the Thames programme with the full weight of its collective, talismanic Insight byline. It was headed 'INADMISSIBLE EVIDENCE', and its general thrust was that *Rock* was based on reporting which was deeply biased and in some respects fraudulent. It began: 'Insight has investigated the documentary's evidence and reports that the picture which emerges actually contradicts many of the programme's claims. Indeed, vital witnesses are now complaining that their views were not accurately reported.'

The high scepticism applied to Thames evidence went with unattributed official information presented as credible, even triumphantly credible:

> Insight understands that the government's lawyers at the Inquest will have evidence that is expected to silence the critics and undermine *This Week*'s evidence. Whitehall sources with access to the official evidence are relishing the prospect. Insight has learnt that the Ministry of Defence believes it can contradict Carmen Proetta's testimony with incontrovertible evidence . . . What started as a 'trial by television' may yet become a trial of television.

The Thames team, according to Insight, had manipulated and bullied witnesses. In some cases it had concealed facts detracting from the credibility of witnesses, and in others it had distorted what was said, by dishonest editing and by suppression of inconsistencies.

397

Three vital witnesses – Stephen Bullock, Josie Celicia and Lieutenant-Colonel George Styles, the explosives expert – had apparently been misquoted in *Death on the Rock*, to an extent that could only be deliberate. Celicia, according to Insight, considered Carmen Proetta's evidence 'ridiculous'. Bullock, a British barrister who had been close to the shooting, contradicted her claim that there had been no verbal challenge. If Dimbleby, Manyon and their team had been guilty of even part of the misconduct alleged in Insight's indictment, they were clearly unfit for employment by any honest media business.

It was trenchant stuff. But it was not risky work in the sense of Insight's reporting in this area during pre-Murdoch days. Neil includes it as an exercise in 'Ruining the Sunday Breakfasts of the Rich and Powerful', but 'INADMISSIBLE EVIDENCE' was distinctly agreeable to the highest breakfast-tables in the land, especially those of the Prime Minister and the Security Service. Indeed, Insight's assertions about Thames and its witnesses strongly resembled the government's own briefings.

To suggest that Thames Television in 1988 was a dangerous power spunkily invigilated by the *Sunday Times* is grotesque. They were in the ordinary way evenly matched media contestants. In the particular *Rock* context Thames was suffering the furious anger of a powerful government – and its executives were feeling understandably exposed. Of course, if a television company or a newspaper lies about the government and its servants, it must be legitimate to report the fact. But the action should not be represented as sticking up for the little fellow, and especial care should be taken with research and interpretation – not because other media professionals are sacred, but because the official capacity to dictate history is an endemic danger.

And there was also the interesting question of Murdoch's own television interests. Sky Television had just been launched, and Andrew Neil was doubling as its chief executive while editing the *Sunday Times*. Murdoch wanted the television market deregulated totally, and the skies opened to commercial satellites. The Independent Broadcasting Authority was an obstacle to his ambitions. The *Sun*, the *News of the World*, *The Times* and the *Sunday Times* were all denouncing the IBA as a barrier to entrepreneurship and enterprise. And now it was not even able to insulate the public from IRA propaganda.

The day after the *Sunday Times'* demolition of *Death on the Rock* Murdoch called Wyatt to suggest how the political lesson could be drawn:

> *Monday 2 May* . . . Rupert rang from Venice yesterday. He said she [Mrs Thatcher] oughtn't to attack the IBA in the way she did because it let all the left-wing people say she is too authoritarian, trying to censor everything . . . He said, 'The real answer is to have lots and lots of channels and no authorities overseeing them and let them all get on with it. It would be like newspapers with different voices and should be the same for the news as well.'

Newspapers with different voices?

The *Sunday Times* took a similar editorial line the next Sunday, 8 May – along with repeated allegations of evidence-faking by Thames. In September, one witness withdrew the evidence he had given to the pro-gramme. On 25 September Wyatt discussed with Mrs Thatcher:

> the appalling situation about Thames Television putting out the programme with bogus evidence making trial by television over Gibraltar. It had been revealed last week that the witness who said he saw the SAS man murdering an IRA terrorist on the ground was lying . . . He said he was pestered to give false evidence by Thames . . .
>
> I said, 'Typical of Ian Trethowan, Chairman of Thames Television, trying to defend the action of the programme team which went out there to find things to discredit the SAS and the government.' I went on, 'And as for the IBA, they are a disgrace in allowing that programme to go ahead when you and Geoffrey Howe were asking them to postpone it . . .'
>
> She said, 'We have to think of who is going to take over from George Thomson at the IBA.'

The inquest did not in the event turn out as the *Sunday Times* had pre-dicted. Carmen Proetta's evidence was not shaken, and the witness who withdrew proved to be peripheral. An open verdict was recorded, which pleased neither the government nor the families of the dead.

But Thames were feeling the weight of the government's anger and the long campaign by the *Sunday Times* and its tabloid running-mate. The company commissioned an independent investigation of *Death on the Rock*, under a Conservative peer, Lord Windlesham, a former Northern Ireland minister. He had been a television executive, and was known as a fair-minded man. Nonetheless, there was now a presumption of guilt against a programme which had questioned the words of authority.

Then in the New Year the case the *Sunday Times* had so long sustained blew up. On 2 January 1989 the *UK Press Gazette* ran a letter from a journalist named Rosie Waterhouse: 'Now that I have resigned from the *Sunday Times* I would like to set the record straight, belatedly, about my involvement in the Insight investigation into . . . *Death on the Rock*.'

She had interviewed two witnesses, Josie Celicia and Stephen Bullock.

Their account of my interviews with them was inaccurate in the *Sunday Times* and had the effect of discrediting parts of the documentary and the evidence of another witness, Carmen Proetta.

In brief, Josie Celicia did not dismiss all of Proetta's evidence as 'ridiculous', only one aspect of it. Stephen Bullock has only one quarrel with his interview on Thames – that he was portrayed as saying no warnings were given before the SAS fired, when in fact he said he told the reporters that he was not in a position to hear if a warning was given. However, Bullock stressed to me, and I quoted him as saying: 'Nothing I saw was inconsistent with what Carmen Proetta said she saw.'

After the story appeared I complained to Robin Morgan [the editor] who compiled the story, that my interviews had been inaccurately represented in the paper, and gave him a full transcript of my interviews with Celicia and Bullock, so the mistakes would not be repeated. I also apologised to Celicia and Bullock for the errors, saying they probably occurred because of the speed with which the story had been put together. But some of the mistakes appeared again the following week.

I came very close to resigning then, but my mortgage got the better of me. I did however send a very detailed memo to Morgan and the features editor who is in charge of 'Insight' listing my complaints. Two other reporters took similar action regarding complaints about how their copy was used.

No further action was taken and I was advised that if I took the matter further I was unlikely to win in any confrontation between an 'Insight' reporter and the Focus editor. I was and still am deeply unhappy that my copy was used to discredit another piece of investigative journalism. A copy of this letter has been sent to Thames TV and Lord Windlesham who is conducting the enquiry into the making of Death on the Rock . . . I resigned over another unconnected matter.

The 'detailed memo' Ms. Waterhouse sent on 5 May to Robin Morgan, the editor in charge of the *Sunday Times* investigation was a formidable document. She told him he had:

left the ST wide open to accusations that we had set out to prove one point of view and misrepresented and misquoted interviews to fit – the very accusations we are levelling at Thames.

You were not interested in any information I obtained which contradicted your apparent premise – that the Thames documentary was wrong, and the official version was right . . . It became almost impossible to make any point which contradicted the official line . . . You then gave me a lecture on how Insight did not have to be like a provincial newspaper, that Harry Evans has told you how Insight had to make a judgment. I said this whole story revolved around conflicting evidence which should be left to a jury to decide.

This Insight investigation was shown to be flawed. The real version allowed – indeed encouraged – an experienced judgment between conflicting strands of evidence (see Chapter 8 above). It never allowed a judgment between the evidence and an editorial premise: the working hypothesis was set always at zero, and subject to veto by reporters on the ground. In the *Rock* case, there was no serious judgment to be made between Proetta, Celicia and Bullock, only between the sum of their evidence and the story the *Sunday Times* desired but ought to have discarded. The false conclusion, as we see, persisted.

Matters of official killing distinguish most sharply between unfree and free societies. In the one case, the state will automatically suppress questioning. In the other, there is an intense risk that it will try to – an attempt somebody must resist. The pattern – it applied to both Bloody Sunday and *Death on the Rock* – is sadly familiar: the culpability of the dead is overstated; the legal system manipulated; any inconvenient witness is rubbished, or slandered; disinformation is circulated unattributably; and high-level political anger dispensed. In short, an official propaganda campaign is mounted against any media team which asks legitimate questions. It is not something the British state does subtly or well, which is greatly to its credit – and the more discredit to anyone who actively assists in – as against falls for – the operation. When it 'investigated' *Death on the Rock* Insight was doing government propaganda, not journalism. Either it could not tell the difference or was reckless about it. This we may expect of the ideal pseudo-newspaper, not to be found in the real type.

Not that the *Sunday Times* travelled quite alone. Several tabloids went with it part of the way; the *Sun*, however, actually took a lead. Carmen Proetta – shown eventually to be an honest witness – was only accused by Insight of anti-British malice, whereas the *Sun* campaign asserted she was a whore. (Lawyers finally extracted an apology from the *Sun*.)

As Wyatt's journal shows, it was quite natural for Murdoch to use the favours done by his newspapers for the state as occasion to request favours from it. The political fury created by Thames Television's alleged sinfulness was not the efficient cause of the dismantling of Britain's system of television regulation – one of the Thatcher government's last acts. But it was contributory to it. Lord Windlesham's report concluded that the claims against *Death on the Rock* were spurious. On the evidence, no other conclusion was possible, but the government refused to abandon the Murdoch version. Mrs Thatcher's belief in Murdoch's 'objectivity' was to be decisive in the rebirth of Sky as the miraculous BSkyB.

The Gibraltar case does not have the historic resonance of Bloody Sunday, and rightly so – the dead, though perhaps mistreated, were never innocent. But as examples together with Westland they show the systemic difference Murdoch control makes to newspapers when something a little out of the ordinary comes along. The effect is different, though, in different papers. For Kelvin MacKenzie's *Sun* the *Death on the Rock* fabrications were by this time almost routine, but they sit less comfortably in the *Sunday Times*; credulousness in sizeable quantity must have been required just to get them into the paper. What was the source of this, in a newspaper formerly characterised by scepticism?

In Andrew Neil's *Full Disclosure* he shows that many of the targets at which he aimed his paper – Thames Television and the IBA were certainly examples – appeared to him as limbs of the 'establishment', a pervasive, shadowy force, inimical to life, liberty and the pursuit of satellite television. Though Rupert Murdoch has not attempted any such connected account, he clearly shares the obsession. Insofar as Newscorp has an ideology and a belief-system it is to be militant against the establishment. And in this there are probable connections to credulousness and authoritarian behaviour.

13

PRESENT NECESSITIES, 1983–2002

It is clear fom this incident what in detestation calumnies should be held in free cities and in every other mode of life and . . . with a view to checking them no institution which serves this end should be neglected.

NICCOLO MACHIAVELLI, *The Discourses*

. . . the notion that papers are impotent in the face of so-called public opinion is a myth that tabloid owners and editors enjoy spreading. They relish their power while denying its existence. So how do we square the circle?

ROY GREENSLADE, in the *Guardian*, 3 February 2003

The way people see politicians is now so awful that some of my colleagues think that you have to pretend you're not a politician and move around at night in camouflage.

NICHOLAS SOAMES, MP, in
Trust Me, I'm a Politician, BBC2, 8 February 2003

This story began with Rupert Murdoch denying suggestions that he might be any kind of wheeler-dealer. Nobody, surely, could suggest he had ever 'asked for anything'? Perhaps we can say that anyone still persuaded of such innocence is persuaded past the reach of evidence. We should now move beyond the basic construction of the Murdoch enterprise to ask other questions. How it has worked is fairly clear. But why should it work – why should politicians yield to Murdoch? And will it go on working?

Newscorp achieved its critical mass – a capacity to be self-sustaining – in the 1980s, as a phenomenon of three Anglophone societies, connected to but remote from each other. The 1990s and the opening of the twenty-first century have seen an extension into other cultures, successful intermittently but without having achieved (as yet) the global scope desired. During these years Newscorp's notoriety has often enabled it to obtain what it needs without explicit request. This is no essential change: we still find instances where it asks, demands and – if tactically necessary – truckles.

My proposal is that understanding Newscorp means understanding first the real workings, in both sickness and health, of our accident-prone media professions – particularly their interaction with authority – as context to the development by the Murdochs – Keith first, then Rupert – of a capacity to traffic with established power, legitimately or otherwise, while pretending to rebel against it. In this the first component is a peculiar personality – or lack of personality – shown in their actions and already somewhat discussed. Second is a kitsch-ideology, sustaining a crusade against the sins of a supposed 'establishment'. Through this, Newscorp retains the loyalty of its psychologically orthodox members. Organisations without that capacity endure only if they can deploy repressive force, which is not the case with Murdoch (though it is with some of his advertised friends). Mainly we need to know what in politics puts services like Murdoch's in demand – increasingly, as it seems.

Newscorp's imperial years have coincided with changes now said to indicate a crisis of rule in democratic society – its Anglophone subdivisions particularly, where electoral apathy engenders political alarm. Is this crisis real, invincible, and perhaps connected to the Murdoch phenomenon – to the tabloid power which as Roy Greenslade says can be both exercised and denied? The core of the story concerns political leverage developed in newspapers and extended into other business – television especially. As Michael Grade, a particularly successful boss of Channel 4 Television, put it, 'If Murdoch didn't own [at the relevant time] 36 per cent of the newspapers, supporting a Conservative Government . . . he would never have got where he is today.'

Grade's statement wasn't comprehensive, of course, in terms of governments involved or of ownership statistics, but it was an otherwise accurate statement of a politico-business model. Its existence Murdoch stoutly denies, typically in 1999 when delivering one of his hectic sermons against state-supported broadcasting (in Western societies):

> We are about change and progress, not about protectionism through legislation and cronyism. We are about vigorous competition, not about whingeing or distorting the market. We are about daring and doing for ourselves, not about riding on someone else's coat tails.

This speech, when placed against a survey of Newscorp's operations in its years of triumph, raises doubt about whether Murdoch possesses any meaningful internal narrative.

The events outlined in Chapter 6 inspired denunciation of Rupert Murdoch's editorial practices throughout Australia, often from Labor voters in the simple class-war terms that their parents had once aimed at Keith. Something, they said, must be done. Labor's leaders – such as Bob Hawke, Paul Keating and Mick Young, busy with political reconstruction – agreed. But, subtle practical fellows, they didn't try to reduce Murdoch's media power. Rather, they assisted its growth. This appeasement exemplifies, without yet explaining, some stubborn curiosities of present-day politics. Murdoch's chief Australian competitors, the Fairfax and Melbourne Herald media groups, they saw as ineluctable enemies and each case involved something other than editorial-page ideology.

The *Herald* of course had exposed the Connor scandal and made Dismissal possible. An ALP legend – which persists – made out that the revelations were engineered by Labor's Liberal enemies, the paper being just a vehicle. Thus Labor fell by dirty tricks, not as a consequence of its own abuses, rightly investigated. And that belief was combined with rage against the *Australian*'s electoral rhetoric, not against its delinquent reporting. Complaint dwelt on subjective, rhetorical items, making a dark victory of propaganda. Somewhat later, Britain's Labour Party blamed its misadventures on propaganda, chiefly Murdoch's, rather than on its own real failings. (F. M. Cornford, an official propagandist in London in 1914–18, called it 'that branch of the art of lying which consists in almost deceiving your friends, and not quite deceiving your enemies'. The health warning continues to be ignored.)

By all its principles, the ALP should have put aside its *Herald* quarrel when Murdoch set out to engulf the group, for nobody by then fancied that editorial independence was in his game-plan. Instead it was joined to the ALP's Fairfax feud – one generated by Fairfax being based in the forest home of Australia's most luminous political tyger, the New South Wales Labor right. The tyger often serves NSW well, but it greatly resents illumination of its doings, and during the 1980s this increased in Fairfax papers, such as the *Sydney Morning Herald*, in step with a decline in the group's traditional anti-labour ideology. Not a second too soon, Fairfax was modernising – using some of the country's best journalists – and in such campaigns professional and political conservatism often perish together. New editorial activism was drawn to Paul Keating and the ALP, as a zoologist turns to vivid fauna (not such sad life-forms as the NSW Liberals). The tyger came to think itself the bleeding underdog. As the ideal types of social science never present ideally, both *Herald*s displayed some propagandist, pseudo-newspaper qualities. But it was their improving tendencies – the true-newspaper component – which the ALP misinterpreted and loathed.

Complexity heats such feuds because journalists and politicians share some activities closely, others hardly at all. Most serious reporters chastely scorn political involvement (even the humblest grass-root service) and can sound like virgin priests offering sex-advice. Most politicians have significant journalistic ability, but in the leader-writing sub-crafts, least consequential in the moments which separate journalism from propaganda. Disclosure to the reporter is an end: to a politician it is a means.

Complexity of course didn't afflict Murdoch. But the ALP, re-elected in 1983, wove itself a Byzantine two-for-one. Fairfax was more noxiously intrusive, but protected from takeover by family holdings. However, if Murdoch ejected the Melbourne Tories by public offer he would control 70 per cent of the metropolitan newspaper trade and could be relied on to undermine Fairfax's ad revenue. Hounding the ALP would then be an over-expensive luxury.

After Fox, a government in office could readily have used the country's foreign-ownership laws to fend off Newscorp's drive towards monopoly. There was no lack of alternative proposals for maintaining diversity and Australian control. But the administration was steadfast for Murdoch. John Menadue took his dismay to his old friend Mick Young, chairman of the ALP, and received a strategic lecture: 'It's more subtle than you think, Jack. The Herald and the Fairfax people – they're always against us. But you know, sometimes Rupert is for us.' Completing the deal in 1987 required such financial firepower as lethally to endanger Murdoch's credit facilities (and we shall find it central to Newscorp's near-death experience in 1991). But it translated into whacking leverage over the Hawke–Keating administrations: enough details of this are known to show just what Murdochspeak like 'doing and daring for ourselves' came to mean at the end of the last century.

Geography and economics make Australia a major aviation market, exploited for many years by the 'two airline' policy – a classic of market distortion and corporatist cronyism. Really there were three firms concerned: Ansett Airlines (controlled by Sir Peter Abeles and Rupert Murdoch); Australian Airlines and Qantas (both owned by the federal government). Qantas flew to and from the country, competing with other long-haul carriers. 'Two airlines' was the official regime under which Ansett and Australian kept all business within the island continent, fixing capacity and prices jointly. Customers paid about 30 per cent above anything seen overseas. In Black Jack's day, when pioneers like Reg Ansett invented airlines, some state protection was defensible. By the 1980s 'two airlines' was pure marketplace abuse and Labor undertook to end it by privatising and deregulating. A hurricane of whingeing struck this wish for change and progress.

After his Tokyo ambassadorship John Menadue became CEO of Qantas, which as a prelude to privatisation was hoping to be allowed to compete on domestic routes. Menadue's executives saw manifest benefits in merging Qantas with Australian Airlines pre-privatisation. But would such a new entity be free to tackle Ansett? Suspecting that the path of ALP aviation policy might not run smooth, Menadue started making notes. In March 1988 Qantas proposed a merger of Qantas, Australian Airlines and Air New Zealand (also government owned), linking the domestic and international networks in both countries. This 'Tricycle' plan would let Ansett expand across the Tasman Sea to New Zealand. But it would involve Ansett in domestic competition.

Initially Air New Zealand liked it, as did the Australian Aviation Minister, Senator Gareth Evans. But Prime Minister Hawke and Treasurer Keating were unsure. They told Evans that changes must 'respect' the wishes of Ansett's owners. Menadue and his colleagues were unsurprised to hear axes grinding. But at first Evans 'kept us briefed on [the] discussions'. Abeles, working with shared capacity in Australia, demanded the same for New Zealand – requiring Qantas actually to *cut* its trans-Tasman flights. The Qantas team were outraged: domestic capacity-fixing was supposed to be ending; what could justify extending it to international routes? The requirement, Evans told Menadue, was 'as solid as the Rock of Gibraltar'. Reluctantly, a formula was calculated.

But appeasement encourages enhanced demands. The unions, accepting the Tricycle deal, guessed it would not be 'sufficient . . . for Peter Abeles', and were soon proved right. During discussions with Evans in Sydney Menadue's team were sent out while a Canberra call came through. 'On our return, Evans described the situation: "Paul Keating said there had to be enough in the arrangement to get the support of Murdoch and Abeles." It was very clear from Evans that it was Murdoch and not Abeles on the Ansett side who was now the prime negotiator.' Immediately, new restrictions hit the Tricycle. It would be too hard on Ansett if Qantas flew its wide-body Boeing 747s within Australia. They had to be excluded.

And while the planners again recalculated the formulas, a fatal blow fell. Evans decreed that the Tricycle must not use its mid-size Boeing 767s within Australia, *though Ansett would use identical aircraft*. The consortium collapsed – Murdoch had taken so much that nothing remained. Though it neatly joined market principle and public interest, the Tricyle wouldn't automatically have survived due-process assessment. But no show was made of any such process: the 767 restriction was bald official endorsement of a market fix. No formal reply came when Qantas asked why it was done 'without talking to us'. But later Evans said to Jim Leslie, the Qantas chairman, 'Rupert was only in town for two days, so I had to make a deal.'

And the Menadue memoirs open a further window on to Newscorp political economy – in its late, highly streamlined form. In this case aviation is outscaled: Telstra (Telecom Australia) is the country's largest business, and the story, as the *Australian Financial Review* put it, concerns the country's 'largest strategic and financial disaster'. (That is, up to publication date in July 1997. Other papers, largely Murdoch's, were less upset.)

In December 1994 Menadue, who had meanwhile left Qantas, got a call from Canberra suggesting he might join the board of Telstra – government owned, but scheduled for part-flotation. It seemed natural that the caller should check his relations with Murdoch, as Telstra was proposing to move into television networking.

> I assumed [he] was asking whether I might have any conflict of interest . . . I said I was not aware of any conflict because, whilst I had worked for Murdoch in the past, my links were [by] then quite tenuous. It became clear to me, however, that I had misinterpreted the question. The caller was wanting to establish whether I would be a supporter of Murdoch on the Telstra board. I kept my counsel, and was appointed . . .

The invitation was from a member of the Keating administration. The caller – a minister named Michael Lee – was unaware of the Tricycle conflict, which was then secret. Menadue, as an ex-News executive, was taken for a Murdoch loyalist. The government was checking for conflicts: *to make sure they existed.*

This is a long way from Black Jack and his whisky bottle, or from Whitehall's constitutional charades with Times Newspapers. By the 1990s Newscorp's rank in the real administration was so eminent, and its terms of trade grasped so well and so discreetly, that the government itself greased its own hidden wheels. (The slight error proves it was not Murdoch's own hand at work – he would have known not to choose Menadue.)

Telstra, via public investment in cable and satellite links, was being readied as a huge pay-TV outlet. Before Menadue's appointment, the search had begun for a content-providing partner, and the choice fell on Newscorp's subsidiary, Foxtel. As the 'world's third largest producer, distributor and owner of films and television programming', the parent could 'guarantee' content. This Telstra would badly need, for two other firms, Optus and Australis, already had Australian rights for all movie sources besides Fox. Outline agreement was made on 11 November 1994 for a partnership between Fox and Telstra, to be called 'Foxtel'.

But the 'guarantee' assumed curious form. At 3 a.m. on Christmas Day Newscorp's primary Australian arm, News Ltd, signed an agreement giving Australis exclusive rights to supply content to the Foxtel joint venture. Telstra was not consulted about this Christmas box, which landed it with prospects of $3.7 billion excess costs over twenty years – to buy from Australis movies made by Fox and others, otherwise available competitively. Foxtel would suffer; Fox itself, upstream of Australis, would collect.

Just after the Australis deal but before ratification of the Foxtel partnership, Menadue joined the Telstra board – seemingly, a Murdoch vote. Unmasking himself, he wrote to the chairman David Hoare that he was not 'persuaded' about the proposed arrangements with News Ltd and Australis. 'My basic problem is understanding how such an agreement could be signed without being satisfied that News Ltd could "guarantee content availability". Didn't we check whether News could and would deliver?' Managing director Frank Blount simply told the directors 'the Government wants us to do the deal with News': ministers were 'better briefed' than they about the likely 'prosperity'. Chairman Hoare asked them for unanimous assent. But when Menadue objected to this 'political pressure' he settled for a majority vote.

The official prosperity was as frail as Newscorp's guarantee: Telstra suffered pay-TV losses of $818 million in 1996–7, and $166 million in 1997–8, whereupon David Potts wrote in the (Fairfax) *Sun-Herald* that Telstra had been 'taken for a ride' by Murdoch – taxpayers were bailing out a 'scandalous' deal. Paul Keating was by then Prime Minister, and – using a famous Keatingism – Potts argued that to permit such a transaction was 'banana republic' stuff, but the government seemingly had 'encouraged' it. Now we know that the government had in fact ordered it.

Telstra escaped larger damage when Australis collapsed, along with its touted 'prosperity'. However, it now seems that the pay-TV network, into which vast public sums have been sunk, can only get by as a Foxtel monopoly. Newscorp has made spacious promises about diverse access to the system. Curiously, they attract scepticism. Newscorp sold out of Ansett in 1999. Ansett went bust in 2001, as the airline recession hit its padded cost-base.

In Britain the transition from late 1980s to early 1990s was Thatcherism's aged evening. But before nightfall Newscorp, strong in the regime's affection, gained an essential benefaction – its way into the Sky monopoly. Central to the relationship was the MacKenzie *Sun*, near its manly noon, promoting superpatriotism as a patent of the Thatcher Tories, and viewed by them as a bulwark of the nation. Journalists, sharing their profession with the *Sun*, have preferred to regard it as a comic masterpiece – and often cite classic instances from the MacKenzie period, such as 'FREDDIE STARR ATE MY HAMSTER'. Few shakier tales have led a newspaper. The *Sun*'s chroniclers Chippindale and Horrie detail the ultra-spin Max Clifford had to apply to clear his comedian-client of pet-molesting without wrecking the fragile concoction – and its otherwise lucrative notoriety. As that was *after* publication, it was certainly a classic of *Sun* technique.

On 6 February 1989, celebrating twenty Murdoch years, the *Sun* identified its own purpose as fundamentally serious. Its commitment was to 'questioning' on behalf of ordinary people, who otherwise would be oppressed by the 'establishment'. Murdoch is reported as having been co-author of this populist credo, which warned against danger from 'a growing band of people in positions of influence and privilege who . . . wish to conceal from their readers' eyes anything they find annoying or embarrassing to themselves'. Such people wanted papers to parrot their views, *Pravda*-like: the *Sun* would always be alert to that. And an opportunity turned up swiftly for the promise to be made good.

On 15 April there was an event which deeply embarrassed people in 'positions of influence and privilege' – the Prime Minister and her spin-doctors. It was the Hillsborough stadium disaster, in which ninety-five Liverpool football fans died. Its general cause was refusal by the booming football industry to take ground-safety seriously. Its immediate cause was callous incompetence by the responsible police force. These truths were unwelcome to the government, which had ignored the specific public-safety issue and resented any criticism of authority apt to reflect on its own. It preferred Hillsborough to be the work of its victims – a 'tanked-up mob' was Bernard Ingham's phrase, shaped by police briefings he and the Prime Minister had received.

This tosh was promoted with a devious vigour unusual for British cops, but authority's signal seemed very legible. Vile, drunken fans became the matter of confidential briefings, off-the-record chats, discreet phone calls. (Most unusually, police evidence statements were corrupted.) By the Monday after the disaster, the news agencies were freighted heavily with lies.

Even skilled news-gatherers may fail in such circumstances, and much Hillsborough coverage was tainted. But on Wednesday the *Sun* distributed the official line with a gullibility all its own. MacKenzie's headline, 'THE TRUTH', flared over untruths such as wartime enemies cannot often have turned against British suffering, offering a level of abuse unique in national terms. 'Animal' behaviour had been universal, with heroic cops attacked incessantly (even when giving the kiss of life). By the *Sun*'s account drunks had robbed inert bodies, spouted obscenities and sprayed urine offensively about (this was presented as special evidence of malice, suggesting that the *Sun*'s sub-editors knew little about traumatic death and its indignities – relaxation of bladder control particularly). Anonymous quotations pictured the crowd as pitiless brutes. Stuff like this reached everyone via the agencies. Too many printed some of it, qualified variously. Only MacKenzie's imagination generated no sceptical reflex. Eventually the propaganda was revealed, exposing 'THE TRUTH' for its sloppy procedure and macho culture. (As Chippindale and Horrie report, papers were more accurate where tears could be shed.)

Now, what response to the impact of accident shows that some collection of people and machines does amount (however roughly) to a newspaper? It must be the thing MacKenzie and Murdoch claimed to be brave exponents of: 'questioning', pressed for the sake of those unable to ask questions for themselves. Clearly it is an extreme accident when people die horribly, and when powerful people – ones perhaps failing in their duty – say the cause is crime by the victims and their friends. In a newspaper this generates questions instantaneously, smothering the claim in ambiguity which must persist while questions stay open. Good papers resolve such ambiguity; poor ones just display it. Sadly, factors like ethnic or geographic distance subtract energy from the process. But at Hillsborough all these, for a British paper, were negligible. In the *Sun*, while questions gaped everywhere, ambiguity was zero. A space existed instead of a newspaper's operational core: official lies simply flowed in, to be parroted out.

'Official' doesn't mean they were a product of the legitimate state itself. On the contrary, Mrs Thatcher's Cabinet asked an eminent judge to investigate, and accepted his findings. (Sir Bernard Ingham has several times offered his personal view that Lord Justice Taylor produced a whitewash, but he has not had many takers.) The propaganda came from office-holders who sought illegitimately to manipulate the state, by spreading disinformation. The *Sun* was their efficient vector, showing itself an official or government organ, as far as that can exist under democracy, where it requires pseudo-newspaper qualities.

In the real world, any democratic government is a Jekyll-and-Hyde duality. It always contains a number of uncomplicated autocrats who believe the media should do what the government says: they are the overt Hyde element. Usually, they are outnumbered by liberal Dr Jekylls, who use and enjoy free media, and to whom government newspapers or government broadcasting would be a grotesque idea – until, of course, Dr Jekyll the politician has the painful experience of being made to look bad by some disclosure by the free media. (This is especially painful when undergone at the hands of public-service broadcasters using liberties specifically granted to them by liberal politicians.)

Democracy survives just as long as the Jekylls of government resist the Hyde which they find within themselves at every moment of stress. And of course it would be a long, long step for the leaders of any industrial democracy to bring newspapers or broadcasters directly under their control. But if the idea can be privatised, it becomes immensely more tempting: pro-government publications run by private corporations, or pseudo-newspapers, on the argument of this book. It remains, so far, a narrow and difficult market. Most pseudo-newspapers contain large journalistic impurities, and cannot be depended on. Many publishing companies decline to offer a product. But News Corporation has developed a remarkably consistent brand, marketed now wherever a demand exists.

No formal orders generated the Hillsborough propaganda. But that was rarely needed in the old *Pravda* days – divining what the powerful desire is rarely taxing. What was taxing for Murdoch and MacKenzie was trying to explain 'THE TRUTH' as the truth itself emerged – their costive apologies illuminated nothing. Comparison of their promises with the *Sun*'s actual behaviour suggests that linkages between words and impact mystified them – and writings from MacKenzie in more expansive mood are suggestive. In 2002 he looked back from his new status as a radio entrepreneur to the legal struggles at the *Sun*, recounting a case when the paper's Bizarre column was headed 'STING: WHY I HAVE TAKEN DRUGS'.

It was run only because Sting was 'a clean-living sort of guy' and 'we didn't have anything else'. At once, the singer's lawyers sent a denial. At once, MacKenzie investigated – that is, allowed his reporter to tell him Sting had confessed on tape. Nobody checked the tape. The lawyers were told 'to get stuffed'. But they persisted, until senior counsel and legal footsoldiers had to gather round the editor and prepare a defence. Now the tape was played, and yielded, says MacKenzie, 'A lot of boring dribble about what great songs he sings, why he sings them and then, finally, the crunch. The Bizarre reporter says: "Tell me Sting, have you ever taken drugs?" Sting pauses and then replies firmly: "No."' Almost any newspaper would have checked it pre-publication. One which wouldn't check after the denial is hard to picture. But this is MacKenzie describing his own unique operation: no verification till the legal paladins saddle up.

At this point cheery reminiscence changes to a flailing assault on libel law – because Sting got £75,000 damages. Outrageous: as much as the payout for losing both arms in a car crash. 'In what way was his reputation so mightily damaged? I saw the Brits the other night and Sting received a lifetime achievement award. He didn't look very damaged to me . . .' In reality, a victim of negligence losing both arms would typically get £750,000, because the law puts damage to the body above damage to reputation. However, the law does hold that words carry responsibilities. On MacKenzie's account they have their uses – dressing up some 'boring dribble' perhaps. But, to judge by the Sting case, that doesn't attach much responsibility to them. People who share his talent for dealing with words usually feel that they matter more. Pseudo-newspapers, therefore are not quite simple to run, and have some scarcity value.

At the time of Hillsborough Newscorp was developing satellite television as a way round the rules which had stopped Murdoch controlling the London Weekend franchise. To him they were a commercially obstructive growth. To the Thatcher administration – as we've seen – they were political obstruction, a forest which shielded unpatriotic enemies. The Sky business, when Murdoch bought it for £1 in 1983, consisted of a small, unprofitable northern European network. But by 1989, when it relaunched as a major British service, Murdoch and his competitors were laying vast financial bets: technical advance was about to make satellite into another 'licence to print money'. Today, that licence remains somewhat elusive. People are often surprised to learn that Sky – though hugely profitable at times – has so far lost money overall. It is one of the things which tell us that monopoly control matters to Newscorp more than profit.

As the Thatcher administration approached its last moments, both Sky and its rival British Satellite Broadcasting were financially moribund, their initial assault on the marketplace having badly misfired. BSB was a joint venture of existing ITV companies and the Pearson group, owners of the *Financial Times* and the *Economist*. Like Sky, and rather like the initial Fox network, BSB was based on Hollywood movie output – an opportunity which appeared because the public-service rules applying to terrestrial broadcasters were largely absent. Even had the government admired the existing television model, applying it to orbiting transponders would have required serious legal ingenuity.

Both BSB and Sky expected a movie-driven audience to generate heavy advertising income (they were not ready to adopt encryption and pay-TV). However, for reasons like those making it hard to regulate, satellite was hard to calibrate. Terrestrial viewing figures were (and are) imperfect, but they provided some credible basis for collecting ad revenue; satellite had no equivalent and collected very little. By mid-1990 Sky was heading for annual operating losses of £95 million (£130 million now) after £120 million launch costs, and BSB was worse. Merger was their sole hope.

It was of course unclear that a new media system should become a monopoly to bail out investors doing and daring unluckily. Unlike the newspaper case, no law specifically required a Sky–BSB merger to be tested for public-interest impact. But many politicians and television executives believed that the Monopolies Commission should investigate the satellite débâcle, and seek a future which might be competitive, fitting the government's theoretical outlook. Monopoly, however, was the government's practical bent – a product of its political afflictions. Prominent among these was the decline of Ingham's media ascendancy. Won over the mid-1980s press, it had bred great over-confidence, and now faced penetrative challenge from the *Independent* – which had not existed when Ingham had the Westminster lobby at his command, and, operating quite outside it, was revealing Tory Party dissent which *The Times* and the *Sun* had once been able obediently to ignore. In this context documentaries which asked questions began to seem intolerable. Loathing for ITV's *Death on the Rock* remained unique, but the BBC was also thought, absurdly, to assist the IRA's operations.

The *Independent* appeared invulnerable, but perhaps not the broadcasters, and substantial blows were aimed at them – if without satisfying effect. The 1990 ITV licensing round was run as a financial auction, which could be expected to trim the funds available for troublesome current-affairs programming. This possibly began the long decline of the ITV audience, but its immediate (unpredicted) effect was to knock out the one licence-holder, London Weekend, which the Prime Minister admired. As for the BBC, hopes did exist that Professor Andrew Peacock, commissioned to look into advertising on the BBC, might suggest ways to privatise the Corporation (eliminating the communist elements Woodrow Wyatt complained of). But the professor, a free-market advocate, judged the economics unworkable, and – disastrously – suggested the BBC should be left alone.

The administration was dying from poll-tax complications, not just from the derelict measure itself – but from the blustering method it exemplified and the consequent Conservative resistance which for some three years it had seemed sagacious and practicable to conceal. These illusions were sustained (until they became incurable) by the Murdoch papers – centrally the *Sun*, providing from the Falklands to Hillsborough facilities for splashing insults over any target apt to inconvenience the regime. It had all been constitutionally frivolous, and also reckless: the Cabinet's collective legitimacy had been shattered with the *Sun*'s aid in 1986, and pretending that no wound existed had naturally made it worse.

Reality's recrudescence the government's loyalists attributed to bias – showing that the long Thatcher–Murdoch alliance had given a new, absurd meaning to the word. For the offending news – though picked up elsewhere – came primarily from the *Independent*, whose editor Andreas Whittam Smith and political editor Anthony Bevins were as remote from real bias as practical journalists have ever been.

Whittam Smith had founded the paper in exact antithesis of Murdoch principles, promising readers that its content represented 'the editorial team's own agenda and nobody else's; neither the advertising department's, nor the owner's, nor any particular political party's, nor any business interests". Bevins hated reporting that was slanted in any partisan direction, and left the Murdoch *Times* because he was asked to favour the government. He received an award as Political Reporter of the Year for 1990 – because he revealed there would be a challenge to the Tory leadership. That the story should be a scoop, and require his talent to uncover it, shows how distorted political circumstances were.

The BBC news department rarely seeks to outdo the most adventurous newspaper work, and did not then. But it strives to be thorough, and to report disclosures in other media once checked out by its own experienced staff. Thatcher loyalists saw this as publicising dissidents far better ignored; Independent Television News offended too. And since 1989 there had been a benchmark to set their sins against: Sky News, which Downing Street thought splendidly impartial. Broadcast news can begin by retailing national and international wire-service copy unchecked, and some channels aspire no further. Sky News today has an editorial framework and presentational pizzazz – its competitors take it seriously. In 1990 it was a scratch team exercised more by its own likely collapse than by the government's collapse. Thus it grappled scarcely at all with the story of the year – and what could show lack of bias better? For Margaret Thatcher, still hopeful of retaining power, Sky was a sturdy addition to the nation's media.

Negotiations to create British Sky Broadcasting (BSkyB) paralleled the political crisis, and on 29 October Murdoch went to Downing Street to explain things to the Prime Minister. As he recalled it to Matthew Horsman in *The Story of Sky*, she was showing out a foreign visitor, and said to him, 'Here is Mr Murdoch, who gives us Sky News, the only un-biased news in the UK.' Murdoch said, 'Well you know it is costing us a lot, and we are going to have to do a merger.' The Prime Minister nodded. And as with the airline and telecom deals in Australia, it was basically that simple.

Still, the hand-stitching was neat. Just then the government was put-ting the Independent Television Commission (ITC) in place of the Independent Broadcasting Authority (IBA). That was to dilute the public-service tradition, but sufficient remained for both the IBA and its successor to say that the deal might need modifying. The Office of Fair Trading also planned to investigate monopoly implications. But none of them knew – as the Cabinet did – that a five-day 'window' would exist before the ITC got control of satellite licences via the Television Act 1990. And within this window the BSB licence passed to BSkyB, with executive control and half the equity in Newscorp. That might have been hard to accomplish with the new law in place. It was one more *fait accompli* from a friendly government.

To begin with, all Murdoch got was a chance to save his skin (and BSkyB still lost £646 million in 1991). But, more important, he got something he would be able to defend as a monopoly should it become profitable (£271 million in 1998, before the plunge into digital losses). Murdoch would be able to control the access of rivals to the satellite plat-form – diversity and competition, as ever, kept at bay. It was a remarkable dispensation, based on Margaret Thatcher's even more remarkable idea of 'impartial' news. Newscorp's media scale and media clout tempt it into expansive gambles – and then help it to escape the consequences. Roughly parallel with the satellite crisis, another such drama occurred in the Australian base territory. Murdoch's acquisition of the Melbourne Herald group imposed costs which were a dangerous element in the 'debt crisis' of 1990–1 – again providing the dispensation which helped Newscorp find a way out.

Murdoch's problem originated in the interlocked Herald group

419

structure which had once allowed his father to exert personal control over a widely held public company. The Melbourne company's Adelaide and Brisbane subsidiaries were also its own biggest (though not majority) shareholders. Murdoch's 1987 purchase of the Herald and Weekly Times Ltd was for A$1.8 billion, a price elevated so far above market values that the existing directors had to recommend it to their shareholders. Two-thirds of the offer was in Newscorp shares – advantageously damping down the share price, and thus the payouts due to Michael Milken's punters (see Chapter 11 above). But a third was in cash, which drove Newscorp debt to the edge of banking tolerance.

It was a deal in the spirit of a high-rolling period, and abruptly one of the high aces joined in: Robert Holmes à Court offered for the 56 per cent publicly held shares in Queensland Press – the Brisbane company. Having paid a vast price for the Herald group, Murdoch might have to share control with a notoriously free spirit. He continued a steamroller approach, countering Holmes à Court with an offer again so far above market price that the Queensland directors had to agree. But this added A$600 million to the cost of the deal for Newscorp, exceeding even the Commonwealth Bank's risk-appetite.

The problem was circumvented by making the Queensland buyout through Cruden Investments, Murdoch's personal vehicle inherited from Keith. It did not have A$600 million, but it got bank credit against the A$1.5 billion value of its controlling share in Newscorp. Then, in the October 1987 stock-market crash, the Commonwealth Bank demanded repayment. The cash was provided by Queensland Press, which bought – in secret – a sufficient tranche of Cruden's Newscorp shares, at roughly 40 per cent above the existing market price. To do so it raised an expensive, long-term loan. For one company to provide clandestinely the finance for its takeover by another would be illegal under American or British law. In this respect the Australian company code was then hazy, though it was actually undergoing the reforms which now make it consistent with US–British practice.

The debt crisis was caused by a huge expansion-and-acquisition spree by Newscorp between 1986 and 1989, the Herald and Sky being just two of the more dramatic examples. Once it was realised that Newscorp could survive only by drastic rescheduling of its debts, there were significant differences in market perception as between Australia, Britain and the US. Everyone knew that the essence of the cure was a debt-override agreement signed in February 1991, forgiving all existing debt in exchange for a new three-year repayment schedule – highly profitable to the syndicate of creditor banks, led by Citicorp in the US and Commonwealth in Australia. Outside Australia not many bankers, let alone lesser souls, realised that debt relief was required for Murdoch personal companies – and especially for Cruden – as well as for the Newscorp business. The aim was not just to revive the prostrate empire, but to resecure simultaneously the system of personal governance which had enabled Murdoch to plunge it into debt.

The paradox of debt-default clearly fills an essential social need, and orderly provision for it may well be capitalism's greatest achievement. But it is less clear that society is well served by leaving the authors of default in control of assets they have accumulated by recklessly embracing it. Bankers' lectures on 'moral hazard' are usually delivered when such a course of events is made obvious. In this case it was adroitly concealed. Even so, the debt-override agreement encountered reluctance, because some American bankers did not like what they heard about the element of Murdoch personal debt contained within it. They would have liked the state of affairs even less had they been aware that an extra A$600 million properly belonged to that part of the tally.

During 1990 the Australian Securities Commission (ASC) was established, as an approximate, much overdue equivalent to the SEC – a response to the lunatic doings of the 1980s. One of its earliest actions was to examine the Queensland Press purchase of Newscorp shares, and in March 1991 the Commission's lawyers concluded that Murdoch had taken over Queensland by making use of Queensland's own financial resources. In any sensible way, so it had. Under the reformed corporate code, powers now existed for ordering the deal to be unravelled – making Cruden repay A$600 million – and the Commission began to consider the case for doing so.

Had the facts of the matter become public – and the prospect of ASC action been reported – then the debt-override agreement, a touch-and-go exercise anyway, would have been likely to blow up. And most of the details were reported to the magazine *Australian Business,* through its

Brisbane correspondent Neil Chenoweth. A two-page spread was prepared for the March issue, but was pulled on the decision of the editor, Trevor Sykes, one of Australia's best-known financial journalists, and something of a mentor to Chenoweth.

Australian Business was not owned by News, but it operated in a market under Murdoch's monopoly influence. (Most definitions of monopoly use a market share well below Newscorp's 70 per cent control of Australian newspapers.) Chenoweth had no doubt that the likely consequence, had his editor chosen to go ahead, would have been to unravel Murdoch's control of Newscorp – putting the override into default and making Murdoch sell News shares in a hostile market. But he also knew what the certain result would be in any lesser outcome. As he put it to me, 'I saw myself becoming an ex-journalist called Neil Chenoweth.' He accepted Sykes' decision, and made no effort to take the story elsewhere – either to Fairfax or to any overseas publication. Chenoweth has since written a valuable book, *Virtual Murdoch*, containing a history of the Queensland Press affair, but nowhere mentioning that the secrecy critical to the affair could and should have been dispelled in 1991, when it constituted vital disclosure. It is scarcely possible to imagine the suppression taking place in an American context. (Enron attempted diligently to stop Bethany McLean of *Fortune* from pricking its bubble, but did not succeed.)

Murdoch's lawyers fought a savage, unpublicised battle with the ASC lawyers until the mid-1990s, their aim being to have Queensland certified as a routine investment decision. They only half succeeded, but their campaign inhibited all action until ASC's overworked staff let the matter drop. The Newscorp case was that Keith McDonald, the News retainer in charge of Queensland, was a coolly independent figure who simply made an independent investment decision in the best interests of his company. But there are no coolly independent figures in the Murdoch empire. His real attitude – and his desire to shield his boss from piddling restraints – was expressed in a claim that 'men of integrity' like Murdoch would always make 'decent, wholesome newspapers' unless held back by 'fool laws' specifying that 'you can't own more than this or that'.

The debt crisis appears in News folklore as something akin to a small boatbuilder fighting off hard-hearted bankers: they were asking us to put our company into liquidation, Murdoch said indignantly. This was hyperbole. What was saved by the bizarre supra-national immunities of Newscorp was not the 'wholesome' businesses within it, but Murdoch's dominion over them.

Chapter 11 showed that Murdoch's operation of the Fox network rested on his becoming personally an American, while retaining an Australian corporate identity. Deformities in the legal skeleton started to show through Fox's corporate pelt in 1993, but by the time they became conspicuous in 1995 Murdoch's Washington power was massive enough to have them patched over without any lasting ill-effect.

A lawyer for the National Association for the Advancement of Coloured People first spotted an SEC filing in which Newscorp listed Fox – supposedly an independent US company – as one of its subsidiaries. Argument on the issue aborted a TV-licence application in Philadelphia, and subsequently Fox asked the Federal Communications Commission to 'clarify' matters, repeating that 76 per cent of Fox voting stock was held by Murdoch and other US citizens. Newscorp admittedly owned some equity. However, '[its] precise dollar value . . . at any given time would appear to be immaterial'. But the FCC staff, having been asked, persisted – and found that it was altogether material. News owned 99 per cent of the real capital, and all real voting control. This, after pressure from the NBC network and other sources, led Reed Hundt, the Clinton-appointed FCC chairman, to launch an investigation in 1995 which might – legally – have revoked Fox's licence.

The counter-attack by Murdoch's Republican allies was judged by observers to be a classic of Washington lobbying (or 'degradation of the legislative process by money', as Hundt put it). The conclusion of the Commission's Republican majority was as remarkable as Margaret Thatcher's thoughts about unbiased news.

It was agreed that News Corporation, a foreign company, had indeed owned Fox ever since 1985. And Fox had not revealed until 1994 that 'alien ownership' was in 'far excess' of the statutory benchmark. But the Commissioners decided that Fox had not 'intentionally lacked candor', had 'reasonably relied on the opinion of its legal counsel', and *did not know* of any 'duty to disclose the amount of equity capital contributed . . . by aliens'. Staggeringly, they could not imagine 'any motive for [Fox] to conceal the facts of ownership in 1985'. They were satisfied that Rupert Murdoch, an American, controlled Fox. Naturally the circumstance that he controlled it via a highly idiosyncratic, supra-national structure – enabling him to borrow more money and pay less tax than American competitors – was, similarly, beyond their imagining.

Murdoch's successes, observes Andrew Schwartzman of the Washington-based Media Access Project, 'are due to political and regulatory help as much as they are to smart investment decisions'. In this context, that is surely a mild assessment. It underlines the point that special market conditions are not an occasional luxury, but a basic necessity for Newscorp.

The next year in Britain was the lead-in to a general election, which it would clearly be difficult for John Major and the Tories to win. The delicate question for Murdoch was to decide if and when to switch his impartial newspapers over to the Labour Party. The stages are recorded in volume three of the Wyatt diaries, and are poignant because the author – a man of loyalties if nothing else – felt confident through 1993–4 that Murdoch would stick to Tory principles and see Major through to a hard-fought victory.

> *Thursday 15 September 1994.* Spoke to Rupert at about twenty past eight in the morning.
> I said 'I think Major's doing very well.' Rupert wasn't quite so sure.
> Anyway he's not going to withdraw his backing.

Doubts, however, occur from time to time (in fact there are too many fluctuations to quote conveniently):

> *24 November 1994.* I know you've been flirting with [Tony] Blair . . . Are you not going to back Major any more? I will if I can [a complaint here about Major's 'weakness'].

There are bad moments in 1995 over the administration's plan for cross-media restrictions. But they are less than swingeing, and by the autumn Murdoch is relaxed:

23 September 1995. Rupert didn't exactly promise to back Major but as good as on the whole . . .

Then some personal alarm as Blair seems to make serious progress with Murdoch:

> *1 December 1995.* He [Murdoch] doesn't seem to value what I did for him. I had all the rules bent for him over the *Sunday Times* and the *Times* when he bought them . . . Rupert's almost coming out for Blair . . . [Wyatt thinks Blair has agreed to protect BSkyB from monopoly investigations, and fears his own columns are being cut back because he criticises Blair.]

All is not lost, however, for Murdoch wants to discuss the Broadcasting Bill with the Prime Minister:

> *14 February 1996.* I think he was impressed by Major in a way he hadn't been before.*

But there is no happy ending:

> *Monday 17 March 1997.* Rupert has behaved like a swine and a pig. He doesn't like backing losers and he thinks Major will lose. Tonight the great announcement has come out that the *Sun* is backing Blair and there'll be huge headlines across the front page tomorrow . . .
>   Irwin [Stelzer] says, of course, that he's not the Rupert we used to know.

It's striking that Wyatt – like Harry Evans, like others – was blind to a record which made the outcome obvious. It is blindness of a type that Machiavelli notices. A prince should not break faith, but need not worry about a perfidious track-record preventing reuse of the tactic. 'Present

---

*Matthew Horsman in *The Story of Sky* says the legislation preserved BSkyB's monopoly substantially untouched.

necessities' in matters like politics ensure that 'he who seeks to deceive' can always find an individual 'who will allow himself to be deceived'.

Murdoch's first significant campaign under the Blair regime was the trashing of the Davies Report on digital television – referred to in the Introduction. At its core the Davies case was that creation of a universal and diverse digital system – popular enough to achieve the desired analogue switch-off – would be frustrated by assigning the commercial sector a decisive role. Though Davies put it a great deal more diplomatically, the report was coloured by a suspicion that the skills of Britain's commercial-TV sector have withered considerably after years of ideologically driven wheezes calculated to accommodate talents no greater – even less sometimes – than Murdoch's.

The paladins of Carlton and Granada joined with Murdoch in furious attack on the Davies plan, which was to put the digital-pioneer responsibility (with safeguards) firmly on the BBC. In terms of pluralism, it was not an ideal solution, but it avoided the delusion that the ITV companies had a surplus of creative energy sufficient to launch a new division of their industry. Notoriously, the Carlton–Granada joint venture failed after doing considerable damage to programme-makers and football clubs. Few analysts were prepared to excuse ITV-Digital, except to note that the battery of anti-competitive practices built into Sky by its original construction and years of political protection could well have made the task impossible for a considerably abler team. The monopoly is now stronger than ever, but still a long distance from profitability.

Nobody reporting the Blair government doubts that its media policies are circumscribed by Newscorp (see below for further illustration). Everyone knows that Murdoch, appeased adequately, will deliver his troops. Though discipline may be ragged, in the way of mercenary bands, the job gets done. But what 'present necessities' have driven so many politicians to make so many grubby, short-sighted accommodations? Machiavelli's iron rule of political survival states that mercenary alliances are worthless. Is the great realist's advice obsolete in this respect? Are tabloid leader-writers really different from *condottieri*?

Over time, ideas about words, power and politics have certainly altered, and something in the present context may explain Newscorp's appeal. We know that Augustan or early-Victorian oligarchs kept an

426

editor or two – plus a shrewd mistress and some discreet thugs – and that they were discommoded when newspapers grew rich and bribery declined. In the last century Stanley Baldwin saw media bosses trying to reverse the trade in power, and repulsed them with the famous courtesan metaphor. His cousin Kipling asked Beaverbrook personally to explain the erratic politics of the *Daily Express*, and was told: 'I want power. Kiss 'em one day, kick 'em the next.' That was when Kipling called Beaverbrook a 'harlot' (the private breach anticipating the Prime Ministerial broadside). However, the subject fairly surely was not 'power' in the orderly, creative sense electoral office-holders prefer; the Beaver meant the 'black arts' of mischief and disorder. Kipling was a prac-titioner – not an impresario – of journalism, and his reporter's intuition saw far past Beaverbrook into the dangerous future of industrial news and entertainment.

Their extreme corruption, Kipling thought, might create lunatic soci-eties – a theme of several intricate parables written prior to August 1914. *The Village That Voted the Earth Was Flat* begins with an irresponsible mag-istrate imposing phoney motoring fines on four newspapermen and a show-business boss – adding moralistic lectures and anti-semitic wit to amuse his rural gallery. Their revenge – hypnotic spin applied to national news and entertainment – turns the village into a world centre for insane cults. Responsibly, the illusionists close the show short of fatal chaos (the takings go to their ace reporter and star singer, riding together into the sunset). But the comedy carries traces of hysteria, amplified in darker tales like *As Easy as A. B. C.* – where isolated survivors of an indescribable ethnic holocaust have learnt to treat populist rhetoric and exploitation of privacy as ultimate felonies. These subtle visions anticipated the totali-tarian regimes which made them crudely real (and perhaps contain other warning hints: look at 'reality TV' in their light). Kipling didn't think constitutional societies were helpless against media corruption, but that only increased his contempt for anyone naively fooling with the defences in time of rising danger. The 'power' Beaverbrook coveted had no legit-imate uses.

More prosaically, political scientists in the inter-war years developed statistical surveys of media influence in societies still relatively healthy. And Paul Lazarsfeld in America attacked a fundamental puzzle.

Republican opinion then dominated newspapers. But it was an era of Democratic electoral supremacy – so what about Northcliffe's 'power of the rotary press'? Lazarsfeld's work showed that, where a valid parliamentary structure coexists with even mildly diverse news media, the masters of huge circulations cannot determine electoral outcomes. Editorial views, however strenuous, are just one element in a manifold; and six decades of work throughout the democratic world supports Lazarsfeld, suggesting that within any nation the legitimacy of politics and of news media interdepend.

Successful newspapers in free societies lean to conservatism, reflecting their character as property. That this makes no decisive impact is for some hard to bear. The right feels that ownership deserves more, but is robbed by liberal conspiracy. The left suspects occult property-effects, which explain the proletarian indifference to Marx. The reality is that media systems don't naturally resemble an irrigation array with pumps and regular conduits. Scientific inquiry suggests something sponge-like – an intricate wetland, with hidden linkages between its primary chan-nels. Many compounds stain its waters – nutrients or pollutants – and diffuse without great respect to the place or purpose of injection.

For almost everyone, primary news comes via broadcasting – still roughly neutral in competent democracies. At least, it doesn't trade char-acteristically in revelations with high partisan potential. These originate chiefly in newspapers, magazines or websites, but their essentials seep cir-cuitously into broadcast channels, and basic facts often survive the journey better than nuances of spin and propaganda. Many people gather only minimal political data first-hand, augmenting it on occasion from personal contact with the zealous few. A nation is a community of micro-communities, trafficking in advice, hints, gossip and ideas – often political – and most individuals possess a relative expertise. (Social science advanced hugely by finding that knowledge of US farm machinery was distributed far better than any relevant literature – because catalogue-buff farmers often shared a jug with others.)

Media grandees sometimes despise the 'punters' – a blank herd accepting 'dumbed-down' propositions. But best-evidence is that modern communities track social and political events alertly, because they consist of individuals with assorted personal and institutional sources. This alertness rises generally with education, and now brings attitudes which trouble office-holders deeply. The best recent study is by the Harvard political scientist Pippa Norris. *A Virtuous Circle* covers all the OECD nations, finding similar core-values in all these industrialised democracies. Her burial of the myth in which television is print media's enemy we cited earlier. Overall, 'dumbing-down' notions make a poor statistical showing.

Data for reading, viewing and political action of course varies by nation, but chief indicators are robustly alike: newspaper sales sustain themselves reasonably well, usually with a trend towards broadsheets; use of current-affairs television links with reading, practices which reinforce each other. Commitment to political and civic action accompanies this, but includes critical perception of the systems involved – that is, 'virtuous circles' stimulate interests which need satisfaction. This means that declining apathy may in time be replaced by disengagement due to unanswered criticism. This, though superficially similar, is dynamic, not inertial, and is also deadlier.

The Norris evidence doesn't say that 'dumbing down' and political necrosis cannot become serious because so far they have not. It may be read as an early warning of stratification in the rich democracies, with high-grade media separating (often profitably) from junk aimed at groups suffering educational or geographic disadvantage (like Americans outside the range of strong metropolitan newspapers). Junk media may well stimulate a psychic analogue of obesity. Britain, with the biggest, most necrotic popular press, has unusual rates of distrust for both its politicians and its news media. But nothing suggests a universal law at work. More likely is that some media operators feed on – and feed – particular ailments overdue for treatment. This is the realm of Murdoch, and perhaps of his imitators.

Surely popular opinion may be wrong, but not in general through frivolity, or through the politician's all-consuming involvement. What detached judgment exists is most likely distributed across the population, and opinion-research records show, in free electorates, a history of sensible perception – supporting Machiavelli's argument that peoples are wiser than princes. The chief gains in public consciousness probably develop from transactions between a detached majority and particular witnesses with imagination vivid enough to survive extreme emotional fields – where prosaic observers suffer overload, forming the inexact images which propaganda magnifies.

The Cuban war Stephen Crane covered after his imaginary Chancellorsville began in a media frenzy, and some US officers claimed that the Spanish were mutilating corpses. Like others, Crane reported the fantasy – one of a type frequent in war. But Crane could create battles of his own (as it were), and he went with a US Army surgeon to examine the dead precisely. Their injuries, it turned out, were made by high-velocity jacketed bullets, a recent advance on lead and black powder. Hearst's editors didn't find time for the rewrite, staying with the fantasy. Before Crane's short career ended he taught them a little better. (Links between emotional capacity and precision were discussed in Chapter 3 above.)

Chris Patten, Hong Kong's last Governor, is not unique among politicians in finding Murdoch's status paradoxical. The aid he provides 'is only available if you don't need it' – a leverage not just unconstitutional, but unuseful in Patten's view. However, the ex-Governor isn't orthodox. Awe of Newscorp colonises most minds in or near office, and sceptics rank about level with advocates of unprotected sex. Patten, as the British Tories' strategist for the 1983 general election, disputed his colleagues' belief that the advertising spend should focus on the *Sun*. His research showed that most *Sun* readers were Labour voters, likely to think it a Labour paper (handy for TV-lists, celebrity-hunts and sport, not political advice). Still, faith in Rupert, steersman of the proletariat, was no less bulletproof than the ALP vision of a biddable monopolist.

So another circle needs squaring. Northcliffe's contemporaries could half justify obeisance, when opinion measurements didn't exist. Today, power like Murdoch's should be recognisably spectral. To be sure, it might become substantive with a modest rise in media-concentration permitted under democracy (modest, because large ones have already occurred). The last century proved that dominion – if rigid, unstable and hysterical – can be imposed under a sufficient monopoly. It also showed the effects of diversity to be highly resilient, with a breakdown point difficult to predict. Doubtless it is short of the Nazi case, where all editors were state censors (even those few with papers not run by the regime). It must vary with the health of law, parliament and related institutions.

Italian democracy has been visibly ailing while Murdoch's friend Silvio Berlusconi controls – privately, or as Prime Minister – most of Italy's television, and much of its newspaper, magazine and book output.

Certainly there are Anglo-American financial engineers eager to take the experimental process further. But, as a witness to the Shawcross Commission suggested, once it's taken to the point of diversity being extinguished, there's unlikely to be a comeback. A glib theory says electronic media are automatically diverse – bilge to drain when we come to Murdoch's China. In present fact, legislators entertain hallucinations about media power such that their behaviour might make it real.

Pure lack of moral fibre can't explain it. Electoral office is no trade for self-seeking fools, especially on pay which CEOs with a tenth of the ability-level would inflate by many powers of ten. Indeed democracy as employer seems both ungenerous and inconstant, which may explain something: Newscorp's fitful acclaim at least gushes. Sir John Kerr found himself an intrepid patriot in the *Australian*, as the Thatcherites stood invincible in the *Sun*; Tony Blair's advisers were delighted when their man scaled the Thatcher plinth in Newscorp's pantheon. Hero-worship certainly is a Newscorp competence, refined internally. If Kelvin MacKenzie can equate Rupert to Mozart, admiring Bob Hawke must be easy work.

Still, this is flimsy comfort. Little in opinion-research is steadier than the popular-trust surveys in which politicians rank bottom with journalists and dealers in real estate. And complexities apply in the media case. Close analysis shows that public contempt concentrates on tabloid practitioners – television newsreaders (journalists after all) rank as high as doctors. Additionally, maverick status may have professional value when convertible loosely to 'iconoclasm' or 'exclusiveness'. But politicians face uncomplex facts. Without some trust-like commodity, convertible formally to votes, their occupation's gone.

If you want a friend in politics, said Harry Truman, 'get a dog'. In this lonely trade a newspaper may do as well, and the radical insecurity which this suggests has increased. Clement Attlee, an effective Prime Minister who ignored newspapers and used the Cabinet news-feed only for cricket scores, was unusual in the 1940s, impossible today. He would be startled by the idea of keeping his occupation a secret. Coexisting with this media-soaked practice is a traditional theory that politicians should find psychic refreshment in national sentiment. There is talk of 'mandates' and of the inspiration a majority brings. We may see a crowd's welcome lift some minister's grey fatigue of office. We hear that 'the people have spoken' (or confided their wishes via focus groups). But this now is a mantra which has lost much of its significance.

Lincoln's words in 1863 – government 'of the people, by the people, for the people' – are not yet empty. Evidently, the people are governed. Evidently, it is done for them, as graft is historically modest. But it is hard to speak with his directness about government *by* the people. Democracies today are explained in layers of proxy and delegation – often sincerely, but what emerges is not the Gettysburg meaning. Something once active is now passive, and what was subject has acquired qualities of object. Of course Lincoln's 'people' was restricted: Roman *populus* rather than *plebs* – that is, free citizens qualified to have a voice in affairs. Lincoln did not require that every man be included identically, nor did he consider women. But more important than qualification – which is anyway broadening – is how Lincoln expected the qualified to act, as participants in a ruling process.

That expectation has a complex past. The Athens of Euripides is distant, but the idealistic debaters in *The Suppliant Women* still appear in school, quoted by Milton in *Areopagitica*. From *The Prince* it arrives with zero idealism. Machiavelli specifies that in a political community people and ruling class are one body, membership being by free will. A prince rules active colleagues, and – banishing mercenaries – is sustained by the people's qualities: courage, reason and above all constancy. Though Machiavelli saw no infinite *virtù* in the people, he judged (expertly) that only treachery would be found by seeking support anywhere else.

Many Florentine texts develop the theme, but 'Of Mixed Principalities', the famous third chapter of *The Prince*, gives its essence – describing the arbitrary regime which lost Milan for Louis XII. Scholarship traces it through Puritan England, then revolutionary and federal America, as the 'Atlantic republican tradition'. What has changed since Lincoln's crystalline definition (apart from slavery, the barbarity he was excising)?

Machiavelli, Milton and Alexander Hamilton experienced nothing of mass society, Lincoln only its dawn. As a Founding Father – of journalism – Hamilton was prophetic about editorial techniques, and how they might shape a national imagination. Mass societies would have abstract qualities – hard to grasp, easy to distort. But not even he foresaw their development under bureaucracy's impact. Abusive labels aside, 'bureaucracy' is Weber's term for extensive rationalistic organisation: corporations, public or private, learning to measure human needs and supply them through complex systems calculated to suppress accident. The years when its most potent form took over European-derived societies were called in Chapter 9 the Age of Normality, after its basic statistical tools.

As a comparison, the old Chinese mandarinate had its bureaucratic qualities, but over centuries the condition of its vast clientele did not alter, or its own minimal presence expand. In the Atlantic case, over a few generations, life changed as never before, and a new domain of methodical structures established itself. Now, just the government's part (the pure bureaucracy, shall we say?) handles some 40 per cent of a total wealth eclipsing Golconda. Ghosts of Marx and Smith dispute which benefits flow from the private manifestations, which from the public. What matters for the interplay of people, rulers and media – Milton's investigation – is that they irresistibly are benefits, including a life-span once considered implausible.

Hamilton's colleague John Adams told his wife that 'light and glory' should turn up some time after 1776. Abigail, sustaining farm and family amid smallpox, monetary chaos and near-famine, correctly judged that posterity would be 'scarcely . . . able to conceive the hardships and sufferings of their ancestors'. Not much machinery of palliation existed in Machiavelli's world or hers. Now it's installed, we rebel against its human components – because they constrict as well as sustain us. But we do not rebel systematically, if only because 'they' now are also 'us'. Brewers and meat inspectors use fund managers; air-traffic controllers seek building consents; an engineer illuminates the hospital where a psychiatric social worker assesses her child for autism.

In exchange for indirect power over the vast apparatus, our politicians become responsible for its workings. No rational harlot – no Florentine prince – would accept this asymmetric prerogative. One of its lesser effects is hugely to centralise guilt, so that the government, like Donne's thief at bar, is questioned 'by all the men that have been robb'd this year'. Still, it provides some administrative legitimacy, and allows politicians some credit should net improvements appear. Thus persuasion – the end-product of partisanship – may convert to executive outcomes, and votes. However, extreme crisis apart, the 'people' – the collective entity – are not involved. Members of our supposed ruling class participate individually, on the occasions when as cogs (maybe eminent ones) they perform a particular task. To update Lincoln, we routinely have government *of* and *for* the people – government *by* the people, perhaps, if push comes at last to shove. The inconsistency between our professions of democracy and the realities of social organisation has not precluded material success. By degrees, though, it is making politicians into vassals of tabloid media.

Reliability is the special additive rational bureaucracy offers, whether the base product is census data, pharmaceuticals, entertainment or fast food. But it has a toxic side-effect: secrecy so addictive, thought Weber, that its 'fanatical' adepts might ruin civilisation. The witness Keynes illuminated this, saying, on inside experience, that every organisational high-command holds that serious events never occur. The view isn't purely false – events once serious and incessant for Abigail Adams are not so now. But it exaggerates. The real difference is that they have become rare enough to be deemed unrepresentative, or accidental, making it possible – dutiful – to conceal them.

Thus events are best kept secret, in case they happen – or secret in principle, and disclosed once they haven't happened. Any experience of press-releases (government or corporate) reveals this numbing doctrine. In purest form, a head of MI5 once said the Official Secrets Act meant that everything not officially public must be secret. Occasionally during the last century the world maybe seemed from Whitehall so news-free that bureaucratic nirvana – utter abolition of events – might be possible under the Act. It wasn't, and – as hiding things from inspection is apt terminally to obscure them – Britain's fine machinery has become not just secret but incomprehensible.

Among the early Atlantic republicans secrecy could not be so potent a contaminant. Tactical deception fascinated Machiavelli personally, but outrageous fortune often ruined execution. Statistics not collected could not be fiddled. And between the decline of alchemy and the rise of high technology, expertise conferred quite modest leverage and created rather few potential secrets. The Founding Americans tended to be polymaths – but by knowing more things than their constituents, not things separate in order. Giving a famous dinner to Nobel Prize winners in 1962, John F. Kennedy said the White House had contained no such concentration of intellect since 'Thomas Jefferson dined alone'. Jefferson – lawyer, scientist, architect, linguist, diplomat and statesman – commanded personally most of the expertise a ruler of his day might need. Today, even Jefferson would need bureaucratic alliances for daily counsel and intellectual logistics.

Few reporters of corporate antics will think Keynes or Weber unjust. Still, secrecy is not simply evil. It may be innocent – as privacy or confidentiality – handy, occasionally indispensable. Expertise now does create executive necessities difficult (or risky) to explain. The real problem is secrecy's dynamism. It circumvents audit, aborts the interbreeding of discovery, immunises ignorance. Errors then demand new secrecy for concealment – darkness by chain-reaction, in which each adept becomes, as Daniel Ellsberg puts it, 'something like a moron . . . incapable of learning'.

This is an especially modern threat, because the powers our organisations deploy originated in *destruction* of secrecy – in the rules of open discourse which grew up beside Atlantic politics, and opened the scientific revelation. That growth was hard: Newton's distaste for scrutiny puts him nearer the common soul than Halley, who made him bear it (the stern astronomer of course was Newton's true friend, and ours). The rules still chafe enough that an urge to operate them with scrutiny somehow disabled remains strong among us. Of the mountainous evidence for this, Daniel Patrick Moynihan's may be most poignant. In *Secrecy*, Senator Moynihan analyses the Western Cold War débâcles caused by untested clandestine fantasy, and concludes that this self-made damage may outrank all the USSR's earnest malice.

Like any addiction, secrecy targets real desires – but stimulates what it offers to satisfy, creating shame. In Britain now its role is often denied except when ex-mandarins lecture on its evils. And a natural defence of

435

the inadmissible is fanaticism – effort, says one philosopher, which intensifies as its aim becomes less visible. Serving mandarins, however, need not make themselves absurd – because elected people are available. To any democrat the 'nation' is a stirring concept. But it is an abstract one, whereas officials are present fact, producing the fodder which government needs for its existence. People who can feel a daily need *and* treat sceptically those supplying it are rare, and so political literature shows that most ministers tell the public the information officials provide to them – typically, fragments of truth, arranged with no general design of truth.

Consequently, and contrary to an erroneous and corrosive belief, today's politicians dissemble very little. Narrow grasp of fact confines them to insistent recitation – the performance we usually see, and a public nuisance by the unsentimental ethic of Lincoln or Machiavelli. Politics for them was speaking what truth the day would bear, so as to permit more later – a flexible purpose, at times requiring untruth. Therefore Machiavelli's theory makes lying a core-competence, while his *practical* discussion concerns its very sparing employment. Because excess will destroy trust – individual ambition may wish to be fooled, but not a people – management of untruth is a delicate personal task.

Over this temperate duty today's practice lays promiscuous obedience to the bureaucratic script – not shrewd personal dissembling but gross concoctions, serving the delusion Keynes sardonically observed, and now earning rising contempt from smarter audiences. Exercise without responsibility of powers still prone to accident – for what narrows error's frequency may widen its impact – is the rigid theme, and denials often interlock. In the 'mad cow' case, not only was there deception over the science of BSE, but Tony Blair's ministers defended deceptive claims that the deception was innocent – fanatically, for the offence was off their watch, and invisible to them. Predictably, honest official science is now distrusted.

Dissembling comes in grades (some are mostly truth, and projects like ending slavery involve a variety). Machiavelli tells us that if falsehood – near or pure – becomes essential, it works only for a credible ruler. And credibility cannot exist when rulers are routinely reckoned false – when 'Why is this lying bastard lying to me?' (Jeremy Paxman of the BBC) is the sub-text of all political interviews. Yet it's a curious proposition. Though casual lying is measurably widespread, the same is not true of systematic major fabrication by individuals on their own account. It seems that most of us want our personal narratives to display consistency of some sort. There are exceptions, to be sure. But why should the public life of politics attract dispositions happiest living amid a jumble of contradictions? Politics is about coherent stories for specific audiences – indeed their absence causes the crisis we observe. Really, the bastards are rarely lying. Rather, it is the machine.

Lord John Russell (we noted earlier) ran a small Victorian prototype of the modern state, thus any misleading concoctions he produced involved the personal quality of a lie. His descendants, ministers nominally commanding the mature juggernaut, retail artefacts generated impersonally – a different moral case. Most of these begin as scattered essays in sectional exculpation (or calumny), gaining the monstrous aspect of lies by self-assembly from parts individually harmless. Mystery may attach to this process, but not to its effect on those presenting the results: politicians as ministers attract more distrust.

And they may serve nobly without altering this, because in 'a good government and in a bad' – Milton observes – 'errors . . . are equally almost incident'. (Indeed, if good means active government, the incidence must be more.) This need not be deadly unless regulation confines 'the liberty of printing' (information) to 'the power of a few' – but that is government's temptation, says Milton. Error then causes confusion no sophistry can dispel.

In the contemporary state Senator Moynihan (social scientist by trade, not poet) found regulation by secrecy capable of wildfire growth. In a single year when US classification authorities contracted sixfold (through Cold War decline) the output of classified documents rose 62 per cent. Moynihan computed that if all America's newspapers used all their pages to print the secret matter created daily by government, nothing else could appear. Britain, naturally more secretive, may well be more absurd. (Complaints of leakage resound in every capital, but then overloaded vessels will be incontinent.)

In specialist histories modern secrecy appears as bred by accident out of national security. Writers like Moynihan ascribe something to

mediocrity, little to malevolence. And if we trust Milton, an almost natural fallacy about administrative action is enough to wreak havoc in
powerful systems. To say that secrecy makes morons is to say it stops
people and groups trafficking ideas with those who don't hold certain
occult currencies – though the unsecret world, as Ellsberg points out,
contains most true experience. Secrecy's outcome, for Moynihan, is
uncomprehending spaces in and between organisations. It seems fair to
guess that these gaps are where things most like lies accumulate – not so
much dishonest by design as designed without honest knowledge of their
parts, without anything like 'joined-up government'.

Secrecy and centralisation – potentiating each other – stop the present
state explaining itself credibly. And this, not personal mendacity, is what
undermines politicians as a professional group. (Harm must occur to a
degree by sometimes telling a free people less than the truth – more,
surely, by insulting their intelligence in the regular way of business.
Certainly Franklin Roosevelt did the first when leading America towards
war, but in relative terms the second offence was then easier to avoid: he
retained sufficient trust.) Thus a crisis of rule can exist without a decay
in popular intellect – which the evidence denies. Nor need we say our
administrators are especially malevolent: only that organisation without
responsibility is a prerogative few spontaneously surrender.

Politicians thus suffer an affliction with deep causes, hard to cure.
And Newscorp has a quack remedy no one else bottles so convincingly.
Tabloid preparations – works of Murdoch genius – are supposed to win
over voters in decisive mass, with alienation and apathy dissipated. The
sale pitch inclines to be minatory: 2003 opened with a statement that it
would be Tony Blair's 'biggest mistake' to ignore the *Sun*'s European
instructions. Mythology about Euro-schemes for banning items like
French mustard, motor scooters, large pizzas, brandy butter, milk bottles,
British toilet pans and fried breakfasts – while enforcing straight bananas
(also cucumbers, rhubarb), water meters, Latin fish-and-chip labels,
school Euro-history and Mother Christmas suits – abound in the *Sun*.
Real accounts of the currency issue don't. Nonetheless its outcome,
stated David Yelland (then editor), 'our readers will decide'.

Blair advisers, notably Alastair Campbell and Philip Gould, accept the
pitch. In a government's media agenda they think the tabloid section is

decisive, and centrally the Murdoch tabloids. That belief motivated their boss's journey to the Barrier Reef resort where News Corporation held its annual intellectual exercises in 1995, and hard work went into presenting New Labour as something ex-exponents of Thatcherism might endorse without lightning striking them.

To be sure Labour worked hard on all media relations, but by any input–output measure – effort and repentance – Newscorp was the Prodigal case. In the 1997 general-election campaign the *Sun* was first out of the trench, and in victory the government bonded closely with the Murdoch papers rather than with the *Guardian* and *Independent*, though they were carrying scars from lengthy conflict with the departed Tories. New Labour media experts often assert there is a tabloid discourse more significant than anything in broadsheets or current-affairs television, one reflecting the 'gut interests' of 'real people'. This usually means misreporting crime and race issues, and spurious concerns that reformist and social-democratic party (or genuine conservatives) cannot exploit – and which some tabloids are moving away from. Massive circulation isn't always critical to political communication with a mass of individual people. In the 1997 campaign Labour revelled in tabloid support, but no serious impact resulted from the sex scandals their new friends aimed at the Tory enemy. But real impact was made by financial-corruption stories, which chiefly originated in the *Guardian*.

The sales-trend of Murdoch's tabloids may show Newscorp profitably managing a declining product, but they do not suggest magic communion with the *zeitgeist*. And measurements of influence are even less inspiring: about 14 per cent of British adults think that papers like the *Sun* are trustworthy. This is within a point or two of politicians themselves, and election studies provide little or no evidence that tabloids can change votes. (People deciding major issues can't be simplified into '*Sun* readers' or '*Financial Times* readers'.) Murdoch's product may be thought of as the trust politicians have lost since (roughly) Baldwin's time. His business is selling it back to them – successfully in spite of high prices and lack of proof that the recycled produce is efficacious. The sale causes further erosion of political authority (via spreading cynicism) and further advances in monopoly – which may terminate the democratic project.

Why do they pay? It's said that the poor get bad bargains, and in a dark corner of economic theory lurks Giffen's Paradox, offering a kind of analogy. This is where sales of a commodity rise when the cost increases. The commodity may be an indispensable food, which can support a (perhaps unhealthy) life on its own. While the economic situation is happy, a proportion of higher-quality non-essentials are bought. But, if prices rise, no high-quality product is affordable. So more of the essential is bought to fill the gap. No case has been observed in economics (though it perhaps occurs in ruinous famines). A political analogue is visible when the nation's least trusted seek the aid of those barely more trusted than themselves. The politician must have something trust-like, however low the quality. Why is trust so scarce and costly – forcing politicians to buy Murdoch's over-priced Giffen Goods? Attempts are being made to increase the supply. But this process is slow and complicated.

Machiavelli did not invent consultation in trust – he analysed them, with indispensable clarity. It made him unpopular both for thinking our honesty defective and for investigating ways to use it while accepting the flaws. Better than perhaps any other writer he deals with the physics of trust. Really accurate human judgment is 'by the hand', but very few people can be intimate enough with a leader to employ it. Most must judge 'by the eye'. So a leader's moral failures, if not gross, may be confined to close friends able to forgive them. Those who judge by sight will continue their trust. But nothing more remote existed in Machiavelli's time. No more than Lincoln did he think of political communities and their leaders as media constructs based loosely if at all on real demeanour. We talk easily now about people – voters, consumers – as existing 'out there' in abstract spaces we don't define.

Machiavelli's assumption is that some corruption may escape close judgment by the eye. Writers of the mass age, like Orwell or Kipling, fear that almost anything may be concealed behind the media image. And certainly it was possible in the last century for sane people to believe that Stalin and Mao were amiable, kindly creatures. Lies of this kind they imagine being imposed on a featureless mass of humans – perhaps David Riesman's 'lonely crowd' – something quite unlike the democratic Lazarsfeld crowd, which on examination turns into a dense structure of sub-groups linking people in complex patterns. They fear the decay of the second into the first, and it is not hard to find evidence which might point that way – electoral non-participation, for example.

Decay, however, is not all the present story. Strenuous efforts – some due directly to government itself, and others to various mixes of popular and legislative action – are being made to illuminate our often mysterious society, to open structures which have been secretive, centralised, unaccountable or all those things. Some are highly successful, some disastrous, many ambiguous.

Most industrial societies now contain politicians, administrators, corporate executives and professional practitioners who have realised (or realise sometimes) that much authority (or its shadow) must be surrendered to regain something of reality. That is quite specifically the motivation behind the British government's devolution of power to Scotland, Wales and Northern Ireland and its decision to make the Bank of England independent (again). Nearly everybody can think of examples they hate – and of examples they admire. In Britain medical institutions are becoming dramatically more open; financial institutions, it might be argued, have furthest to go. Privatisation is part of this. The left suspects, probably with good reason, that much of this is mercenary, but would be foolish not to see that it is only saleable politically because other attractions are involved.

Ways are being found to understand the dimensions of our society which are beyond the reach of hand or eye, though progress is hampered by misapprehension and confusion. A sophisticated writer celebrating the American Revolution in 2002 showed that the intimate past still has a ghostly existence among us by asking whether today's politicians would have the resolve of Washington and his colleagues – who did not feel the need to consult ritually abused focus groups before taking action. But they (like the Florentines) had direct knowledge of their intimate communities, and certainly of specialised groups within them. The use of opinion polls and survey data of various kinds – yes, even focus groups – are steps towards understanding what goes on 'out there'.

Naturally this is a picture full of complex movements. In America the decay of national voting has gone further than in Britain and much further than in Europe generally. (It cannot formally happen in Australia, where poll attendance is legally enforced, perhaps masking apathy.) But many processes of civil participation are stronger in America, notably local responsibility and jury trial. Whitehall's attempt to limit jury rights to ease the task of incompetent police and prosecutors would meet stern resistance in the USA. Everywhere consultation often turns out to be 'consultation' and crucial promises – such as Britain's Freedom of Information Act – are stalled, sidelined or emasculated.

The development of structured, interlinked communities is obviously possible within a mass society. Much of this structure already exists, even if tremendously increased complexity has made some of it hard to understand. It obviously isn't possible for everyone to participate equally throughout a very large society. But if there are decent levels of participation within devolved groups which interact with each other, there will not be very many degrees of separation between people, and in those circumstances trust indeed will be manufactured in enhanced quantities. While it will not be maintained by accident, it is not more or less implausible than the lonely crowd.

Repair of the political process therefore isn't impossible. But the decisive issues are interlocking ones of news-media regulation and administrative disclosure, and they have yet to be addressed seriously. Genuinely competitive media operating in a world with official secrecy largely dismantled – a strengthened set of 'virtuous circles' – would eliminate any need for politicians to have mercenary help in communicating with their constituents.

But there would be discomfort, as in Halley's regime for Newton. The politico-bureaucratic nexus which dominates the practical constitution in every present-day industrial democracy would be shattered, and ministers would find themselves using their own words (truthfully or otherwise) in response to demands for information. And Machiavelli's last service is to show that life would be strenuous for the media as well as for bureaucrats.

Secrecy, even in the minimal quantity of his times, Machiavelli considered deadly. Rule, being based on perception and reputation, is undermined by 'detestable calumnies' – hence his enthusiasm for suppressing them quoted at the head of this chapter. But not with an Official Secrets Act. *The Discourses*, observing that calumny is 'practised more where accusations are used less', says society must ensure 'that it is

442

possible to accuse every citizen without any fear and without any suspicion'. Political health depends on the whistleblower and investigator. *The
Discourses* doesn't argue for people's courts or privileged denunciation,
rather for a public process using legally admissible evidence. This is 'justified defamation' in modern terms. Clearly Machiavelli would back it up
with a swingeing Freedom of Information Act.

'Calumnies' then equate to libel or slander in modern terms – defam-
ations which cannot be proved. And – in his drastic way – Machiavelli
demands even-handed peril. As there will be no anonymity or immunity,
but retribution, for those who are successfully accused, there must be
tough consequences for accusers who cannot prove their case. A
MacKenzie theory of libel is far from his mind. The Roman practice of
tossing calumniators off the Tarpeian Rock would be worth reviving, he
considers.

What this is saying is that disclosure lies at the centre of all political
communication, and should tell us that any useful reform of media legislation has to relate increasingly powerful Freedom of Information
legislation to questions of libel and privacy, and relate both of them to
the issues of media ownership, competition, control and organisation.

There is a very powerful argument, with strong historical evidence
behind it, which says that the most successful media systems up to now
have contained a principle of nationality. Roughly speaking this means
that effective ownership of media businesses should be in the hands of
citizens of the countries in which they operate. The view is taken very
strongly by the United States, and less comprehensively elsewhere. A
good deal of our story has concerned Rupert Murdoch's unrelenting
campaign to erode all such inhibitions – one of his specific targets being
the British legislation confining commercial television ownership to
British companies. His arguments are usually characterised by being
selected purely for reasons of tactical opportunism, and are thus incoherent. The point here is that virtually nobody seriously committed to the
future of the British media considers them convincing – even as a poor
conclusion reached by interesting means.

Before devising and publishing its new Media Bill in 2002, the British
government asked for submissions of evidence from interested organisations and individuals. Twenty-four documents were received, many of

which rejected in some detail the idea that the British-ownership rule should be relaxed. Others dismissed it quite briefly, influenced by the fact that the relevant Minister, Tessa Jowell, both explicitly and by way of extensive briefing off the record over several months, had indicated that the government was not interested in the idea. Two submissions argued vehemently for the restriction to be completely abolished: News International (the UK division of Newscorp) and Arthur Ardersen, then Newscorp's auditors but of course no longer able to continue the discussion.

The Bill then emerged with a clause repealing the British-ownership requirement. The supporting documents and briefings from Downing Street did not engage in any substance with the arguments made in the 'consultation' documents, most of which were wholly ignored, along with the majority of media-reform issues discussed in recent years. Apart from reversing Ms Jowell's earlier statements about the ownership clause, most of the Bill was concerned with attempts to revive the prospects for terrestrial digital television – shattered by taking the advice a few years earlier of Rupert Murdoch and the (then) ITV companies. Professor Patrick Barwise of the London Business School, author of the standard book on television and its audience, said that the 'consultation' was entirely spurious. 'They might as well have just said at the start: "We are going to do what News International want", and saved everybody a good deal of time.' This amounted to a blunt statement that modest shoots of reform are just that, and that the old diseased vegetation – bureaucratic orthodoxy plus tabloid appeasement – won't easily be cleared away.

The problem of rule which the Murdochs have exploited is entirely available for others to follow. A favourite Downing Street line just now is to say that it would be wrong to write media laws to deal with just one man, Murdoch. After all, he will soon be gone like all mortals. This is cover for having written a media bill just for him, which is remarkable double-think. But the more important point is that Murdoch's operation may well be, after a little refinement, the general model of media empires which live in corporatist bliss with slowly degrading national governments.

14

RUPERT'S ESTABLISHMENT, 1910–2003

A journal that gave utterance to nothing but untruths would loose [sic] its influence with its character; but there are none so ignorant as not to see the necessity of occasionally issuing truths. It is only in cases in which the editor has a direct interest in the contrary, in which he has not had the leisure or the means of ascertaining the facts, or in which he is himself misled by the passions, cupidity and interests of others, that untruths find a place in his columns. Still, these instances may, perhaps, include a majority of the cases.

JAMES FENIMORE COOPER, *The American Democrat*

antimetabolite

noun:

A substance that closely resembles an essential metabolite and therefore interferes with physiological reactions involving it.

The American Heritage Dictionary of the English Language

The Murdoch enterprise has prospered through some nine decades from a peculiar ability to penetrate democracy's imperfect immune system. Its relationship with totalitarianism has been shorter, and also easier. There being no immune system under such governments, Newscorp bonds simply to communist China.

Democratic elites honour Newscorp uneasily. When an editor of the

445

Sun – one who suggested that a gay mafia ran the British Cabinet – hands over to an editor of the *News of the World* – one who excited the country's most recent vigilante outbreak – ministers attend the corporate ritual, along with such eminent bureaucrats as the chief of national security. But fear moves them as fully as admiration.

The chiefs of Beijing are warmer. They praise the 'objectivity' of Murdoch's journalism, calling him an 'intellectual'. Jiang Zemin (when President) stood in once as supreme movie critic, to assure Chinese audiences they would find in *Titanic* a noble tale of proletarian heroes versus 'capitalist lapdogs and stooges'. And these people – though they fear many things – don't fear Murdoch. Rather they grant Newscorp unique trading concessions. What they do fear is disruption of their grand historical project – erasing the criminal record of their Party. Among modern terrors, only the Nazi and Soviet examples resemble it in scale. The difference is that its crimes are officially secret.

Though ebullient tyrants and frail democracies abound, authoritarian systems, for various reasons, have found present times increasingly fatal. The Nazi and Soviet organisms are defunct; in the nations they infested, free memory is prophylactic. But not so in China, where power brutally seized remains in the Party's grip, along with a resolve to legitimise it – means to that end being, necessarily, amnesia. Beijing intends nothing less than to prove (though the words are Murdoch's) that 'authoritarian countries can work'. This, if it can after all be shown – and on such a scale – will be a profound discovery.

Given Murdoch's personal ductility, we may expect him to be meek and gentle with these business partners and remain a self-advertised libertarian. However, a media organisation, even so protean a one as Newscorp, must somewhat disguise the contortions involved. Partly it's been done by misrepresenting China – using such standard means as suggestio falsi and suppressio veri.

Subtler processes are ideological – and apply to the Archipelago generally. A Murdoch ideology may seem implausible, but it exists, as just the thing Marx and Engels initially discussed: a means to sculpt reality, to pull wool over half-shut eyes. And anyway an organisation in plural democracy – still Newscorp's chief habitat – needs some defining beliefs: the Murdoch ideology, verbally populist, centres on assaulting something called the establishment. Newscorp befriends the populace everywhere against the elitist, snobbish masters of the world. They, consequently, envy Murdoch's bond with the workers whose values and interests his tabloids celebrate.

That this rhetoric achieves noticeable (if tinny) resonance is due to present unease – sometimes guilt – about democratic command and elite responsibility. Our erotically intrepid society treats the facts of rule and class like the Victorians who supposedly dressed up their piano-legs. But social passions, like sex, are irrepressible. Though Britain may seem to disguise it least, exploitation of privilege in Australia and America is quite as energetic – justifying working-class resentments which, tickled with a little philistinism, make easy game for populist flattery. (That Alexander Hamilton's *New York Post* should be devoted to this is ironic. As we have seen, he thought republics should especially mistrust anyone paying 'obsequious court' to the people.)

The ideology is financially libertarian, militantly so whenever a visionary is restrained from enriching the people. It was very soon after Enron's colossal bankruptcy that Murdoch's veteran economic counsellor Irwin Stelzer appeared for the defence in the *Weekly Standard*, Newscorp's journal of intellects. Enron may have sinned – here Stelzer briefly resembled a fastidious Maoist chiding over-zealous Red Guards – but its 'anti-Establishment entrepreneurs' made war on great boardrooms, terrified Wall Street, galvanised markets, re-endowed consumers. Like Michael Milken in the 1980s, it had made economic revolution. (Milken's insurrection of course produced the 'junk equity' to float Fox.) For Milken fans his fraud sentence almost outdoes the martyrdom of Bartholomew, and Stelzer was pleading against any similar flaying. That plea may fail, Enron's lust actually to mulct consumers having been exposed. But his rhetoric – Enron the populist crusade – remains imposing.

This outfit was advised by McKinsey, grandest of consultancies. Its auditors were Arthur Andersen – ruined now by criminal guilt, but pre-eminent when hired. The rococo tax-shelters at Enron's heart were erected by Wall Street's finest (notably J. P. Morgan Chase and Citicorp), in exchange for monumental fees. Enron the war against big business is as grotesque as the socialist–realist content of *Titanic*. But in a willing subject all sense of the grotesque is blocked by invocation of the 'establishment', enabling the revolutionary disguise of Newscorp and its sympathisers to be sustained. Kipling tells us that words are drugs, and such a potion's origins deserve inquiry. The idea of the establishment is in fact a derivative of McCarthyism – one its inventor, Henry Fairlie, took off the intellectual market because of vile side-effects.

McCarthyism itself was a product of 1950s secretiveness and Stalin's espionage against the West. The subversion was hardly remarkable, but the efficacy of US counter-intelligence certainly was: the 'Venona' decrypts provided both proof of the danger and the means to contain it. Zeal for security – excessive, in hindsight – entirely hid these victories from the public, and also from President Truman.

The sufficiently sobering truth being secret, valid distrust of the USSR became morbid obsession and Senator McCarthy found that, where official silence inhibited accusation and disproof, smears ('calumnies' in Machiavelli) would luxuriate. When the spies Burgess and Maclean escaped to Moscow, pandemic treachery developed a British potential tapped by Fairlie's *Spectator* column in September 1955. The traitors, he suggested, belonged to a connection pervading all society's institutions – even ostensible competitors – which he named the 'establishment'. It was not communist. But it protected from the popular mass its privileged practices and members – communism, communists and other unspecified mischiefs included. Today, the spies' getaway is known, straightforwardly, as Kim Philby's work. Then, notions of a numinous, eminent conspiracy explosively outgrew the *Spectator* audience, and have since outlived the USSR. The naming of its members (bishops, bankers, union leaders and so on) makes a gossipy parlour-game along with speculating on the network's crimes – the railroading of Milken by the US chapter, causing the Second World War (via Appeasement, prior to the unmasking), blocking Princess Margaret's marriage, inventing AIDS (and more, more).

But there's always a dark potential to this game. Its original players, indeed, urged a magnitude of snooping as extensive as that carried out by the supposed establishment, and called for open season to be declared on individuals they named for suspicious connection to communists. 'Treason and sedition' made 'niceties of protocol' obsolete, declared the ultra-Tory MP Harold Soref – and was applauded by the *Daily Telegraph*, where Malcolm Muggeridge was assistant editor for inquisitions.

For various reasons, they failed to create a proof-strength British McCarthyism, and one was that an idea launched in an intellectual weekly may be torpedoed there. Establishment-hunters, wrote the historian Hugh Trevor-Roper – a Tory, and an MI5 veteran – implied that to defend a suspected communist was to become a communist conspirator. The *Spectator*, surely, wouldn't say that 'citizens have personal rights [but] suspected communists have not'? He went on to expose the persistent nature of this brand of thought – its hybrid intellectual tissue. Muggeridge's followers, said Trevor-Roper, were attacking under 'the name of an abstraction' – of the vaguest sort – things far from abstract: 'human rights' expressed as 'personal loyalties' to particular people.

This abstractness many find seductive. Out of a few ecclesiastical overtones Fairlie had conjured a thrilling, vacuous term, in which portent overwhelms content. Targets of infinite opportunity (persons or policies) may therefore be framed in it, and implications attached to individuals with immense economy of evidence. Where the usage is accepted, the effect of accusation may be had without law's long-grown requirement to be concrete and consistent.

Abstraction is not inescapably vague, but it is labile in ways impossible for the concrete – which a standard dictionary will define as 'relating to an actual, specific thing or instance' (as in 'the concrete evidence needed to convict'). For that reason analysis mixes them circumspectly. Fairlie was more phrasemaker than analyst. But he was also a Tory of the type intuitively hostile to witch-hunts and he withdrew his invention from the McCarthy cause. Rather than abusing influence, the establishment restrained it.

> One must thank whichever gods control Britain's destiny that it is there . . . Men of power need to be checked by a collective opinion which is stable and which they cannot override: public opinion needs its counter; new opinion must be tested. These the Establishment provides: the check, the counter and the test.

But that possibly was its last favourable reference. Though the term occurs regularly in discussion of institutions, it attracts scorn, even loathing. Establishments are what other people belong to.

In no culture is the usage more insistent than Newscorp's. Irwin Stelzer, still an admirer, sees conflict with the establishment as defining Rupert the Rebel. John Menadue, long disillusioned, recalls being initially attracted by Murdoch and Rivett 'thumbing their noses' at the Adelaide establishment, and supposed the Profumo exploitation and its successors to be similarly healthful irreverence. A frequent assumption is that the tabloid style – Murdoch's speciality – is intrinsically rebellious, and thus a counter-establishment force. The columnist William Safire, when expressing unease about Murdoch's reconstituted patriotism, still assumed that the new-minted fellow American would 'challenge the powerful'. An editorial writer in the *Wall Street Journal*, saddened by recent toadying to China in the *Post*, expressed surprise. Surely anti-establishment Murdoch sheets didn't do such things? Many journalists know the midnight session when troubled Murdoch rankers plead that the boss – 'whatever you say' – does pitilessly stick it to the establishment. For Newscorp Anzacs, England is the establishment's imperial fortress, ripe for plunder. Andrew Neil, as we saw in Chapter 12, observed the establishment's coils everywhere (Newscorp almost uniquely keeping a foot somehow on the monstrous throat).

This widespread usage might plausibly be linked to the opacity of social and political mechanisms which the previous chapter analysed. But it is better included in a larger proposition: that even in fantasies like Stelzer's the term refers – if with superb imprecision – to things with real existence, that is, the 'ruling classes', or the 'governing classes'. Those were once labels people wore cheerfully to display status and power. 'Establishment', then, somewhat resembles a euphemism for older, blunter language.

If society's rulers are indeed the people as a whole, then the 'ruling class' must always be a committee, or perhaps a network of sub-committees, deputed for the sake of praxis to choose courses and exercise powers. Life doubtless departs from that ideal, but the presence all the same of some sort of ruling class, as Trevor-Roper said to Fairlie, is 'hardly a novel discovery'; he called it 'a necessary condition of social existence', which is true whatever unease its real name evokes, however corrupt the praxis. Few theorists find anarchism a genuine option.

Unease isn't unreasonable. Rhetoric connecting 'rule' to exploitative barbarism – if partisan – isn't baseless. Also, rule requires discrimination; which in whatever cause seems 'no more just and rational to those discriminated against, than racial discrimination,' as Randall Jarrell said of cultural choice. And unease is too slight a word if the question is whether those practising rule are genuine agents of a ruling people, or kleptocratic principals like the Soviet nomenklatura – extremes with ambiguous states between. Not even qualification is simple: 500 years after the close of the Middle Ages the meritocratic West still admits power got by birth. These are not even all the reasons people might like to dispense with the ruling class, or anyway not pronounce its name, as primitive folk hope to neutralise an evil spirit. But, short of a failed state, the best reality is that our ruling class, or establishment, should not be 'so held together by conscious or institutional solidarity that it escapes competition and criticism, as in some countries it does' (Trevor-Roper's words).

This may be compressed into saying that in all societies the 'ruling class' has one meaning at least, and a democracy is a society where it has two: the people and their delegated executive, distinct in somewhat the way of shareholders and directors. In accurate discourse 'ruling class' should take the second meaning until stated otherwise. 'Establishment' only obscures issues of competition and criticism. Obviously a ruling class exercises power. But it may be forgotten – the quotation from Fairlie shows him remembering it – that a parallel function is restraint of power, particularly that of its own members. In a modern state it has many components, most of which are expected to invigilate each other specifically while collaborating generally.

This idea of a ruling class is not the same thing as an upper class – the picture in crude Marxism – or a propertied class or, come to that, a proletariat attempting dictatorship. Personnel will overlap if such categories exist, but, when motives overlap, corruption begins. Effective rule involves acceptance of standards which in a modern state are sure to be complex, fast-changing and hard to apply consistently. (Complexity is not least due to the present state's painful, contradictory struggle with its addiction to centralism, discussed in Chapter 13 above.) In an ideal politics there might be no reason for members of the ruling elite to accumulate privilege, rewards or status, only powers and burdens. But that would require us to live for ever, as R. G. Collingwood showed (in

451

The Three Laws of Politics, work incomplete at his own death). Under mortality, privilege and status must be allowed for, their price being rigorous transparency.

But ruling-class privilege without a ruling-class price (yes, Kipling's 'power without responsibility') is seductive. And here the establishment ideology may be applied, by insisting that real power doesn't reside in anyone visible, like yourself, but in an occult conspiracy from which you are excluded with the herd. Penetrating investigation enables you intermittently to expose and pillory particular conspirators. In Murdoch's case they have often turned out to be sub-committee members tasked with upholding television's political independence, restraining monopoly or sustaining tedious financial shibboleths. But the power-centre remains obscure – even from Newscorp's best agents. Never, of course, has Murdoch been excluded – except in 'establishment' pantomime – from the ruling class. Nobody holding such possessions could be, however recalcitrant about consistency and obligations.

Several reasons exist for Rupert to prefer appearing as other than the hereditary ruling-class member he is. But a major one is that media bosses are entitled only to restricted membership. A general conflict of interest properly excludes them from every significant executive subcommittee – even from transactions with such bodies. News media are there to invigilate the total process of delegation and agency, thus legitimising it, thus keeping the first meaning alive. That is why the wish of the twentieth-century *Times* to be a newspaper 'for the governing class' (a second-meaning synonym) was corrupt as well as pompous. Democracy is fictional if media are *for* anyone but the primary ruling class (which includes all socio-economic layers). This is Milton's meaning, and Jefferson's: only when media are transparent can the essential qualities of the intimate republic be realised in post-industrial society, where abstract data must supplement the intimate – but may well distort it.

The radical anti-establishment come-on is necessary camouflage for a business specialising in privatised government propaganda. But it also stimulates the peculiar journalistic uselessness which makes Newscorp supreme within the field. (Other proprietors, as we've said, may be tempted, but are outclassed.) If you can believe, on the strength of some tosh about establishments, that Murdoch isn't a ruling-class comprador, but rather a rebellious outsider – this being an element in your recruitment and indoctrination – you might believe anything. Something of this was seen with *Death on the Rock*, but the classical example is the *Sunday Times*, AIDS and the establishment.

Acquired Immune Deficiency Syndrome is one of humanity's deepest challenges. Its cause, Human Immunodeficiency Virus (HIV), is that rare, unnerving phenomenon, a retrovirus. Life is a pattern which must pass accurately from existing to new generations and it succeeds because DNA, holding the code, isn't involved in transmission to new cells: RNA carries the message. The Central Dogma of reproduction (as life-science calls it) requires this process to be one-way, so that errors only occur 'downstream'. Retroviruses defy the dogma. Like other viruses they consist of RNA junk, and have no DNA. But HIV, somehow using the enzyme 'reverse transcriptase', copies itself, sloppily, into the DNA of its host's cells. It may remain long inactive. But when cells divide (to create growth) billions of alien offspring appear. The host's immune system crashes – having evolved to suppress transmission errors and external attack, not a corrupted original pattern. Without antiretroviral drugs, the host must die of opportunistic infections.

Since its recognition in 1981 AIDS has acquire a densely emotional history. Initially terror was widespread, then there was relief when HIV's role was identified in 1984 and Margaret M. Heckler, the US Secretary of Health and Human Services, estimated two years for delivery of a vaccine. Given medicine's war-record against plagues it didn't then seem hubristic. Since then, bitter lessons have been taught, amid failure, despair and scandal. Now, with usable drugs, some victories for containment and some ideas about vaccines, we might be near the end of the beginning.

A sad strand in this history is that a fine scientist named Peter Duesberg asserted that the HIV/AIDS model of an efficient retrovirus was false. He was far from alone. Many people resisted the model, for it made sexual orientation irrelevant, and a new sexual civility indispensable. (Some fundamentalists lickerishly fancied AIDS to be retribution for sodomy.) But he was almost alone among capable scientists.

Duesberg thought HIV immunologically trivial, and that various agents were causing distinct afflictions wrongly conflated as AIDS.

Sympathetic critics think he just miscalculated the dreadful retroviral leverage. His work, anyway, is the persistent core of the proposition that HIV/AIDS doesn't exist, still taking fatal effect around the world – spectacularly, in South Africa. The *Sunday Times* in the 1990s built it into a crusade to save humanity from the disastrous 'myth' of AIDS: few newspaper investigations have been as fiercely wrong-headed. Had its counsel against AIDS measures prevailed, disaster would be no adequate description.

AIDS delusions rest on pseudo-science which caricatures the real thing as a one-dimensional reductive process, where every investigator interrogates every fact individually, and scepticism zaps anything logically incomplete. This antique vision – formally captioned 'epistemological individualism' – decorates naive websites, though it has been properly laid to rest now by work like Steven Shapin's (*A Social History of Truth*, and so on). Realistically, science's major dimension is trust, with judicious scepticism a vital supplementary. Realistically, potent science may be logically insecure – the grand example being calculus, flawed as Newton and Leibniz designed it because they could not explain infinitesimals. Bishop Berkeley cleverly showed that it was all nonsense. Calculus nonetheless created the basis of modern life, and afterwards, in mid-Victorian times, it was completed logically by 'limits'. The subject was right, as Alfred North Whitehead put it; it was just that the explanations had been wrong. And 'this possibility of being right, albeit with entirely wrong explanations', often makes external criticism of science 'singularly barren and futile . . . The instinct of trained observers, and their sense of curiosity, due to the fact that they are obviously getting at something, are far safer guides . . .'

At the time the *Sunday Times* campaign took off, the collective instinct of trained AIDS observers was that the HIV model was 'getting at something' – this was ten years ago, ahead of the strongest evidence – and Duesberg's ideas were not. Research interest in them was fading; scientific publications largely ignored them; newspapers and television saw nothing to report. *Nature*, the most powerful journal in world science, considered them not worth further significant resources. And this, the *Sunday Times* asserted, was a gigantic scandal: a process of censorship, suppression – and boondoggling – only possible if the whole world of life-sciences – corporate, official and academic – had been corrupted. Neville Hodgkinson, the paper's science correspondent, undertook to end this outrage, with the zealous backing of his editor, Andrew Neil.

Their thesis was that Duesberg had been silenced because his work proved that AIDS – in the sense of a pandemic, caused by HIV, and killing millions of men, women and children – didn't exist. AIDS was sustaining a vested interest of great power, which was consuming immense revenues. But it was an illusion: as one of their headlines said, yet another case of 'THE EMPEROR'S CLOTHES'. The reality behind the AIDS illusion was just an ailment of homosexual men and heroin-users. To be sure it was mysterious, and lethal. But it was inflated by confusing it with diseases always suffered by peoples outside mainstream Western society. The causal agent was certainly transmitted in blood, but only in the practice of buggery (the sturdy vagina would exclude it) or in the sharing of needles by addicts. Those avoiding such habits were scarcely endangered. And to hide such unprofitable, unfashionable truths, immunologists (aided by many others, journalists particularly) were risking the whole fabric of normal Western life. If true, this might have been the most significant disclosure ever made by one newspaper.

To most people working on AIDS, however, it was worse than shouting 'Fire' in a crowded theatre. It was more like telling people in a bushfire to relax and make toast. At that time, with no effective medication, containment was vital. The government was responding, but everything rested on making it plain that sex, even if rigorously orthodox, may infect either partner with HIV. *Nature*'s editor, John Maddox, wrote a leader bitterly accusing the *Sunday Times* of recklessly logic-chopping scientific evidence – which was certainly incomplete, but just as certainly compelling – and of 'recruiting young and adult people' to the avoidance of safe sex. He was accused in return of censorship: the world's leading scientific journal was 'playing in a sinister game'.

At this point the *Sunday Times* came generally into dispute with other newspapers, and selectively with its own older self. It considered that most papers were betraying their readers and joining the 'sinister game' because they were trapped in soggy, conventional thought, and pre-Murdoch the *Sunday Times* had been like that too. But even then it had broken free once, to expose the thalidomide scandal – an advance manifestation of the intellectual liberation now systematically installed, and significant as a prior example of the evil done by ruthless application of scientific orthodoxy. This was a curious statement, however, because what the thalidomide investigation uncovered was evil done because application of scientific orthodoxy didn't occur at all (see Chapter 8 above).

Though not undamaged, AIDS science survived two years of frantic assault from one of the world's major newspapers. When for distinct reasons Neil left the *Sunday Times* – he authentically revealed certain misdeeds by the Thatcher government, stuck admirably to his story and terminally alienated Murdoch – zeal collapsed. The life of the contrarian hypothesis ended by increment rather than breakthrough – though elimination of HIV fragments from American donor blood had great impact, for the problem of AIDS by transfusion went with it.

Journalistic delusions as such are not rare. What made this one truly rare was its scale, its persistent, paranoid inflation into something that could only be true with the pressure of a vicious, ramified, international conspiracy. Nothing remotely fit to support such a proposition was produced then or has been since. And it was not a case of devil-may-care *Sun* or *Post* gullibility. It happened to a substantial newspaper run by people professing serious aspirations. What made it credible to them? The paranoid ingredient was their General Theory of Establishment – of IRA pollution in ITV, of protection enfolding thalidomide's developers. Here was the establishment, riding again. Headlines and text expounding the Emperor's Clothes AIDS thesis were spattered insistently with references to the establishment. The 'sinister' aspect of things was that the establishment's scientific chapter (or division) had awesome clout, having been able to suppress evidence about AIDS worldwide. It would have utter victory in sight once it could stop the *Sunday Times*. According to Neil's memoirs he spent much time 'locked in hand-to-hand combat with various parts of the Establishment', and this must have been a testing bout.

Anyone equipped with such assumptions knows a lot before starting corruption investigations. An establishment, as it rules us in secret, is by description corrupt conspiracy at the top level – so that's clear straight off. Investigators sure of conspiracies readily see one, because evidence trivial to others yields them significance. But a potent establishment can suppress evidence, so absence of evidence may itself become evidence (as in the scientific depredations above). Now reporting admittedly can't start in a mental blank. Coleridge, for instance, said all inquiry lacking an intellectual 'prerogative' was futile. But Coleridge added a proviso, relevant to conspiracy cases. When 'the prerogative of the mind is stretched into despotism, the discourse may degenerate in the grotesque or the fantastical . . .'

What reality underlay the grotesque, fantastical campaign? What should be called the scientific ruling class was culling dud ideas – that is, discriminating. This is always happening, and is always a hard call, because knowledge is incomplete, causing a kind of natural unfairness. AIDS remains a deeply emotive problem, seeming at times insoluble. But on the HIV model doubt seems sufficiently eliminated, so the rulers of science probably got that about right.

Was conspiracy even likely? Broadsheet pundits like to see events as 'cock-up, not conspiracy'; tabloid headline-writers see conspiracies proliferating ('gay mafias' and the rest). The first attitude is the sillier, being a false antithesis (and a licence for lazy journalism). Cock-up, mostly, is conspiracy's outcome, the outcome of enterprise run on a hidden and thus confusing plan. As confusion is endemic there is always a cock-up rate, which conspiracy drives up. 'Successful' conspiracies seem mostly to be crimes or counter-productive wars. They rarely conquer disease, establish peace or win gold at the Olympics.

Exploding them is an ongoing news-media function (and if it's properly performed most detonations are scarcely noticed). But a good working assumption is that conspiracy, though frequent and serious, is unordinary and uncomprehensive in a free country. This makes a-priori sense: conspiracy being mostly uncreative and incompetent, a society in which it is truly routine will get into terrible trouble under modern conditions. Soviet history demonstrates this, though it also shows that the trouble can be suppressed until large sympathetic detonations occur, with vast destructive effect.

Can conspiracies occur in science? Yes, of course, but not easily. The rules of publication and peer review are robust, crossing national or cultural borders easily (unlike, say, accounting rules). Cases of the scientific ruling class behaving with the kind of lunatic solidarity the *Sunday Times* alleged are hard to find. A scientific ruling class tends to be, in Trevor-Roper's words, 'loose . . . and fissile'. That was the case with thalidomide. The rulers, persuaded by ruthless commercial lobbyists, fell into an error. But, once it was unearthed, they did not hang together long to defend it; some expertly assisted the excavation. The risk in science's ruling class is that it lacks one of Trevor-Roper's democratic attributes: it is not 'heterogeneous', but selective and specialist. Discourse is nominally open, but few of us rate as 'peers', therefore penetrating a potentially corrupt argument is arduous and often expensive. That said, corruption and conspiracy in science has mostly occurred at corporate or political interfaces – tobacco and BSE are examples – where superior levels of the ruling class predominate.

The 'establishment' concept might usefully be dispensed with before its fiftieth birthday. It has exhibited enough of the hallucinations likely when a potentially clear term, 'ruling class', is replaced by one inherently deceptive. As we must deal with the amazing privileges our financial rulers have awarded themselves, it might be timely once more to speak frankly about the realities of social status and advantage.

Murdoch's kitsch-ideology is unusual in attributing general influence to conspiracy inside democracy. (The view has few scholarly exponents, though the economist Vilfredo Pareto was one.) But conspiracy can be considered as the form the authoritarian principle assumes in a free society – as against a society where it can operate untrammelled. This is implicit in the maxim that force and fraud are equivalent. If you believe one authoritarian manifestation can work, you will presumably think likewise of the other.

But much rests on what 'working' means. At the end of 2002, Nicholas D. Kristof of the *New York Times* investigated the appalling results of China's determination to deal with its AIDS epidemic by authoritarian means – that is, keeping it quiet – and drew a sad historical comparison.

Thirteen years ago I watched the Chinese Army turn its machine guns on pro-democracy protesters, killing hundreds and outraging the world. I couldn't imagine the Chinese government doing anything worse. But here in Henan, it looks like a slow-motion slaughter on an even more horrifying scale.

What is the story of Newscorp's connection with Chinese social and political experiments?

Two circumstances pervade it. First, it opened when Newscorp's libertarianism was triumphal. Murdoch and his followers reckoned they had fought 'shoulder to shoulder' (as one put it) to vanquish the USSR and other tyrannies. In this sense the *Victory*'s parrot fought at Trafalgar, but anyway Newscorp was feisty. Bring on the Chinese seems to have been the mood. Second is the condition just then of the Chinese nation and its government. It was the aftermath of Tiananmen, an event like Peterloo or Bloody Sunday, intensely revealing as domestic political massacre is bound to be – though, allowing for population size, Tiananmen was about three times more lethal than Peterloo.

Among individuals, the taboo against killing fails most often among those entangled with each other both emotionally and legally. Such ordinary murderers rarely harm people unconnected with them. Governments, of course, are different. They usually kill foreigners, not their own legal connections. Disorientation is natural when these norms collapse. People may prefer not to think about governments which are murderous in the domestic sphere, for their motivations are paradoxical. Inhibitions against homicide fail only when overwhelming emotions are present – or none, as in the psychopathic serial killer. But between government and citizen there should be no passion sufficient to dissolve taboos. Citizens are not lovers, the great conservative Michael Oakeshott tells us, 'and civil association is not a relationship of love'. This makes it a reliable bar to homicide. Moreover, in civil society the general attributes of the lethal psychopath bar their carrier from power. Thus a government which kills its own must be one where the psychopath's emotional blankness is well represented, and civil association absent. Convenience may restrain its actions, but little else. Consistent with this we can understand settled democracies having developed some halting concern about their own rulers' use of lethal force against foreigners. And, of course, the fact that a homicidal government has no legitimacy.

For China, the problem of legitimacy applies with special power. No one really knows which was the 'worst' of the great genocides, but the Nazi and Soviet examples at least exist historically. Russian terror between 1917 and the 1990s sought to erase memory and 'engineer the

soul'. But the engineers were up against writers remarkable even as successors to Pushkin, Dostoevsky and Tolstoy: Osip Mandelstam,
Aleksandr Solzhenitsyn, Anna Akhmatova and others still.

Akhmatova's dedication to the famous poem 'Requiem' says that
when Leningrad 'swung like a useless appendage . . . from its prisons' she
spent seventeen months in prison queues.

> One day somebody 'identified' me. Beside me . . . there was a
> woman with blue lips. She had, of course, never heard of me; but
> she suddenly came out of that trance so common to us all and
> whispered in my ear (everybody spoke in whispers there): 'Can you
> describe this?' And I said: 'Yes, I can.' And then something like the
> shadow of a smile crossed what had once been her face.

'Requiem', 200 lines of crystalline understatement, is the description
the woman wanted. It works, says the poet's translator D. M. Thomas, by
means opposite to the piled detail of Solzhenitsyn's *Gulag Archipelago*, but
both are works of invincible recall. Of the inhabitants of the prison
queues and gulags, Akhmatova says simply: 'I have woven for them a
great shroud.'

In China this cannot happen, as even the need for a descriptive shroud
is unmentionable: history is contraband. To be sure, the Party can't
wholly hide the epic mortality of Mao's era. But the Helmsman made
'mistakes'; let them fade away as such. The peoples of the former USSR
may slip back to the simulated order and deadly chaos of the past, but
not in ignorance of its nature. Khrushchev in his first account called
Stalin's actions 'crimes', and Russians do not confuse them with errors
any more than Germans in the case of Hitler.

Where does this connect with the trade of newspaper and television
offices? First, Akhmatova's account should inter the myth of the
detached reporter. The writer's task, at any time, is not detachment; it is
to engage without being consumed, and describe what calls for description. At Akhmatova's level it demands nerve hard to imagine. 'Requiem'
was made in a society swamped by mania, of which she and her family
were victims ('son in irons and husband clay'). Too dangerous for paper,
over seventeen years it existed only in the memory of Akhmatova and

certain friends. Second, commonplace reporting exists to reduce the call for feats which so outshine it. While news media and politics remain transparent, a society may avoid such lethal spirals as need 'Requiem', and an Akhmatova, to unwind them. We shouldn't ask it to be done again.

It's often reckoned (if not out loud) that flaws in the civil liberties of foreigners don't impact on us. Certainly, wealthy democracies have often done business with despotic regimes – selling them weapons, indeed, until they (allegedly) point them at us and need taking out. Though there is high language at such moments, the liberties of the liberated do not seem indispensable.

China challenges such comfy notions. Changing the Beijing regime by physical force is hardly an option. But the way in which China solves the complicated difficulties it faces – or fails to solve them – may well decide how much freedom our own societies will maintain in the twenty-first century. This is because of the stupendous scale of those problems, and the extent to which they have been home-grown and artificial. Edward O. Wilson, widely considered the greatest of practising biologists, has written that however much progress the other nations make in moderating human impact on the world's ecology China, as an 'unsteady giant', may helplessly cancel out all of it.

Westerners once imagined China as equable, a 'perfect instance (in de Tocqueville's words) of that species of well-being which a highly centralised administration may furnish . . . The condition of society there is always tolerable, never excellent.' Reality rather was tolerable intervals in a turbulent penury. For generations the huge, rich, temperate land failed to generate a satisfactory life for its people. Subsistence agriculture under a thin web of bureaucracy was maybe an inevitable dead-end. Whatever the cause, it wasn't Chinese DNA, since Taiwan, Hong Kong and Singapore (in its harsh way) are rich.

Ancient notions of environmental harmony did exist. But Mao replaced them with a violent assault on nature – originating a pollution syndrome which is now desperate, and shattering a brilliant generation of Chinese scholars and technologists who resisted his dogmatism. Chapter 9 suggested that modern states are built on statistical techniques – Quetelet's 'advance enumeration of births and deaths'. All such science

Mao brushed aside: the Great Leap Forward consequently was an insane vault into famine. When Ma Yinchu, president of Beijing University, computed the impending demographic disaster, he was denounced and dismissed. The famine the Party made took thirty, perhaps fifty million lives in 1959–61, amid cannibalism and infanticide – ghastly evidence for Amartya Sen's thesis that repression and secrecy are famine's essential allies. Those knowing the truth at the time may have been as few as 300, for no realistic news media existed. 'Writing about the bright side' was safe, 'writing about the dark side' a delinquency.

Abuse both of individuals and of resources – particularly water – runs through the Party's half-century in command. After the hydraulic engineer Huang Wanli was arrested for refusing to approve the Sanmenxia dam, Mao personally asked him to retract, and was told that 'stifling of views . . . was China's real problem'. Huang was sent to hard labour on Sanmenxia itself – admitted eventually to be useless. But even after attention from the Red Guards he declined the Party's request for some emollient words on its technological record. 'The earth,' he said, 'will always circle the sun . . . This will not change because of anything you have to say.' When almost ninety, he told Judith Shapiro, author of *Mao's War against Nature*, that 'Mao was the greatest criminal in history . . .'

China's secret history is filled with the recollections of men and women who won't accept euphemisms about 'error', and whose evidence proves that the Party's authoritarian actions have consistently generated catastrophes with no substantial cause, and intensified those arising naturally. Mao's successors fear, rightly, that their present argument – it says the Party's power monopoly is essential to China's survival – would not survive the nation's reconnection to its past.

China is a state which carefully limits accusations, but licenses itself to use calumnies freely. There is widespread mental stress, some of it officially manipulated, and some of it giving motivation to mystic cults such as Falun Gong. It is also very poor, with a per-capita GNP of £840, below South Africa (£3,020), Russia (£1,660) and Albania (£1,120). Deng Xiaoping's 1980s slogan 'To Get Rich Is Glorious' gave new, astonishing form to the socio-ecological pressures inherited from the Cultural Revolution. Trashing most of the Party's corroded philosophy, Deng began the present charge for industrial growth.

It is the shift from agrarian to industrial life on a China-wide scale that makes Wilson's 'unsteady giant'. Though it now ranks beside America as the largest of grain producers, China is close to using more than it can grow. By 2030 annual imports of 200 million tons are likely to be wanted, roughly the world's export total today. Getting rich now is crucial. Output must meet consumer demand, plus import bills – doing so within the capacity of a re-engineered but over-stressed water supply.

Eminent as Wilson is, many would challenge his details. But few would doubt his judgment that no simplicities apply. Paradoxically: grain shortage might be best met by moving China's effort into fruit and vegetables (huge labour resources giving export advantage, though at high cost in social reconstruction). Certainly: industrialists, growers and consumers will have to achieve amazing water-efficiency. Generally: stress, clashes of interest and income-volatility will confront dress designers, subsistence farmers, cops, doctors, soldiers. Nothing says it's impossible. Everything points to vast forces, unguessed effects and outrageous fortune intervening freely.

And this vast programme is to be accomplished without the open discourse free nations have required to moderate situations that were never as complex. Rather, the secretive authority which has serially betrayed China is serially awarding itself more – and more – chances. The Party maintains the tactics implicit in its last threadbare ideas – bribing consumers, denouncing 'split-ists' – because its record compels it to treat the people as political dead weight, devoid of reason and constancy, incapable of using free news media. It is the obvious course for satraps with no alternative. Less obvious is that a libertarian newspaperman – as Murdoch calls himself – should offer them comfort ('objective support').

The Tiananmen demonstrations were the climax to an increasingly manifest discontent with the elite's indifference to its own offences. The Party chiefs knew that, however intemperate, the students intended no challenge to the state. There was a challenge to monopoly over the state, and the Party chose murder to deflect it – expelling colleagues who had the humanity to demur. For some years rigorous leftists had been admiring a replacement USSR, and Western democrats had hoped for cautious progress towards pluralism. Guns in the square made clear it was not so easy.

Murdoch, when entering this situation four years later, was coming from the direction of a liberator. Something additional to commerce was involved in Newscorp's payment of £525 million, in July 1993, for 63.6 per cent of a company called Satellite Television Asia Region (Star T-V), with large satellite cover on the Chinese mainland (it was based in Hong Kong, where British colonialism was expiring). Satellite television, Murdoch maintained, was a means to improve the world, just as subsidising the *New York Post* was about enabling tabloid journalism to make the world 'a better place'. His stance offered nothing to compromise. It was that of the man of conscience, one of the last century's important, overworked figures, converse of totalitarianism's limp allies, the 'fellow travellers' and 'useful idiots'.

Fellow travellers, of course, sometimes have excuses. Liberals such as Maynard Keynes saw through the Bolsheviks immediately, but for years afterwards eminent British intellectuals were fooled by the façade of the Moscow trials. Many businessmen traversed apartheid South Africa blind to the repression delineated by James Cameron, Anthony Sampson, Ruth First and others. But it isn't compulsory to have the intuition of Keynes, or even the tradecraft of a trainee reporter. Aptitude, instruction and disappointment usually go into learning that cabbies and barmen at the smart end of town don't model political conditions reliably; shrewd businessmen may be simpletons in such matters, and even admit it.

Rupert might cast himself as a simpleton, unskilled in complex truths – certainly, the recreator of the *New York Post* could plead that his improvements to the world don't run mainly to such things. But he insistently volunteers expertise in international causes – as when deciding that Harry Evans was not a man of conscience, or of enough conscience, and needed to be replaced at *The Times* by someone properly matched with the cause of Akhmatova and Solzhenitsyn. And Evans' deficiency was merely scepticism about plans for prompt social implosion in the Soviet territory (see Chapter 10 above). Like many life-long anti-communists at the time, conservatives and liberals, Evans was tinged with gradualism to that extent. Not so Murdoch. Freedom to him was one shaft, and he was its spearhead; the causes of totalitarianism destroyed, of unregulated (largely tabloid) television, of union-free workplaces and innovative finance were not divisible. Revelations since Russia's advance towards freedom suggest that grand Western chest-drumming probably stiffened communism's resistance somewhat. But passion might excuse it. It is hard not to think the anti-compromisers had a point, for the Soviet case teaches lessons on political monopoly that even idiots should have been able get in a single pass.

Murdoch also had liberation cred from an image that seemed macho to both admirers and detractors. The right-hand version could come out of Ayn Rand – the prose-poet of 'objective individualism', whose novels (such as *Atlas Shrugged*) depict titans eliminating collectivist foes of human excellence. In Murdoch's case these would be 'elitist' and 'snobbish' editors (of his own and other papers), Luddite unions and the ubiquitous agents of something he has called 'liberal totalitarianism'.

That usage is not unusual among right-wing voices, but Murdoch applies it particularly to rules and institutions involved with news and entertainment. Totalitarians of this kind permeate the Australian Broadcasting Commission, the Independent Broadcasting Authority (and its successors), the Office of Fair Trading, the BBC and the staff of the Federal Communications Commission (FCC). Oddly enough, outfits like these are rarely caught lending a hand to the vanilla totalitarians who run prison camps or have people shot in the neck by secret policemen. The BBC and ABC indeed are among those who drive them nuts most often. Still, Murdoch's typology has found supporters. We have seen the FCC's political masters accepting Murdoch as freedom's partisan, with happy results for Newscorp.

On the left hand are critics alleged to 'demonise' him, and perhaps they do. Michael Foot's description, 'an evil genius', has been influential, and sounds something like a demon – macho, surely, ex officio. Numerous enemies credit him with demonic skill in exploiting the popular lust for his output (seeming almost as keen as he is to to exaggerate it). Some judge the machismo invincible, and Newscorp so demonically logical an expression of capitalism that only replacement of the entire system will change anything; meanwhile, realists might as well join the payroll. This, a snug fit with establishment theory, is another happy result for Newscorp.

Sky and Fox, Times Newspapers, the monopolisation of Australian journalism and lesser coups in parallel amounted by the early 1990s to sweeping victory for Murdoch over structures devised by democratic states and intended to limit abuses in news media. Each carried its own business justification, but the overall pitch presented them as campaigns in a crusade. The rhetoric of 'liberal totalitarianism' perched the democracies on a continuum with the authoritarian states – not at the Evil Empire end, to be sure, but liable to move towards it without the vigilance of Murdoch and other friends of liberty.

To proceed from this to the idea of freedom as negation of the state is just shuffle-ball-change. It's a proposition which holds when an authoritarian government monopolises power; then its local retreat advances local liberty, and nothing else can. But in a democracy, where the state's power is constitutionally restrained, no one-dimensional continuum exists. Constitutional action narrows some freedoms and widens others – something that is especially clear in the case of media systems. More freedom from defamation is less freedom of speech; freedom of information reduces freedom of bureaucratic diktat; less freedom to create monopoly is more freedom to compete. Under democracy, government is always a problem and always a possible (not automatic) solution. Simplifications like the Reagan one-liner 'Government is not the solution, government is the problem' in reality confuse the issue, like the oxymoronic 'liberal totalitarianism' formula, or the relabelling of the ruling class.

Not everyone believed in theories of Murdoch the freedom crusader (the practice in Newscorp's operations having rather been to eliminate or marginalise competitive and other problems by seeking political advantage). Still, they were clothed in free-market economic arguments by Stelzer and others, while Murdoch himself acquired the badges of American right-wing principle: supporting the Cato Institute (named for the two Romans who were antiquity's most unyielding champions of freedom and financial purity) and subsidising conservative intellectual journalism of the right. But all this was laid over a programme much in the style of Black Jack McEwen, who saw the state as a business association (if not a personal property) and would have found the *Weekly Standard* a trifle precious. Some contradictions were therefore visible. The Murdoch Doctrine, however, carried a saving guarantee. Every inhibition on liberty was to be liquidated by revolutionary technologies, installed under Newscorp's direction.

In September 1993, three months after taking control of Star T-V, Murdoch delivered the remarkable speech in London – written according to Newscorp insiders by Stelzer – in which he seemed to say that his company's operations would shortly be putting an end to authoritarian politics everywhere in the world.

Advances in the technology of communications have proved an unambiguous threat to totalitarian regimes: fax machines enable dissidents to bypass state-controlled print media; direct-dial telephone makes it difficult for a state to control interpersonal voice communication; and satellite broadcasting makes it possible for information-hungry residents of many closed societies to bypass state-controlled television channels.

The effect was partly to re-emphasise that the Western media regulators he had overcome represented the liberal brand of repression. But they were the old frontier and Star the new, so his remarks were taken as a challenge to Beijing, and Murdoch seemed sincerely happy with that. Satellite television, having saved Britain from 'snobbery', would save the Middle Kingdom from tyranny.

A Newscorp employee who found this particularly interesting was Jonathan Mirsky, whom *The Times* had just appointed to Hong Kong. Mirsky, an American, was expert in Chinese culture, driven powerfully by conscience and trusted by many brave dissidents: he may have been the Western journalist most loathed by Beijing. Dispatches from Tiananmen Square to the *Observer* had won him a British Press Award as foreign reporter of 1989 – and unlimited exclusion from mainland China. For *The Times* to embed him, as it were, in Chris Patten's forthcoming attempt to fortify democracy before the Hong Kong handover was to slap a glove down in front of the Communist Party, in just the bold spirit the boss had been showing.

The Party saw the problem. Promises of economic advance required Western co-operation, and thus required the tranquil absorption of Hong Kong. Force at Tiananmen had worked, but foreign sensibilities could not be outraged again. (The book Patten was later to write contains an unwelcome message for the Party: that the West had no need to assist its search for legitimacy.) Study of the Soviet collapse seems to have convinced Party leaders that changes need not undermine their power so long as they could hang on to media control – that is, explode Murdoch's thesis.

Belief that communications technology brings liberty without moral choice contains just enough truth to mislead. There is an argument that maritime communications promoted freedom in Europe (as against land-locked armies). This looks neat from a British perspective; for West Africans it promoted intercontinental slavery. Technologies differ tactically from the government-control viewpoint. Transistor radios, giving cheap, inconspicuous access to Ayatollah Khomeini's revolutionary harangues, contributed to the Shah of Iran's downfall. Murdoch probably overestimated fax. On 4 June 1989, as the army moved on Tiananmen Square, government monitors were deployed at every fax machine. Fax can be tapped as readily as telephones. Printing has some good resistance qualities, for no traceable plant need be held by the audience, and personal networks amplify its effects remarkably. But it can be marginalised by sufficient control of fast machinery. The Internet then was a consideration for the future.

Probably it did not take Beijing's propaganda specialist Guangen Ding long to assess satellite television. The reception plant is bulky, and generates an electro-magnetic 'signature' (used in Britain, that closed society, to detect licence-fee evasion). The dish, from a political policeman's viewpoint, is delightfully conspicuous, and transmits significant amounts of information only if sophisticated resources are available.

Star had been active since 1991, and when Murdoch arrived was running five twenty-four-hour channels: Viacom's MTV Asia; Prime Time Sports (a joint venture with the Denver-based Prime Network); entertainment and cultural programmes through Star Plus; a Mandarin Chinese channel; and the BBC's World Service Television, WSTV. It would be hard to think of anything 'information-hungry residents' of a closed society like China would want on their screens more than WSTV (now BBC World). It was set up in 1991 as a twenty-four-hour service for Asia and the Middle East, promising to keep viewers 'not just informed, but well informed, with in-depth analysis and cutting-edge interviews – the story from all sides'. That promise the channel is generally judged to fulfil. It is the visual partner of BBC Radio's World Service, a byword for international reporting with wide range and reliability. It runs many of the high-value features produced at the Television Centre in London, one of which in 1993 was *The Last Emperor*, a biography of Mao. This was highly critical, and, though it didn't use Huang Wanli's term 'criminal', Mao's horrible sexual behaviour was frankly disclosed. Quite credibly, it is said to have rocked the Party.

Also there were numerous references to Tiananmen on the World news bulletins – as there still are: the BBC website lists more than a hundred a year. Chinese media of course must respect official amnesia, but the BBC uses ordinary newsdesk practice and, after 400 people have been killed in such a fashion, reverberations persist. Tremors from Bloody Sunday, threefold more distant in time, and rather less mortal, still register with comparable frequency. 'It was driving them nuts,' said Murdoch, meaning the masters of Beijing. But then it was a new experience for them.

Dishes on the mainland were still few, and their status undecided. Early in 1994 the Propaganda Ministry told Murdoch that, unless Star's programming started conforming with their idea of good television, they would ban dishes wherever Star's 'footprint' reached in China. There would be no advertising revenue from Western firms in pursuit of the Chinese consumer. Star's potential, and value, could sink to nothing. Of course that was a new kind of experience too.

Television regulation is complicated and hard to enforce. The notion under democratic government is that you should have a television operation only if you allow independent editorial and creative judgment within it. This roughly is the BBC/ITV model, for which Murdoch has constantly displayed his loathing. He prefers editors who consider his word sacred, practises arbitrary dismissal widely, and thinks entertainment a product distinct from news, and essentially more attractive. (There is nothing to suggest he knows anything about real news, except that it gets out of control, which to others is its great fascination.) Naturally Murdoch doesn't put it like that, but argues generally that regulation of course means rules, and society should have the least rules possible.

Satellite television in the West has certainly eroded a great many of the rules. Murdoch based his original Sky transmission system in Luxembourg, targeted at British audiences but outside the jurisdiction of British regulators. He was able to press this advantage, and get the sort of system he likes, not because the regulators were totalitarian or authoritarian – just the reverse. In Britain there would be profound legal difficulties about preventing people from having aerials to receive signals from space: a free country of course isn't lawless. (Also, the regulators were responsible to politicians whom Murdoch professed to support, and certainly not to threaten.)

Murdoch is not greatly troubled by law that tends to circumscribe his media operations. His method is to signal acceptance, and afterwards to find exceptions and loopholes – gun-jumping or foot-dragging – then, if he gets stuck, he seeks political aid. But loophole-drilling works only if others – especially the servants of the state – hold laws generally in respect. Trouncing the institutions of the constitutional West isn't good training for going a few rounds with career totalitarians. One cannot say the leaders of China care little for law – they care absolutely nothing for it. People capable of Tiananmen would find it simple to create a situation in which no sane individual would go anywhere near a satellite dish.

Murdoch promptly set about 'trying to make peace with the Chinese government'. He claims to have been puzzled by Ding's attitude – curiously, it was that of a man responding to a threat. After all, as he told *Forbes* later in 1994, there had not been anything in the London speech beyond 'a few standard clichés'. He agreed to remove the BBC channel from Star's satellite AsiaSat-1, and it was done by April 1994. This stopped it from reaching the few mainland viewers who had seen *The Last Emperor* and the unhinging Tiananmen reports, and simultaneously chopped off substantial audiences in Hong Kong (then independent of Beijing) and Taiwan (which remains independent, as a pluralist democracy). He also agreed to put $5.4 million into the *People's Daily*, which is the central element in China's totalitarian media apparatus, and so pure a pseudo-newspaper that Weber might rethink his dictum that ideal types never appear exactly in the real world.

The crusade in China had lasted roughly six months. It would be hard to explain such a surrender in terms of ordinary psychology – how a long-serving media executive could have sufficient credulity to be so mistaken about the nature of totalitarianism. Clearly Murdoch must have some over for believing people who say what a demon he is. He had of course seen off the British print unions, in the previous decade, but that was with a friendly state protecting him (he felt 'very safe', he told Woodrow Wyatt then). The rugged images – hero and anti-hero – jointly produce the idea of the boss of Newscorp as an uncompromising character. This is true only if 'uncompromising' is used to mean flipping between aggression and submission without intervening tension.

After his long and successful campaign against the excessive governing rules in Western society, Murdoch agreed to a reduced set of one: just obey the government. Ayn Rand's reaction is hard to imagine, but there is something applicable in a commentator who received his Nobel Prize just after Murdoch's speech consigning government authority to history: the US economic historian Douglas C. North.

> The evolution of government from its medieval, Mafia-like character to that embodying modern legal institutions and instruments is a major part of the history of freedom. It is a part that tends to be obscured or ignored because of the myopic vision of many economists, who persist in modeling government as nothing more than a gigantic form of theft and income distribution.

Murdoch and his supporters, probably without understanding much about them, had taken the most myopic of these free-market doctrines, mixed them with some incantations about new media, and declared that a pathway to the future was open. In fact it was a wormhole leading back to the Mafia state. But perhaps Murdoch hardly noticed. By October 1994 he was telling a Melbourne lecture audience that Orwell had got it all wrong and that political monopoly had been eliminated by technology. In view of what had happened and has happened since in China, this was almost superb. (He had by then bought Star's remaining equity.)

Admittedly the business has expanded physically, though like BSkyB its profits are only potential. Xing Kong Wei Shi (Starry Sky Satellite TV) received permission late in 2002 to begin national distribution in China, and claims great success for products such as its male beauty-contest *Woman in Charge*. But if it has information-hungry customers they are in worse shape than ten years back. 'Star is steering clear of news alto-gether,' wrote the *Financial Times* Beijing correspondent James Kynge, reporting the new concession – the first for a foreign-owned network. It was a reward for:

> the strategy of Rupert Murdoch, News Corp's boss, who has assid-uously courted the Chinese government for more than a decade, trying to convince it that Star TV programming will do nothing to upset Beijing's authoritarian rule.
>
> 'Everything in China is about relationships and about mutual benefit,' said Jamie Davis, head of Star TV in China . . . 'I think Rupert Murdoch has a very good relationship with the Chinese government . . . and we work hard at it,' he added.
>
> Consistent with this, Xing Kong Wei Shi's apolitical content is reviewed twice to make sure it is inoffensive.

Perhaps Orwell didn't think of material already apolitical by construction needing to go through two more processes to ensure Big Brother's good-will. Mr Davis, of course, was neatly illustrating Professor North's point.

By reversing the one-dimensional model, this story could be made to show the 'state-run' BBC as custodian of liberty and private capitalism as the enemy. But it makes no more sense reversed. Neither ownership nor partisan alignment is the real issue here. Liberals may bridle somewhat, but the lesson properly to be drawn is that in an essential way the polit-ically neutral BBC, the liberal *Guardian*, the illiberal *Daily Mail* and the conservative *Wall Street Journal* all resemble each other more than any of them resemble Newscorp media output. All, in utterly dissimilar ways, have worked within the constitution of the state to consolidate their independence from it. Newscorp is about eroding the boundaries between the state power and media operations, meanwhile cloaking this process in fantasies which – necessarily – feed back into and distort its journalism. Keith Murdoch's conscription propaganda in 1915, the *Sunday Times'* crackpot assault on the 'AIDS establishment', the abject his-tory of Satellite Television Asia Region are all manifestations of something which makes itself marvellously comfortable in Beijing. There are plenty of other distortions of journalism, but none of them matter nearly as much. A good thing about Murdoch's Chinese activities is that no democratic politician who agrees to examine them can entertain honest doubt about the character of the operation.

We shall never know what might have happened if Murdoch had used a robust Australian expression (there is a wide choice) when Ding threatened what was (and remains) an outpost of his empire financially, however congenial culturally. We shall never know what would have happened to the United States if Kay Graham and her colleagues had surrendered to a far more serious threat.

We may be sure Ding and friends remain pleased with the deal. Indeed, it has given them confidence: they think they know now how to handle Western corporations (in particular, they have been able to get hold of enough firewall technology to keep the Internet fairly well in hand). Murdoch of course no longer alleges that there is an unequivocal threat from satellite television, but he has aired the notion that Western-style entertainment, separated from Western-style news, may incrementally bring change to China, and so make it 'work'.

But neither China, nor the world, has the time for adaptations of *Buffy the Vampire Slayer* to take subtle effect. During the ten years which Murdoch has spent assuring the Communist Party that media systems need not be contaminated at all with reality, AIDS has been disseminating in China. As near as can now be worked out, it had attacked about 10,000 people by the period of the *Sunday Times*' unsuccessful attempt to persuade the British government there was no such thing. Official refusal to admit its existence in China has given appalling impetus to HIV infection and the least alarming projections by outside analysts now predict nineteen million deaths during the first quarter of this century. Severe Acute Respiratory Syndrome (SARS) is a not dissimilar case of disastrous secrecy: the rest of the world is beginning to understand what Professor Wilson meant by his phrase 'the unsteady giant'.

To the extent that official China acknowledges that AIDS is a problem, this is mostly due to Elizabeth Rosenthal of the *New York Times*, who in 2000 exposed the scandal of the infected commercial blood-banks in Henan province. Her colleague Nicholas Kristof was following up the story, and judging that the government's response was still so grudging as to be 'tantamount to murder'. Nobody who knows anything about

Newscorp's investigative capability, anywhere in the world, would think it likely to produce work like Rosenthal's. But the arrangement Starry Sky Satellite TV has with the government actually makes it impossible. In that sense, totalitarian societies 'work'. If they continue doing so long enough, the results will be something beyond even Akhmatova's capacity to describe.

When the story of Murdoch's surrender broke in 1994, Jonathan Mirsky filed the story – but *The Times* did not run it. 'We don't run Murdoch stories,' said the deputy foreign editor, David Watts. 'We', it turned out, meant the foreign pages. The practice was to confine stories about the boss within the business pages. Mirsky kept trying, and filed ten more stories about the eclipse of the BBC, including a report of Chris Patten's speech on the matter, which was not friendly to Murdoch. None of them made the paper anywhere.

A little later, both Patten and Mirsky found their accounts of China anathema to Newscorp subsidiaries which had commissioned them: Patten's book *East and West* unwanted by HarperCollins; Mirsky's journalism by *The Times*. During the consequent arguments over censorship Neil wrote that Murdoch terrorised his subordinates, and Mirsky remembered being told, on joining *The Times*, that it was an office dominated by 'fear'.

Qualities of demonic genius may inspire terror, but to some observers these are no more visible than Murdoch's celebrated charm. Patten, like Gough Whitlam, found the leader of Newscorp mildly tedious – with unique access to China, and off-the-peg ideas.

Murdoch's style doesn't include the swagger seen sometimes at the top of a media business, nor is the (usually dubious) epithet 'larger than life' applied to him: this is just a sinewy man of middle height, with a casual gait (one shoulder carried a little forward) and the unaffected demeanour of his class. Overtly, Australian privilege likes to keep the egalitarian faith, and Murdoch was bred in that culture by good tutors and a careful mother. The sages certifying him later as a *Times* proprietor were wrong to consider 'colonial aristocrat' a full description. But what they chose to see was itself real. Today he is leaner, lined, and more irritable, but the easy manners remain effective in small, uncontentious groups: there, charm is still reported. As a listener he outclasses many media bosses, and to Margaret Thatcher seemed an admirable conversational-ist. (Wyatt's diaries say that Murdoch spoke little in their meetings. With a Patten or Whitlam, conversation is always something of an all-comers joust.) In another mode, however, Murdoch may pour sudden abuse over some individual target within a group.

Media companies, of course, don't resemble a Household Cavalry officers' Mess. Still, the rule against dumping on people in front of their colleagues is roughly respected, and even in Old Fleet Street many of the famous 'bollockings' were only louche horseplay. In Newscorp they have a regular disciplinary character – of a piece with the notorious silent phone calls. Nor would loyalists of the MacKenzie type, considering Murdoch a genius, deplore it – 'bollocking' is a stripe of honour, to hand down to lower ranks. Outside the tabloid newsrooms, self-respect is not quite so plastic, but shrewder courtiers can apply evasive tactics. Simon Jenkins (editor of *The Times*, from 1989 to 1992) noted outbursts to be rarer one-on-one: contention should be avoided in group settings. Veterans tend to stress their own resistance to treatment visited on others: Neil, explaining the method of silences to a television audience, said that he managed one day to contain himself till *Murdoch* broke into speech. Jenkins says he suffered no tirades himself, but that Andrew Knight, when chief executive of the British division (News International), submitted 'like a butler'. John Menadue, however, states frankly that individual survival tactics leave the culture of autocracy undisturbed.

It confers tactical advantage in deal-making. Murdoch – therefore Newscorp – switches briskly between attack and retreat, or walkout and handshake. He sees here a principle that media companies, being in 'the ideas business', can't be 'run by committee'. But if the ideas are to be real ones, such companies can be run no other way, for any worthwhile check is in principle a committee. A classic illustration is the 'Hitler Diaries' case, which also reminded Hugh Trevor-Roper how correct he had been about restraints on power.

He was by then Lord Dacre and a national director of Times Newspapers; he was also the one source of intellectual credit for the his-torical coup Murdoch desired. That eclipse of a scholar's judgment was transient, and ended when he wrote a *Times* article to certify the 'diaries'.

Writers often know the sick realisation that expounding an argument has revealed it as bilge: sadly, due to frantic deadlines, this came to Dacre after it was printed. Steeling himself, he told *The Times* editor Charles Douglas Home that embarrassing retreat was necessary.

The Hitler-fakers had expected gloriously to exploit the world's publishers – but they did not know Murdoch. Once he had built them up, cut them down and cracked their nerve, the expectation vanished: converting to a belief at Times Newspapers that the boss was bringing in, as one hit, the scoop and bargain of the age. To be a corporate nay-sayer in such circumstances was unappetizing, and Douglas Home avoided passing Dacre's news to the *Sunday Times* team busy on the ersatz journals. By chance they found out just as their own print-run began.

For a paper like theirs the sole professional option was to replace the edition – stripped of world-scoop claims – and put checks in hand. For most of them, only the word of a one-time Regius Professor of Modern History had held back scepticism: using Dacre's better judgment – acting, indeed, in committee fashion – they might have saved some intellectual capital.

But it was Murdoch's call – though he was in New York, and not entitled legally to influence any *Sunday Times* editorial decision. Brian MacArthur, deputy editor, phoned to say Dacre thought the diaries phoney after all.

'Fuck Dacre,' said the boss.

Whereas Starry Sky Satellite TV concerns censorship within China the Patten/Mirsky incidents were about western censorship appeasing Beijing. Patten's *East and West* argued that for democracies to accommodate political monopoly in China was not honourable, prudent or necessary: Mirsky's complaint was that *The Times*, having once been bold, was restricting his accounts of dissidence in China, particularly any involving Tiananmen.

Newscorp denial took various forms. Peter Stothard, then editor of *The Times*, boldly declared that Murdoch never influenced – had never once dictated to him – any item of policy. Promptly John Izbicki, a former *Times* man, described in the *Daily Telegraph* an act of dictation he had seen taking place. Stothard surely convinced himself, but few others.

Subtler colleagues rebutted charges not seriously made, such as the existence of efficient conspiracies to keep Murdoch-unfriendly matter off the news pages. Admittedly the Patten scandal didn't make *The Times* until it had been well ventilated elsewhere, wrote the media editor, Raymond Snoddy – but that was cock-up, disproving conspiracy. Presumably he wasn't in on the conspiratorial little rule on Murdoch stories once explained to Mirsky. But that's a cock-up for you.

HarperCollins tried first to suggest *East and West* wasn't fit for publication. Its subsequent, most successful publication by Macmillan was then cited by Murdoch fans as proof that it had not truly been censored (that this torpedoed the initial argument didn't trouble them). Of course the book was censored as completely as lies in the power of any enormous publisher, and doubtless the Chinese leadership took it very kindly. That Western publishing maintains diversity is hardly Newscorp's fault.

Naturally the real issue was (and is) self-censorship, better called auto-censorship. This, everyone knows, is unlike administered censorship – something barely legal in liberal states, and unusual in authoritarian ones. China, following its minimal bureaucratic tradition, uses little of the Nazi's egregious machinery. Speech and assembly are quite free – so long as Marxist-Leninist-Maoist thought, the dictatorship of the proletariat and the incumbent satraps aren't disturbed.

Auto-censorship works through faculties its subjects must possess to merit restraint: only part of a reporter's ability is needed to estimate (or over-estimate) the desires of the powerful. Like Adam Smith's invisible hand, auto-censorship then responds to contingencies which planned suppression cannot reach. To understand the Chinese application, says the American scholar Perry Link, imagine that writers work under a chandelier in which lives a huge anaconda. Coils drop occasionally to crush a victim. But much activity the snake ignores. No serious effort is made to disguise the menace of this situation; still less to explain it. 'You decide,' is the anaconda's message.

The West requires disguises – some of which we've examined – and explanations, commonly supplied as pseudo-technicalities. When Mirsky quit *The Times* in 1997 over rejection of his China writings, Brian MacArthur – now an elder columnist for the paper – assured its readers that censorship wasn't involved, just issues of professional method. As an ex-academic, Mirsky could not fashion the 'telling "intros"' *The Times* required, and the subs could not 'disentangle' his copy. It had been just the same at the *Observer*.

Though Mirsky had indeed been a professor, it hadn't stopped *The Times* expensively poaching him (nor does Donald Trelford, his editor at the *Observer*, recall missing intros and tangled text). But essentials were involved here as much as presentational zip. Mirsky failed to understand how his 'obsession' with the state of democracy in Hong Kong interfered with something MacArthur called 'normal news reporting'. Although it wasn't stated, readers aware of Mirsky's record could infer that his qualities might be useful at such moments as Tiananmen, and for winning prizes. But real journalism was about 'prosaic' considerations.

'Normal news' is the oxymoron which in a free society helps make auto-censorship tolerable to its practitioners. 'Normality' implicitly takes the high moral ground. In many activities such usage is legitimate, but in media work it is a seductive delusion to suppose that the mass of normal, prosaic stuff has a value of its own. With the abnormal subtracted, it's deadly rubbish, and China is an exemplary case. The exiled poet Bei Ling has written of the bright normality which clad China's capital during George Bush's presidential visit in February 2002:

> On this day of the lunar New Year . . . Beijing's Avenue of Heavenly Peace throngs with the last of holiday revelers. The highways are crowded with evidence of new wealth. Customers at a Starbucks in Shanghai pay $3 for a caffé mocha and never feel the sting. And there are writers in prison simply because they are writers. Printing a commentary piece like this could bring a death sentence in China. The sun shone as President Bush's motorcade made its way through Beijing's burgeoning streets, but looks can be deceiving.

James Fenimore Cooper saw (in the epigraph to this chapter) that journalists of his day were truthful intermittently, and routinely untruthful by circumstance. Allowing a bit for corruption, he judged their activities predominantly indefensible. Method and technology have changed those statistics: the routine bulk of a broadsheet paper now has little reason to be grossly untruthful, and not much is. Its staff can count their particular actions as mostly honest and this comfort applies in normal circumstances to Newscorp titles like *The Times* or the *Australian*. If – abnormally – the passions, cupidity or interests of Newscorp obtrude, 'obsessive' reactions only imperil the good work done otherwise.

Most newspapers of Cooper's time were visibly untrustworthy. So today are the *Sun* and the *New York Post*, which therefore aren't trusted. There would scarcely be any need to worry about such outfits except that our elected leaders – still struggling to design an open, efficient and modern statecraft – revolve with them in a dance of folly which has at least the potential to be a dance of death for democracy. But the broadsheet newspaper (and its electronic offspring) will be dangerous even if politicians can kick their tabloid habit. Its normal mode seems trustworthy. And as democracies only place real stress on their essential institutions now and then, they may discover too late which ones do nothing more than seem.

After MacArthur's rebuke to Mirsky, *The Times'* reporting of China achieved consummate normality for several more years – being perhaps least obsessive in the first half of 2001, the period when James Murdoch stated that investors in China should have a 'strong stomach' like his father's (and his own); also the climactic phase in Beijing's world-respectability campaign (via the Olympic Games and the World Trade Organisation); and Newscorp's crucial acquisition of shares in China Netcom, the broadband business run by President Jiang Zemin's son. This last the *China Daily* called 'revolutionary' and 'not entirely legal'. The law in fact forbad any such foreign ownership, so the real meaning was that for purposes of Beijing corporatism – of regulation 'by man rather than law' – Newscorp had achieved solid insider status, and was no longer foreign.

Many things have shifted since Murdoch's prediction of regime change in Beijing. Its rulers are now better entrenched – with Newscorp right alongside. There are cosmetic changes in China, but no challenge to the monopoly. A less impoverished normality is visible since 2002 in *The Times'* reporting of China – Rupert and James can't have much fear of defenestration now – but nothing obsessive. Nothing like what should come from a major media concern deeply linked to the country.

What has not shifted any more than the Chinese regime is the character of the Murdoch operation. It remains one where journalists are uniquely ready to 'march in step'. Not incessantly, but in 'Cooper's Moment', as it were: when the proprietor's passions, cupidity and interest are in play.

A present commonplace holds that war is disastrously dividing democratic opinion. But history surely suggests that war never inflicts its worst damage on democracies until it ceases to divide. Uniformity – doubtless because it tends to the spurious – has restricted application in constitutional systems: a great turn-up of the last century was the resilience, military and civil, of disputatious, disunited free societies, and the propensity of monoliths to shatter.

It's therefore striking that Newscorp's contribution to the Iraq war of 2003 was a unanimity scarcely matched by any other body – involved – not, for instance, the Pentagon. Soldiers in America and in Britain acknowledged agreements and disagreements, volubly, and quite often on the record. Within Newscorp there were great variations in style, from the elegant *Australian* to the oafish *Post*, but everything kept in phase: the intellectual equivalent of synchronised swimming. From the tabloid members there was a true whiff of Great War brimstone – a reminder that one good Newscorp question asks how much of it is survival from 1914–18, and how much portent of tomorrow. The unanimity, anyway, was phenomenal in twenty-first-century terms and Roy Greenslade, former *Daily Mirror* editor and professor of journalism at City University in London, thought it worth examination. But no Murdoch editors responded to his calls or e-mails – their achievement was not one they cared to discuss. And when journalists are more tight-lipped than soldiers, auto-censorship is at work.

Though tracts of normality exist, fear and conformity – sufficiently attested – do set Newscorp apart from other companies. The mechanism depends essentially on the characteristics of media work: people must always court uncertainty, making themselves vulnerable to the authoritarian's spurious assurance. Those tough enough to confront it are sidelined or ejected. Sophisticated defences of Newscorp hardly bother to deny this. The abuses submitted to are mostly voluntary, absurd or trivial, and cock-up frustrates much of the corporate purpose. Isn't it over-reaction to find Gulag qualities in *The Times* subs' desk?

Yes, but the question is misguided. Indeed, the Murdochs aren't running in the west a copy of the Chief Administration of Correctional Labour Camps. Here, the lawful state and its countervailing institutions are a dynamic structure which excludes such abuses. The question is whether Newscorp is one of the organisations contributing strength to that structure, or whether its net effect is just parasitic weight – and, if the second is true, how much it matters.

Aleksandr Solzhenitsyn gave in *The Gulag Archipelago* a famous warning to those who fancy there are places perfectly immune to the things it describes. 'All the evil of the twentieth century,' he says, 'is possible everywhere on earth,' and obviously a millennium doesn't alter that. Explaining how repression diffused itself in a scattered system (archipelago) linked by subjection to an arbitrary will, his 'literary investigation' deals harshly with himself. Showing how much was voluntary, absurd and trivial, he records the grotesque fact that the men arresting him couldn't find the Lubyanka, and that he showed them the way, fancying it might improve his situation. At times he was about to resist, 'or at least cry out' – but things were never quite so acute, or the audience quite suitable. Opportunities were hard to discern: especially ones sure to improve one's own position. And things happened under appearances of normality, among non-witnesses occupied with 'studying the safe secrets of the atomic nucleus, researching the influence of Heidegger on Sartre, or collecting Picasso reproductions; [who] rode off in . . . railroad sleeping compartments to vacation resorts, or finished building . . . [a] country house near Moscow'.

What our own inquiry adds is that in a well-ordered society – anyway, one better ordered than the old USSR – a media business may present still fewer choices, certainly fewer than excuses to overlook them. But of course a structure is not more resilient for being checked and tested less often.

Max Weber was not surprised that journalists should be corrupt. What he thought remarkable, given their circumstances, is that many are not, and this applies – with everything said about choices – to those have worked for Murdoch, or still do. Among them are some who have sought to rebel – or at least not to compete in toadying – and have taken the consequences. Journalists as a group have paid dues – have recognised that

481

diversity has costs – and if some have paid heavily, some little, and others nothing, that is scarcely novel.

Nowhere in the democratic societies where Murdoch operates can this yet be said of the elected political class. On the contrary – and irrespective of partisan alignment – they have smoothed Murdoch's way, so regularly as to imply that media chieftains who don't emulate him (not yet a majority) are simpletons. An attempt has been made here to avoid rhetoric about politicians' moral fibre, and comprehend their present necessities. Still, these can't be reduced by easing the ambitions of Murdoch and those ready to follow him: canvassing their goodwill, the record shows, is helping the jailers to find the jail.

By prevailing assumption the left considers Newscorp profit-driven, but the record suggests that this reaction oversimplifies. A striking financial point about Newscorp in the last decade of the last century is not that it made huge profits, but that it scarcely paid tax. In 1999 *The Economist* calculated that the group's operations in Britain had generated £1.4 billion profit since 1978 – a strong but not startling performance – and paid net British corporation tax of zero, which is startling. It is unlikely that any major company outdid this kind of performance.

Basic corporate tax rates are 36, 35 and 30 per cent in Australia, by America and Britain. Investigating Newscorp's worldwide operations over four years to 1999 *The Economist* found profits of A$5.4 billion and A$325 million paid in corporate taxes: roughly a 6 per cent rate. Disney, a comparable megacorporation, paid 31 per cent over the same years. With vast cashflow and minimal tax bills, profit and dividend don't have quite the significance found elsewhere in capitalism.

China provides a cross-bearing: Newscorp clearly hasn't profited by injecting some $2 billion there. This comes not from Newscorp accounts, but from analysis in the authoritative *China Economic Quarterly*, showing that few resident western firms make money in China, and Newscorp (*CEQ,* May 2003) is not one of them. For foreign capital, the present reality is trivial margins, chaos and surrounding corruption. Murdoch's personal diligence, nonetheless, suggests China remains congenial to the Newscorp core-competence: swapping approval with the controllers of the state. Progress here is solid. And once the Party has made China work, with Newscorp a close partner, vistas of exceptional profit insulated from competitive attack doubtless open. Similar speculation, if less epic, has gratified Newscorp previously: cash and patience 'making the world a better place'. But such fixation on the exceptional is exceptional in profit-seekers.

Profit excites moral reflexes. But its pursuit is not identical with pursuit of market dominion – indeed, for entrepreneurs generally, the two are incompatible. No route to profit is as direct as fortunate trading in a market which expands through competition centred on quality. Qualifications abound, but the statement matches neatly with economic theory, and not badly with large tracts of commercial life. Sub-texts include step-changes in technology and operational peculiarities – media businesses exhibit many – and from such complexities are born ingenious plans to generate exceptional profits, or super-profits (often some form of short, victorious war involving price). In theory, none pay off over time in a fair market. In practice, fixing large markets is a costly game, rich in counter-productive potential (even if you are Bill Gates). It is simpler to accept the uncertainties of living with assorted competitors on roughly equal terms. In business rhetoric, competition resembles apple pie. Nobody eulogising apple pie sounds wholly sincere. Many people, all the same, quite like it.

Profit-seeking may have its evils. But its virtue, for the freedoms discussed here, is that it works naturally with diversity. For market dominion – and whatever it sustains – diversity is a silver bullet.

A necessary memory is that profit funded the first real media freedom – that is, made newspapers independent of patronage and political subsidy. Practices of independence, once developed, proved adaptable to different systems – remarkably, even to government-funded ones. Consistent with all this is that market dominion in modern states is unsustainable without political protection or collaboration.

Interaction with competitive markets naturally excites the authoritarian need for dominion. The contest of rough equals, a stimulus tolerable for most people – seductive for a few – irritates the authoritarian by its ambiguity. But the qualities which make competition a burden adapt neatly to reducing it: to marching media teams in and out of political alliances which offer a less stressful future.

This set of reactions is destructively unlike those a free political system needs. But the use of liberty to disguise them as healthy cannot be prevented – only discredited.

Product gaps will occur: the authoritarian can control, but not opti-mise journalistic performance. Newscorp can recruit passion adequate to editing the *Sun* or *News of the World* – low-grade products in secular, lucrative decline – or maintaining well-established acquisitions. Profound challenges – say, re-creating *The Times*, a high-grade product now gutted by Newscorp's reckless price warfare – demands something far more intense.

The British newspaper market's outstanding product of the last quarter-century is the *Daily Mail*: under Paul Dacre's editorship its sales grew 44 per cent between 1992 and 2002. It was not ripped off from anything existing, nor expanded by price-war. Liberals see vividly the vices – traceable back to Christiansen's *Express*: loathing of its passionate Thatcherism obscures virtues descended similarly. It has investigative force, and its targets – like the rich, fanatical Moonies, the Real IRA's bombers, genetic-engineering corporations, and racist gangsters – show the eclectic, risky nature pseudo-journalism lacks.

Murdoch offered Dacre *The Times* in 1992. Doubtless to Newscorp this was a marriage made in heaven, and to media liberals hell; but a real talent is rarely so predictable. Had Dacre done it, and made it, a *Times* would have appeared unlike either the *Mail* or the present-day *Times*: we can be sure only that it would not have marched for Blair in 1997.

Few journalists could outdo Dacre as avatar of the profit-seeking market or be closer philosophically to the Thatcherite Murdoch of 1992. He was certainly drawn to the task, aware perhaps of abilities suitable at least in scale. Still, he refused, from conviction that the independence essential for success was something Murdoch could not provide: 'I believe passionately that editors must be free to edit and that if they have a pro-prietor above telling them what to do, it all goes wrong.'

The market permits and even encourages this freedom, but provides no complete defence of it. The cause is visible in a famous statement from Rosa Luxemburg (and use of an eloquent Marxist voice may emphasise the irrelevance of partisan tribalism in this business):

Freedom only for the supporters of the government, only for the members of one party – however numerous they may be – is no freedom at all. Freedom is always and exclusively freedom for the

484

one who thinks differently . . . because all that is instructive, whole-some and purifying in political freedom depends on this essential characteristic, and its effectiveness vanishes when 'freedom' becomes a special privilege.

Freedom on this account is part of the system of public goods, which free riders – who cannot penetrate a market system directly – may desta-bilise. In our economic system the amount we will pay for something shows how much we desire it. The mathematical demonstrations don't convince everyone, but as market economies blow up less than planned ones it is hard to say it's all nonsense. The outcome is that those who express no preferences enjoy no goods.

Except with public goods. In a free country, for instance, everyone gets freedom regardless of preference. Of course public goods have to be paid for, but free riders who deny any preference for the goods – and don't pay – get the same benefits as those who contribute. Defence is a favourite illustration, partly because it is an instance where a compulsory 'preference' is politically acceptable. The issue is central to the construc-tion of tax systems, and their effectiveness depends on carefully balancing compulsion with voluntary disclosure.

Determined free riders do not seem to be numerous (societies in which they are become dilapidated). As a commercial example, few if any of Newscorp's competitors make similarly rigorous pursuit of negligible tax bills: perhaps because a complicated corporate structure brings many disadvantages. Compulsion of course does exist in tax systems, and nobody suggests that public goods could be financed without it being present as an option.

Naturally, when the goods in question are freedom as Luxemburg defined it, compulsion has limited use. People can't in principle be made to use the freedom of the press or compelled to contribute to the real cost – in which the crucial components have never been monetary. The First Amendment bargain mentioned early in this book is principally a compact of honour, only enforceable via indirect details – though these are not negligible items.

Freedom is exactly like other public goods, in that the rational indi-vidual action is to subscribe nothing personally but to make all convenient use of what others pay for. As it happens, human beings are not perfectly rational about this, and the reasons are not well understood. We can name them – honour, compassion, folly, rebelliousness – but these are labels more than explanation. From writers like Solzhenitsyn we can piece together some understanding, particularly of the costs.

Murdoch's record suggests he is perfectly rational. When pressed over non-publication of Chris Patten's *East and West* he said, 'Let somebody else annoy them' – that is, the Chinese Government, with which he was making peace. The free-rider ethic could not be more neatly put. But Murdoch isn't the text-book free rider, who conceals a preference for something actually desired, only to make use of it when others have paid. If he were that, he could not have made the progress we have seen. Murdoch, loudly and more consistently than any other Western publisher, presented himself for thirty years as gripped by an overmastering preference for freedom. Nobody could have ridden the theme harder. And without some such appearance, he would not have been able to extract from democratic systems the assistance, the special permissions, the waivers on which his operations rely. Political assistance alone would not have been sufficient.

It is the nature of a free society – in Luxemburg's account – that its members cannot be made to reveal their preferences. Not even someone who uses freedom to persuade people that he should be allowed to turn a free and diverse market into a monopoly. There is nothing to pay. But where freedom is a 'special privilege', preferences are starkly displayed. The China story reveals that Murdoch's preference for freedom only holds when the cost to himself is effectively zero. It demonstrates that the newspapers, television networks and book firms Murdoch controls – a substantial part of democracy's seeming armament – must be reckoned useless against any risk which might impose real costs on the boss. But there is also a message for the future.

Governments cannot allocate freedom, and perhaps can't do much themselves to protect this least dispensable of public goods. But governments can and must allocate the control and use of other public goods which give liberties material expression. This function is the reason Newscorp is interested in governments. The 'First Amendment bargain' is not overall enforceable. But governments do not have to – and must not be allowed to – hand over those goods to conspicuous free riders. It is unlikely there are very many of them about – at least, rigorous ones – or our world would not have got this far. But if we have created a society in which free riders are hard to detect, it would be suicidal for us to take no notice when they expose themselves.

NOTES

INTRODUCTION: DYNASTS IN CYBERSPACE

Epigraph. *The Jew of Malta*, Act IV, scene 1.

Shawcross interview. *Vanity Fair*, October 1999.

Davies Committee. Very few politicians and officials connected with the Blair government will discuss Murdoch's influence openly: many insist, like the Prime Minister himself, that it does not exist. These denials are treated as ritualistic by everybody in the media industries, but government sources will only discuss the real situation unattributably. Wherever possible this book uses attributable sources, but some exceptions must be made when describing power-networks still operating at full force.

Redstone. *Fortune*, 26 October 1998, 'The Rules According to Rupert'.

Coolly denied in public. J. G. A. Pocock in *The Machiavellian Moment* gives a more comprehensive statement which can hardly be improved. He translates Giovanni Cavalcanti as describing how:

> in the last phases of pre-Medicean rule, there came to be a strange discrepancy between what was said and who was elected in public assemblies of the republic, and what was determined and how it was determined in the political backrooms where things were actually done. Many were called and few were chosen, he observed; many were called to office and few to real power . . . Cavalcanti believed he was witnessing the decline of government by participation. Rule by the citizens themselves, on a footing of absolute or proportionate equality, was being replaced by the government of a courthouse gang, of which the Medicean machine politics that replaced it was only the culmination.

News and opinions. Fair Trading Act 1973, Part V, section 59(3).

Conventional politicians. For all three, their politics were essentially – even maniacally – open, and not a means to any other end. Beaverbrook was the Unionist MP for Ashton-under-Lyme from 1911 until 1916, when he was one of the power-brokers who replaced Asquith with Lloyd George. He was bitterly disappointed not to win Cabinet rank as a reward. He was persuaded for party loyalty's sake to shift to the House of Lords, and it was afterwards that he devoted himself principally to newspapers. (A. J. P. Taylor, *Beaverbrook*.) Hearst was elected to Congress as a Democrat in 1902, tried energetically to start a new, more radical (Independent) party, and having returned to the Democrats was considered as a Presidential candidate in 1912; his representative ambitions only slowly faded away. (David Nasaw, *The Chief*) Northcliffe never submitted himself to election, but considered his peerage acknowledgment of his standing as a leader of the nation: he was both overt and sincere, however deluded.

Japanese agent. See Chapter 4. Foot as KGB agent: Chapter 10 notes.

Scott. *Manchester Guardian*, 6 May 1926.

Murdoch. *A Current Affair* (date missing).

Slavery. From Professor Lessig's book *Code and Other Laws of Cyberspace*.

Independence. Andreas Whittam Smith, *Independent*, 9 October 2001.

1: A CONTINENT OF NEWSPAPERS

Epigraph 1, Bigelow. Quoted by Michael Schudson, *The Power of News*.

Epigraph 2, Wright. *Collected Verse*.

Improbable, etc. Blainey's most famous account of Australia is *The Tyranny of Distance* (1966) which made a powerful theme of remoteness. Later writers have criticised him in detail – and seen a lack of sympathy for the Aboriginal Australians. But his general point about the Australian achievement still has its strengths.

Anglo-Celtic tensions. Though 'only a small part of total emigration from Ireland, Irish immigrants were a higher proportion of the Australian population than in any other Irish migrant destination . . . [and possessed] confidence beyond their fellow Irish in North America and elsewhere (Professor Eric Richards in Davison et al., *The Oxford Companion to Australian History*). Some religious and ethnic hostility can be traced in almost every part of national life. It has been said that within the 'Invincibles', the great cricketing combination of the 1940s and 1950s, Bill O'Reilly and other Catholic (Irish) players were at odds with the Protestant Bradman. If such disunity existed, their opponents were never able to benefit from it.

***Tera nullius*, whispering.** The full story is given by Henry Reynolds, *The Law of the Land* (1987) and *This Whispering in Our Hearts* (1991). The Mabo decision in the High Court of Australia (1992) struck down the *terra nullius* principle, but the issue of land rights is modified rather than settled.

Melbourne. *The Rise and Fall of Marvellous Melbourne* by Graeme Davison describes the sudden transformation of an illegal settlement into a hectic metropolis. For this story Michael Cannon's *The Land Boomers* has maximum relevance as it is revealing about Theodore Fink, initial developer of the Herald newspaper empire.

Trollope made his first visit in 1871. *Australia* remains in print (University of Queensland Press; also Sutton Press Pocket Classics) and is well worth reading, if some appalling remarks about Aboriginal people can be overlooked.

Zenger. *The Press and America* by Michael Emery and others is probably the most accessible of numerous American references to this case. It deals with the issue of criminal libel, central to the relationship of press and state – a major theme of this story.

'No linear process . . .' is my own phrase, which I hope properly encapsulates Schudson's subtle account of the growth of press liberties.

Port Phillip Herald. Quotation from a collection of facsimiles published by Herald and Weekly Times in 1990.

Federal Commonwealth. *Our Future's Past*, written for the centenary, demonstrates the Australian and popular character of the constitutional debate – burying the curious myth of an imposition from London.

D. H. Lawrence. Cited by Humphrey McQueen in *Temper Democratic*. Lawrence is generally reckoned to have caught the physical environment of Australia brilliantly in *Kangaroo* (1925).

Twopeny succeeded as a journalist in Australia, but regarded himself as English, with a friendly but critical attitude to local institutions. He was also involved in Melbourne business, which he thought highly corrupt.

600 newspapers. Elizabeth Morrison in the Davison et al., *Oxford Companion to Australian History* cites the *Australasian Newspaper Directory* produced by the Gordon and Gotch advertising agency in 1888.

Cricket. Twopeny gives the cost at 10s 6d per word, which roughly converts to A$300. The central event of the tour was the initial 'Ashes Test' at the Oval.

Ned Kelly. The execution, and demonstrations against it, are reported in the *Herald* edition of 11 November 1880. Nobody wishing to survey the Kelly legend will have difficulty finding material. The most recent item, Peter Carey's novel *The True History of the Kelly Gang* (2001), has been read extensively in Britain and the US.

'Rivers of gold'. The first use of this phrase is hard to find, but its currency continues.

Words and drugs. Kipling's address to the Royal College of Surgeons, 1923.

Fink's career. Theodore Fink left his papers to Melbourne University, but nothing was done about them until the mid-1990s when Professor Don Garden was persuaded to take them in hand – perhaps rather against his will. However the result, *A Talent for Ubiquity*, is an intriguing account of a complex Australian. I have followed with gratitude in Professor Garden's track.

Secret compositions. This is Michael Cannon's special territory in *The Land Boomers*.

***Economist* on Newscorp finances.** Issue dated 18 May 1999.

Murdoch family, Scottish antecedents and David Syme. The basic biographical facts are well known and well stated by Shawcross, in *Murdoch*, and others, including the connection of Syme as Keith Murdoch's first employer. They don't record the deplorable character of the *Age* as an editorial environment, for which a primary source is Geoff Sparrow (ed.), *Crusade for Journalism*, the first official history of the Australian Journalists Association. Syme is a puzzling figure, described in detail by C. E. Sayers under the title *A Colonial Liberalism* – though he was an advocate of protection and of state socialism. Gaps between theory and practice were large: Syme supported the Anti-Sweating League, but sweated his own editorial employees (as Keith Murdoch made clear in later years). The AJA history is concerned with the setting up of the union in Melbourne in the early twentieth century. The central message is that the *Argus* and Fink's Herald group, though never enthusiasts of unionism, were businesslike and reasonable, whereas the *Age* victimised anyone suspected of union activity, a practice continued after Syme's death in 1908. Syme strove to repulse another wave of the future – federalism – until Theodore Fink assembled a group of Melbourne worthies which persuaded him that resistance was hopeless.

Printing technology. Emery et al., *The Press and America* deals concisely with the introduction of automatic typesetting and web printing. Kipling evokes web machinery through the names of two of the famous manufacturers ('The Harrild and the Hoe . . .') in 'The Press', verse epigraph for *The Village That Voted the Earth Was Flat*, a story about the Edwardian growth of mass communications.

Stringers, news philosophy etc. Max Frankel, *The Times of My Life – and My Life with The Times* (1999), a classic account of the reporter's work.

***Herald* machinery.** On 26 February 1923 the *Herald* published a special edition for its move into state-of-the-art offices in Flinders Street. This described the Hoe web installation of 1912, which was modernised and much expanded on the new site, giving at the same time details of the facilities for news reporting and processing of graphics.

2: THE CONSPIRATOR AS HERO

Epigraph. The famous equivocal essay in which Bacon says honesty is valued even by those who don't practise it but 'A mixture of a Lie doth ever add Pleasure'.

From a place . . . Weir's movie is available on video (VHR 3019) and the basic publicity material is repeated on the box. 'First and Second English officers' who demand the suicidal charge in which the hero dies are walk-on villains with exaggerated accents: their role is essentially fabrication.

Rupert was a backer. Murray Sayle, *Spectator*, 10 October 1981. The basic story, with variations, appears in many sources, including Shawcross, *Murdoch*. Sayle's version is cooler than most written from an Australian perspective.

Blood, etc. Figures and volunteer details are given later in this chapter.

Fink and the war. This follows Garden in *A Talent for Ubiquity*.

Gallipoli Peninsula campaign, etc. The literature on Gallipoli is huge, and often superb, including the latest comprehensive account, Les Carlyon's compassionate *Gallipoli*. This came out immediately after my own research, and I was glad to find that it reconciled the British, Australian and other versions, after decades of bitterness, as I have tried to do on a narrower scale – that is, where Keith Murdoch is involved. The basic facts are of course in the report of the Dardanelles Commission (1917) and the Australian and British official histories (Bean, *Anzac to Amiens*; Aspinall-Oglander, *Military Operations Gallipoli*). Bean's extraordinary bestseller *The Anzac Book* (1916), a kind of scrapbook of the campaign, made a strong impact on me as a Melbourne schoolboy around 1950, and probably still does so for others today. Alan Moorehead's *Gallipoli* is still good for atmosphere, and for scepticism about Keith Murdoch from a Melbourne *Herald* alumnus. Moorehead is criticised in Robert Rhodes James' *Gallipoli*, which was probably the first attempt at a balanced account – generally successful, though Rhodes James seems not to have found Australians very likeable. Geoffrey Serle's *Monash* is authoritative for his subject's period on the Peninsula and (temporary) lack of success. Topography and details of combat are synthesised from these and other sources (see below) but have been reviewed against Rhodes James and Carlyon, to be as consistent with them as possible. Many sidelights come from diaries, memoirs and polemics, principally General Hamilton's *Gallipoli Diary*, Ellis Ashmead-Bartlett's *Uncensored Dardanelles*, Compton Mackenzie's *Gallipoli Memories* and H. W. Nevinson's journalistic autobiography *Fire of Life*.

Two days later, etc. This sequence is uncontroversial, being given by Desmond Zwar, *In Search of Sir Keith Murdoch* and elsewhere.

Military innocent. That this notion should exist at all may seem curious, and is corrected by Peter Firkins, *The Australians in Nine Wars: Waikato to Long Tan*. It is partly explained by the social-democratic fabric of Australian society, where military and pacifist strands are closely interwoven. Eric Andrews, *The Anzac Illusion*, gives details of Australian military ambitions pre-1914.

Syd Deamer. Personal acquaintance with the Deamer family.

NOTES

Golden age of lying. This remark is usually attributed to the Labour MP Arthur Ponsonby, probably abbreviated from a sentence in his book *Falsehood in Wartime* (1928): 'There must have been more deliberate lying in the world from 1914 to 1918 than in any other period of the world's history.' Within a few years totalitarian regimes went much further, but the statement probably remains true of liberal-democratic societies.

Ashmead-Bartlett and the Anzacs. Andrews reproduces a cartoon of an elderly English lady asking two Anzacs which tribe they belong to.

Flowing robe. Nevinson, *Fire of Life*.

Light of battle. Melbourne *Herald*, September 1915.

The letter. Nevinson, *Fire of Life*, doesn't name Murdoch, but Ashmead-Bartlett, *Uncensored Dardanelles*, gives all these details.

Cabinet already knew. Sir Edward Cook, author of *Delane of The Times*, was the British censor 1914–18 and wrote a brief memoir, *The Press in War-Time* (1920). 'Sometimes the candour of the commanders and the Government was overborne by the optimism of the newspapers.' He quotes Bonar Law:

> After the . . . attack of August 6 all the papers were speaking as if we had won a great victory. We knew that we had, compared with what we aimed at, suffered a great failure . . . and it was decided at the Cabinet that a true and careful account of exactly what had happened should be prepared and issued to the Press. This was done . . . But what did we see? Coming down to the office next morning I saw on all the posters in big headlines, 'Gain of 800 yards at Gallipoli'.

Northcliffe's career is outlined generally in many works: Francis Williams, *Dangerous Estate* sets out the context well. References here to his military views and dealings with Keith Murdoch come from Reginald Pound and Geoffrey Harmsworth, *Northcliffe* (1959). This is the family version, based on Northcliffe's own papers – admiring, but not mendacious.

Northcliffe and Germany. *The Scaremongers* by A. J. A. Morris describes pre-1914 agitation for a showdown with Germany.

Haunted. Pound and Harmsworth, *Northcliffe*.

Murdoch Letter. The Public Record Office in London has the version printed for the Cabinet. The Australian National Library contains the version addressed to Fisher, which differs only in format.

Old brigadiers. Pearce letter: Australian National Library.

Monash not responsible. Serle, *Monash*.

August battles. This highly compressed account of intricate events synthesises Rhodes James, Serle, Carlyon and the official histories – see note on campaign above. Firkins, *Australians in Nine Wars*, and others have moving accounts of The Nek, which Weir handles brilliantly as the climax to his film.

Hamilton's staff, Dawnay's mission. Rhodes James' account in *Gallipoli* can be expanded from Dawnay's correspondence and notes in the Imperial War Museum, recording his departure from Imbros on 2 September 1915, his arrival in London on 10 September, and then almost daily meetings, official and social, with the King, Prime Minister, Kitchener, Cabinet ministers and senior officers. It is clear that his sober optimism about the campaign was decisively reversed in mid-August, due not to defeat alone, but to unrealistic reactions to it. A handwritten note from Asquith illuminates his relationship with the Prime Minister:

> 10 Downing Street
> Whitehall SW
> 2 Oct 1915
>
> My dear Dawnay
> Here at last is your Bridge debt.
> On reflection, I think it better not to trouble Sir Ian Hamilton with the text of the Australian letter, of which I spoke to you. It is largely composed of gossip and second-hand statements, and the antecedents of the writer are not such as to command much confidence.
> It may, however, do mischief in Australia, and there are certain specific points upon which we shall no doubt ask Sir I. Hamilton for explanation & comment.

Withdrawal. Dates recounted by Rhodes James, *Gallipoli*. Dawnay's letters to his wife make clear that he believed the campaign irreversibly lost, but feared to the last it might be restarted.

Ashmead-Bartlett interview and report of letter. *Sunday Times*, 22 October and 26 December 1915.

The Chief, etc. Pound and Harmsworth, *Northcliffe*. Northcliffe, if deluded, remained splendidly cool under German fire. One of his staff who proposed baling out of the house at midnight was told: 'I propose to be killed in my own bed, and I suggest you return to yours and do the same.' The authors spell out his military policy and his faith in Haig's tactics quite uncritically. Murdoch's intimacy with Northcliffe is described by Shawcross, *Murdoch*, and others; Andrews, *Anzac Illusion*, adds detail from Murdoch correspondence in the Australian National Library.

Somme and Arras campaigns 1916 and 1917. Peter Charlton's *Pozières* is often said to describe Australia's most harrowing action in 1914–18, but Andrews, *Anzac Illusion*, calls Bullecourt the 'nadir'. The Raws letter is quoted by Firkins, *Australians in Nine Wars*, who describes both fights in some detail. Melbourne *Herald* files were checked in the Public Library of Victoria, but there is a nearly complete run in the newspaper section of the British Library. Many fine British histories of the Somme campaign exist: I have used that of General A. H. Farrar-Hockley (*The Somme*), which is good on the interrelationship of the subsidiary battles which constitute the whole Somme (the moment, for instance, when the Australians handed over the 'subliminal dust' of Pozières to the Canadians. He makes clear in respect of Arras Gough's inadequacies and the ill-repute of his staff.

Killing-matches. This compresses a major controversy about the competence of the 1914–18 generals, and especially Haig. John Terraine appeared for Haig's defence in 1963 (*Douglas Haig: The Educated Soldier*) and Robin Neillands in *The Great War Generals on the Western Front* passionately represented virtually all of them in 1999. I have worked on the basis that, if they (especially Neillands) can find nothing to say, the case is hopeless. Neillands largely abandons Gough, for instance. Terraine retrieves a great deal for Haig the human being: Haig the general he acknowledges mistaken, but capable of backing people better than himself. Professional historians now think simplistic the idea that all 1914–18 generals were monsters, and my account accepts this.

Conscription campaign. This of course is a major passage of Australian history, recounted in the principal biography of Billy Hughes (Fitzhardinge). Eric Andrews' contribution in *Anzac Illusion* is to make clear the extent of Keith Murdoch's involvement in the campaigns as Hughes' ruthless agent. The Fitzhardinge account is sympathetic and treats Hughes as a dedicated if harsh Australian nationalist.

Everything I have. Murdoch was one of many witnesses called before the Dardanelles Commission which in 1917 investigated the conduct of the campaign, with results permanently injurious to Winston Churchill, its chief author. Murdoch repeated some of the allegations in his (unpublished) letter of 1915 but could not substantiate them.

Haig and Germany. Terraine, *Haig*.

Kaiserschlacht. The last German offensive is described in all general accounts of the First World War. Neillands' version in *Great War Generals* leans as far as respectably possible towards excusing Gough (and Haig) by blaming Lloyd George for holding back reinforcements. Terraine, *Haig*, is more emphatic than most Australian sources on the critical role of the AIF. Monash's own account, *The Australian Victories in France*, describes the tense moments before the halting of the German advance. Murdoch's 'advice' to Hughes is quoted by Serle, *Monash*.

Cost of heroism. Australia's population in 1914–18 was about 3.7 million. Figures from the Australian National War Memorial show that 416,809 men volunteered for service, of whom 331,781 went to war and 59,342 were killed – a rate against population of 16.04 per thousand. British Isles deaths per thousand were slightly higher, but roughly 50 per cent were conscripted. The 8,000 Australians killed at Gallipoli were 13 per cent of the total killed during the war. Canada's dead were 56,639 and New Zealand's 16,302.

Breaking the front. For brilliant exposition of military detail Monash's own account is unsurpassable, though the reader may not realise how much Currie and Plumer contributed. Neillands, *Great War Generals*, is a good corrective, and Plumer's entry in the *Dictionary of National Biography* helps.

Deamer's flight. Deamer family.

The Bean–Murdoch plot. The story was first exposed by Serle, *Monash*, but received little attention on publication in 1990. It is an intricate narrative which (happily) turned out to have little significance for Monash's career – the main concern of a substantial book. Of course it reveals appalling flaws in Bean and Murdoch – difficult subject matter for Australian-based writers. The estimate of Murdoch given by Phillip Knightley (*The First Casualty*) remains conventionally heroic.

3: THE SOUTHCLIFFE INHERITANCE

Epigraph 1, Lyons to Keith Murdoch. National Library of Australia, cited in George Munster, *Rupert Murdoch: A Paper Prince*.

Epigraph 2, Eugene Meyer. Cited by Katharine Graham in *Personal History*.

Biographical details of the Murdoch family are on record in numerous sources. William Shawcross received substantial assistance from Rupert Murdoch for his biography (*Murdoch*, 1992), and his account is generally the most detailed. The text was read (and to some extent edited) by Woodrow Wyatt as Murdoch's representative (see Wyatt, *Journals*, vol. 3). I have therefore treated it as being reasonably close to an official version.

Towering figure. John Grigg's volume in *The History of The Times* (vol. 6: *1966–1981*).

Comatose, expertise etc. This version appears in Shawcross, *Murdoch*, and to a lesser extent in other versions: Shawcross saying that the *Herald* was so loosely sub-edited that press releases were put straight into the paper. This story was told of the *Age* during its decrepit 1950s, but is highly unlikely to be true under the editorial system set up by J. C. Davidson (not that public-relations handouts were very common then). *Northcliffe* by Reginald Pound and Geoffrey Harmsworth (1959) is filial, but with access to family papers gives detail about Northcliffe's rise and discusses his eventual breakdown rather frankly.

Opinions of Northcliffe. Most standard accounts of British politics 1900–20 give similar accounts of the way Lloyd George and others saw Northcliffe.

Fink, Davidson, Murdoch, Innes. Don Garden, *A Talent for Ubiquity* (see notes to Chapters 1 and 2) remains the principal source for Fink's role at the Herald group. Professor Garden also made use of the Murdoch Papers in the National Library of Australia. References to Fink are from Garden unless otherwise stated.

Herald business, design etc. Munster, *Murdoch*, which takes the story to 1985, is much the best informed of previous accounts, especially on Australian background and newspaper economics generally. Garden comments on the *Herald*'s editorial development as seen in the Fink papers and describes manoeuvres over the editorship in 1920. Some of the financial details are supported by the (sadly incomplete) Melbourne Stock Exchange files at Melbourne University. The British Library contains a nearly complete run of the Melbourne *Herald* from 1890 to the present *Herald-Sun* which incorporates the once separate morning paper. Gaps in 1914–18 have been filled from the complete run in the Public Library of Victoria. Simple inspection shows a reasonably sophisticated broadsheet layout developing before the First World War, certainly far in advance of *The Times*, where Murdoch received some production training before returning to Melbourne. A *Herald* special supplement, *The Herald's New Home*, 26 February 1923, gave much detail of the new building and its equipment, which together with Garden's account shows that it must have been conceived by Fink and Wise. Garden cites Newscorp in 1995 attributing the work to Keith.

Murdoch arrives in Melbourne. Garden quotes *Smith's Weekly* on the Northcliffe–Murdoch golfing partnership and the discomfort of Wise.

Support by Northcliffe. Shawcross, *Murdoch*, describes the meeting with the Herald directors but does not mention Northcliffe's mental derangement. Garden quotes Murdoch's letter to Northcliffe giving thanks and describing lobbying.

'Chief', marriage etc. Murdoch's urbanity is common ground in Munster, *Murdoch*, Shawcross, *Murdoch*, and other accounts. Serle makes clear in *Monash* the hostility of both Monash and White to Murdoch continued (cloaked in outward correctness). Murdoch's attempt to decide the form of the state's war memorial was defeated by Monash after a long campaign.

'Greatest editor', etc. This is from Grigg, *History of The Times*, vol. 6, but is echoed in Shawcross, *Murdoch*, and others. Munster points out that Keith Murdoch published little or no serious journalism, and was mainly interested in using inside information for political and commercial purposes.

'Monty' Grover and A. N. Smith are well described in a study by the Department of Journalism at the Royal Melbourne Institute of Technology, which lists major Australian journalists and their distinctive publications.

Corporate manoeuvres in Western Australia, South Australia and

Queensland were described by Munster in *Murdoch* in 1985 and Shawcross' biography follows them in outline. Neither had use of the Fink papers available to Garden for his *Talent for Ubiquity*, which make clear that Fink was in overall command of the South Australian campaign in particular. Syd Deamer's role is mentioned by Munster and was amplified in personal interview (2000) by Adrian Deamer. Standard history is Henry Mayer, *The Press in Australia*.

John Wren and 'Red Ted' Theodore. The main facts about 'Red Queensland' in the 1920s are in several standard histories and summarised under various headings in the *Oxford Companion to Australian History*. Details of Wren's extraordinary quasi-criminal career and his involvement with Labor politicians and the Catholic Church continue to emerge. There is a wide range of academic material posted on the Net. *Power without Glory* (secretly published in 1950) is still worth attention. The impression left by Garden in *Talent for Ubiquity* is that Fink would not have taken the lead himself in dealing with so notorious a character as Wren, but was content to benefit personally if the younger and hungrier Murdoch chose to. As noted elsewhere, Fink had been ready to cut corners in his own early days.

Murdoch and Lyons. The lunch exchange is quoted by Munster in his *Murdoch* from Enid Lyons' memoirs (*Among the Carrion Crows*). Munster then discusses the subsequent relationship between Murdoch and the Prime Minister in detail, especially the argument over radio licences. Most Australian political sources agree on the closeness of the relationship between Lyons and the Herald group under Murdoch leadership.

Menzies, Murdoch and censorship. This bizarre story is visited very briefly in most accounts of Keith Murdoch's life, and there is very little trace of it in the Herald files. However, the basic facts were recorded at the time in non-Murdoch papers (*Sydney Morning Herald*, *Age* and so on) and are detailed by Garden in *Talent for Ubiquity* from the Fink papers.

Disappearance of Fink. Again, Garden's *Talent for Ubiquity* provides details. Melbourne University Press filed all the reviews of Garden's book, and there are none in Newscorp papers. John Fitzgerald in a personal interview described the 'absence' of the newspaper's founder. In my own time I never heard of Fink, which would be like training on the *Guardian* without hearing of C. P. Scott.

Rupert's youth, influences etc. This follows what he told Shawcross, who also interviewed Darling. The teacher (now deceased) quoted an extremely hostile portrait of a Murdoch-like baron from the Australian novelist Martin Boyd (in *Lucinda Brayford*, 1948). Web postings by ex-students of Darling's suggest that he evoked admiration from most of them.

498

Michael Schudson holds a chair of sociology at San Diego, and has published much scholarly work on media systems. The quotation is from *The Power of News*, in which most of his principal ideas appear, including the 'professional–commercial' model of American journalism. Schudson of course does not regard this as an ideal system, but convincingly shows that deliberate partisanship has declined with the development of professional journalistic education in university departments.

Professional development in Australia. Sparrow, *Crusade for Journalism*.

'God-given' gift. In Graham, *Personal History*.

The Red Badge of Courage. Crane's gifts are brilliantly discussed by Michael Robertson in *Stephen Crane: Journalism and the Making of Modern American Literature*, which cites the remark to Conrad. The *New York Times* on 27 August 2002, reporting memorial work at the Chancellorsville battlefield, referred matter-of-factly to Crane having fought there.

Fright, nausea etc. This is in Christiansen's autobiography *Headlines All My Life*. He is certainly not the only celebrated editor who admits to having found reporting extremely difficult and emotionally disturbing. Graham feels she was only adequate, and Christiansen perhaps rates himself lower – emphasising admiration for his betters.

Stenography, mental devices etc. Personal experience. The estimate of Australian reporters is in Christiansen, *Headlines All My Life*. Scott is cited above.

Britain's news system. Donald Read, *The Power of News*, the official Reuter history (not to be confused with Schudson above), gives details of the rise of news agencies in the second half of the nineteenth century.

Rupert and the *Herald* and *Birmingham Post*. The Shawcross and Munster Murdoch biographies square up reasonably. During the 1950s there was no awareness in the *Herald* newsroom that Rupert Murdoch had done any significant work on the paper – indeed, had been present at all. For separate reasons neither Shawcross nor Munster was familiar with the then Australian training system, though it indelibly marked anyone who experienced it.

Australian Broadcasting Tribunal records for Murdoch evidence (cited in Chapter 11).

'Keeping one's cool'. Jane M. Richards and James J. Gross, Department of Psychology Stanford University, in *Journal of Personality and Social Psychology*, September 2000. The abstract (which does inadequate justice to this brilliant paper) states:

> A process model of emotion suggests that expressive suppression should reduce memory for emotional events but that reappraisal should not. Three studies tested this hypothesis. Study 1 experimentally manipulated expressive

suppression during film viewing, showing that suppression led to poorer memory for the details of the film. Study 2 manipulated expressive suppression and reappraisal during slide viewing. Only suppression led to poorer slide memory. Study 3 examined individual differences in typical expressive suppression and reappraisal and found that suppression was associated with poorer self-reported and objective memory but that reappraisal was not. Together, these studies suggest that the cognitive costs of keeping one's cool may vary according to how this is done.

Self-assurance, accident. This is from Max Weber's celebrated essay, *The Profession of Politics*, 1919 (trans. Simona Dragici, 1989). Weber (1864–1920), a central figure in rigorous social science, is best known for *The Protestant Ethic and the Spirit of Capitalism* (1905). It is not widely realised that the 1919 essay is only a fragment of Weber's work on journalism and newspapers, in which he was deeply interested from 1905 onwards. Weber himself wrote for a variety of newspapers, and planned a major study on the press in Europe and America. The 1914–18 war and his early death frustrated this, but his journalistic work is being collected and published in German. *The Cambridge Companion to Weber*, ed. Stephen Turner, helps in tracking references to news-media issues which are scattered throughout his existing publications.

Rivett and family relationships. The *Oxford Companion to Australian History* is excellent on the persistent influence of distinguished families in Australian life and culture, somewhat modifying the stock notion of Australia as a proletarian enclave. The main facts of Rivett's life and the details of his relationship with the Murdochs are drawn from the Rivett family papers in the National Library of Australia, supplemented by personal interviews with Mrs Nancy Rivett, Professor Ken Inglis, David Bowman and others.

Rupert the Fear. Andrew Neil (*Sunday Times* editor 1982–92) in the *Guardian*, 2 March 1998.

Plato, *The Republic*, Book IX, 'On Right and Wrong Government: The Tyrannical Man'. This famous passage has been much discussed. The British philosopher R. G. Collingwood was one of the first to stress the labile, fluid quality of the tyrannical character ('jetsam, floating on the surface of the waves he pretends to control') as against the resolute despot ('The Three Laws of Politics', 1943, in his *Essays in Political Philosophy*).

Charm. There are innumerable references to Murdoch's charm and persuasiveness: a fairly detailed (and rueful) account is in Harold Evans, *Good Times, Bad Times*. Neil Chenoweth in *Virtual Murdoch* says his subject is the most persuasive force in the world.

Modern investigations. T. W. Adorno, Else Frenkel-Brunswik, Daniel J. Levinson and R. Nevitt Sanford, *The Authoritarian Personality* (1950) was initially funded by the American Jewish Committee as part of a series studying the origins of extreme right-wing regimes. The literature on the development of the Frankfurt School is of course part of the foundation material of modern social science. *Strength and Weakness: The Authoritarian Personality Today* by William F. Stone, Gerda Lederer and Richard Christie collects essays reviewing the vast literature which has criticised and developed *TAP* in the years 1950–92, including the extension to left-wing authoritarianism. Christie worked on the original surveys under Frenkel-Brunswik. Links between gullibility and authoritarianism are emphasised by Frenkel-Brunswick.

Rebel, outsider etc. Stelzer, an economist and columnist for Newscorp's *Sunday Times*, is quoted extensively in the Wyatt *Journals*, where Murdoch's supposedly rebellious character is presented as a refreshment to British society.

Oxford's 'extraordinary success . . .' Professor John Kay in the University Council, 1999.

Lenin, etc. The anecdote of the bust is well known, and confirmed by Murdoch to Shawcross. As stated, Murdoch's activity in the Cole Group appears in his correspondence with Rivett. Cole (1889–1959) was Chichele Professor of Social and Political Theory. The Group was 'recruited each year from the Oxford University Labour Party and Ruskin College by the previous year's group . . . it met one evening a week during term-time and discussed the social, economic and political ideas that interested the members . . . [it] helped prevent radical people from following the Communists into the political wasteland' (L. P. Carpenter, *G. D. H. Cole: An Intellectual Biography*, 1973). The essence of the Group was an interest in the realities of political power. Cole's wife Margaret (a Cambridge alumnus) thought it might be over-successful in establishing a grip over British Labour politics (*Growing Up into Revolution*, 1949).

'Help bring about the inevitable' was Karl Popper's caustic version of much socialist motivation prior to the fall of communism. Leszek Kolakowski in *Main Currents of Marxism* (1978) discusses the attraction of Marxism during the first half of the twentieth century as a route to power and prestige likely to appeal to ambitious authoritarians. Eric Beecher (editor Melbourne *Herald* 1978–82) interviewed by Christopher Hird (*Murdoch*, 1990) thought Rupert developed a fascination with political power-figures early in life through the example of his father (who also displayed left-wing attitudes when Labor dominated Australian politics pre-1917).

Pickering and the *Express*. Shawcross, Munster and other sources mention this connection. A fine account of the rise of the *Express* is in Francis (Lord) Williams, *Dangerous Estate*. This is supplemented by Christiansen (*Headlines All My Life*) and by the author's personal observation of Fleet Street (*Evening*

Standard 1960–2; *Daily Herald* 1962–4), by discussion with Michael Foot, Adrian Deamer and others, together with accounts in A. J. P. Taylor, *Beaverbrook*; Michael Davie and Anne Chisholm, *Beaverbrook*; William Barkley, *Reporter's Notebook*; James Cameron, *Point of Departure*; René MacColl, *Deadline and Dateline*. The decline of the *Express* is brilliantly evoked by Anthony Delano in *Slip-Up*.

Bribes, etc. This point is made in Williams, *Dangerous Estate*, and the honesty of Australian papers is described by Twopeny, *Town Life in Australia*. Copper in *Scoop* (1938) by Evelyn Waugh is generally reckoned a composite caricature of Northcliffe and Rothermere.

See you to the devil. Captain Stevens' conversion is in Dennis Griffiths' history *Plant Here The Standard* (1996).

More powerful. There is ample evidence in Pound and Harmsworth, *Northcliffe*, for Northcliffe's belief that he enjoyed more power as a newspaper magnate than he could as a Cabinet minister. But there is also much evidence for his delusionary cast of mind.

Legendary Baldwin oration. The best account is in Keith Middlemas and John Barnes, *Baldwin: The Unknown Prime Minister*. Kipling and Baldwin were connected through the Burne-Jones family (Pre-Raphaelites). Kipling first used the 'harlot' phrase as a rebuke to Beaverbrook in a personal argument: the *Kipling Journal* (2002) quotes Baldwin's letter asking permission to use it in public.

Hot-metal technology. Compresses press history references with my own personal experience as reporter and production executive on several newspapers. Christiansen's role is described (admiringly) by Williams in *Dangerous Estate* and (modestly) by Christiansen himself in *Headlines All My Life*.

Hardware, bandwidth limits. 'High-speed' (56k/byte) modems are the present maximum for analogue telephone installations and are borderline for real Web access. The spread of ADSL and cable-modems offering data-transfer speeds up to ten times higher increases the possibility of real Internet newspapers. But many issues remain – the size and weight of monitors, resolution and refresh rates and so on. Possibilities for the electronic newspaper are important but most prophecies inspired by the Internet bubble have collapsed with it.

Electronic print technology. Even standard word-processors can perform instantaneously type-management operations which were arduous in hot-metal. Comparison is truly dramatic with publishing systems like QuarkXPress or Adobe InDesign.

Christiansen's disciples. Williams, *Dangerous Estate* and personal observation. James Cameron in *Point of Departure* describes vividly the barrier many good journalists found in hot-metal editorial technology. He was appointed mistakenly as an *Express* sub in 1940, and was dysfunctional, but as he had been exempted from military service (also mistakenly, as it turned out) the *Express* would not let him go. Only after 1945 did Christiansen agree that 'I would never be able to work out a heading across four columns in 48-point Cheltenham Bold without using my fingers' and allow Cameron to become a brave and eloquent foreign correspondent.

British subs best. Murdoch has repeatedly made this point during interviews, especially in disparagement of American newspapers (see Chapter 7).

Big toad. Quoted in David Dary, *Red Blood and Black Ink: Journalism in the Old West*.

Page-one purpose. Quoted in Williams, *Dangerous Estate*.

Hard, bright expertise and its fascination. Adrian Deamer taped biographical interview, Australian National Library, and personal discussions with him at various times.

The 'newcomer' memo referred to the *Daily Express* front-page lead on 21 October 1951.

Northcliffe considering readers were 'only ten'. Williams, *Dangerous Estate*.

'Up-market shit'. Murdoch discussion with Godfrey Hodgson c.1975 re Mirrorscope feature in *Daily Mirror* (personal from Hodgson).

No subject etc . . . Christiansen in *Headlines All My Life*; similar statements from Greeley, are in Emery et al., *The Press and America*. Synecdoche and the avoidance of numerical reality is analysed further in Chapter 9. Real decline in child murder being accompanied by a popular belief in its increased danger culminates with the tabloid (especially *News of the World*) coverage of the Sarah Payne case in 2001.

'Tabloidization'. David C. Krajicek in *Scooped! Media Miss Real Story of Crime while Chasing Sex, Sleaze and Celebrities*.

'Faraway country'. Christiansen in *Headlines All My Life*. Beaverbrook and the *Express* supported Appeasement (Richard Cockett, *Twilight of the Truth*) but changed dramatically when war broke out. Michael Foot, a socialist anti-appeaser, was made editor of the *Evening Standard*; he and Beaverbrook (intimate friends) agreed that they would inevitably become political opponents some time after the war. Many gifted journalists covered the war for the *Express*, pre-eminently Alan Moorehead. Not the least of Christiansen's achievements was packing Moorehead's dispatches into four or six pages of rationed newsprint. Moorehead's own account is *African Trilogy*, comparable with the best of Crane. The Library of America offers two superb volumes: *American Journalism: Reporting World War II: 1938–1944* and *1944–1946*. Sadly no British collection is as thorough.

'**Common Market' attacks.** Personal knowledge of the journalist who was hired for this task.

'**I picked it up . . .**' Barkley in *Reporter's Notebook*. However, in 1953, when Murdoch was there, the *Express* was still dauntingly slick in the production technology of the time. Nobody was taken on to the subs' desk with the trivial experience Murdoch then had – or would have survived had it occurred. Cameron's wartime experience was special to the time.

Ease of writing leaders. Pringle's autobiography *Have Pen Will Travel*.

Parents, children and independence. The Adorno analysis of authoritarianism is extended and refined in the work of Erich Fromm, particularly *The Anatomy of Human Destructiveness* (1974), which discusses the need to develop independently from parents. Material from his earlier *Fear of Freedom* (1942) is encapsulated, recording the Frankfurt School's pioneer studies among working-class Germans in the 1930s. The historian Richard Hofstadter summarised much of this (using language perhaps more graceful than that of the psychologists) in *The Paranoid Style in American Politics* where he connects authoritarian attitudes to 'pseudo-conservative' politics, which lack the essential moderation of traditional conservatives (like Eisenhower or Macmillan):

> Among those (Adorno) found . . . to have strong ethnic prejudices and pseudo-conservative tendencies, there is a high proportion of persons who have been unable to develop the capacity to criticise justly and in moderation the failings of parents and who are profoundly intolerant of the ambiguities of thought and feeling that one is so likely to find in real-life situations. For pseudo-conservatism is among other things a disorder in relation to authority, characterised by an inability to find other modes for human relationship than those of more or less complete domination or submission. The conservative always imagines himself to be dominated and imposed upon because he feels that he is not dominant, and knows no other way of interpreting his position.

Fromm emphasises that authoritarianism is rare. Of German workers surveyed in 1932 the majority (78 per cent) were not authoritarian. About 12 per cent had solidly tolerant principles, and only 10 per cent seemed likely to become ardent Nazis (the contemporary authoritarian option). Also Fromm is highly critical of the famous 'punishment' experiment of Stanley Milgram (1965) and of Phillip Zimbardo's 'Stanford Prison Experiment' (1971), both of which have been taken to show that majorities are authoritarian and perhaps sadistic. Fromm is emphatic that most people mature without major authoritarian damage, and that society usually contains a leavening of ruggedly tolerant individuals. (In 2001 the BBC abandoned an attempt to restage the Zimbardo experiment after heavy criticism of its methodology.) 'The main result of Milgram's study,' Fromm observes, 'seems to be one he does not stress: the presence of conscience in most subjects . . . The Nazis had to use an elaborate system of camouflage of atrocities in order to cope with the conscience of the average man.'

Inheritance. Sir Keith Murdoch's will is an involved document due to numerous codicils and alterations.

'I think he's got it'. This anecdote is in Shawcross, *Murdoch*, and other versions.

'His ideals'. *British Journalism Review*, January 2000: Rupert Murdoch interviewed by Bill Hagerty.

Table talk. Woodrow Wyatt, *Journals*, vols 1 and 2.

Courtiers. Neil, *Guardian*, 2 March 1998.

Each man for himself. Stevens quoted in Hobson et al., *The Pearl of Days*, official history of the *Sunday Times*.

4: BLACK JACK AND THE STUDENT PRINCE

Epigraphs. Rochefoucauld's style (1613–80) was unlike that of the third man in the Kelly–Nash–Arvey machine which ran Chicago in Roosevelt's time; both, however, saw politics as a trade in favours. Charles B. Cleveland's profile of Arvey is in *Illinois Issues* 34 (November 1977), Sangamon State University (http://www.lib.niu.edu/ipo/ii7711tc.html).

Sir Keith installed etc. Acquisition of the *News* and appointment of Rivett is recounted by Munster, *Murdoch*, and largely followed by Shawcross, *Murdoch*, and others.

'Great comfort' is from Lady Murdoch's letter to Rivett 1960 (dated only 'Sunday' but probably 17 July 1960), Box 5 Rohan Rivett MS8049/2/19, Rivett family papers in the National Library of Australia.

Not the easiest man. David Bowman letter to Rivett, 1960 (Rivett papers), expanded by interview, 18 November 2002.

The *Bulletin*, founded 1880, carried the White Australia banner for most of its independent career. Donald Horne became editor on the Packer takeover in 1961 and removed it.

Playford's dominion over South Australia is described in Munster, *Murdoch*, following standard sources. Professor Ken Inglis, who was on the Adelaide faculty when he wrote *The Stuart Case* (1961), neatly conveys its extension into academic life.

Murder at Ceduna. This generally follows Munster, *Murdoch*, and Inglis, *Stuart Case*, taking account of Professor Inglis' revised edition (2002) which includes interviews with Stuart (see below).

Williams, Henderson, Menzies. Commercial television and journalism. Munster's account in his *Murdoch* is supplemented by personal recollection.

Rivett's challenge to the South Australian authorities was a striking example to my generation of Melbourne *Herald* trainees. Many of us wished to think well of Rupert Murdoch.

Cultural detonators. Henry Fairlie's initial 'establishment' articles were in the *Spectator*, 23 and 30 September 1955, and their resonance continues. Chapter 14 analyses this influential coinage and its importance to Murdoch's business.)

'Surged and fought'. Professor Inglis supplied a copy of this letter written to him by Reid, 25 July 1961, in which he says he takes no offence at references to him in Inglis' coverage of the Stuart case in *Nation Review*. The material of those reports provided a basis for *The Stuart Case*, which is the chief descriptive source.

Status of judges. Australian Associated Press, 8 November 1999, reported a solicitor in a Melbourne property case as saying that the judge 'has got his hand on his dick'. Mr Justice Philip Cummins ruled: 'It may be offensive, but it is not contempt of court for a person to describe a judge as a wanker.'

Royal Commission crisis. The basic facts are common to Inglis, *Stuart Case*; Munster, *Murdoch*; and Shawcross, *Murdoch* – the latter leaning towards Murdoch's own interpretation that Rivett's judgment was eccentric. There seems no real doubt that the news-bill which went too far was Murdoch's – exactly the kind of error inexperienced headline-writers make. David Bowman, who was reporting the case, realised at once that the *News* would be in trouble – not because the error was serious, but because the authorities would attack on any pretext.

Zenger. *The Press and America*, describes Andrew Hamilton's defence of Zenger. In Chapter 7 we come to *Alexander* Hamilton's follow-up blow against criminal libel. Essentially this law died at the hands of the US Supreme Court in 1812, but here and in Chapter 6 we are concerned with the corpse still twitching in twentieth-century Australia.

Bid for the *Advertiser*. Munster, *Murdoch*, describes Murdoch's attempt to ally himself with the powers of Adelaide and Sir Mellis Napier's proposed role. A note by Professor Inglis should not be forgotten: Sir Mellis supported Inglis' promotion within the university, though he is unlikely to have enjoyed *The Stuart Case*.

Mirror Group Newspapers. Inglis describes Murdoch's elation in his historical essay about *Nation Review* (*Nation: The Life of an Independent Journal of Opinion*).

John Norton and *Truth*. Cyril Pearl's *Wild Men of Sydney* often beggars belief but is generally accepted as realistic.

Murdoch sacks Rivett. This is Rivett's own typescript in his papers at the

National Library (Rohan Rivett MS8049/2/19) headed 'The Australia [Hotel] Melbourne, Sunday July 17 1960' and addressed to Sir Stanley Murray Chairman of Directors News Ltd Adelaide SA. It runs to about 900 words, cleanly typed, going into detail about handover arrangements and farewells to colleagues, then commenting on the two dismissal notes, particularly Murdoch's failure to make any personal contact in spite of the suggestion that he means to do so:

> Mr Murdoch has spoken vaguely of talks and specifically of having 'many reasons'. There have been no talks in the 10 days since my dismissal nor any reasons advanced. In the 12 days since the letters were written he has not contacted me although I . . . could have been reached in a matter of minutes.
>
> This seemed to me – and to everyone who has expressed an opinion on it – a strange course of action, firstly in view of a friendship lasting 14 years, secondly in view of the very firm partnership which had existed especially following the death of Sir Keith Murdoch in October, 1952 and continued and developed mostly long before . . .

The document is unsigned, and is presumably not the version sent to Murray. Possibly it was superseded by advice Murray gave to Rivett (see below) and not sent at all.

The two dismissal notes are also in the Rivett papers, along with the numerous letters expressing regret, amazement and incredulity, among them Professor Walter Murdoch (26 July 1960 and 3 August 1960) saying he has heard various stories, 'all of them ugly', about Rupert's behaviour.

No protest by Rivett. Mrs Nan Rivett explained to me in several conversations in 1999 the advice Sir Stanley Murray gave her husband.

Changing editorial course. The *News* (Adelaide), 15 and 29 July 1960, *Daily Mirror* (Sydney), 29 July 1960. David Bowman (18 November 2002) said that Rivett's successor Ron Boland instituted a practice of having *Mirror* editorials transmitted to Adelaide: the time-gap enabled him to ensure against the *News* getting out of line.

Meeting the Queen. *Canberra Times*, 3 May 2000.

Forgetting. Quoted by Olivier Todd, *Albert Camus*. At the end of 2002 the national memory was powerfully revived when Stuart's story was turned into a movie, *Black and White*, by Craig Lahiff – one in a series of productions (including *Rabbit Proof Fence*) revisiting the oppression of black Australians. David Ngoombujarra played Stuart; Ben Mendelsohn, Rupert Murdoch; John Gregg, Rohan Rivett; Robert Carlyle, the defence lawyer David O'Sullivan). This also was the occasion for Professor Inglis' new edition, with extensive material on Stuart's after-life. Having become literate in jail and overcome (eventually) his drinking problems, Stuart now ranks as a stable and respected elder of the Arrernte community, able to point out in retirement that his life-history doesn't resemble that of the violent paedophile, where recidivism is the usual case. Murdoch, in Adelaide for News Corporation's AGM, produced a curious memory for an ABC radio show (*The 7.30 Report*, 30 October 2002). There had been pride at the *News*, he said, for circulation maintained, as Stuart 'was not a popular cause'. And, with apparent seriousness: 'I remember being tried for treason.' David Bowman was astonished that anyone should remember a treason trial – many steps past even Tom Playford's imagination – or assume Stuart's cause necessarily unpopular. Circulation of the *News* rose consistently under Rivett. But Max Stuart, in the same programme, was understandably happy to overlook any oddities of memory: 'If we hadn't had Rupert Murdoch, I would have been down Adelaide jail now, been buried there in an unmarked grave.'

Boland obituary. The *Australian*, 28 April 2000. This baldly records his appointment to the *News* as consequent on his predecessor's departure 'in the wake of a judicial and criminal justice controversy which led to complex libel actions successfully defended by the company'. During his seventeen years as editor there seems to have been no journalistic achievement that needed recording (the swimsuit campaign predated WWII).

Television manoeuvres, Murdoch, Frank Packer and others. This is a compression of Munster's superb analytical narrative in *Murdoch*, which demonstrates that the prizes sought were essentially monopolies and quasi-monopolies distributed by the state – though public-service obligations were to be minimal compared to those imposed on the state's own monopoly (the ABC) and fairly simply avoided.

McEwen connection. Eric Walsh, still very much a presence in Australian politics, outlined this to me in January 1999. Peter Golding's *Black Jack McEwen: Political Gladiator* is the essential overall source for this remarkable life, and discusses the 'surrogate parent' relationship with Murdoch. Both Walsh and Golding are supplemented from John Menadue's memoir, *Things You Learn Along the Way*, amplified by discussion with Menadue himself. As a young reporter I heard political experts discussing McEwen's combination of factional skill and pragmatism; some referred to him as 'the man who had to screw his hat on', which Walsh and Menadue consider harsh.

Corporatism has a rather modest literature, but Keith Middlemas, *Politics in Industrial Society* (1979) describes some of the characteristics from British experience. Ralph H. Bowen in *German Theories of the Corporate State* describes early manifestations in the first half of the last century.

Campaigning for McEwen. Eric Walsh has entertaining memories of attempts to promote the Country Party in the *Daily Mirror*, puzzling its Sydney working-class clientele. Murdoch realised that he needed a paper which Canberra politicians would read.

The *Australian* – intentions and early difficulties. Again, Munster, *Murdoch*, gives the main story. John Pringle, editor of the rival *Canberra Times*, describes the other side of the hill in his memoir *Have Pen Will Travel*. Accounts in interview from David Bowman and the late Adrian Deamer confirm the general picture of a newspaper in deep disarray.

Wrong date. Walsh tells this story with some relish.

Launch, defective news coverage and falling sales. Munster, *Murdoch*, gives the sales figures and expert critique of the *Australian*'s news coverage.

Maxwell Newton. The biographical note in the National Library of Australia outlines a remarkable career. Born in Perth in 1929 he was a brilliant student at the University of Western Australia, the Sorbonne and Cambridge (where he graduated with a first in Economics in 1953). He was an economist for the Commonwealth Treasury until 1960 when John Pringle hired him as a political correspondent for the *Sydney Morning Herald*. In 1963 he launched the very successful *Australian Financial Review* for Fairfax. He was essentially a freelance after breaking with Murdoch, but in 1980 they were reconciled and he became a columnist for the *New York Post*. He died in Florida in 1990. His libertarian viewpoint implied that corporatism contained seeds of fascism. But he made himself ridiculous by asserting that Australia actually became fascist in the 1980s.

Catholic children, etc. Munster quotes this statement in *Murdoch* – never a decent comment on Australian Catholicism, but grossly out of touch in 1960s and the era of Vatican II.

Anti-semitism of the intellectuals. No exact citation of this has been found, but Professor Peter Viereck's colleagues at Mt. Holyoake College are sure that he originated it.

Newton's letter is quoted in Munster, *Paper Prince*. Pringle clearly enjoyed publishing it. 'Leaving the field to us' is from *Have Pen Will Travel*.

'Disaster'. Menadue, who was general manager of the *Australian*, thought Murdoch was near to closing the paper in 1967.

Harold Holt and succession struggle. This episode, concluding with the *Australian*'s contribution to McEwen's victory after the death of Holt, has been described often – notably by Munster. But the version here goes further in making clear the undercover role of the Australian intelligence services, disclosed by Alan Ramsey of the *Sydney Morning Herald* (23 September 2000). Menadue's memoirs, *Things You Learn Along the Way*, and discussion with him and Adrian Deamer, added detail and corroboration; Alan Ramsey added more from his long personal knowledge of Canberra politics.

ASIO history and the 'Scorpion'. Brian Toohey and William Pinwill recount some hair-raising episodes in *Oyster*.

ASIO documents. Ramsey in *Sydney Morning Herald*, as above. The circumstances in which Ramsey got them from the Australian National Archives are described below.

McMahon's suspicions. Ramsey had many discussions at the time with McMahon, who often demanded late-night street meetings, and limited his telephone conversations.

Death of Holt. Kim Torney's note in the *Oxford Companion to Australian History*, ed. Davison et al., records the currency of the Chinese submarine, but naturally treats it as fantasy.

McEwen's manoeuvres. Ramsey reconstructed these from the Scorpion's pedantic notes, which exactly accord with the public facts but of course add a dimension wholly invisible at the time.

'Disclosure' in the *Australian*. Munster describes this and hints at ASIO involvement – but had no proof at the time he wrote (1984). Menadue, *Things You Learn Along the Way*, describes the story as 'a terrible beat-up' (newsroom language for 'wild exaggeration') produced by Murdoch. Deamer thought it unprofessional rubbish, but had only just joined the paper and had no editorial authority.

Ramsey's disclosure. Ramsay went to the archives to check files which he knew to exist – the police files relating to the notorious raids on Newton. The story ran during the Sydney Olympics – Australians usually take note of tales of political skulduggery, but would ignore the Second Coming during a major sporting occasion.

***News of the World*.** The mechanics of the Sunday popular market which it dominated were always well known in Old Fleet Street, and are described with a certain relish in *The News of the World Story* by Cyril Bainbridge and Roy Stockdale, beginning with its nineteenth-century origins and extending to the early Murdoch period.

'Hansard of the sleazy'. Reg Cudlipp, Hugh's brother, one-time *NoW* editor, quoted by Bainbridge and Stockdale.

***News of the World* takeover.** Bainbridge and Stockdale, Shawcross (*Murdoch*) and Munster all give roughly similar accounts of divisions in the Carr family, unscrupulous attacks on the unscrupulous Maxwell and so on and other public facts of this notorious City duel. 'Bumptious swindler' is a personal judgment based on extensive contemporary investigations of Maxwell which I carried out with colleagues from the *Sunday Times* (1969 onwards). Tom Bower looked still further into the story in later years, and his *Maxwell: The Outsider* is definitive.

Script by Catto. Dominic Hobson, in *The Pride of Lucifer* (1990), records the rising arrogance and subsequent fall of Morgan Grenfell, with interesting details on the *NoW* affair (see below).

Defeat of Maxwell. Files of the *Financial Times*, December 1968 to January 1969, show almost daily coverage up to the decisive meeting, with criticism of the rival bidders' behaviour and suggestions that the City authorities should have restrained them.

Out of Scotch. The details are given by Golding in *Black Jack McEwen*. Walsh recalls driving Murdoch to The Lodge (official Canberra residence of the Prime Minister) for a celebration drink with Gorton on the successful conclusion of the *NoW* deal.

'Jungle'. Hobson, *Pride of Lucifer*, cites the agreement of an unnamed Morgan director as an example of the bank's contempt for the City's contemporary regulators.

Bushwhacking Murdoch. Maxwell was an early case of a now notorious phenomenon in which auditors allow bogus transactions to transform the bottom line. 'THE ANATOMY OF A PERGAMON PROFIT' (*Sunday Times*, 1969) led to an official inquiry which judged Maxwell unfit to run a public company. He was allowed nonetheless to take over the London *Daily Mirror*, with disastrous consequences for newspaper competition.

Sober after lunch. Murdoch to the author in 1969, during interview for Maxwell investigations (see above).

Trade in prurience. Bainbridge and Stockwell, *News of the World Story*. Details of the defence deals with murderers show the London criminal bar in a very dubious light.

Backlash. Harry Evans, then editor of the *Sunday Times*, describes in *Good Times, Bad Times* inviting Rupert and Anna Murdoch to dinner and finding both of them resentful and puzzled by the chorus of denunciation.

Low work in high places. Murdoch gave the annual A. N. Smith Memorial Lecture in Journalism at Melbourne University on 15 November 1972. Smith, a founder of the Australian Journalists Association (1910), was an exponent of non-partisan political analysis. On his death in 1935 the lecture was set up to give journalists (and sometimes politicians) an opportunity to discuss their work with intellectual rigour. Murdoch is in a list that includes John Pringle, Adrian Deamer, Laurie Oakes, Michelle Grattan, Bob Hawke, Mary Delahunty and Kim Beazley. His Profumo assertions may have been the lecture's least distinguished moment.

London Weekend Television. Jeremy Potter's official history, *Independent Television in Britain*, vol. 3: *Politics and Controls* (1989), is the basic source.

'I have given my word', etc. Personal discussion with Dr Tom Margerison, 13 October 1999, reconfirmed subsequently.

Character assassination. Sir Brian Young, then head of the IBA, and David Glencross concede that Murdoch was under attack in the press but firmly deny that the IBA was responsible for the fact or influenced by it. Murdoch quite clearly was taking control, and nobody with such significant newspaper holdings could legally do so: issues of residence and character were never discussed. Anthony Pragnell, who wrote that LWT's licence might be invalidated, was unable for health reasons to discuss the episode with me, but Glencross, present at the time, was clear on the sequence of events. Sir Brian Young (9 May 2001) said he did not believe there was any basis to Murdoch's claim that Margerison was incompetent.

5: TRADING TABLOID PLACES

Rise of the *Sun*. The indispensable history is Peter Chippindale and Chris Horrie's *Stick It Up Your Punter*, which reflects much personal experience. There are passages in which it comes close to falling for the 'boys (and girls) will be boys' defence, and/or for the 'down with snobs' defence, but mostly the authors are ruthlessly clear-eyed. Larry Lamb's *Sunrise* covers the same early ground, but naturally with more self-congratulation. Roy Greenslade's memoir of his part in the *Sun*'s first night (*Guardian*, 15 November 1999) explains clearly why the initial crew-members were on board.

Cudlipp's champagne. The sad complacency of the *Mirror*'s top brass is a famous legend of Fleet Street. Mike Molloy and Tony Miles (both editors of the *Mirror* subsequently) described this in similar terms. My account of the *Mirror*'s decline was much helped by recollections from them and from Tony Delano.

Circulation figures. Unless otherwise stated, all these are drawn from the database of the Audit Bureau of Circulations. Records back to the 1930s have now been converted to electronic form, but are inevitably sketchy in the early periods, when major newspapers like the *Daily Telegraph* refused to take part. Now it is impossible to run a newspaper business without audited sales figures. Many imperfections remain, as the ABC staff readily admit, but at least the system is good enough to smooth out misleading short-term trends.

Tabloids. Northcliffe is supposed to have adapted the term from pharmaceutical marketing. David C. Krajicek's concern in *Scooped! Media Miss Real Story of Crime while Chasing Sex, Sleaze and Celebrities* is that of an experienced crime reporter anxious to show that popular journalism can and should be serious.

Spiked with invective. A representative comment is Anthony Lewis of the *New York Times* covering a British general election, and seeing journalism of 'a kind now hardly known in the United States; grotesquely partisan, shamelessly advancing one party's cause' (*International Herald Tribune*, 3 April 1992).

Daily Herald. Francis (Lord) Williams, at one time its editor, gives most of its history in *Dangerous Estate*. I worked there in 1962 and found it depressing after a rather exhilarating period on Beaverbrook's *Evening Standard*. There was no temptation to remain for IPC's relaunch of it as the *Sun* – because this, while based on interesting sociology, included no provision for effective news-gathering, which I was trained to consider indispensable.

Devious Briginshaw. Chippindale and Horrie's account in *Stick It Up Your Punter* is confirmed by Geoffrey Goodman, then industrial editor of the *Mirror*.

Early *Sun*, premises, content etc. Greenslade adds some detail to the Chippindale–Horrie picture. Jacqueline Susann's remarkable work is still in print.

Murdoch the reformer. This comes from Menadue (*Things You Learn Along the Way*), a severe Murdoch critic, and sympathisers usually take the idea much further. The element of truth in the generalisation was corruption in industrial relations – an important one, but as shown by the cynical manoeuvre with Briginshaw (see above) one that Murdoch was then far from challenging.

Bartholomew, Cudlipp and the *Mirror*. Williams in *Dangerous Estate* describes Bartholomew's career from personal acquaintance. Hugh Cudlipp in *Walking on the Water* adds some rather chilling personal insights. Mike Molloy pointed out the *Mirror*'s Little Rock coverage to me.

Mark Abrams. The work Dr Abrams did for IPC's *Sun* launch was the basis for a large presentation at the Café Royal in 1963: this is well remembered by Geoffrey Goodman, Molloy and other *Mirror* veterans. The documents on which it was based do not appear to be among Abrams' voluminous papers in Churchill College, Cambridge but there is no doubt about the basic thrust, which was in tune with his general outlook, reflected in political works such as *Must Labour Lose?* (1960) written with Professor Richard Rose. Professor Harry Henry, a pioneer of newspaper marketing for Roy Thomson, recalls Abrams as a 'visionary'. Masterman's observation is in *The Double-Cross System*, a history of intelligence in WWII.

Mirrorscope **and Larry Lamb.** Chippindale and Horrie, *Stick It Up Your Punter*, report this largely from Lamb's view – as he does himself in *Sunrise*. Delano, Miles, Molloy and other *Mirror* veterans take a variety of views, but agree that for it to have succeeded much more time and determination would have been needed.

Recruitment. Godfrey Hodgson, after joining Times Newspapers in 1957, received a questionnaire asking him to list his school, college, regiment and clubs – and state whether he had a private income. Nicholas (Nico) Colchester, of the *Financial Times*, died sadly young in 1996; his obituary said that he had felt 'drawn' to journalism after Oxford and 'had an interview with

Gordon Newton, the *Financial Times* editor who . . . asked him to sit outside his office and write an article on the current state of British Leyland. Colchester did the piece and got the job.' Colchester had a distinguished career. But one should try to see how this kind of thing might look to a Larry Lamb – especially when put against John Douglas Pringle's evidence in Chapter 3 about the very modest difficulty of such a task.

Tabloid ambitions. Greenslade on 'wannabes' in the *Guardian*, cited above; Anthony Delano in *Slip-Up*, on upward mobility.

Dick Dinsdale. Personal to the author, many times. But perhaps not his own coinage.

Cudlipp and his (one) reporter. A very characteristic remark according to Mike Molloy.

Son of Cassandra, etc. Chippindale and Horrie in *Stick It Up Your Punter*, who bluntly describe the *Sun* as a wholly unoriginal 'rip-off' from the *Mirror*.

Michael Christiansen quoted by Chippindale and Horrie, *Stick It Up Your Punter*. He and all the other *Mirror* executives cited are open to the accusation of being bad losers. Nonetheless, it may be doubted whether editorial genius could have made itself effective in face of the commercial handicaps they describe. A truism of media history is that commercial and editorial creativity rarely appear separately from each other.

Lamb's achievement. Michael Leapman, obituary, *Independent*, 20 May 2000.

Columbia Journalism Review. See Chapter 7.

'Fantasy factory'. Raymond Snoddy in *The Good, the Bad and the Unacceptable: The Hard News about the British Press* (1993).

Techniques of control and domination. Admirers (e.g. Kelvin MacKenzie), neutrals (Simon Jenkins) and critics (John Menadue) describe very similar phenomena: the silent interrogation by phone and the intolerance of multi-sided discussion. This passage collates evidence from Menadue, *Things You Learn Along the Way*, and from Chippindale and Horrie, *Stick It Up Your Punter*. In Channel 4's 1998 film *The Real Rupert Murdoch* Andrew Neil described one of these phone calls which was memorable to him because he successfully determined to make Murdoch break the silence.

Deamer's *Australian*. Once again, Munster (*Murdoch*) and Menadue (*Things You Learn Along the Way*) give a generally similar story. But the chief source here is personal conversation with Deamer, supplemented by his tape-recorded memoir in the National Library of Australia. One handicap in this was a curious Deamer characteristic: that of becoming irascible if he felt he was being tempted into anything like boasting. But apart from Professor Mayer (*The Press in Australia*) there is ample evidence from observers like David Bowman of the *Australian*'s startling improvement under Deamer.

Dismissal of Deamer. This is pieced together from Menadue, Munster, Deamer himself and Professor Ken Inglis, who was close to the late Tom Fitzgerald. Deamer was not bitter about Murdoch, for whom he never felt any respect, but he could not forgive Fitzgerald's failure to tell him what was happening.

Campaigning for the ALP. This is Menadue's evidence in *Things You Learn Along the Way*: again, a story outlined by Munster in his *Murdoch* is amplified from inside knowledge, putting Murdoch's aims and motivation beyond sensible doubt.

6: MR MURDOCH CHANGES TRAINS

Global ambitions. Menadue, *Things You Learn Along the Way*.

Local and international. Max Frankel in *The Times of My Life* has an illuminating passage on how the *New York Times* (the most sophisticated world-citizen among newspapers) remains at heart a local sheet which never loses sight of the New York parish pump. A reading of Downie and Kaiser, *The News About the News*, provides more evidence for a proposal that the US papers which cover the world best enjoy a strong municipal base: among other things, classified ad revenue can buy a lot of foreign travel. Britain's 'national' newspapers are something of an exception, formed by London's extraordinary dominance over a fairly small island.

American beginnings. Shawcross, *Murdoch*, conveys the strenuous character of the *Star* campaign, and Murdoch's angry claim that only snobs would doubt the value of supermarket tabloids.

The CIA and the Coalition. Toohey and Pinwill, *Oyster*, explain this delusion – one very characteristic of intelligence agencies.

Gough stands Rupert up. An interview with Walsh conveys the impression that organising a Whitlam schedule was like steering a skittish supertanker: extra turbulence appears to have set in whenever it was necessary to bring him alongside Murdoch.

Alwest. Munster's account in *Murdoch*, which Whitlam elaborates in *The Truth of the Matter*.

Pentagon Papers content. Frankel's summary in *The Times of My Life*.

Pentagon Papers, Watergate and the *Washington Post*. The principal sources are the memoirs of Katharine Graham (*Personal History*) and Benjamin C. Bradlee (*A Good Life*), with important background from Frankel and from Bernstein and Woodward (*All the President's Men*).

Cantankerous press. In this instance quoted from Frankel (*The Times of My Life*), but Google will find it in many places on the Web.

NOTES

Thomson and the gun-runners. Personal knowledge, as writer of the story. Further details in an obituary note on Denis Hamilton (*Independent*, 9 April 1988) as editor of the *Sunday Times*.

Delane and disclosure. Williams makes this point in *Dangerous Estate*.

Tits in the mangle. This was Attorney-General John Mitchell's phrase aimed at Mrs Graham. *Personal History* records her pleasure, after Mr Mitchell's downfall, at her editorial colleagues' presentation to her of a small brass mangle.

'Crash through or crash' makes an intriguing credo for a former air force navigator: it is cited by Menadue, and most writers mentioning Whitlam. His unique blend of aggrandisement and self-mockery is caught by an interview with the *Age* (9 March 2002) in which he suggests he ought to depart the earth via a blazing Viking funeral in Sydney Harbour, were it not for inconvenience to the commuter ferries. During the three years of his government 'the things we launched and also the ones we tried to launch were extraordinarily well conceived and well executed'. (He did abolish university fees, reform the school system, give welfare payments to single-parent families and the homeless, set the voting age to eighteen, end Australia's military presence in Vietnam, and open diplomatic relations with China.) Patrick White's autobiography *Flaws in the Glass* gives entertaining details of the new honours system and a scathing view of the Dismissal.

Constitutional crisis. Surely the reason this story is little known outside Australia is the sheer complexity of events and sources. Again, using the particular material in Munster's *Murdoch* and Menadue's *Things You Learn Along the Way*, together with well-regarded general accounts such as Paul Kelly's *November 1975* and the ABC's documentary reconstruction in 1995 (for which Malcolm Fraser was interviewed at length) and David Marr's life of the Chief Justice Sir Garfield Barwick, I have assembled a basic narrative which attempts to be consistent with the carefully balanced judgments of Davison et al., *Oxford Companion to Australian History*. I have spliced into this a strand which seems to have been much neglected but is vital to media history: the Melbourne *Herald*'s independent and persistent investigation which uncovered the basic abuses committed by Senator Connor. John Fitzgerald, then editor of the *Herald*, was a patient guide to this complex pre-history of the main crisis. Other sources include the late Sir John Kerr's *Matters for Judgement*, Richard Hall's *The Real John Kerr: His Brilliant Career* and Whitlam's *Truth of the Matter*.

Play it down the middle. Munster, *Paper Prince*.

Menadue's recruitment is of course his own account in *Things You Learn Along the Way*, in which he convincingly describes conservative resistance, or obstruction, to Whitlam's government.

Cavan gathering is described by Munster. Menadue, *Things You Learn Along the Way*, adds detail – emphasising that the Governor-General's behaviour was never reported until after the Dismissal (and remained secret from the Prime Minister).

'Torn down'. Murdoch told the ABC documentary in 1995 that Labor supporters saw him as the man who had done that to their leader, though in his own view he had done no more than stand up for constitutional principles.

Government iniquity etc. Munster makes the point about lack of real investigation by Murdoch's papers; this sparked my examination of the *Herald*'s role.

Criminal libel. This appears to have been the last spasm of the unlovely corpse. Connor's writ was not seen as threatening the *Herald*'s survival in the way the Nixon administration's legal assault threatened the *Washington Post*. But there was no doubt in the mind of John Fitzgerald, up to the moment of Connor's surrender, that he and several of his colleagues were putting their careers on the line.

Senator Withers explained the fragility of his position in the 1995 ABC documentary.

C. P. Scott (1846–1932) lived through the period which created the industrial newspaper.

Sir Martin Charteris is dead. The source for the quotation is John Menadue's 1975 note of a discussion with Tim McDonald, Official Secretary at Australia House, London. Sir William Heseltine, then Assistant Private Secretary at Buckingham Palace, has since confirmed that Kerr's action was kept secret from the Queen and her staff, and was not at all admired (*Sydney Morning Herald*, 10 March 2001).

Kerr's decision. David Marr (*Barwick*) establishes this in his account of the elaborate process the Governor-General set in train for secretly visiting Chief Justice Barwick.

Cutler made this clear in the 1995 ABC documentary.

Lunch with Murdoch. This is from Menadue, *Things You Learn Along the Way*, amplified by personal discussion with Menadue himself. He is certainly convinced that Fraser's change of attitude on his employment was part of a strategy; this view was expressed by Peter Bowers in the *Sydney Morning Herald*, 4 November 1995. Sir Malcolm Fraser declined my request for an interview.

Election and aftermath. The evidence of bias is cited by Munster, who does not suggest it materially affected the outcome. Menadue thought Fraser did not fulfil his potential as Prime Minister, finding that the country's economic problems were indeed exogenous, not primarily due to ALP sins (which he seems to recognise in his 1995 ABC interview).

7: AN AMERICAN NIGHTMARE

Epigraph 1. *The Uncelestial City*, a long narrative poem, had a sizeable success in 1930, taking a view of journalism (and other institutions) which was widely shared.

Epigraph 2. *Federalist No. 1*, 27 October 1787 by 'Publius' (Alexander Hamilton).

Fortunes of the *Post*. Newscorp doesn't publish separate accounts for any of its papers. But the unprofitability of the *Post* is freely described in the memoirs of its veterans, such as Steven Cuozzo, *It's Alive*.

World a better place. Cuozzo, *It's Alive*.

Force for evil. *Columbia Journalism Review*, June 1980.

Yellow journal office. Emery et al., *The Press and America*. This is the general, if much compressed, account of American newspaper development.

Dark playfulness. Cuozzo, *It's Alive*. Compare with Chippindale and Horrie, *Stick It Up Your Punter*.

Snake. Sheridan of course was familiar with the real-life Snakes of London journalism.

***The Times* and the news.** Harold Evans (*Good Times, Bad Times*) and Williams (*Dangerous Estate*) explain the context well, using basic facts from Grigg, *History of The Times*, vol. 1.

***The American Democrat*.** Cooper also thought that plenty of material was deliberately misleading.

***Our Press Gang*.** Wilmer's fine diatribe remains available in the British Library.

Pulitzer. *The Press and America* of course provides a substantial account, but additional details come from Professor Seymour Topping's history on the Pulitzer Prize website at www.pulitzer.org.

Schudson, *Power of News*, was cited in Chapters 1 and 3.

Weber and news media. Peter Lasswell's essay in Stephen Turner (ed.), *The Cambridge Companion to Weber* discusses plans and refers to this extensive journalism and proposed studies of journalism.

Objective journalism. Everyone who comes into contact with American newspapers encounters something of this debate. A later passage quotes Frankel (*Times of My Life*) on the editorial crisis caused by a kind of pseudo-objectivity at the *New York Times* in the 1960s. The discussion in *The Press and America* is extensive.

'Let's not be too technical'. Cuozzo, *It's Alive*, gives much further evidences of his admiration for Dunleavy.

Murdoch's attack on 'elite' journalism was made at the American Newspaper Publishers Convention, 1977.

Muckrakers, etc. A. N. Smith Lecture, Melbourne University, 1972.

Murdoch's notion that the Muckrakers were close kin to his own tabloid operations doubtless testifies to the cunning of President Theodore Roosevelt's attack on them (launched because their criticisms stung his administration). They were like the man sweeping a floor in Part II of *The Pilgrim's Progress*, who forgets to look up at the heavens. Murdoch gives the impression that their work was salacious, which was not true at all. He also told his audience: 'It was not the serious press which first campaigned for the Negro in America: it was the small, obscure newspapers of the Deep South.' This nonsense he must have snatched out of the air.

Presentational ingenuity. This is supported in great detail by Anthony Delano's unpublished PhD thesis, which combines extensive historical inquiry with questionnaire results from recent surveys of British, American and Australian journalists.

Cameron quits. He tells this and other stories brilliantly in his autobiography *Point of Departure*. His first employers, in twentieth-century Scotland, would have chilled Pulitzer, let alone Godkin. He later wrote, 'British journalism at its best is literate and lightweight and fundamentally ineffectual; American journalism at its best is ponderous and excellent and occasionally anaesthetic.' This does less than justice to the present quality of papers like the *Guardian*, the *Independent* and – in a contrasting manner – the *Daily Mail*. But it is still truer than it ought to be.

Brady on Dunleavy. Quoted by Krajicek, *Scooped*.

Journalists and sources. In *The Times of My Life* Frankel comments on a tension which few journalists can maintain unbroken. Relaxing into the arms of the sources is always comfortable. When I. F. Stone said of Theodore H. White that 'a man with a prose style like that need never lunch alone', he was omitting the fact that White as a young foreign correspondent had stood up for unpopular truths. But he accurately portrayed a temptation.

Pulitzer Prize awards are admirably documented at www.pulitzer.org.

Dorothy Schiff's *Post*. Working in New York in the late 1960s, one saw the good qualities of the *Post*, and equally saw that its news coverage of the New York area was at best thin, and sometimes lamentable.

Felker and Murdoch. Described in Shawcross, *Murdoch*. I talked with Felker at the time, and he said Murdoch had 'changed his ideas about the nature of friendship'.

Valuing the *Post*. Jerome Tuccille, *Rupert Murdoch* (1989), gives a clear and coherent account of newspaper values, US accounting conventions and the purchase of the *Post* and (earlier) the San Antonio papers.

Son of Sam. The essential facts of David Berkowitz's killings are easily found and checked by numerous Web postings. I have kept the underlying narrative within the agreed record, then laid over it an analysis of the *Post*'s antics. Cuozzo, who was present throughout (*It's Alive*), provides a devotional account of the activities of his colleagues. Thomas Kiernan, who witnessed Murdoch's involvement, provides a more sober perspective in *Citizen Murdoch*. Material quoted from the *Post*'s files is identified in the text.

Brawlers. Cuozzo, *It's Alive*, misses no opportunities to sound a macho note. Rupert Murdoch seems to have had a background role in a famous Sydney battle (1962) where Kerry and Clyde Packer were the stars (details are in Munster, *Murdoch*). Otherwise his personal demeanour seems usually to have been circumspect. Criminal violence (such as rape and muggings) was prevalent at various times in twentieth-century New York. But if 'street-brawling' means large-scale riot and disorder other cities in America and Europe are more notable.

Gold watch and tears. This is Cuozzo in *It's Alive*, heart nailed to sleeve.

America and the news. We cannot be sure Hamilton personally wrote these words, as the paper's launch edition (in the way of the times) did not carry bylines. But what is well established (see *The Press and America*) is that while Hamilton lived the paper was in every way an expression of his own powerful intellect. No such major statement would have appeared in the *Post*'s birth unless it expressed the General's outlook.

8: TIMES AND VALUES

Denials. Lord Biffen and Baroness Oppenheim interviewed 15 June 1999 and 26 May 1999 by Bruce Page and Elaine Potter. There are many others, variously explicit: Chris Mullin MP wrote personally to Biffen in 1998 and found the denial impressive, as bound by Parliamentary honour. Peter Stothard, then editor of *The Times*, gave a representative News Corporation view on Radio 4 in the same year (*Guardian*, 10 February 1998).

People and government. Harold Evans recounts Barnes' achievement in *Good Times, Bad Times*; Grigg, *History of The Times*, vol. 6, and Barnes' entry in the *Dictionary of National Biography* supplement the story. Florentine political theory is analysed further in Chapter 13.

The Times under Barnes and Delane. Francis Williams in *Dangerous Estate* is another excellent account in parallel to Evans, *Good Times, Bad Times*, and others.

'Last analysis and journalism'. Claud Cockburn's first volume of autobiography, *In Time of Trouble*.

Appeasement. Williams and many others describe *The Times*' abject role. Richard Cockett in *Twilight of the Truth* gives what may be the definitive version (showing that *The Times* was far from alone in its offence). Cockett makes the point that *The Times*' pro-Soviet bias deserves, but has not yet received, proper investigation. The historian E. H. Carr, active as a leader-writer during the war years, appears to have seen Stalin as a high-minded Fabian reformer whose circumstances justified a degree of ruthlessness.

Cabinet committees. Professor Peter Hennessy, James Cameron Memorial Lecture 2000.

Cruickshank. Personal interview, 28 April 1999.

News on the front page. For many years a reproduction of this blunder was framed in *The Times*' New York office. Visiting American reporters found it hard to believe that it was a proud souvenir rather than a hideous warning.

***Sunday Times* pre-Thomson.** Hobson et al., *Pearl of Days*, covers this period gracefully.

Suez circulation figures. From the Audit Bureau of Circulations database. The fact that the *Guardian* and *Daily Mirror*, both highly critical of the Suez expedition, do not seem to have lost sales need not detract from the courage of the *Observer*'s editorial team. Often the cause of circulation loss is not immediately known. But it is always a confidence-sapping experience, and particularly so when there are other pressures.

Higher duty. Charles Moore writing in *Guardian Media*, 1998.

Victorian lies. Randall Jarrell, *A Sad Heart at the Supermarket*.

Objective fallacy and the *Telegraph*. Personal from Don Berry, managing editor 1986–91.

'Never happier'. Andrew Neil, *Full Disclosure*.

'Sure [Maxwell] was lying'. Tony Jackson, Lombard column, *Financial Times*, 30 January 1992.

Philby investigation. Details can be found in *The Philby Conspiracy* (1966) by Bruce Page, David Leitch and Phillip Knightley. In subsequent inquiries others have much improved the record, but basic factual disclosure stands as it was. Lord Chalfont's warning was issued to David Leitch and me at an interview in the Foreign Office early in 1966. Direct evidence of Whitehall's whispered counter-strike surfaced a year or two later through the paper's diplomatic correspondent, who in tradition with the period acted almost as a member of the diplomatic service. When the Foreign Secretary was invited to lunch at the paper, another colleague asked why I hadn't been invited. 'Oh, we thought it would be embarrassing for a member of the [Communist] Party to have to meet the Foreign Secretary,' said the diplomatic correspondent kindly. Later, Donald Maclean invited me to interview him in Moscow, but correctly predicted I would not get a visa as the KGB were sure I worked for the CIA.

'Tightly knit group of politically motivated men'. Harold Wilson produced this famous phrase in the House of Commons, 20 June 1966. It was intended to overcome the difficulty of labelling the Seamen's Union as being under communist control when there were no communists at all on its executive.

Thalidomide. For various reasons (mostly legal) thalidomide's pharmacological and teratogenic history could not be set out fully in the *Sunday Times*. A detailed account is given in Bruce Page, 'A defence of "low" journalism', *British Journalism Review*, 9.1 (1998).

Gun-running in Aden. *Sunday Times*, 1964. Author's obituary note on Denis Hamilton, *Independent*, 14 April 1988.

Mussolini Diaries. The 'six figure' account is in the *Sunday Times*, 1967. More details are given by Phillip Knightley, *A Hack's Progress*, though this does not mention the role of Colin Simpson in uncovering the fraud.

Northern Ireland. Any account of the events since the mid-1960s will be disputed from some viewpoint, and no volume of references will change that. I have written down the way it looked to me and to a good many of my colleagues. Many of us felt that we – and academics like Professor Richard Rose – were sounding warnings which the Labour government of the day was determined to ignore. Certainly the *Sunday Times* was not alone, but I think the article 'JOHN BULL'S POLITICAL SLUM' (3/7/1966) by Stephen Fay, Cal McCrystal and Lewis Chester had the basic qualities of a firebell in the night.

Old woman on a street corner. There is no way to trace the television news programme in which this remark was made. But John Barry, Eamonn McCann and I all participated, and recall it in similar terms. It was only unusual in being explicit.

Bloody Sunday. At the time of writing the Inquiry under Lord Phillips is still at work and expected to report some time in 2004, at an estimated cost of £120 million. It seems clear that the Widgery findings will be discredited; indeed, the general tenor of evidence suggests that the *Sunday Times*' account will be broadly confirmed. Edward Heath (*Guardian*, 15 January 2003) in his evidence to the Inquiry said that he had warned Lord Widgery that the government was fighting 'a propaganda war as well as a military one' in Northern Ireland. He denied that this amounted to a 'steer'. But this does confirm, as we felt at the time, that the government was determined to find support for its claim that the Paratroops had been under serious attack. Peter Pringle and Philip Jacobson, members of the Insight team who did the original work, have written an excellent re-examination using much new evidence (*Those Are Real Bullets, Aren't They?*).

Massacres. At Sharpeville near Johannesburg on 21 March 1960, police opened fire without provocation on Africans protesting against repressive 'pass laws' and sixty-nine people (eight women, ten children) died. At Tlatelolco, Mexico City, on 2 October 1968 a student demonstration ended in a storm of bullets and several hundred people were killed and wounded; details and causes have yet to be fully understood. At Lhasa in Tibet during March 1989, People's Armed Police, specially trained to crush anti-Chinese sentiment, killed between 80 and 150 unarmed demonstrators. At Kent State University, Ohio, on 4 May 1970, the National Guard fired on students protesting against the bombing of Cambodia, and four were killed. Peterloo: the same facts are in any standard history of Britain. Some very wild figures were at times cited for Tiananmen: Jonathan Mirsky of the *Observer* was present, and his immediate estimate of 400 dead seems now to be mainstream. Croke Park (Dublin 1920) has been mentioned as a precedent for Bloody Sunday: the Black and Tans killed thirteen people by firing on a football crowd. But this had more the character of a wartime atrocity – the crowd itself was not political. The Amritsar massacre in India, in which 400 Sikh nationalists died, was certainly an attack on a political gathering. But it was not on Britain's own soil (and Winston Churchill, the Colonial Secretary, disowned General Dyer's action in passionate terms).

Peaceably to assemble. This is of course from the first of the ten amendments to the US Constitution which were ratified on 15 December 1791 and which together form the Bill of Rights.

Low levels of competition. Monopolies Commission reports on press mergers.

Jay and Barber. House of Commons, Monopolies and Mergers Bill, second reading, 29 March 1965.

Monopolies Commission Report on Thomson takeover of *The Times*. 1966.

History of The Times. Some Times Newspapers veterans (including Harold Evans) are critical of this work. But its author John Grigg (1924–2001) was a distinguished biographer and historian, whose life of Lloyd George is recognised as a scholarly masterpiece.

Harry Henry confirmed and amplified what he had told John Grigg when interviewed for this book (2 August 1999). Professor Henry clearly thought the Monopolies Commission were naive.

Blundering amateur. The author was a witness to this pronouncement, and the awful silence following it. It may seem a harsh judgment on an amiable man, but should be compared with Michael Grade's review of Lord Hussey's autobiography (*British Journalism Review*, 13.1 (2002)), which describes Hussey's period as Chairman of the BBC. 'It displays what those of us who had to work for him suspected from the beginning – he was under-qualified and overrated . . . simply a placeman.'

Merry Christmas. Fitzpatrick to author, 8 September 1999.

Unattractive characters. It was usual at Times Newspapers in the 1970s for executives to demonise local union officials (somewhat before the word itself became fashionable). Some of them carried a flavour of brimstone, but it was difficult to take the complaints seriously because (a) most of the speakers had no personal acquaintance with the 'demons', and (b) it was conventional also to insist on the statesmanlike qualities of Duke Hussey (see above), which made it hard to see what benchmark, if any, was in use.

James Evans. Interview 8 July 1999.

Prior canvassed. Lord Prior, interview 20 August 1999.

Thatcher Cabinet. The account of Margaret Thatcher beginning her Premiership as leader of a minority within her own government is supported by opponents (such as Lord Gilmour, *Dancing with Dogma*), supporters (such as Lord Wyatt in his *Journals*) and independent observers like Hugo Young (*One of Us*). Lord Prior's account (*A Balance of Power*) and Lord Howe's (*Conflict of Loyalty*) were amplified by interviews (Prior, 20 August 1999; Howe 15 February 2001).

Pessimism. Sir John Hoskyns to Sir Alfred Sherman, 22 December 1980, in Sir Alfred's papers at Royal Holloway College.

Thomson decision. In interview James Evans (8 July 1999) and Sir Gordon Brunton (20 October 1999) describe the meeting, phone call and so on, and do so in terms fundamentally similar to Grigg, *History of The Times*, vol. 6.

Sale of the papers. The same basic narrative facts occur in Grigg, *History of The Times*, vol. 6; in Harold Evans, *Good Times, Bad Times*; and other sources. Generally the major events (e.g. Gordon Brunton's announcement of the sale on 22 October and his complaints against the unions) were reported in *The Times* next day, and regularly followed up. Charles Raw and other journalists on the *Sunday Times* enabled Elaine Potter and me to collect most of the Thomson press releases, union resolutions and so on which marked the progress of the sale. Financial disclosure was minimal throughout, but we obtained a copy of the Warburg sale prospectus which contains most of the important figures.

Shawcross Court is in the Royal Commission's report.

Loss-making company. Strongly emphasised by Harold Evans, *Good Times, Bad Times*. Sir Gordon Brunton when interviewed did not concede any importance to the distinction.

Evans' lost opportunity. He has made his regrets very clear in *Good Times, Bad Times* and in other contexts.

***Sunday Times* profitability.** The figures in the Warburg prospectus are discussed by Harold Evans, and are in essence quite straightforward. As the text suggests, both Don Cruickshank and Ian Clubb (interview, 8 October

1999) were absolutely emphatic that a loss-making picture could only be artificial.

Evans, Maxwell etc. Personal experience while running the *Sunday Times* investigation of Maxwell.

Lord Donoughue. Tom Bower in *Maxwell: The Outsider* shows Donoughue as excessively reluctant to accept the evidence of Maxwell's savage dishonesty.

Vetting Panel. In *Good Times, Bad Times*, Harold Evans describes this ludicrous procedure without sparing himself.

Public interest. This is the crucial provision in the Fair Trading Act 1973: Part V, section 59(3).

Wyatt *Journals*. Jane Reed, head of corporate affairs at News International (i.e. Newscorp UK) has attempted to discredit the Wyatt material: 'I am afraid this is a case of Woodrow being extremely readable but wrong' (*Guardian*, 19 October 1998). The *Journals* contain some strange judgments about science and history, but carry great conviction in their detailed account of Wyatt's dealings with Murdoch and Thatcher. It's unlikely anyone reading Wyatt thoroughly will find Ms Reed convincing.

'Substantial inquiry'. Sir Keneth Clucas, interview 4 August 1999.

Further information, etc. Brunton, interview 20 October 1999.

Sold as a going concern. Thomson British Holdings press release, 22 January 1981.

Altering the proof. This incident was described by Bruce Page in the *New Statesman* ('Into the Arms of Count Dracula', 30 January 1981) on the basis of discussions with several of those present.

Bid could go forward. Letter, Lord Biffen to Bruce Page, 28 June 1999.

Parliamentary dress. House of Commons, 27 January 1981.

Linklater, etc. All were interviewed at various times in 1999.

Legal advisers. Arthur Marriott QC and Geoffrey Robertson QC, interviewed in 1999, remembered most of the circumstances clearly and in similar terms. Robertson had copies of the notes made in negotiations after the application was withdrawn. Marriott produced a copy of his letter to the Attorney-General. Lord Hoffman could not remember the case at all, which he said was always usual of periods when he was very busy giving opinions.

Twelve people voted against. Malcolm Crawford, Peter Dunn, Tony Geraghty, Isabel Hilton, Philip Jacobson, Peter Lennon, Magnus Linklater, Linda Melvern, Gwen Nuttall, Elaine Potter, Charles Raw, Claire Tomalin.

9: VIRTUALLY NORMAL

Epigraph 2, Christiansen. Quoted in Francis Williams, *Dangerous Estate*.

New York office. Harold Evans in *Good Times, Bad Times*.

Running newspapers. James Evans has made this point on a number of informal occasions. Many financial analysts say something similar.

Benchmarking editors. In 2002 the *British Journalism Review* and the *UK Press Gazette* asked their readers to vote for the 'greatest newspaper editor of all time'. The readers took this in effect as greatest British editor (demonstrating that newspapers are national phenomena). Few ballots can have been less rigorous psephologically, and like those assessing musicians and historical figures (Mozart, say) were on the same footing as current practitioners. Only eight editors received a worthwhile number of votes. Arthur Christiansen (*Daily Express* 1932–56), Hugh Cudlipp (*Sunday Pictorial* later *Sunday Mirror* 1937–40, 1946–9, editorial director of Mirror group 1952–63) and Larry Lamb (*Sun* 1969–81) were grouped together with Thomas Barnes (*The Times* 1817–41). Kelvin MacKenzie (*Sun* 1981–94) shared third place with David English (*Daily Mail* 1971–92). C. P. Scott (*Manchester Guardian* 1872–1929) was a long way ahead of them in second place – and Harold Evans a very easy winner. No active editor received any significant support. It's not likely that a more scientific survey would have produced any very different result.

Gresham's Law. According to the *New Palgrave Dictionary of Economics*, MacLeod thought the statement 'bad money drives out good' was expressed by Aristophanes in *The Frogs*. Thomas Gresham (c.1519–79) was concerned about forgery and corrupt coinage but did not state such a general principle. Collingwood's essay 'Economics as a Philosophical Science' (1925, in his *Essays in Political Philosophy*) should have eliminated it as a quasi-scientific metaphor for decay, but it has lived on, sometimes in elaborate dress. While it is true that forgery and so on have caused many currency problems, economists have found it hard to state a consistent rule from the complex historical record (*Palgrave* lists plenty of starting points for anyone who wants to keep trying). The Cape Town Museum is one which has a collection of tradable cannons imported by the long-established Malay community.

Heading texts. It shouldn't be thought that Steven Shapin's remarkable book, because it focuses on the gentlemanly scientists of the seventeenth-century Royal Society, is remote from the contemporary issues. Shapin worked as a biologist before he became a sociologist and historian (University of California, San Diego). As he writes (letter to Bruce Page, 23 April 2001), 'my work is partly motivated by a general concern about the grounds of integrity. Gentility in the C17 was ONE solution to identifying integrity – and therefore grounds of belief – but solutions differ from one setting to another.' His 'social' history challenges the idea that scientific knowledge comes entirely from 'epistemological individualism', and shows that networks of trust are always necessary, in addition to the personal confrontation with fact. The Locke paraphrase is easily confirmed from the *Essay*. Christiansen and Keynes illustrate the fact that some people have an interest in struggling against Locke's vision of a predictable world, and others find it suits them very well.

Child murder. In the early 1970s it was found that in an average month four children were murdered in England and Wales: seventeen died in road accidents. Both rates are declining, though people fear otherwise. In 1970 England and Wales had the developed world's fourth highest rate of child murder, equal with Japan, Germany and America. In that year the care and protection professions were shocked by a public inquiry into the dreadful death of a child named Maria Colwell. Since then, serious (doubtless imperfect) efforts have been made to co-ordinate the activities of police, doctors and social workers, and in England and Wales the child murder rate has fallen to one of the lowest in the world. Professor Colin Pritchard of Southampton University made an international comparison (*British Journal of Social Work* 32 (2002), 495–502) by summing the period 1974–8 and 1993–7 and constructing an index of reduction. In this a low index figure means a sharp reduction. The index for England and Wales was 0.41: only Japan (0.35) did better within the period, though Germany (0.56) and the Netherlands (0.58) were impressive. Over the same time Italy (1.08), Spain (1.10), USA (1.40) and France (1.58) grew significantly worse. By no means are such changes well understood, though Professor Pritchard points out that British child-care budgets were better protected during the period than America's – suggesting that the Thatcher and Reagan administrations were not always alike. But whatever prevented it, late-twentieth-century Britain did not suffer the rising tide of violence against children which news media seemed to describe. Nor, when violence did occur, was it often done by a stalking tabloid monster such as 'no one is safe from'. Children are unsafe principally from their mothers (and frequently the mother's male partner); they belong to families suffering mental and and social damage which methodical care services can detect and repair before effects are fatal, and that is why improvement can be made. Ferociously dangerous paedophiles certainly exist, says Pritchard. But no useful purpose is served by giving the impression that they are other than rare, and likely to remain so.

Northern Ireland. Violent death in Northern Ireland has never been high by some standards – the Balkans have been much worse since the collapse of Yugoslavia, and others more horrifying still. Only in 1972 did the Troubles cause more deaths than road accidents. But the point is that their media impact, broadly, was inversely related to their frequency.

Famine. Amartya Sen in *Development as Freedom*.

Astrology. Augustine's attack on the astrologers is devastating, particularly their attempts to explain how twins born seconds apart could receive wholly different treatment from the stars. But he is a recovering astrologer – that is, before his conversion he was close to the Manichees, who were astrologers, and offered a significant alternative to Mediterranean Christianity.

Hostpur and Glendower. *Henry IV, Part 1*, Act III, scene 1.

Gauss and normality. The literature on this subject is of course gigantic and often highly specialised. But Jan Gullberg's elegant compression of the history in *Mathematics from the Birth of Numbers* provides the essence of what is needed here:

> In the early 18th century it became apparent to scientists who studied the distribution of errors in repeated measurements that observations of a great number of different measurements often tend to show a similar form of distribution, now called the normal or Gaussian distribution. In 1733 its mathematical equation was formulated by the mathematician and statistician Abraham de Moivre . . . The mathematical properties of the normal distribution were studied and explained by Pierre Simon Laplace, Siméon-Denis Poisson and Carl Friedrich Gauss . . .
>
> The Belgian astronomer, mathematician and statistician Adolphe Quetelet had studied astronomy and probability with Laplace in Paris and was the first to apply normal distribution to the study of sociology. Quetelet presented his concept of the 'average human being' (*l'homme moyen*) around whom measurements of human traits were grouped in normal probability distributions. His observations of the numerical consistency of what had been supposed to be voluntary acts of crime provoked extensive discussions about free will versus social determinism; such studies are still an important subject for research on social behaviour and criminology.

At http:/www.wikipedia.org/wiki/Carl_Friedrich_Gauss on the Web there is a biographical note which lists and describes all of Gauss' achievements, among them: 'In 1818, Gauss started a geodesic survey of the state of Hanover, work which later led to the development of the normal distribution for describing measurement errors.'

Quetelet, 'law of large numbers', polls etc. Professor John Allen Paulos (*A Mathematician Reads the Newspaper*) provides an excellent brief account of the ubiquity of Quetelet. Doubtless he is right to say that economics may be considered as 'social statistical mechanics': my opinion is that the best economists are those who know when the analogy between the human and the mechanical will break down. Reporters can still be found who think they can sniff the air during a by-election and produce a better analysis than an opinion-poll can do, but mostly they are wrong. To take a reliable sample of (say) people's voting intentions needs several hundred respondents randomly selected, and even if a single reporter could do it the first data would be obsolete before the collection of the last. A reporter with really powerful intuition may be able to assess opinion in exceptional cases where survey technique isn't applicable, but that person will be far too intelligent to do something extremely difficult when a good a result can be obtained by a simple team procedure.

'Out of the ordinary'. Many writers record Northcliffe as giving this definition – and his saying 'News is something someone wants to suppress' and 'When a dog bites a man, that's not news – news is man bites dog.' I have not found any record of Northcliffe claiming these as original perceptions, but the official life by Pound and Harmsworth makes it plain that he believed them. Today, somewhat more sophisticated ideas about news and probability are beginning to be discussed – stimulated by cot deaths, vaccination risks and so on. However, many people still find it difficult to grapple with probabilities, and distinguish the random from the significant in daily events. The mathematician and financial trader Nassim Nicholas Taleb suggests (*Fooled by Randomness: The Hidden Role of Chance in the Markets and in Life*) that this is something we owe to human origins in a simpler and less abstract world:

> a natural habitat does not include much information. An efficient computation of the odds was never necessary until very recently. This explains why we had to wait until the emergence of the gambling literature to see the growth of the mathematics of probability. Popular belief holds that the religious backdrop of the first and second millennium blocked the growth of tools that hint at the absence of determinism, and caused the delays in probability research. The idea is extremely dubious; we simply did not compute probabilities because we did not dare to? Surely the reason is rather that we did not need to. Much of our problem comes from the fact that we have evolved out of such a habitat faster, much faster than our genes. Even worse; our genes have not changed at all.

The biologist Edward O. Wilson (quoted in Chapter 11) suggests from a different direction that human rationality is limited by the small scope of the societies in which it developed. Chapter 13 refers again to Taleb and Wilson in discussing contemporary attempts to broaden the framework of social decision-making.

'Small Earthquake' etc. Harry Evans comments on Morison with great restraint, but with some impatience. Claud Cockburn (*In Time of Trouble*) tells the 'small earthquake' story saying that it won an informal competition among *Times* sub-editors to write the most boring headline possible.

Weber's 'ideal types'. Weber worked on an expansive scale, and most of his commentators go the same way. But a clear and economical account of his ideal types by Professor Frank Elwell is at www.faculty.rsu.edu/~felwell/Theorists/.

10: CASES OF CONSCIENCE

Unless stated otherwise, quotations and documents are from Harry Evans' account, which forms the major part of his memoir *Good Times, Bad Times*. Nowhere else is there any substantial quantity of quoted documents and contemporary recollection. Inevitably Evans' account, being written essentially in defence of his own reputation, has been criticised as self-serving: there are two main groups who take this view. Some people essentially accept the Murdoch version, and there is little to be said to them. Another group I refer to in the text as 'the Old Times'. They were not necessarily old at that time by the calendar, or generally of one mind, except in considering themselves opponents of the journalistic values they saw in Rupert Murdoch. They then persuaded themselves that Evans' values were essentially the same – that he was the tyrant's agent and deserved no better than one of Tamburlaine's discredited lieutenants.

I believe that Evans is accurate as to fact, and restrained – even excessively – as to judgment. Indeed, I doubt we have any better or more detailed evidence of power corruptly at work in British society: instances may well have been worse, but we know very much less about them. Brilliant as Evans' account is, he had to describe a débâcle which was set moving by his own decision. This restrains him from putting his own evidence as clearly as he might – but never clearly enough, of course, to prevent Mr Worldly Wiseman (a reliable Murdoch ally) from discounting it altogether.

I followed the story at the time and reported some of it in the *New Statesman*, from a viewpoint strongly critical of Murdoch, and not much less critical of Evans. He was after all maintaining publicly that all was well with Times Newspapers and that those of us who said otherwise were cynics. The corporate smokescreen was not thick enough to disguise altogether what was really happening, and *Good Times, Bad Times* later confirmed that. There can be no doubt that it would have been far more comfortable for Evans simply to accede to Murdoch's demand, or simply to make a settlement and run away with the money. Fortunately, he chose to give us the record.

I have checked my own recollection and the Evans account by discussion with others then close to the events, particularly Peter Hennessy, Hugh Stephenson and Richard Davy.

A complicating factor in the story is that people who were close friends of the late Charles Douglas Home generally cannot accept the Evans version of his behaviour. One must respect their loyalty, but there is separate evidence – in, for instance, the Hitler Diaries case – which suggests they were mistaken about his character.

Lamb and *The Times*. Larry Lamb in *Sunrise*.

An upturn could be seen. Figures from the Audit Bureau of Circulations.

Striking against the Guarantees. The bare facts of this matter emerged at the time, though the people Murdoch struck at and through chose to make no protest. In 1992 the *Sunday Times* quite grotesquely accused Michael Foot of being a KGB spy, and Foot sued for libel. Foot's lawyers intended to subpoena Rupert Murdoch to cross-examine him on the degree of control he exerted over Times Newspapers, and the means by which he gained it. They were able to obtain statements from Frank Giles and Ron Hall about the subversion of the guarantees. When this was disclosed to Newscorp's lawyers they displayed a sudden readiness to settle the matter, and Foot – chiefly because he was then in poor health – was advised to accept. On Foot's instruction his solicitors showed me the papers in the case, and they suggest that determined pursuit of the issue in 1982 would have posed serious problems for Murdoch.

The paper has no conscience, etc. Richard Davy was the leader-writer who dealt with Eastern Europe and the USSR, and was in place when Evans arrived. Davy argued, with support from Evans, that Nato's policy of detente, involving negotiation and multi-level contacts with the USSR and its allies within a balance of power, was more likely to keep the peace and erode the Soviet empire than the confrontation Ronald Reagan at first proposed (and later modified). Davy is well known separately from *The Times* as a writer on Soviet and European history. Scarcely anyone would accuse him of supporting a position in which conscience played no part.

11: PATRIOTIC LIKE A FOX

Epigraph. In *The Meaning of Treason* West studied British citizens who committed acts of treachery on behalf of Nazi Germany (such as Joyce) and of the Soviet Union (such as Nunn May). Her notion of patriotism as contributing to moral equilibrium has never quite gone out of fashion.

Citizenship. More of less the same story is told in most accounts: Chenoweth in *Virtual Murdoch* stresses the private and privileged nature of the hearing.

Safire. *New York Times*, 16 May 1985.

Breslin. *Daily News.*

Failure of the *Post*. The financial woes of the paper are very frankly acknowledged in Cuozzo's *It's Alive*. To Cuozzo Murdoch's willingness to keep the paper going amid heavy losses is a proof of his unselfish qualities. Thomas Kiernan in *Citizen Murdoch* is quite dry-eyed, suggesting that Murdoch's motivation had more to do with political power-broking than with editorial romanticism. Kiernan surveys the two Reagan campaigns and emphasises the prevalence of sound and fury over substance.

Lamb *Sun* v. MacKenzie *Sun*. Lamb's memoir *Sunrise*, having celebrated the 'rise and rise of the Soaraway *Sun*' concludes on a bitter note. He suggests that during his editorial regime there was a degree of restraint absent from the MacKenzie case. Many journalists are prepared to agree.

MacKenzie and the Falklands. The *Sun*'s activities during the Falklands War have been much discussed in terms of bias and jingoism. The editorial incompetence which emerges from Chippindale and Horrie's account in *Stick It Up Your Punter* has been less noticed.

TEN-10 licence hearings. These were held by the Australian Broadcasting Tribunal. Its records (and those of its predecessor, the Australian Broadcasting Authority) are held now by the Australian Broadcasting Authority, set up in 1992.

Inoculation. Orwell, 'Notes on Nationalism', in *Collected Essays*.

Paleolithic heritage. *Scientific American*, 24 February 2002. Professor Wilson is probably the greatest living biologist – recipient of the US National Medal of Science, the Pulitzer Prize for literature, and the Craoord Prize given by the Royal Swedish Academy for sciences not covered in the Nobel awards. In this article he shows that group loyalty is an indispensable human asset, but one developed within limited horizons. If narrowly exploited it blocks the co-operation needed to save the human world from irreversible damage.

Burke. *Reflections on the Revolution in France*. Burke's defence of national feeling accompanies a famous distaste for generalised hatred of any nation: 'I do not know the method of drawing up an indictment against an whole people' ('Speech on Conciliation of America', in *On Empire, Liberty, and Reform*, edited by David Bromwich.

Rancid chauvinism. Without being so consistent, other British tabloids sometimes merit the description, but British broadsheets, almost never – apart from *The Times* and the *Sunday Times*. Thus, a *Times* leader (27 March 1998) on the Ardennes:

> The Germans have been uniquely handicapped in exploiting nostalgia to sell automobiles. The image of classic German engineering which persists in many minds is of adaptable off-road vehicles crashing through the Ardennes. But now that more than 50 years have passed since the last Panzer fired a shot in anger, the time is ripe for a revival of an earlier, more elegant tradition in German engineering . . .

The subject was Volkswagen's plan to revive the Horch luxury-car brand to compete with Mercedes (whose usage of a glamorous past hardly seems inhibited by Battle of the Bulge memories, whatever *The Times* might fancy). The leader-writer encouraged Germans to revisit automotive history extensively: 'By appreciating anew why countries have an attachment to their native traditions, Germans might better understand the reluctance of some to travel on an autobahn without exit to another's Utopia.'

Then there was the response when Germany's ambassador protested mildly about a *Sunday Times* article headed 'WHY I HATE THE GERMANS' (18 July 1999) saying no German paper would run anything similar about Britain: 'It's not our style.' Quite right, came back the writer A. A. Gill: 'Their style is to send the panzers over the border at dawn and shoot the editor.' Gill, having found that method which eluded Burke, of indicting a whole people, said that his critics (German and British) must grasp that the free press (represented by himself) never worked 'to a secret agenda', and wasn't 'biddable one way or another'. Certain British were out to impose 'happy-clappy' friendship throughout Europe – such people he could 'hate more than the Germans'. With this went a picture of the author wearing a *Stahlhelm*.

Personal advantage. Burke, *Reflections on the Revolution*.

Fox network construction. The outline of this story is well known, and told largely in Murdoch's own terms by Shawcross in *Murdoch*. The analysis which cast new light on it in 2001 was Neil Chenoweth's book *Virtual Murdoch*, showing how the deal was paid for by redefining the nature of debt. Most of the gross figures cited were on the record before Chenoweth's work, but he puts them into an entirely fresh context. The other principal source for the foundation of Fox is Thomas Kiernan (*Citizen Murdoch*), who at this time was working on what was to be an approved biography of Murdoch. Kiernan eventually found that he could not sympathise with Murdoch's view of editorial ethics and published without approval. But, before the break, his access to Murdoch enabled him to secure several remarkably frank and important admissions.

Michael Milken. The rank of Milken among titans of speculative excess has been reduced somewhat by the Enron epoch and by Milken's own image-reconstruction subsequent to release from jail. A detailed reminder of the facts is provided by Edward Cohn, 'The Resurrection of Michael Milken' in the *American Prospect*, 11.9 (13 March 2000).

'Unusual financing'. *American Lawyer*, December 1993. In this interview Siskind does not really explain the legerdemain involved (see below).

Concentrations of power, etc. Kiernan, *Citizen Murdoch*, on the basic technique and resemblance to the Times Newspapers case.

Financing Fox. Chenoweth, *Virtual Murdoch*, on the phenomenal expansion of News Corporation credit.

In truth the money was a loan. Though Siskind (noted above) purported to explain the curiosity, there does not seem to be any specific feature of Australian commercial law or accounting principle under which a debt can be treated as shareholders' equity. It seems more likely that News Corporation's auditors, Arthur Andersen, simply did not challenge the point, and there was at that time no Australian regulatory body to do so.

12: MARGARET THATCHER'S HEROES

Woodrow Wyatt. The three volumes of Lord Wyatt's *Journals* are an essential source for the real relationship between News Corporation and Margaret Thatcher's government.

Wyatt–Murdoch introduction. Stated by Evans in *Good Times, Bad Times*.

Communism and the Electricians. Some idea of the scale of the battle Wyatt and his allies had to fight can be gained from *All Those in Favour* by C. H. Rolph (with a foreword by John Freeman), which is an account of the fiercely contested legal actions which eventually settled the matter.

Voices (Joan of Arc). Lord Howe's *Conflict of Loyalties* was published in 1994. We now know that Wyatt was indeed a regular telephonic voice. In the early days of the Thatcher regime Sir Geoffrey Howe (as he then was) was himself one of the group very close to the Prime Minister. Every government has a 'kitchen cabinet', usually including some members of the Cabinet. In Margaret Thatcher's case, however, the members seem to have been unusually prone to form sub-groups – which traded contempt with each other – and mostly to have departed thinking her either too extreme, or insufficiently so. Wyatt was one of the few loyal to the end. John Ranelagh, an ex-member of the Conservative Research Department, listed a formidable number of intellectual influences and back-room volunteers in *Thatcher's People* (1991): major economists like Friedrich von Hayek and Milton Friedman, middling economists like Sir Alan Walters; minor economists (Ralph [Lord] Harris); PR experts (Sir Tim Bell, Sir Bernard Ingham); Tory MPs (Ian Gow and Airey Neave); grand Tory MPs (Sir Keith Joseph, John [Lord] Biffen); businessmen and consultants (Sir John Hoskyns, Norman Strauss); civil servants (Sir Charles Powell); journalists (Sir Alfred Sherman, Wyatt). Norman Strauss left her Policy Unit because he could not persuade her to more extensive reforms. John Hoskyns left, in part, because he feared that strategic clarity was being lost, and partly because he felt he had done the job he'd come to do. James (Lord) Prior – never part of the inner circle – thought both of them mischievous cranks. Lord Howe – originally part of the inner circle – seems to have felt that the Prime Minister eventually took on something of that quality. Biffen doubtless spoke for most ex-Thatcherites when he told Ranelagh that she had lost 'the real, genuine Thatcherites like myself'. Perhaps Joan rather than Gloriana was the apter parallel: nobody thought Elizabeth Tudor was hearing voices.

BBC as state monopoly. Cited by Wyatt, *Journals*, vol. 2; also in Sherman papers at Royal Holloway College.

Sherman as communist. Born in 1919, he joined the Party in his teens, and fought in the Spanish Civil War. He told the *Guardian* (10 November 2000) that he was expelled in 1947 for challenging Stalin's hostility to Tito. Knighted in 1983. Subsequently *Daily Telegraph* leader-writer, adviser to Radovan Karadzic, etc.

The Times' new direction. Notes from Richard Davy, with further background from interviews 24 May 2001 and subsequently. A similar text by Davy was published in the *Independent*, 9 March 1998. See also note to Chapter 8.

Hussey's encore. See Michael Grade's review of Hussey memoirs in notes to Chapter 8.

Sanskrit. MacKenzie interviewed in *The Real Rupert Murdoch* (Channel 4, 1998).

Sunday Times: editorial trouble. Elaine Potter worked on the paper during this period, seeing the effect of the Hitler Diaries fake on her colleagues. Andrew Neil in *Full Disclosure* rightly says that mental energy was low, but attributes this to pre-Thatcherite social attitudes. A more realistic diagnosis would have been professional disorientation: to Magnus Linklater the impact of the Hitler blunder was intensified by Murdoch's lack of apparent concern (personal communication). Neil first met Murdoch just after the fake collapsed. He gathered that Murdoch (a) had essentially imposed the Diaries on the paper, and (b) still thought it 60 per cent probable they were real. Neil doesn't record any concern about the journalistic competence of the man who shortly afterwards made him editor.

Rebellious youth. Neil cites as evidence of rebel qualities his refusal to smoke cannabis as a Glasgow University student. *Full Disclosure* doesn't disclose who sought to force the spliffs upon him.

Insight and Christopher Hird. In the period before his formal takeover Neil rightly studied the paper's editorial pipeline, and says (*Full Disclosure*):

> I asked Hird to let me see his file of current investigations; he did not need both hands to carry it. It consisted of a few slips of paper summarising a series of second-rate investigations that were going nowhere and a general disposition to 'look at local government . . .'

Hird comments (11 October 2001):

> This is quite untrue. I did not produce a 'few slips of paper' but a document of (I recall) about six single typed pages, which covered a number of proposed investigations, which had been drawn up following discussions with the senior execs . . . he did not – so far as I recall – express any disgruntlement at the proposed list of investigations.

In a separate discussion of investigative potential, Hird asked Neil whether he would publish a detailed, highly challenging study of Sir James Goldsmith's finances, which the departing editor had kept on hold. Neil declined to say: this investigation by Charles Raw never was published. (Goldsmith died in 1997.) Hird says that on his first day as editor Neil disbanded Insight without commenting on its editorial plans:

> On his own ideas of investigations, there is the notorious story of the two chauffeurs. On his appointment Rupert gave him two chauffeurs. Neil wanted two parking permits for outside his flat in Kensington and Chelsea but council rules only allowed one permit per person. So he wrote to the council asking if he could have two permits but – because the chauffeurs worked shifts – he could guarantee that there would never be more than one car parked outside his flat at the same time. The council refused his request. On their letter of refusal, he scribbled 'Set Insight on to this' and got his secretary to give it to me.

The letter reached *Private Eye*. Neil then rang Hird, whom he had just sacked, to say it was just a joke. Hird later founded Fulcrum TV, which ever since has produced successful investigative programmes for all major UK channels.

Response from Downing Street. According to Donald Trelford, then editor of the *Observer*, the Downing Street press officer, under Bernard Ingham tried to bury the story by (a) persistently refusing to discuss it in public, and (b) accusing David Leigh, Trelford and the *Observer* in off-the-record briefings of fabrication and 'irresponsibility'. Dire, unspecified consequences were projected for papers which might follow the story up. Trelford received phone calls from a variety of senior Tories about the damage he was doing to himself and the *Observer*. Generally, Trelford says, publishing material the Thatcher administration disliked was a lonely business (interview, 20 October 2001). For several weeks there was no support from the *Sunday Times* or any other paper. A still more startling piece of misattribution occurs in Neil's *Full Disclosure* with the suggestion that the *Sunday Times* revealed the Matabeleland atrocities committed by Robert Mugabe's Zimbabwean government. This disclosure (obtained by Trelford himself at some personal risk) was in the *Observer*.

Lobby set-up. Cockett's thorough account in *Twilight of the Truth* gives no indication that journalists or their largely Tory bosses were at all concerned about MacDonald's schemes. Hunter Davies' remark, I like to think, was tongue in cheek.

I may not be Prime Minister. Howe, *Conflict of Loyalty*. But see below.

Helping the Foreign Secretary. Interview with Lord Howe (15 February 2001).

Ingham and the law. Linklater and Leigh quote this in *Not with Honour*. But see below.

Elective dictatorship. Margaret Thatcher inspired some ironic smiles when just before the general election of 2001 (*Daily Telegraph*, 1 June) she warned that the Prime Minister's office had such a potential. Lord Hailsham, she said, had pointed it out in 1975.

Collective responsibility. There are several variants of Lord Melborne's remark, but all reflect his belief that actions rarely turn out well, and blame should therefore be equitably distributed. Many studies of Cabinet responsibility have followed in Bagehot's track, but in this context a useful if unexciting one is Patrick Gordon Walker, *The Cabinet: Political Authority in Britain*. Published in 1970 on the basis of recent experience, it argues effectively that the institution was then in tolerable health. In a highly regarded standard text (*The British Cabinet*) John P. Mackintosh MP stated the responsibility principle neatly: 'If a minister is doing too much on his own, or even if the Prime Minister is acting too often without prior agreement, it is in the name of Cabinet responsibility that his colleagues will venture to object and request that the matter be reopened.'

Leak-driven world. Howe, *Conflict of Loyalty*. Similar points are being made by senior politicians in almost every democratic system, with increasing frequency.

Revolutionary jacquerie. The words, quoted by Howe in *Conflict of Loyalty*, are those of Sir Oliver Wright (born 1921, Solihull School, Cambridge, Foreign Office 1945–86, Ambassador to US, various directorships, trustee British Museum etc).

Developed as an autocracy. Hugo Young describes the process in *One of Us*.

Westland story. This matter appeared to spring out of nothing in the midwinter of 1985–6, achieve a brief, ferocious intensity and then vanish. Only one substantial effort was made to put the facts on public record at the time: *Not with Honour*, by Magnus Linklater and David Leigh, then on the *Observer*. This summarised and extended the paper's coverage (in which Leigh worked with Paul Lashmar). However, Woodrow Wyatt was making numerous entries in his journals as he joined battle on behalf of the Prime Minister, and on behalf of her ally Rupert Murdoch. My reconstruction chiefly draws on Lord Wyatt, on *Not with Honour*, and again on Lord Howe's *Conflict of Loyalty* (amplified and confirmed by interview on 16 November 1999).

Tension racked up at Wapping. Linda Melvern's *The End of the Street* gives a highly detailed narrative of the Wapping confrontation. The story was clarified by interviews with Baroness Dean (20 July 1999) then general secretary of the Society of Graphical and Allied Trades (SOGAT), Barry Fitzpatrick (8

September 1999), also of SOGAT, and Alf Parrish (3 September 1999) of the National Graphical Association (NGA).

She should tell Bernard Ingham. Wyatt, *Journals*, vol. 1.

Exchange of letters ('material inaccuracies'). This sequence of events, down to the 'LIAR' headline, is based on Linklater and Leigh, *Not with Honour*. The general outline is confirmed by Michael Heseltine in *Life in the Jungle*, and in interview.

Provoke a conflict. Baroness Dean (20 July 1999).

Concessions on offer. Wyatt's account in his *Journals*, vol. 1, suggests that Murdoch was turning well-waxed ears to anything Dean had to say.

TNT's purchase. Linklater and Leigh, *Not with Honour*. TNT no longer exists and it has not been possible to trace Mortimore.

Courtiers. Andrew Neil in the *Guardian*, 2 March 1998.

Oxygen of publicity. Margaret Thatcher addressed the American Bar Association in London on 15 July 1985, and referring to the role of the media in the Northern Ireland conflict said that it would be necessary to starve paramilitary organisations of 'the oxygen of publicity'. Drastic action to that end was taken on 19 October 1988, when the Home Secretary Douglas Hurd used powers under the broadcasting licensing legislation to prevent transmission of interviews with paramilitary organisations and political groups deemed to be their allies. (The government of course had no such power to restrict press activity.) The ban did not apply to election communications. It had no discernible effect on support for paramilitaries of either side, and was an international embarrassment to Britain. It was lifted in September 1994. The Charter 88 website (http://www.charter88.org.uk/pubs/violations/hall.html) provides a historical note (25 October 2002) by Tony Hall, BBC Managing Director of News and Current Affairs. Hall points out that contradictory rationales were given for the ban: such interviews were supposed to 'give offence', but also to be capable of seducing public opinion. There are few equivalents to such a use of law in a free country, and there can be no doubt that the makers of *Death on the Rock* were operating in a climate of very serious official hostility.

At 3.30pm . . . The Windlesham–Rampton Report is used as the best guide to the sequence of events identified with the television documentary *Death on the Rock*. David (Lord) Windlesham PC was commissioned to investigate the making of the programme – its motivation and its accuracy – because he had been a Conservative Minister of State for Northern Ireland (later a Cabinet minister) in addition to having had a substantial career in commercial television (managing director, later chairman, of the ATV network, etc.). He brought in as co-author Richard Rampton QC, an expert in defamation law.

Thames Television developed . . . The Windlesham–Rampton report includes a complete transcript of the programme.

Press attacks. Windlesham–Rampton made a collection of press responses to *Death on the Rock*, but confined itself to items of a fairly orthodox type – though sometimes very hostile – in the *Telegraph*, *Guardian*, *Mail* and other papers. The more remarkable material in the *Sun*, some other tabloids and the *Sunday Times* was collected by Roger Bolton, producer of the programme. These he collected in his book *Death on the Rock and Other Stories* – which attracted surprisingly little notice when published in 1990.

UK Press Gazette. Rosie Waterhouse sent the same material to Windlesham and Rampton at the same time. Not surprisingly, their report gave no credence to the *Sunday Times'* attacks on *Death on the Rock*. In his chapter 'Ruining Sunday Breakfasts', Neil says that in 'a series of articles amounting to 16,000 words he amassed evidence to show that if the SAS had killed these bombers in cold blood Thames TV was very far from proving it'. Thames had never claimed to have done so.

13: PRESENT NECESSITIES

Crisis of rule. Fears of a degeneration in the political process – one somehow connected with the media – have been acute in Britain since the 2001 general election produced a very low turnout. But a chronic ailment has been worsening since the 1960s. *Trust Me, I'm a Politician* (quoted in the epigraph) felt no need to prove the existence of a problem: description was enough. An article by Philip Stephens, political editor at the *Financial Times* (21 June 2002: 'The Lie at the Heart of Politics'), is representative of many others.

> Public cynicism has rarely been greater. Relations between the government and swathes of the press have never been worse. The politicians blame the journalists, the journalists the politicians.
>
> The people who matter, the voters, look on with disdain. Whichever way the question is asked, politicians and journalists are anchored at the bottom of every league table measuring public esteem. Used car salesmen rate more highly. Only estate agents compete . . . Ask leaders from around the world what most vexes them and the answer is likely to be the ingrained assumption of their domestic media that they are crooks and charlatans. Participation in elections is falling everywhere. Abstentions are the new protest votes.

Grade on ownership. Quoted by Matthew Horsman, *Sky High*. Grade also wrote to the *Guardian*, 24 May 1995:

> Not only do we learn (from Rupert Murdoch's *Money Programme* interview) that he will use the nation's best-selling daily newspaper as a conduit for his own views

at the next General Election, but also that Messrs Major and Blair are now on notice that he will be pondering the 'difference' between them before deciding which one to support . . . During the period of consultation which now follows the publication of the Government's thoughts on cross-media ownership, Mr Murdoch will doubtless pay close attention to any 'differences' between them on ownership matters before deciding how to cast the *Sun*'s vote. Perhaps we should not be too surprised that the Green Paper has no views on his effective monopoly of encryption technology.

Doing and daring. Presentation by Rupert Murdoch to the European Audiovisual Conference, Birmingham, 6 April 1998 (http://europa.eu.int/eac/speeches/murdoch_en.html).

Engineered by Labor's enemies. John Fitzgerald, then editor of the *Herald*, to Bruce Page (27 February 2003): 'I'm aware that people put about it was all a Liberal fix. That's absolutely untrue. We deliberately kept clear of pollies altho' once they got a whiff of our success a couple of them tried to get themselves into the loop.'

British Labour's misadventures. Roy Greenslade (*Guardian*, 24 June 2002), citing his own observations and those of Andrew Rawnsley in the *Observer* and Matthew d'Ancona in the *Sunday Telegraph*, wrote that the New Labour campaigning of the 1990s had been shaped by a belief that tabloid antagonism had brought about Neil Kinnock's defeat: 'Everything about the way today's Labour party handles the press grew out of a single, ferocious decade at the hands of newspapers.'

Art of lying. F. M. Cornford in *Microcosmographia Academica* (1922).

Feuding. Gavin Souter in *Heralds and Angels* says the now defunct *National Times* was loathed more than any other Fairfax paper, recording an occasion when Paul Keating, 'after finding himself the unwilling subject of a detailed but inconclusive article in the *National Times*, said with characteristically vivid imagery: "It's a jungle out there. And I'm a tiger. Where do you shoot a tiger? Between the eyes, that's where. Well, they missed, they only wounded me."'

But the *Sydney Morning Herald* offended also, as in a three-page survey of abuses in the NSW justice system:

> At about 10 a.m. . . . . the group general manager received a phone call from the federal Treasurer, Paul Keating, saying he was absolutely shocked by the first three pages of the paper . . . [Neville] Wran [Labor Premier of NSW] would go for it with a vengeance, and Federal Labor would put its back into his efforts to crush the company . . .

Wran shortly after rang to amplify the message: 'Fairfax was going to pay the price for this. All of its interests at some time wanted something from the Government. He could assure Gardiner that he did not forget easily and that he would devote a lifetime to bring Fairfax and the [*Sydney Morning*] *Herald* down.'

More subtle than you think. Menadue in *Things You Learn Along the Way*.

Two airlines. This narrative is condensed from Menadue. A draft was shown to former Senator Evans (now head of the International Crisis Group in Brussels). He was kind enough to read and confirm the details, in spite of distressing events on the day of the interview (11 September 2001).

Telstra and Fox. Again set out with documentation by Menadue in *Things You Learn Along the Way*.

Freddie Starr. Chippindale and Horrie, *Stick It Up Your Punter*, make clear that the supposed incident was already three years old when it reached the *Sun* as a rumour.

Influence and privilege. *Sun*, 6 February 1989.

Hillsborough. Chippindale and Horrie, *Stick It Up Your Punter*, say that MacKenzie, with a kind of caution, substituted 'THE TRUTH' for his first idea, 'YOU SCUM'. Phil Scraton, Professor of Criminology at Edge Hill College, Ormskirk, who has produced two detailed studies of the catastrophe and its aftermath (*No Last Rights*, written with others, and *Hillsborough: The Truth*) suggests that some of the most inflammatory 'briefing' came from Police Federation officials. In *Hillsborough* he wrote of the Taylor *Interim Report*:

> Sixty-five police officers gave evidence to the inquiry and Taylor found the 'quality of their evidence' to be 'in inverse proportion to their rank' . . . most senior officers 'were defensive and evasive witnesses' . . .
>
> Taylor also recognised that there had been a police-led campaign of vilification against Liverpool fans. He listed the allegations [urinating on police, robbery and so on]. He concluded, 'not a single witness' supported 'any of those allegations although every opportunity was afforded for any of the represented parties to have any witness called . . . those who made them, and those who disseminated them, would have done better to hold their peace'.

Lord Justice Taylor's findings caused shock and official surprise, indicating how confident the authorities had been of making their allegations stick. Ingham furiously denounced the judge's work as a 'whitewash', but could produce no proof. Murdoch and MacKenzie suggested that the *Sun* had made an unusual mistake, but 'THE TRUTH' seems unusual only in the extreme gravity of the accusations it chose to accept. What remains unusual in Britain is for authority to make such ruthless use of press gullibility. See Lord Justice Taylor, *Interim Report into the Hillsborough Stadium Disaster* (1989), and *Final Report into the Hillsborough Stadium Disaster* (1990).

Sting. MacKenzie in the *Guardian*, 11 March 2002.

Development of Sky. Horsman, *Sky High*.

Professor Peacock. The Independent Review Panel (chairman Gavyn Davies) which examined the financing of the BBC in 1999 looked back in these terms:

> The Government established the Peacock Committee in 1985 with the hope that it would recommend in favour of advertising on BBC television. [But] Alan Peacock wisely rejected the advertising option. He said that it would trigger head-to-head competition for audience share with ITV, and that this would be ruinous to the UK'S broadcasting 'ecology'. Instead, though, he predicted that technological advance would end the problem of spectrum scarcity, and with it the issue of market failure in broadcasting would largely disappear. Accordingly, he recommended that the BBC should become more dependent on subscription revenue in the new world of plentiful supply. This recommendation fell by the wayside, for various technical and political reasons . . . Nevertheless, a key watershed had been passed – the forces of radical change got bogged down . . . [and] the supporters of the BBC re-asserted themselves. Some of these, in the private broadcasting industry, were alarmed by the threat of advertising on the BBC, and therefore rallied behind the licence fee. But more generally, the public's respect and affection for the organisation proved deep-seated . . . Even Mrs Thatcher, increasingly irate about the BBC, never felt able to overcome this silent force.

The offending _Independent_. Basic timing of the paper's launch is in Michael Crozier, _The Making of the Independent_. The motivation in some of its best staff – an urge to escape from government subservience at _The Times_ – is visible in 'Rat Pack', by Anthony Bevins and Colin Hughes (unpublished MS, Queen Mary College, London). The remarkable career of Tony Bevins is described in several obituary notices: Jonathan Fenby, _Observer_, 25 March 2001; Colin Hughes, _Guardian_ and Andrew Marr, _Independent_, both 26 March. The basic concept of the paper is well explained in Whittam Smith's fifteenth-anniversary article (_Independent_, 9 October 2001).

Here is Mr Murdoch. Horsman, _Sky High_. The remarkable sequence of events in the changeover from IBA to ITC was recalled by David Glencross (interview 10 February 2002), who worked for both organisations. The 'impartial' quality of Sky News, he confirms, was less noticeable than the very small scale of its operation.

Debt crisis. John D'Arcy, formerly CEO of the Melbourne Herald group, was on the News Corporation board between 1987 and 1990, when Murdoch dismissed him without giving specific reasons. D'Arcy (interview 18 January 1999) said in several board meetings that Murdoch's acquisition programme of the late 1980s was financially unsustainable – which of course proved correct. The manoeuvres which enabled Murdoch to escape the consequences are brilliantly set out in Chenoweth, _Virtual Murdoch_.

Ex-journalist. Neil Chenoweth interview, Sydney, 25 January 1999.

Fox's corporate pelt, etc. David Honig was the fiercely determined Washington-based volunteer lawyer for the National Association for the Advancement of Coloured People who ignited the FCC inquiry into Fox Ownership. Murdoch's jubilation at the outcome was matched by Honig's disgust at what he saw as a process 'tainted . . . Murdoch's Republican cohorts blackmailed the FCC by threatening its existence'. See Ken Auletta, *The Highwaymen*.

Present necessities. Machiavelli, *The Prince*, chapter 18.

Digital television. The Independent Review Panel recommended that:

> the BBC should retain a central role in the provision of public service broadcasting in the early years of the digital age, at least up to Charter Review in 2006 . . . and should receive additional funding for the purpose. The preferred method was by an additional licence fee for digital television users . . . amounting to an average of £1.57 a month over the seven years to 2006, and falling to 99p a month at the end of the period.

This was bitterly attacked by Murdoch and other commercial broadcasters as a 'poll tax' which would inhibit the development of digital television (though detailed econometric evidence in the Panel's report demonstrated that the reverse case was probable). Civil servants at the Department of Media, Culture and Sport made it plain in off-the-record conversations that 10 Downing Street refused to consider the digital licence fee, though additional funds (somewhat less than the Panel recommendation) were provided by other means.

Mercenaries. They are only useful, says Machiavelli, when there is no danger to hand. He insists on the point repeatedly in *The Art of War* and in *The Prince*, e.g. chapter 13: 'The wise prince . . . has always avoided these arms and turned to his own; and has been willing rather to lose with them than to conquer with others, not deeming that a real victory which is gained with the arms of others.'

Kiss and kick. *Kipling Journal*, December 2002.

Lazarsfeld and his team first published in 1944, providing the basis of the 'two-step flow of communication' theory, in which 'opinion leaders' first receive, then disseminate (and modify), data produced by news media. *The American Voter* developed the argument further in the 1960s. Present-day investigations like *The Emerging Democratic Majority* (by John B. Judis and Ruy Teixeira), *Why Americans Don't Vote* (by Ruy Teixeira) and *Wealth and Democracy* (by Kevin Phillips) don't replace the model, but consider its potential success (or failure) under conditions of rising inequality and fast social change – where face-to-face communication remains essential to the formation of political and other opinions.

Robert M. Worcester, chairman of Market and Opinion Research International (MORI), in a private conference 21–22 June 1995 described public opinion as working through a 'diffusion process', subject to Lazarsfeld's crucial demonstration that 'opinion leaders' exist in all social categories, 'distinguishing themselves primarily by a higher consumption of media, and exerting an active influence on the opinions of people in their social surroundings'. Much work in the 1990s reflected a desire in advertising and marketing to discover just how much gender and age and education affect the influence of opinion leaders in consumer issues (such as cars and health) as much as in public affairs. Today, 'however it is to be measured, we have a model of voter behaviour that is dependent upon a complex system of influences, local and national, direct and indirect, affecting the individual personally, affecting family/friends, and sometimes not touching his/her life directly . . .'. Pippa Norris, *Virtuous Circle*, provides an up-to-date picture of the interaction between news media and politics.

Machiavelli's argument. *The Discourses*, chapter 58:

> in the matter of prudence and stability, I say, that a people is more prudent, more stable, and of sounder judgement than a Prince. Not without good reason is the voice of the populace likened to that of God, for public opinion is remarkably accurate in its prognostications, so much so that it seems as if the populace by some hidden faculty discerned the evil and the good that was to befall it . . .

In present-day polling it is found that the general public forecasts the election outcomes with great accuracy.

Patten on Murdoch. Interview, 11 September 2001.

Nazi media. Roger Manvell in Thomas Parrish (ed.), *The Simon and Schuster Encyclopedia of World War II* (in part):

> On October 4, 1933, a decree was issued which made every editor an 'official', forbidden to publish anything deemed injurious to the state or to act or write independently; the editor became a censor and all journalists had to hold a license to practice their profession. Conferences were constantly called to give editors 'guidance'. By 1939, Max Amann (secretary of Goebbels' press office) employed 600 editors in chief; by 1944, 82 per cent of the German press had come directly under Amann's control.

Berlusconi's media control. Tobias Jones, *The Dark Heart of Italy*:

> In Italy there's no fourth estate: newspapers, with a few exceptions, are divided among the oligarchies . . . Besides owning Juventus the Agnelli group owns one-quarter of all national or provincial papers (and, more importantly, controls 13% of all advertising revenue in the country). Berlusconi, besides AC Milan, owns the Mondadori publishing house, and therefore the copyright on a quarter of all

Italian books. *Il Giornale*, a national newspaper, is his (or, technically, his brother's) . . . as are three out of seven national TV channels. By now the most convincing explanation, albeit the most mundane, for Berlusconi's political appeal is the simple fact that he controls three television channels. Having a politician who controls three television channels turns any election into the equivalent of a football match in which one team kicks off with a three-goal advantage.

Berlusconi's Mediaset, says Jones, is not so much biassd as 'a-political'. He adds a postscript: 'The riddle of television ownership is still unsolved. Rather than sell his own channels, Berlusconi has suggested the sell-off of RAI, effectively its privatisation. By now, every news programme on every channel will run two or three long, admiring items on Il Presidente. No critical voice can be heard.'

Extinction of diversity. *Royal Commission on the Press 1961–62.*

Mozart. MacKenzie interviewed for *The Real Rupert Murdoch*, Channel 4 (1998).

Popular trust. A survey for Lord Nolan's Committee on Standards in Public Life asked people to say which professions could be trusted to tell the truth. Its 1995 report was bad news for politicians and journalists (figures are percentages): clergymen/priests, 80; doctors, 84; teachers, 84; television news readers, 72; professors, 70; judges, 68; the police, 63; ordinary people in the street, 64; pollsters, 52; civil servants, 37; business leaders, 32; trade union officials, 32; politicians generally, 14; journalists, 10; government ministers, 11. Surveys carried out since have seen ups and downs, but no real movement at the bottom. In 2002 doctors had moved up to 91 per cent; journalists were at 13 per cent, below politicians (19 per cent). Government ministers, who usually rank below politicians generally, were for once effectively level at 20 per cent. Rather less frequently, institutional trust is surveyed, and this produces different results. For instance, NOP asked at roughly the same time as Nolan:

Q. Do the following have a good influence on life in Britain today, a bad influence, or no influence on life in Britain today?

	Good	Bad	None/ DK	Good less bad
The BBC	63	11	26	+52
The Church of England	45	13	42	+32
Broadsheet newspapers (*Guardian, Telegraph, Times*)	42	13	42	+29
Trade unions	38	25	37	+13
Royal family	36	33	31	+3
British pop singers	31	31	38	0
The legal system	37	38	25	–1
The national lottery	38	42	20	–4

Members of Parliament	27	38	35	−11
The big banks	27	38	35	−11
Satellite and cable TV	25	40	35	−15
Football players	24	49	27	−25
Tabloid newspapers				
(*Sun, Mirror, News of the World*)	19	61	20	−42

Source: NOP for *Sunday Times*, 30 November and 1 December 1995.

Again, ups and downs occur, but the BBC and the broadsheet newspapers are fairly clearly among the best trusted of national institutions. And even Parliament did a lot better than the tabloids, comprehensively loathed.

Attlee and the media. Williams, *Dangerous Estate.*

Lincoln of course spoke before the Fifteenth Amendment (1870) sought to stop individual states limiting the right to vote. As Judith N. Shklar points out (*American Citizenship*) it did very little for Southern blacks 'and . . . it did nothing at all for women'. Even the Voting Rights Act 1965 leaves room for improvement if compared to Australia or some European examples.

Participant rulers. Google finds more than 5,000 Web references to Milton's 1644 essay against censorship. If the First Amendment marks *Areopagitica*'s establishment in democratic law, then it was 147 years taking effect. (The Areopagus hill north-west of the Acropolis was a traditional meeting-place supposedly democratised by Pericles.) Milton opens with his own translation of words from *The Suppliant Women* rendered today as 'Liberty speaks in these words: "Who with good counsel for the city wishes to address this gathering?" Anyone who wishes to do this gains distinction; whoever does not keeps silent. Where could a city enjoy greater equality than this?'

The plot concerns a debate over going to war to help the women of the losing side in the Theban civil war to get their dead buried – an apparently selfless gesture. (Milton, a stout republican, omits that Euripides' Athens is a constitutional monarchy, and his quote is from Theseus, the king.) In 'Three Laws of Politics' R. G. Collingwood describes Machiavelli as setting the moment in which:

> political science recognised what I will call the positive function of the ruled in the life of a body politic. To be a mere recipient of a ruler's behests, an obedient subject, is to have a merely negative function; to have a positive function is to have a will of your own which your ruler must take into account. The chief lesson which Machiavelli learned from his famous study of the fortunes of Louis XII on his Italian campaign, and set forth in the third chapter of *The Prince*: 'Concerning Mixed Principalities', concerns the way in which a prince may use his subjects as a reservoir of strength; they thus become no longer negative or passive partners in the work of government but active participants in it.

Puritan England to America. Shklar in *American Citizenship*:

> the ideas presented at the state constitutional conventions [of the early nine-teenth century] which were called to deal with the demands for political democratization were far older than the American republic. Like so much else in American political thought, these had their origins in Puritan England, and especially in the Putney Debates of 1647 . . . 'We judge,' one of the officers said, 'that all inhabitants that have not lost their birthright should have an equal voice in elections.' Moreover, they '[did] think that the poorest man in England is not at all bound in a strict sense to that government that he has not had a voice to put himself under.'

Shklar points to the unique stress produced by the juxtaposition of constitu-tional liberty with modern slavery. J. G. A. Pocock, *The Machiavellian Moment: Florentine Political Thought and the Atlantic Republican Tradition* is a famous, subtle account of the republic's confrontation with corruption.

Hamilton and mass society. See Chapter 7 above.

Chinese bureaucracy. An impression still exists that pre-communist China was run by an extensive mandarinate. Professor John King Fairbank of Harvard insisted with great pertinacity that the opposite was true, and virtu-ally all scholars seem now to accept this – though how so few ruled so many remains somewhat unclear.

John to Abigail Adams. America Past and Present Online.

Toxicity. Weber never fancies that modern life is possible without bureaucracy but fears 'the disenchantment of the world' through its insistence on secrecy and irresponsible control. Mommsen, *Political and Social Theory of Max Weber*, quotes his belief that 'together with the inanimate machine it is busy fabri-cating the cage of serfdom which men will perhaps be forced to inhabit some day, as powerless as the fellahs of ancient Egypt'. And H. H. Gerth and C. Wright Mills translated a still darker passage from Weber's *Economy and Society*:

> Bureaucratic administration always tends to be an administration on 'secret ses-sions': in so far as it can, it hides its knowledge and action from criticism . . . The concept of the 'official secret' is the specific invention of bureaucracy, and noth-ing is so fanatically defended by the bureaucracy as this attitude, which cannot be substantially justified beyond these specifically qualified areas. In facing a par-liament, the bureaucracy, out of a sure power instinct, fights every attempt of the parliament to gain knowledge by means of its own experts or from interest groups . . .

Jefferson dined alone. The John F. Kennedy Library and Museum in Boston has an exhibit concerning the dinner which took place on 29 April 1962.

Like a moron. Daniel Ellsberg, *Secrets*.

Cold war débâcles. Moynihan is not so naive as to suggest in *Secrecy* that an exact measure can be made. But he points out that by the time communism collapsed the US budget was so badly ravaged by expenditure aimed at a wildly overestimated threat that assistance like that given to the defeated of 1945 could not be contemplated.

BSE. House of Commons, 26 October 2000. The Minister of Agriculture, Fisheries and Food (Nick Brown) endorsed the Phillips inquiry in its statement that those who misled the public over BSE acted 'in accordance with what they conceived to be the proper performance of their duties'. This was repeated many times by government spokespeople.

Lying bastards. John Rentoul, *Independent*, 16 November 2002, reviewing *The Political Animal* by Jeremy Paxman.

Errors. Milton, *Areopagitica*, last paragraph.

Expansion of secrecy. Summarised by Richard Gid Powers in his introduction to Moynihan, *Secrecy*.

Sales pitch. David Yelland interviewed by the *Financial Times*, 15 October 2002.

Euroschemes. These and many others are collated at http://www.cec.org.uk/press/myths/r.

Serious impact. The *Observer* ran three ICM constituency polls during the 1997 election. Two Tory MPs (Allan Stewart and Piers Merchant) who had been the subject of tabloid sex-scandal stories were found to have support at least as strong as any candidates of their party. But in the previously safe Tory seat of Tatton there was massive hostility to Neil Hamilton – exposed in the *Guardian* as taking money to ask questions for the boss of Harrods. Hamilton lost the seat on a huge swing to Martin Bell.

'By the hand'. Machiavelli, *The Prince*, chapter 18, 'Concerning the Way in Which Princes Should Keep Faith'.

Indictments and calumies. Machiavelli, *Discourses*, chapters 7 and 8.

Media bill and media ownership. Professor Barwise in *Financial Times*, 15 October 2002. Extended in discussion.

14: RUPERT'S ESTABLISHMENT

Editors. Rebekah Wade moved from the *News of the World* to the *Sun* in January 2003, replacing David Yelland, who left to prepare at business school for an unspecified role in Newscorp management (*Guardian* and others, 13 January 2003). He led the *Sun* on 8 November 1998 with the story about homosexual ministers controlling the Cabinet ('TELL US THE TRUTH TONY: ARE WE BEING RUN BY A GAY MAFIA?') . Reports of Wade's appointment recalled her 'name and shame' campaign against paedophiles run in the *News of the World* during

July 2000 when public anxiety was high because of the murder of schoolgirl Sarah Payne, and noted that the chief constable of Gloucestershire and others had called her 'grossly irresponsible' (e.g. BBC, 13 January 2003). The handover party attracted (among others) Tony and Cherie Blair, Gordon and Sarah Brown, the Home Secretary, the Education Secretary, the US Ambassador William Farish and MI5 Director-General Elizabeth Manningham-Buller. (*Guardian*, 25 February 2003).

Titanic in China. On 9 March 1998 the *New York Post* revealed that Fox's *Titanic* had become the first Hollywood film endorsed by a Chinese leader. The masses consequently were 'clamoring for the film' in advance of release. The *Evening Standard* reported Jiang's assessment on 24 April, noting that Disney and MGM had earned disfavour by making films about the Dalai Lama.

Objectivity, etc. Reuters on 11 December 1998 reported Jiang and Murdoch meeting to celebrate a new Newscorp office in Beijing (*China Daily* carrying a large picture of the two clasping hands). This report is typical of many which treated the occasion as a breakthrough for Murdoch in terms of Beijing acceptance. The President 'expressed appreciation of the efforts made by world media mogul Rupert Murdoch in presenting China objectively and cooperating with the Chinese press over the last two years'. Co-operation has continued, especially helpful against 'wild lies' about Chinese repression in Tibet. Beijing's news service for overseas Chinese, Zhongguo Xinwen She, said (BBC Monitoring Service, 7 July 2000) that the main author of those lies, the Dalai Lama, had happily been subjected to intellectual analysis in the West and 'exposed as "an old lama very interested in politics, who is going canvassing among many countries in a pair of Italian-made Gucci leather shoes." This penetrating portrait of Dalai Lama, given by Mr Murdoch, the media king, is the most vivid of all.' In other dispatches Murdoch's aperçu is called 'profound' as well as 'vivid'. Its basis is the Shawcross *Vanity Fair* interview (October 1999: see Introduction) in which Murdoch revealed considerable misunderstanding of Tibetan religion and recited notorious Beijing propaganda about Tibetan society prior to the Chinese invasion. The Dalai, of course, is younger than Murdoch.

Authoritarian countries. Ken Auletta published a substantial article about Murdoch in the *New Yorker*, 13 November 1995 ('The Pirate'), one of a series dealing with principal media operators (republished in book form as *The Highwaymen*). He quoted Murdoch as follows: 'The Chinese government is "scared to death of what happened in Tiananmen Square," he says. "The truth is – and we Americans don't like to admit it – that authoritarian countries can work."'

In ordinary speech 'authoritarian' and 'totalitarian' are treated as synonyms, and justifiably so. They differ slightly because the one, 'totalitarian', is derived from the other to express exclusiveness (see below from *The American Heritage Dictionary of the English Language*). Thus 'authoritarian' may be used to qualify description of governments which are not totalitarian. There can be 'a democracy, but with some authoritarian characteristics'; there cannot be a democracy with some totalitarian characteristics. An authoritarian country where there is no democracy qualifies as totalitarian, and is the case of the Chinese People's Republic, in spite of cosmetic modification.

> **Authoritarian:** 'ADJECTIVE: 1. Characterized by or favouring absolute obedience to authority, as against individual freedom: an authoritarian regime. 2. Of, relating to, or expecting unquestioning obedience.'
> **Totalitarian:** 'ADJECTIVE: Of, relating to, being, or imposing a form of government in which the political authority exercises absolute and centralised control over all aspects of life, the individual is subordinated to the state, and opposing political and cultural expression is suppressed: "A totalitarian regime crushes all autonomous institutions in its drive to seize the human souls" (Arthur M. Schlesinger, Jr.). ETYMOLOGY: total + (author)itarian.'

Ideology. The word may in itself be neutral, merely denoting the existence of systematic beliefs. For instance (Douglass C. North, Nobel Prize Lecture, 1993): 'Ideologies are shared frameworks of mental models that groups of individuals possess that provide both an interpretation of the environment and a prescription as to how that environment should be ordered.' To have no ideology may be equivalent to having no coherent convictions. But Marx and Engels applied a sceptical twist which Anthony Flew describes (*A Dictionary of Philosophy*, Pan Macmillan, 1983):

> ... in *The German Ideology* (written in 1845–6 but published first in 1932) the word refers to such general systems only insofar as they are recognised to contain falsehood and distortion generated by more or less unconscious motivations. In this sense the writers did not, of course, consider their own work ideological.

Obsequious court. This is from the *Federalist Papers*, eloquent working documents produced during the creation of the US Constitution. Hamilton wrote in *The Federalist*, No. 1, 27 October 1787, that:

> a dangerous ambition more often lurks behind the specious mask of zeal for the rights of the people than under the forbidden appearance of zeal for the firmness and efficiency of government.

Stelzer. 'The Rise and Fall of Enron', *Weekly Standard*, 26 November 2001 –

reprinted in the *Guardian*, 29 January 2002 ('Why Enron deserves our gratitude: The biggest corporate bankrupt was a champion of the consumer').

Milken. The financier's defenders are discussed sceptically by Edward Cohn (cited above). Milken was jailed for fraud in 1990, and as the New Economy boom raised steam he was portrayed as a mistreated prophet of true financial religion. Some of the arguments used were found less impressive after the crash at the century's end.

Enron. It is hard to recall how illustrious the company was before its collapse in December 2001: for some time its plea of tragic error worked. But after inquiries by Congress, federal prosecutors and others, the *Financial Times* (16 October 2000) pronounced that the 'greed, corruption and fraudulent behaviour' characterising its operations in various markets were an embarrassment to all of corporate America. It may be a long time before individual responsibilities are fully pinned down, but there is no longer any doubt that fraud and related habits were endemic in Enron. The *New York Times*, 2 May 2003, reported a battery of indictments: HOUSTON, May 1 – Federal prosecutors unsealed indictments today against 11 former Enron executives, including charges that the once-vaunted success of the company's high-speed Internet business was largely an illusion.' Its energy sales in California were anything but consumer-friendly, according to the state's Governor, Gray Davis, who wrote in the *New York Times* on 11 May 2002 ('Enron's Lessons for the Energy Market') that documents disclosed by the Federal Energy Regulatory Commission amounted to 'a confession by Enron of its efforts to exploit the system. Residential ratepayers and small businesses were among the victims . . . through its greed and possibly illegal manipulation, Enron did incalculable damage to California's economy and to the national economy.'

The involvement of major banks with Enron's bizarre financial operation is a matter of public record, though their executives assert generally that their own organisations did nothing illegal. The *Financial Times*, 25 July 2002, reported: 'Congressional investigators released evidence this week that they said showed bankers from Citigroup and JPMorgan Chase helped Enron disguise debts as energy trades.' McKinsey & Co: *Business Week*, 8 July 2002, reported (similar accounts appearing elsewhere) that the world's 'most prestigious consultant' provided advice on 'basic strategy' to Enron – where CEO Jeffrey K. Skilling was a former McKinsey partner. Many of Enron's 'intellectual underpinnings' came from the consultancy and received praise in the *McKinsey Quarterly*, which *Business Week* quoted to embarrassing effect.

McCarthyism and Venona. This amazing story is set out by the late Senator Moynihan in *Secrecy: The American Experience*. The cryptographic system used by Soviet spies in the US used one-time pads, theoretically unbreakable.

American cryptanalysts made brilliant use of tiny procedural flaws and opened up the system sufficiently to prove the extent of the attack and evolve tactics to defeat it, though not before some Soviet gains. ('Venona' is a meaningless code-name.) Obviously much had to remain secret, but persistent suppression of the real facts enabled two partisan fantasies to establish themselves. The left held that Soviet subversion was a myth constructed in Washington; the right that it had comprehensively undermined the security of the Western alliance.

The establishment. In May 1951 Guy Burgess and Donald Maclean vanished from the Foreign Office in London. Their defection to Moscow was not confirmed until 1955. Meanwhile official disclosure was so minimal as to approximate to disinformation, and this was the theme of Henry Fairlie's political column in the *Spectator* of 25 September 1955, where he said that a 'subtle influence which is exercised by the members of what I call the "Establishment"' created 'an attitude of mind to the whole question of the disappearance of Burgess and Maclean'. This attitude was represented in the Liberal politician Lady Violet Bonham Carter and the editor of the *Observer*, David Astor – who alleged that press pursuit of Maclean's wife Melinda, particularly by the *Daily Express* and *Daily Telegraph*, had descended to witch-hunting. Melinda had been left behind by the escapers, joining Maclean much later. In sympathetic accounts she seemed like a refugee from vigilantism more than a communist defector. Lady Violet was a longtime friend of the Maclean family. Both she and Astor were immaculately upper-class and influential. The implication of Fairlie's piece, perhaps not deliberately, was that influence had in some way protected the spies and assisted their escape, subsequently protecting Melinda from journalistic pressure which might have extracted important counter-espionage information from her. Responses included furious communications from Astor and Bonham Carter, ready to go to court unless the *Spectator* renounced all suggestion that they were communist sympathisers (which it did). Hugh Trevor-Roper wrote on 21 October to say that, if wrong about Mrs Maclean, they had been right about witch-hunting:

> . . . did the newspapers, which pursued Mrs Maclean and her children so uncivilly, pursue them (as they now virtuously claim) because they knew or suspected that she was a Communist, or was it merely because they regarded her as a source of news about Maclean – in which case their retrospective virtue vanishes? And secondly, even if they did suspect Mrs Maclean of Communism, does such suspicion justify such persecution? . . . [They] seem to argue that even if other citizens have personal rights, suspected Communists have not . . . The theory of an outlaw party seems to me worse than the supposed fact of an 'Establishment'.

He went on to argue the points given in the text about the existence and real nature of a governing class (democratic or otherwise) and the danger of abstract allegations. Trevor-Roper (later Lord Dacre) knew at this time about the un-abstract role of Philby in the Burgess–Maclean affair, which he later helped the *Sunday Times* to reveal (see Chapter 9). Fairlie's view of 'establishments' grew more benign as he learnt about McCarthyite abuses in the US. The passage cited was written in the *Spectator* of 25 May 1956, reviewing *The Power Elite* by C. Wright Mills, and it concluded: 'The Establishment has to be watched . . . But Senator McCarthy would not have thrown professors out of their jobs here . . . That may not be much, but it is something.'

Newscorp and the establishment. Menadue (*Things You Learn Along the Way*) in addition to the Adelaide establishment refers to a belief by Murdoch that 'the Melbourne establishment, which his father was very much a part of, had denied him his rightful inheritance in the Melbourne Herald group'. Sir Keith died before Fairlie's unmasking article, but such retrospective sightings are not unusual. The late Lord Boothby wrote to the *Spectator* suggesting that the Appeasement-seeking 'Cliveden Set' was the establishment not yet named. William Safire's assumption about Murdoch's attitude to power was in the *New York Times*, 16 May 1985 ('Citizen of the World'). Tunku Varadarajan lamented the reverence for China of the supposedly irreverent *New York Post* in his *Wall Street Journal* column, 9 April 2001 ('Where's the Chinese Wall?'). Reference to Newscorp Anzacs and so on draws on personal exchanges. Andrew Neil's memoirs (*Full Disclosure*), in which he extensively reviews establishment phenomena, says that only his rebellious personality saved him from membership of it.

Discrimination. The poet and critic Randall Jarrell wrote a novel of college life, *Pictures from an Institution*, where there's an English teacher who agonises every year over bright students being published in the annual magazine more extensively than stupid ones.

> Miss Batterson was perfectly good-hearted in this: if you cannot discriminate between good and bad yourself, it cannot help seeming somewhat poor-spirited and arbitrary of other people to do so. Aesthetic discrimination is no pleasanter, seems no more just and rational to those discriminated against, than racial discrimination; the popular novelist would be satisfied with his income from serials and scenarios and pocket books if people would only see that he is a better writer than Thomas Mann.

'The Three Laws of Politics' is the title of R. G. Collingwood's 1941 Hobhouse Lecture at the London School of Economics. His first law of politics says that a body politic is divided at any moment into rulers and ruled. The second law 'describes this division as *permeable*': all of those ruled are potential rulers, and individuals move between the divisions as circumstance requires. The third law deals with the need for rulers who are currently in command to avoid intellectual corruption – and the lethal effect if they slide into tyranny. (Collingwood wrote at a time when a victory of fascism over civilisation was widely expected; he sought to show why it was improbable.

AIDS and HIV. The literature, technical and popular, is of course gigantic. I share the widespread admiration for *ABC of AIDS* by Michael W. Adler, and rely on its technical analysis. (He is Professor of Sexually Transmitted Diseases at the Royal Free and University College Medical School, London.) The intensive stage of the *Sunday Times* campaign ran from early 1993 to late spring 1994. There are too many items to cite separately, but the issue of 28 November 1993 is representative. Much of it consists of a reply to an article in the *Sunday Telegraph* (20 November 1993) questioning the Hodgkinson–Neil project and saying that while criticism of orthodox science was legitimate, 'claiming that the risk does not exist at all is an act of indescribable folly'. Because Paul Eddy, co-author of the piece, formerly worked on the *Sunday Times*, Neil regarded the article as betrayal (personal communication from Eddy), and this elicited the thalidomide comparison which Neil extends in *Full Disclosure*. The *Nature* editorial ('New-style abuse of press freedom') appeared on 9 December 1993. Whitehead's account of the history of calculus is in *An Introduction to Mathematics*. Coleridge on despotism of the mind is in the essay 'Shakespeare and the Science of Method', appearing in various collections of his work.

Conspiracy. Pareto's thoughts about ruling elites can be found in Professor S. E. Finer's *Sociological Writings of Vilfredo Pareto*: their superiority over the mass justifies considerable skulduggery. Pareto despised Italian democracy, but died (in 1923) with slight experience of its replacement.

AIDS in China. Kristof's article ('China's Deadly Cover-Up') was in the *New York Times*, 29 November 2002.

Shoulder to shoulder. Andrew Neil in 'Rupert the Fear', *Guardian*, 2 March 1998.

Tiananmen mortality compared. Simple arithmetic tells only a fraction of the story when a popular assembly is repressed by violence. But calculation does assist comparison between Tiananmen and two British tragedies because of China's human scale. The Peterloo death-toll was inflicted on a small population; Bloody Sunday, though much less than Tiananmen in absolute terms, was not far away in proportion. Political response is of course very different in each case.

Total population

China 2000	1,261,000,000
UK 1821	15,471,000
UK 1971	55,515,000

Killed by official action

Tiananmen 1989 (approximate)	400
Peterloo 1819	11
Bloody Sunday 1972	13

Deaths per million people

Tiananmen	0.31
Peterloo	0.71
Bloody Sunday	0.23

Citizens and lovers. This is in Oakeshott's essay 'On the Civil Condition', part of his final book *On Human Conduct* (1975).

Akhmatova. This is from *Requiem and Poem without a Hero*, translation and introduction by D. M. Thomas.

Unsteady giant. Wilson's analysis is summarised in *Scientific American*, February 2002, and extended in his book *The Future of Life*. Other details of ecological and demographic disaster are in Shapiro, *Mao's War on Nature*, and Sen, *Development as Freedom*.

Delinquent writing. This is described in a note to Jonathan Mirsky from Perry Link, Professor of East Asian Studies at Princeton:

> 'Writing about the dark side' (*xie yinanmian*) may have been first used (but I'm not sure) in the 1954 campaign against Hu Feng, whose transgression precisely was this. The opposite, correct, behavior was called *xie guangmingmian* 'writing about the bright side'. From the 50s through 80s these terms appeared in all kinds of places. Did Mao personally initiate the terms? Must have, I would guess, even if we can't find them in his published works.

GDP per-capita figures are from the 2002 World Bank World Development Indicators.

Star-TV organisation. Details from archives of the Museum of Broadcast Communications, Chicago Cultural Center, 78 East Washington Street, Chicago, Illinois 60602 (www.museum.tv/archives/etv/S/htmlS/startvhong/startvhong.htm).

Liberal totalitarianism. Murdoch expounds this concept in the biography by William Shawcross (*Murdoch*) giving his temporary loss of the *New York Post* as a case in point. He had to sell the paper (later being able to repurchase it) when his television operations expanded into New York: Federal Communications Commission regulations do not allow ownership of newspaper and television assets within a single market. Murdoch sought a waiver, which was resisted by Senator Edward Kennedy, a notorious liberal, and in Murdoch's view a totalitarian because he insisted on compliance with the law.

Michael Foot restated the 'evil genius' notion in giving the author a comparison with Beaverbrook, a capitalist he could admire as well as oppose.

Technology and totalitarian governments. Museum of Broadcast Communications archive (see above).

Mirsky's recruitment. Personal communication.

Patten's book *East and West* was notoriously excised from the list of the Newscorp publishing subsidiary HarperCollins on Murdoch's demand (and was published instead by Macmillan).

BBC World is described on the BBC website. The BBC confirms that *The Last Emperor* was distributed on WSTV in 1993 and so must have been seen by some viewers in China, but it is impossible now to know the number.

Making peace. Murdoch described his discussions with the Chinese authorities in an interview with *Forbes* (January 1994). He thought his London speech had been drawn to Beijing's attention by his 'enemies'.

Mafia government. Quoted by Kevin Phillips in *Wealth and Democracy*. See also North's Nobel Prize acceptance speech, 1993.

Orwell's errors. Murdoch gave the 11th John Bonython Lecture, Melbourne, 20 October 1994.

Star-TV and the Chinese government. When announcements were made about Star being permitted to broadcast nationwide, its executives were happy to tell financial journalists of the favoured status of the channel, and that this was based on rigorous exclusion of material which might offend the government. 'Star TV rises on a promising eastern horizon': Rahul Jacob, *Financial Times*, 6 December 2002. 'News Corp's wooing of Beijing pays off': James Kynge, *Financial Times*, 9 January 2003. Clearly these accounts should be read alongside Nicholas Kristof's report on the same government's suppression of facts about AIDS ('China's Deadly Cover-Up', *New York Times*, 29 November 2002).

Not making the paper. Personal from Mirsky.

Mildly tedious. Patten, interview cited above.

Hitler Diaries. Robert Harris' *Selling Hitler* is a classic account of journalistic fantasy-mongering. Several participants assisted with further details, but prefer understandably not to be cited.

Snoddy and the Cockup. Interview, BBC Radio 4 on 1 March 1998.

China and self-censorship. Perry Link, 'The Anaconda in the Chandelier', *New York Review of Books*, 11 April, 2002.

'Normal' journalism. MacArthur in *The Times*, 27 March 1998. When used in the sense of a columnist's attack on Mirsky, 'normality' often means something

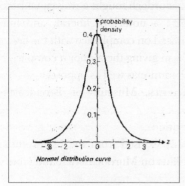

Bell curve

even more restricted than a normal distribution. The 'bell curve' does include some rare events – 'outliers' – in the slim 'tails' of the bell. In *Fooled by Randomness* the financial trader and mathematician Nassim Nicholas Taleb notes that people often choose to disregard the tails – and that there are many activities, administrative ones particularly, where this causes no serious problem because 'the difference in payoff between different outcomes is not significant'. This is generally the case in education and in medicine:

> A professor who computes the average of his students' grades removes the highest and lowest observations, which he would call outliers, and takes the average of the remaining ones, without this being an unsound practice. A casual weather forecaster does the same with extreme temperatures – an unusual occurrence might be deemed to skew the overall result (though we will see that this may turn out to be a mistake when it comes to forecasting future properties of the ice cap). So people in finance . . . ignore infrequent events, not noticing that the effect of a rare event can bankrupt a company.

Real journalism has many similarities with finance.

Normality in Beijing. Bei Ling and Andrea Huss, 'Warming Up to China, Neglecting Democracy', *New York Times*, 23 February 2002.

Munro's investigation. 'Judicial Psychiatry in China and its Political Abuses', by Robin Munro, *Columbia Journal of Asian Law*, Vol 14, No 1.

James Murdoch's strong stomach, etc. 'News Corp. Heir Woos China With Show of Support', *Los Angeles Times*, 23 March 2001. Also *Daily Telegraph*, 26 March 2001.

Most costly blunder: 'SARS In The Hinterland', Joshua Muldavin, *International Herald Tribune*, 8 May 2003.

Newscorp's Iraq war. Roy Greenslade, 'Their Master's Voice', *Guardian*, 17 February 2000.

Deamer wake. Personal from Tony Clifton, Alan Ramsey.

Surely it isn't evil? Personal from Newscorp veterans, over the years.

Newscorp and taxation. *Economist*, 18 March, 1999.

No profit in China. *China Economic Quarterly*, Q2 2003.

Dacre. Interview with Bill Hagerty, *British Journalism Review*, 13 March 2002.

Luxemburg. This is from her 1918 pamphlet *The Russian Revolution*, warning that Lenin and Trotsky, by suppressing democracy, were taking a catastrophic direction.

BIBLIOGRAPHY

Abrams, Mark and Rose, Richard, *Must Labour Lose?* Penguin, 1960.

Adler, Michael W., *ABC of AIDS* (fifth edition). BMJ Books, 2001.

Adorno, T. W., Frenkel-Brunswik, Else, Levinson, Daniel J. and Sanford, R. Nevitt, *The Authoritarian Personality*. Harper, 1950.

Akhmatova, Anna, *Requiem and Poem Without a Hero*, trans. D. M. Thomas. Paul Elek, 1976.

Andrews, Eric, *The Anzac Illusion*. Cambridge University Press, 1993.

Ashmead-Bartlett, E., *The Uncensored Dardanelles*. Hutchinson, 1920.

Aspinall-Oglander, C. F., *Military Operations Gallipoli*, vols 1–2 (1932). Battery Press, 1992.

Auletta, Ken, *The Highwaymen: Warriors of the Information Superhighway*. Harcourt Brace, 1998.

Bacon, Sir Francis, *The Essayes or Counsels, Civill and Morall*, ed. Michael Kiernan. Oxford University Press, 1985.

Bagehot, Walter, *The English Constitution* (1867), ed. R. H. S. Crossman. Fontana, 1963.

Bainbridge, Cyril and Stockdale, Roy, *The News of the World Story*. HarperCollins, 1993.

Barkley, William, *Reporter's Notebook*. Oldbourne, 1958.

Barry, Paul, *The Rise and Rise of Kerry Packer*. Bantam, 1993.

Barwise, Patrick and Ehrenburg, Andrew, *Television and its Audience*. Sage, 1988, 1996.

Bean, Charles (ed.), *The Anzac Book*. Cassell, 1916.

Bean, Charles, *Anzac to Amiens* (condensed from the 20-volume official history of Australia in the Great War). Australian War Memorial, 1946.

Belfield, Richard, Hird, Christopher and Kelly, Sharon, *Murdoch, the Decline of an Empire*. Macdonald, 1991.

Belfield, Richard, Hird, Christopher and Kelly, Sharon, *Murdoch, the Great Escape*. Warner Books, 1994.

Ben Block, Alex, *Outfoxed*. St Martin's Press, 1990.

Bendix, Reinhard, *Max Weber: An Intellectual Portrait*. Methuen, 1966.

Benfey, Christopher E. G., *The Double Life of Stephen Crane*. Deutsch, 1993.

Bernstein, Carl and Woodward, Bob, *All the President's Men*. Touchstone, 1987.

Bevins, Anthony and Hughes, Colin, 'Rat Pack' (unpublished MS). Queen Mary College London.

Blainey, Geoffrey, *The Tyranny of Distance*. Sun Books, 1966.

Bok, Sissela, *Lying: Moral Choice in Public and Private Life*. Vintage, 1989.

Bolton, Roger, *Death on the Rock, and Other Stories*. W. H. Allen, 1990.

Bowen, Ralph H., *German Theories of the Corporate State*. McGraw-Hill, 1947.

Bower, Tom, *Maxwell: The Outsider*. Aurum, 1988; Mandarin, 1991.

Bradlee, Ben, *A Good Life*. Simon & Schuster, 1995.

Brogan, Hugh, *The Pelican History of the United States of America*. Pelican, 1986.

Burke, Edmund, *Reflections on the Revolution in France* (1790), ed. Conor Cruise O'Brien. Penguin, 1968.

Burke, Edmund, *On Empire, Liberty, and Reform: Speeches and Letters*, ed. David Bromwich. Yale University Press, 2000.

Buruma, Ian, *Bad Elements: Chinese Rebels from Los Angeles to Beijing*. Random House, 2001.

Butler, David and others, *Failure in British Government: The Politics of the Poll Tax*. Oxford University Press, 1994.

Button, John, *As It Happened*. Text Publishing, 1998.

Cameron, James, *Point of Departure*. Sphere, 1969.

Campbell, Angus, Converse, Philip E., Miller, Warren E. and Stokes, Donald E., *The American Voter*. Wiley 1960, 1966.

Camus, Albert, *The Fall (La Chute)*, trans. Justin O'Brien. Penguin, 1963.

Cannon, Michael, *The Land Boomers*. Nelson, 1976.

Carlyon, Les, *Gallipoli*. Macmillan, 2001.

Carpenter, L. P., *G. D. H . Cole: An Intellectual Biography*. City University NY Press, 1973.

Carroll, V. J., *The Man Who Couldn't Wait*. Heinemann, 1990.

Chadwick, Paul, *Media Mates: Carving Up Australia's Media*. Macmillan, 1989.

Charlton, Peter (foreword John Terraine), *Pozières 1916*. Leo Cooper, 1986.

Chenoweth, Neil, *Virtual Murdoch: Reality Wars on the Information Highway*. Secker & Warburg, 2001.

Chippindale, Peter and Horrie, Chris, *Stick It Up Your Punter: The Story of the Sun*. Simon & Schuster, 1999.

Christiansen, Arthur, *Headlines All My Life*. Heinemann, 1961.

Cockburn, Claud, *In Time of Trouble*. Hart-Davis, 1956.

Cockerell, Michael, Hennessy, Peter and Walker, David, *Sources Close to the Prime Minister*. Macmillan, 1985.

Cockett, Richard, *Twilight of the Truth*. Weidenfeld & Nicolson, 1989.

Cole, Margaret, *Growing Up into Revolution*. (s.n. in British Library catalogue) 1949.

Collingwood, R. G., *An Autobiography*. Oxford University Press, 1939.

Collingwood, R. G., *Essays in Political Philosophy* (inc. 'The Three Laws of Politics', 'Economics as a Philosophical Science'), ed. David Boucher. Oxford University Press, 1989.

Conn, David, *The Football Business*. Mainstream, 1997.

Cook, Sir Edward, *The Press in War-Time: With Some Account of the Official Press Bureau*. Macmillan, 1920.

Cooper, Guy (ed.), *American Journalism: Reporting Vietnam 1959–1975*. Library of America, 2000.

Cooper, James Fenimore, *The American Democrat* (1832), ed. G. Dekker and L. Johnston. Penguin, 1969.

Cornford, F. M., *Microcosmographia Academica*. Bowes & Bowes, 1922.

Crozier, Michael, *The Making of the Independent*. Gordon Fraser, 1988.

Cudlipp, Hugh, *Walking on the Water*. Bodley Head, 1976.

Cuozzo, Steven, *It's Alive: How America's Oldest Newspaper Cheated Death and Why It Matters*. Times Books, 1996.

Dardanelles Commission, 'Final Report'. PRO CAB 19/1 (1917–18).

Dary, David, *Red Blood and Black Ink – Journalism in the Old West*. Knopf, 1998.

Davie, Michael and Chisholm, Anne, *Beaverbrook*. Hutchinson, 1992.

Davison, Graeme, *The Rise and Fall of Marvellous Melbourne*. Melbourne University Press, 1978.

Davison, Graeme, Hirst, John and Macintyre, Stuart, *The Oxford Companion to Australian History*. Oxford University Press, 1998.

Deamer, Adrian, Audio tape TRV 2984, Oral History Collection. National Library of Australia.

Delano, Anthony, *Slip-Up: How Fleet Street Caught Ronnie Biggs and Scotland Yard Lost Him*. Coronet, 1986.

Delano, Anthony, 'The Formation of the British Journalist 1900–2000'. PhD thesis, University of Westminster, 2002.

Divine, Robert A., Breen, T. H., Fredrickson, George M. and Williams, R. Hal, *America Past and Present*. Addison-Wesley, 2002.

Downie, Leonard Jr and Kaiser, Robert G., *The News About the News: American Journalism in Peril*. Knopf, 2002.

Eisenstein, Elizabeth L., *The Printing Revolution in Early Modern Europe*. Cambridge University Press, 1983.

Ellsberg, Daniel, *Secrets: A Memoir of Vietnam and the Pentagon Papers*. Viking, 2002.

Emery, Michael, Emery, Edwin and Roberts, Nancy L., *The Press and America*. Allyn & Bacon, 2000.

560

BIBLIOGRAPHY

Euripides (introduction Richard Rutherford), *Electra and Other Plays* (inc. *Suppliant Women*), trans. John Davie. Penguin, 1998.

Evans, Harold, *Good Times, Bad Times* (3rd edition). Phoenix, 1994.

Evans, Richard J., *In Defence of History*. Granta, 1999.

Fairfax, James, *My Regards to Broadway*. Angus & Robertson, 1991.

Farrar-Hockley, A. H., *The Somme*. Batsford, 1964.

Firkins, Peter, *The Australians in Nine Wars: Waikato to Long Tan*. Robert Hale, 1972.

Fitzgerald, T. M., Audio tape TRC 2247, Oral History Collection. National Library of Australia.

Fitzhardinge, L. F., *William Morris Hughes: A Political Biography*, vol. 2: *The Little Digger 1914–1952*. Angus & Robertson, 1979.

Ford, H. A. J., Austin, R. P. and Ramsay, I. M., *Principles of Corporations Law*. Butterworth, 1999.

Fordham, Michael, *Judicial Review Handbook* (2nd edition). Wiley, 1997.

Frankel, Max, *The Times of My Life – and My Life with The Times*. Random House, 1999.

Fromm, Erich, *The Anatomy of Human Destructiveness*. Cape, 1974.

Fromm, Erich, *The Fear of Freedom* (1942). Ark, 1984.

Garden, Don, *A Talent for Ubiquity: The Life of Theodore Fink*. Melbourne University Press, 1998.

Gibbs, Philip, *Adventures in Journalism*. Heinemann, 1923.

Giles, Frank, *Sundry Times*. John Murray, 1986.

Gilmour, Ian, *Dancing with Dogma: Britain under Thatcherism*. Simon & Schuster, 1992.

Glover, Stephen (ed.), *Secrets of the Press*. Allen Lane, 1999.

Golding, Peter, *Black Jack McEwen, Political Gladiator*. Melbourne University Press, 1996.

Gordon Walker, Patrick, *The Cabinet: Political Authority in Britain*. Basic Books, 1970.

Graham, Andrew and others, *Public Purpose in Broadcasting: Funding the BBC*. University of Luton Press, 1999.

Graham, Katharine, *Personal History* (1997). Vintage, 1998.

Griffiths, Dennis, *Plant Here The Standard*. Macmillan, 1996.

Grigg, John, *The History of The Times*, vol. 6: *1966–1981*. Times Books, 1993.

Gullberg, Jan, *Mathematics: From the Birth of Numbers*. Norton, 1997.

Hall, Richard, *The Real John Kerr: His Brilliant Career*. Angus & Robertson, 1978.

Hamilton, C. D. (Sir Denis), *Editor in Chief: The Fleet Street Memoirs of Denis Hamilton*. Hamish Hamilton, 1989.

Hamilton, Sir Ian, *Gallipoli Diary* (2 volumes). Edward Arnold, 1920.

Hardy, Frank, *Power Without Glory* (1950). Panther, 1975.

Harris, Robert, *Gotcha! The Media, the Government and the Falklands Crisis.* Faber, 1986.

Harris, Robert, *Selling Hitler.* Faber, 1986.

Harris, Robert, *Good and Faithful Servant: The Unauthorised Biography of Bernard Ingham.* Faber, 1990.

Held, David and others, *Global Transformations.* Stanford University Press, 1999.

Heller, Joseph, *Catch-22.* Vintage, 1994.

Hennessy, Peter, *Cabinet.* Blackwell, 1986.

Hennessy, Peter, *The Hidden Wiring.* Gollancz, 1995.

Hentoff, Nat, *Speaking Freely: A Memoir.* Knopf, 1997.

Heseltine, Michael, *Life in the Jungle: My Autobiography.* Hodder, 2000.

Hilton, Isabel, *The Search for the Panchen Lama.* Viking, 1999.

Hirst, J. B., *The Strange Birth of Colonial Democracy.* Allen & Unwin, 1988.

Hobbes, Thomas (introduction C. B. Macpherson), *Leviathan* (1651). Pelican, 1968.

Hobson, Dominic, *The Pride of Lucifer.* Hamish Hamilton, 1990.

Hobson, Harold, Knightley, Phillip and Russell, Leonard, *The Pearl of Days: An Intimate Memoir of the Sunday Times.* Hamish Hamilton, 1972.

Hochschild, Adam, *King Leopold's Ghost.* Macmillan, 1999.

Hodgson, Godfrey, *The World Turned Right Side Up.* Mariner Books, 1996.

Hofstadter, Richard, *Anti-Intellectualism in American Life.* Cape, 1964.

Hofstadter, Richard, *The Paranoid Style in American Politics.* Cape, 1966.

Holmes, Stephen and Sunstein, Cass, *The Cost of Rights: Why Liberty Depends on Taxes.* Norton, 1999.

Horsman, Matthew, *Sky High.* Orion Business Books, 1998.

Hoskyns, Sir John, *Just in Time.* Aurum, 2000.

Howe, Sir Geoffrey, *Conflict of Loyalty.* Macmillan, 1994.

Hundt, Reed, *You Say You Want a Revolution.* Yale University Press, 2000.

Hussey, Roger, *The Oxford Dictionary of Accounting.* Oxford University Press, 2000.

Hynes, Samuel (ed.), *American Journalism: Reporting World War II 1939–1946.* Library of America.

Independent Review Panel, *The Future Funding of the BBC: Chairman Gavyn Davies.* DCMS, 1999.

Inglis, K. S., *Nation: The Life of an Independent Journal of Opinion 1958–1972.* Melbourne University Press, 1989.

Inglis, K. S., *The Stuart Case.* Melbourne University Press, 1961; Black Ink, 2002.

Insight (*Sunday Times* editorial staff), *The Thalidomide Children and the Law.* Deutsch, 1973.

Insight (*Sunday Times* editorial staff), *Suffer the Children.* Viking, 1979.

Isherwood, Christopher, *Mr Norris Changes Trains.* Vintage Classics, 1999.

Jacobs, Eric, *Stop Press: The Inside Story of the Times Dispute.* Deutsch, 1980.

BIBLIOGRAPHY

Jarrell, Randall, *A Sad Heart at the Supermarket* (inc. 'The Taste of the Age'). Eyre & Spottiswoode, 1965.

Jarrell, Randall, *Pictures from an Institution* (1953). Phoenix Fiction Chicago University Press, 1986.

Jones, Tobias, *The Dark Heart of Italy*. Faber, 2003.

Judis, John B. and Teixeira, Ruy, *The Emerging Democratic Majority*. Scribner, 2002.

Kaplan, Justin, *Lincoln Steffens: The Father of Modern Muckraking*. Cape, 1974.

Kaplan, Robert, *The Nothing That Is: A Natural History of Zero*. Allen Lane, 1999.

Kearns, Burt, *Tabloid Baby*. Celebrity Books, 1999.

Kelly, Paul, *The End of Certainty*. Allen & Unwin, 1994.

Kelly, Paul, *November 1975*. Allen & Unwin, 1995.

Kerr, Sir John, *Matters for Judgement*. Macmillan, 1979.

Kiernan, Thomas, *Citizen Murdoch*. Dodd, Mead & Co., 1986.

Kipling, Rudyard, *A Diversity of Creatures* (inc. 'The Village That Voted the Earth Was Flat' and 'The Press') (1913). Penguin, 1987.

Kipling, Rudyard, *Something of Myself* (1937). Penguin, 1977.

Knightley, Phillip, *The First Casualty*. Harcourt Brace, 1975.

Knightley, Phillip, *A Hack's Progress*. Cape, 1997.

Kolakowski, Leszek, *Main Currents of Marxism: Its Rise, Growth and Dissolution*, trans. P. S. Falla. Oxford University Press, 1978.

Krajicek, David C., *Scooped! Media Miss Real Story of Crime While Chasing Sex, Sleaze and Celebrities*. Columbia University Press, 1999.

Kuttner, Robert, *Everything for Sale: The Virtues and Limits of Markets*. Knopf, 1996.

Lamb, Larry, *Sunrise: The Remarkable Rise and Rise of the Best-selling Soaraway Sun*. Papermac, 1989.

La Nauze. J. A., *Walter Murdoch: A Biographical Memoir*. Melbourne University Press, 1977.

Lawrenson, John and Barber, Lionel, *Reuters: The Price of Truth*. Mainline, 1985.

Lawson, Nigel, *The View from No. 11*. Bantam, 1992.

Lazarsfeld, Paul, Berelson, Bernard and Gaudett, Hazel, *The People's Choice* (1944). Columbia University Press, 1968.

Leapman, Michael, *Barefaced Cheek*. Hodder, 1983.

Lessig, Lawrence, *Code, and Other Laws of Cyberspace*. Basic Books, 1999.

Linklater, Magnus and Leigh, David, *Not with Honour: The Inside Story of the Westland Scandal*. Sphere, 1986.

Locke, John, *An Essay Concerning Human Understanding* (1690). Penguin, 1998.

Lyons, Dame Enid, *Among the Carrion Crows*. Rigby, 1972.

MacColl, René, *Deadline and Dateline*. Oldbourne, 1956.

Machiavelli, Niccolo, *The Prince* (1532). Penguin, 1970.

Machiavelli, Niccolo, *The Discourses*, ed. Bernard Crick. Penguin, 1970.

BIBLIOGRAPHY

Machiavelli, Niccolo (introduction Neal Wood), *The Art of War* (1521), trans. Ellis Farneworth. Da Capo, undated.

Mackenzie, Compton, *Gallipoli Memories* (1929). Panther, 1965.

Mackintosh, John P., *The British Cabinet*. Stevens & Sons, 1968.

McQueen, Humphrey, *Temper Democratic*. Wakefield, 1998.

Marr, David, *Barwick*. Allen & Unwin, 1980.

Masterman, J. C., *The Double-Cross System*. Yale University Press, 1972.

Mayer, Henry, *The Press in Australia*. Lansdowne Press, 1968.

Mayer, Jane and Abramson, Jill, *Strange Justice: The selling of Clarence Thomas*. Houghton Mifflin, 1994.

Melvern, Linda, *The End of the Street*. Methuen, 1986.

Menadue, John, *Things You Learn Along the Way*. David Lovell, 1999.

Middlemas, Keith, *Politics in Industrial Society*. Deutsch, 1979.

Middlemas, Keith and Barnes, John, *Baldwin: The Unknown Prime Minister*. Weidenfeld & Nicolson, 1969.

Mills, C. Wright, *The Power Elite*. Oxford University Press, 1956.

Milton, John, *Prose Writings* (inc. *Areopagitica*) (1644), ed. K. M. Burton. Dent, 1958.

Mommsen, Wolfgang J., *The Political and Social Theory of Max Weber*. Polity Press, 1989.

Monash, Lt Gen. Sir John, *The Australian Victories in France in 1918*. Hutchinson, 1920.

Moorehead, Alan (with Anne Moyal), *Gallipoli*. Macmillan, 1975.

Morris, A. J. A., *The Scaremongers*. Routledge, 1994.

Moynihan, Daniel Patrick, *Secrecy: The American Experience*. Yale University Press, 1998.

Munster, George, *Rupert Murdoch: A Paper Prince*. Penguin, 1987.

Nasaw, David, *The Chief: The Life of William Randolph Hearst*. Houghton Mifflin, 2001.

Neil, Andrew, *Full Disclosure*. Macmillan, 1996.

Neillands, Robin, *The Great War Generals on the Western Front 1914–18*. Robinson, 1999.

Nevinson, Henry W., *Fire of Life*. Nisbet/Gollancz, 1935.

Nolan, Lord, *Committee on Standards in Public Life: First Report*. Cmnd 2850-I, HMSO, 1995.

Norris, Pippa, *A Virtuous Circle: Political Communications in Post-industrial Societies*. Cambridge University Press, 2000.

Oakeshott, Michael, *On Human Conduct*. Oxford University Press, 1975.

Orwell, George, *Collected Essays*. Mercury Books, 1961.

Page, Bruce, Leitch, David and Knightley, Phillip (introduction John le Carré), *The Philby Conspiracy*. Ballantine, 1981.

Pareto, Vilfredo, *Sociological Writings*, ed. S. E. Finer. Blackwell, 1976.

Parrish, Thomas (ed.), *The Simon & Schuster Encyclopedia of World War II*. Simon & Schuster, 1978.

Patten, Chris, *East and West*. Pan, 1999.

Paulos, John Allen, *A Mathematician Reads the Newspaper*. Basic Books, 1995.

Pearl, Cyril, *Wild Men of Sydney*. W. H. Allen, 1958.

Phillips, Kevin, *Wealth and Democracy*. Broadway Books, 2002.

Plato, *The Republic*, ed. Desmond Lee. Penguin, 2003.

Pocock, J. G. A., *The Machiavellian Moment: Florentine Political Thought and the Atlantic Republican Tradition*. Princeton University Press, 1975.

Pocock, Tom, *Alan Moorehead*. Bodley Head, 1970.

Potter, Jeremy, *Independent Television in Britain*, vol. 3. Macmillan, 1989.

Pound, Reginald and Harmsworth, Geoffrey, *Northcliffe*. Cassell, 1959.

Pringle, John Douglas, *Have Pen Will Travel*. Chatto, 1974.

Pringle, John Douglas, *Australian Accent* (1958). Rigby, 1978.

Pringle, Peter and Jacobson, Philip, *Those Are Real Bullets, Aren't They?* Fourth Estate, 2000.

Prior, James (Lord Prior), *A Balance of Power*. Hamish Hamilton, 1986.

Ranelagh, John, *Thatcher's People*. HarperCollins, 1991.

Read, Donald, *The Power of News: The History of Reuters 1849–1989*. Oxford University Press, 1992.

Reynolds, Henry, *The Law of the Land*. Penguin, 1987.

Reynolds, Henry, *This Whispering in Our Hearts*. Allen & Unwin, 1998.

Rhodes James, Robert, *Gallipoli*. Pimlico, 1999.

Riesman, David (with Nathan Glazer and Reuel Denney), *The Lonely Crowd*. Yale University Press, 1950, 1961.

Robertson, Michael, *Stephen Crane, Journalism and the Making of Modern American Literature*. Columbia University Press, 1997.

Robson, L. L., *The First AIF: A Study of its Recruitment 1914–18*. Melbourne University Press, 1982.

Rolph, C. H., *All Those in Favour*. Deutsch, 1962.

Royal Commission on the Press, *Chairman Lord Shawcross: 1961–1962*. Cmnd 1811, HMSO, 1962.

Royal Commission on the Press, *Chairman O. R. McGregor: 1973–1976*. Cmnd 6433, HMSO, 1976.

Schudson, Michael, *The Power of News*. Harvard University Press, 1995.

Scraton, Phil, *Hillsborough: The Truth*. Mainstream, 1999.

Scraton, Phil, Jemphrey, Ann and Coleman, Sheila, *No Last Rights: The Denial of Justice and the Promotion of Myth in the Aftermath of Hillsborough*. Liverpool City Council, 1995.

Seaton, Jean (ed.), *Politics and the Media: Harlots and Prerogatives at the Turn of the Millennium*. Blackwell, 1998.

Sekuless, Peter, *A Handful of Hacks: Chester Wilmot, Lorraine Stumm, Kenneth Slessor, Alan Moorehead*. Allen & Unwin, 1999.

Sen, Amartya, *Development as Freedom*. Oxford University Press, 2001.

Serle, Geoffrey, *John Monash: A Life*. Melbourne University Press, 1990.

Seymour-Ure, Colin, *The British Press and Broadcasting since 1945* (2nd edition). Blackwell, 1997.

Shapin, Steven, *A Social History of Truth*. Chicago, 1994.

Shapiro, Judith, *Mao's War Against Nature: Politics and the Environment in Revolutionary China*. Cambridge University Press, 2001.

Shawcross, William, *Murdoch*. Chatto, 1992.

Sheridan, Richard Brinsley, *The School for Scandal* (1777). Oxford University Press, 1998.

Shklar, Judith N., *American Citizenship: The Quest for Inclusion*. Harvard University Press, 1991.

Snoddy, Raymond, *The Good, the Bad and the Unacceptable: The Hard News about the British Press*. Faber, 1993.

Solzhenitsyn, Aleksandr, *The Gulag Archipelago*. Harvill Press, 1999.

Sophocles, *The Three Theban Plays: Antigone, Oedipus the King, Oedipus at Colonus*, trans. Robert Fagles, ed. Bernard Knox. Penguin, 1984.

Souter, Gavin, *Heralds and Angels*. Melbourne University Press, 1991.

Sparrow, Geoff (ed.), *Crusade for Journalism: Official History of the Australian Journalists Association*. Federal Council of the AJA, 1960.

Steinberg, S. H., *Five Hundred Years of Printing*. Penguin, 1969.

Stephens, Mitchell, *A History of News*. Harcourt Brace, 1997.

Stone, William F., Lederer, Gerda, and Christie, Richard, *Strength and Weakness: The Authoritarian Personality Today*. Springer-Verlag, 1992.

Sykes, Trevor, *Two Centuries of Panic*. Allen & Unwin, 1999.

Taleb, Nassim Nicholas, *Fooled by Randomness: The Hidden Role of Chance in the Markets and in Life*. Texere, 2001.

Taylor, A. J. P., *Beaverbrook*. Hamish Hamilton, 1972.

Taylor, Sir Henry, *The Statesman* (1836), ed. David Lewis and Robert Rubel Schaeffer. Praeger, 1992.

Taylor, Rt Hon. Lord Justice, *Final Report into the Hillsborough Stadium Disaster*. HMSO, 1990.

Taylor, Rt Hon. Lord Justice, *Interim Report into the Hillsborough Stadium Disaster*. Cmnd 765, HMSO, 1989.

Taylor, S. J., *The Reluctant Press Lord: Esmond Rothermere and the Daily Mail*. Weidenfeld & Nicolson, 1998.

BIBLIOGRAPHY

Teixeira, Ruy, *Why Americans Don't Vote: Turnout Decline in the US 1960–1984*. Greenwood, 1987.

Terraine, John, *Douglas Haig, the Educated Soldier*. Hutchinson, 1963.

The Times, *The History of The Times*: Vol. 1, *The Thunderer in the Making 1785–1841*. The Times, 1935.

Thomas, David, *Alan Sugar: The Amstrad Story*. Century, 1990.

Thompson, J. Lee, *Northcliffe: Press Baron in Politics 1865–1922*. John Murray, 2000.

Thompson, J. Lee, *Politicians, the Press and Propaganda: Northcliffe and the Great War*. Kent State University Press, 2000.

Todd, Olivier, *Albert Camus*. Knopf, 1997.

Toohey, Brian and Pinwill, William, *Oyster*. Heinemann, 1989.

Trollope, Anthony, *Australia and New Zealand* (1873). Sutton, 1967.

Tuccille, Jerome, *Rupert Murdoch*. Donald I. Fine, 1989.

Tunstall, Jeremy, *The Westminster Lobby Correspondents*. Routledge, 1970.

Tunstall, Jeremy, *Newspaper Power: The New National Press in Britain*. Oxford University Press, 1996.

Tunstall, Jeremy, *The Media are American*. Constable, 1999.

Tunstall, Jeremy and Machin, David, *The Anglo-American Media Connection*. Oxford University Press, 1999.

Turner, Stephen (ed.), *The Cambridge Companion to Weber*. Cambridge University Press, 2000.

Twopeny, Richard, *Town Life in Australia*. E. Stock, 1883.

Weber, Max, *General Economic History*, trans. Frank H. Knight. Allen & Unwin, 1923.

Weber, Max, *The Profession of Politics* (1919), trans. Simona Dragici. Plutarch, 1999.

Weber, Max, ed. Peter Baehr, trs. Baehr & Gordon C. Wills, *The Protestant Ethic and the Spirit of Capitalism and Other Writings*. Penguin, 2002.

West, Rebecca, *The Meaning of Treason* (1949). Phoenix, 2000.

White, Patrick, *Flaws in the Glass*. Cape, 1981.

Whitehead, Alfred N., *An Introduction to Mathematics*. Oxford University Press, 1948.

Wilkinson-Latham, R. J., *From Our Special Correspondent: Victorian War Correspondents*. Hodder, 1979.

Williams, Francis, *Dangerous Estate*. Longmans, 1957.

Williamson, Audrey, *Wilkes: A Friend of Liberty*. Allen & Unwin, 1974.

Wilmer, Lambert A., *Our Press Gang; or, an exposition of the corruptions and crimes of the American Newspapers*. Philadelphia 1859 (no imprint).

Wilson, Edward O, *The Future of Life*. Little Brown, 2002.

Windlesham, P. and Rampton, R., QC, *The Windlesham/Rampton Report on 'Death on the Rock'*. Faber, 1989.

BIBLIOGRAPHY

Wiskemann, Elizabeth, *The Europe I Saw*. Collins, 1968.

Wolfe, Humbert, *The Uncelestial City*. Gollancz, 1930.

Worcester, Robert and Mortimore, Roger, *Explaining Labour's Landslide*. Politico's, 1994.

Wyatt, Woodrow, *The Journals of Woodrow Wyatt* (3 volumes), ed. Sarah Curtis. Macmillan, 1998–2000.

Young, Hugo, *One of Us*. Pan, 1990.

Zwar, Desmond, *In Search of Sir Keith Murdoch*. Macmillan, 1980.

INDEX

INDEX